INTERIOR DESIGN MATERIALS AND SPECIFICATIONS

INTERIOR DESIGN MATERIALS AND SPECIFICATIONS

2ND EDITION

LISA GODSEY
LEED AP, ASID, IDEC, IESNA, IIDA

Fairchild Books
An imprint of Bloomsbury Publishing Inc

BLOOMSBURY
NEW YORK • LONDON • NEW DELHI • SYDNEY

Fairchild Books
An imprint of Bloomsbury Publishing Inc

1385 Broadway
New York
NY 10018
USA

50 Bedford Square
London
WC1B 3DP
UK

www.bloomsbury.com

FAIRCHILD BOOKS, BLOOMSBURY and the Diana logo are trademarks of Bloomsbury Publishing Plc

First published 2013
Reprinted 2015

Library of Congress Cataloging-in-Publication Data
A catalog record for this book is available from the Library of Congress.

2012938422

ISBN: PB: 978-1-6090-1229-8
ePDF: 978-1-6090-1805-4

Typeset by Tom Helleberg
Cover Design by Carly Grafstein
Cover Art: © Ocean Photography/Veer; © paulmaguire/Veer; © PiLens/Veer; © Ronen/Veer; © c/Veer; © Danilin/Veer; © Andrey Volokhatiuk/Veer; © c/Veer
Chapter 1 Opener Art: © Owen Price/iStockphoto Chapter 14 Opener Art: © Michelle Gibson/iStockphoto

Printed and bound in the United States of America

TABLE OF CONTENTS

EXTENDED TABLE OF CONTENTS

Chapter 8: Glass 235

Chapter 9: Metals 251

Chapter 10: Tile and Brick 269

PREFACE

Interior design students are required to understand many more issues in their work than ever before—methods for best practice, software platforms for developing and communicating design, strategies for researching and incorporating new ideas and approaches, and new materials. To best serve the needs of students who must assimilate a lot of content, this second edition has undergone tremendous changes relative to the first.

The format of the information has been somewhat compartmentalized, allowing students to revisit portions of the various materials chapters and find the information there complete for that issue of that material. Much information has been streamlined—converted to tables and charts for fast assimilation—and topics edited to address the materials more concisely and comprehensively.

New pedagogical features allow for quick introduction to concepts and information that can be presented in smaller chunks, and do not require lengthy background information to comprehend. These features appear as *Helpful Hints*, *Points of Emphasis*, *What Would You Do?*, *For the Connoisseur*, and *Cautionary Tales*. *Helpful Hints* are quick tips for managing a portion of the process. They are related to, but distinct within, the materials presented. *Points of Emphasis* further explain some nuance or expand on a specific instance within the topic. *For the Connoisseur* tidbits share some popularly held valuations or preferences. *Cautionary Tales* are just that, stories of what has gone wrong with an installation and why. These tales are an opportunity to see the often hidden implications for material characteristics. *Web Search Activities* and *Personal Activities* for each chapter encourage students to apply newly gained knowledge and ending *Summary Questions* test comprehension of topics discussed in the chapter. This new edition also introduces a glossary of definitions for important *Key Terms* that are listed at the beginning of each chapter and bolded at first mention within the text.

A textiles section has been added to address the needs of students in programs where textiles is not a separate course or an elective. It gives students a working knowledge of fiber chemistry and the various characteristics of fabrics that affect performance. This chapter will also be a good overview for students who intend to study fabrics in more depth in a class devoted to fabrics alone.

Other new features engage students' curiosity by suggesting consideration of possible outcomes of selections and requesting that the student form an educated opinion about an issue, or think of a resolution to a possible problem, in the *What Would You Do?* feature. *Shop Visits* have been moved out of the CD and into the book proper so students are not required to switch media to access the material. Each of these features, *Helpful Hints*, *Points of Emphasis*, *Cautionary Tales*, *Shop Visits*, and *What Would You Do?*, contain important and specific information, succinctly put forth with little extraneous explication. Streamlining the materials will help busy students get the gist of these topics quickly and, at times, even visually.

This is a nuts-and-bolts subject that deserves the most straightforward presentation. The idea behind the book is to give the new designer a working knowledge of surfacing materials and the basis for a logical investigation when selecting and specifying. Globalization, sustainability, and toxicity are important conversations within the material topics and are integrated into the materials chapters to help students make direct connections between the material and these issues.

The specification format that has been adopted by the industry is used in every materials chapter so students can comprehend the universality of the format and how it is adapted to every material that they read about. The chapters have been rearranged so that they ease students into the topics with materials that are familiar to most people, such as wallcoverings and carpeting, to expand on the understanding that they have likely acquired before starting their interior design studies.

The book provides a background that will be the basis of material selections from a performance standpoint, making this valuable information to have acquired prior to studio classes.

ACKNOWLEDGMENTS

I am very grateful to the reviewers for their critique of the first edition: Bill Beitz, Oklahoma State University; LuAnn Nissen, University of Nevada, Reno; Linda Nussbaumer, South Dakota State University; Petra Probstner, Columbia College Chicago; Erin Speck, George Washington University; Elizabeth Stokes, The Art Institute of Portland; Maruja Torres-Antonini, University of Florida; Meghan Woodcock, Savannah College of Art and Design. Their comments became the basis for many of the improvements that we made to meet the changes in student needs for simplicity and streamlined focus. Thank you, Olga Kontzias, for all of your suggestions for organization, especially regarding the new format of the chapters. Maureen Grealish, development editor, and Joe Miranda, senior development editor, contributed mightily to the organization and guided the process through a couple of iterations as we arranged and rearranged for ever more logical presentation. The beautiful new cover was designed by Carly Grafstein. Last, but not least, thank you to Gale, still my best sounding board and friend.

Chapter 1

MAKING MATERIAL SELECTIONS

Key Terms

Air changes per hour (ACH)
Best practices
Carcinogens
Coefficient of friction
Commissioning agents
Critical radiant flux (CRF)
Ecosystems
Flammability
Green
Leadership in Energy and Environmental Design (LEED)
Low-E glass
Outgas
Particulates
Passive solar
Sick building syndrome
Specification
Specify
Sustainable
Synthesis
Third-party
Trombe wall
Volatile organic compounds (VOCs)

Objectives

After reading this chapter, you should be able to:

- Learn about general material characteristics that will pertain to the design goals in your project's design program.
- Identify the different characteristics that are required by law as distinguished from characteristics that you must define for your project.
- Understand characteristics that apply to many material types so you can make good selections.
- Understand how to evaluate testing data that you will encounter when researching materials for your jobs.

Understanding the content of this chapter will give you a foothold on how to evaluate the material selections that you make for your clients' projects.

Entry-level designers are typically the ones responsible for researching and comparing material selections and working with their project manager to determine the best from among all options discovered. For this reason it is very important for your career that you understand how to evaluate options so you are presenting the best choices to the rest of your design team. There are reasons provided by codes and standards as well as reasons defined by your specific project that will indicate which materials are the best for your job.

Understanding the content of and the difference between codes, standards, and guidelines helps you prioritize your criteria for making material selections. Codes are required conditions on completed project sites. Building safety and fire codes are examples of these mandatory characteristics. Standards are consistent methods for testing or performance measurements. The American National Standards Institute (ANSI), American Society of Heating, Refrigerating and Air-Conditioning Engineers (ASHRAE), and American Society for Testing and Materials (ASTM) are just a few examples of organizations that develop standards you will reference. Guidelines are a way of configuring or detailing your designs to achieve a desired result. The Americans with Disabilities Act (ADA) mandates that you incorporate the ADA Accessibility Guidelines in your designs for public spaces. The National Kitchen and Bath Association (NKBA) also has guidelines for best practices when designing kitchens and baths. There is no law mandating that you must use NKBA standards, as there is in the case of the ADA, but when you design kitchens and baths your designs will be more functional if you do. We cannot always satisfy all our requirements for a material. We need to prioritize characteristics in order of importance so we can make the best decisions. You must satisfy those conditions that are mandated by law and, after those mandates are satisfied, you will also include other standards and guidelines among your considerations.

Evaluating materials is complicated business. Interior designers rely on testing and recommendations of numerous parties before they finalize the decision that they must personally stand behind in providing for the health, safety, and welfare of their clients. **Third-party** testing data and recommendations must be carefully scrutinized by the designer on a daily basis. Is the source of the information upon which you base these important decisions reliable and objective?

Designs that you create will only be implemented if they fall within budget constraints. It is something of a juggling act to distribute project resources among hundreds of project decisions in order to complete the project. Completed projects meet your client needs and also build your reputation. Projects that run out of money not only fail to satisfy your clients' needs but damage your reputation and cast a bad light on interior designers generally, so it is imperative that you fulfill project goals while managing client budgets responsibly.

GUIDELINES

There are many influences beyond client preference that guide the designer's selections and it is helpful to understand the distinctions between the various guidelines that you will reference. While codes are always mandatory and are considered to be the minimum standard of practice, and rating systems are usually voluntary, guidelines are often referenced to help designers exceed the minimum and work toward **best practices**. Guidelines are frequently referenced in code and rating system requirements. To understand this better, consider the International Building Code (IBC). It is a guideline that was developed as a model code and it references standards in other guidelines to explain certain performance minimums that it requires. Individual jurisdictions may adopt parts of the IBC for their own local codes. A building must comply with local building codes but guidelines may be voluntary.

Building Code Structures

Designers **specify** materials for surfaces and items that are installed in spaces that are governed by building codes and accessibility requirements as stipulated by the ADA. Both codes and the ADA are mandatory for your selections

Most local codes are based on model codes like the IBC. The IBC is the most commonly used model code that individual jurisdictions have utilized to create their own local building codes. It was developed by the International Code Council (ICC), a nonprofit, nongovernmental organization.

Lightly regulated:	Heavily regulated:
Private space (like a residence) in stand-alone buildings (vs. an apartment or condo building)	Public spaces shared by a variety of people both publicly owned (like schools) and privately owned (like restaurants)
Used by able-bodied adults who are familiar with the premises (inhabitants stay for long duration)	Spaces that serve vulnerable populations (like children or sick people)
Use presents no exceptional hazards	Hazardous materials or processes are contained

FIGURE 1.1 The spectrum of code stringency makes logical sense. This makes it easy to wrap your brain around the material restrictions that will apply to your project.

Codes also vary in stringency by location and occupancy class (building use, like lodging or mercantile), increasing in stringency when risk goes up. Spaces where users may be unfamiliar with the building and its exits, where vulnerable populations exist (such as the young or infirm), and that contain high-hazard areas (like restaurant kitchens) are subject to codes that are stricter than for low-risk spaces like a residential dining room. Figure 1.1 illustrates the gradation.

Your career may take you into areas of design where you will evaluate selections for their resistance to impact and explosions and other less common hazards that are also governed by code, but for the purposes of this general topic we will be addressing the most typical situations. Remember that every jurisdiction develops its own code, so codes vary slightly from one jurisdiction to another. You will need to get a copy of the local code for the project location.

Your commercial project must comply with the Americans with Disabilities Act (ADA). The ADA defines mandatory guidelines that must be met to accommodate people with disabilities. These guidelines do not vary with jurisdiction; the same requirements apply across the nation.

There are many guidelines pertaining to interior design work that govern size and configuration of spaces but our focus here is on finishes and items that designers specify.

Guidelines that pertain to materials:

- Fire resistance
- Slip resistance
- Ability to be cleaned or sanitized

Guidelines that pertain to items:

- Ease of use (particularly in panic situations)
- Visibility
- Air quality

Fire safety codes stipulate resistance to flame. Flame spread ratings vary through Classes A, B, and C with Class A being the most stringent against flame development and C being the least. All building and surfacing materials are governed by codes for commercial installations and codes also govern many residential surfaces as well. Testing that proves the material you specify meets minimum code standards should be done by third-party organizations such as Underwriters Laboratory (UL). Third-party testers should have no connection to the company's products so they are impartial. Building code, also referred to as life/safety code, includes items and surfaces that you specify, things like floors, walls, ceiling surfaces, doors, stairs, ramps, and furnishings. **Flammability** is one of the biggest concerns for designers specifying surfacing.

Test methods include the following:

Methenamine pill: The methenamine pill test tests materials' resistance to a burning object that falls on them. A pill is placed on the material and ignited. Seven out of eight samples must resist burning out from the center. Measured from center to the edge of the burn, the flame must be extinguished in less than eight inches.

Steiner tunnel test: The Steiner tunnel test involves a 25-foot chamber and gas jets. The material is adhered to the top of the chamber and gas jets burn for 10 minutes. The distance of burn indicates the rating from 0 to 200. Asbestos is 0; oak flooring is 100, considered a moderate burn rate. Class A materials have a flame spread rating of 0 to 25; Class B, from 26 to 75; and Class C, from 76 to 200. Class D ranges from 200 to 500. Class D material is not permitted even in one-family and two-family dwellings. Class D decorative paneling has been implicated in a number of fatal fires. Carpet manufacturers object to this test because the carpet is not tested in a manner imitating typical use, since it is tested on the ceiling instead of the floor.

Chamber test: The chamber test is similar to the Steiner tunnel test but material is placed on the floor of the chamber. The rating system has only two classifications, B and C, so a descriptive scale is difficult. Also the relationship between the rating and fire spread has not been proven.

Radiant panel test: The radiant panel test entails placing a sample on the floor of the test chamber and heating the sample by a gas-fired panel mounted at an angle over it. The amount of energy required to sustain flame in the sample is measured and described as **critical radiant flux** or **CRF** (*flux* here refers to the flow of heat energy). The greater the energy required, the higher the number, meaning more resistance to flame, so low numbers indicate higher flammability. This test is usually used for flooring materials.

ADA REQUIREMENTS

In addition to regulating space planning and clearances issues, the ADA governs product and material selection with the aim of creating environments that can be safely used by people with disabilities. The following are examples of how product selections that you will make to complete your project will be governed by the ADA.

Flooring materials:

- Must be level and flush with surrounding surfaces.
- Slip resistance must meet a **coefficient of friction** greater than 0.6.
- Changes in height ¼ inch or less require no transition but changes up to ½ inch require a beveled transition, and changes greater than ½ inch require a ramp.
- Carpet may have a maximum pile height of ½ inch and must be fastened along all edges.

Sustainability

Green design includes **sustainable** site planning, preventing pollution, restoration of urban and habitat sites, accessibility of public or alternative transportation options by building occupants, storm water runoff management, reduction of heat island effects, maximization of open space, reduction of light pollution, water-use reduction, energy conservation, recycling, conservation of materials, sustainable practices and materials, attention to toxicity and general occupant health, and utilization of daylight in interior spaces. Material considerations are important, not just in the sustainable characteristics of the materials themselves but also in the assembly of the materials into building components that work together to create sustainable options. Energy-efficient windows are an example of such a construction: two panes of specially formulated or coated **low-E glass** are separated by an insulating space. Material considerations are also part of integrated design elements interacting with each other in the environment. For instance, high-albedo or light reflective materials reduce light absorption if a designer wants to reduce heat gain or utilize daylight more effectively. Dense materials assist **passive solar** systems by absorbing radiant heat from the sun during the day and releasing it at night, evening out the load on heating systems with constructions such as a **trombe wall** or dense flooring material. Building in accordance with sustainable principles used to be an option but changes in the International Building Code (IBC) will make such considerations mandatory, as sustainable building makes its way into local code requirements.

The United States Green Building Council (USGBC) has been a leader in defining sustainable principles, having developed the **Leadership in Energy and**

Environmental Design (LEED) system for evaluating the effectiveness of building designs in achieving sustainability. This system is separate from building codes and compliance with LEED standards is optional. The LEED system awards points for meeting specified criteria. Buildings can achieve a silver, gold, or platinum certification depending on how many sustainable characteristics are incorporated into the design.

Green, or sustainable, materials and products you specify will have one or more of the characteristics from Table 1.1. The more green characteristics that a product exemplifies, the greener it is. Few products can satisfy every category.

Table 1.1
Several characteristics contribute to a material's sustainability. An ideal material would meet all criteria but such a material is rare.

Characteristic	Meaning	Examples
Renewable	More of the material can be produced. Plant or animal based so can grow more. Recycled content that will continue to become available.	Lumber, jute, leather
Sustainable	The time and resources needed to produce the material.	Managed forestry
Recyclable	The material can be put to some other use at the end of its current use.	Used concrete can be broken and become aggregate in new concrete work
Recycled	Material that would have gone to a landfill is used as an ingredient in new products.	
	Down-cycling—Used products are turned into items of less value than the original item.	Old carpet turned into car bumpers for parking lots
	Up-cycling—Used products are turned into items of greater value than the original item.	Recycled newspaper turned into solid surfacing for countertops
	Cradle-to-cradle—Old products turned into new versions of themselves.	Carpet fiber reclaimed and turned into new carpet fiber
	Postconsumer—The item has been used and was destined for a landfill when it was diverted from the waste stream into a new purpose.	Aluminum cans recycled into aluminum for storm doors
	Preconsumer—Scraps from production are cycled back into the material stream at a fabricator's place of manufacture.	Glass trimmings from production are melted into new batches of glass
Durable	This refers to the physical fitness of the material for its intended location as well as the longevity of its design.	Stone mosaics in the Pantheon
Adaptability	The item can be reused in its current form in a new location.	Carpet tiles moved to a new facility
Low-embodied energy	Little energy was consumed in producing and transporting the item. Materials that are regionally manufactured or regionally harvested.	Using stone from a local quarry rather than an overseas source
Sustainably maintained	The material does not require excessive maintenance for its location.	Porcelain tile that can be easily maintained without the use of noxious chemicals
Nontoxic	Compounds that are unhealthy for humans and the environment are not used.	Specify inert components that do not off-gas VOCs so they do not affect indoor air quality (IAQ)
Biodegradable	Material that will deteriorate harmlessly into safe components.	Specify plant-based materials that are not treated with toxic chemicals and will degrade into harmless components when exposed to living organisms if possible
Carbon neutral	Production of the material does not increase the amount of greenhouse gas in the atmosphere.	Select materials that have low energy use or manufacturers that offset carbon dioxide by, say, planting trees
Remanufactured	Material that is reworked to extend its life.	Carpeting is one example of a material that can be overprinted to refresh its appearance if it "uglies out" before it wears out
Reuse	Secondhand items salvaged from other sites.	Architectural salvage and furniture have established markets so convenient reuse of some product categories is available

When researching how green a product is, consider not just the product characteristics; consider the manufacture, installation, use and maintenance, and removal and disposal. Is it green along the course of its entire life? The life of the goods includes the following:

- Manufacturing—Were environmental considerations such as pollution and water and energy use addressed in the manufacturing process?
- Packing and shipping—Was minimal packaging used and were shipping distances short?
- Preparation and installation—Was minimal site prep required and was it free of chemicals that **outgas**?
- Use and maintenance—Can it be used without damaging people and the environment and be maintained without solvents?
- Removal and disposal—Can it be removed without excessive damage and reused or recycled?

Nontoxic Materials

Green design has quite naturally assumed the issue of toxicity (the degree to which a substance is poisonous) within its domain, since what is bad for our systems is often also bad for **ecosystems**. This materials topic centers on **volatile organic compounds (VOCs)**, the chemical sensitivities of individuals, and **carcinogens**.

Because VOCs are volatile, they can change states from a solid or liquid to a gas. These gasses and **particulates** together affect indoor air quality (IAQ), frequently referred to only as IAQ in literature. The solvents in paint thinner are an example of such compounds. You would never dream of sipping these solvents from a cup, but you are ingesting them when you breathe the fumes of these volatile compounds after they have changed from a liquid to a gas. Because these compounds are organic, they can interact with our bodies' processes and mechanisms. There is a wide range of tolerance among different people. While some people exhibit dramatic evidence of the negative effect of particular chemicals in their environment, others report no ill effects because of their bodies' current ability to achieve a healthy stasis. While IAQ or indoor air quality can be improved with more sophisticated ventilation equipment that manages how much fresh air is provided, **air changes per hour** or **ACH**, it is much better to specify materials that do not emit these organic compounds. **Sick building syndrome** is another issue related to air quality. For a variety of reasons, some buildings have a higher incidence of illness among the people who work or live in them. Often the culprit is mold in HVAC ducts but chemicals in the air are also frequently to blame.

Common Carcinogens

While the following list is not exhaustive, carcinogens and other toxic materials often specified by interior designers include the following:

- *Antimony*—Found in fire-retardant finishes—is an ingredient in halides, used in flame retardants.
- *Arsenic*—Found in pressure-treated lumber—is a naturally occurring heavy metal used as a preservative. Long-term exposure to arsenic has been linked to cancer of the bladder, lungs, skin, kidneys, nasal passages, liver, and prostate.
- *Bisphenol A (BPA)*—Found in paints, coatings, and adhesives—is responsible for reproductive dysfunction.
- *Cadmium*—Found in plastics and pigments—is a heavy metal used in pigments for red, orange, and yellow and causes brittle bones and kidney damage.
- *Chlorofluorocarbons (CFCs)*—Found in solvents—is a synthetic chemical that reacts with chemicals high in the atmosphere resulting in the depletion of the earth's protective ozone layer.
- *Dioxin*—Generated during the manufacture of materials containing polyvinyl chloride (flooring, wallcoverings, paint, plastic liners, etc.) and in bleaching and incineration as part of the production of materials used in interiors—is a component of plastic released when it breaks down or is burned in landfills. Dioxin is toxic and bioaccumulative and causes endocrine problems.
- *Formaldehydes*—Found in sheet building products, textile resins, and glues—is a cancer-causing, volatile organic compound outgassed in paints, glue adhesives, and laminates.
- *Furans*—Found in some grouting products, in the energy derived from burning fuel, and used in the **synthesis** of nylon—are bioaccumulative toxins that are also suspected carcinogens.

- *Halogenated compounds*—Commonly used to make flame retardants and in polyurethane foam for upholstery—are persistent bioaccumulative toxic chemicals thought to cause neurological and reproductive problems and are banned by the EU.
- *Lead*—Found in existing paint finishes—is a toxic, bioaccumulative heavy metal.
- *Mercury*—Found in electrical switches and fluorescent lamps—is a toxic, bioaccumulative heavy metal.
- *Perfluorinated chemicals (PFCs)*—Found in stain repellents—are thought to cause thyroid problems and some cancers.
- *Polychlorinated biphenyls (PCBs)*—Used in paint, plastic, and rubber—are bioaccumulative (are not flushed from our bodies and do not break down in the food chain) and are cancer-causing in humans.
- *Polyvinyl chloride (PVC)*—Common plastic, 70 percent of which is used in building industries and found in fabric, furniture, and finishes—is linked to the production of dioxin in the atmosphere and requires many harmful additives (heavy metals and plasticizers like phthalates).

According to the Environmental Protection Agency (EPA), volatile organic compounds are up to ten times more concentrated in interior environments than in the open. Another problem being encountered comes from the synergy or interaction between two or more different chemicals. Two chemicals that may outgas are not problematic by themselves, but when they meet each other they bond forming a chemical with different properties than the two original constituents and this third chemical can be problematic.

Protection Against Toxins

Vigilance against toxins prompts us to:

1. Specify inert material that will not chemically react or interact with organic systems; material with no VOCs.
2. Specify material that will outgas quickly or has had enough time to outgas sufficiently.
3. Encapsulate the material in a nontoxic material.

Environmental Costs

Design and building decisions are always price driven. The value of the result is compared to the cost of acquiring it. This cost is typically evaluated in terms of dollars alone, which is incomplete for obvious reasons. When comparing two materials you should consider a number of factors beyond cost. For example, materials and finishes that outgas not only harm end users, they harm the fabricators who handle them and they poison the environment.

> **Point of Emphasis 1.1**
> What is the difference between green design and toxicity?
>
> Toxicity directly addresses the affect that the product's "ingredients" have on the human body but, interestingly enough, oftentimes the things that are bad for human beings are also bad for ecosystems. When you avoid toxic materials for your client's sake you are usually preserving the health of the environment as well.

When calculating the full costs, consider not only the price in dollars but also the sustainability (minimization of harm to the ecological balance of the earth) and social impacts. Sometimes companies circumvent high environmental safety standards and workplace safety standards in the U.S. by moving manufacturing to places where polluters are not prosecuted and workers are not protected by laws requiring a living wage or safe working conditions. Companies may locate facilities in impoverished areas where they provide jobs, but if they do not contribute to the formation of a stable community in the process, they may pull out of that area to find workers who will work for lower pay, for instance, leaving it impoverished once more. Companies committed to sustainability also build stable communities around them; it is not enough to say they are improving an area just because they are currently providing people with jobs. Costs in dollars, environmental impact, and social costs should all be part of your accounting when you compare potential materials and products for your projects.

THIRD-PARTY ORGANIZATIONS

When you are evaluating products and materials you will look beyond claims made by manufacturers themselves, searching for third-party verification of claims of sustainability, safety, and quality. There is a distinction among first-party organizations that have an immediate interest in a product, secondary organizations that have an association with a product, and third-party organizations that have no interest in a particular product. For example, for wood flooring a first-party agent would be the manufacturer of the flooring. A second-party agent would be the National Wood Association, whose members are people in the wood flooring industry. A third-party agent would be an organization like the Forest Stewardship Council (FSC), an independent, nonprofit association established to promote the responsible management of the world's forests. Third-party agents play a crucial role in the selection and evaluation of surfaces and items that you'll specify. Independent organizations that test materials for sustainable and safety characteristics should be free of bias as they develop quality standards, make educational resources available, or evaluate products. Sometimes industry organizations fulfill this role. There are numerous organizations, each with its own mission and emphasis, contributing to product data serving the design industry. Table 1.2 (opposite) lists second- and third-party organizations that pertain to materials for interior design. This list is a sampling of a vast organization structure supporting the building industries. For instance, a couple of organizations focused on wood are included here, however there are over 50 such organizations in the U.S. devoted to wood products.

> **Point of Emphasis 1.2**
> Even if testing is performed by objective third parties, it will be ordered and paid for by the manufacturer, who will specify the tests they would like to have performed.

Environmental costs are more complicated to calculate and evaluate than costs in dollars. Remember that third-party evaluation of these, and other costs, may be more reliable than calculations performed by the manufacturer of a product that you are considering for your project. See Table 1.3 for costs that may be global, regional, or local.

Table 1.3
Environmental costs for mismanagement of resources affect the earth and people at all scales.

Global Costs	Regional Costs	Local Costs
Ozone depletion	Land degradation	Eutrophication (oxygen depletion in water)
Global warming potential	Acidification potential (acid rain)	Toxicity in soil or water
Resource depletion	Upsetting ecosystems	Creation of photochemical oxidation (smog)
		Pollution (air, water, sound)

BUDGETS AND ESTIMATES

Once a reasonable budget has been drawn up, it is another guide to selections and design details as the project develops. Designers who specialize in a narrowly defined area of expertise are often very accurate when they estimate. Kitchen designers, for example, depend on good "guesses" because they proceed with the detailed design work *after* the contract has been executed (signed by the parties) with dollar amounts included. Office landscape designers have developed a similar expertise. Other kinds of designers prefer to wait until some of the design work has been completed and approved by the client before beginning to budget.

Clients are naturally interested in the expected cost of their project at the outset. Generally speaking there are three degrees of exactness to meet the nature of the need that prompted the request: (1) ballpark estimates; (2) cost comparisons; and (3) actual costs for purchase. You will want to appropriately match the estimate that you discuss with them to the phase of the project so you are as accurate as possible. In the early stages there are too many unknowns to be exact and in the later stages, your estimates are understood as a firm price. Ballpark estimates, cost comparisons, and these three degrees of exactness all have their proper place in the discussion.

Table 1.2
Designers are like the conductor in an orchestra assembling all the parts of the piece. You will rely on experts of all kinds to make the best decisions for your client. There are many second- and third-party organizations that are experts in their own topics that you will want to know about in order to get the information you need to make selections.

Organization	Function	References Include	Industry Affiliation	Information for You
American Association of Textile Chemists and Colorists (AATCC) www.aatcc.org	Provides test method development for quality control	Research papers and student resources	People in textile industry	Explains tests for textiles
American Concrete Institute (ACI) www.concrete.org	Produces concrete-related codes, specifications, and reports; administers certification programs in the concrete industry	Concrete products and installation	Contractors, suppliers, and manufacturers	Extensive research on materials and best practices
American National Standards Institute (ANSI) www.ansi.org	Development of standard for materials and associated practices	Independent third party focused on a broad range of materials and products	None	Description of the organization
American Society for Testing and Materials (ASTM) www.astm.org	Tests materials and describes quality standards	Variety of building and finishing materials	None	Research abstracts
Americans with Disabilities Act (ADA) www.ada.gov	Defines configurations for places that will be accessible to people with disabilities	Info-rich site includes the act in its entirety and related issues	None	The site is not restricted and all info is accessible, including checklists for your projects
Architectural Woodwork Institute (AWI) www.awinet.org	Development of quality standards and education of members	Architectural woodwork and case goods	Manufacturers and suppliers	Podcasts about LEED, back issues of magazine
Association for Contract Textiles (ACT) www.contracttextiles.org	Education and promotion of voluntary performance and sustainability guidelines	Contract textiles	Wholesalers and contract textile trades	Whitepapers, numerous links
Brick Industry Association (BIA) www.gobrick.com	Technical, business, and legislative information	Brick and related products	Brick producers, suppliers, and installers	Extensive information on many aspects of brick industry
Building Stone Institute (BSI) www.buildingstoneinstitute.org	Provides information to design and building trades as well as suppliers of natural stone	Natural stone	Importers and tradespeople	Sustainability research, general stone info
Business and Institutional Furniture Manufacturer's Association (BIFMA) www.bifma.org	Develops standards for North American office furniture	Office furniture	Manufacturers, suppliers, and service providers associated with commercial furniture	Industry news from practice issues to legislation in archived newsletters
Carpet and Rug Institute (CRI) www.carpet-rug.org	Disseminates information to consumers and industry professionals	Textile floor coverings	Textile floor-covering manufacturers	Extensive research on material and installation guidelines
Ceramic Tile Institute of America (CTIOA) www.ctioa.org	Educates installers and relays manufacturer information to the public	All tile products	Members are manufacturers, suppliers, and installers	Extensive research on materials and construction best practices

(continued)

Table 1.2 (continued)

Designers are like the conductor in an orchestra assembling all the parts of the piece. You will rely on experts of all kinds to make the best decisions for your client. There are many second- and third-party organizations that are experts in their own topics that you will want to know about in order to get the information you need to make selections.

Organization	Function	References Include	Industry Affiliation	Information for You
Concrete Countertop Institute (CCI) www.concretecountertopinstitute.com	Provides consumer info and training for fabricators	Concrete countertops and stone	Concrete fabricators	Information-rich site includes videos of production
Concrete Network www.concretenetwork.com	Provides information about technical and design issues related to concrete	Concrete in all forms, interior and exterior	All trades and vendors supplying concrete product and labor	Lots of information and videos related to concrete work
Construction Specifications Institute (CSI) www.csinet.org	Indexing system for specifications	Many varied products indexed for specification writers	None	Master format numbering system and other info
Energy Star www.energystar.gov	Rates appliances on energy consumption	Electrical appliances	None	All kinds of tips for saving energy
Glass Association of North America (GANA) www.glasswebsite.com	Technical information and education to glass trades	Flat glass and safety glass	Members are glass manufacturers	Full technical papers related to glass
Greenguard Environmental Institute www.greenguard.org	Educates building trades and consumers about indoor air quality (IAQ)	Materials and installation products and practices that affect indoor air quality	None	Numerous research papers on broad spectrum of topics
Green Seal www.greenseal.org	Promotes the manufacture, purchase, and use of environmentally responsible products and services	Products and processes that are sustainable	None	Lots of information about sustainable products and methods for sustainable management
Hardwood Plywood and Veneer Association (HPVA) www.hpva.org	Information and sampling for hardwood	Suppliers of hardwood products	Represents hardwood, veneer, and plywood suppliers, specifiers, and producers	Reasonably priced information for sale
Hardwood Manufacturers Association www.hardwoodcouncil.com	Hardwood flooring	Information about hardwood species, floors, and finishes	Hardwood producers	Information for professional CEU training with self-test at end of each lesson
International Organization for Standardization (ISO) www.iso.org	Development of common international standards for materials and associated practices	Numerous organizations developing standards in individual countries contribute	Third party as well as organizations with an interest in developing trade	Information about ISO
International Code Council (ICC) www.iccsafe.org	Develops guidelines that are often adopted by jurisdictions developing their local codes	Building, safety, sustainability, and accessibility guidelines	Third-party agencies such as ASTM and USGBC	Information-rich site covering governance of numerous areas of interest to designers
Leadership in Energy and Environmental Design (LEED) www.usgbc.org	Establishes standards for sustainable design	Material and installation practices as well as building configuration suggestions	United States Green Building Council (USGBC)	Information pertaining to becoming a LEED professional
Marble Institute of America (MIA) www.marble-institute.com	Provides consumers and industry with information about natural stone materials and installation	Natural stone	Suppliers and installers	Information-rich site with research papers and videos

Mason Contractors Association of America (MCAA) www.masoncontractors.org	Political advocates for and education of masonry installers sponsoring certification programs	Brick and natural stone installation	Stone installers	Extensive basic information about brick masonry
Masonry Veneer Manufacturers Association (MVMA) www.masonryveneer.org	Develops technical, market, and performance information for the stone industry	Stone and brick veneer products	Stone and related products suppliers	Product and installation information
National Association of Architectural Metal Manufacturers (NAAMM) www.naamm.org	Education of metal fabricators, development of performance standards and advocacy	Metal fabricators, architectural metal (like doors), and furniture	Manufacturers and suppliers	Information about metal products, production, and finishing
National Ornamental and Miscellaneous Metals Association (NOMMA) www.nomma.org	Education of metalworkers and advocacy for metal industries	Metals and metal finishes	Metalworkers	Basic and consumer-oriented info
National Terrazzo and Mosaic Association (NTMA) www.ntma.com	Establishes specifications and standards	Terrazzo and mosaic installation	Installers and fabricators of terrazzo surfaces	Literature of promotional nature
National Wood Flooring Association (NOFMA or NWFA) www.nwfa.org	Defines standards for quality wood products and their installation	General information about wood species, definitions of quality standards for material, and best practices for installation	Wood flooring suppliers and installers	Few student resources but an important organization
North American Laminate Flooring Association (NALFA) www.nalfa.com	Established to define and maintain standards of quality for laminate floors	Laminate flooring products and installation	Laminate flooring manufacturers and installers	Explanation of quality determinants by ASTM
Resilient Floor Covering Institute (RFCI) www.rfci.com	Technical and best practices information	Resilient flooring	Manufactures and suppliers	Full technical papers
Tile Council of North America (TCNA) www.tileusa.com	Current info on best practices and legislation for tile industry	Rigid tile materials and installation	Manufacturers, suppliers, and installers	Research and information
Underwriters Laboratory (UL) www.ul.com	Third-party safety testing of material products	Broad variety of products	None	Few student resources but an important organization
United States Hide, Skin and Leather Association (USHSLA) www.ushsla.org	Government organization promoting leather trade	Legislative and business information related to leather	Leather suppliers	Legislative and business information
Wallcoverings Association (WA) www.wallcoverings.org	Distribution of information in the wallcovering industry	Wallcovering	Manufacturers, distributors, and suppliers	Technical data, estimating guides
World Floor Covering Association (WFCA) www.wfca.org	Provides industry partners and consumers with information about floor coverings	Both product and installation standards	Floor-covering manufacturers, sellers, and installers	Consumer information and visualization tools

Ballpark Estimates

A ballpark estimate is delivered when a client is considering whether or not to pursue a particular notion. It is logically delivered as a range and is based on past experience with similar projects. You may be able to simply tell your client that such-and-such a project is likely to cost between $60 to $90 per square foot (SF) for furnishing and soft goods; that a kitchen remodeling can cost between $100 and $300 per SF, etc. This may be enough information for your client to make a decision about whether to proceed with a project.

> **Helpful Hint 1.1**
>
> Over time you will get a sense of how much certain installation tasks cost. These costs are usually estimated based on time required to complete the installation. They are often calculated on half-day increments that include travel time. There are construction estimating software packages used by many contractors but rather than take the time to learn and set them up you might want to purchase (or borrow from your library) the *RSMeans Cost Data* book or a similar publication. Keep in mind that labor prices per man hour vary across the country so labor prices in New York City will be higher than in Jellico, Tennessee.

If you do not have personal experience that you can rely on because the project is not like anything that you have done before, you may need to do some research to come up with some usable figures for consideration, but if it leads to your winning a job, you will certainly be glad that your numbers were fairly accurate.

Cost Comparisons

You may make cost comparisons between material options to get the client headed in the right direction. These comparisons can help your client as they approve selections during the design phase.

Life-Cycle Costs

Life-cycle costing includes the cost of the material and installation along with maintenance costs over the expected life of the material, the cost of removal and disposal of existing material, and eventually removing and disposing of the material currently under consideration. When accounting for life-cycle costs, add together the cost of:

- Material
- Prepwork required
- Installation
- Maintenance per year multiplied by the number of years the material is predicted to last
- Cost of removing and disposing of the material
- Cost of restoring surfaces to receive other materials after removal

Divide that total cost over the life of the material by the number of years the material is likely to last to derive an annual cost for the material. This number can form a valid basis for comparing two materials to see which one will be the more economical over its life.

Actual Costs for Purchase

When your client is ready to implement plans that you have produced and selections that you have made, you will produce contracts, proposals, work orders, specifications, requests for bids, or other documents that will eventually cause the work to occur. Unlike the other two kinds of estimates you provide, these documents of actual costs for purchase are legally binding. They must be very complete and precise. Once they have been agreed to, the work must be provided and paid for as stipulated in the document. Your specification is the basis for the purchase contract. Materials are sold in units of measure. The unit of measure varies; materials are sold by the square foot, lineal foot, roll, etc. When calculating the purchase cost you will need to know how the material is sold in order to estimate for your budget.

PROGRAMMING CONSIDERATIONS

In addition to the influence of codes, standards, guidelines, and costs, designers take into account numerous considerations that are particular to their clients' unique sites. Aesthetic expression is often foremost in their minds as they finalize a selection. Approaches

Table 1.4 Typical units of measure for items you will estimate and specify.

Unit of Measure	Items Sold in Such Units
Each	FF&E (furniture, fixtures, and equipment): desks and kitchen cabinets, toilets, light fixtures
	Fittings like faucets, component parts to systems such as accessory parts for light fixtures
	Optional trims like decorative tile pieces
Square foot	Most types of flooring (except carpet), field tile for walls and floors; paint coverage is estimated this way although paint is actually sold by the liquid measure, like pint, quart, or gallon
Lineal foot	Millwork trim, vinyl base
Square yard	Carpeting
Lineal yard	Fabric and most commercial wallcovering
Roll	Wallpaper, particularly for the residential market, is priced by the roll (but often sold in two-roll increments as a continuous piece)
Bolt	Fabric and commercial wall covering that you need in large quantities may be sold to you in full bolts at a lower price than when you are buying yards cut from full bolts
Job	Any material may be specified and defined as including all material required. For example if you sold "carpet installed in multipurpose room" it would be assumed that however much carpet was required, it would be provided under the agreement.

undertaken to select appropriate materials may be as generalized as principles of design or include more complex considerations involving marketing efforts or brand expression (marketing image of a product). You might want to ask yourself questions like the following:

- Where do I want visual emphasis?
- How can materials alter the distribution of visual weight throughout the space to balance it?
- How can sustainability be addressed with materials?
- How can material selections assist effective use of natural daylight, reflecting light, and minimizing glare?
- How can I specify to minimize toxins in the environment?
- How can I use materials to visually organize spaces to improve way-finding or to demarcate distinct functional areas within a large open area?
- How can material selections create the specific atmosphere called for in the space or express the brand to coincide with marketing efforts? How can they work to enhance a theme?
- How can materials be used to manage noise or direct sound functionally as would be desired for my project?
- Which materials will work with the kind of maintenance the facility is likely to receive?

Other considerations are implied by life-cycle cost factors. Issues like durability are obvious considerations. Logical assumptions pertaining to maintenance are also accounted for. Even though the lobby of a park district building and a fine hotel have many program points in common, the level of care that the park building would receive relative to the lobby of the hotel would not be equal, so material selections for each would vary. The hotel is a 24-hour facility operating 365 days a year, which also has implications for appropriate maintenance methods. Similarly, the emergency room at a hospital must be maintained while occupied, so materials that can be easily cleaned while people are present would be a programmatic consideration for facilities like these.

Material Units and Estimating

Material is sold in varying unit measures (increments in which a material is sold or estimated). Table 1.4 lists some materials that come in units you will use to estimate. Square-foot estimates are easy: measure the length and width of a surface and multiply both numbers together. Lineal feet and lineal yards are also simple to estimate. No matter how wide the material, it is sold by the lineal yard, so you will only measure how much length you need. Square yards are similarly uncomplicated. Determine the square-foot measurement and divide by nine to calculate square yards. Remember, when budgeting you should account for both the installation and the product in the price, either in the construction budget or as a separate line item accompanying the material proposal, because installation prices vary. For example, a stone tile and a porcelain tile may be comparable in price for the material but the stone tile will cost nearly twice as much to install.

GLOBAL CONSIDERATIONS

Global considerations, or issues pertaining to design that affect people and places beyond the immediate area, are defined from different angles. Business, humanitarian, and design considerations are prominent in discussions of global thinking. A designer who is working on a project that assembles people and material resources from around the globe is involved in "global design." This will require an understanding of how climate varies because that will indicate particular design solutions. An understanding of other cultures is important for the configuration of your plan, as is an understanding of the indigenous materials, those native to the area, which you might specify and how the people in that culture are likely to interact with you during the implementation phase of your project. Another critical component of designing globally is being able to predict how end users will respond to your designs. This angle of global thinking requires that you set aside your own preferences and frame of reference.

A designer who is thinking globally will not simply transport a western aesthetic to a distant culture and imagine that they have truly accounted for all global implications inherent in the project. The designer who is thinking globally may also reference design solutions that originate in neither the designer's home base nor the project site, but rather in another locale entirely. For instance, a designer working on a project site for a hot climate may look at solutions for keeping cold air out in a cold climate, in order to meet the needs of their project's design program. You will perform research on culture, vernacular architecture, climate, local materials, and many other topics so that your own horizons are broadened to include options beyond what is familiar to you from your experience in your home country.

Humanitarian considerations will hone your focus onto conditions of production in the locale where you will be sourcing material. What are the conditions under which the material is produced? Are they safe for workers and the environment, or are working conditions hazardous and waste from production disposed of carelessly, damaging the environment where the workers live? What kind of contribution does production make to the local economy? Does production strengthen the local economy and raise the standard of living in a sustainable way, or is it likely that foreign manufacturing concerns could divert business to a different locale to pursue lower labor costs, devastating any gains that might have been realized? This investigation is complicated when a product that you are specifying is processed in several different places along its production route, having been harvested in one place, formed in another, and finished in yet another. As an example of the issues that you might encounter in such an investigation, according to the United Nations International Children's Emergency Fund (UNICEF), approximately 158 million children participate in child labor, often working in hazardous conditions.

Helpful Hint 1.2

Third-party organizations are often a good source of information about industry-specific considerations that you should keep in mind while determining what your criteria should be as you search for appropriate products.

Another prominent angle on global thinking pertains to design. How would not only local designers approach and solve the problem at hand, but what would be the approach of people from distant places as well? Sometimes when you break a design program down into component parts, rather than approaching it only in the broadest strokes, you have access to more ideas. For instance, you may find a water-conservation idea used in a northern area that pertains to your subtropic client site.

The design history of a client's locale, as it spans time and distance, will be reviewed by the designer who is thinking globally. You will employ materials and methods that may be new to you and explore solutions from outside your own building culture and the building culture of the project site. You will access potential solutions from around the globe.

MANAGING THE SPECIFICATION

After you have selected materials for your project, you must evaluate and manage information about them. We tend to think of structuring the **specification** as something that occurs after the selection has been finalized but if, from the start, you think of your selection in terms of what must be communicated about it, the specification can also be used as a thinking tool. As you proceed from first contact with a likely material to detailing the installation, you might realize that complications inherent in the selection make it less feasible. Whether you use checklists or specifications to organize your thinking, you will need a framework for analyzing selections. Thinking of each selection as an eventual specification will help you organize information that you will need anyway as the selection process moves forward.

Table 1.5
Specification content will vary with your project needs and governing mandates from stakeholders.

Open	Generic specification that identifies a product and describes the installation process and/or results but does not list a specific vendor or manufacturer.
Closed	Provides all the information that is included in an open spec but in addition to that, a particular supplier or manufacturer is identified and the supplier's/manufacturer's product that is to be used on the project is identified.
Performance	Describes what the completed installation must accomplish. For example if the completed installation of floor surfacing must provide a certain level of slip resistance or emit a restricted amount of VOCs, those standards will be described along with how the installation is to be tested to prove that the requirement has been met.
Reference	If material must comply with standardized testing, which is to be performed prior to installation, you may reference the test and the score that must be achieved. For instance, if a coating must meet an NFPA 286, UL 1715, and 2009 IBC 803.1.2 you would reference those tests in your spec.

The "Spec"

You will need to describe the products and labor required to complete the installation. Specifications ("specs") break down into basic types that may be combined into a single spec. An open specification describes the material and installation but omits mention of any specific manufacturer. This allows the bidders to provide the most economical materials. An open specification is typically required for governmental projects or other instances where the lowest cost for the installation is more important than a particular product solution. A closed specification also lists labor and materials but will reference a particular manufactured product. A performance specification lists the functional outcomes desired, but no product is described. It would be very unusual for a designer to write a specification this way but you will likely include performance stipulations in any spec that you write. For instance, an open or closed spec might include performance specifications or make reference to testing that is to be performed.

Table 1.5 distinguishes between the different kinds of specs that designers might write. The open spec requires the most description but is necessary for government work or other work where you want to give all parties an equal opportunity to bid. The closed spec gives you the most control over the product used. There is a semi-open spec that relies on the description of a unique item by manufacture item number but then with the addition of the words *or approved equal* it can be opened up to alternative product suggestions to control costs or product lead times.

Specification books for projects can have hundreds of specifications and can be several hundred pages in length. Large spec books are organized like other kinds of books, with a table of contents. The Construction Specifications Institute (CSI) has devised an organizational structure for project specification books that has been adopted by many firms that design large building projects. It suggests an "order of appearance" for material specifications. According to this system, the sequence that orders your specs will be listed as a series of three pairs of numbers that move from broadest scope to narrowest. So, early in the design process you know that a wall will be painted but you have not yet determined what decorative finish you will eventually specify. So you know that it is division 09 (finishes) and that decorative finishes are subgroup 94, so your spec will be CSI # 09 94 until you decide that it will be, for example, faux finish, which is 16. Now you can complete the numbering as 09 94 16 and locate it in your spec book between stained finishes (09 93 23) and antigraffiti finishes (09 96 23). Contractors and other parties to your project will know where to look for that specification.

The CSI format includes labor and materials so it simplifies the connection between specifications and construction management. Building Information Modeling or Management (BIM) connects computer-aided drafting (CAD) drawings to specs and to construction scheduling information, simplifying, somewhat, building construction management.

Master Specification

In addition to the CSI format you may work for a firm that structures individual specifications based on a master specification, prepared by the manufacturer or spec writer for modification by the designer in order to meet the unique needs of a client's job, commonly called a master spec. Specifications are more than a description of what you need for a portion of your project. They are also understood to define a contract, so precise language is required when composing a spec. You don't want to leave anything out or leave anything open to interpretation. Because specifications span the topics of selections and contracts, many designers use master specifications or specification formats. Some of the master specs that you will find and use are simply templates that you "fill in" to complete a specification. Other master specs that you will use will be generated by product manufacturers to help you specify their product. Even though these specs are more complete than master spec templates, you will still modify them for your specific job requirements and you will still be responsible for their clarity and completeness. Never issue a spec that you do not fully comprehend or one that contains references that you have not looked up.

Master or template specifications are generic specifications that are modified by individual firms to describe materials that are part of a specific client project. They are sometimes prepared by organizations. For example, the National Wood Flooring Association (NOFMA) has prepared generic specs pertaining to wood flooring products. The master spec that you might use as a guide for writing your own spec might have been written by a company like the Association of Researchers in Construction Management (ARCOM), whose business is writing specs that they sell to others, usually to manufacturers who pay ARCOM to write a specification for their unique product.

SPECIFYING

Dissecting the master spec: The general organization of master specs varies slightly but information that you provide in a spec may include any of that contained in Sample Spec 1.1 that follows.

PROCESS

The interior designer is often the hub of the materials selection, so coordination between all parties often falls on the designer. The organization of the process may take different forms that affect how much detail is required for specification records. Table 1.6 sums up the differences distinguishing each type of organization. As you move down the list from design-bid-build to owner-build there is some likelihood that your level of responsibility for managing selections will decrease. More responsibility = more time = higher design fees.

Table 1.6 The structure of job contracts affects your approach to the work and project management.

Contract Organization	Characteristics	Implications for Materials Management
Design-bid-build	Custom design completed prior to bidding by multiple bidders	• Selections completed prior to bidding • More work performed "up front" • Detailed spec records
Design-negotiate-build	Custom design completed prior to contract with single bidder	• Selections may be made during bidding • Management of selections may be shared • Detailed spec records for all materials selected by designer
Design-build	The contractor and designer are the same entity and custom design is documented only as necessary to communicate with tradespeople	• Selections may be made even during construction • Designer/contractor manages selections • Specifications for owner approval
Owner-build	Custom design is built by resourceful owner acting as general contractor	• Selections will be completed per your contract • Owner manages selections • Specifications prepared for client approval

SAMPLE SPEC 1.1

Part 1 General Information

1.1 Related Documents

A. This includes references that must be accessed in order to comprehend the entirety of the spec. The items that you describe here might be drawings or data that is to be kept as part of the definitions of the spec.

1.2 Summary

A. Describe any work that is related to the work in the spec. If another trade must perform part of the work you would identify that work as Related Work Specified Elsewhere. An example of this would be the electrical work required to complete an order for motorized drapery. The electrical work is part of the installation but is provided by the electrician, not the drapery workroom. However, the drapery workroom has an interest in the specifications that the electrician is receiving about the electrical work to be provided, so you would reference the specification to the electrician in this spec as related work.

B. Describe the scope of the project defining the work to be performed and the identity of the party that will be responsible for each item mentioned and the materials that are to be provided as part of the contract.

C. Related work describing the work of other trades that must precede the work described or will come after, affecting the work described.

1.3 References

A. If codes or best practices standards defined by trade or third-party organizations are to be part of the required work, reference them here.

1.4 Contractor Submittals

A. If you require shop drawings, samples, or mock-ups describe them here. If samples or mock-ups may become part of the completed work say so in this section.

B. If verification data must be provided to certify that the installation conforms to fire code, meets LEED requirements, proves that the workroom is insured, or meets other certification, describe the documents that will satisfy this condition.

C. Other paperwork that may be required by others pertaining to the installation such as installation instructions or recommended maintenance.

1.5 Quality Assurance

A. Describe the minimum experience the workers who will be providing the material and installation are required to have, credentials that they must hold, the minimum performance threshold that the installation must achieve in testing.

B. It is typical to require that materials be delivered to the site in the manufacturers' unopened containers so you can be sure there are not substitutions that would compromise the quality of your installation.

1.6 Delivery, Storage, and Handling

A. Describe how to get the materials on-site in a condition that renders them suitable for a quality installation. Some materials are damaged by freezing temperatures, moisture, or other environmental conditions that you want to prevent. Material may have to acclimate to site conditions for a specified period of time or be protected from dust, dirt, or other potential damage, so use this section to describe all the conditions that must be maintained in order to ensure the material is in good condition throughout the installation.

1.7 Maintenance of Installation

A. The material will likely have to be protected from damage after installation until the owner takes possession of it, usually upon completion of all the work. Describe the conditions that are required. You might describe how to cover the material, how long it is to remain protected, if a minimum temperature must be maintained at the site or other conditions must be present until the owner takes possession. Describe those conditions here.

Part 2 Products

2.1 General Information

A. List all materials that are to be provided as part of the contract including materials unique to your job as well as materials required to complete the installation. For example, all fasteners and adhesives required for installation should be identified as being included in the contract.

B. Installers are expected to provide their own "tools of the trade" and come equipped with their own ladders, shims, braces, etc., required to complete the installation.

C. The quality of each material provided should be described, including any reference specifications or testing standards. An ASTM standard is an example of a reference that you might include in this section.

2.2 Manufacturers

A. List acceptable manufacturers. You may list only one manufacturer if you are writing a closed specification.

SAMPLE SPEC 1.1 (continued)

2.3 Products

A. Describe the product to be installed; include any item numbers.

B. Describe any related products that will be required, such as trims, sealants, membranes, etc.

C. Describe any work that must be performed on the material before, during, and after the installation. If the material must be cut to fit, polished, and sealed, such instructions would be part of your product description.

Part 3 Execution

3.1 Examination

A. Describe the condition that the material must be in if it is to be considered acceptable upon completion of the job. If it must be free of defect, acclimated to the site, or in another condition in order to ensure a satisfactory installation, describe it here so the installer can confirm prior to installing that the material will be acceptable. In the building industry, installation constitutes acceptance and there is no recourse for an unsatisfactory material after it has been installed.

B. Describe the condition that the site must be in before the installation can begin. Should the heating plant be fully functional? What work by others must be completed before the work described in this specification can commence?

3.2 Preparation

A. Describe work that must be performed under this contract (not related contracts mentioned earlier) to get the material or the site ready for installation.

3.3 Installation

A. There are different approaches that you might take for this section. You might describe the process to be followed or might describe the result that you require, or you may combine them. For example: You may say that the installer is to use a bubble level in the center of the unit to check that the installation is level. You might simply say that the installed material is to be level. You may combine the two and say that the material is to be demonstrably level by testing with a bubble level placed in the center of the installed unit.

B. If there are allowable tolerances describe them. In the above example you might say something like "do not exceed $3/32$" deviance from level in 10 feet or more."

3.4 Post Installation

A. Describe the condition that the installation should be in before the installer leaves the job site. If the materials must be cleaned to a certain standard, sealed, or protected, or other work performed under this contract, describe those conditions in precise language.

B. If scraps and waste are to be disposed of by persons executing this contract describe those procedures.

C. If you must sign off on the installation before it is to be considered to be complete, describe how that is to be arranged.

For the Connoisseur 1.1

Just as your client may purchase top-of-the-line products or economy products, he or she will also find that the marketplace provides varying degrees of project management service to go along with the provision of design ideas. Some design firms are simply furniture specifiers and others will produce novel design ideas and details. Your client may want "full-service" design and expect you to detail, specify, and manage the implementation of the design. Other clients understand that limiting your service will also limit your fees and may decide to economize there. It is crucial that both you and your client understand the scope of work in the same way or you may find yourself expected to deliver service that you did not mean to include in your agreement.

Some firms will only work on full-service contracts as a way of protecting their reputations by controlling every aspect of the job. These firms become known for their excellence and high prices. Other firms build a reputation out of providing only those services that they are uniquely qualified to provide and leave all the purchasing and implementation of the design to resellers and contractors.

The way you work must jibe with your price structure or you will find yourself waiting tables to support your design habit!

COLLABORATING

Collaboration begins very early in the design process, and in addition to designers, architects, clients, and contractors, design teams may include LEED-accredited professionals and **commissioning agents**, facility managers, manufacturers' reps, and others. Once your client has decided to proceed with the project, you may find yourself collaborating with varying combinations of tradespeople and professionals to complete the installation. It is a good idea to have a general idea of who bears what responsibility so you are addressing issues with the most logical person.

In order to keep the material selections moving forward, to ensure they are installed on time and properly, each party to the project has to meet his or her responsibilities as they pertain to the specifications of surfaces and items. Review Table 1.7 for the various parties to the project.

THE SUPPLY CHAIN

The supply of materials for a job is handled by a number of people. It's a good idea to understand who does what along the supply chain so you are interacting with the appropriate person depending on where you are in the selection process. The various suppliers include:

- *Manufacturers*—Make a product; assemble or fabricate materials for use in interiors.
- *Manufacturers representatives ("reps")*—Promote the use of these materials to designers and architects and may provide other services to promote the use of the products they represent, such as custom details and specification formats. Some reps do not sell product and will refer you to a dealer when you are ready to purchase.

Table 1.7
Projects are collaborative efforts. Even though roles are generally defined for all parties, the contract will clarify areas of overlap.

Who You'll Collaborate with as You Manage Material Selections	How? and/or Why?
Architect	Installation details and specifications will be transferred into the architect's documents so a single set is referenced rather than multiple drawings by different offices; collaborate on decisions about surfaces.
General contractor	The general will determine which trades will be required to install the surfacing materials that you select; you'll meet and answer questions and render decisions all along the production process.
Subcontractors	The subs will install the materials according to your directions, including following manufacturer recommendations you forward to them as well as your custom installation details.
Other designers	If there are specialists on the job, you'll collaborate with them in the selection of materials. These specialists include those listed here.
	Acoustic consultants will have special material requirements for their systems and you will make selections from among their recommendations or find new materials that comply with their needs.
	Lighting consultants depend on reflectivity of surface for successful designs so you will interact with them as you select colors and finishes.
	LEED consultants advise and document the project's sustainability. You will submit information about your selections for their records as well as work with them to locate appropriate materials.
	Office systems suppliers will organize the components of panel and desk systems. You will make your selections for these items from their standard offerings.
	Kitchen or millwork designers must coordinate their materials and finishes with the rest of your project so you will select from standard offerings or work with them to develop custom finishes
Client	The client approves of all materials and finishes prior to incorporating that material into the specs. Some firms have the client sign an acknowledgment of their approval.

- *Dealers/distributors/vendors*—Sell material to trades (including designers, architects, contractors, and retailers). The distributor may offer the service of reviewing the materials list to ensure that it has all the required pieces to complete the installation. These are the people who respond to the designer's request for proposal (RFP). Some distributors do not provide services other than managing the sale to the trades but most will not sell to end users.
- *Resellers and retailers*—Sell material to end users. Retailers may also offer design services or may only sell product. They may sell to end users and designers or contractors. Designers and contractors prefer to do business with vendors who extend a trade discount (or charge the end users a higher price).

Some supply chains are short, such as the millworker making cabinetry sold directly to the end user. When this happens, all of the above functions are performed by one person; your millworker is the manufacturer, the rep, the distributor, and retailer. Some supply chains are long; a resin panel material may be represented by each of the different individuals described above in the chain. When you contact a manufacturer about their product they may refer you to a rep who will educate you about the product and then pass you along to a dealer to work on the particulars required for pricing. If the dealer does not install, they may recommend installers who have experience with their product so you can assemble the labor costs along with the material costs for the product. If it is common for a particular material to be sold as part of an assembly as is the case for glass, wood, and other such materials, you may contract with the fabricator who will sell the material, fabrication, and installation for a lump sum. In the case of the above-mentioned resin panels, you may never learn the cost of the material, it will be buried in the cost of the whole job.

PROJECT ORGANIZATION

After reviewing the above information, it is easy to see that this industry is complex and that in addition to the people who you see at the job site, there are many other participants, each with their own interests and responsibilities. The designer will constantly evaluate the need for, and form of, communication with the different participants while managing selections. Some of the product information that you collect must be shared with the client, other information with the contractors, etc. Review the example in Figure 1.2 showing a rather generic manufacturer's spec for carpet indicating who in the project would be likely to receive what information listed there. Some of the information is for you, to help you make a decision, other information is of interest to your client, some to the vendor, etc. Realize that the type of information that you share with the various parties will vary from job to job. On a given job, it may be the case that your client demands a lot of information and on another job, you may be working with a client who is only interested in the broad strokes and prefers not to get bogged down with minute details of the spec. Some installers prefer to have more information than others. This content and organization may be your call, or may be determined by office protocol. In any case, you will be responsible for determining how much information is required and where to draw the line to avoid "oversaturating" the people who will receive the information that you compile.

There are a number of tasks that the designer performs to manage the specifications, beginning with the options that the designer presents to the client and ending with the completion of the punch list. Material options will be selected that meet the criteria established in the design program. They are presented to the client and recommendations are made to help the client to make a good selection from the choices presented.

After the selection has been finalized, pricing will be confirmed. It may be the case that up to this point the designer's material estimates, called takeoffs, have been used for price comparisons and a ballpark estimate from one installer has been used as the installation cost. If the pricing for purposes of comparison has been assembled this way you will now meet with the selected installer, review the site conditions, and receive a firm price for the work, along with the precise quantity of material that the installer needs to complete the job. If your firm will be ordering the material, you will order the quantity requested by the installer. If the installer will order the material, they are likely to deliver the bid as material installed. With all the firm price quotes on hand, the material order can now proceed.

Regardless of who places the order for the materials, the designer is responsible for reviewing and approving samples and shop drawings. The shop drawings are drawings for custom items and custom constructions that document all the details that must be worked out before fabrication can begin. Custom work frequently requires the production of shop drawings.

Specifications

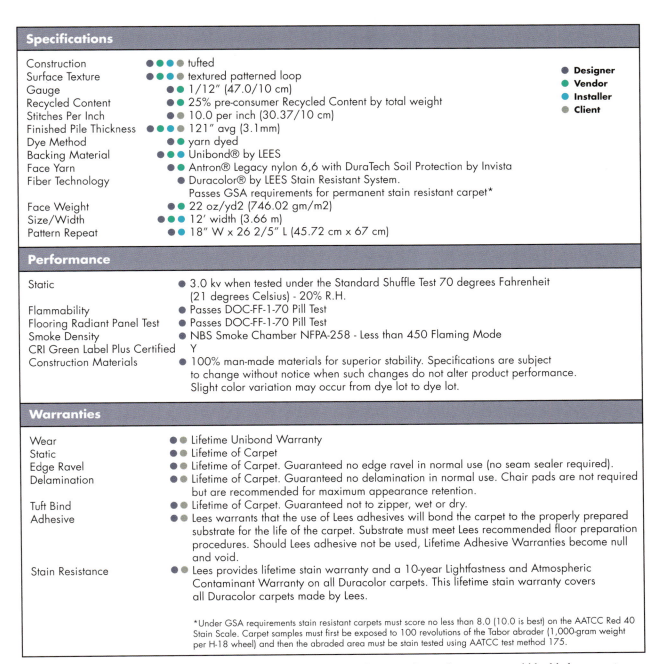

Legend: ● Designer ● Vendor ● Installer ● Client

Construction	●●●● (Designer, Vendor, Installer, Client)	tufted
Surface Texture	●●●● (Designer, Vendor, Installer, Client)	textured patterned loop
Gauge	●● (Designer, Vendor)	1/12″ (47.0/10 cm)
Recycled Content	●● (Designer, Vendor)	25% pre-consumer Recycled Content by total weight
Stitches Per Inch	●● (Designer, Client)	10.0 per inch (30.37/10 cm)
Finished Pile Thickness	●●●● (Designer, Vendor, Installer, Client)	121″ avg (3.1mm)
Dye Method	●● (Designer, Vendor)	yarn dyed
Backing Material	●●● (Designer, Vendor, Installer)	Unibond® by LEES
Face Yarn	●● (Designer, Vendor)	Antron® Legacy nylon 6,6 with DuraTech Soil Protection by Invista
Fiber Technology	● (Designer)	Duracolor® by LEES Stain Resistant System. Passes GSA requirements for permanent stain resistant carpet*
Face Weight	●● (Designer, Vendor)	22 oz/yd2 (746.02 gm/m2)
Size/Width	●●● (Designer, Vendor, Installer)	12′ width (3.66 m)
Pattern Repeat	●● (Designer, Installer)	18″ W x 26 2/5″ L (45.72 cm x 67 cm)

Performance

Static	● (Designer)	3.0 kv when tested under the Standard Shuffle Test 70 degrees Fahrenheit (21 degrees Celsius) - 20% R.H.
Flammability	● (Designer)	Passes DOC-FF-1-70 Pill Test
Flooring Radiant Panel Test	● (Designer)	Passes DOC-FF-1-70 Pill Test
Smoke Density	● (Designer)	NBS Smoke Chamber NFPA-258 - Less than 450 Flaming Mode
CRI Green Label Plus Certified		Y
Construction Materials	● (Designer)	100% man-made materials for superior stability. Specifications are subject to change without notice when such changes do not alter product performance. Slight color variation may occur from dye lot to dye lot.

Warranties

Wear	●● (Designer, Client)	Lifetime Unibond Warranty
Static	●● (Designer, Client)	Lifetime of Carpet
Edge Ravel	●● (Designer, Client)	Lifetime of Carpet. Guaranteed no edge ravel in normal use (no seam sealer required).
Delamination	●● (Designer, Client)	Lifetime of Carpet. Guaranteed no delamination in normal use. Chair pads are not required but are recommended for maximum appearance retention.
Tuft Bind	●● (Designer, Client)	Lifetime of Carpet. Guaranteed not to zipper, wet or dry.
Adhesive	●● (Designer, Client)	Lees warrants that the use of Lees adhesives will bond the carpet to the properly prepared substrate for the life of the carpet. Substrate must meet Lees recommended floor preparation procedures. Should Lees adhesive not be used, Lifetime Adhesive Warranties become null and void.
Stain Resistance	●● (Designer, Client)	Lees provides lifetime stain warranty and a 10-year Lightfastness and Atmospheric Contaminant Warranty on all Duracolor carpets. This lifetime stain warranty covers all Duracolor carpets made by Lees.

*Under GSA requirements stain resistant carpets must score no less than 8.0 (10.0 is best) on the AATCC Red 40 Stain Scale. Carpet samples must first be exposed to 100 revolutions of the Tabor abrader (1,000-gram weight per H-18 wheel) and then the abraded area must be stain tested using AATCC test method 175.

FIGURE 1.2 Example of a generic manufacturer's spec for carpet, indicating who in the project would be likely to receive what information.

There are a number of sample types that you may review. One common sample is a finish sample. Finish samples are reviewed for wood finishes, sealants for tile and stone, as well as color samples of many different kinds. Another kind of sample is called a mock-up, which is a life-size construction. A cabinet door and drawer face may be constructed full scale to allow you to check proportions and details; a few pieces of tile may be adhered to a board and grouted so you can confirm the visual compatibility of the two materials installed, and possibly sealed as well. It will frequently be the case that production will not proceed until the samples, shop drawings, and mock-ups are approved or "signed off" (this sometimes means

Table 1.8
Interior designers must manage all phases of production from initial selection through inspection to close the punch list. Notice the flow of the management tasks and the time required. Some materials are staged in accordance with other work, such as plumbing. Plumbing valves and pipe, "roughs," go in when the project is in studs and the rest of the assembly, the faucets and handles, called the "trim," must wait until the walls are finished.

	Month											
	1	2	3	4	5	6	7	8	9	10	11	12
Light/Electrical												
Architectural			Select	Bid		Contract				Inspection	Punch list complete	
Decorative						Select		Bid, Contract	Sample		Inspection	Punch list complete
Plumbing	Select, Bid, Contract		Inspection					Contract			Inspection, Punch list complete	
Flooring												
Wood	Select				Bid	Contract	Sample	Inspection, Punch list complete				
Tile				Select, Bid	Select, Bid	Sample, Contract		Inspection	Punch list complete			
Stone	Select		Bid	Contract		Inspection	Punch list complete					
Resilient				Select	Bid	Contract, Sample		Inspection	Punch list complete			
Carpet						Select, Sample	Bid	Contract				Inspection, Punch list complete
Walls												
Paint							Select, Bid	Contract		Sample		Inspection, Punch list complete
Wallpaper							Select	Sample	Bid, Contract		Inspection	Punch list complete
Tile					Select, Bid	Sample, Contract		Inspection	Punch list complete			
Stone	Select		Bid	Contract, Sample		Inspection	Punch list complete					
Wood			Select		Bid	Contract, Sample		Inspection, Punch list complete				
Millwork												
Trim			Select		Bid	Contract, Sample		Inspection	Punch list complete			
Cabinetry		Select			Contract		Bid			Inspection	Punch list complete	
Window Coverings						Select	Bid	Contract				Inspection, Punch list complete
Furniture					Select		Bid, Contract					Inspection, Punch list complete

• Select • Bid • Contract • Sample • Inspection • Punch list complete

an actual signature and date in permanent marker on the sample itself).

After the samples are approved and the fabricators have permission to proceed, the work will be put into production as soon as possible. If a shop has other customers whose orders predate yours, you will wait until your job comes up in their production schedule before your material will be produced. Sometimes shops have a lot of work in house (they have contracted with many other purchasers) so lead times spanning months are not unusual for some manufacturers and workrooms. That is why it is a good idea to inquire about lead times when you are making your initial material selection. The material will be produced and shipped when the order is complete and the balance on the material has been paid.

The contractor will need to have material on the job site by a particular time in order to meet the deadlines in the construction schedule. You will track the progression of the materials selected as the job moves forward so you know when you should block out time to inspect material which is being installed. Some materials should be inspected on-site before, during, and after installation. To be proactive in managing your selections, find a way of keeping track of the management tasks that you must perform at each phase in order to keep your jobs on track. Table 1.8 is a simplified version of one way of managing this task. Notice at the bottom of the form there is a legend defining the various tasks that the designer must perform to manage selections.

SUMMARY

In this chapter we discussed a variety of standards, guides, and recommendations that contribute to our design goals for the materials and installations we devise for our clients' projects. They included mandatory and best practices considerations that were developed by a number of second- and third-party organizations, including both private and public entities. One of the most prominent set of guidelines, which is becoming mandatory in many code jurisdictions, relates to sustainable building practices. Global considerations are increasingly important in design and this chapter reviewed some considerations that the conscientious designer analyzes when specifying for the global emphasis of a project; an emphasis that will vary in importance with the scope and location of the project but global considerations are appropriate for all design projects. Another important consideration during the selection and specification of materials is the client's budget. Designers develop different kinds of estimates during the various stages of a project for project management.

Designers manage selections from initial generic selection to identifying the precise materials to be used to writing the specification and monitoring the installation. During the process, designers will collaborate with several entities along the supply chain to orchestrate the process.

WEB SEARCH ACTIVITIES

1. Go to the International Code Council Web site, www.iccsafe.org, and notice the number of communities that are part of the guidelines developed by the ICC. The ICC reviews its various guidelines on a continuous basis and changes its recommendations every three years or so.

   Keeping in mind that the ICC is often referenced by jurisdictions as they develop their local code mandates, you can understand that the ICC is a place to see what future codes will require. Anticipating the future is part of the programming process. Select one area of interest (such as disabilities or sustainability) and see what is being considered by ICC right now and will likely become a requirement in local codes in the future.

   Save the location on your computer so you can quickly browse these topics as you work on your design projects. You will want the projects in your portfolio to be aligned with current thinking when you hit the streets and look for your first job, and this is one tool that you can use to anticipate the future.

2. Go to the Americans with Disabilities Act Web site, www.ada.gov. Find the Guidelines document and notice the topics that pertain to material surfaces, such as ground and floor surfaces and ramps and steps. Also notice resources for specific kinds of facilities such as small businesses and lodging facilities. These brochures were written with business owners in mind and they provide clear explanations of requirements that are likely to pertain to those kinds of businesses. You may want to review one or two of the brochures that pertain to your areas of interest in interior design.

3. As a designer entrusted with the health, safety, and welfare of your clients and the public, you will weigh the health effects of your decisions along with other programming issues. Manufacturers serving the design industry will respond to demands from designers to create safe products, but you must be vigilant and create that demand by only specifying safe products for your clients, especially if you are creating designs for vulnerable populations. Vulnerable populations include children whose immune systems are not fully developed, the elderly, whose immune systems are often suppressed, and people with illnesses whose immune systems are compromised.

   Go to www.EPA.gov and search for the health effects of the chemicals listed here in the text. You may prefer to use a search engine directly instead of starting at the EPA Web site but if you do, make sure your source is reliable and objective.

4. Go to the USGBC Web site, www.usgbc.org. Under Resources you will find presentations that are succinct and self-explanatory introductions to the importance of LEED and how the system works. All of the presentations are worth perusing, so pick at least one and spend the couple of minutes required to learn about it.

5. Choose a material that you would like to use in your selected project and note the price. Then perform a search for installation cost information for the material. For instance, let's say you picked ceramic tile, search for *installation cost ceramic tile*.

   Measure the area of the surface to receive the material that you select and see how much money you would likely have to budget for the material and installation as you managed your client's budget.

6. Go to the Construction Specifications Institute Web site (www.csinet.org) and search for information about MasterFormat. One of the free PowerPoint presentations is called "What Is MasterFormat?" View the slides for a more in-depth explanation of MasterFormat.

   If you cannot find this information on the CSI Web site, search for *What's MasterFormat? PPT*.

7. Go to the Construction Specifications Institute Web site. Under the Common Questions tab there is a choice to see an answer to "What's My MasterFormat Number?" Click on that choice and find the link to download the numbers and titles. You might want to reference the numbers on any specifications you write while studying this topic. Save the PDF to your computer so you don't have to find it again since the site is not the easiest to use.

   If you cannot find it on the CSI Web site perform a general search to find the *MasterFormat index* numbers.

   Peruse the divisions. Division 9 has many materials of particular interest to interior designers.

8. Search for a master spec for a selected product. For example, you might search for *master spec wood flooring*. Save or print the document and reference it as you review pages 16–18.

   You will probably notice in the master spec you find online for a specific material that there are numerous places where you must customize the spec. Look for brackets like [this] and <this>, which indicate you need to confirm or insert information. Also keep your eyes open for numbered lists. When you see a numbered list it will frequently mean you must pick one option from the list as items numbered there are exclusive choices and to have a number of them in your spec would present confusing contradictions.

9. Search for an example of each step in the supply chain for a single kind of material.

10. Professional designers must acquire continuing education units as part of activities required to maintain their membership in professional design organizations. Many CEU learning opportunities are free of charge—presented live by vendors or online through sites like AEC Daily.

    Go to www.aecdaily.com and click *Continuing Education*. Notice that the courses are arranged according to the CSI index. Look in Division 9 (Finishes) for topics that you might like to view related to this material.

    There will be an opportunity to take a test at the end of each presentation. The test is required of professionals seeking CEUs but is just for fun for you; however, when you pass the test you might want to print or save the certificate as documentation of the experience (especially if your instructor has you keep a class notebook of information related to this topic).

PERSONAL ACTIVITIES

1. Find images of a variety of interior places in magazines or online. A hospital room, hotel lobby, restaurant, classroom, and an office would allow for a good variety of programmatic considerations.

   What considerations would you account for if you were the designer responsible for making material selections for each place?

   In your opinion, are the selections shown appropriate? If there are some materials shown that you would not have specified what would you have used instead?

   If you deem that the materials shown are appropriate, what makes them so?

SUMMARY QUESTIONS

1. Why is it important for you to leave school with enough understanding of materials to make appropriate selections, rather than wait until you are on the job to learn how to approach materials?

2. What is the difference between codes and standards or guidelines?

3. Why can't you use the IBC for your guide on all of your projects?

4. What are examples of a standard or a guideline?
5. Why are third parties so important in developing standards and guidelines?
6. What is a model code and what is it used for?
7. How are local codes developed?
8. What is the meaning of occupancy classification?
9. Which populations are more vulnerable requiring more stringent safety standards?
10. What is the purpose of the Americans with Disabilities Act?
11. What are the characteristics of sustainable products?
12. When making selections for a commercial interior, what flame resistance is generally required for the materials that you select?
13. What are VOCs?
14. How can you specify to reduce toxins in spaces that you design?
15. What is the role of third-party organizations and how can you evaluate their objectivity?
16. Under what system are sustainability guidelines organized and accounted for? What organization developed these guidelines? What is the relationship of these guidelines to building codes?
17. What are characteristics of sustainable materials?
18. What chemicals are you likely to encounter as you select materials for your clients that you should try to avoid?
19. What is accounted for in a life-cycle cost analysis?
20. Why should a designer know the unit increments for the various materials specified?
21. What are some of the ways to approach the task of "thinking globally"?
22. What does social sustainability mean?
23. Why are third-party organizations critical to objectivity? What are the benefits of objectivity in the development of guidelines and standards?
24. How would different design practices approach developing initial budgets for their clients' projects?
25. When would you produce a ballpark figure for your client? A cost comparison? At what point is it appropriate to invest the time to develop complete costs? Why wouldn't you develop complete costs during the design development phase?
26. Come up with an example of a material that is sold by the square foot; by the lineal foot; by the lineal yard. What kinds of things will you specify that are priced as "per each"?
27. What is the form and function of the Construction Specification Institute indexing system?
28. What is a master specification and how will you use them?
29. What is the difference between a manufacturer's rep, a dealer, and a reseller?
30. What is the difference between the manufacturer's spec and the designer's spec?
31. How does your task change depending on the way the contracts are structured (such as design-build vs. design-bid-build, etc.)?
32. How can you keep track of the production of the materials required for a job?
33. What is the importance of a shop drawing?

Chapter 2

PAINTS, COATINGS, AND WALLCOVERINGS

Key Terms

Alkali burn
Alkyd
Alligatoring
Biocide
Bleed
Bleeding
Block fillers
Blooming
Chalking
Checking
Commercial/contract wallcovering
Companion/correlated wallcovering
Crocking
Embossed
Epoxy coatings
Faux finish
Feathered
Flash
Flocking
Foil
Glaze
Grain raising
Ground
Laminated
Lap
Mylar
Prepasted
Pretrimmed
Register
Repeat
Sags
Selvage
Shellac
Sizing
Stock
Striaé
Substrate
Water-modified alkyd

Objectives

After completing this chapter, you should be able to:

- Select paints, primers, and wallcoverings with characteristics appropriate to your job conditions and design program, addressing formula, sheen level, and price point.
- Avoid common problems with paints and coatings.
- Specify for conditions that require special primers and paints.
- Make decisions about what kind of prepwork and painting quality is needed for your client's job.
- Collaborate with suppliers of stock and custom wallcoverings.
- Select the right painter or paperhanger for your client's job.
- Manage the process for regular painting and paint techniques.
- Evaluate safety and budget considerations.
- Specify paint and wallcovering products and labor.
- Inspect completed painting and wallcovering work.

You are probably somewhat familiar with the form of the paints and coatings that are covered in this chapter and may have applied some of them yourself. If so, you have already had to make evaluative decisions when you selected the paint or coating that you used, thus your personal experience will help you visualize the things that will be discussed in this chapter. A deeper understanding of the product category will make you a better specifier, able to solve and avert problems.

PAINT MATERIALS

When approaching a topic it is sometimes helpful to break it down into its simplest distinctions, and in the case of paints and coatings, it is useful to consider a base coat versus a top coat and **alkyd** or oil-based products in contrast to water-based products using latex or acrylic. The products will also indicate the kind of thinner that should be used if the paint must flow on differently than the formula was originally designed to do.

Primers

A primer is the performance-improving base coat for paint. Its job is to hold the finish coats to the surface, preventing them from soaking into the surface and causing the gloss level to **flash** or otherwise produce an inconsistent top coat. If the **substrate** is **chalking**, or a previous coat of paint is **checking** or **alligatoring**, it must be cleaned and primed with an appropriate sealer. Primers create a good bond between the substrate and the paint.

Two categories of primer are sealers and underbodies. Sealers hold back anything on the substrate that might **bleed** through the finish coats. They also prevent damage from the chemical reaction of alkaline "hot spots" in plaster substrates. Underbodies are selected to conceal minor imperfections. These primers have more pigment than sealers and can be easily sanded. They are sometimes called **block fillers**.

Primers may be alkyd (oil-based) or water-based (latex or acrylic) primers or a hybrid, **water-modified alkyd** that uses plant-based oil instead of petroleum. Latex is more flexible than acrylic and acrylic is a little harder than latex. Both will cause **grain raising** of bare woodwork (because water makes the grain swell) so they are sanded after they are dry or tack free. Oil-based coatings are no longer allowable on wood although alkyds are permissible on materials that are not compatible with water, such as on metal that requires a coating. Manufacturers have been developing hybrid primer technologies and paints to come up with waterborne coatings that will not raise the grain.

> Point of Emphasis 2.1
> Sometimes different categories of finishes will be used in tandem. Paint and shellac have their differences but they are often used together when woodwork is shellacked before painting to seal knots and sap.

Paint

Paint is the top coat. It is a performance coating but it is also decorative. Like primers, paint may also be oil- or alkyd-based or water-based. Generally the recommended paint-primer system will behave similarly. However, even though water and oil don't willingly mix, there will be circumstances where performance requirements demand that they do, and paint technology can address many tricky problems with specific chemistry.

Paint for Special Surfaces

Other paint formulas are designed for special use. Even though oil is increasingly illegal for walls and trims, paint for metal is still oil-based (water corrodes metal). High-performance **epoxy coatings** are used for high-traffic floors, and additives are introduced to paints for antifungal, antimicrobial, mildewcide or other **biocide** properties. Some companies will produce custom coatings for large quantities, working with you to define the necessary characteristics and developing a formula to meet your needs. The many surfaces specified for paint finish require a variety of paint formulations.

Many designers mistakenly restrict their specs to manufacturer, color, and gloss level, but you should always include the formula in your specification. Formulations recommended for various surfaces include:

- Cement: Cementitious paint (like a thin mortar).
- Cement floors (high traffic): Urethane coating or epoxy polyamide.
- Concrete block (above grade): Cementitious latex specially formulated for use on concrete blocks with a filler finish, epoxy polyester, or below-grade cementitious only.
- Wallboard, particleboard, or flake board: Alkyd undercoat with a latex top coat or alkyd undercoat and top coat.
- Wood: Water-based top coat or water-modified alkyd undercoat and top coat.
- Metals: Alkyd- or urethane-based paint.
- Impervious surfaces that need to be meticulously cleaned: Urethane.

CHARACTERISTICS

Product characteristics vary, making some materials better suited for your site conditions and program goals. A mere awareness of the differences will help you as you investigate options, but a designer is expected to have a working knowledge of the differences between product types and when to select from among them.

Primers

A primer's main job is to prepare the specific surface in question for the paint specified. The substrate, site conditions, paint formula, and planned use will indicate the proper primer (and paint). Different materials (metals, brick, wood, plaster, concrete, etc.) require primers having specific characteristics. Whether the job is above or below grade also influences the selection of primer, as can the planned use (heavy traffic floor paint, spaces with temperature fluctuations, etc.). **Shellac** is sometimes used to seal resinous wood or knots in wood before the wood is primed to further seal the surface so the resins or pitch will not work to the surface.

If the surface is particularly absorbent it will need a different primer than if it is not. Sealers can be especially formulated for particular situations like sealing knots in wood, or suppressing stains on existing surfaces if you must cover graffiti or ink, or creating compatibility between a substrate and a finish, such as painting plastic laminate or other nearly impervious surfaces.

Some primers will work with many paints but work best with particular paints and others will not work at all for certain kinds of paints. One manufacturer's acrylic paint will not be utterly identical to another's, so it is common to specify the entire system, primer/sealer and paint, from the same manufacturer. As you investigate different formulations you will notice some combination products that are paint and primer in one.

If the surface to be painted has previously been painted a color that is similar to the color you have specified, you may not need to prime at all. Test the surface by spritzing a little water on it; if the water soaks in you should specify that the walls be primed or specify a self-priming paint. If it does not soak in, priming may be optional.

Paint

Components in paint are orchestrated to produce desired properties. Paint is essentially a combination of pigment and binder in a carrier that removes itself as the paint dries, but the sophistication of the product category allows paint to do more than simply color surfaces. Table 2.1 shows a more realistic picture of the basic paint recipe.

Table 2.1
A simplified recipe for paint.

Pigments	Powders, usually minerals that impart color but also affect gloss levels.
Binders	Responsible for the toughness of the paint, bind the other ingredients into a film after the diluents "go away."
Diluents	The thinner or carrier that makes the paint liquid enough to spread.
Additives	Change the characteristics, making paint viscous, stable, fast-drying, increase "open time," mildew resistant, flame retardant (remember, these additives are all chemicals and will change the toxicity of the formulas to which they are added).
Emulsifiers	Fuse materials together by breaking down chemical "walls" that keep each ingredient distinct from the others.

Grades

Paint has quality distinctions that affect pricing. While the designer always prefers to specify the highest available quality, price is often a consideration as you manage client budgets. There are varying qualities at varying price points available from most manufacturers; however, some specialty products do not offer different quality grades.

Contractor grade is generally a lower price and lower quality paint; it tends to have lower sheen levels than the same sheen level designation at higher quality grades such as specification grade paint. Understanding why this is so will help you make better decisions regarding these two grades. Contractors bid competitively for work and would like to have the lowest possible material cost in the bid, so they bid lower quality paint, unless a different formula is specified. One of the characteristics of contractor-grade paint is that it has a lower resin content. This lowers the price, lowers the sheen level, and lowers the washability. This may be ideal for your client, especially if the client is a commercial client who prefers to touch up rather than wash their walls. In such a case, the lack of washability is not a problem and low sheen levels allow for better blended spot touch-ups, so the low grade agrees with their maintenance preference. See Table 2.2 for a comparison of specification and contractor grades.

Table 2.2
Comparison of two quality levels of paint.

Specification Grade	Contractor Grade
Geared to residential market	Geared to commercial market
Higher resin improves washability	Lower resin results in lower sheen for easier touch-ups
Higher cost	Economical compared to specification grade
Higher sheen level	The gloss level will be lower for each sheen level designator (e.g., satin will be less shiny than for specification grade)

Formulations

Water-based and oil-based paint are the two broad categories of formulation commonly referenced. Oil-based paints can still be understood by the traditional meaning: the solvent is oil. The solvent in water-based paints may be latex or acrylic.

Oils traditionally used in paint include linseed, tung, and soya oil but now the designation oil paint usually refers to alkyds (modified oils). Alkyds dry harder and faster than traditional oils. Oil paint does not simply dry but oxidizes in a way that produces extra hardness, which is referred to as surface tack. This characteristic is preferred for moving parts, such as window sashes, which must slide without sticking.

To limit the introduction of VOCs into the environment, oil-based paints using solvents that will off-gas VOCs are being replaced by water-based paints. Water-based systems include acrylic, vinyl acrylic, styrene acrylic, polyvinyl acetate, and waterborne epoxies and waterborne alkyds. Water-based paints are less toxic. See Table 2.3 for characteristics of the different formulas.

Table 2.3
Characteristics of different paint formula ingredients.

Acrylics	Good adhesion Thermoplastic Flexible Resist damage from moisture
Vinyl acrylics	Form a breathable film Thermoplastic Non-yellowing Alkali resistant
Styrene acrylics	Good film strength Resist moisture
Polyvinyl acetate	Forms a breathable film Nearly odorless Good alkali resistance
Waterborne epoxies	Non-yellowing Have low VOCs
Waterborne alkyds	High-sheen formulas Crisp details

Water-based paint is easy to use; painters don't have to keep stirring it and it cleans up with water. It does not emit solvent fumes (although it does have an odor and many latex formulas off-gas VOCs). VOC levels are identified as parts per volume using the metric measurement of grams per liter (g/l), even though paint is still sold by the gallon in the U.S. Some latex paint formulations claim zero VOCs and are virtually odor-free. There may still be some toxicity related to colorants and additives but getting the solvent down to zero is a big step toward healthier environments.

Water-based paint dries faster than oil and, therefore, must be applied very quickly with as little rework-

Table 2.4
Description of sheen-level terms.

Gloss Level	Measurable Sheen	Considerations
High gloss	85% or even more	Every surface imperfection will be highlighted
		Expert preparation of the surface is necessary
		Prepwork will be easily judged by the perfection of reflection in the surface
Gloss paint	75 to 85%	Surface imperfections will be visible
		Expert preparation of the surface
		In utility spaces, where washability is more important than appearance, it is usually acceptable to use gloss paint on less-than-perfect surfaces
Semigloss paint	40 to 75%	A little less shiny, a little less washable
		Less of a need for a perfect surface
		Specified more often than gloss paint
		Frequently used on millwork trim and as accent areas
Satin	25 to 40%	Soft sheen Can be cleaned with a soft cloth and mild soap
Eggshell	10 to 25%	Close to the sheen of satin
		View samples side-by-side in order to discern the difference (for example, eggshell on the walls and satin on the trim)
		Still washable
Matte	5 to 10%	Good at hiding imperfections
		Affords some washability but not rigorous
		Also referred to as velvet and suede finish
Flat	Less than 5%	Not washable; touch-ups only
		Hides more imperfections than other sheen levels
		Touches up easily

ing over the surface as possible to avoid brush and roller marks. When latex paint is to be used on woodwork, some painting contractors mask off the entire room, leaving only the millwork exposed, and they spray the paint on. No brushing means no brush marks; however, you still must watch for drips and **sags**.

Gloss Level

In addition to formula and color, paint cannot be adequately described without designating a sheen level. Standard designations break down into the following: gloss, semigloss, satin, eggshell, and flat. Manufacturers have proprietary formulas for sheen levels. Generally speaking, as sheen increases so does washability and the tendency to show surface imperfections. The surface under gloss paint must be very well prepared and flawless. Matte or flat paint will be much less washable but the soft reflection will be very forgiving of imperfections. Sheen level is a measurable characteristic, but since the reflectivity of each sheen level will vary with manufacturer and with formula (remember the difference between contractor grade and specification grade) there is a range in the sheen levels described in Table 2.4.

> **Point of Emphasis 2.2**
> Manufacturers may designate their own descriptive names for some sheen levels, so you will occasionally run across other sheen-level names like Benjamin Moore's "Pearl," which is not a sheen level referenced by all manufacturers.

RELATED WORK

The quality of your paint job is dependent upon the surface, paint selection, and the skill of the painting labor. No part of the system is independent of the others. If the surface was previously painted, the painter may have to correct problems left by the previous painting such as drips and globs, dents or roughness under the paint, and areas where the paint did not cover completely. It is unlikely that drywall has been nailed to the studs in new construction but in buildings that were built before the late 1970s, nails were used, and you will need to look for nail pops (where the nail is working its way out of the surface, making a bump), which should be pulled, replaced with screws, and spackled.

Your job may require that a textured surface be created. These surfaces are often formed with special products that are applied as a paste and worked to build up a textured base that is then painted. Some of these products are colorant and texture in one. They are usually applied by the painting contractor, unlike a **faux finish** or **glaze** that is applied by painters that have special fine arts training.

QUALIFYING INSTALLERS

Painters tend to learn their trade on the job. Trade unions often have a formalized system of advancement beginning with Apprentice and advancing to Journeyman. Not all painters (or plasterers) join a union, but if you are working on a job site where other union workers are employed (or working in a building that employs union elevator operators) you will want to hire union painters. You will qualify both union and nonunion painters the same way. Review photos of previous, similar work, visit a job site where the painting crew worked, and call references. When you are hiring a large crew through a painting contractor you will not qualify individual workers; it is the company that you are hiring. A company may be as small as one painter with a helper, so in that instance you are, of course, qualifying the individual.

INSTALLATION

New substrates will usually be in more predictable condition than substrates that have been in use for years. The older the surface material is, the more likely it is that the surface will require repair. While you are in the early planning stages and preparing budgets for your client you should draft a rough idea of the work involved in bringing surfaces to acceptable condition so that you can formulate sensible plans for the quality and timing of the completed work. List conditions you notice on the job site that should be repaired, so you will be organized when you talk to bidders.

A job like a residential living room may require a high level of finish, but you don't need top-notch painting labor for every circumstance. The boiler room in a school, for instance, will not be subject to the same high expectations as the living room, so the meticulous attention given to the living room would be inappropriate for the boiler room. Different levels of finish quality can be specified to accommodate the different needs of these situations. Table 2.5 describes the different qualities of wall finish application that you can specify.

Prepwork

Before painting can begin, preparatory work, or prepwork, is usually required. Even if the wall or trim surfaces are new they must be filled or spackled, primed, and sanded. Walls that have been in use should be washed and sanded and sometimes primed before they can be painted.

Walls

The substrate for painted walls is usually drywall or plaster. If new plaster walls are to be painted they must cure completely before painting work begins or problems with adhesion may occur due to **alkali burn**. Different plaster formulas and site conditions will vary curing time. Allow a couple of weeks for cure time in your schedule and have the painter perform an alkalinity test. After the drywallers have installed the drywall sheets and the corner beads, and have taped and spackled the seams and out-corners, the spackle is **feathered** out and sanded smooth. The walls may also be fully skim coated with a special kind of plaster coat. This is, of course, more costly because where this special kind of plaster coat normally covers only screw and seam locations, skim coating covers the entire wall. The material list is slightly different too. The seams may be taped and spackled, but a special coat that cures like plaster (called hot mud) may be used to skim coat. The surface is worked and troweled like a plaster wall finish coat.

Table 2.5
Use these descriptors in your spec so painters can bid accurately and provide the level of finish most appropriate to your client's needs.

Level	How Wallboard Is Finished	When to Specify this Level of Finish	Finishing
Level 0	No finishing.	Temporary partitions that shield areas from construction dirt. When finishes will be determined by others under separate contract.	No finishing.
Level 1	Joints and interior angles are taped with tape set in joint compound, but compound not smoothed, excess compound removed.	In hidden areas, such as in plenum above ceilings.	Primed.
Level 2	Fastener heads and tape covered in (not just set in) joint compound at taping, excess compound removed, not smoothed.	When surface will be covered with tile or other material not requiring smooth surface.	Primed with two coats of paint.
Level 3	Fastener heads and tape covered in (not just set in) joint compound at taping, second layer of joint compound, excess compound removed, compound is free of tool marks and ridges.	If textured skim coat or heavy-duty and textured wallcovering is to be applied.	Primed and painted two coats. The paint application may appear inconsistent but that should not be due to painters' work.
Level 4	As level 3 but two separate coats of joint compound applied to flat areas and one to interior corners, fastener heads covered with three coats, excess compound removed, compound free of tool marks and ridges.	Where flat paints or medium-texture finishes or wallcoverings are planned.	Primed with two coats of paint. This is the most common level of finish for visible surfaces.
Level 5	As level 4 but a thin skim coat of joint compound or other plaster veneer applied to entire surface, excess compound removed, compound free of tool marks and ridges.	Higher sheen paint finishes, non-textured surfaces, and where lighting conditions will exaggerate defects, such as side-lighting conditions.	Primed and painted at least two coats, sanded between coats. This is the highest level of perfection.

Point of Emphasis 2.3

Both the material and labor costs are increased for skim coating, but if the budget allows for it, it is more durable and more solid sounding. We experience spaces with all our senses and can hear quality construction in the way sound moves, or doesn't move, through spaces.

In either drywall or plaster installations you may encounter water damage or settling cracks. Plaster may have come loose over time and needs to be tightened down to the lath with special plaster screws (Figure 2.1). There is no point in repairing the surface and painting if the cause of the problem has not been corrected; thus, the repair should be done first and then the resulting damage corrected. If the painters will not be taping and spackling because a taping crew has been hired for that work, it is a good idea to include instruction in your paint specs mandating that the painter must approve the tapers' work prior

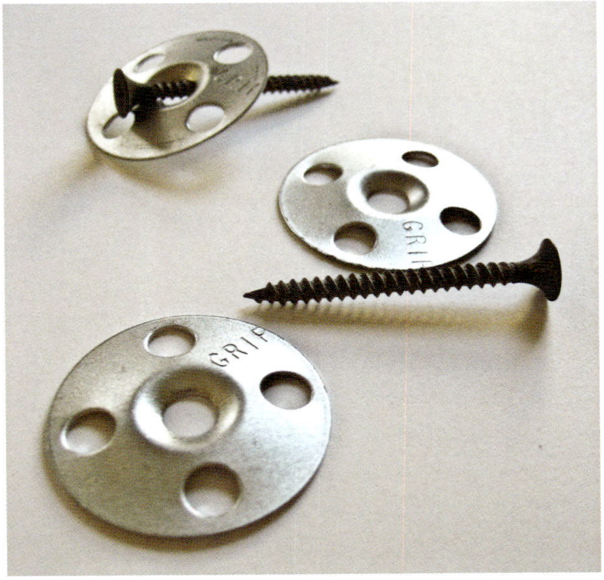

FIGURE 2.1 Plaster washers from Rodenhouse are used to tighten plaster to the lath if some of the fingers/keys have broken off.

to painting to maintain control over the quality of the finished job.

> **Helpful Hint 2.1**
>
> It is especially tricky to locate the source of leaks, so clients should be prepared for a couple of wrong guesses as to the source of the water. Be sure to allow time in the schedule for this sleuthing to be complete before the work proceeds.

New paint formulations are available with built-in primer so you may select such a finish and not require a primer. Ideally the primer color should be similar to the finished wall color, even though painters frequently use white. White primer is usually fine for pale paint colors, but if you intend to use a very dark or bright color you may request that the primer be tinted to within 75 percent of the finished color. This allows for better presentation of the final color while still allowing the painter to confirm that all the primer is covered by the finish paint.

> **Helpful Hint 2.2**
>
> Changing a pale color to a dark one or a bright color to a pale one often requires multiple coats of paint (unless you have specified one of the new formulations that have super coverage). I once read a spec by a designer who I admired for their meticulous attention to detail. For a dark paint color that would require a tinted primer and multiple coats the designer specified that the primer would be tinted to 75 percent of the color and each successive coat of paint should be 10 percent deeper than the previous. The designer wanted to make sure that the color was absolutely consistent upon completion and the succession of deeper coats allowed the painters to see where the current coat was a little too thin.

Once the primer coat has been applied, it is easier to see any surface imperfections before the final coats of paint are applied. Many good painters will graze the wall surface with a bright light to check the quality of the prepwork before proceeding with painting. You can do the same kind of check with a flashlight if your painter is disinclined to check his or her own work, and indicate with a pencil mark where additional filling or sanding is required.

> **Helpful Hint 2.3**
>
> Use pencil to make any notations on primed walls to instruct painters after your inspection of the prepwork. Only write things like "sand," "fill," and other work they should perform before painting with pencil because pen will bleed through paint and through all but special, stain-killing primers as well.

Trims

Millwork trims may have many layers of old paint on them. If the woodwork finish is in bad condition, it should be stripped or replaced. Stripping paint is costly but makes sense if the damaged paint is confined to a small area of a large job having fine, consistent trim throughout. If the paint is in poor condition throughout the entire job it is, unfortunately, cheaper and sometimes healthier (in cases where lead paint would have to be removed or chemical strippers used) to remove all trim and replace it with new trim. If paint is flaking in a few places, specially shaped tools are used to drag the loose paint off the woodwork profiles. This work must be carefully done by experienced tradespeople because these tools are sharp enough to cut into the wood (Figure 2.2a and b). The woodwork is then hand-sanded to try to minimize the differences at the junction between the painted and scraped portions (although you will still be able to see subtle ridges under the new paint). The successive layers of new paint will further work to minimize the difference between areas with many layers of old paint and those with bare wood where all paint has been removed. This is less costly (money and environmental) than stripping or replacing wood trim. If only a few sections of the trim will be replaced on a job having old original woodwork, the existing woodwork is likely to have several layers of old paint. The new work will look "crisper and newer" compared to the existing areas unless you specify extra layers of paint for the new work.

Helpful Hint 2.4

If woodwork has been stripped down to bare wood, there may be areas that should be sealed to prevent sap from rising through the paint.

Typical Process

The following hypothetical scenario outlines the steps in working with a painter: Imagine that you want to hire a painter. You define the scope of work with the client and select all the finishes and colors, then:

1. Meet your prequalified painting contractor(s) on-site for a walk-through (even if the job was bid from a set of plans there will eventually be a walk-through to confirm all presumptions made during bidding). The painter will want to inspect the surfaces to be painted to make sure they are in the condition expected (and thus in condition upon which the bid was based). The painter may make suggestions regarding proper preparation of the surfaces for the painting work described in the scope of work. The painter will be able to perform many of the required prepwork tasks and may include them in the bid.
2. After contract terms are confirmed, the painter will be hired and paid a deposit (often the payouts are one-third, one-third, and one-third, but sometimes they are half down and half upon completion if the job will not take long).
3. The color is selected or custom mixed with the painter. It is a good idea to check the color on the site with the painter, who should have universal pigments on hand to adjust the color as needed. Have all of your material samples in hand for color comparison at this meeting. Review a large (18-inch or larger) square of dried sample. If the color should be adjusted, the painter will add pigments as needed, drying the samples with a blow dryer or heat gun so you can see the final, dried color.
4. When you believe you have mixed the correct color, the painter should paint it on several surfaces throughout the area so you can check it in bright light, diffuse, and indirect light, and in shadow as well as in natural and artificial light and all lighting conditions that you can effect. If it still looks right, and your client approves, the painter will purchase all the paint needed for the job, custom mixed by his or her supplier to match the color that you just created.

FIGURE 2.2A–B These tools that scrape loose paint from trim profiles are very sharp and inexpert handling can create gouges in wood.

Point of Emphasis 2.4

Some painters refuse to mix color and in many instances this results in a compromise: a color that is *almost* right. You should prefer to work with painters who can "nudge" a color a little.

5. Take a painted sample away with you after the mixing meeting for your records. You may want to check the color of the batch mixed by the supplier; sometimes they are slightly off, which may or may not be a material difference. If it is not a dead-on match but is still a good color, you may choose to accept the batch even if it is a little off.

Helpful Hint 2.5

It is a good idea to prepare for your sample of a custom-mixed color by taking a piece of board, like poster board or foam core, and a drop cloth for your trunk. The sample will need to dry someplace where it won't be disturbed. Even if you are having other meetings while at the site, it is a good idea to put the paint sample in your trunk so you don't forget it and it is not disturbed while drying.

6. The painter will perform all the prepwork described in the contract. If a large quantity of paint will be required, you should specify to the painter that he or she should box the paint (mix up the batches to even out any slight variation in colors of each). After the prepwork is completed and approved the painter will apply primer and paint as specified. If a high-quality paint job is required, the painter is likely to sand the walls and trim between coats. When each coat is dry to touch, you will be able to see the final color, but it must dry even further in order to hold up to sanding.

If you require a glaze technique (a faux finish or sponge, for example) the proceedings are just slightly different. The painter will create large (18" × 18") samples on poster board. Check this sample at the site by carrying it into several different lighting conditions available there. Request any adjustments necessary and have the painter make a new sample if the change is significant.

Accessories that are to be painted (switch-plate covers, outlet covers, floor or wall vents) must be lightly textured metal if they are to hold paint.

For the Connoisseur 2.1

Your expert painter can "faux grain" the floor vents to blend with a wood floor or faux paint outlet covers that are on stone backsplashes so, like a chameleon, they blend in and are not eye-catching on the fine surfaces that you have specified.

SPECIAL FINISHES

Paint techniques are very popular now and are achieved by a variety of methods. Some techniques that you will specify may require a textured undercoat. This undercoat may be as delicate as tissue paper (Figure 2.3) or as bold as a buildup of a composite (Figure 2.4). Many techniques require multiple steps to achieve (Figure 2.5). They range from random spatters to a tightly controlled trompe l'oeil. Textural effects are possible when paint layers of differing formulations react to each other in controlled ways, such as this alligator finish (Figure 2.6). Commonly used techniques include **striaé** (Figure 2.7), a simulated wood grain called faux bois (Figure 2.8), or other simulated materials. Many of these finishes, certainly the multiple-layer techniques, employ the use of a glaze, a thinned-down paint that is applied by some

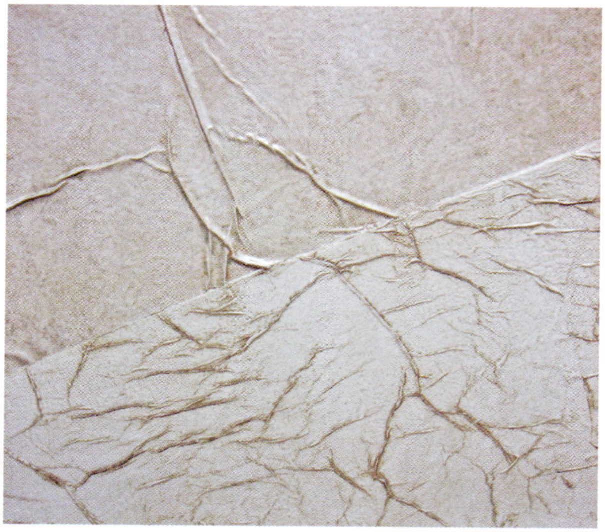

FIGURE 2.3 Regular paper forms the underlayer of the sample on top and tissue paper forms the underlayer of the sample on the bottom. *Both samples by Hester Painting and Decorating in Skokie, IL.*

FIGURE 2.4 A composite material was used to create a very heavily textured surface for a metallic paint coat. *Sample by Hester Painting and Decorating in Skokie, IL.*

FIGURE 2.5 Many techniques require more than one coat. Here, a lightly textured base coat was ragged with two successive layers of glaze. *Sample by Hester Painting and Decorating in Skokie, IL.*

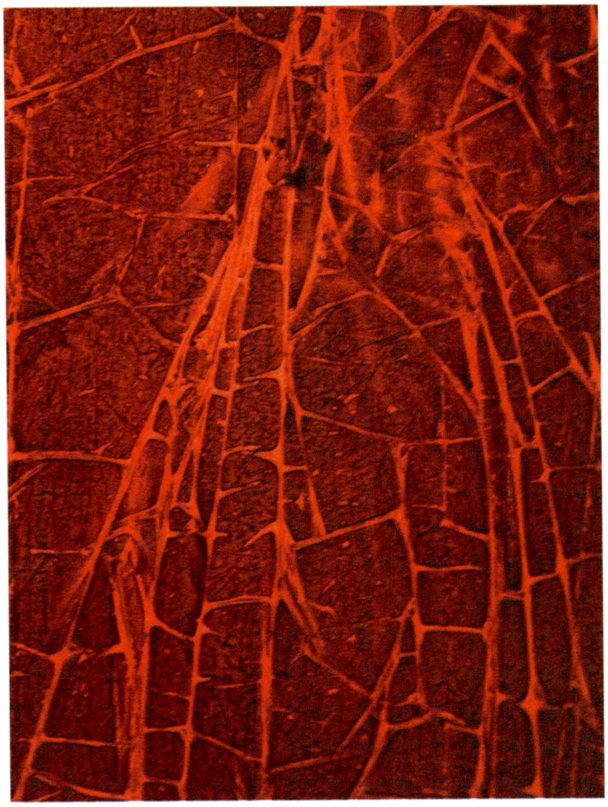

FIGURE 2.6 This alligator skin technique requires careful management of two paint formulations, which create this visual texture. *Sample by Hester Painting and Decorating in Skokie, IL.*

FIGURE 2.7 A classic technique called striaé (pronounced: *stree-ay*) drags the over glaze in one direction. *Sample by Hester Painting and Decorating in Skokie, IL.*

FIGURE 2.8 Faux bois (pronounced: *foe bwah*) techniques imitate wood surfaces. *Sample by Hester Painting and Decorating in Skokie, IL.*

FIGURE 2.9 Stencils may be cut to create crisp patterns with a heavy application of paint or delicate patterns as shown here with a glaze. *Sample by Hester Painting and Decorating in Skokie, IL.*

FIGURE 2.10 Metal leaf will be super-thin metal that the painter must remove from its tissue paper backing and apply to the surface by burnishing. Actual metal is used so characteristics of the metal will remain constant—meaning oxidizing metals must be sealed.

method over a solid base color. The glaze can be any formulation that allows the painter to work the medium as necessary to achieve the finish desired. For instance, faux tortoise technique depends on the incompatibility of two or more glazes that repel each other rather than combine with one another.

The use of stencils (Figure 2.9) allows for a repetition that resembles printed patterns on wallpaper. Metal leaf (Figure 2.10) is not paint, but is included here because it is a surfacing material employed for the same function and it would be applied by the painter. These thin foils are small (less than 6 inch square) and so fine that the painter cannot handle them with bare hands—the heat from your skin is enough to attach the leaf to your fingers. The material and labor are expensive for metal leaf surfaces. Metallic paints can be substituted. Recall that metal will retain its characteristics regardless of the application, so the properties of metal leaf and metallic paint include the tendency for some metals to oxidize.

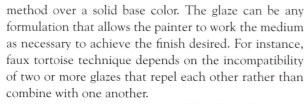

A Cautionary Tale 2.1

About two weeks after the painter had finished a custom surface with metallic paint, I got a call from the client to come and see a change that had taken place on the ceiling where the paint had been applied. In four-foot spacing, the silver paint had tarnished in narrow stripes. We quickly realized that the stripes corresponded to spackled joints in the drywall ceiling. The spackle had reacted chemically with the metal flakes in the paint. The painter repaired the problem by repainting the oxidized areas with a sealer/primer and dabbed in the new paint to blend with the other areas. If the finish had been rolled on smoothly instead of dabbed in squares and rectangles, he would have had to recoat the whole ceiling to repair the oxidized stripes.

PROTECTION/MAINTENANCE

Painting labor is one of the last tasks to be performed. If a floor required a final coat of sealant, that work would follow the painting work. After that, carpeting and window treatments go in, followed by furniture. The installation of carpet typically will scuff and mar small areas and it is very typical for the painters' contract to include these touch-ups in their contract price. Higher sheens are more durable against abrasion and are more washable; they are harder to touch up than low sheens. If you are worried that a specialty paint technique or a painted floor will be subject to soiling or wear, you may specify a clear coat over it to protect it.

SAFETY

Pale colors often contain titanium dioxide. This material is dangerous if inhaled, so workers who are preparing and sanding previously painted surfaces should wear masks. Select paint with low or no VOC formulas when appropriate and consider coatings with as few chemical additives as will be functional at your client's site. Old paint may contain lead.

SUSTAINABILITY

Coatings often emit volatile organic compounds (VOCs), reducing indoor air quality (IAQ). Water-based finishes generally emit fewer parts per liter of known VOCs but VOCs are not the whole story. Designers should look at other chemicals that are present because other kinds of poisons are not, strictly speaking, VOCs, so they are not necessarily accounted for as VOCs. Check the specific paint's material safety data sheet.

As you navigate this important area of environmental considerations you will encounter organizations that have been instrumental in promoting clean air. They have developed guidelines and limits on emissions and their standards are often listed in performance specs that manufacturers provide for their products. They are also referenced in project requirements; an example of such a requirement would be the LEED standards. Some important organizations issuing standards are the EPA (Environmental Protection Agency), AIM (Architectural and Industrial Maintenance Coatings rule), CARB (the California Air Resources Board), SCAQMD (South Coast Air Quality Management District), OTC (Ozone Transportation Commission—northeastern states), and LADCO (Lake Michigan Air Directors Consortium). Green Seal has established criteria for sustainable paint and couples that with standards for performance identified by ASTM. Greenguard has also established guidelines for emissions.

Unused paint must be disposed of properly, preferably taken to a paint recycling or remanufacturing facility where the paint will become part of a batch that will be used on someone else's job (usually these colors are pretty nice neutrals). Empty paint cans are to be entirely dry inside before disposing of them. Small amounts of paint (less than a quarter of a can, for instance) should be left open in a well-ventilated place and allowed to dry before being thrown away.

MANAGING BUDGETS

When work is released for bids, price differences can be startling if there are differences among the skill levels of the bidders. You get what you pay for and it is an unspoken expectation that the college kid painting houses over summer break will not be expected to provide the same quality work as skilled, full-time craftsmen.

Because painting work comes toward the end of the job, there is a temptation to skimp on the quality of the painting labor (resulting from the ever-present cost overruns during construction) and compared to other kinds of work that you will specify, painting is fairly easily redone at a later date. In the hierarchy of the building process the most important work is the preparation of the substrate. The substrate should allow for no compromise. It is easy to understand client hierarchies that occasionally shortchange painting quality. The unfortunate thing is that the walls are very visible and poor paint and painting is quite evident after good paint and painting has been distinguished. It is fair to expect top quality from a low bidder only if your specifications have been quite explicit in the matter.

A wide range of skill levels are available for hire. If you are managing rental property and need a lot of area sprayed white, you would not hire a highly skilled painter as the quality expectations do not indicate that level of expertise (or expense). Painting is one area where it is possible to cut costs if necessary. Unlike structural work, painting can always be done again and properly when funds become available. However, if you plan to paint twice to achieve appropriate quality, consider the cost of the initial job *plus* the final job as the real cost when opting to cut this corner. New construction settles and a few of my clients over the years have elected to delay the "real" paint job for two to three years in cases where I suggested using the paint techniques described above.

There is a quality difference between paints, even those from the same manufacturer. Manufacturers will produce different quality levels to meet various price points so they can compete in more markets and don't get priced out of budgets. There is a quality compromise when you downgrade the paint quality so make sure you will still get the performance you need if you drop down from specification grade to contractor grade. Also understand that some manufacturers target low-end or high-end markets, so one manufacturer's high-grade product will be comparable to another's low-grade product. The quality of paint includes many factors but a shortcut for discerning quality if you are not sure is to look at coverage. High-quality paint will cover more square feet than low-quality paint. Paint that has more opacity from solids per volume of paint will provide better coverage.

ORGANIZATION OF THE INDUSTRY

As described above, there are different kinds of painting laborers specializing in different aspects of the work. Training may be formalized or very informal on-the-job training. Both routes produce painters of varying commitment and refinement. Shops specializing in large-scale commercial painting don't want to be bothered with small fastidious jobs and small painting contractors are incapable of completing large-scale work on time or even on budget. You will want to do a thoughtful job of matching your job with the right painting contractor.

It is most typical for painters to supply the materials used on the job and some will have their own preferred brands for paint characteristics and pricing. If you specify the color and sheen only, you run the risk that the painter will provide the lowest quality paint. You will match the scale of your work to the companies that you contact for bids.

A Cautionary Tale 2.2

After receiving bids from two of my good-quality, professional painting contractors for comparison, my client decided to find a third on their own. My painters came in at $25,000 and $27,500 and the client's third bidder came in at $17,000. My specifications for the bid were a little "loose" because I had worked with both of my bidders before and knew their commitment to quality. I explained that the quality might not be as good but my client really felt that there could not be an $8,000 or $10,500 difference no matter how poor the third company was and reminded me that, per my contract, I would be instructing and inspecting so they should theoretically be able to get the same quality from the last bidder anyway.

The prepwork completed, I swung by after the end of the workday to graze my flashlight against the wall, highlighting every imperfection, circling it and writing my note for more work required (it was considerable and took hours to complete). The next day the work described was performed in the most perfunctory way, not to make it right but to say it had been done, even though results would not support the fact that any effort had been made. The relationship became contentious and I was not surprised; I know that you get what you pay for when it comes to painting labor and it was not fair to insist on the high standards that we expected when it was not made clear to the bidder before the bid was finalized.

So what finally happened? We fell to the bottom of the work list because my client's job became a money-losing proposition for the contractor, who would throw a couple of guys onto it when he could spare them from more profitable jobs. The painting work took three months to complete instead of one and the job became chaotic as other trades could not complete their work as expected.

A Cautionary Tale 2.3

I had a client who "knew a guy" who represented one of the large paint manufacturing companies. This client had the cost of the paint itself removed from the contract, the painter estimated quantity, and it was delivered to the site. This painter was in the habit of simply stopping for more paint on the way to the job site when he ran low, and having to wait for paint to be delivered by this third party caused a delay as well as a nuisance for my client, who had to be the go-between for each of three additional requests for paint of one color or another (and undoubtedly for "the guy" who had to have a gallon delivered on three separate occasions). This is one of many penny-wise, pound-foolish instances to explain to your clients to dissuade them if they imagine that they can afford to "save" some small sums of money at the expense of job organization.

SELECTION CRITERIA

As you organize your priorities for these finishes it will become clear what kinds of products and labor you require. Some considerations to get you started are presented in Table 2.6.

SPECIFYING

Let's presume that your client is an eye surgeon with a small suite in a medical building. You have decided that it makes sense to use color to help patients who have difficulty seeing detail and reading signage to locate themselves in the suite using color cues. Each of three exam room doors is to be a unique color. Open waiting areas are to be a color that is distinct from corridor walls, etc. You imagine that elderly people, who comprise a large percentage of the doctor's patients, may steady themselves by touching walls, so you balance your desire to omit any possibility of glare with the desire to occasionally wash smudges from walls and doors. For this client, your spec may resemble the following spec.

Table 2.6
Organize your selection criteria to help with your paint formula selection.

Condition	Program Implications
How will this site be maintained?	If the client prefers to touch up, specify matte or flat; if they prefer to wash, specify eggshell or higher sheen.
Is this a high-traffic location?	Higher sheens are more durable but require better prepwork because they show every imperfection.
What needs are there for visual organization and wayfinding?	Color selection and distribution can be used to create meaningful contrasts to organize the space and indicate direction.
What kind of lighting will be present?	Tune and adjust your color palette to be attractive under the selected lighting conditions. If lighting is cool, select colors with cool notes even if they are warm, e.g., brick red vs. tomato red.
Are there several kinds of surfaces requiring different paint formulas in a single area?	The identical color in different formulas will have a noticeably different appearance due to chemistry and sheen variation. If this will be disturbing you may decide to purposely call different painted surfaces out in different colors since they will never match.
Will you be trying to maximize daylighting?	Reflectance for walls should be between 40% and 70% and for floors 25% to 40%.
How interested is your client in sustainability?	Consider an alternative surface like tinted lime plaster, clay plaster, or milk paint. If sticking with typical paint products select low- or no-VOC formulas with few added chemicals.
Are specialty finishes required?	This work is often performed by different painting contractors on the job site and always by different workers, who need to be coordinated, especially if the painters prepare the base coat for the specialty painter, as product compatibility must be managed.

SAMPLE SPEC 2.1

Part 1 General Information

1.1 Related Documents

A. Refer to finish schedule for location of each paint specified.

1.2 Summary

A. Prime and paint newly constructed partitions, ceilings, doors, trims in suite 105.

B. Ten wall colors located as specified, to be washable matte finish. Six trim colors, located as specified, to be satin. One ceiling color throughout to be flat.

1.3 References

A. Comply with local regulations pertaining to disposal of leftover paint.

B. Comply with OSHA regulations for ventilation of work site.

1.4 Contractor Submittals

A. Two sets of material safety data sheets for all paint and compounds used.

B. Samples demonstrating color and sheen for each paint specified, minimum size 18" × 18" labeled with the paint formula and color.

1.5 Quality Assurance

A. Contractor to have a minimum of 5 years of proven satisfactory experience.

B. Qualified journeypersons to perform painting labor and supervise apprentice labor.

C. Work to be inspected and approved by designer when priming is complete and upon completion of painting labor or at the end of each of two weeks estimated as duration of painting work.

1.6 Delivery, Storage, and Handling

A. Deliver all paint in sealed, original containers bearing the manufacturer's name and product identification.

B. All product to be stored in accordance with manufacturer's recommendations.

1.7 Maintenance of Installation

A. Prevent paint from falling on items that are not to be painted with painter-supplied drop cloths and tape.

B. Remove all spatter from unpainted surfaces.

Part 2 Products

2.1 General Information

A. This contract includes all contractor-supplied equipment required to complete the work described, sufficient quantities of all materials to provide the specified number of coats, all drop cloths, ladders, and safety equipment.

B. ASTM D476 titanium dioxode

C. ASTM D332 hiding power

2.2 Manufacturers

A. Ecopaint Inc., 1234 Industrial Drive, Anytown, ST 45678.

B. Smoothseal Caulk Corp., 5678 Industrial Drive, Anytown, ST 45678.

2.3 Products

A. Ecopaint No-VOC Tenacity formula primer

B. Ecopaint No-VOC Tenacity formula paint in washable matte for walls as noted below and on finish plan:

1. PNT-1 Moorefield Gray
2. PNT-2 Moorefield Lichen
3. PNT-3 Moorefield Heather
4. PNT-4 Moorefield Moss
5. PNT-5 Seaspray Lilac
6. PNT-6 Seaspray Deep Water
7. PNT-7 Seaspray Tidal Sand
8. PNT-8 Hilltop Hay
9. PNT-9 Hilltop Coneflower
10. PNT-10 Hilltop Phlox

C. Ecopaint No-VOC Tinman paint in washable satin for metal or wood doors and trim:

1. PNT-11 Moorefield Slate
2. PNT-12 Moorefield Bottlefly
3. PNT-13 Moorefield Amethyst
4. PNT-14 Seaspray Lieutenant
5. PNT-15 Seaspray Keel
6. PNT-16 Hilltop Winter Wheat

D. Ecopaint No-VOC flat wall paint for ceilings:

1. PNT-17 Hilltop Snowdrift

E. Smoothseal low-odor, paintable caulk.

Part 3 Execution

3.1 Examination

A. Do not paint any surface that, upon inspection, is not properly prepared for quality level 4 finish. Painting a surface constitutes acceptance of surface quality and painter shall not be relieved of providing work of acceptable quality.

B. No dust is to be generated by others during the duration of the painting labor.

C. Ensure adequate ventilation to comply with OSHA standards.

3.2 Preparation

A. Describe work that must be performed under this contract (not related contracts mentioned earlier) to get the material or the site ready for installation.

3.3 Installation

A. Apply primer in accordance with manufacturer's conditions and recommendations in workmanlike manner, sand and vacuum.

B. Apply a minimum of two coats of finish paint color, sanding and vacuuming between coats.

3.4 Post Installation

A. Upon completion, work is to be free of brush or roller marks, **lap** marks, sags, drips, stippling, missed areas, and foreign materials.

B. All defects visible at 30 degrees to surface to be corrected.

C. Contractor responsible for protecting painted surfaces until curing time stated in manufacturers literature has passed.

D. Clean site of all equipment and debris and leave ready to present to owner.

Table 2.7
Watch out for some of these common problems when you inspect completed paint jobs.

Problem	What Probably Caused It	What to Do
Roller marks	The wrong roller or low-end paint lacking the chemistry to level out	Sand walls, repaint with correct roller nap, painter should dampen roller before starting to paint with water-based paint; specify better quality paint for recoating
Lap marks	Not working with a wet edge (painting in long strips that dry before adjacent area is coated)	Recoat
Hatbanding (area cut in around ceiling looks different from walls)	May be similar to lap marking or may be poor priming	Recoat with one more layer of paint, rolling and if necessary, feathering in at cut-in areas; worst case: may need to prime and recoat
Subtle cracking to "mud-cracking"	Paint applied too thickly, perhaps over a too porous surface	Sand or scrape and sand if cracks are larger; recoat with high-quality latex paint
Poor leveling	Inferior brush or roller with nap too deep for paint formula or working back into paint that has started to set	Sand and recoat with good quality paint; correct brush and roller nap; do not rework surface
Inconsistent sheen	Poor primer/priming or not working with wet edge	Recoat
Sagging (paint slides down surface)	Paint applied too thick in areas or it was thinned	Sand and recoat
Wrinkles	Second coat applied before first coat was dry enough	Scrape and sand, then recoat
Spatter (paint drops appear on surfaces that were not painted)	Too much paint on roller, rolled too fast	Use proper nap; roll in small sections not long swaths; specify wall paint for ceilings (lower-spatter formulas)
Bubbles/foam leaves tiny craters	Old paint may have been used and shaken instead of stirred; paint may have been applied too quickly, "frothing" it up	Sand and recoat properly
Blisters	Moisture is coming from below; maybe the first coat was not dry enough or the problem may be with the substrate	Scrape and sand; fix the problem; prime; recoat

INSPECTION

You may find it beneficial to evaluate the paint work in process. Aside from confirming that everything is still on schedule, you are looking at the same things that you would check at the end of the job: that the prepwork has proved to be adequate, the color is correct, the level of gloss is as specified, the work is being neatly done, and all areas to be painted are being painted. After the job has been completed, recheck all of these features as well as the clean-up on windows and hardware (check hinges especially) and other finished surfaces. Make sure there are no runs or drips or "globs" on the painted surfaces. Arrange to have all artwork, window coverings, and anything else that was removed for the paint work reinstalled if necessary. Table 2.7 lists some problems that you might notice if the painting that you are inspecting is not just right; possible solutions are included.

RELATED MATERIALS

Other products are used to coat and color surfaces. Special sustainable surfacing plasters and paints and finishes for wood are related to this topic. You can find similar product information about these related materials in Chapter 5, Wood.

Paints and Plasters

Special kinds of paints developed for sensitive client populations include milk paints that use the casein from milk as a binder. It produces a generally matte surface that can be buffed to a satin sheen. It is recommended that it be sealed for damp areas like bathrooms or where condensation might occur due to temperature, such as adjacent to large, older windows, and in skylight wells.

Table 2.8 Top Coats for Shop Finish Wood Products
You will hear mention of these finishing options when talking to your finisher.
The general descriptions of performance issues will help you discuss options as you work with your finisher to determine the best one.

Formula	Contents	Characteristics	Uses
Nitrocellulose lacquer	Solvent based, strong acids dissolve cellulose source material	Fair scratch resistance; easy to repair; only fair chemical and water resistance, yellows with age; "thin" (multiple thin coats generally better than thick coats), flexible; forgiving formula	Architectural trims, furniture, paneling, ornamental carving
Acrylic lacquer	Water- or solvent-based clear coating	Non-yellowing; relatively soft; low resistance to heat and chemicals; good stain resistance; low VOCs	Furniture, casework, paneling, blinds and shutters
Catalyzed lacquer	Hybrid formulas cure chemically via acidic additives	Good resistance to abrasion, staining and chemicals; yellows over time; finish must be sprayed on	Furniture, casework, stairs, blinds and shutters, architectural trim work, doors
Precatalyzed lacquer	Chemically cures; precatalyzed just means the catalyst is part of the formula	Fast drying; better abrasion resistance than nitrocellulosic; medium buildup; slight ambering over time	Furniture, paneling, trim work, ornamental carving, vertical stair parts (not treads), doors, window frames, shutters and blinds
Postcatalyzed lacquer	Chemically cures; catalyst is added at the time of use; small shops prefer because they mix what they need when they need it	Fast drying; easy to apply; better abrasion resistance than cellulosic; good clarity; slight ambering over time	Furniture, paneling, trim work, ornamental carving, vertical stair parts (not treads), doors, window frames, shutters and blinds
Polyester	Catalyzed finish	Waterproof; builds thick coat quickly; among the most durable finishes	Formal furniture with a "thick" finish with closed pores and slick gloss
Varnishes	Resins and oils combined, such as alkyd, phenolic, and urethane, often combined with oils like linseed, tung, safflower, and soybean	Varnishes combined with oils dry harder than oils alone and build up a surface with fewer coats Alkyd is a broadly used, general purpose varnish Phenolic is usually combined with tung oil; durable and somewhat flexible so often used on exterior work Urethane and polyurethane offers the best abrasion, solvent, and heat resistance	Casework, paneling, stairs, windows and doors, blinds and shutters, furniture, architectural trim work, countertops
Polyurethane	A varnish with urethane as the resin	Solvent-based; easy to apply, plastic finish; nonflexible; ambers with age; does not bond as easily with subsequent coats as lacquer (harder to repair than lacquers); can be applied with a brush; slow drying time: cures for approximately 30 days	Floors, furniture, paneling, trims
Conversion varnish	Catalyzed varnish cure chemically via acidic acid	Resistant to damage from scratching, heat, and solvents	Furniture, casework, stairs, blinds and shutters, architectural trim work, doors
Water-based finishes	Many of the same ingredients as oil-based but water used as a vehicle; requires emulsifiers	The ingredients of the varnishes and lacquers determine properties so variable characteristics with slight diminishment in heat and solvent resistance	Furniture, casework, stairs, blinds and shutters, architectural trim work, doors
Water-based urethane		Resin; easy to apply; nonflexible; does not amber with age; low fumes; one- and two-component formulas	Furniture, paneling, trim work, floors; two-component formulas are suitable for commercial floors
Moisture-cure urethane		Very durable, very moisture resistant; some formulas yellow with age, odorous and difficult to apply; solvent base so use is restricted	Furniture, paneling, trim work, floors
Waxes	Carnauba or beeswax	Penetrates into wood; typically used as a polish on top of another finish; damaged by water; buffing after applying wax forms a surface seal that is soft but repairable	Furniture, case goods
Oils: tung or linseed	Reactive material cures vs. hardens through evaporation of solvent	Too soft to build up much of a surface coat; low sheen; "natural" look; repairable; water spots; tung oil is a little more durable	Furniture, architectural millwork, floors
Shellac	Insect secretions form a basic ingredient combined with denatured alcohol	Not very durable; easily tinted; easy to apply; removable with alcohol; easy to touch up because new coats soften and bond with previous coats of shellac; easily damaged by water; ambers with age; select clear versions for pale wood	Beneath other finishes to seal surface and French polishing

Other coating surfaces for walls can be substituted for paints. Products like clay plasters and lime paints and plasters with pigment added are applied as a finish coat. Clay and lime plasters are generally inert and remain inert if mineral pigments are used to color them. It is common practice to wax these surfaces to protect them from soiling. The wax can also be tinted so complex color subtleties can be developed. Milk paint will often have lime in it but it is different from lime paint. Lime paint used to be called whitewash. It is less washable than regular paint.

Top Coatings for Wood

As mentioned in chapters pertaining to wood, wood is vulnerable to soiling, staining, and expansion and contraction due to changes in humidity. Top coats seal the wood, minimizing these problems. Table 2.8 breaks the finish types down by formula and characteristics.

Other Coatings

Paints and coatings are used on many surfaces, not just walls. Substrates, such as MDF and particleboard, metal, and plastics are coated with specific formulations. You are probably already aware that there is no such thing as a universal coating that can be applied to any surface. Coatings have been developed to meet a variety of needs and surfaces. Research will be required any time you specify a coating so you are sure you understand the characteristics of the coating you are specifying and confirm that it will adhere to the substrate and provide the performance that you need.

WALLCOVERINGS

Any material that can be adhered to walls, and later removed without damage to the wall, can be used as "wallpaper." The following discussion reviews materials commonly sold specifically for that purpose. However, with proper sizing and preparation, followed by careful and durable installation, your creativity can expand beyond these materials. Table 2.9 shows the various material combinations that are used to make commonly available wallcoverings.

Table 2.9
Wallcovering assembly.

Backing	Decorative Layer	Coating	Use and Care
Paper	None	None	Line walls before applying other paper
	Printed onto backing	None	Light use Dry clean
	Material (string, cork) laminated to backing		
	Printed onto paper laminated to backing		
	Printed onto paper laminated to backing	Light vinyl sprayed on	Moderate use Damp sponge
		Vinyl sheet laminated to face	Heavy residential use in kitchens and baths; light commercial use Washable
	Vinyl laminated to backing	None	Heavy residential use in kitchens and baths; commercial use varies with thickness of vinyl Washable or scrubbable
Nonwoven	Vinyl laminated to backing	None	Heavy residential use in kitchens and baths; commercial use varies with thickness of vinyl Washable or scrubbable
Scrim	Vinyl laminated to backing	None	Heavy use Washable or scrubbable
	Fabric	Teflon or Nano-Tex	Light use
	Material (string, cork) laminated to backing		
Drill	Vinyl laminated to backing	None	Heavy use Washable or scrubbable
	Fabric	Teflon or Nano-Tex	Light Damp sponge

WALLCOVERING MATERIALS

Just as paints have functional and decorative variety that is derived from the precise materials used, wallcoverings serve a variety of aesthetics and functions that are also derived from the materials used to create them.

Paper

Printed paper is the simplest form of wallcovering and is exactly what its name implies. Wallpaper is usually two kinds of paper **laminated** together with a paper that has good characteristics for printing on the front and good characteristics for adhesion on the back. Colors are printed onto the face via screens, blocks, or cylinders to produce the image on the surface. Each additional color requires an additional "screen" and the number of colors used is typically diagrammed as little squares on the **selvage** that the paperhanger trims off when installing the wallcovering. The more colors and the more complex a pattern, the higher the cost will be because of the difficulty in perfectly aligning each color with the others to form the pattern. If the successive colors are not perfectly aligned, the pattern is said to be out of **register**. Figure 2.11a and b show off-register prints. The "looser" quality of 2.11b renders the registration less important than for 2.11a. This distinction

Point of Emphasis 2.5

Not all prints are produced by screen printing; the number of colors is often called the "number of screens."

Screen print Hand-screening a pattern of different-colored inks onto the paper through mesh fabric that has portions of the mesh stopped (so no ink can get through, thus controlling the pattern) with a separate screen used for each color.

Block print A carved block (traditionally wood) has ink applied with a roller. The portions of the block that have been carved away will, of course, receive no ink, so when the block is positioned facedown on the paper, only the parts of the block that were inked will transfer color to the paper.

Cylinder print A roller is carved with a pattern; similar to the block print, ink is dispersed onto the roller, which is then rolled over the wallcovering to transfer the colors in the pattern.

FIGURE 2.11A–B Hand-blocked wallcovering will display some off-register markings because the human hand is not as precise as a machine. In this precise pattern (a) the misalignment is easy to find in the white border next to color areas. This pattern utilizes a moderately large number of screens; 11 different color layers create this pattern. In this less-precise pattern (b) the off-register marks are not as noticeable. If you are hoping to find the imperfection in the product as evidence of its hand-produced nature you may want to consider how the pattern displays, or does not display, the evidence.

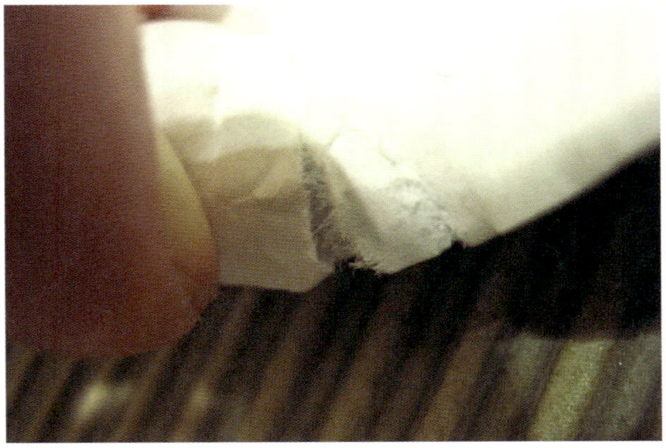

FIGURE 2.12 When the backing tears before the vinyl face, the wallcovering will be more durable against moisture and stains.

is part of your quality evaluation during selection because some kinds of patterns will require tighter registration than other designs.

Hand-printed paper is increasingly rare and most printing is now done by machine. Small defects and irregularities are to be expected on hand-blocked papers. These are considered to be the charming quirkiness of a handmade product, but a gross defect—a large, noticeable, unattractive, off-register lot—is cause for rejection of goods. You should retain all samples and strike-offs to support your point, in case of defective goods or a quality dispute.

Coated paper has a thin layer of vinyl or acrylic sprayed on. This layer of acrylic provides protection and light washability but is not to be mistaken for a more durable vinyl coating. Figure 2.12 is a zoomed-in shot of the backing paper tearing while the vinyl face merely stretched. This wallcovering is more serviceable than one where the vinyl coating tears along with the paper backing.

Small shop production and collaborative process make unique designs relatively simple to produce within reasonable price ranges. These papers may not conform to industry standards for size or installation procedures. When a special paper is being handcrafted for your client, you will meet with the fabricator and your installer and figure out how to produce a durable installation. If you are deviating from the products that are typically offered as wallpaper, you may have to invest more in labor to prepare the wall surface with special **sizing** and you may decide to seal the installation after the wallcovering has been installed.

Facing Materials Other than Paper

Any materials, backed with paper, a textile, or left unbacked, that can be glued to the wall can be used as wallcovering. Among the many commonly available choices are grass- and string-faced papers, veneers, foils, cloth, and vinyl.

FIGURE 2.13 Grass cloth has vegetable fibers glued to a paper substrate. The seams on this paper will always show, so it is important to consider the seaming plan with the hanger so the rhythm of panels is acceptable.

Grass Cloth

Grass cloth is paper faced with long woven grasses that are left natural or dyed (Figure 2.13). Paperhangers can avoid an uneven appearance by rotating every other panel as they install. The seams between panels of grass cloth always show. Special clear paste is required to avoid staining the face of the goods. Because some grass cloths will shrink as the glue cures, the hanger may not trim the top and bottom of the sheets until the glue is dry.

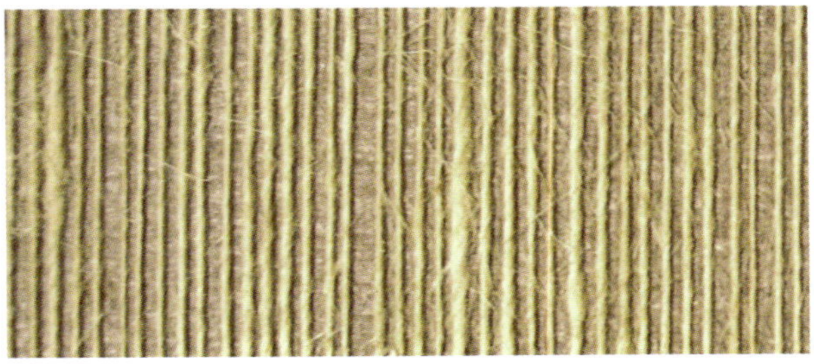

FIGURE 2.14 String paper has string glued to the paper substrate. This paper will not show its seams as readily as grass cloth.

String

String paper has continuous rows of strings laid side-by-side on a paper backing (Figure 2.14). Because the strings relate to the vertical seams, the seams can be well hidden. These coverings are especially porous and vulnerable to soiling (and cats cannot resist clawing them).

FIGURE 2.15 Cork veneer on a paper backing. The voids in the cork sample on an angle allow contrasting paper to show through to decorative effect.

Wood and Cork Veneer

Wood and cork veneer wallcoverings are real wood or cork veneers that are backed with paper or mesh, providing flexible wallcovering (Figure 2.15). They are available in different unit dimensions, so check with the manufacturer before estimating. Three feet wide is fairly common but narrower and wider widths are also available. Some manufacturers sell this material by the panel (eight or nine feet long), others by the roll. The veneer surface is ready for finishing on-site or may come prefinished.

Foil and Mylar

Foil, **Mylar**, and metalized plastic wallcoverings, backed with paper, are reflective and can show every imperfection in the wall surface, so prepwork may be more intensive than merely sizing the walls, including filling and sanding or the installation of a lining paper. These products require a level 5 finish. (For prepwork levels, refer back to Table 2.5.) Foils are actual metals and can oxidize under the wrong conditions. Mylar (DuPont trademark for their metalized polyester film) and other metalized plastics are reflective and imitate foils but will not oxidize.

> **Point of Emphasis 2.6**
> Liner paper is used as a substrate for wallpaper. It has the characteristics of the backing used for paper wallcoverings.

Flocked

Flocking is utilized by manufacturers of wallcoverings, carpeting, and fabric so the same process that you have or will encounter in other chapters applies here too. Flocked wallcovering has had glue applied, usually in some kind of pattern, in a manner similar to applying ink to printed wallcoverings. Small fibers are then sprinkled onto the glue so the wallcovering is "fuzzy" in those areas.

Cloth

Cloth can be backed with paper, knit backing, foam backing, acrylic backing, or left unbacked (Figure 2.16). If the backing is laminated rather than sprayed on, the backing process may stretch some sections of the facing material more than others. If you use a third party to back your fabric (rather than select fabric that is already backed by the manufacturer) your fabric may not arrive at the paperhanger's precisely on grain (with warp and weft at right angles to each other). Paper backing does not allow for any movement, if the hanger should have to "fudge" the alignment of a pattern, for instance. A knit-backed or acrylic-backed fabric will allow for some movement, if necessary.

Textile wallcoverings (cloth, grass cloth, and string) should be treated with a stain-repellent finish to make it easier to remove any adhesive from the face after installation. Cloth-faced wallcoverings can also have vinyl laminated over them, which will improve washability and protect the fabric from damage.

FIGURE 2.16 Fabric can be purchased paper-backed or can be laminated to paper. When you select fabric already adhered to the paper substrate you are more assured of consistency in the application than when you have fabric laminated per order by a third party.

Vinyl

Vinyl wallcoverings are usually the most cleanable. Vinyl won't be damaged by a little water. Many vinyl wallcoverings are considered to be scrubbable and can withstand more aggressive cleaning and sanitizing products, so vinyl is a good choice for areas subject to slight moisture and dirt. Vinyl can be laminated over paper or a textile. Some vinyl coverings are heavily textured expanded foam material or lightly textured **embossed** product to add texture for visual appeal and acoustic control. Another form of vinyl wallcovering is a vinyl-impregnated cloth on paper. Different classifications of vinyl are:

- *Paper-backed vinyl* is a paper substrate with two-to-five-milliliter solid vinyl layer applied to substrate in liquid form. The decorative layer is printed on the vinyl.
- *Fabric-backed vinyl* has a woven or nonwoven substrate to which up to ten milliliters of vinyl is applied in liquid form. The vinyl may be printed or embossed.
- *Solid vinyl* consists of film vinyl that is laminated to a paper or fabric substrate. It is more durable than paper-backed or fabric-backed vinyl, where the vinyl or acrylic is a coating.

Vinyl wallcoverings have been the standard for many kinds of commercial locations because they have been engineered to withstand impact and their highly cleanable surfaces can be sanitized with vigorous cleansers without damage. Vinyl presents some problems however as it off-gasses VOCs, contains PVC and plasticizers, and some colorants contain toxic metals.

Other Product Characteristics

Wallcoverings can be very durable if properly selected for your client's site but eventually they must be removed as they become worn or fashion changes and looks must be updated. This will sometimes necessitate tedious work and steaming equipment to loosen the covering from the wall. If the wall was not properly sized before installing the covering, the wall is likely to be damaged as the wallcovering is removed. Some wallcoverings are designed to be strippable, meaning they can be dry-stripped from the wall (no steaming required) leaving only traces of adhesive that can be easily washed off. If you anticipate that your client will always want wallpaper for that surface, you might specify a peelable wallcovering. This means that when the wallpaper is removed the decorative face delaminates from the backing paper. The backing paper stays on the wall providing a perfect surface for a new wallcovering.

Some designs are developed for special uses. Borders are narrower wallcoverings designed to hang with a horizontal orientation. A unit of border paper is referred to as a spool instead of a roll. Ceiling papers are designs that are nondirectional and look correct from any angle. Mural papers are panels that must be hung in precise consecutive order to complete a scene. These costly papers are often installed with restoration techniques so that they are removable intact for reinstallation elsewhere.

Custom Colorways for Wallcovering

Some manufacturers will custom color any of their designs on a **ground** (the paper or vinyl that is the base material for the patterned wallpaper). Minimum quantities usually apply and often there is a setup charge in addition to the usual costs. Custom colors and patterns can also be hand-blocked onto any suitable ground.

The custom process will increase the delivery time of the order. You will need time to investigate possible design impact of color combinations in relation to the pattern selected. You may need more than one strike-off (sample) as color combinations may have unexpected results. Include the time for production of the strike-off as well as transportation of the strike-off between the fabricator, your office, and your client. It is advisable to have the unit cost per strike-off stated up front if there is a limit to the number of strike-offs that will be produced as part of the order cost.

> **Point of Emphasis 2.7**
> Color theory effects, such as simultaneous contrast and color vibration/phantom color, are often exhibited in various color combinations on wallcoverings. As intriguing as these effects are to encounter, they are best avoided in your wallcovering designs.

For the Connoisseur 2.2

Wallcovering often serves functional purposes; vinyl provides a more durable surface than paint. It also must serve an aesthetic function, and pattern and color are central to such considerations. But what is it that makes some wallcoverings command such a high price? There are several categories where the designer can look to find a product that would earn the descriptor "exquisite." Things that your client might value enough to pay a high price include:

Historical accuracy Some people seek a connection to the past and will pay more for a special archival pattern.

Material Patterns printed on silk or delicate handmade paper are especially satisfying to some clients. The difficulty in handling such materials commands a high price.

Exclusivity Hand-blocked (meaning the pattern is stamped on by hand rather than by machines) with its inherent unique presentation is more one-of-a-kind than untouched-by-human-hands machine perfection. A custom-designed wallcovering made by an artist will have similar value.

Novelty Unusual surfaces that surprise people also delight them.

Backings

Products offered for sale as wallcoverings are typically backed with a material that is compatible with the covering. If you are selecting a backing for a product that is not sold as a wallcovering but you intend to use it that way, the different characteristics of various backings should be considered.

- *Woven* (light = scrim, heavy = drill/cotton twill) backings allow for flexibility so the paperhanger can make minor adjustments, if necessary, while hanging. The various weights should correspond to the material being backed. The backing should be lighter in weight than the face.
- *Nonwoven* backings will be dimensionally stable because of the randomized orientation of the fiber and fiber content of the backing. This backing will also be flexible, allowing for adjustment.
- *Knit* backing is a fine open knit and allows for adjustment at the site since it is so flexible.
- *Paper* backing fixes the dimensions of the covering and is not flexible, so the paperhanger cannot make adjustments on-site. This selection should be reserved for coverings that are also very stable, such as tightly woven chintz, or materials that do not require any pattern matching.
- *Contact paper* is an engineered substrate of cellulose, polyester, and a synthetic polymeric backing designed especially to stabilize patterns. These products feel like paper but have improved performance and are a more expensive option.
- *Acrylic or latex* backing maintains flexibility and, because it is applied in liquid form, it bonds fibers together. This backing would be selected for a fabric likely to unravel at the cut edges where you expected that adjustments would be needed at the site.
- *Lining paper* is a backing that is not yet adhered to a facing material. It may be installed on the wall and then the decorative wallcovering would be installed over it rather than being adhered to the wallcovering. Special bridging lining would be selected to mask texture on the wall if necessary.

Helpful Hint 2.6

Minor imperfections can be concealed by adhering lining paper to the walls if you intend to install another wallcovering. If you intend to paint, lining paper is not the best, so consult with your painter, who will likely recommend a fine canvas instead.

RATINGS APPLICABLE TO WALLCOVERINGS

There are a couple of different rating systems serving the industry and familiarity with them can help you narrow your search. One relates to all wallcovering and the other describes **commercial/contract wallcovering** specifically.

Ratings for All Wallcoverings

- Class I: Decorative
- Class II: Decorative and serviceable (more washable and colorfast)
- Class III: Decorative with good serviceability; medium use for abrasion and stain resistance; meets strength and crocking resistant standards
- Class IV: Decorative with full serviceability, heavy consumer and light commercial use; meets strength, crocking, and tear-resistance criteria
- Class V: Medium commercial serviceability; high-abrasion and crocking resistance; colorfast and tear resistant
- Class VI: full commercial serviceability; in addition to above criteria, resists cold cracking, heat aging, and shrinkage

Ratings for Commercial Vinyl Wallcoverings

These wallcoverings are all fire-rated.

- Type I: Light duty for offices, hotel rooms, patient rooms; 12 to 18 ounces per lineal yard
- Type II: Medium duty for reception areas, corridors, classrooms; 18 to 24 ounces per lineal yard
- Type III: Heavy duty for hospital corridors and other heavy uses with moving equipment; heavier than 24 ounces per lineal yard

PRODUCTION

Patterns are often produced in several different color combinations called colorways. A **stock** pattern may also be printed on a variety of different grounds that are available coated or uncoated, so there are often many different ways you can specify a given pattern. The manufacturer will produce one colorway and then the printing machinery will undergo a color change where some or all of the ink colors will be replaced with different colors and a new production run will be printed. Pattern and run numbers are printed along the edge of the wallcovering. The color run is akin to the fabric dye lot, so another run of the same pattern in the same colorway may not match another run. (This edge is trimmed off during installation.) Wallcoverings shipped for your order must all come from the same run to ensure uniform appearance.

Table 2.10
Standard wallcovering sizes.

Type of Covering	Width	Length	Coverage	Sold
American rolls	27"	4.5 to 5 yards per single roll	30–33 SF/roll	Double or triple
European rolls	20.5"	5.5 yards per single roll	27.5 SF/roll	Single or double
English rolls	20.5"	11 yards per single roll	55 SF/roll	Single
Borders	No standard	5 yards per spool	5 lineal yards	Spool
Vinyl	54"	Sold by the yard in 30- to 35-yard-long bolts	13.5 SF/yard	Per yard

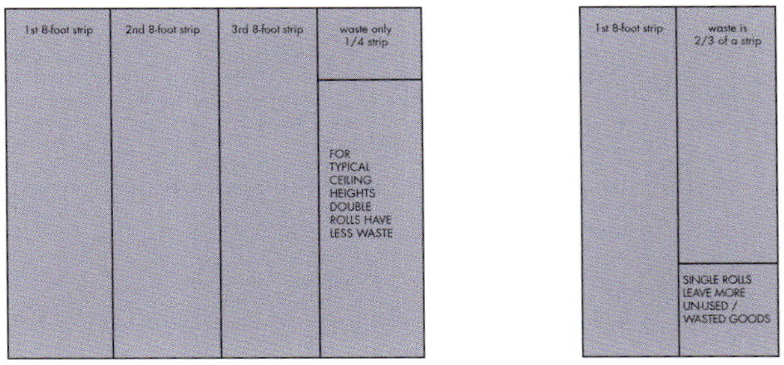

FIGURE 2.17 Single versus double roll yields demonstrate the material savings for two rolls of wallcovering left contiguous rather than cut into separate rolls. It is priced by the single roll but shipped in doubles.

SIZES AND ESTIMATING

Standard wallcoverings come in a variety of forms and sizes and are generally proportioned similarly, as shown in Table 2.10, so these sizes can be used for purposes of estimating and budgeting.

Wallcoverings are manufactured in several standard sizes. American single rolls are 27 inches wide, European rolls are 22 inches wide, grass cloths are usually 36 inches wide, and vinyl is typically 54 inches wide. Most papers produced for the residential market are priced by the single roll but sold in double or triple rolls to reduce waste. Wallcoverings are produced in lengths longer than the lengths shipped. A long strip of wallpaper coming off the machine is cut into single, double, or triple rolls. When the wallpaper is priced by the single roll but shipped in doubles or triples this means that two or three rolls will be left together rather than be cut apart. Figure 2.17 demonstrates the coverage of a single versus a double roll. Unless a cutting charge is offered, allowing you to purchase an odd number of rolls, you have to round up to the nearest multiple.

Commercial vinyls are often sold by the yard or the bolt. Bolts commonly contain 30, 50, or 60 yards depending on their weight. The best way to know for sure how much wallcovering comes in a single unit for any wallcovering product (bolt, roll, double roll) is to ask the supplier. The number will probably be stated in terms of yards for commercial vinyl or in terms of square feet for residential rolls, so you may have to perform a little math to deduce the length by dividing the width (in feet) into the square feet to arrive at the length.

Estimating

General rules can be used if the roughest of take-offs is sufficient. For example, an American roll will usually cover about 30 square feet of wall surface. Subtract a half roll for every door or window of similar size. If the wallcovering is metric add an extra roll for every four American rolls. Patterned wallcovering will result in some waste. For a **repeat** up to 6 inches, reduce the 30-square-feet coverage rule to 25; for 7 to 12 inches, the coverage will be closer to 22 square feet; for 13 to 18 inches it drops to 20 square feet and for 19 to 23 inches it will be about 18 square feet.

Calculating Quantities for Cost Comparisons

The most precise way to estimate wallcovering is to use the strip method. It is the method that most paperhangers use when estimating quantity.

1. Measure the perimeter of the room and divide by the width of the paper to determine the number of panels or alternately, tick off the panel widths on your to-scale plans illustrated in Figure 2.18. The benefit of looking at a plan while you determine the panel count is that you can understand where the seams will fall. If you are using a grass cloth or other materials where the seams will be apparent you may decide to shift the layout and will then know what additional instructions you should give the installer. The pattern will not match up where the first strip meets the last one. So identify on your plan where this mismatch will be least noticeable and note where the installation should begin.

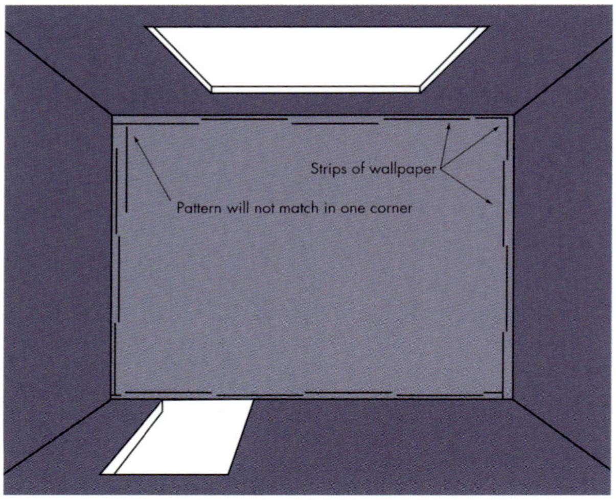

FIGURE 2.18 The most precise way to estimate the quantity of wallcovering required is the strip method. It will also help you to visualize how the pattern of seams may lay out if you have a wallcovering where the seams will not hide well.

2. Calculate the total running length of paper required by multiplying the number of panels times the length of the panels. Recall that the quick calculation instruction above directed you to deduct a roll for every two openings, but Figure 2.19 diagrams a configuration that disallows any subtraction of material for an opening, so that kind of deduction is for the quick take-off to produce a ballpark estimate only.
3. Repeats are important in determining the quantity of wallcovering required. The kind of match—drop match or side match (Figure 2.20)—does not cause as much difference on quantity as does the length of the repeat, but the kind of match should also be relayed to the paperhanger before finalizing quantity. Divide the size of the vertical length of the repeat into the height of the wall and round up to the next full repeat. Multiply that number by the vertical length of the repeat. This will give you a cut length.
4. Divide the cut length required by the length available in a single unit (single roll if sold by the roll, bolt if sold by the bolt, in a single yard if sold by the yard, etc.) to arrive at the number of units required. Add one full repeat per roll to your order so you can start the first cut where you want it.

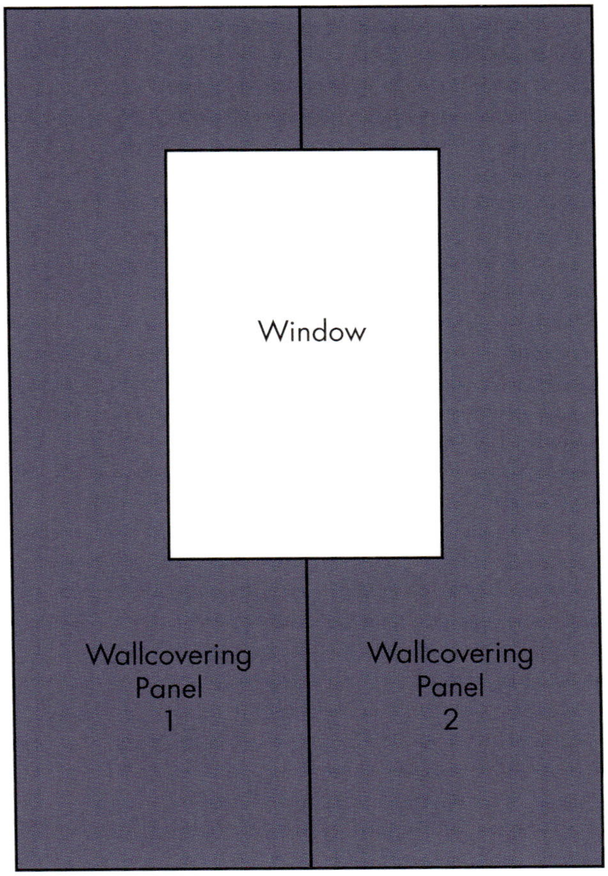

FIGURE 2.19 Formulas do not always yield accurate information. The formula may tell you that you can deduct so much wallcovering for openings but if the full length of wallcovering only partly intersects with the window you cannot reduce your order per formula and receive enough paper.

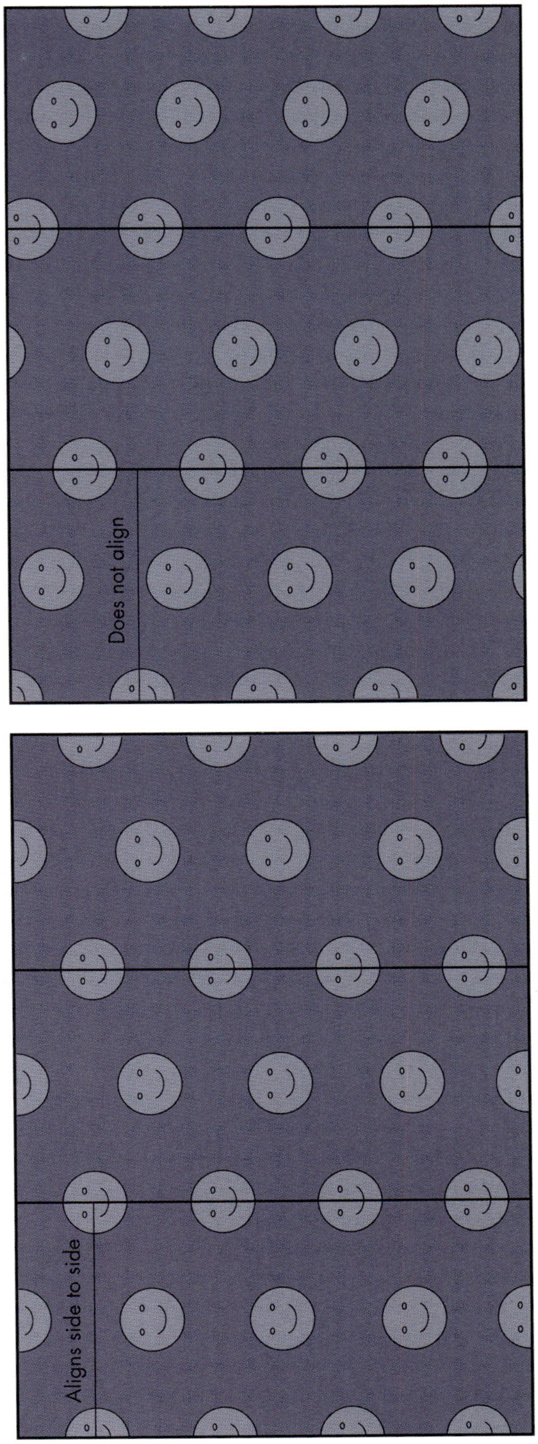

FIGURE 2.20 The match may be described as a straight/side match or it may be a half-drop or other match. This info should be given to the estimator when you are ready to place the order. It does not always mean more paper than estimated will be required but better to have overage on hand than come up short.

QUALIFYING INSTALLERS

You will interview the installer about similar work that he or she has done in the past and ask how the work was done, what issues came up in the hanging and how they were handled. If possible, you should review photos of similar installations. If the job is especially tricky and the material is costly (if you are hanging a hand-blocked fabric with some inconsistency in the match for instance) you may ask to see a completed installation of a similar material, even if it is not recent. While inspecting the installation you should evaluate:

1. How neatly the matching was done and if an exact match was not possible, whether the seams are inconspicuous.

2. Whether the seams are clean (with no glue, wrinkles, etc.).
3. Whether the overall job appears to run on grain and the pattern is well placed relative to architectural details.

You should also interview previous clients of the hanger and ask about the quality of the installation, the accuracy of the estimates for material and time, and the professionalism of the workers (i.e., their general tidiness and courtesy).

OBTAINING AN ESTIMATE

When it is time to draft the proposal to your client, you will obtain written estimates from one or more paperhangers. The installer will tell you how much paper to deliver to the job site or their receiving room. Along with your request for bid, you should forward:

- A description of the job: Location, room name, condition.
- Scope of work: Washing, sizing, other work required for the walls, in addition to hanging the paper. Include any special instruction from the manufacturer in the scope of work list.
- Description of the material: Type of wallcovering (paper-faced vinyl, paper, etc.), unit of measure (yard, American roll, etc.), width, and repeat. Tell the installer if the paper is **prepasted** or **pretrimmed**.
- Description of any other work that will have to be done: Will old wallcovering have to be stripped from the walls first? Will the walls have to be sized, primed, deglossed, or otherwise prepared?

Include a to-scale plan and information on how to gain access if the hanger wants to inspect the job site before bidding. If you need the bid by a certain date or if there is a deadline for completing the work, you should also include that information with your request for bid.

INSTALLATION

Wallcovering is typically one of the last materials to be installed and if it is a delicate, decorative product you will make sure that the hanger is the last trade to work in the area. Preparation varies with the product and site conditions, so you will review manufacturers' installation instructions before you approve them for your job.

Prepwork

In addition to the prepwork required for painting (including priming with the recommended primer, traditionally an alkyd-modified primer) you will need to bring the surface to a particular quality level that will often be specified by the wallcovering manufacturer. The metalized wallcovering mentioned earlier typically requires a level 5 finish. Other products, like grass cloth, string paper, and textured vinyls, are very good at camouflaging a level 3 surface quality. It is a waste of money to bring a surface to a higher finish level than required, so if you are specifying for new work confirm requirements.

On an existing site, old wallpaper may have to be removed, walls may need to be deglossed or sanded so that the adhesive will stick. All holes and cracks must be repaired. Walls may have to be sized so the paper can be stripped off without damage at the end of its life and to limit absorbency of the wall surface and allow for a good bond between the wall and the wallcovering. If the walls are not smooth enough, a bridging primer may be recommended or a liner paper may be installed.

If walls have a textured finish they may be able to be sanded or you may instruct the installer to apply a skim coat of a plaster product. If the walls are primed with a color similar to the color of the wallcovering, any small opening that develops from paper shrinkage as the glue dries will be less noticeable.

In order to minimize the visual presence of HVAC grilles and electrical device cover plates, you may want to have them covered as well. This works better with wallcoverings that are thin than it would for coverings that are heavy, commercial wallcoverings with a drill or foam back. Since these covers likely start out as a flat sheet of metal, wallcoverings can be sliced for vent openings or have their corners notched to eliminate bulk and adhered to the face of these covers. Return grilles tend to soil more and a covered grille is a little harder to clean, so you may decide to selectively paint those covers to match the wallcovering ground even if you decide to paper supply and electrical device covers.

Wallcovering is usually installed from the bottom of any crown molding to the top of base molding and does not extend behind these millwork trims because that would make it difficult to remove wallcovering in the future.

FIGURE 2.21 International symbols for characteristics and performance of wallcoverings are a necessity in today's world market.

PROTECTION/MAINTENANCE

Instructions pertaining to the handling, installation, and maintenance of wallcoverings are usually included with the shipment and may be given in the form of international symbols as shown in Figure 2.21.

If the face of a wallcovering is likely to be marred by adhesive, it is a good idea to have the face sealed prior to the installation so any stray adhesive can be removed. This goes for fabric and string papers and textured absorbent material like cork or unsealed wood veneers. Painting work on trims and ceilings required in the space should be completed before the wallcovering goes up.

SAFETY

Wallcoverings are generally safe to use. Some products are antimicrobial or have biocides to combat problems in the job environment, such as microorganisms or mold. There has been some discussion about the contribution that wallcoverings make to the growth of mold. Wallcoverings generally offer no special nutritive environment for mold growth but it will not correct moisture problems inherent in the building structure that might promote the growth of mold. If you have a concern about potential for mold growth because of the climate in your job area you can ask the manufacturer of your nonbreathable wallcovering (breathable coverings are less likely to grow mold than nonbreathable) for microvented product. Microventing is invisible when the wallcovering is installed and you can only see the small perforations when you hold the wallcovering up to the light.

SUSTAINABILITY

The material specified may have recycled content in it. The use of vinyls should be carefully evaluated weighing their serviceability against the negative environmental affects. Heavy vinyl protects wall surfaces against damage in places where wheeled carts are used (hospitals, hotels, etc.) and they can be easily sanitized. As much as designers would like to stop specifying vinyl, it is still frequently selected for those advantages. All considerations of your design program must be weighed as you evaluate materials with potential negative sustainability characteristics but remember that the least sustainable material is the one that does not endure. Select water-based inks, limit coatings and additives to adhesives that could emit VOCs. While never forgetting that an appropriate specification (in terms of aesthetics as well as function) will endure longer than an inappropriate one, so a sustainable material that does not perform may be replaced before the end of its useful life and that is not a sustainable outcome. Look for recycled content in vinyl and shop for PVC-free materials.

Our long-standing love affair with the practicalities of vinyl leave us with a sustainability quandary. Vinyl is not an ecologically sound material; thermoplastic olefin is a possible substitute. It is low emitting and does not have other chemical components that we worry about with vinyl wallcovering.

MANAGING BUDGETS

Materials are likely to represent the greatest price variation from one job to another. Materials that are rare or difficult to handle can increase the cost of producing the material. Printed wallcoverings that have multiple screens are more difficult to produce and can raise the price of the material significantly. Exclusive designs and sometimes historical designs can command premium pricing.

Most wallpapers are so consistent in their form and matching that paperhangers will often figure their installation costs on a flat fee per roll or yard of covering hung. If a hand-blocked fabric is being used, the hanger may charge on a time and materials basis to allow for degrees of possible variation. Highly specialized wallcoverings that are difficult to handle (silk textile wallcovering or other materials that cannot be easily cleaned) will require a slow and careful installation and installers will usually account for that in their pricing. When you are subject to a time and materials fee, try to obtain a "not-to-exceed price." Keep in mind that the maximum agreed-on price that will be charged often becomes the final fee.

ORGANIZATION OF THE INDUSTRY

The industry is quite varied in supply of wallcoverings, from the small custom hand-block shop to the large manufacturer. It is quite common for **companion** or **correlated wallcovering** products to be produced, designed to be used together on a job site with several distinct areas. These correlated suites of patterns often share a common color scheme and are designed in patterns that will enhance each other or will at least not fight with one another. As you browse the wallpaper books at the vendor, these companion wallcoverings are shown together. Product originates in many countries but in order to achieve any market share, the manufacturer must have representation in the country where it is to be sold. The wallpaper is somewhat segmented between trade and "street" sources but less so than for other products. Exclusivity is disappearing in this product category as the Internet gives your clients access to product that once upon a time could only be accessed through a designer. If you have structured your business with a markup versus a fee for services, you will want to restrict your search to those products that are available only through the trade.

Discontinued product on hand is often sold at a reduced price. The quantity is referred to as a job-lot and is often available at a reduced price. You will want to be sure you have enough to complete your order because, even if another vendor also has it on hand, the likelihood that you can find it and that it will be from the same run is very slim. Retail vendors will also sell room lots, sale units consisting of enough rolls of a pattern for a typical room, with a set quantity, but the professional designer is unlikely to specify a random quantity that way. Retail and Internet sources will also sell off-grade, not first quality, wallcoverings at deep discounts. The defects that you will find in them are often minor and a room that is of little importance, such as a laundry room, may be the kind of place that you would make the unusual decision to specify an inferior quality to save money.

Paperhangers generally receive their training on the job but may attend classes to learn how to hang wallcoverings. Many small-shop painters also hang wallcovering and many large-shop painters have a division for paperhanging specialists, but the single-person shop that has years of experience is well suited to a small job, especially if meticulous details are part of the plan.

SELECTION CRITERIA

Your design program should define material performance characteristics in enough detail to use it to determine choice of wallcovering that you might select. Organize your own unique program points to indicate a list of options, perhaps in the manner shown in Table 2.11.

SPECIFYING

Let's imagine that you are the lead designer for a nightclub in Jackson Hole, Wyoming, that is to be a tongue-in-cheek tribute to painter Jackson Pollock. At one point in his career Pollock painted by dropping and dripping paint on canvases, incorporating cigarette butts and other detritus into the surface, where it adhered to the paint. You have decided that for one accent wall in the club you are going to commission a local artist to create a wallcovering that incorporates small mementos from other local venues, such as ticket stubs, signature swizzle sticks, etc., into the surface. This wallcovering will cover a wall that is 18 feet wide and 9 feet tall with a continuous effect that does not look like individual strips of canvas. So you have decided to have the canvas paper-backed by a backer that serves the design trade applying various kinds of backing and coating to fabric as well as chemically treating the flammable material for use in commercial environments. Then your paperhanger will cut the panels to fit (with a few inches extra top and bottom to allow for a surface that might be out of square). The fabricator, who is a huge fan of Pollock, will lay the paper-backed canvas panels out and hopes to "channel" Pollock while creating the panels. The following spec would be addressed to the fabricator painting the custom wallcovering.

Table 2.11
Possible organization for your wallcovering selection criteria.

Condition	Program Implications
Is this a high-traffic commercial space?	Select type III wallcovering.
Is this a brainstorming space?	Consider dry-erase wallcovering.
What needs are there for visual organization and wayfinding?	Select directional patterns or color-cue with selection.
Is there a concern that the building configuration could foster the growth of mold?	Consider microventilated wallcovering and a biocide installation system.
Will acoustics be a concern for the design of this area?	Select acoustical wallcovering with a high NRC rating.
Will you be trying to maximize daylighting?	Reflectance for walls should be between 40% and 70%.
How interested is your client in sustainability?	Consider materials other than vinyl but perform LCA (life cycle cost analysis) to be sure you don't compromise durability (which could tip your scale in the opposite direction).
Are you attempting to give an institutional building a residential atmosphere?	Residential wallcoverings are often used in light-traffic areas for that reason. Residential rooms in a nursing home are generally light-traffic places where you can use residential products.
How cleanable must the covering be?	Match cleanability with your design program for an appropriate choice.

SAMPLE SPEC 2.2

Part 1 General Information

1.1 Related Documents

A. Refer to finish plan for location of material to be installed by others.

B. Refer to books about Pollock by Emmerling, Lanchner, Namuth, and Karmel with pages tagged by designer for technique and color.

1.2 Summary

A. Paper-backed canvas to be supplied (backing applied by others), cut to approximate size by the installer. Painting technique discussed to be utilized to create the appearance upon installation (by others) of a continuous canvas, with a pattern of drips and drops continuing from one piece to the next.

B. Dominant, color-contrasted swoops to be used to emphasize continuity of panels.

1.3 References

A. No solvents to be applied or use of any chemical that will diminish effectiveness of fire-resistive chemical treatment applied by others.

1.4 Contractor Submittals

A. Provide daily pictorial diary of job progress with series of close-ups at junction between one panel and the next to confirm that illusion of continuity and imitation of technique accomplish all goals listed in these specifications.

1.5 Quality Assurance

A. As a Jackson Pollock fan, fabricator to strive to create wallcovering that closely imitates Pollock's technique and decision processes.

B. Panels to be laid out in the artist's studio in order of installation with no spaces in between consecutive panels for the painting.

C. Final review and approval to be performed by designer upon completion of canvases.

1.6 Delivery, Storage, and Handling

A. Upon completion, and when panels have cured sufficiently to roll and transport, a moving company will deliver them to the site. Numbering of panels to be visible on panel backs when panels are rolled.

1.7 Maintenance of Installation

A. Installation to be performed by INstallexperts, who will maintain order noted as well as visually confirm that texture of painting is contiguous before installation.

Part 2 Products

2.1 General Information

A. Installation materials and tools required to complete the installation to be provided by INstallexperts.

SAMPLE SPEC 2.2 (continued)

2.2 Manufacturers

A. Backing and fireproofing to be provided by Back Me Up, 1234 Industrial Drive, Anytown, ST 45678.

B. Painting of custom wallcovering to be provided by Lee Smith, 1234 Student Ghetto, Anytown, ST 45678.

C. Installation by INstallexperts, 3456 Industrial Drive, Anytown, ST 45678.

2.3 Products

A. Unsized canvas to be paper-backed for wall application and fireproofed before delivery.

B. Custom-painted canvas to have acrylic paint dropped onto canvas for color and texture and also to adhere mementos (provided by designer) unevenly distributed as discussed.

Part 3 Execution

3.1 Examination

A. Fabricator to confirm that canvas is thoroughly adhered to paper backing across entire surface and that no bleeding of adhesive will interfere with tight bond between acrylic paint and canvas.

B. No frayed edges or damaged fabric is to be painted; notify designer immediately regarding any damage or defect.

C. Installer to confirm that walls are primed (by others) and ready to receive sizing and canvas by INstallexperts.

3.2 Preparation

A. Using the general colors and techniques identified by the designer and tagged in books, and litter and mementos provided, fabricator to create a facsimile of large Pollock canvas.

B. Final product is to appear to be a contiguous canvas.

3.3 Installation

A. Installer to size walls and install panels in sequence, trimming top to align with top of partition and bottom to be neatly trimmed along top of baseboard. Care is to be used when abutting panels side-by-side to ensure that continuity of paint technique is maintained to create illusion of contiguous canvas.

3.4 Post Installation

A. Remove all scraps and debris.

INSPECTION

Your paperhanger is the one who will likely be responsible for checking the quality of the material delivered for the job as you will ship the product directly to the hanger. That is why you will want to send a memo or piece of your strike-off with your installation order. The hanger will be able to spot defects like **bleeding**, **blooming**, color **crocking**, off-register prints, and the like but will not be able to judge quality without a sample. The hanger will compare the quality of the sample to the goods delivered as they are hung, so unless you specify that the wall covering is to be inspected upon arrival, problems will not be discovered until the installation. If a construction delay causes a lag time between delivery and installation you may want to request that a roll be inspected.

You will inspect the installation to check the seams for a tight, accurate match and make sure there is no adhesive on the face of the paper. Make sure that natural material (cork, grass cloth, etc.) was installed so as to minimize the effect of variations in the panels and that fabric orientation is consistent (fabric may reflect light differently depending on which way it is hung). There should be no bubbles or crush marks. All cuts should be straight and neat.

If HVAC grilles are covered, be sure:

1. The slices are straight and neat.
2. The covering is adhering tightly to the entire surface.
3. The corners of covered plates and grilles are neatly folded and tightly adhered.
4. On fabric or string wallcovering, cuts do not show fraying or loose edges.

For restoration of historic places, installation techniques that were originally used are followed with the addition of one more step, installing acid-free liner paper. Historically, the plaster was sized with diluted glue and a lining paper was installed using cooked wheat paste. Then a layer of 100 percent cotton muslin was installed on top of the blank lining paper and the decorative wallpaper was installed on top of that. Today we add a second layer of acid-free lining paper beneath the decorative paper to ensure longevity of the installation.

RELATED MATERIAL

Specialty painting is often used in place of patterned or textured wallcovering. Linen-painted textures, stencil patterns, and graphic appliqué function in a similar manner aesthetically if not functionally. Another closely related material application would be custom-upholstered wall panels.

Like custom-wood wall panels, upholstered panels will be drawn up in elevation and put out to bid. It will probably be your preference to have the fabricator also handle installation. Drapery workrooms often supply this kind of service and some upholstery shops also do this kind of work. Panels will require some kind of stable substrate. Homasote is often used; it can be backed with MDF or other material to strengthen it if necessary. Panels can be padded with a layer of foam or polyester batting. They can be hung on the wall with cleats or Velcro or some other concealed method that is demountable. The panels should probably not be glued since this would make it impossible to change the fabric without damage to the panel substrate and the wall. Walls may be padded out and fabric panels tacked top and bottom and a millwork trim or fabric welt added to cover all tack locations and seams between panel widths.

More consideration to service outlets must be given to upholstered panels than for wood panels. The same issues apply but are compounded by maintenance considerations. HVAC vents (returns as well as supplies) and switch plates will be areas subject to soiling. HVAC grilles are problematic because wherever a lot of air is moving past a textile there will be extra soiling. Switch plates will accumulate dirt from hands. Areas adjacent to windows that open are vulnerable to soiling as well. Cleats for hanging artwork will have to be modified so the artwork does not "dimple" the wall upholstery.

The fabric width should exceed the panel width to avoid having a seam on the face of the panel. Repeats will have to be figured into the planning and placement and all of this information must be clearly communicated to the fabricator in drawings and notes. You may want to inspect the panels at the shop prior to their delivery to the site to make sure that the panels are covered as instructed, on grain and free of unwanted tucks and puckers, and that the padding is smooth and of the proper puffiness. It will be easier to correct or adjust panels at the shop than on-site.

There are experimental materials that use heat-reactive ink that changes color with temperature and coverings that incorporate LEDs or glow-in-the-dark inks that emit light. Light-reactive plastic films and other new material technologies have enlivened this material category.

SUMMARY

In this chapter we covered the selection of paints, primers, and wallcoverings, addressed paint formula, sheen level for paint, and quality distinctions and product types for wallcoverings. We reviewed sustainable and safety considerations for paint and wallcoverings. We reviewed potential problems with site conditions, materials, and labor. We learned how the coatings industry is organized and how wallcoverings are produced, distributed, and installed. We reviewed considerations for selecting product and tradespeople and specifying labor and materials. We reviewed typical job progression for standard and custom installations. We reviewed budget considerations and how to make decisions appropriate for your site conditions and design program. We reviewed punch list items for coatings and wallcovering installations.

WEB SEARCH ACTIVITIES

1. Visit a paint manufacturer's Web site and go to the section for architects and designers. Imagine a surface that you might paint in your home or at your job. Go to the product section pertaining to primers and then to the section with paint formulas. Select products that you would specify based on performance characteristics of this particular formula.

2. Perform an image or video search for *repair old plaster walls* or *patch plaster walls*. You will likely be able to understand the processes described in step-by-step photos with descriptions. If you search for videos, try to find a professionally made video from one of the popular TV shows (the amateur videos can give you vertigo).

3. Search for *painters union* and add your zip code after the string to see what kind of community is available to painters in your area. Check for educational opportunities and apprentice programs. What skill level for painters is promoted by resources in your area?

4. Go to a major paint manufacturer's Web site and locate a material safety data sheet (MSDS) for one of their primers or paints. Review the ingredients and cautions and decide if you would use this product on a job site and under what conditions.

5. Find a master spec for a painted surface on the Internet and review it for comprehension.

6. Go to a commercial wallcoverings Web site (you can access some through the Wallcoverings Association Web site: www.wallcoverings.org) and search for a commercial wallcovering product that contains no PVC, chlorine, or heavy metals. Review its spec sheet for other attributes such as light fastness, flame resistance, cleaning recommendations, and other characteristics that you would consider if you were specifying wallcovering for the corridors in a hospital or hotel.

7. Search for *specialty wallpaper*, *custom wallcovering manufacturers*, or some similar string. Notice the breadth of resources available. If you have time, click on some to see their product offerings and potential for truly custom work.

8. Go to an international sourcing site such as www.alibaba.com and enter *wallpaper* in the Products bar and select different countries from the Origin drop-down menu. Notice that there are wallcoverings available on the international market produced in many countries. As an alternative search you could use the word *wallcovering* followed by individual countries you are curious about to see what kinds of wallcovering products are being produced in those locations.

9. Locate a material safety data sheet (MSDS) for a commercial wallcovering.

10. Go to www.wallcoverings.org and select a manufacturer. Visit a few manufacturers' Web sites. Compare the information that you are able to find out about residential wallcoverings versus commercial wallcoverings. It is likely that there will be much more information available to the commercial designer than the residential designer.

PERSONAL ACTIVITIES

1. Go to a store that sells paint and look for a sample card that shows different sheen levels. If samples are made available to take, take one; if not, notice the differences and take some notes to help you remember such as:

   Flat—has no gloss from any angle
   Eggshell—looks flat when viewed head-on but has a sheen when seen from an angle (and so on)

   Or contact a manufacturer and request a sheen-level card.

   Use the card as a reference to determine the sheen level on walls to trim to furniture—as many as you can notice. Consider in each instance if that sheen level makes sense to you. Also notice how the finish is holding up. Can it be kept clean? Does it show fingerprints? Is it abrading (wearing off)?

2. Consider an area in your own plan where you might use a painted surface or find a picture of an installation of a painted surface in an interior space. Select a product and, using the spec template in Chapter 2, write a spec for the item or surface.

3. Imagine a highly custom wallcovering. It could be as simple as the pages of your favorite book laminated to blank stock (undecorated wallpaper) or cigarette butts à la Jackson Pollock adhered with acrylic paint to canvas or items stitched to fabric that is glued to paper, etc. Where would you find the materials you need? Who could you hire to make it—or would you make it yourself?

   You just finished reading about qualifying installers, installing, inspecting, specifying, and the rest—think of how your custom wallcovering relates to each part of this process.

4. Select a wallpaper that you can imagine using in your plan (or in the to-scale plan that you have found for this exercise). Select a place in one of the rooms where it will be the least noticeable if the pattern does not match up (a corner behind a door is a good choice). See how many panels you will need and perform a take-off of the length you will need. Just presume a nine-foot ceiling if there is no ceiling height given. Using any method, calculate the quantity of the wallcovering that you have selected, calculating for the stated repeat (if any), and adding 10 percent waste factor to your quantity.

SUMMARY QUESTIONS

1. Describe the difference between primer formulations.
2. How are primers different from paints?
3. Describe the different paint formulas, highlighting their differences.
4. Rank sheen level in order from lowest to highest using standard industry terminology.
5. Which materials require an alkyd base?
6. What characteristics can be provided by special primer formulas?
7. How can you determine which primer and which paint to use?
8. How would you approach the repair for a plaster wall with fine surface cracks throughout?
9. How would you approach the repair of a plaster surface with large, loose sections?
10. How would you approach the repair of a settling crack?
11. How would you explain to your client why one contractor's bid is higher than another's?
12. What would you inspect for when the walls are primed?
13. What would be on your checklist to inspect for when the walls are painted?
14. What is skim coating? What are the benefits of it?
15. What conditions would you account for when evaluating existing trim to determine the scope of work in repainting it?
16. How are faux finishes created?
17. What sustainability issues pertain to paint and painting?
18. What are some alternative materials if you want lower toxicity and more sustainability than is typical?
19. What organizations issue guidelines pertaining to air quality with regards to paints and coatings?
20. How are painters trained?
21. What are some common problems with coatings and how can they be resolved?
22. What are the different decorative faces used for wallcoverings and what are the differences in their performance?
23. What backings are used and what circumstances indicate the use of which wallcovering?
24. What is the distinction between custom wallcovering and custom colorways?
25. What is the difference between vinyl and vinyl-coated wallcovering?
26. What are the two rating systems that pertain to wallcoverings and what does each of the numbered ratings mean?
27. What steps are necessary to estimate the quantity of wallcovering needed for purposes of budgeting?
28. What information should you give the installer when you are ready for an actual estimate of quantity of wallcovering and labor price?
29. What kind of prepwork prepares walls for wallcovering?
30. When would you use an antimicrobial system? A biocide? Microvented vinyl?
31. What is the difference between strippable and peelable?
32. What sustainability issues pertain to wallcovering?
33. What characteristics can add to your price for the job?
34. When inspecting a completed job what kinds of things will you look for?

Chapter 3

TEXTILES, WINDOW TREATMENTS, AND SOFT GOODS

Key Terms

Biodiversity
Calendering
Cellulosic
Chintz
Crimped
Denier
Economies of scale
Felted
Filaments
Floats
Greige goods
Hand
Inside mount
Memo sample
Mercerizing
Monoculture
Nap
Off-grain
Pile
Protein
Seam slippage
Stackback
Synthetic
Twill
Worsted

Objectives

After completing this chapter, you should be able to:

- Specify how yarn, weave, and finish processes define the characteristics of a textile.
- Understand how the chemistry of the fiber affects performance.
- Know what to consider when selecting and specifying a textile for a specific use.
- Explain how leather is used in place of textiles and how to evaluate leather for your client's job.
- Understand soft goods, their uses and design considerations, and installation.
- Understand upholstery production and evaluation.
- Relate to sustainability issues associated with fabric and leather.
- Select from related materials, such as manufactured window coverings.
- Understand working with other materials used for window coverings and upholstery.

Your clients may respond to fabrics and wallcoverings with more enthusiasm than they do for any other material you present to them. This is because we come into physical contact with them, so they are especially personal. They must be visually appealing (and appropriate) and tactilely pleasant. You may even find that your client is more involved in the evaluation of the fabrics that you present than they are in the furniture they go on!

Your evaluation of fabrics will address your program goals for cleanability, acoustical control, flame resistance, durability, fade resistance, sustainability, global markets, and other factors that will make the fabric serviceable and long lived in the environment. You don't need a textbook to tell you that a huge variety of fabric types has been developed to provide performance and aesthetic characteristics to interior design. Your client is likely to have a personal reaction to the fabrics you suggest, even though you are suggesting a fabric not only to please them, but to create a look that is congruent with their brand or their project's concept. These visceral responses also play part in your selection.

As you select and evaluate fabric, keep in mind that characteristics are influenced by several factors. For example: a crisp hand may be due to the fiber type, like linen. Linen fiber is described as crisp; it comes from the stem of the plant (called bast fiber). Knowing its function on the plant makes it easy to understand why it is stiff. A high twist can also make a fabric feel more crisp, so a fiber that is not characterized as crisp can still be used to make a crisp fabric. A tight weave can also affect the hand of the fabric and make it feel crisper. A **twill** weave can have more body than a plain weave. Finishing processes such as starching or glazing (part of the finishing process for cotton **chintz**) lend crispness to fabric. The versatility that is created by the great number of materials and processes used to make fabrics results in myriad fabric choices that you must evaluate when you select fabrics for your jobs. The characteristics of a fabric cannot ever be attributed to a single element of its fiber, construction, or finishing, as they all work together to define the nature of a particular fabric.

MATERIAL

Fabrics are woven from yarns and yarns are constructed of fiber. Fiber sources can either be natural or **synthetic**. Some natural fiber sources provide fiber directly. Cotton and wool are such natural sources, so these fibers are referred to as natural fibers. Cotton is a natural **cellulosic** fiber and wool is a **protein** fiber. Other natural sources for cellulosic fiber are wood or bamboo. Wood and bamboo are often deconstructed into their chemical constituents and the chemicals are then recombined in forms that are more appropriate for textile production. You could imagine that the cellulosic material is chemically "melted" with other chemicals, the molecules rearranged and then extruded into **filaments**. These fibers have natural sources but they are still man-made, since they are extruded into fibers. These fibers are called man-made fibers.

Wool is one of two protein fibers, the other being silk. Wool is a category encompassing the hair from any animal. When we think "wool," we immediately think of sheep. There are many kinds of sheep with varying wool characteristics: some sheep have heavy lanolin production that makes their hair good for carpeting. Some sheep have long, fine hair and their wool is used to make **worsted** wool, which has a smooth, fine surface and good drape. Some sheep have short, curly hair, which is good for fabrics that are woven to produce hefty fabrics with a "warm" hand.

The hair of any animal can be made into wool textiles. The luxury fibers from alpaca, camels, or cashmere and Angora goats can be found in blends for the furnishings industry, but because of the larger quantities required for furnishings versus clothing, it is not as common to see these fibers used in fabrics for furniture and drapes as it is to find them in apparel.

Although there are a few different species of silkworms, most of the silk that you will specify comes from one kind of caterpillar that eats mulberry leaves. Since this silk represents over 90 percent of the commercial silk industry, it is usually not distinguished from other kinds of silk and will be simply known as silk. Only when needing to distinguish from other kinds of silk will anyone refer to this silk as mulberry silk. The other kind of silk that you are likely to specify is called tussah (or less commonly, tassar) silk. It is not as lustrous as mulberry silk and has a crisper hand. Silk from silkworm cocoons will be in longer strands if the insects are not permitted to chew their way out of the cocoon.

Other fibers are derived from constituents that do not come from plants. These fibers are synthesized from chemicals and extruded into fiber the way the man-made fibers are extruded, but since they are composed of chemicals that were not grown in nature they are called synthetic fiber. Table 3.1 categorizes these fiber origins.

Table 3.1
Fiber characteristics.

Natural Fiber			
Protein Fiber	**Properties**	**Hand and Appearance**	**Uses and Implications**
Silk	Good tensile strength, may water spot, yellows with age, degraded by UV rays	Smooth or slubby, lustrous, crisp drapability	Drapery, light upholstery, used in blends
Wool	Resists wrinkling, absorbent, resilient, burns slowly in direct flame, self-extinguishes	Worsted, smooth, drapable, short, staple, springy; varies by animal	Carpeting, upholstery, and drapery
Cellulosic Fiber	**Properties**	**Hand and Appearance**	**Uses and Implications**
Cotton	Absorbent, dyes well, flammable unless treated with chemicals; hydrophilic	Soft and drapable, tends to wrinkle and soil	Drapery and multipurpose in blends; difficult to keep clean without treatments or use in blends
Linen	Absorbent, dyes well, resists piling and degradation from UV, wrinkles, reacts to moisture in air	Crisp, smooth	Upholstery wrinkles, drapery elongates and shrinks with changes in humidity, some use in carpeting, dry-clean only
Jute	Absorbent, dyes well	Crisp, coarse	Floor covering, novelty
Hemp	Absorbent, dyes well	Crisp, coarse	Floor covering, novelty
Bamboo	Very absorbent, antibacterial	Crisp, coarse	Multipurpose
Man-made Fiber			
Cellulosic	**Properties**	**Hand and Appearance**	**Uses and Implications**
Rayon and lyocell	Absorbent, easy to dye; from wood pulp	Artificial silk; drapes well	Multipurpose and light upholstery
Acetate	Resists shrinking, moths, from wood pulp; cross-dyed with cotton or rayon	Soft and drapable, variety of lusters possible	Multipurpose and light upholstery use
Lyocell	Dyeability, wrinkle resistance, biodegradable	Good drapability, varying construction simulates silk or leather	Multipurpose fabrics
PLA	Good wicking, low absorption, light fiber, low smoke and flame; renewable from sugar crops, corn, and beets		Multipurpose fabrics
Bamboo	Very absorbent, antibacterial	Soft and drapable	Multipurpose, novelty
Noncellulosic	**Properties**	**Hand and Appearance**	**Uses and Implications**
Polyester	Springy hand, resists wrinkling, shrinkage, mildew; melts, self-extinguishes; oleophillic	Pleats and creases must be heat set; crisp hand	Carpet, multipurpose, used in blends for upholstery
Nylon	Strong, elastic, abrasion resistant, resists damage by many chemicals, low absorbency; hydrophobic	Lustrous, can be fine or coarse depending on fiber cross section and size	Carpet, upholstery, drapery, blends may pill
Acrylic	Low absorbency, dyeable, resists winkling, soiling, and damage from UV	Can resemble cotton or wool	Carpeting, upholstery, novelty; may pill unless continuous fiber
Polypropylene	High bulk, resists abrasion, moisture, UV, chemicals; low melting temperature, oleophilic	Springy, waxy feel	Carpeting, upholstery, used in blends
Glass	Fiberglass is nonabsorbent, flame resistant	Heavy, can cause skin irritation if handled excessively; the term *glass curtains* is also used in place of the term *sheers*, which may be made of another fiber	Window covering

Selection of the correct fabric for your job begins with your design program. You will determine the characteristics that the textile must have for each location on your client's job. During your evaluation, and throughout this chapter, you should keep in mind that a fabric's characteristics are created by manipulating a number of elements in the construction and each of these elements is independent of the others. These characteristics are independent of one another. For instance if you had two fabrics that were identical in every way except for the density of the weave, the looser weave would have superior drape to a denser weave. If two fabrics were identical in every way except the degree of twist given to the yarn, the fabric woven from the high-twist yarn would have more body. Designers must make evaluations of each fabric selected by noticing its characteristics. Some of these characteristics can be seen and felt, others are measurable and you will review the test results when selecting textiles for commercial use. Table 3.2 lists these measurable characteristics for which you will be able to locate testing data.

Point of Emphasis 3.1

To really comprehend some of the subtle distinctions between the characteristics that you read about in this chapter, you will need to have access to different kinds of fabric for interior design. Options here would be to purchase a swatch kit intended for interior design studies. You can find such a swatch kit online—make sure it clearly states that it is for interior design because there are fashion studies kits as well and they will not serve your purposes. Another option is to keep a list of characteristics that you read about and then go to a fabric shop or an upholstery shop that has sample books and locate physical examples of those characteristics that you can cement in your brain with direct contact. If you identify yourself as a student, shops will sometimes save their discontinued books for your projects.

The goal is to have direct contact with fabric so that you become actively aware of the implication of the various characteristics on performance. You can tell a lot about how a fabric will be likely to perform *just by touching it.*

Table 3.2
Characteristics to evaluate for your textile selections.

Resistance To	Important Because
Flame	Textiles in commercial interiors especially should not support flame
Smoke generation	Even if a textile does not flame up it can obscure an exit route with smoke or release toxic chemicals
Abrasion	Fabric that abrades will wear through from friction, limiting its useful life
Stains	Fabrics that look soiled will be discarded even if they are still serviceable otherwise
Static	Sensitive equipment such as hospital monitors can be disrupted, moving drapery can transfer electrons and develop static cling
Crushing	Fiber can flatten out where weight is applied (from people sitting) and appear worn out even if it is still structurally sound
Moisture	Absorbent fibers may change with humidity, shrinking and growing in length; fiber with high moisture-regain properties are more comfortable
Chemicals	Affects cleanability
Tear strength and burst strength	If fibers break, fabric will be likely to pill or even tear; upholstery endures "foot sitters" and sharp objects
Seam slippage	Stressed seams, like on upholstered seats, will split open if the fabric unravels at the seams

Fabric intended for the residential market will not always have testing data immediately available. This means that you will be expected to make a determination of the suitability of the fabric with only the barest information about it. Often you have only the fiber content and width of the bolt provided and the rest you must evaluate by looking and handling the fabric. Luckily many of the characteristics in the list above can be discerned by a physical inspection of a **memo sample.** Table 3.3 lists some of the characteristics inherent in the fiber chemistry, so you can see that this information is very important as many properties vary with chemical makeup. These are properties that you could not be expected to discern by looking at and handling the fabric, so this is information that you will have to remember or look up when you are a working designer evaluating fabric for your client's jobs.

COMPONENTS

Fabric characteristics depend on the entire fabric construction with each component interacting with the others, creating the way each fabric feels, looks, and performs. The components that you will evaluate, not just individually, but as parts of the whole structure, include fibers, yarn, and weaves.

Fiber

Fibers have their own inherent properties created by their chemistry and their form. For instance, the chemistry of nylon makes it resist abrasion and when spun into a trilobal, meaning it has three lobes in cross section (Figure 3.1), it also conceals soiling.

FIGURE 3.1 *Trilobal* simply means "three lobes" and that describes the cross section of the fiber.

Table 3.3
Characteristics of fiber chemistry compared. (L = Low, M = Medium, H = High)

	Wool	Silk	Cotton	Linen	Jute	Hemp	Bamboo	Rayon	Acetate	Lyocell	PLA	Polyester	Nylon	Acrylic	Polypropylene	Glass
Flame resistance	H	H	L	L	L	L	L	L	M	L	L	H	M	M	L	H
Moisture regain—comfort	H	M	M	M	M	M	M-L	M-H	L	M-H	L	L	M-L	M-L	L	L
Abrasion resistance—durability	H	M	M	M	M	M	M	M	L	M	L	H	H	M	H	L
Tensile strength—breakage	L	H	H	H	H	H	M	L	L	H	M-H	M-H	M-H	M	H	H
Elasticity—recovery after stress	H	H	L	L	L	L	M	H	L	M	H	L	H	H	H	L
UV resistance	L	L	M	M	H	H	H	M	M	M	H	H	L	H	M	H
Resiliency—wrinkle resistance	H	H	L	L	L	L	M	L	M-L	M-L	H	H	M-H	M-H	M-H	H
Density (low density = coverage)	M	M-L	H	M-H	M-H	M	H	M-H	M	M-H	L	M	L	L	L	H

Fibers that are long and fine will produce smooth fabrics; worsted wool made from longer hair with a high twist to the yarn is smooth and fine but wool that is spun and woven from shorter hair is fuzzy and warm. Fibers that are kinked or **crimped** will produce fabric that has a little "give"; conversely, fiber that has no elongation can produce a more stable fabric, provided the weave is tight. Fiber characteristics are a very critical consideration when evaluating a fabric for your job. Table 3.4 has a quick comparison of some characteristics of different fibers.

What Would You Do? 3.1

If you wanted a fiber for a senator's waiting area in a government building that was flame resistant and comfortable to sit on, what fiber would you pick? Why?

If you wanted a fiber that was UV and wrinkle resistant, what would you pick? Why?

If you wanted a fiber that dried quickly and resisted breaking, what would you pick? Why?

Reasons for selecting textiles include functional and aesthetic considerations. There are many highly subjective reasons for choosing aesthetic characteristics but some considerations that seem to be aesthetic are also functional. Table 3.5 illustrates some seemingly aesthetic choices that have functional outcomes.

Fibers are used alone and in blends. The reasons for blending two fibers together include:

1. Properties of two fibers will contribute to the characteristics of the finished textile. Sometimes these blends are motivated by price, as when acrylic is blended with wool to reduce the price of wool fabric while changing the hand and appearance as little as possible. Sometimes it is motivated by performance, as when nylon and polyester are combined to lend nylon's improved elasticity or polyester's superior fade resistance to the blended fabric.
2. Different dying methods are possible with multiple fibers because different fibers react to dyestuffs in different ways creating an ombre effect.

Table 3.4
Functional outcomes of various properties.

Fabric Component	Characteristic
What the fiber is made of will affect many properties	Some fibers are naturally slippery, stiff, springy, flammable, or flame resistant, etc. Different fibers have different characteristics.
Fiber characteristic—length	Fibers that are long may feel smoother whereas short fibers will have the ends "poke out" of the yarn, possibly imparting a warmer hand.
Fiber characteristic—kink	Fiber that has some kink or curl has some potential to elongate just due to the fact that the kink makes extra material available to stretch out.
Yarn characteristic—thickness	A thick denier puts more fiber into the construction so even if some wears away, there is still fiber holding the structure of the cloth together. The hand will be more "plump." The opposite is true for a fine yarn.
Yarn characteristic—twist	A high-twist yarn will produce more "body."
Density of the weave	The more tightly the yarns are packed together the firmer and more stable the fabric will be.
Weave construction	Some weaves are more durable and stable than others.
Processes	Treatments and chemicals applied to fibers or to fabrics alter the characteristics and performance of the fabric.

Table 3.5
Functional outcomes of aesthetic choices.

Characteristic	Functional Outcome
Fabric weight	Serviceability is affected; heavy fabrics with more fiber in them will last longer
Texture	Coarse textures will attract more soiling; smooth textures may be finer and therefore less durable yarns
Color	Light and dark fabrics show different kinds of soiling; medium tone fabrics are most successful at concealing soiling
Luster	Reflect more light, show more surface dirt
Pattern	Some patterns conceal soiling

For the Connoisseur 3.1

Even though synthetic fiber has been developed to solve a lot of problems that cannot be overcome by natural fiber, natural fiber is still preferred by the connoisseurs. Fabric constructions that feature long staple, high-twist, small denier yarns in natural fiber are likely to meet with approval among the connoisseur crowd.

Yarn

The character of the yarn comes from the fiber properties (see Table 3.5, opposite) and processes that have been used on the fiber. Natural fibers like cotton and wool are shorter in length than long fibers unwound from the cocoon of a silkworm. The long length of silk fiber is partly responsible for the smooth surface and luster of silk fabric. Man-made fibers are spun into similarly long filaments. These filaments are typically given a crimp or texture so that they mat together, creating a more stable and resilient yarn. When long filaments are texturized they are referred to as bulked continuous filament (BCF). The yarn made from these filaments is smoother because it does not have the ends of short fibers projecting out of the yarn that would make it "fuzzy." Short staple yarns like wool (Figure 3.2) and cotton have their short ends poking out so they are fuzzier than silk and BCF yarns. Figure 3.3 shows the silhouettes of two fabric yarns. The top one is made from fiber cut to staple length and crimped before being spun into yarn and the bottom one is only crimped. Both will have a slightly warmer hand and have more resilience and elasticity than BCF left uncrimped, but the fabric woven from staple length will have a warmer hand than the fabric woven from long fiber.

The degree of twist as the fibers are spun into yarn also contributes to the characteristics of the fabric. Tightly twisted yarn, called high-twist yarns, have more body, and are more stable than low-twist, "blown" yarns. More than one yarn may be twisted together to make the complete yarn used to weave a fabric. Each strand of yarn is called a ply and a single-ply yarn is only one yarn twisted into a strand to be woven while a two-ply yarn has two yarn strands twisted together and so on. Figure 3.4 diagrams a two-ply yarn: two yarns twisted around each other after they were spun.

FIGURE 3.2 Most natural fiber is staple fiber, meaning shorter pieces like the length of a sheep's hair or the height of the stalk that linen comes from. One of the yarn characteristics that comes from this staple length is that fuzzy ends protrude from the spun yarn.

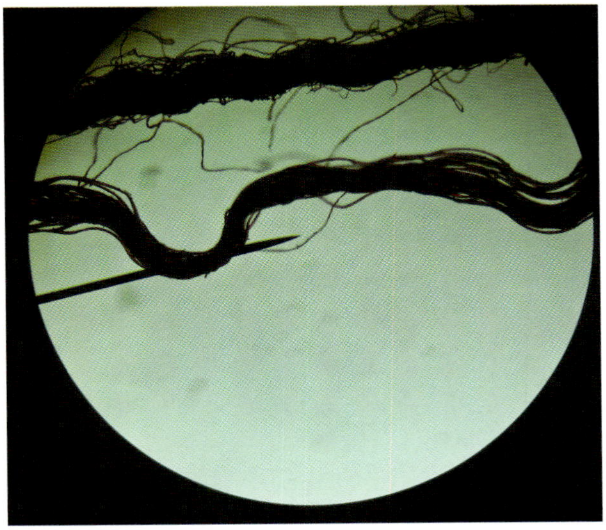

FIGURE 3.3 Man-made fiber can be much longer than staple length. Long fiber is called filament, as in staple yarn versus filament yarn. When man-made fiber is modified to make a fabric that resembles natural fiber it will be cut to staple length and crimped to give it texture, as in the silhouette at the top of the image. The filament yarn at the bottom of the image does not have the small ends poking out of the yarn.

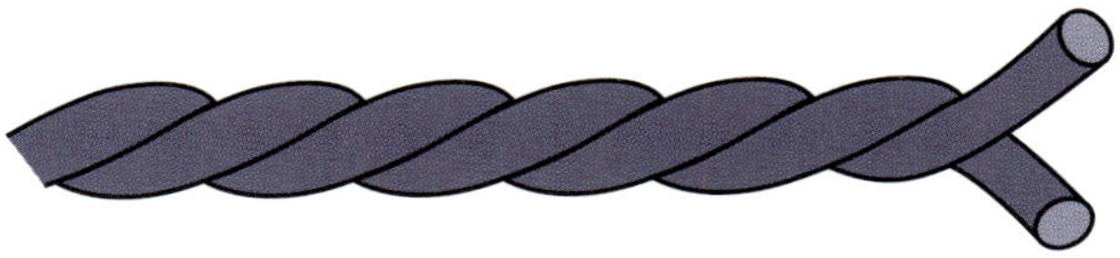

FIGURE 3.4 *Ply* means the number of yarns twisted together. This two-ply yarn illustrates the concept but many more plies are possible.

The thickness of the yarn makes a difference too. The thickness of the yarn is described as a measurement of its **denier**. A high-denier yarn is a thick yarn. Thick yarn may be more durable because it has more fiber to wear away before it wears through. All else being equal, fabrics woven of heavy-denier (thick) yarn will have more fiber in them so they will not wear out as fast as those made from the same fiber but spun into a finer yarn. The fine denier of a yarn used to weave a batiste and the heavy yarn used to weave a commercial-grade hopsacking demonstrate this distinction (Figure 3.5).

There are novelty yarns that are an inconsistent diameter with some portions tight, smooth, and fine and other parts along the length of the same yarn being thicker and less tightly spun. These yarns are called slub yarns. There are special yarn constructions, called bouclé yarns that are two-ply or more, with one yarn for stability and the other for texture. Figure 3.6 shows a bouclé and Figure 3.7 shows a fabric woven with a bouclé yarn. If you look closely at the bouclé yarn shown in Figure 3.7 you can easily imagine that a looped bouclé yarn could be vulnerable to catching and pulling if not woven in tightly or adhered to a backing. The slub yarn in Figure 3.6 has, alternately, a loose, "blown" structure and a more tightly twisted structure. You can imagine that these special yarn constructions affect the appearance and performance of the fabric.

Simply varying the denier of the yarn used throughout the weave can introduce subtle textural changes. Figure 3.8 shows a series of weaves called filling rib weaves because they have weft yarns that are of a heavier denier than the warp yarns. The fine denier of the faille fabric on the left of Figure 3.8 is different from the wide denier of the ottoman fabric on the right. Bengaline and rep in the center of Figure 3.8

FIGURE 3.5 The denier of the yarn, its thickness, has a significant effect on the characteristics of the fabric woven from it. This wool hopsacking cloth on the left and the batiste on the right utilize the same weave pattern but anyone would guess that their performance and hand will be quite different.

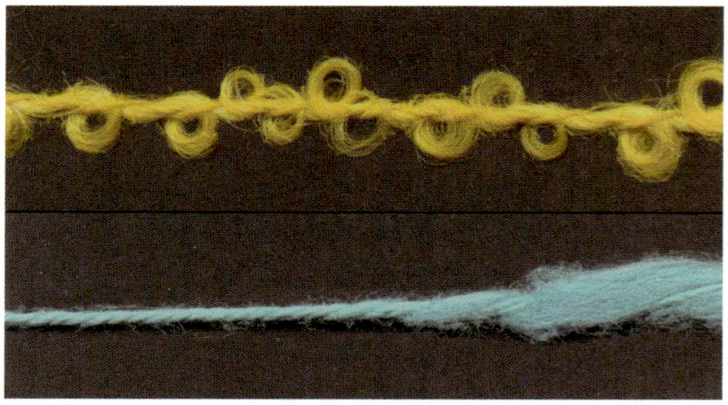

FIGURE 3.6 Specialty yarns lend additional texture to fabric weaves. This bouclé yarn at the top is a multiple-ply yarn that retains a little loop in its construction. The slub yarn at the bottom has more fiber, or more loosely spun fiber at isolated sections of its length.

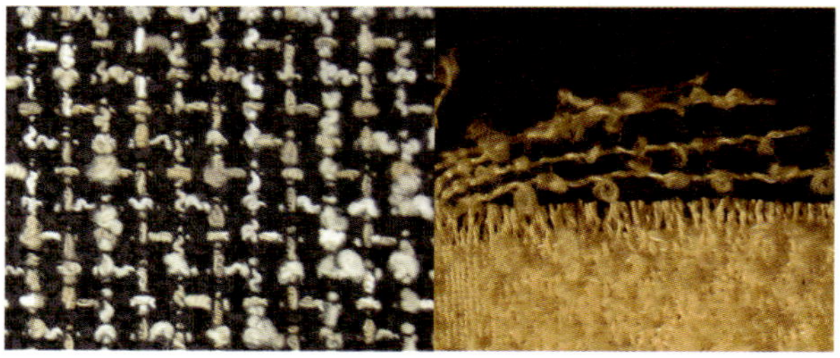

FIGURE 3.7 The loops of bouclé yarn lend texture to the surface. Be sure to specify a bouclé only for areas where the fabric is not likely to be snagged or pulled.

FIGURE 3.8 The filling-rib weave produces a horizontal (selvage to selvage) rib. The size of the rib is variable and, depending on the size, would be categorized as a faille, bengaline, rep, or ottoman weave.

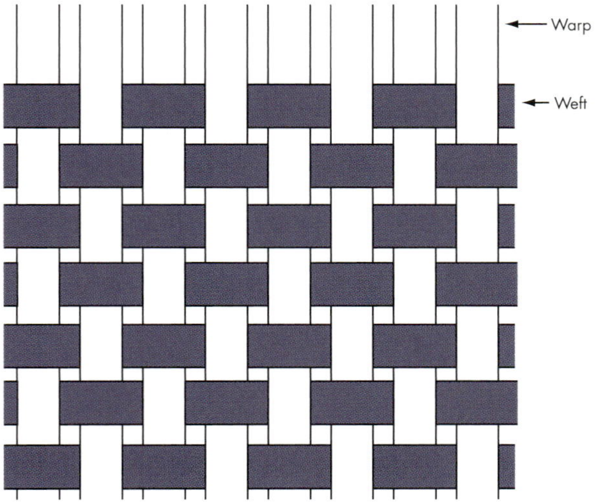

FIGURE 3.9 Hopsacking versus batiste comparison in Figure 3.5 shows a plain weave with a simple over-under structure.

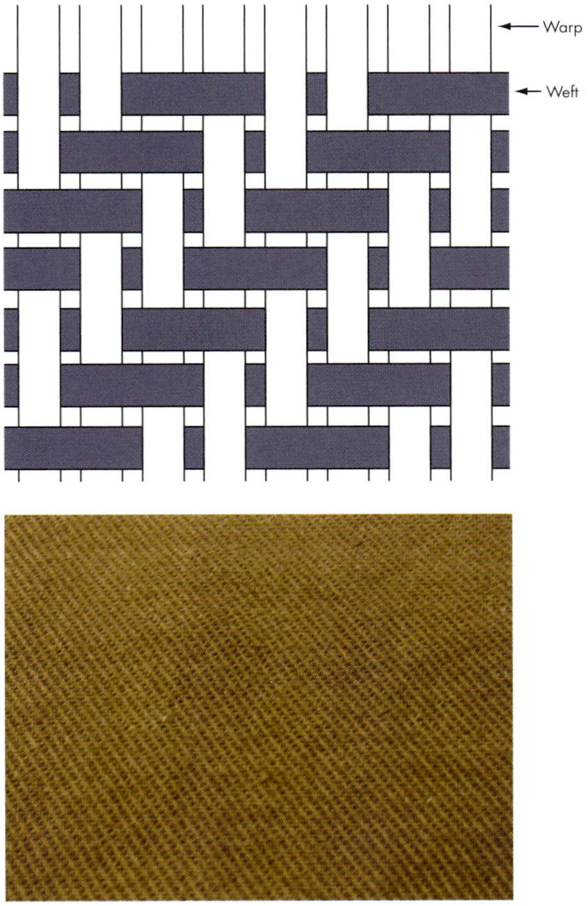

FIGURE 3.11A–B The twill weave is a durable weave that appears to have a diagonal construction although the warp and weft are still perpendicular to each other.

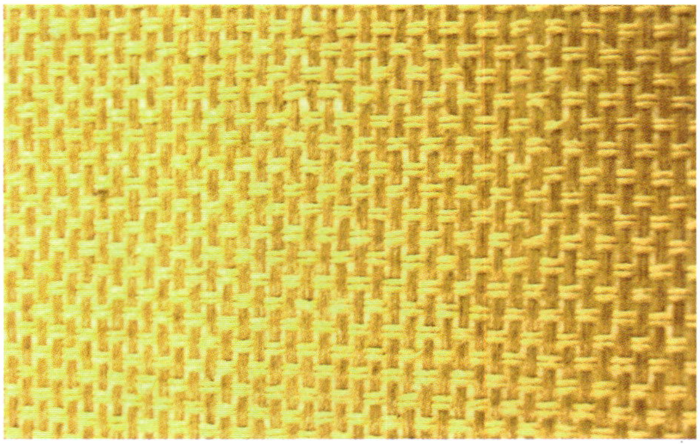

FIGURE 3.10 The basketweave utilizes an over-over-under-under construction. This structure can be durable if densely woven but does not lock the structure in as surely as the plain weave.

also have the pronounced horizontal filling ribs from having heavier yarns used in a horizontal direction. You will notice (if you look very close) the yarns that are horizontal filling ribs are not visible; they are entirely encased in the warp yarns.

CONSTRUCTION

No single attribute is responsible for the characteristics of a fabric, so if the yarns are tightly packed in the weave it will be more durable than a loosely woven fabric (it may also have more body and less drape). Fabrics may be woven, felted, knitted or knotted, or created from a film.

Weave

The simplest weave is a plain weave (Figure 3.9). The woven pattern is not just about the texture and aesthetics of your fabric. Some woven patterns are more durable and stable than others. For example, a basketweave (Figure 3.10) is a simple variation on a plain weave. Instead of an over-under pattern it is over-over-under-under. It is not as durable or stable as a plain weave because yarns will "float" across the face before interlacing, so if your fabric must endure hard wear, a plain weave that locks the yarns down in the weave is a better choice than a basketweave.

A twill weave (Figure 3.11a and b) is more durable than a basketweave or a satin weave (Figure 3.12a and b); the satin weave is more luxurious and delicate than a plain weave, among other subtle performance differ-

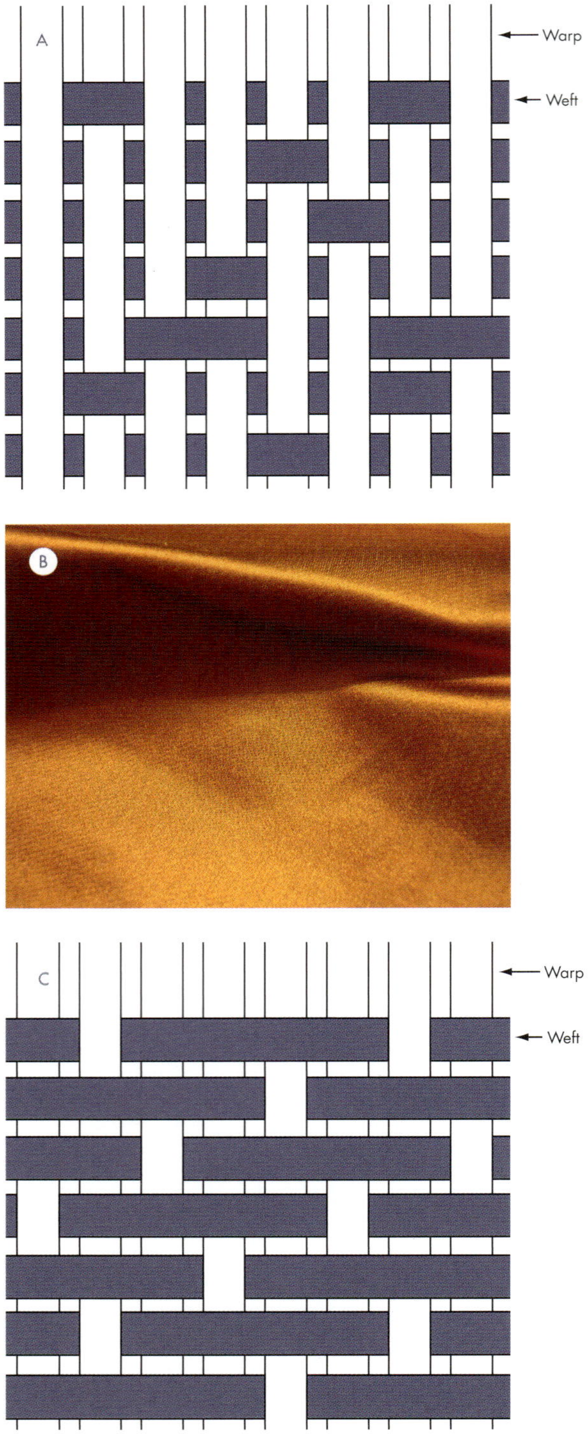

FIGURE 3.12A–C Satin weave (a) "floats" the warp yarn over several weft yarns before diving under and locking itself down. This makes it vulnerable to snagging but creates a fabric that has a high luster (b). Sateen weave (c) is similar except the weft yarns float over several warp yarns before diving under.

FIGURE 3.13A–B Herringbone is an example of a modified weave; it is a twill that changes direction creating a repeating chevron.

ences. The long **floats** on a satin weave are vulnerable to catching and snagging to a greater extent than a weave that secures the yarns in more closely. Satin fabrics will be lustrous (have a sheen) but are not as abrasion resistant because vulnerable threads are traveling unsupported along the face. A sateen weave also has long floats for a lustrous appearance. Sateen has floats in the horizontal weft direction (Figure 3.12c) and most of the sateen that you find will be cotton or a cotton blend.

These basic constructions are subject to yet further modifications. Herringbone is a modification of twill (Figure 3.13a and b) and has properties similar to twill but if you look closely, you will see that the twill weave here reverses and creates a zigzag rather than a diagonal that runs across the full width. The twill and herringbone weaves are composed of perpendicular warp and weft yarns and the diagonal is visual only.

These weave modifications are not just decorative. As mentioned above, the basketweave is not as stable as a plain weave, but a modification of the basketweave shown in Figure 3.14 has the coarse, loose appearance of a traditional basketweave but is much more stable than a typical basketweave. If you look very closely, you can see the brown yarns that form the background occasionally loop over the yarns that form the basketweave pattern on the face. These yarns stabilize the weave and improve its performance.

As you learn more about how all the materials and constructions work together, you could randomly draw a fiber composition, a yarn construction, and weave characteristics "out of a hat" and predict how that fabric would perform, what it would look like, and how it would feel to touch it.

FIGURE 3.14 This modification of a basketweave is more stable than its initial appearance would suggest. If you look closely at the construction you will notice that there is a sturdy ground (brown yarns at back) and every so often they come forward and grasp what appear to be long floats, but locking them down to make a more stable fabric.

Point of Emphasis 3.2

Upholstery weight, drapery weight, and multipurpose weight are three general designators implying appropriate use of the fabric and their names make it pretty obvious what you might use them for. The multipurpose weight is often used for soft goods such as bedding, drapery, and tight, light-use upholstered pieces; think dining chair or bench at the foot of the bed. Drapery weight may also be used for bedding but not for light upholstery. Even if it seems heavy enough, it may not have a tight enough weave to withstand the stress of taut upholstery details. Upholstery weight can be used for drapery but often has too much body to stack neatly and may have a fiber content, perfect for upholstery, that resists wrinkling, but the flip side of this characteristic is that the fabric is unlikely to hold a pleat. Pleating is what makes drapery hang, move, and stack neatly.

There are a great number of woven constructions—so many that there is little point in naming all of them—but the above are basic woven constructions that are common and the basis for other, elaborated and modified weaves. No matter what the weave pattern is, the warp and the weft must be perpendicular to each other. Twill looks like the construction is a diagonal but this is an illusion created by the pattern; all the warp and weft yarns are still perpendicular, as they must be for the fabric to be on-grain. Fabric that is **off-grain** will not hang correctly and will pucker on upholstery.

Complex Weaves

Looms are modified to create these different patterns. Computer-driven looms that have an intricate system for manipulating the warp yarns can create patterns that have even more complexity. The leno weave (Figure 3.15a) is produced on a loom that has an extra piece of equipment attached. Notice that the warp yarns are twisted back and forth, locking the weft yarns into position. The next time you come across a very open weave that you can see through, look closely and see if it is a leno weave that prohibits yarn slippage because the weft is caught tightly in a twisted warp. If you look very closely at a chenille fabric you will notice that that the "yarns" forming the weft are not spun yarns but are leno-woven strips with small fibers caught in the twisted pair

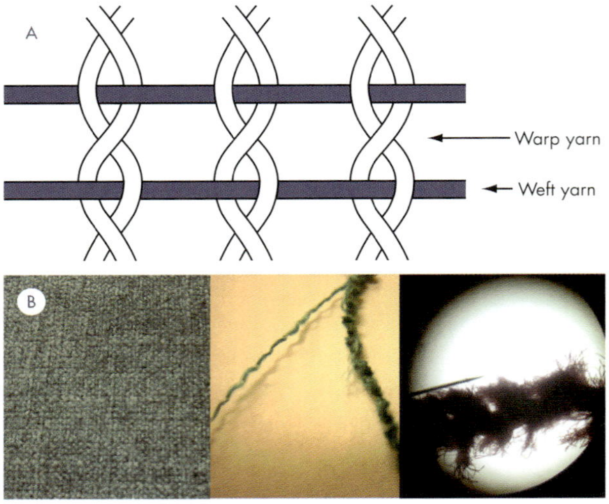

FIGURE 3.15A–B A leno weave (a) can create a stable netting or mesh because pairs of warp yarns grasp the weft yarns, holding them in position. Chenille fabric (b) is called that because it is woven from chenille yarns which are not spun but are made by slicing a leno weave into strips. When you look closely at the silhouette of the yarn you can see that small fibers are wound into crisscrossing warp threads.

of warp yarns. The leno fabric was woven, then sliced into "yarns" and these yarns were again woven into fabric. Figure 3.15b shows the face of a chenille fabric; this fabric was woven with alternating leno and spun yarn and if you zoomed in with a microscope, you would see in the silhouette of a single chenille yarn small tufts caught in the twisted leno warp pairs.

Some weaves must be produced on Jacquard looms because they require especially complex computer commands and more manipulation of the warp yarns, raising and lowering them in intricate sequences to create elaborate woven patterns. The word *tapestry* refers most strictly to a plain weave that is based on hand-loomed techniques that have a long history. The weave was common for flat-weave rugs and wall hangings (Figure 3.16). Modern, machine-made tapestries undergo numerous color changes like their hand-woven ancestors to create intricate patterns based not on the complexity of the weave patterns but on the numerous color changes (Figure 3.17). But you may find that people casually refer to any multicolored pattern with a complex, motif presentation as a tapestry or they may lump all such patterns together and call them Jacquard, even though that is technically a loom and not a weave.

Brocades (Figure 3.18) and damask weaves (Figure 3.19a) are also woven on Jacquard looms. Damask has been defined as having only one or two colors and is

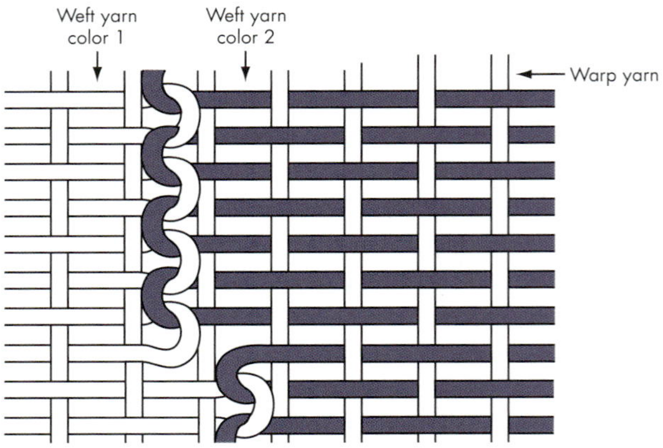

FIGURE 3.16 A tapestry has traditionally been a pictorial fabric with a plain weave, usually exhibiting numerous color changes. The hand-woven tapestry interlocked the colors as they changed or left a slit between. Many flat-woven rugs utilizing the technique are called slit tapestry.

FIGURE 3.17 Machine-woven tapestry is plain weave like hand-woven tapestries were. Their color changes produce a pattern that is intended to be seen from one side, meaning, even though they are a plain weave and the weave has no front and back, the tapestry does.

FIGURE 3.18 Brocade fabric utilizes a complex weave. When you look closely at this fabric you can notice several different woven patterns.

FIGURE 3.19A–B Damask relies on a variety of weaves; in the case of the fabric in (a), the changing play of light off the different woven textures is responsible for making the pattern visible.

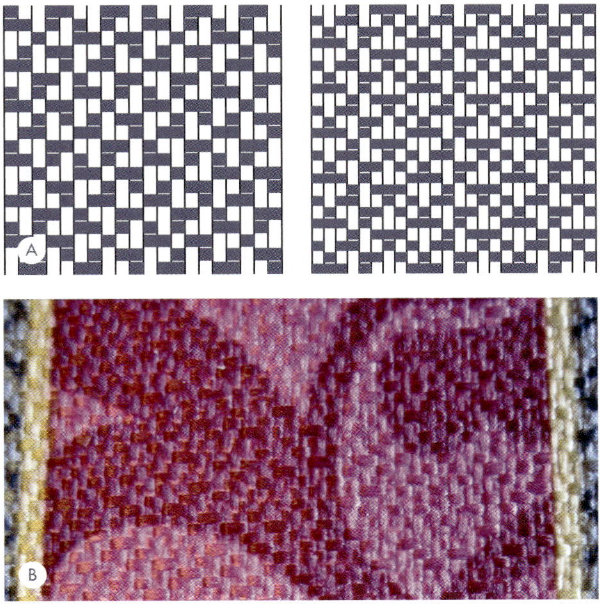

FIGURE 3.20A–B Crepe weave is intended to appear random, without pattern. There are many patterns that produce a random look. Figure (a) shows different crepe weaves. The result is a fine, pebbled appearance rather than a repeating pattern as shown in (b). This crepe fabric has a printed pattern as well.

FIGURE 3.21 The dot-spot weave floats yarn across the back until required on the face for a surface motif.

most typically a one- or two-color pattern, but Figure 3.19b illustrates yet another variation on a theme with a variety of damask weaves having four colors. Even though its back is like a negative of the front (as is typical of tapestry), it is not a tapestry weave and neither is it typical damask (too many colors) but is something in between the two. Look closely at the photo of this "in-between" fabric and notice that these looms are capable of incorporating more than one woven pattern in a single fabric. You can see plain weaves (flat, straightforward, in-and-out), modified twill (diagonal appearance) and sateen weaves (long floats) in a single fabric.

Another complex weave requiring a sophisticated loom appears to be quite simple until you look very closely at the crepe weave and see how randomized the pattern is. The goal of a crepe weave is to appear to have no pattern or directionality. Figure 3.20a diagrams a couple of different crepe weaves (there are many). Figure 3.20b zooms in on a crepe weave so you can see the pattern of the weave, which is nicely random so it doesn't look like a pattern at all, just a pebbled surface. You will also encounter the word *crepe* applied to yarn. Crepe yarn has a very high twist so that it has a highly textured, kinked appearance.

Notice the long floats on the back of the fabric in Figure 3.21. These yarns are only visible on the face in the motif but see that the yarns travel along the back. It is not the intention of the textile designer that these yarns, traveling across the back, should be visible from the front, but if you use this fabric for drapery, the backlighting of sunlight will cause these yarns to "shadow" on the face. If you intend to use this fabric for tight upholstery, pull it

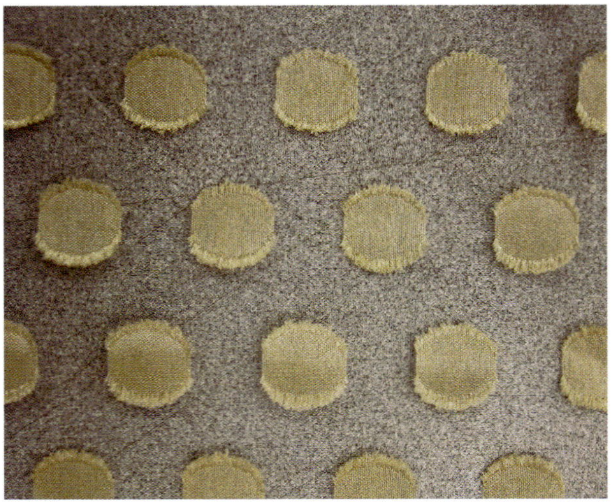

FIGURE 3.22 This clipped dot-spot weave has small fringed ends sticking out where the long floats were trimmed away.

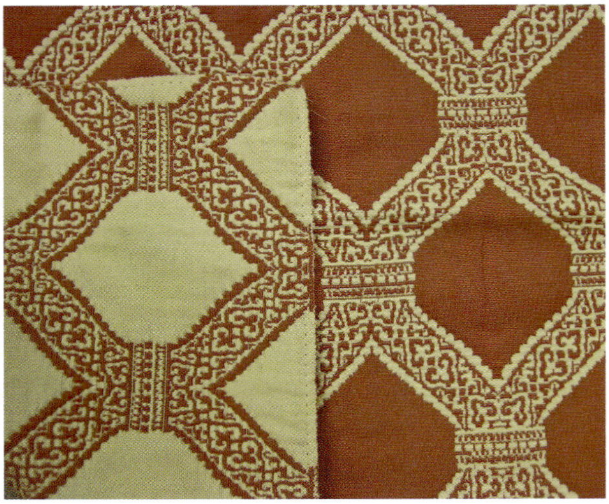

FIGURE 3.23 Matelassé is woven to be reversible with a back that is a perfect negative of the front.

taut and confirm that theses long floats on the back do not ghost through to the face. Sometimes even yarns that do not show when the fabric lays loose as a memo will show up if the fabric is pressed flat as when it is tightly upholstered on the frame of a piece of furniture. This is especially true if the fabric ground is a paler color than the floats on the back. Hold your memo up to the light if you intend to use the fabric for drapery or pull it taut against a white surface (like the muslin or Dacron in upholstery) to

FIGURE 3.24 A cloque has a pillowed appearance like a matelassé but it is not reversible. It appears to be a quilted fabric but if you look closely where the front and back are joined you can see that it is a weave that interlaces the two faces together, not quilting.

make sure these floats do not show through the ground. The dot-spot weave shown in Figure 3.22 has been clipped so the long loose floats have been removed and only the slightest fringe along the edges of the champagne dots indicates they were once there.

You will often have to look at the back of fabrics to really understand their construction. Figure 3.23 shows a matelassé. It is a pocket cloth construction, meaning that if you grasped the large rose section on the face and the corresponding large ivory section on the back you would find they pull apart from each other, completely independent, flat-weave faces. Matelassé fabrics are the only fabrics that are guaranteed to be reversible, with both faces free of defects. Recall that the tapestry is also a negative, front to back, but it has a designated face and any broken yarns that occur during weaving are pulled through to the back and allowed to remain there like little "tails." A matelassé is a pocket cloth that is intended to be used on either side, so it will not have defects in the weave showing up on the "wrong" side because there is no wrong side. The corner turned over in the photo reveals a usable side as perfect as the face. This is not true of all pocket cloths. A cloque is also a pocket weave, but if you examine the back of Figure 3.24 you will see that this fabric has a definite wrong side. The turned-up corner shows the back to be a loose, coarse weave that would not be durable for the face of the fabric. Both the matelassé and cloque are pocket cloths but their construction is not exactly the same. Figure 3.25 shows yet another pocket cloth showing the pocket construction. The two faces of a pocket cloth are only attached into a single cloth at the pattern junctions, as the matelassé, but a cloque is not designed to be used front and back. One consideration that they share is that, even though they may be thick fabrics and you might presume they are very durable, remember that the thickness of one layer will determine the durability of the fabric. When the face layer wears away, the fabric will be ruined, so it is only serviceable to the thickness of the top layer. Matelassé and cloque are weaves that are somewhat dimensional, meaning that they have varying thickness; you can see the slightly "pillowed" face of these double-layer constructions. They resemble quilted fabric (more later, under Finishing) but, unlike quilting, the pillowed surface is the result of the weave.

The dobby weave is also subtly dimensional (Figure 3.26a and b). These small geometric patterns are quite complex and the construction and tension of the yarn used in the pattern can create a 3D effect, as shown in 3.26a, or a repeated geometric pattern, as shown in the multicolored example in 3.26b.

FIGURE 3.25 Pocket cloths have two layers that are occasionally interlaced in the weaving. *Photo courtesy of Amy Willbanks, Textile Fabric Consultants, Inc.*

You are likely familiar with **pile** fabrics like velvet, velveteen, and corduroy. Many pile fabrics are directional. When you run your hand in one direction the fabric feels smooth but when you rub it in the opposite direction it feels rough. The short fibers that create the pile are "leaning" in one direction. Figure 3.27 shows a directional corduroy with an area of the fabric brushed

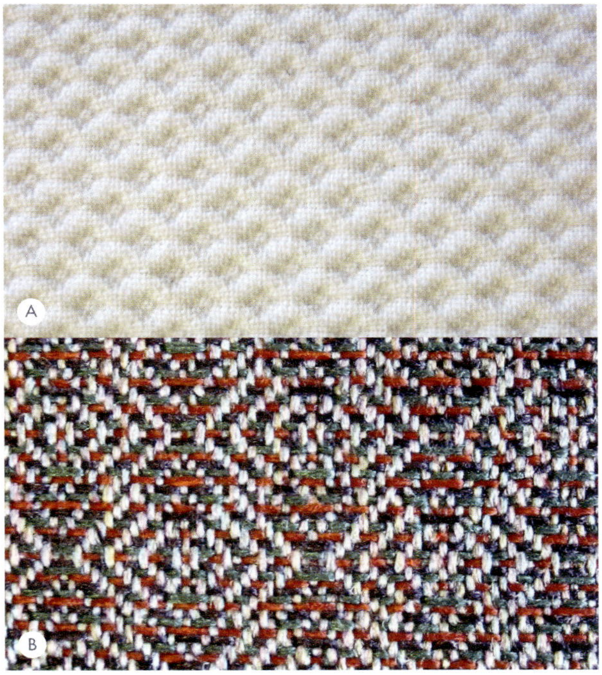

FIGURE 3.26A–B Dobby weaves are complex little geometrics that are often somewhat dimensional.

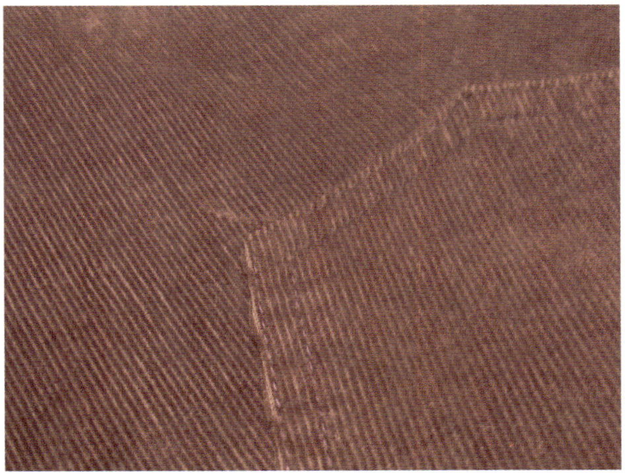

FIGURE 3.27 Pile fabrics may be directional. The pile of this corduroy leans in one direction and looks scruffy when brushed in the opposite direction.

in the "wrong" direction. If you use a directional pile for upholstery remember the phrase *down and out*. When a directional fabric is applied to a sofa, as shown in Figure 3.28, the smooth direction should be in the *down* direction on the vertical parts and the *out* direction on the horizontal parts or the scruffy appearance of the area of corduroy that was brushed the wrong way will show up on the furniture when it is in use. When we exit a piece of furniture we tend to slide forward, and if the pile goes in the direction that we slide, we will smooth the fabric as we leave the furniture. If the **nap** goes in the opposite direction, people leaving the furniture will raise the pile. Not only will the furniture be harder to get out of (as you have to "fight" your way out against the direction of the pile) but it will always look scruffy where people were sitting. Some pile fabrics are woven without a direction so they do not scuff this way or shade (the pile looks darker in one direction than another). Many velvet pile fabrics are woven to be nondirectional.

This directionality of some pile fabrics means not all of these fabrics can be railroaded. When your upholstered item is wider than the fabric, you may want to run the fabric along the length of the item; this is known as railroading the fabric. Figure 3.29 shows the difference between running the fabric off the bolt so you can apply the pile down and out, but you can imagine there will have to be seams on the frame because it is wider than the fabric. Your nondirectional pile selection can be railroaded to avoid these seams.

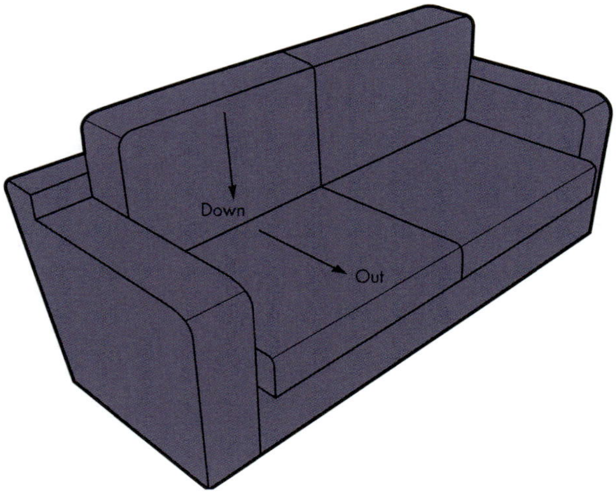

FIGURER 3.28 When applying a directional pile to a piece of furniture the smooth pile should lay down and out.

Not all pile fabrics have cut pile. A loop pile fabric that you may be familiar with is terry cloth; bath towels often have looped construction for their faces. You may not specify much terry cloth for your interior design clients but frieze fabrics have looped faces, or combine loops with other surfaces as shown in Figure 3.30. Frieze yarn is tightly twisted and is often woven into very tight, durable fabrics. Another looped pile construction is called gros point (Figure 3.31). This fabric has a very consistent loop.

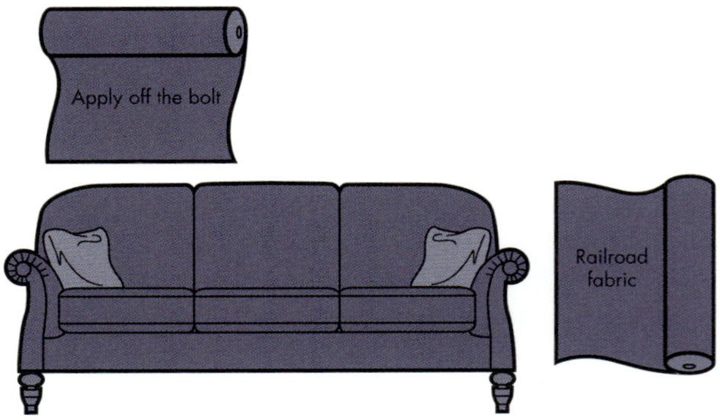

FIGURE 3.29 If your fabric has no direction, you may choose to railroad it to eliminate seams.

FIGURE 3.30 The frieze has a small, regular looped pile face.

FIGURE 3.31 The gros point has larger loops than the frieze. *Photo courtesy of Amy Willbanks, Textile Fabric Consultants, Inc.*

FIGURE 3.32 This plain weave fabric is similar to a tapestry in its woven construction, but is a classic pattern, so is referred to by its unique pattern name, flame stitch.

FIGURE 3.33 Another classic pattern, the plaid, may be constructed from a variety of weaves. If you look closely at this plaid you can see the diagonal pattern of a twill.

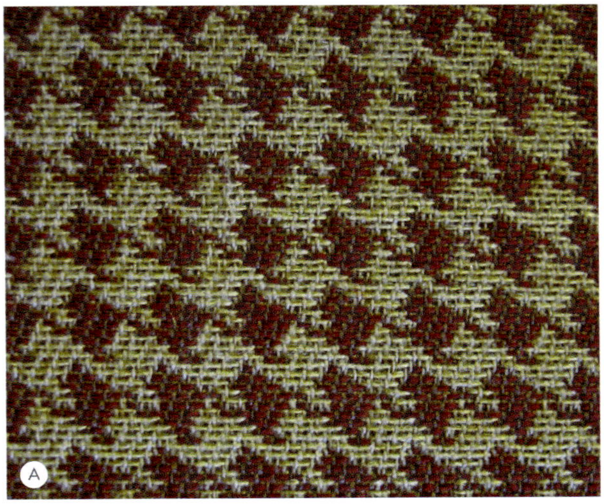

FIGURE 3.34A–B Patterns created from color changes are not dependent on a particular woven pattern. The houndstooth pattern shown in (a) and (b) is at different scales and is produced by different woven structures.

Some woven patterns are identified by the arrangement of colored yarns used in the weave, whatever the weave pattern may be. A classic woven flame stitch (Figure 3.32) has a lot in common with tapestry but the pattern name is more important than the kind of weave. This happens with many classic woven patterns. If you look closely at the plaid in Figure 3.33 you will notice that it is a twill weave, but if you asked any designer what this fabric is called, they will say it is a plaid. They will call the fabrics in Figure 3.34a and b houndstooth, even though they are clearly different weaves.

The compactness of the weave will also affect the fabric. A more compact, tighter weave will be stiffer and more stable. So the weave construction and the density or compactness of the construction affects the hand and durability.

Point of Emphasis 3.3

Drape means the way a fabric falls when held loosely. Fabrics that are densely woven will not fall in graceful folds and fabrics that are woven too loosely will be limp. A fabric that falls in between will have acceptable drape.

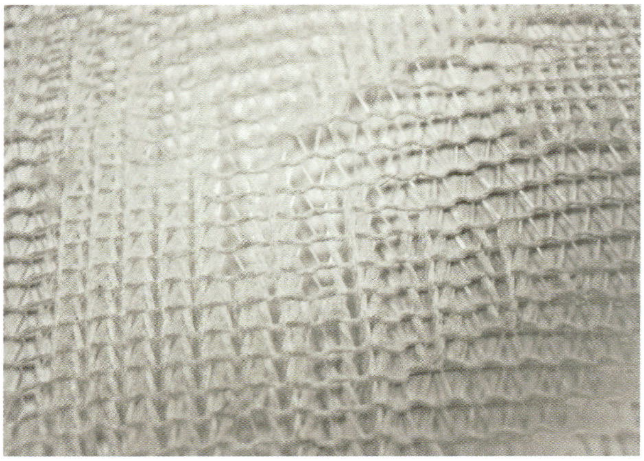

FIGURE 3.35 This fabric is knitted, not woven.

Knits and Felted Fabrics

Not all fabrics are woven; Figure 3.35 shows a knitted fabric used for window covering. Knitted fabrics rely on looping yarn together rather than weaving. Other fabric constructions are produced by flocking wherein small fibers are glued onto the surface of a woven backing. **Felted** fabrics are nonwoven and are made of loose fiber rather than spun yarn. Felted fabrics are made of fibers that are matted or tangled together.

These are just a few examples to illustrate the way the fibers, yarns, and weaves all contribute to the characteristics of the fabrics. This is not to be mistaken for an all-inclusive list of fabric constructions, just the basics of what you will be expected to know and understand.

FINISHING

In addition to the construction of the fabric, textiles may undergo additional processes called finishing. Finishing includes printing, dyeing, applying optical brighteners, mercerizing, soil guard, fire-resistance treatments, and other treatments. Finishing will affect the performance and appearance of the textile.

Mercerizing

Mercerizing is performed on cotton. It increases the luster. Usually yarns that are intended for mercerizing are made of longer cotton fibers, so they are already more lustrous than yarn made form shorter fibers. A caustic soda is used to treat the cotton, and it may also be singed to remove any fiber ends projecting beyond the yarn face.

Helpful Hint 3.1

The most immediate judgment of the characteristics of a fabric is always close at hand because it is, literally, your hand. Many important judgments that you make about a fabric are things that you can feel (and then verify through examination of the specs). The compactness of the weave and the density of the yarn will be apparent when you hold a fabric. With some practice you will not be surprised to learn that the fabric you thought would be serviceable when you picked it up does indeed meet the abrasion-resistance criteria required for your job. The smoothness of the yarn that will shed soiling will be apparent to the touch. The stiffness will affect drapeability and comfort. Squeeze the fabric for 10 seconds and notice the hardness of the wrinkles in the crumpled area, indicating resilience; this will give you clues about its appearance retention. Understanding the connection between hand and performance will save you time as you make selections. You will know instinctively which fabrics warrant closer inspection and which ones do not warrant reading the spec data as you move quickly through fabric displays as you shop for your clients.

Bleaching

Bleaching removes color from the fiber. It is applied throughout or selectively in discharge printing. Discharge printing "prints" with bleach by forcing bleach through a fabric that was previously dyed a color, removing the color only where the bleach was forced through. More often, fabrics are bleached in order to control the final color for white or dyed fabrics. The faille fabric in Figure 3.8 was discharge printed.

Dyeing

Dyeing fabric imparts color to the piece. In the case of a single fiber, the color may be evenly distributed. Sometimes blends are used because the two different fibers will react differently to the same dye bath and create a heathery or varied appearance. Dyes can be used at several stages of production. Man-made fiber can be solution dyed, when dye is dumped into the vat before the fiber is extruded. Solution-dyed fabrics are very fade resistant because color is part of the very fiber. They can usually be bleached and left out in the sun. After the fiber is spun, or removed from the plant or animal and cleaned, it may be stock dyed or staple dyed. In this case the loose fibers are soaked in a dye bath before being spun into yarns. Dye can be used after fiber is spun into yarn. This process is called skein dyeing or yarn dyeing. After the yarns have been woven into fabric, the cloth can be piece dyed. See Table 3.6 for a quick comparison.

Printing

Printing creates an applied pattern rather than an integral pattern that is woven in (like a plaid). The typical methods are rotary or cylinder printing, block printing, and screen printing. Registration is important for clear patterns; multiple colors should meet up precisely without overlapping or leaving unprinted areas of the ground fabric showing through. The more colors involved, the more precise the process must be, so patterns with lots of different color in the print will cost more. Figure 3.36 shows how the number of screens are documented on the selvage of the fabric. Printing sits on the surface of the fabric and may wear off, unlike dyeing that is integrated into the fiber so it will last (except for possible fading) until the fiber itself wears out. The more saturated the dyed area is, the more durable the color retention. The amount of color forced through to the back of the fabric is an indication of the saturation of the dye through the fabric. See Table 3.7.

FIGURE 3.36 Printed fabric will identify the number and color content of each screen used to create the pattern.

Table 3.6
Dyeing methods.

Phase of Production	What Occurs	What This Means for Your Selection
Solution dyeing	Pigment is added to solution before fibers are spun	These fabrics will resist fading; they are likely to be hydrophobic as well, so will resist waterborne stains
Fiber or stock dyeing	Fibers are dyed	Color goes throughout fiber structure, not just on surface; different colors can be spun together in heathered or ombre effects
Yarn dyeing	After fiber is spun into yarn	A single color is evenly distributed throughout the yarn
	Package dyed Beam dyed	Yarn is wound on a spool or beam and immersed in dye bath; dye may be forced through to saturate yarn for even color
	Skein dyed	Unwound skeins are dunked into dye bath; small quantities can be dyed this way for custom color
	Space dyeing	Yarn is printed in colors and the pattern of the printing gets randomized when fabric is made
Piece dyeing	Fabric is dyed after it has been woven	If a single fiber is used, fabric will be a single color; if two different fibers respond differently to the dye used, various effects can be achieved

Hand-Printed

Hand-printed fabrics are less common because they are labor intensive and expensive, but they are the only way to produce a small quantity or custom order. Hand-printed fabrics are appreciated for their imperfections denoting the handmade process. Block-printed fabrics use a block of wood and cut away all but the pattern area for each color in the print. The blocks are inked and pressed facedown on the fabric to transfer the ink to the fabric. The alignment of the colors is called the registration. Hand-printed fabrics are often just ever so slightly out of register, and that belies their handmade origin. The same is true for hand-screened fabrics. A fine mesh has areas blocked off with a resin. When ink is squeezed through the open parts, the pattern is printed. A separate screen is required for every color in the print.

Table 3.7
Printing methods.

Type	How	What It Means for Your Selection
Handmade		
Block printing	Carved blocks are inked then pressed down onto fabric; carved away portion applies no ink	Expensive but makes small quantities possible; registration and saturation are not perfect but this handmade quality is considered to be the charm of the process
Screen printing	Mesh screens are painted to allow ink to only pass through areas intended to receive color	Expensive but makes small quantities possible; registration and saturation are not perfect but this handmade quality is considered to be the charm of the process
Resist printing	Fabric is tied or painted with (removable) solution that prevents dye from being absorbed where tied or painted and fabric is then dyed	Expensive but makes small quantities possible; registration and saturation are not perfect but this handmade quality is considered to be the charm of the process
Machine Made		
Roller printing	Ink is continuously supplied to a roller with the pattern incised on it; the part carved away holds ink and transfers it to the fabric	Large quantity of goods makes this economical; precise registration is more easily achieved so different colors used align accurately; considered by some to be the highest quality fast method of printing
Rotary screen printing	Similar to flatbed-screen printing but ink inside a cylinder is forced out	Large quantity of goods makes this economical; precise registration is more easily achieved so different colors used align accurately; fastest method
Flatbed-screen printing	Automated screen printing with flat screens; the fabric moves along a conveyer belt	Faster than hand-screened but not as fast as rotary screen
Warp printing	The warp yarns are dyed, then strung on the loom	Pattern is irregular at top and bottom of motif but crisp on left and right
Discharge printing	Fabric that was piece dyed is selectively bleached to remove color from some areas, creating pattern	Motif will be white or very pale and ground will retain color
Digital printing	Prints images similarly to ink-jet printers for documents	Uncommon for fabric, used more frequently for carpeting
Heat transfer	Design is printed on paper that is placed facedown on fabric and when heated, transfers to fabric	Customization is easier than for roller and warp printing

For the Connoisseur 3.2

Hand-printed textiles are more highly valued by some discerning consumers. Precision is more difficult in patterns printed by hand and these small imperfections in registration are a hallmark of hand-printed patterns. Your connoisseur client may prefer a less-than-perfect product if it is hand-printed.

The need for multiple applications of ink, one for each color, holds true for machine-printed fabric as well. Mechanized versions of blocks and screens use carved rollers or perforated cylinders to continuously roll the pattern colors onto fabric. See Figure 3.37 for a diagram of how these mechanized screens and blocks differ. The successive rollers or cylinders, each holding a different color of ink, do not have to be lifted, inked, and moved the way hand-printing blocks must be stamped and lifted for every repeat. Rotary screen and flat-bed screen printing push ink through perforations as hand-screened printing does. Roller printing is less like block printing. Remember that blocks for hand-printing are carved so that the design rises above the block to be inked for printing. With roller screens, the design to be printed is incised and ink is removed from the rest of the roller so only the incised areas carry ink to the fabric. See Figure 3.38 for an idea of how this works.

Prints will require pattern matching and large prints require special attention. Take a look at Figure 3.39. Even if this pattern is nondirectional (has no up-down/right-left) you may decide to not railroad it, even though the fabric will now have to be seamed on your wide sofa frame. See how the position of the large motif must be carefully positioned on the sofa's form?

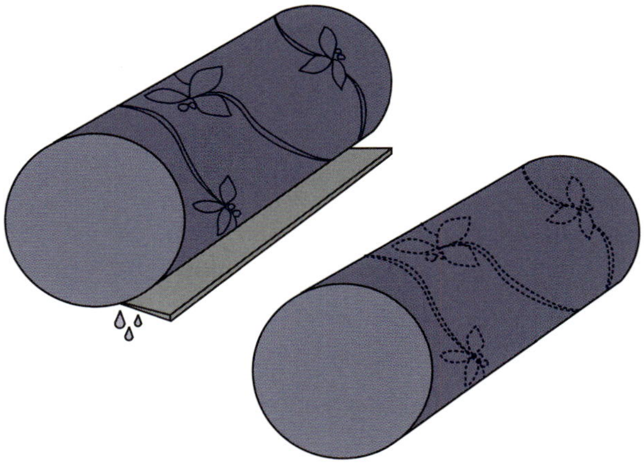

FIGURE 3.37 Imitating hand-print techniques, drums are either incised or perforated to selectively distribute ink.

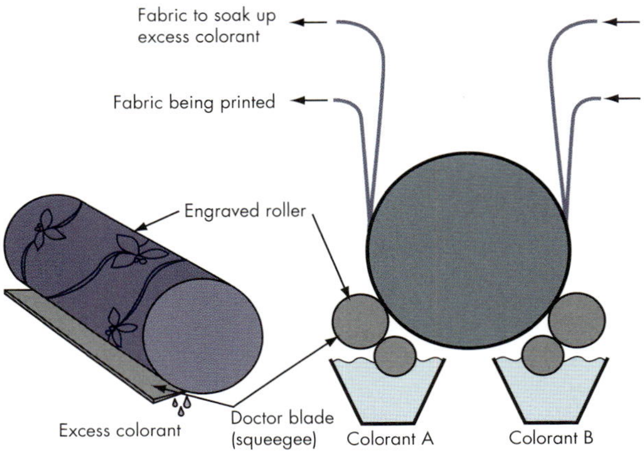

FIGURE 3.38 The drums are positioned to apply the individual colors in perfect registration. The incised groove holds ink until it comes in contact with the fabric and then the ink is transferred to the fabric.

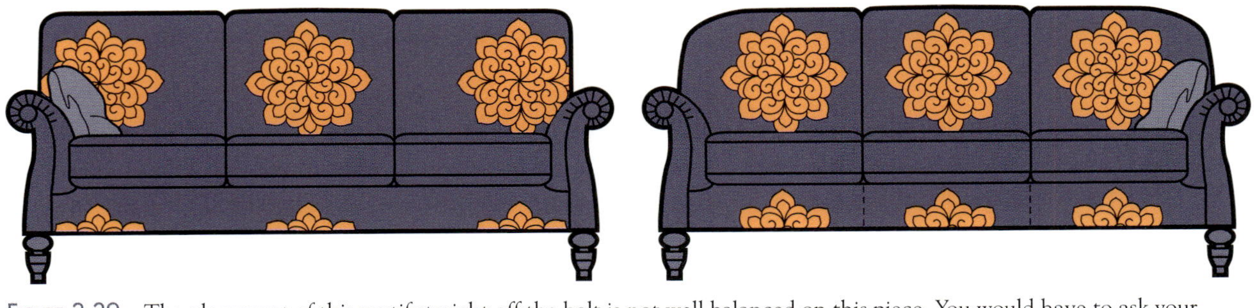

FIGURE 3.39 The placement of this motif straight off the bolt is not well balanced on this piece. You would have to ask your upholster to cut the fabric more often than the style of the sofa would require to achieve better positioning of this motif.

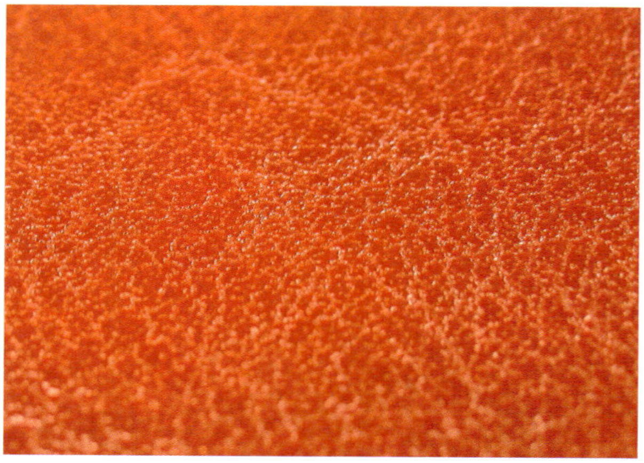

FIGURE 3.40 A plastic film is embossed to impart a skin texture to imitate leather.

Embossing

Embossing forces a texture onto the structure of the fabric. This is very common in faux leathers where the fine wrinkles on animal skin are imitated by pressing a texture onto the surface (Figure 3.40).

FIGURE 3.41 Dotted swiss can be made with a clipped dot-spot weave or flocked as this one was. Small drops of glue hold the fibers that were sprinkled on the surface.

Flocking

Dotted swiss fabric can be constructed as a dot-spot weave (as shown in Figures 3.21 and 3.22) or the small fuzzy dots can be flocked. A machine deposits dots of glue onto a batiste and small fibers are sprinkled over it to imitate a clipped dot-spot weave. If you look closely at Figure 3.41 you can tell that these random fibers are glued on and are not part of the woven structure.

Calendering

Calendering is similar to embossing, in that the face of the fabric is subject to pressure and heat to flatten out some areas. Chintz fabrics are calendered to give them a smooth, flat, lustrous face. Moiré has been calendered to impart a subtle marking that resembles a watermark or wood grain surface that gives moiré its name (Figure 3.42). Related processes of beetling and schreinering are also done with the aim or imparting more luster. Beetling flattens the fibers so they present a flatter, more reflective face and schreinering embosses a fine diagonal onto the surface, also with the aim of reflecting more light. None of these calendering processes is permanent and improper cleaning or abrasion can remove them.

FIGURE 3.42 Calendering alters the profile of the yarn; in the case of this moiré calendering a texture that looks like wood grain or a watermark shows up in certain angles of light.

Crushing

Purposely heat-set wrinkles in fabric are called crushed. Crushed velvet (Figure 3.43) exploits the shading that is normally part of a pile fabric to enhance the crushed appearance and it becomes randomly reflective in a way that really shows off the crushing.

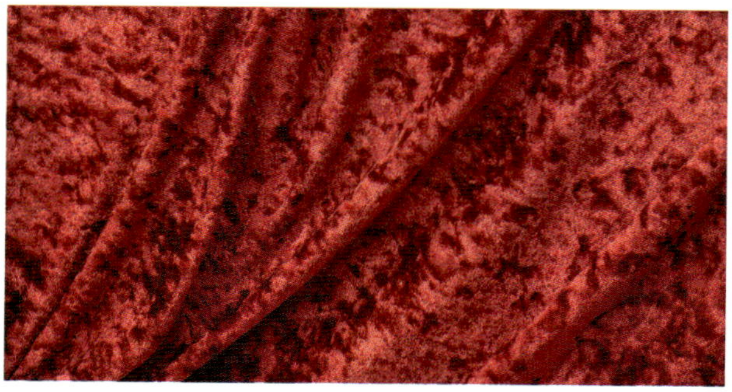

FIGURE 3.43 Crushed velvet interacts with the light in a very different way from velvet left uncrushed.

Glazing

Glazing adds a resin to the surface to make the fabric shinier. The glaze is also likely to make the fabric stiffer and give it a crisper hand. Resins vary in their permanence and they can be worn away or accidentally removed when the fabric is cleaned.

Optical Brighteners

Optical brighteners are sometimes applied to white fabrics to further brighten them beyond what can be achieved by bleaching. These brighteners react to light and fluoresce, appearing brighter still. In clubs that use black lights you can see the optical brighteners of white clothing glowing blue.

Soil Retardants

Soil retardant formulas may coat the fiber, laying on the surface, or they may bond molecularly with the fiber in the case of nanocoatings. In both instances soiling is repelled. Nanoprotectants also repel water and odors.

Heat Setting

Heat setting is required for some fibers and fabrics to keep them from relaxing out of shape. One example of heat setting is the crimp added to synthetic yarns. Filaments are smooth when initially spun and in order to make the fabric more resilient, the fiber is given some curl or crimp that is heat set to make it permanent.

Flame Retardants and Antimicrobial Finishes

Flame retardants are applied to fabrics that would not otherwise meet fire code. Antimicrobial finishes are required for fabrics used in health care applications.

Singed

Fabric may be singed to remove small ends that project beyond the yarn surface to make it smoother. Actual flame is used for cellulosic fibers; hot plates are used for thermoplastic synthetics. Protein fibers cannot be acceptably singed. Converse to singeing, napping the surface of a woven fabric will bring these loose ends to the surface.

FIGURE 3.44 This flannel fabric has been so thoroughly brushed or napped that it looks like felt.

Napping or Brushing

Flannel fabric has a woven construction made with staple fiber. After weaving, the surface is brushed to bring the short staple ends to the surface. If the surface is really worked over it can be hard to tell that there is a woven structure at the foundation of the fabric. Figure 3.44 shows a flannel that is so napped that it looks like felt. It is not until the structure is picked apart (see close-up of corner) that you can see the warp and weft yarns that indicate that this is not felt but flannel napped on both sides.

Quilting

Recall how the cloque fabric construction (Figure 3.45) looked quilted but the pillowing was actually the result of the weave. Actual quilting bonds two or

FIGURE 3.45 The cloque fabric looks quilted but the effect is a characteristic of the weave.

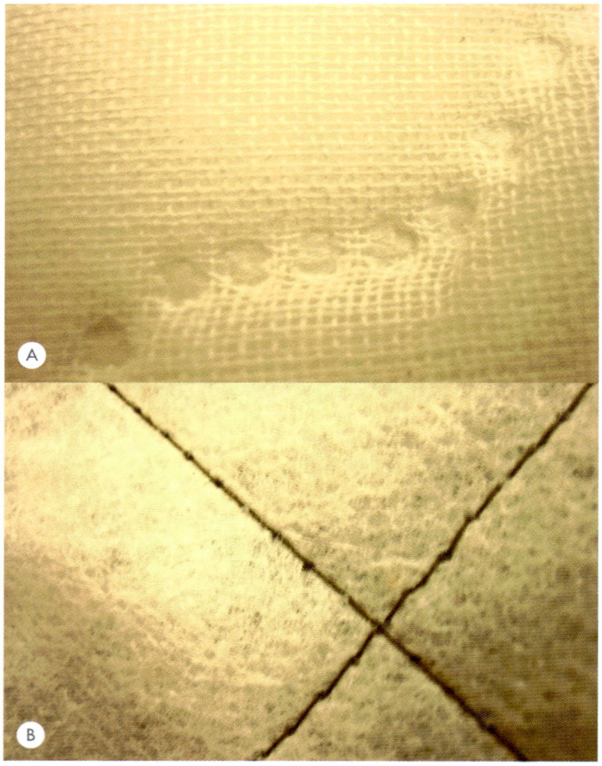

FIGURE 3.46A–B These quilted constructions bind three layers together: (a) by means of fusing and (b) with stitching.

three layers of fabric together. Whether done by fusing (Figure 3.46a) or stitching (Figure 3.46b), quilting binds fabric to a layer of padding. The padding is usually fiberfill or foam products that are formed into sheets, not loose fill like ground foam, feathers, or kapok. The stitching or fusing can follow the outline of a pattern printed on one of the fabrics, follow a straight grid or diamond trellis or a random, curving pattern called vermicelli.

Embroidery

You are likely familiar with this needlework as a handicraft. Machine-embroidered goods are commonly available in silk, wool, and polyester. When you are comparing embroidered silk to the embroidered polyester options, developed to save money over silk options, you will notice that the silk options tend to pucker around the embroidered areas whereas the polyester fabric tends to lay flat.

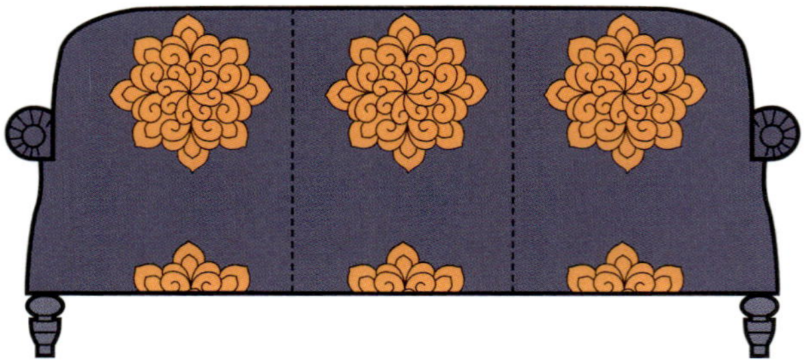

FIGURE 3.47 Large patterns must be carefully positioned. A to-scale drawing is a good tool for confirming the appropriateness of your selection.

Uses and Implications for Selections

If the fabric cannot be railroaded (applied to the piece horizontally) there will be seams on a wide sofa back (Figure 3.47). Seams will occur along the back as well as on any wide seat cushions, or on a tight back. Seams should be aligned with cushions or relate to the design. You should always plan the seam locations, rather than being driven by the fabric width alone.

When shopping for drapery fabric you will see a lot of polyester options. Consider that polyester does not pleat well, the flip side of not creasing is a memory for its untrained state. When drapery is tied up to "train the pleats" these pleats will be temporary for polyester fabrics. Your design should decrease in fullness and still look good with a looser structure. Tailored drapery will not be satisfactory if made up in polyester.

For the Connoisseur 3.3

Oddly, there are instances where a defect is actually preferred. Take the example of the puckering around embroidered motifs on silk fabric. The lower-priced imitators made of polyester do not pucker and it is the puckering that indicates that the fabric is the higher-priced silk option, considered more exquisite. Another example is an off-register, hand-blocked print. Hand-blocking to apply a pattern to a fabric is labor intensive and costly. Machine-printed goods are carefully calibrated to make sure that each color area is aligned accurately with other colors in the pattern. Hand-blocked prints display misalignment that is understood to mean that the print was handmade. This indicator of hand-blocking makes the product desirable.

PROTECTION AND MAINTENANCE

Laminating other materials to a fabric can make the fabric better suited to the installation. Fabric may receive a sheet of vinyl on its face to make it impervious to moisture and easy to wipe down in a family restaurant. A knit backing applied to a less durable fabric construction, like a chenille, can strengthen the fabric for upholstery use. Many chenille fabrics are also latex-backed by the manufacturer, to lock the yarns in formation to prevent **seam slippage**. These processes are not just for chenille though, many fabric constructions can be reinforced with a backing. Fabrics are also laminated to paper for use as wallcoverings.

A Cautionary Tale 3.1

I found a most intriguing casement fabric for a client that was woven out of polyester. A casement fabric is not good for anything except a drapery because it is loosely woven like a net and is intended to be seen through. I figured that, because it was certainly intended for drapery it had, somehow, been engineered to hang gracefully, even though polyester typically does not hold a pleat.

After having drapes made up for a client in the casement fabric, they were tied up to "train" them to hang gracefully. The client dutifully waited two weeks to untie them and they reported that they thought the drapery looked great. However, a few days later my client called and said the drapes pouffed out "like a prom dress." When I saw them for myself I could not disagree. Polyester is polyester no matter what form you fashion it into and it has not been engineered to pleat well. With greater and greater desperation, I instructed the workroom to heat set such a hard crease in them that they would have no choice but to conform to shape. Eventually they were ruined, with hard pointy creases separated by springy sections of fabric that still pouffed out like a prom dress. We replaced them at our expense.

Backings

Companies that apply these backings will offer a few different kinds to meet the needs of unique jobs. The process is typically something like this: Fabrics are forwarded from a number of designers to receive specific types of backings. The fabrics that are to receive the same type of backing are stitched together and run through the laminator (or stitched together to have the latex or acrylic spread down the length of the fabrics) in a continuous piece. The fabrics are then cut apart and each is shipped to the fabricator of the upholstery, drapery, or wallcovering. This is one reason why the backers require that you ship more yardage to them than will be required by your fabricator; there is some waste when the fabrics are stitched together and then cut apart.

If your fabric is not dimensionally stable there is a possibility that it will be off-grain when you receive it from the laminator/backer. Since your fabric is stitched to another designer's fabric, there is also the possibility that an unstable fabric stitched to yours will pull your fabric off-grain for some short distance as well. Send a piece of your fabric to the baker/laminator before you finalize your specification to get their advice on how successful the backing process will likely be. They see the response of fabric to lamination all day every day and you should take advantage of their expertise and ask their advice.

Helpful Hint 3.2

It is a good idea to include a small piece of the fabric with your order to the workroom so they know what it looks like. A busy shop will receive dozens of fabrics every day and if the manufacturer has not tagged it with your name and order number your fabricator may set it aside until someone calls asking about it. This will delay your production.

In addition to letting them know what the fabric looks like, I will also write on samples I send the word *Face* on the front of the fabric and the word *Back* on the wrong side so there is no confusion about which side is to go out.

Polymerization Treatments

Polymerization is related to backings, because it is applied in a similar manner, and effectively inhibits stains, and fungal and microbe growth. These proprietary processes are, most simply, a bath of different liquors that are pressure-forced into the fibers of a woven fabric and then heat set to bind permanently to the fibers. Other characteristics that can be imparted with this technology include antiodor, antimicrobial, enhanced water resistance, abrasion resistance, antistatic, insect repellent, infrared reflection, UV reflectance, wicking, and enhanced absorbency. In a separate process, a waterproof backing can be applied to the fabric. This second step makes it impossible for moisture to leak through or to be drawn through the fabric and into the padding and cushion of upholstered furniture (except at seams). These processes are most often specified for locations that will have spilled liquid (such as beverages or urine) threatening the cleanliness and appearance of the installation.

Nanotechnology

A new kind of technology is showing up in fabrics. It is called nanotechnology because it works on a molecular level. Materials are bonded, molecularly, with the fibers, becoming part of the fiber itself. Silver nanoparticles are the ones that you are likely to encounter most frequently because silver is a natural antimicrobial that is believed to not affect human health even though the particles can migrate into our bodies through contact with materials. Nanocoatings are applied after the fabric is woven and finished. They can make fabric easier to clean and in some cases, increase abrasion resistance. These coatings can be applied to most fabrics but not to heat-sensitive fabric like olefin.

Cleaning Codes

Investigate the recommended cleaning procedures provided by manufacturers. If you want to maintain a low-toxicity environment, product maintenance is going to figure prominently in your selection criteria.

- W—Means the fabric should be cleaned with water. For general cleaning, your client's maintenance staff will whip a mild detergent to create a soap foam to clean light soiling. Any residue remaining after the fabric has dried should be lightly brushed and vacuumed away.
- S—Means the fabric should be dry-cleaned, so solvents, not water should be the basis for the cleaning products used.
- W-S—Means that the fabric can be cleaned with either water-based or solvent cleansers.
- X—Means do not use cleansers of any kind; brush and vacuum the fabric only. This is also recommended for drapery regardless of the fabric cleaning code. There will be instances where you must have the drapery cleaned (dry-cleaning is best) but if you can avoid taking the drapes down, having them cleaned, and then reinstalled, try to design and specify to allow for this most conservative approach. Why would this be true of drapery and not other fabric uses? It is because drapery is more dependent on the fabric properties than any other item that you specify. It has no other "structure" to support it and maintain its shape and there is frequently a lot of fabric in the construction. Recall that many materials will change with time and environmental conditions and when they do so it is as a percentage of their size. The long length of many drapery styles will naturally indicate that any change that takes place as a reaction to cleaning will be more significant than if it is used on a sofa, where the largest piece of fabric used is much smaller.

SAFETY

The safety issues that are most prominent for textiles are risks associated with fire and finishes. The use of flammable products in commercial interiors is restricted to small percentages of overall surface. A variety of test methods have been devised to test the flame resistance of fabrics as well as constructions that are covered in fabric, like furniture and mattresses. Loose-hanging fabric, like drapery, has a lot more air available for combustion than a fabric used as a wallcovering, and the upholstery padding under the fabric, made of a foamed petroleum product, could also be a source of fuel. Tested fire-rated materials are a legal mandate for most occupancies, and even in occupancies where fire codes are less stringent, such as single-family homes, fire safety should be part of your design program and you should design to exceed the safety of code mandates whenever possible because codes are the minimum standard of safety allowable.

Safety Codes

Local codes that will govern your project will reference a class distinction for fire-resistive properties. Classes may be defined as A, B, C, or D or they may be defined as Class I, II, III, IV depending on the test method used. Several different agencies have devised tests that are referenced by municipalities and jurisdictions as they craft fire safety codes for their areas. Some of the tests that will be referenced in the code book that applies to your specific job have tested materials only; others have tested typical assemblies (ignited a piece of furniture or left a lit cigarette to smolder on a mattress, for example). Interior designers do not perform testing of materials; we rely on testing data provided by others. You will use test data to help you make the best selections for your client's job; even when the exact assembly that you intend to use has not been tested, the materials that you will specify for your commercial job must have been tested and must meet the standards defined by the code governing your client's site.

MANAGING BUDGETS

Fabric pricing ranges widely and additional processes can add to the cost. When you are purchasing a large quantity there may be a bolt discount or bolt price that is lower than the cut yardage price, but you will generally have to ask for the special pricing.

There are some small compromises that you might make to bring prices in line with a restricted budget even if quantity discounts do not apply. For alternatives to expensive fibers like silk and wool, specify rayon or mercerized cotton for silk and polyester or acrylic in place of wool. When you specify a synthetic fiber, make sure you give preferred status to manufacturers who have recycled and recyclable options. These fibers will not decompose as will natural fibers.

If you are using a printed pattern, the more colors there are in the print, the higher the price will be. Cotton chintz with 8 screens will be less costly than cotton chintz with 38 screens. To compound the price discrepancy, the cotton chintz with 38 screens is likely to be printed on better quality cotton—who would waste all the effort of orchestrating 38 screens on cheap cotton?

Avoid pronounced trends that are likely to go out of fashion or that do not jibe with your client's style or cannot be reconciled to the architecture in any other way but to say "this is the current trend." If your client's site will have to be freshened up frequently because they must demonstrate current style in their facility or if they will experience hard use, it is even more critical that you perform life-cycle cost analysis on your selections and seek out sustainable options.

ORGANIZATION OF THE INDUSTRY

Let's trace the steps of your fabric from the textile designer to the product installed in your client's project site. A textile designer employed by a mill or by a fabric company designs a textile, or resurrects a historical textile, and develops a palette of color schemes they believe will work with current market preferences. If a historical colorway does not work with current market colors, it may be appealing, but it will be difficult to work it into a scheme with fabrics currently on the market, and it will end up not being specified by designers who must build an entire scheme for their jobs.

The mill will weave a "blanket," which is the new (or resurrected) pattern, in several different color combinations called colorways. This blanket will travel to textile shows where mills and wholesalers will place orders with the manufacturer for selected colorways. Some colorways in the pattern will be open, meaning anyone can buy them. For other colorways the manufacturer will grant exclusivity so no other seller will represent that colorway among their offerings, although others may have the pattern in a different colorway.

Point of Emphasis 3.4

The fabric market is somewhat synchronized across all textile manufacturers. If one fabric in a scheme wears out prematurely and you have to replace it, you might find it is difficult to match a color that was popular a few years ago. Color preferences are constantly shifting; one year reds tend to be more orange and the next, more blue. Companies pay a lot of attention to the predictions of color forecasters and align their products with what experts expect to be the preferred colors in the upcoming years, and if a color combination does not fit with those predictions, it will be hard to work into schemes with other fabrics.

The danger to the designer from an open line is that you may specify a fabric that you find for an item for your client—say a custom duvet envelope. You may be unaware that the fabric that you selected from your trade resource is part of an open line—until the day your client tells you that they saw a bed-in-a-bag at a big box store in the same fabric as their own custom (and costly) bedding. So as a designer you will want to specify exclusive patterns and colorways.

You will purchase the fabric from your trade resource and request a cutting of the current dye lot, called a cutting for approval (CFA). In your specification to the workroom that is going to make the item, you will state that the COM fabric (customer's own material—meaning the workroom will not provide the fabric to make the item) is to arrive from such-and-such manufacturer and you will include a brief description in your order. Most workrooms will start counting the stated lead time from receipt of fabric, so you do not get in line for production until the fabric arrives at the workroom or manufacturer.

Helpful Hint 3.3

If you are going to have a fabric or other material backed for use on walls, send a couple of yards to the backer to test prior to shipping the whole order to make sure the fabric stays on grain and the effect is what you are after. When you proceed with the order, don't forget to treat the surface with a stain repellant before installing it so that any glue that finds its way onto the face of the material can be more easily cleaned away.

A Cautionary Tale 3.2

I got a call from a friend of mine, who is also a designer, explaining that she had just gone to the warehouse to see a sofa that had come in for her client and the fabric was inside out. If she had noted on her swatch to the manufacturer which side was the face of the goods, they would have been obligated to re-cover the sofa. It is a very simple matter to take a ballpoint pen and write the word *face* on the outside/front of the fabric swatch that you include with your order and the word *back* on the wrong side. Since she had not done this it was left up to interpretation and she had to negotiate a resolution. The deal that she finally struck with the manufacturer was that she would replace the fabric and they would pay for all the shipping and re-cover the sofa at no charge. It still cost her thousands of dollars to skip this little step.

This simple version of the flow of fabric from the textile designer to your workroom may or may not have additional parties to the process represented. All fabrics are milled, but not all go through converters; most, but not all, are handled by jobbers. There will be some kind of representation before it comes to the attention of the designer and in many cases this will be someone affiliated with the trade resource from whom you specify.

- Mill—Makes the fabric and sells it in large quantities called minimums. The minimums vary but generally conform to market expectations of at least 1,000 yards in Europe, 3,000 yards in Asia, and 5,000 yards in the U.S.
- Converter—Buys **greige goods** directly from a fabric mill, and dyes, finishes, prints, or otherwise alters the greige goods and sells them in smaller quantities, often around 500 yards or so, to jobbers or wholesalers.
- Jobber—Purchases large quantities of excess finished fabrics from mills and converters and then sells them wholesale, in even smaller quantities, to design firms, manufacturers, and retail fabric stores.
- Rep—A sales representative or "rep" shows fabrics from one or more mills and is the link between manufacturers and wholesalers or resellers.
- Wholesalers—Sell the fabric to resellers like designers, fabric stores, smaller manufacturers, and other links to the end users.

SELECTION CRITERIA

Testing data available to the interior designer will include a variety of measures, some more important to your planned use than others. Depending on your program needs you may look for the following for a commercial interior.

The American Association of Textile Chemists and Colorists (AATCC) is a well-respected, second-party organization that performs unbiased testing of textile characteristics. You may notice references to AATCC ratings on commercial fabrics. They generally rate textiles on a five-point scale with five being excellent and one being poor. The American Society for Testing and Materials (ASTM) is a nonprofit, third-party organization with testing procedures covering many materials, not just textiles. You may also see references to ASTM data on fabric information. ASTM data that you will find will list the testing method and the results. The results may be all inclusive, such as "resists fungal growth," or they may list a numerical result like "seam slippage 25 lbs for warp and weft per ASTM D 4034." You may decide to organize your thinking about your program's selection criteria in a manner similar to that in Table 3.8.

Table 3.8
Selection criteria.

Characteristic	Examples	Select
Flammability	Danger of fire when users may not be familiar with closest exit location; consider application (i.e., adhered with no air space or loose like drapery?)	Class A or Class 1 fire-rated fabric generally; drapery should also list NFPA 701-Pass
Germs	Health-care providers, child care spaces	Antimicrobial treatments
Abrasion	High-use interiors	Select heavy-duty fabric surviving minimum 30,000 double rubs Wyzenbeek or 40,000 on the Martindale test scale; 50,000 double rubs or more for 24-hour facilities
Fade resistance	Exposed to sunlight	Grade 4 or 5; Grade 4 at 40 hours generally or Grade 4 at 60 hours for drapery; depending on exposure, for outdoor use specify Class 5 only
Tear strength	Upholstery fabric that will be subject to high or rough use (recall the children who stand and walk on airport seating) or where fabric might become caught in a hinge or cart, or a brief-case with pointy corners might be set on upholstery	50 lb minimum in warp or weft generally or 35 lb for panel fabrics
Pilling	Abrasion and yarn characteristics combine to create abrasion problems when the short ends of a staple fiber stick and get matted together from abrasion	Class 3 minimum
Seam slippage	Stress at stitched seams causes fabric to open up in the direction of the stress; if the seam runs parallel to the warp the warp threads will slide over leaving only the weft threads for some distance	25 lb in warp and weft direction
Crocking	Colorant rubs off	Generally Grade 3 minimum wet or dry but upholstery should be Grade 4 minimum
Stain resistance	If a fiber is oleophilic, it will tend to soak up oil-based stains; if it is hydrophilic it will soak up water-based stains, so you will consider the fiber chemistry as well as the test method to make sure fabric resists what it must for your client's site	Grade 4 or 5; coatings can enhance fabric stain resistance; chemical or molecular (nano) coatings perform differently so compare properties before specifying to match best to your client's needs
Toxicity	Toxins in location of production as well as in your client's site	Check for heavy metals used in colorants as well as finishes that use formaldehyde and other toxins; check for VOCs in manufacturing and in use
Sustainability	A consideration for all environments but especially those where wear indicates the materials will be replaced one day	Recycled content; ease of recycling and existence of a program for recycling; water use and recycling in production; recommended cleaning methods

Many of the above are recommendations from the Association for Contract Textiles (ACT).

RELATED MATERIAL

Materials that are similar to textiles include leather, which is used in place of fabric in installations and items to which textiles are applied. Each of these topics require a fair amount of information in order to understand them and so are covered rather extensively here. The application of textiles to items is restricted in this chapter to soft goods. Because soft goods have little structure beyond that supplied by the fabric (unlike upholstered furniture for instance) they are heavily dependent on the textile used to make them.

Leather

While leather is not, strictly speaking, a textile, it is used in many of the same instances where we specify fabric; so this is a logical place to consider leather as a material for your interiors. Although we may automatically think of cowhides as the source of all the leather we specify, leather may be harvested from pigs, deer, snakes, calves, and many other animals. Leather is priced by the square foot but sold by the hide or half-hide. The conversion rate is 18 square feet of leather for every yard of 54-inch-wide fabric required for your client's job. This means that a single hide of approximately 50 square feet is about as much covering as provided by 2.75 yards of fabric. Hides vary in size and they are not neat rectangles (Figure 3.48) so you should err on the generous side when estimating how much leather will be required for your job.

There are numerous quality differences between leathers, some arising from conditions in which the cow was raised. Its nutrition plays a small role in the quality of the skin as do scars acquired during life, which remain visible on some kinds of hides. If the cow was raised in a safe environment and was not scarred or injured, the hide will be relatively free of such blemishes. It will still have natural skin wrinkles in some places—like at the neck, and "fat wrinkles" (creases that soak up dye differently than surrounding skin)—but will not be scarred from barbed wire or bug bites. Many will claim that European hides are superior to the free-range hides from cows grown for the meat industry in the U.S. because European cows are raised in safer, cleaner environments and they are generally free of these scars. European hides are more expensive to buy, but the fabricator does not have to cut around damaged areas, so some of the cost is offset by a reduction in waste.

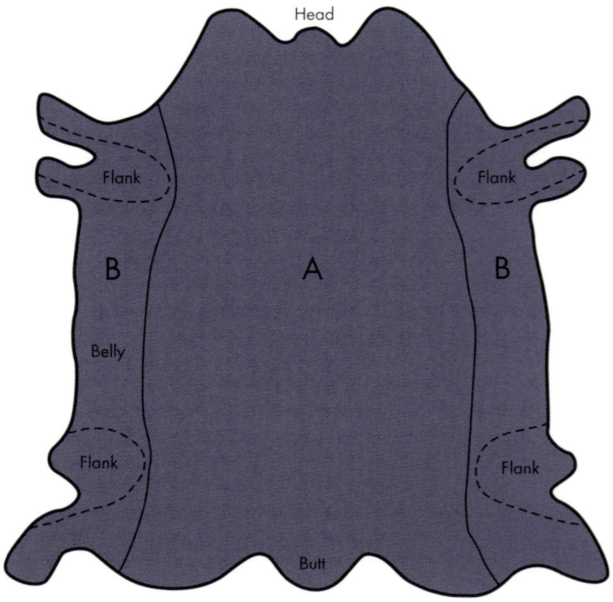

FIGURE 3.48 Hides are not neat rectangles of consistent material, so estimating quantity of leather required gets a little tricky. Ordering returnable overage is often a good idea.

Grades

Although it is not information that interior designers use directly, tanneries grade the skins they process according to their quality and the presence of damage to the skin.

- 41 hide—A 41 hide is a hide free from holes, cuts, deep scores, or gouges more than halfway through the hide, visible grain defects, and broken grain (over one inch long) and has a correct pattern. An exception would be rear shanks containing one hole or cut below the hock that measures less than one inch in length and holes less than four inches from the edge of the hide, which can be trimmed without spoiling the pattern of the hide and not result in a downgrade.
- 42 hide—A 42 hide is a hide that contains either one to four holes, cuts, deep scores or gouges in an area located inside a straight line drawn through the break in the hair of the fore and hind shanks, or a great break over one inch, or an area of warts no longer than one square foot, or a hole regardless of size within the confines of a brand.

- 43 hide—A 43 hide is a hide that contains either five or more holes, cuts, deep scores, or gouges in an area located inside a straight line drawn through the break in the hair of the fore and hind shanks, or one hole or cut over six inches, or an area of warts or open grub holes larger than one square foot. A machine-damaged hide will be considered a 43 hide if at least 50 percent of the surface area of the hide is present and usable for leather manufacture. If less than 50 percent is present the hide will be considered untannable.

Skins are processed through a short series of steps to turn them into nonperishable leather hides. The raw hides (stiff and hard like a dog's rawhide bone) are either vegetable tanned or chromium tanned. The vegetable-tanned hides are rolled in a drum with tree bark, fish oil, and other natural vegetable and mineral ingredients.

> Point of Emphasis 3.5
> Vegetable-tanned hides feel stiffer and crisper than chromium-tanned hides.

Chromium-tanned leather is also rolled in a drum but with mineral salts. Chromium-tanned leather is softer than vegetable-tanned leather. Leather that is only tanned is called crust. Crust leathers are completely "naked," and therefore vulnerable to soiling, so from this stage it will receive other processes and materials altering its delicate characteristics. See Figure 3.49.

Grain

The texture of the skin is called the grain of the leather. Top grain may sound like the best quality but it is second best. The real grain of top grain leather has been sanded away and an imitation grain is stamped into the leather. When the genuine grain remains, the leather is called full grain, or full top grain, not simply top grain. Top grain leather will typically be more resistant to soiling because of its unnatural surface. For leather chairs where people will be eating and drinking, top grain is a better choice than the better quality full grain.

Full grain leather displays the natural markings and grain characteristics of the animal from which it was taken. They are dyed through with transparent aniline dyes. Because the full, natural grain is retained, you should be able to see the fat wrinkles and the feel, or **hand**, should be natural to the touch.

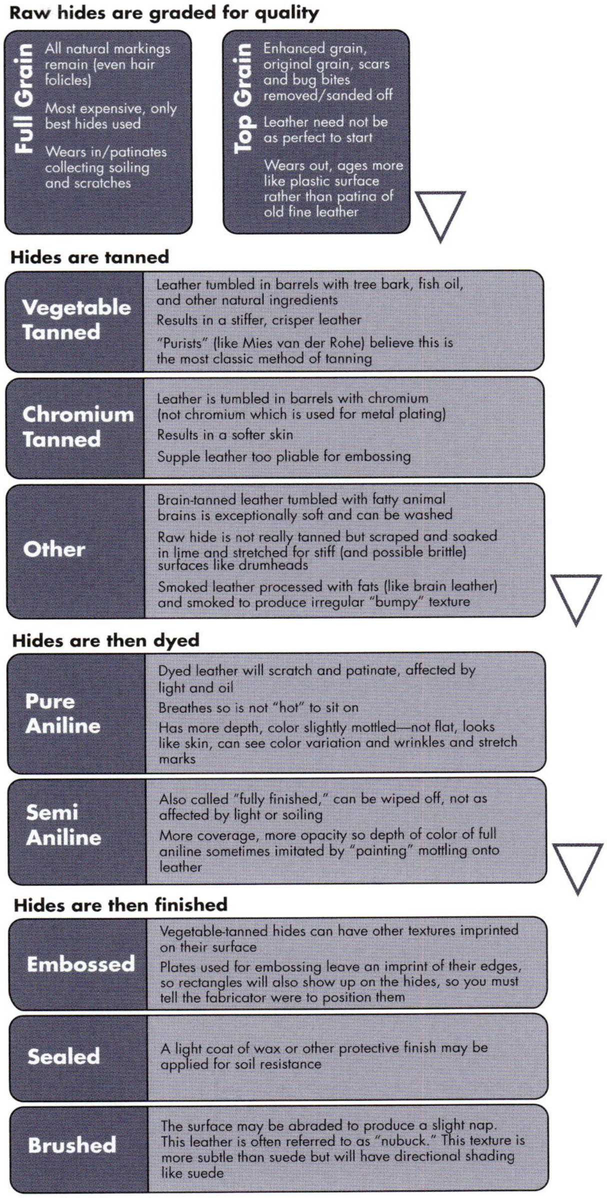
Raw hides are graded for quality
Full Grain
All natural markings remain (even hair folicles)
Most expensive, only best hides used
Wears in/patinates collecting soiling and scratches
Top Grain
Enhanced grain, original grain, scars and bug bites removed/sanded off
Leather need not be as perfect to start
Wears out, ages more like plastic surface rather than patina of old fine leather
Hides are tanned
Vegetable Tanned
Leather tumbled in barrels with tree bark, fish oil, and other natural ingredients
Results in a stiffer, crisper leather
"Purists" (like Mies van der Rohe) believe this is the most classic method of tanning
Chromium Tanned
Leather is tumbled in barrels with chromium (not chromium which is used for metal plating)
Results in a softer skin
Supple leather too pliable for embossing
Other
Brain-tanned leather tumbled with fatty animal brains is exceptionally soft and can be washed
Raw hide is not really tanned but scraped and soaked in lime and stretched for stiff (and possible brittle) surfaces like drumheads
Smoked leather processed with fats (like brain leather) and smoked to produce irregular "bumpy" texture
Hides are then dyed
Pure Aniline
Dyed leather will scratch and patinate, affected by light and oil
Breathes so is not "hot" to sit on
Has more depth, color slightly mottled—not flat, looks like skin, can see color variation and wrinkles and stretch marks
Semi Aniline
Also called "fully finished," can be wiped off, not as affected by light or soiling
More coverage, more opacity so depth of color of full aniline sometimes imitated by "painting" mottling onto leather
Hides are then finished
Embossed
Vegetable-tanned hides can have other textures imprinted on their surface
Plates used for embossing leave an imprint of their edges, so rectangles will also show up on the hides, so you must tell the fabricator were to position them
Sealed
A light coat of wax or other protective finish may be applied for soil resistance
Brushed
The surface may be abraded to produce a slight nap. This leather is often referred to as "nubuck." This texture is more subtle than suede but will have directional shading like suede

FIGURE 3.49 Numerous processes may be applied to leather. Not all of these processes are used on any single hide but the combinations of processes alter the performance and appearance of the hide.

The highest quality skins with the fewest blemishes will be processed as full grain leather; lower quality hides will be processed as top grain. Full grain hides do not conceal any of the natural markings or hair follicles that will be removed or concealed by more extensive processing of top grain hides. Both full grain and top grain hides may be dyed with either vegetable or chromium dyes.

For the Connoisseur 3.4

While your specification should address all functional needs of the program there will be times when you want to specify leather that is considered to be "classic." Vegetable-tanned leather is considered to be just such an instance and full grain is a given as well. Vegetable-tanned leather will be more light sensitive and has a stiffer hand than chromium-tanned leather but the connoisseur is willing to live with these frailties in order to have classic leather for their upholstery.

Full grain hides are processed as full aniline and top grain hides are processed as semi-aniline.

Full Aniline or Pure Aniline:

- Only the finest hides in the world fall in this category. It may be only dyed and has no other finish applied other than a light protective wax.
- This type of leather scratches, picks up oil and soiling, and develops a patina.
- Only 5 percent of the total world hide supply are clean (clear of marks and scars) enough to fall in this category.

Semi-Aniline:

- More processed than pure and full aniline: dyeing in large drums like full aniline, but then also finished on top; spray pigments are applied to the hides to even out the finish and camouflage naturally occurring imperfections.
- These leathers are light and scratch resistant and are more easily cleaned.
- Provides 10 to 15 percent of the worldwide hide supply.

What Would You Do? 3.2

Review the different attributes of leather and consider what might be a proper specification for an airport lounge, a plastic surgeon's waiting area, a bachelor who has a connoisseur's perspective on materials, and a family room for a family that has dogs and children. Assume logical budgetary constraints.

Cow leather is the split hide, meaning the skin was double the thickness of the tanned hide because during processing it was split to half of its thickness. The outside of the skin is used for leather; the meat side of the skin is used for suede. Suede retains a nap after processing. Nubuck is a leather (the outside of the hide) product that also presents a nap but the nap on nubuck has been raised by sanding the leather.

Helpful Hint 3.4

When ordering leather for your job it is better to err on the side of too much leather rather than not enough, especially if you are using full grain leather; here's why: Leather is sold by the hide (or half hide), though estimated and priced by the square foot. Even hides of similar size may yield different amounts of usable leather—it depends on the quality of the skin and on the size of the cuts that the upholsterer needs to complete the job. Some hides may have more unusable leather than others and the upholsterer cannot know this until the leather is in the shop.

Full grain leather is the most natural: it is tanned and dyed and very few additional processes are applied to it. This means that natural variation from one lot or batch to another cannot be cosmetically modified to make one batch look like the next. Top grain leather is typically more processed and more processes yield more opportunity to modify the appearance and achieve a match between two different lots.

What to do: Ask your leather supplier if you can return any uncut hides (many will allow this) and add an extra 10 percent to your fabricator's estimated quantity instructing the fabricator to return any uncut hides to you so you can ship them back to your supplier for a refund.

Hides that still have their hair, called hair-on hides, are also dyed sometimes they are selectively dyed to resemble other animal pelts, such as zebra or leopard.

SOFT GOODS

Fabric is fashioned into a product that the industry refers to as soft goods. These are products that do not have a rigid framework to support the shape of the

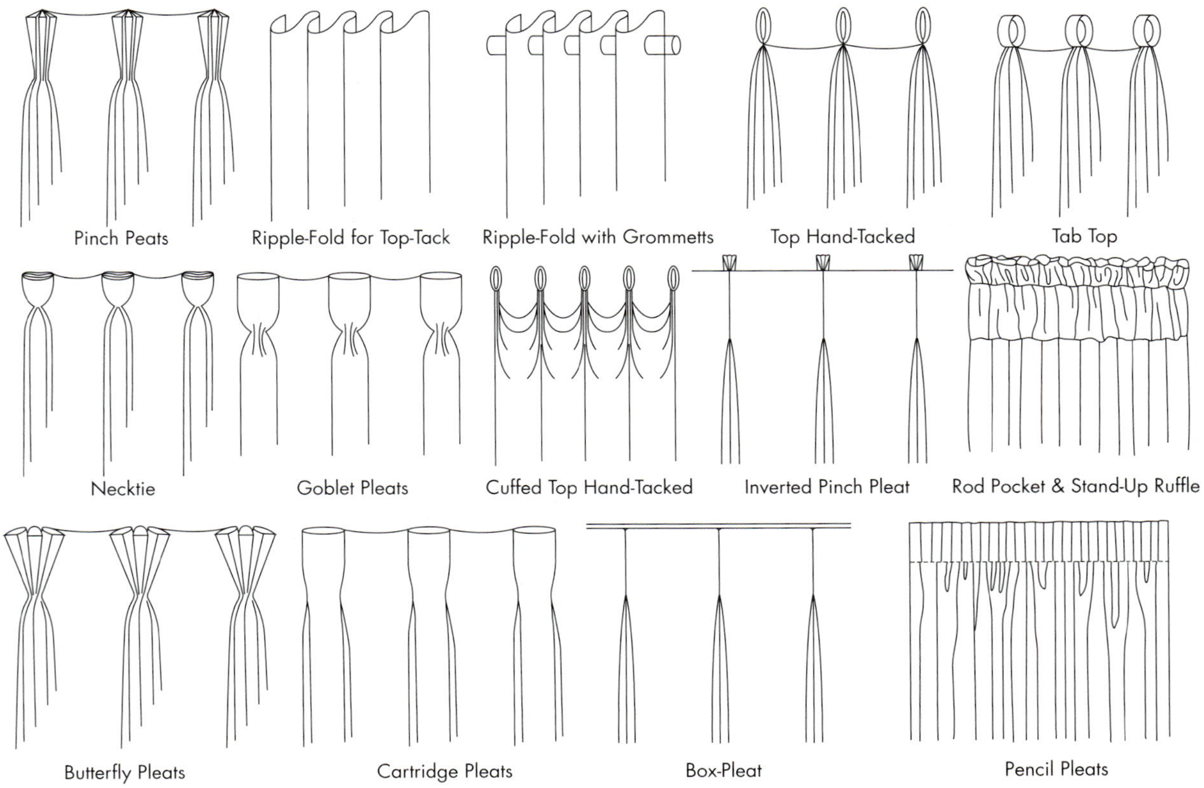

FIGURE 3.50 The top of the drapery is called the header. It not only fastens the drapery to the support that holds the drape up, it adds fullness to the construction. Some headers must be movable so the drapes can draw, others are stationary. Movable drapery will hold hooks or fasten to rings at the pleat location.

fabric product, they rely on sewing and padding alone to present their forms. Window treatments, bedding, table linens, pillows, and the like are considered soft goods. The drapery workroom will also fabricate simple furniture items such as upholstered headboards and will upholster walls. The distinctions between these various soft goods are sometimes loosely defined because there will be items that resemble more than one category.

Window Treatments

There are many issues of style that you will orchestrate according to your design program. Basic categories of treatments that you will utilize or combine might include drapes, curtains, toppers (both hard and soft), custom fabric shades, or manufactured blinds (not technically soft goods but the function is strongly related).

Drapery

Drapery is often assumed to mean treatments that draw open and closed via rigging controlled by a pull cord or motor. *Drapery* and *curtain* are terms sometimes used interchangeably, although the implication of curtains is that they are simpler than drapes and have nonmechanical hardware.

Drapery headers (the hem at the top) are pleated so that even when the drapery is closed over the window, it still has some fullness and ruffling. The hooks that latch the drapery to the rod are fastened to the pleat. There are many different pleat styles (Figure 3.50). Some of them are fatter than others. This will affect how much space the treatment must have when open.

Café curtains, for instance, cover only the lower half of the window and are not strung on movable rigging. They are often assumed to include a companion valence of some sort. Dress curtains are stationary panels that frame the window opening but do not draw across it. So curtains do not require moving hardware.

A Cautionary Tale 3.3

Just as wood expands and contracts due to changes in humidity, fabrics that are made of plant-based fibers will shrink and grow in response to humidity. Rayon was selected for this drapery because, although silk was desired, it was recognized that silk would rot from exposure to sunlight. Since the idea was to use the drapes as sheers, without lining, there would be nothing to protect the silk from the sun.

Rayon is a man-made cellulosic fiber, meaning it started its life as wood. Wood expands and contracts with changes in humidity as a percentage of its size and the rayon fiber here did the same. Because the drop from hem to hem is over nine feet the 1.75 inches of shrinkage that occurred (the angle of the photograph visually exaggerates the shrinkage) is only 1.6 percent of the height. It doesn't sound like a lot when discussed in terms of such a small percentage but it is certainly enough to make a difference in this installation.

Possible solutions:

(1) Lower the rod and repaint the wall.
(2) Take the hem down and hem the drapes with a small "handkerchief" hem with a weighted, beaded chain sewn in so the drapes still hang properly.
(3) Select a similar rayon fabric in a contrasting color to make a decorative band along the bottom.
(4) Select a similar rayon in a similar color, sew it to the bottom, and then turn the new fabric up as the hem.

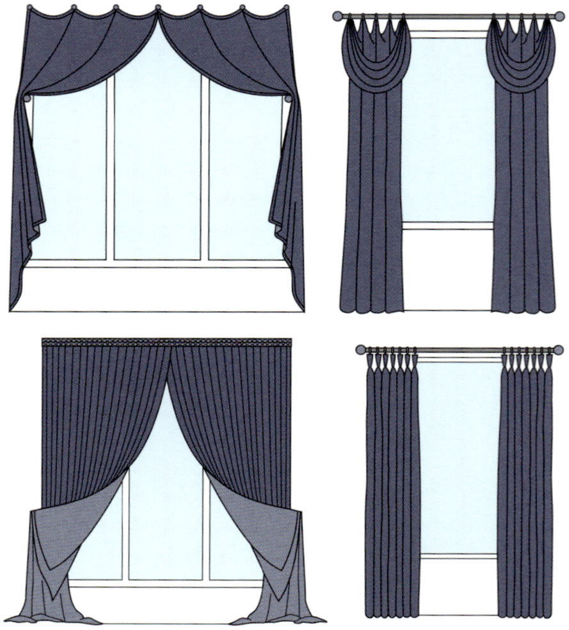

FIGURE 3.51 Dress curtains are stationary.

Dress Curtains Dress curtains are also stationary panels that look like functional draperies (Figure 3.51). You might use them if your client would like the softening look of draperies but the window does not require covering and the cost of drapes is too high. Because dress curtains are not meant to draw, they are often detailed with a tieback (Figure 3.52). If your client intended to use this curtain to cover the window, you would not specify this dress curtain for a couple of reasons. When the tieback is released, the fabric will be wrinkled where it had been held by the tieback. Arranging the pleating flows out of the tieback takes skill and is not as easy as you might think, so it is likely that only your experienced installer can get such perfect results as shown in Figure 3.53.

You also have more options for the header (top of the treatment) because they do not have to move along the rod (Figure 3.54). You may elect to use a header that could potentially move (like the last two on the second row) but that is not required for stationary panels. Figure 3.55 shows stationary panels with tiebacks suspended from rosettes since the drape need not move. Make sure that the dress curtains have sufficient width to maintain attractive proportions. This can be determined with a scale drawing or even more quickly with a to-scale sketch. Remember that after side hems, a 54-inch-wide panel pleats to less than 20 inches. This looks skimpy on windows wider than 2½ or 3 feet.

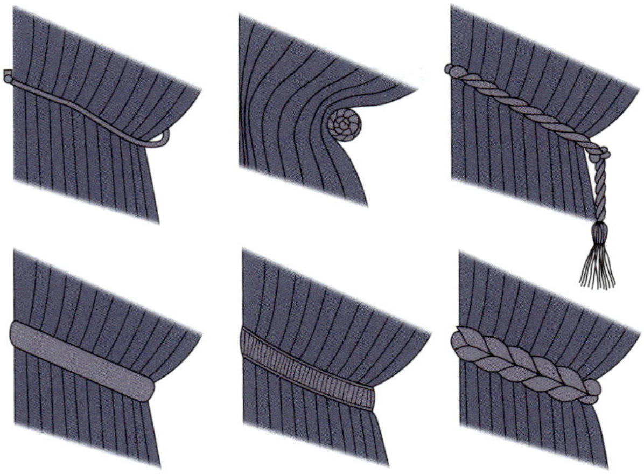

FIGURE 3.52 Stationary panes may be held back. While this looks functional, it is really decorative; the panels may even be hemmed so that they are only the correct length when drawn back.

FIGURE 3.53 This pencil-pleated header and tieback work best on a stationary pane. Notice that a decorative lining has been used on the leading edge instead of the standard white or ivory. This is because it shows when the curtain is drawn back.

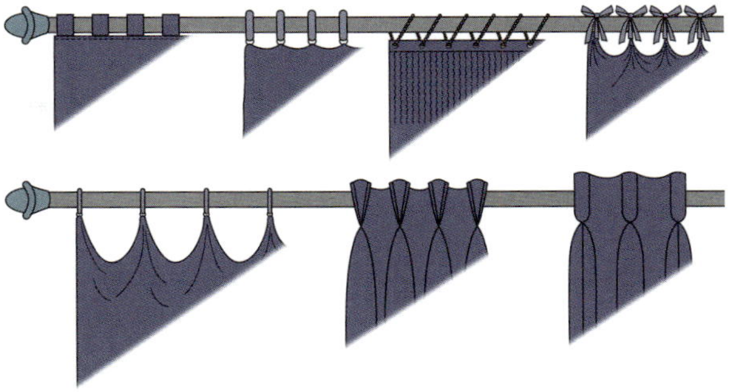

FIGURE 3.54 You have more options for headers when the drape does not draw. Some of these means of fastening would not move easily enough.

FIGURE 3.55 This stationary panel can easily conform to the arch as it hangs from individual rosettes.

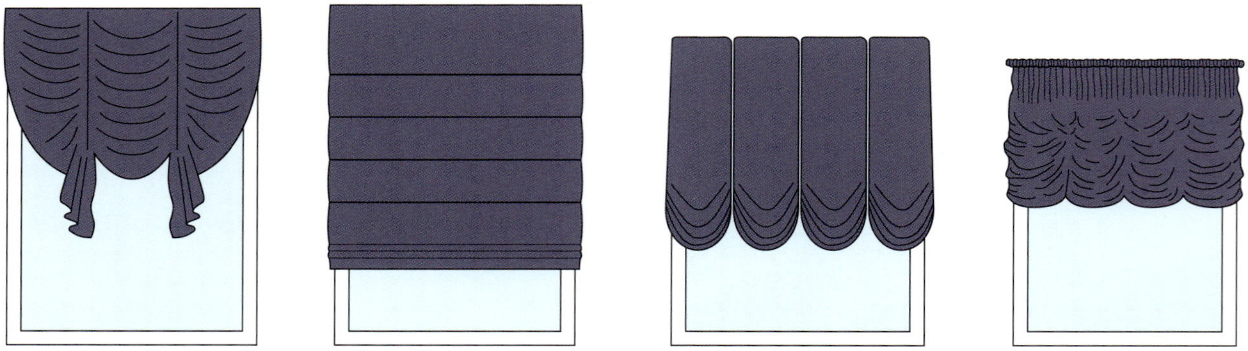

FIGURE 3.56 Custom shades are frequently constructed from selected fabrics.

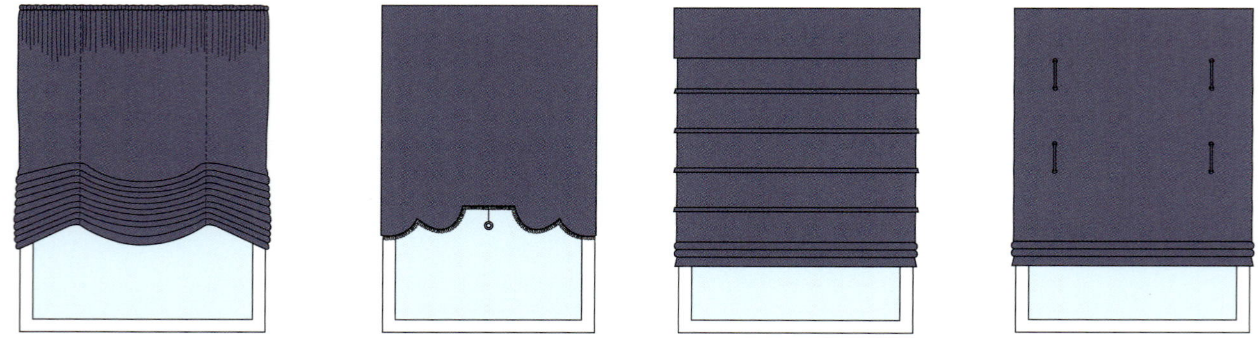

FIGURE 3.57 Shade styles may draw up or roll up.

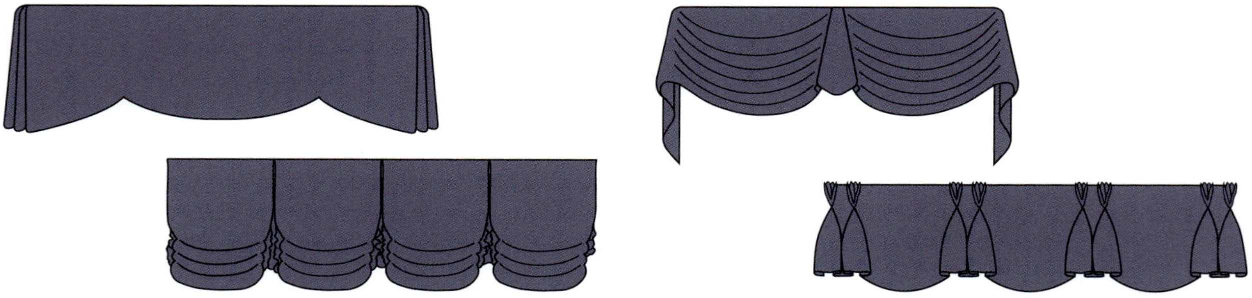

FIGURE 3.58 Valences are soft treatments, meaning they may hang from a board but their structure comes from the shape given to the fabric when stitched rather than by a stiff material underneath.

Top Treatments Top treatments such as swags and jabots or valances are softly constructed, decorative drapery treatments of fabric, often combined with other coverings (drapes, shades, blinds, etc.). Custom shades can be made up in your selected fabric. See Figures 3.56 and 3.57 for custom blinds and shades. If you elect to cover the window with a shade or blind and install stationary panels at the sides, you can save money. This approach requires less fabric, and less labor cost and no rigging, saving labor and fabric requirements.

Soft top treatments include valances (Figure 3.58) and swags (Figure 3.59). Swags look the best if they are cut on the bias, so keep this in mind when selecting fabric that will hang on grain for all of the treatment except the swag. Swags can be cut on grain but they do not hang as gracefully. Notice how smoothly the curves flow in the drape of the swags shown in Figure 3.60; this is only possible if the fabric is cut on the bias or is a very loose weave that can be blocked into shape. Valances are cut on the grain (Figure 3.61 shows a custom valance used above a manufactured grass shade).

Top treatments also include upholstered items (Figure 3.62), cornice boards, lambrequins, and cantoneers, which are often constructed of plywood or

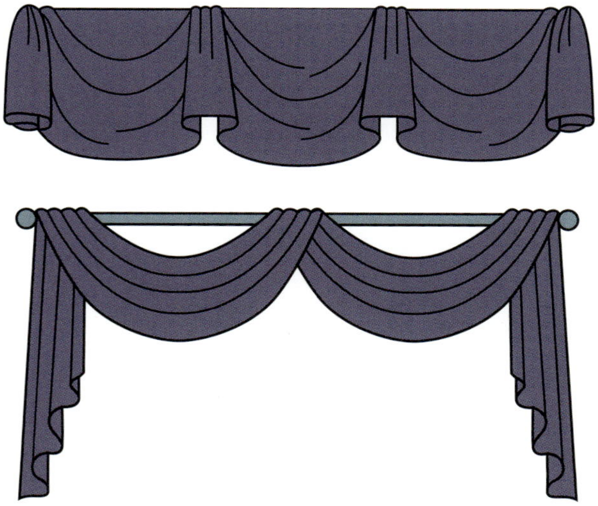

FIGURE 3.59 Swags look very casual but they are highly constructed, so much so that if removed from their support they would stay in shape.

FIGURE 3.60 These swags were cut on the bias so the sweep of their folds is unkinked. *Photograph by author at Baird's Drapery Services, Chicago, IL.*

FIGURE 3.61 A manufactured grass shade is paired with a custom valence. *Design by Tracy Hickman of Chicago, IL.*

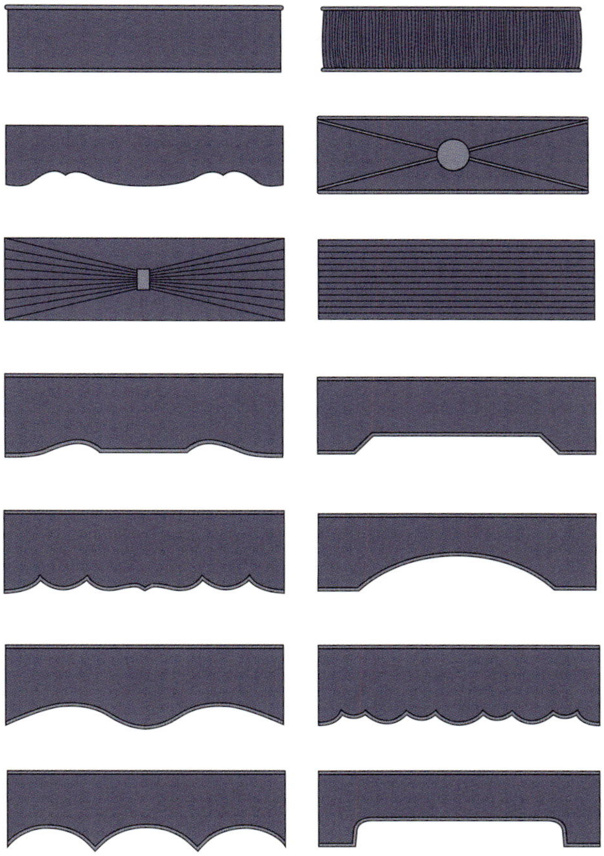

FIGURE 3.62 Cornice boards are fabric-upholstered boards, padded out and covered.

FIGURE 3.63 Window treatment that relies on a stiff substrate to give it shape spans the distance between architecture and soft goods. *Design by Joan Schlagenhaft, Mequon, WI.*

FIGURE 3.64 Lambrequin can lend architectural detail to spaces. *Design by Deutsch Parker, Chicago, IL.*

another engineered substrate, are padded and covered with fabric. They usually have a complementary relationship to the architecture as they transition from structure to window treatment but they are sometimes used to lend a little architectural interest. Cornice boards (Figure 3.63) cover the top of the window, lambrequins (Figure 3.64) cover the top and some portion, or all, of the sides, and cantoneers frame the window completely on all four sides.

Lining When supplied by the workroom, linings will be a standard lining in white, black, or ivory, a black-out lining, or a thermal lining (Figure 3.65). Interlining (a fabric of a variable weight sandwiched between the face fabric and the lining, often a flannel) can be used to give a treatment more body or better thermal properties if necessary.

White or ivory lining became a standard to accommodate the exterior presentation of the building and because it does not alter the color of the treatment when the light shines through it. If the face fabric has a strong color it may be apparent from the outside when drapery is closed at night and lights are turned on inside. Ivory may add a little bit of yellow to the face fabric when the light shines through it; this is most noticeable if the field color of the finish fabric is pale. If you are supplying your own lining, because the design planned will allow the back to show, remember that the seams on the lining should line up with the drapery seams so ideally you purchase the same width as the face fabric or wider and then pay the labor charges to have the workroom cut it to width. Select lining fabric that is most similar to or most compatible with the face fabric so that it reacts the same. You can also supply a special lining or interlining if your treatment calls for it. Figure 3.66 has jabots that are lined with a finish fabric rather than the workroom lining because the design reveals the back of the jabot.

FIGURE 3.65 Standard lining offerings available through your workroom. *Image courtesy of Baird's Decorating Services, Chicago, IL.*

Fitting the Window Treatments to the Space

A simple draw drape on a traverse or other rod could be specified with a written specification alone, but most window treatment designs are best communicated with drawings that show the treatment in plan and elevation showing all pertinent dimensions, alignments to architectural features, and information to the installer. Included in the dimensions are the height, the treatment in relation to the floor or window frame, and the width of the treatment, including stackbacks. The depth of a multilayered treatment or a treatment where the projection would become an issue (bay windows, drapery pockets, or any close proximity) should also be shown on the plans. The location of the control cord or wand should be noted on a plan view.

The plan view that you forward to the workroom will show the depth of the treatment and the anticipated size of the stackback; the location of the pull cord or wand will be noted along with the correct location of floor vents, switch plates, and other service controls.

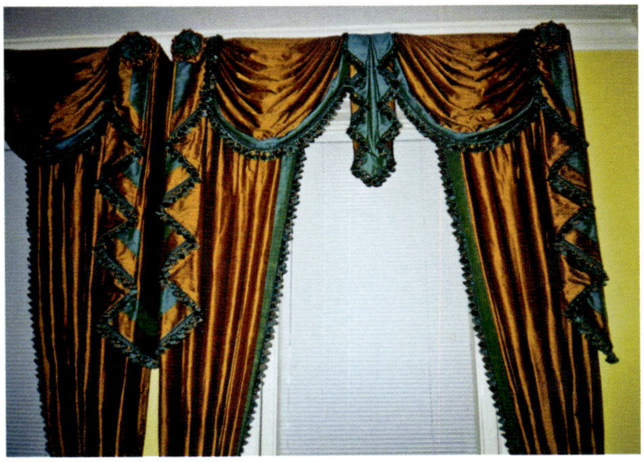

FIGURE 3.66 Swags and jabots are lined with the same fabric as the face when the back will show. *Design by Art and Design, Chicago, IL.*

Depth of the Treatment Estimate that each layer of drapery will project six inches and consult the manufacturer's stack chart for purchased shades and blinds. Some woven grass and bamboo Roman blinds require up to a foot of depth projection to stack up. This can eliminate them from consideration in a situation where two windows meet in a corner or in a bay window. A lambrequin, cornice, or valance adds a couple of inches more to the depth. Show all these layers in your plan view so you can confirm furniture locations and to fully comprehend the scale of the 3D treatment in location. Sometimes it's quite a massive presence. If the drapery will retract into a pocket, there should be room on front and back so the fabric does not drag and snag; in which case, add two or three more inches.

Width of the Stackback The **stackback** is the width required for the open drapery to stand, either off the glass covering wall space or on the glass covering part of the window. It is typically one-third the width of the entire treatment but you can control for some variation. There are a few factors influencing the size of the stackback. One is the fullness. Typical minimal fullness for multipurpose fabric (medium-light drapery weight) is 2.75 times the fullness. Heavier fabric can look okay with 2.5 times fullness; that is fortunate if the stackback is getting too wide, because heavy fabric needs more room to stack. So the second factor influencing the size of the stackback is fabric fullness. The number of pleats and kind of pleats also contributes to how tightly the treatment can stack. You can adjust the fullness and the

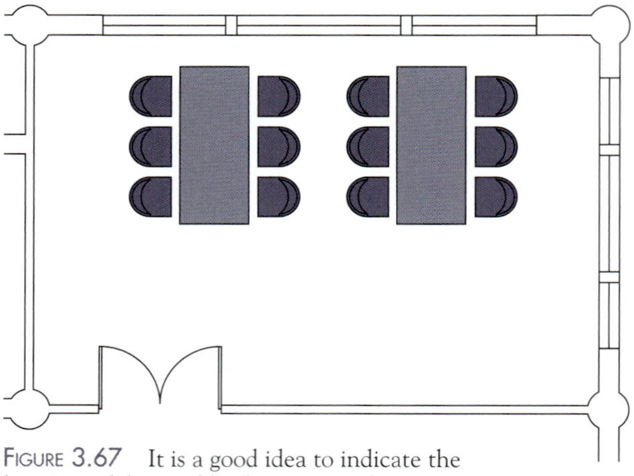

FIGURE 3.67 It is a good idea to indicate the location of the stackbacks on your plans so you account for the space they will take up.

FIGURE 3.68 These goblet pleats take up more space than pinch pleats so the stackback will be wider for this treatment. *Design by Tracy Hickman.*

number of pleats independently of each other. Fewer fuller pleats can reduce the stackback without making the drapes look skimpy. Lining will add to the bulk of the stacked treatment; lining and interlining (as is irresistible for taffeta and other thin solids) doubles the contribution of the bulk from lining. The kind of pleat selected contributes to the stackback (Figure 3.67). Some of the pleat styles shown in Figure 3.50 are so fat, such as the goblet (Figure 3.68), that you might only consider them for stationary panels. They just need too much stackback for most locations.

Size and Mounting Location The mounting height can best be determined on elevation with all casings and moldings indicated in correct scale. A general rule is that treatments should rise minimally 4 inches above the top of the window and extend 4 inches beyond the side of the window, so that is a good place to start when you make your to-scale sketch showing the treatment. If the treatment does not go to the floor (½ inch above finished floor) it should fall 2 to 4 inches below the apron.

Location and Type of Control Also on your plan view will be the control location and type. The location of a wand at the leading edge or a pull cord for the rigging at the outside should be indicated on your plans so that the workroom and the client can comprehend the logistics of getting behind furniture to reach the wands or pull cords.

Location of Room Features There will be times when you complete your plan view to discover that some of the existing room features are in conflict. For new construction, the light switch can be precisely located beyond the stackback, HVAC vents can be positioned so they don't billow drapery, and windows can be located to provide enough wall space for stackbacks. In existing construction, the client may have to make the determination as to whether such conflicts will be a nuisance, in which case the plan of the architecture should be modified. It may be most convenient to open and close them with the flick of a switch, so you'll need to add information to the electrical plan and locate the place in the wall cavity where you can position the motors to drive each rod. You may require an outlet behind the stackback for each pair of drapes that use a motor.

Hardware Drapes can traverse on a track rigged with cords to open and close them or can hang from a rod and be pulled by hand or by a wand hidden behind the leading edge of a drape (so the client isn't tugging on the fabric when moving the drapes). Decorative options for hardware with rigging are limited, and if traversing drapes are desired, you might select one of the hollow-back estate rods or plan to cover the economical white traverse rods with an architectural or soft goods detail. Drapery headers might be pleated, requiring one kind of hanging system, or ripple-fold, requiring ripple-fold hardware. Some treatments are stationary (that is they do not move). Such treatments can be hung on a rod or mounted on a board.

Other Window Treatments

In addition to custom drapery, window treatments include manufactured shutters, blinds, and shades that are made of or incorporate special fabrics, perhaps along with other materials.

Shutters Shutters are bulky treatments unless you can **inside mount** them, so detail how they can be integrated into the architecture. If the site has complicated architectural construction at the windows, it is a good idea to meet the installer at the site or review the plans.

Good shutters are constructed with the same considerations that you would give to cabinet doors. As with cabinet doors, the stiles must be a minimum 2 inches wide on their faces and 1 to 1¼ inch thick for stability. The joints are ideally a slotted joint construction (like mortise and tenon). Shutters should be made of kiln-dried hardwood for transparent finish but could be an engineered wood product if they will be painted. In high-moisture situations (pool houses exposed to a lot of weather conditions and not always controlled with the same tenacity as the air inside the main house) you may want to consider vinyl. Vinyl has standard sizes, and you will adjust the opening or framing to accommodate the standards. Purchase shutters from shops that specialize in them.

Materials for shutters include the following:

- *Engineered hardwood*—A great surface for paint; molded edges are crisp; surface is smooth.
- *Alderwood*—A good choice for paint and stain applications.
- *Basswood*—A good choice for stain and acceptable for paint; it does not have a high surface hardness.
- *Poplar*—A less stable wood than other choices.
- *Polys, PVCs, cellulars, vinyls, hollow fills, vinyl clad*—Suitable for use in high-moisture situations, but they discolor and sag over time in hot, south-facing windows.

Blinds Your supplier or installer is likely to represent product from many manufacturers. Because this product is considered to be something of a commodity, the manufacturers rely on proprietary colors and textures as well as quality specifications to differentiate among the many product offerings. Most manufacturers offer a couple of different price points so that blinds that will not be handled by the end user on a consistent basis don't have the same rigorous specs as blinds that they will adjust frequently. These blinds will not cost as much as blinds with superior construction but there is a quality difference, and you do get what you pay for.

Options that you will encounter among blinds manufacturers' offerings will include width of slats; kind of control (cords, continuous pulley, motorized on a battery or hardwired); decorative considerations (color, surface, decorative tapes, special valance profiles to conceal the mechanics at the top of the blinds); and the option to locate controls left or right.

Qualifying Installers and Fabricators

Find prequalified installers by word of mouth. Interview fabricators and installers, and review their work and their standard specifications. Ask them how long they have been in business. Review of their standard specifications should include quality construction and attention to detail.

Drapes for example:

- The workroom is to take all of its own measurements.
- All fabric is to be inspected with bright light shining through it before it is cut, ideally when it is received at the workroom. If the fabricator waits until it is time to cut the fabric before inspecting it, you will have lost valuable time for getting replacement goods in hand if the goods are flawed.
- They always construct double hems and headers 4 to 6 inches deep.
- They blind-stitch hems (1½-inch double-side hems are standard).
- All seams are serged and over locked.
- All corners are weighted.
- Lightweight fabrics have beaded weights in hem for improved draping.
- Pleating of multiple-width fabric should always conceal seams.
- Draperies should be fan-folded for transport and steamed and tied on-site.

It is preferable for suppliers to have their own workroom and their own installers but successful relationships can be maintained as long as the supplier always assumes full responsibility for their subcontractors.

Shop Visit

Our visit to Baird's Drapery workroom in Chicago begins in their showroom. Not all workrooms will have a showroom. This workroom maintains a showroom as a resource for designers. They are a to-the-trade resource (they do not work directly with end users and their contracts are with design professionals only).

From the showroom we proceed into the workroom.

When requests for quotes come in from designers, a file is created to organize the information sent with the request for quote and to keep track of the information that supports the quote generated. When the job moves into production, the job file will also contain copies of work orders, cuttings, and a record of conversations pertaining to the order.

When the fabric comes in, it is checked for flaws using a light table. You can see small slubs in the fabric, which may not be visible until the light shines through them. This is an important step for two reasons. Unless the drapes are blackout-lined, they will have light shine through them when they are installed, so the light table duplicates that condition. The fabric is checked upon receipt so that there will be time to order replacement goods if there is something wrong with the shipment. Drapery workrooms typically have a lead time that is weeks long so defective fabric can be replaced before the job comes up for production.

Fabric is rerolled onto the shipping tube, tagged with the job number, and stored until the job comes up on the production schedule.

Shop Visit *(continued)*

When the job goes into production, the fabric is cut to length. This measuring and cutting takes place on another light table. If the workroom wanted to avoid the slubs noticed upon arrival they would need to be able to find them so they could cut around them as they cut the fabric into panels. The panels would be the "cut length," which means the finished length from the top of the pleats to the floor plus the header and hem.

The finish fabric and the lining will be cut together and the cut panels for each job hang on racks waiting for assembly. You can see the work ticket, which contains instructions for each phase of production, hangs on the fabric for the job. A small swatch of the face or finish fabric will identify the work ticket if it becomes separated from the fabric panels. Long side seams are stitched to create the fabric width needed for the drapery. The same step will be performed for the lining and then the lining will be fastened to the finish fabric.

This table is the first of its kind, custom built for Baird's to allow the fabric to "hang out" on the tilt surface before the hems are cut. Fabric is not a solid material, it is a sheet composed of warp and weft threads, and up to this point it has been rolled then wrestled under the machine as the side seams were sewn. On the tilt table the fabrics can assume a natural position for drapery as gravity can help approximate the condition of the drapery in the installation. The drapes relax into position, then the panels are cut to length. The top of the panel is on the low end of the table. You will see why in the next picture.

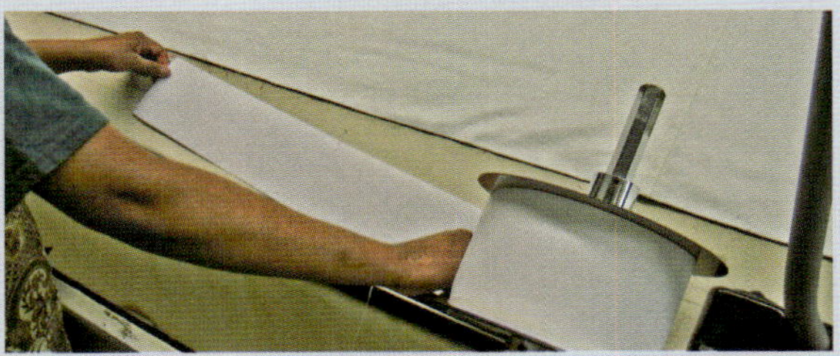

The header, which contains the pleats, must have a little extra body. Here you can see the roll of buckram, which is applied to the header (the top hem).

After the header has been formed, the drapery panel is moved to the pleater table. You can see a series of small rulers, which will guide the amount of fabric pleated at each pleat location. These guides must be set by hand and the spacing confirmed for each job. It varies with the width of the finished drapery treatment, the fullness of the fabric, and the kind of pleat specified.

Shop Visit *(continued)*

After the pleats are marked they will be tacked to hold their form. These pleats are being tacked on a machine. Some pleat styles are tacked by hand.

The hem of this sheer panel is being sewn by hand. Some hems are sewn by machine.

Drapery installations require hardware. Special hardware such as decorative rods and finials are ordered especially for the job. The utilitarian brackets and pins, traverse rods, etc., are on hand at the workroom. The sheer variety of hardware kept on hand is an indication of the number of options available from custom drapery styles.

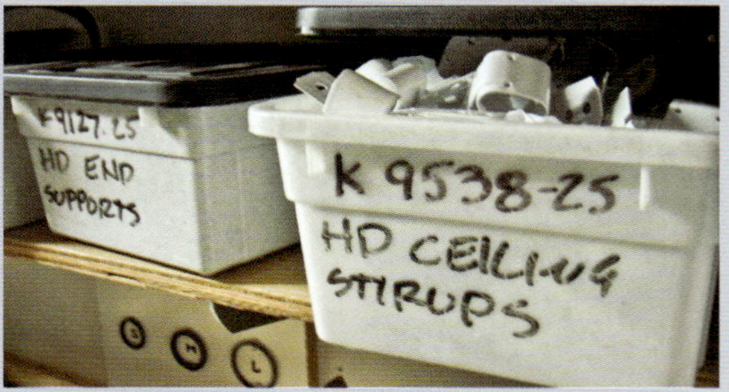

The hardware is organized by type and the storage bins labeled.

Custom valences and cornices were being constructed. The valence under construction here is based on a detailed drawing produced by the designer used in conjunction with measurements taken at the job site (after the contract had been awarded).

A paisley swag that was to be mounted to a cornice board was also being worked on. Here its top has been finished and pleated and the bottom edge is receiving a fringe trim.

The cornice board is constructed of particleboard; it is then padded and covered with the finish fabric. Here you can see that a self-piping (a cord covered in the same fabric as the cornice board) is being applied to the top edge.

Its form is checked on a padded pinup board before it is fastened to the cornice board.

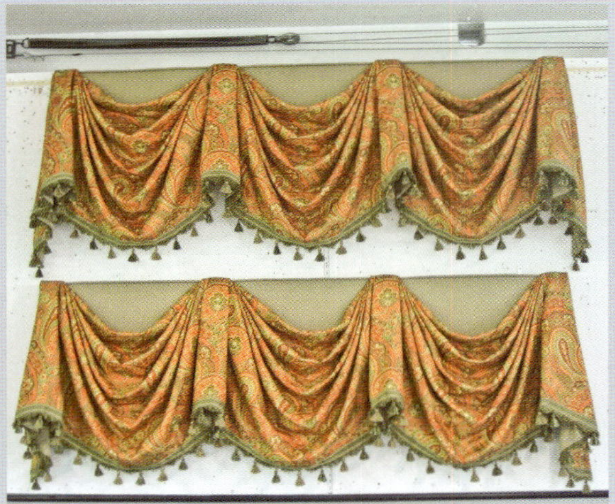

Here are a couple of swagged cornice boards already completed and "hanging out." The swags can relax into shape for a while before they are removed (Velcro tabs hold them on so they can come down for cleaning in the future) and hung on hangers for transporting to the job site.

UPHOLSTERY

Fabric and leather are frequently applied to furniture and, as mentioned in the passage pertaining to fire safety on pages 88–89, fabric and the construction that it covers are inextricably bound together when selecting the appropriate fabric for your client's space.

Bedding and Pillows

Among the many kinds of items that you will have constructed out of fabric, or covered in fabric, for jobs are headboards and upholstered box springs, pillows, and bedding. It's a good idea to sketch these items to scale during the planning stage to confirm proportions and sizes. A sketch with fabric identified for each area clarifies the details for the client and the workroom and locates multiple fabrics, if used. If the spread has piped seams, a banded edge, and a contrasting backing fabric, a drawing will confirm everyone's understanding of where those four different fabrics will be positioned in the final construction. The same can be true for pillows. Include swatches keyed to the sketch. It is a good idea to identify on the swatch which side is to be the face (even if it is obvious). It is very labor-intensive (therefore expensive) to pick the seams apart and flip the fabric right-side out—if it can even be done.

Cushions

Cushions may have foam, down, spring-down (springs wrapped with a down blanket), a Marshall unit, or even cotton padding at their core. Cushions with a foam or spring core will likely be wrapped in a layer of polyester batting (poly-batt) or down. Cushions may be 20 percent down and 80 percent feather (designated as 20/80).

Foam cushions will be described in a couple of different ways. Pounds per cubic foot will be listed and foam categorized by a two-digit number from 10 to 32 relating to the weights. Number 10 is 1 pound per cubic foot, number 18 is 1.8 pounds per cubic foot. More to the point is the indentation load deflection (ILD). If a cushion is described as being 30-pound foam that means that it requires 30 pounds of force to indent the cushion by 25 percent of its total height. A 4-inch cushion of 30-pound foam requires 30 pounds of force to compress it down to 3 inches. The preferred range for comfort is generally 30 to 33; 26 is considered soft and over 40 is considered firm and used for things like church kneelers and car seats. The two measurements are not directly correlated because a low density can be chemically engineered to be firm. If a tufted design is planned (the top of an ottoman, for instance), the foam padding should have a triple-layer laminated construction that is firm on the bottom, medium in the middle, and soft at the top to properly pad the piece and allow for good tufting details. Padding on the frame should be firmer than that used for seat cushion cores.

The fabric that covers the cushions will affect the way the construction feels. Leather upholstery is stiff compared to fabric upholstery, especially vegetable-tanned leather. Thin fabric or fabric with a soft hand will be less firm than heavy or densely woven fabric. Custom upholstery is often covered in muslin for a "test sit" before applying the finished fabric. Be sure to consider the difference between the thin, loose muslin and your selected finish fabric.

Look for new sustainable options; soy-based plastics are being used for inserts.

Inspecting the Fabric Application

Fabric application should be taut, smooth, and consistent. The tucks and seams should be neat, the location of seams consistent (especially relative to their location on the frame), and the seams should be precisely positioned at the corners, not shifted around to the front side of one corner and the back of another. The pattern must match consistently from top to bottom and side to side. The motifs should be well positioned and balanced. Welting should be straight, even in dimension, and smooth on cushions and frames. If the fabric cannot be railroaded, the seams that will occur along the back as well as on any continuous seat cushions or on the tight back should be aligned with cushions or relate to the design, rather than being driven by the fabric width alone.

SUSTAINABILITY OF FABRICS AND LEATHER

The Association for Contract Textiles (ACT) is voluntarily working to assemble a set of guidelines that can be used to evaluate the sustainability of textiles. The guidelines include such considerations that are as applicable to leather as they are to other textiles. Figure 3.69 lists the considerations for determining just how sustainable a textile or leather material is.

You will notice that the guidelines address production as well as content for textiles. Sometimes leather and textiles are produced in areas that do not adhere to our ideas of environmental protection or human rights. In addition to inquiring about the chemistry of the fibers, dyes and finishes, look into country of origin. Labor practices in some countries are more likely to ensure safe production conditions than in other areas. Clean air and water mandates vary around the world. Select textiles that are produced as near to your job site as practicable to reduce transportation fuel. Not all issues are as easy to confirm as recycled content and it will take some investment of time to select textiles conscientiously.

The triple bottom line of *people*, *profits*, and *planet* is important to remember in a world market, because some of the products that you might specify are produced in countries that do not enforce equally high standards for all three *Ps* in that equation. As always, look for reliable third-party confirmation that the products you are considering are sustainable according to triple bottom-line principles. NSF International along with ANSI developed NSF/ANSI 336 Sustainability Assessment for Commercial Furnishings Fabric. The National Center for Sustainability Standards (NCSS), in collaboration with the Association for Contract Textiles (ACT) and GreenBlue, has developed various approaches to sustainability and would provide food for thought as you devise your own criteria on the job. The LEED point system also has standards for sustainability that can contribute to your considerations as you select fabric for your jobs.

You must evaluate all aspects of production and disposal to really analyze sustainability of textiles. For example, with bamboo you would certainly account for the exceptional renewability of bamboo. As a quick-growing grass that requires minimal pesticide use, it has that point in its favor. However, chemically processed bamboo used for fabric (rather than mechanically processed) may use chemicals that can cause nerve damage to the workers who are exposed to them. You will want to find out what kinds of environmental and worker protection standards were in place for the production of the fabric you are specifying if you are doing a full sustainability analysis. Don't forget that this same chemical production also applies to rayon and acetate, which are made of chemically modified plant fiber (often wood) too, so this is not unique to bamboo.

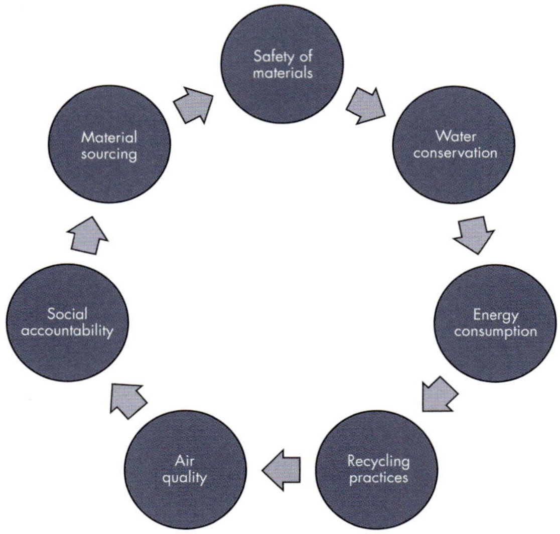

FIGURE 3.69 Considerations when analyzing the sustainability of a textile choice.

As a general guideline, look to manufacturers that limit the application of additional chemicals (retardants, sizing, etc.) by selecting fibers that are inherently suitable to your program needs. Undyed wool and organic plant-based fibers, grown without pesticides, are more sustainable choices. The fewer processes that a leather or textile undergoes, the more sustainable it is likely to be.

Modern cotton production presents a number of sustainability challenges. In order to make this fiber cheaply, **economies of scale** have encouraged a **monoculture** that intrinsically limits **biodiversity**. Balanced ecosystems require less chemical maintenance than monocultures. A biodiverse area can support a variety of insect and animal life. In the expanded acreage devoted solely to cotton production, birds that eat harmful insects have no habitat to live in, so cotton farmers rely on pesticides instead of the bird to control harmful bugs. These chemicals do not discriminate and will kill beneficial insects, like ladybugs, along with the pests. This chemical solution is damaging to ecosystems and to the workers who apply the chemicals and harvest the cotton. Cottonseeds are used for animal food and cottonseed oil is consumed by people. The residual toxins that remain when animals and people eat the cottonseeds and oils is stored in fat cells in the body. Alternative pest control that uses repellents derived from chili oil and other nontoxic ingredients is being tested in parts of the world. A better solution would be to have balanced ecosystems, but this interferes with the economies of scale that keep cotton cheap. Thus, it is easy to envision the ongoing dilemma that challenges the sustainability of cotton.

Recycled material is used to make some synthetic fibers and used natural fiber is now being unwoven and converted into new yarn. Old leather is reduced to fiber and mixed with resins to produce recycled leather sheet goods. Look for sustainable options in production; leather that is chromium tanned is often mistakenly assumed to be more harmful to the environment than vegetable-tanned leather but the environmental effects are very nearly equal. Chromium tanning does not use the toxic chromium VI; chromium III is safe if reasonable precautions are used to keep it out of the environment around the tannery. Heavy metals used in colorants are more likely to be environmentally and physiologically problematic.

SUMMARY

In this chapter we looked at how yarn, weave, and finish processes define the characteristics of a textile and how the chemistry of the fiber affects performance.

You took a look at what to consider when selecting and specifying a textile for a certain use. We reviewed leather used in place of textiles and how to evaluate leather for your client's job. Soft goods are so dependent on textiles for their characteristics it is important to understand their use and design as well as forms and installation; thus soft goods were considered at some length, as was upholstery. The organization of the various industries involved in the production of items using textiles was reviewed. Sustainability issues associated with fabric and leather as well as some considerations for related materials were also reviewed.

WEB SEARCH ACTIVITIES

1. Perform an image search for pictures of each of the yarn constructions mentioned in the section about novelty yarn on page 70 to see what they look like.

2. Perform an image search for pictures of *machine quilting* and notice the variety of patterns that are possible.

3. Using the ACT sustainability guidelines, evaluate leather. Go to www.treehugger.com as well as vendor Web sites to get alternative views on the subject.

4. Go to the Web sites for NSF, ANSI, USGBC, and ACT, to become familiar with the resources available at each site.

5. Go to a fabric manufacturer's Web site and search as you would if you were working for a client. Find the information that you would need regarding fiber chemistry, construction, durability, maintenance, sustainability, flame resistance, etc.

PERSONAL ACTIVITIES

1. If you have a to-scale plan elevation of a project that you designed, imagine that you would upholster one of the walls in leather. Go to a supplier's Web site and select hides that you would use, noting the size of the hide. Sketch an elevation and layout for the seam locations. Consider the details that you would use to conceal seams and make the product removable without damage to the walls beneath.

2. Find a picture of a piece of furniture covered in a large print. Analyze the quality of the fabric application and the positioning of the pattern. Do you agree with the decisions made? Why or why not?

3. Find a picture of an interior that you think would have benefitted from a different kind of window treatment. Using a tracing paper overlay, design a treatment that you think would have improved the interior a little more than what was used.

SUMMARY QUESTIONS

1. What kinds of effects can each component of fabric have on its properties—the fiber, the yarn, and the weave?
2. What kinds of finishing processes are common for fabric?
3. What are novelty yarn constructions and what are the implications for fabric, or what kind of fabrics will each produce?
4. What other processes might be applied to fabric after it has been woven and finished?
5. What is the implication of pile for application on fabric? What does *down and out* mean?
6. What processes are applied to protect fabrics?
7. What kinds of things will add cost to your fabric budget?
8. What is the significance of an open line and exclusive patterns?
9. What is the difference between full grain and top grain leather? What is their connection to full aniline and semi-aniline?
10. What sustainability considerations pertain to textiles and leather?
11. What third-party resources help designers sort out sustainability considerations?
12. What does the *triple bottom line* mean for textile selection?
13. Which soft goods are made by sewing fabrics together and which ones require another support underneath the fabric?

Chapter 4

CARPETING AND AREA RUGS

Key Terms

Access flooring
Carded
Carved nap
Denier
Flat weaves
Heat set
High-density foam
Hot melt
Luster
Metallic fiber
Overtufting
Poms
Random sheared
Stretched
Tip sheared

Objectives

After reading this chapter, you should be able to:

- Understand the various materials, production methods, and characteristics of the various carpet and rug products specified by interior designers.
- Have a basis for evaluating products based on performance, sustainability, and cost considerations.
- Understand the effect that the material components have on the floor covering produced from those materials.
- Know how the carpet and rug industries are organized and how the sequence of selecting through installing varies with the kind of product used.
- Know what maintenance and protection requirements apply to the various types of material products in the category.
- Have an idea of how to work collaboratively on custom product and how to search for the right ready-made product to meet your project's program goals.

This chapter covers carpets and area rugs. The distinction between the two topics lies partly in the predominant methods of manufacture. There is also the assumption that carpet is fastened wall-to-wall as a surfacing material and that area rugs are loose-lay. Carpet that is installed wall-to-wall is often called broadloom for having been woven on looms wider than the looms that are typical for fabric. Traditionally, carpet looms were 27 inches wide, so the 12-foot-wide looms that were developed later were indeed broad looms. Some looms that produce woven goods, versus tufted goods, a topic further explored on page 119, are narrower than fabric looms, but these carpets are still typically installed wall-to-wall. Conversely, floor covering that is loose-laid and does not extend to the perimeter of the room, but rather defines an area, is often referred to as an area rug. There is a little crossover between the two, such as area rugs that are made of broadloom carpet that has been cut to size and had the edges bound and finished, but these distinctions should help you organize the information generally in your mind.

CARPET

Estimates vary slightly but it is safe to say that over 1.5 billion square yards of carpet are installed annually and that over 70 percent of all floors in the U.S., commercial and residential combined, are covered with carpet. There may not be another flooring product that you will specify as frequently as carpet. There are few materials that can compete with carpet's acoustical, thermal, or aesthetic characteristics.

Material and Characteristics

Carpet provides sound absorbency and thermal insulation superior to other floor surfacing materials. It is considered to be a textile and is made from the same fibers that other textiles are made from. The specific characteristics of any given carpet will depend on the fiber and yarn characteristics and its construction. All components of the carpeting, and the type of installation, will work together to characterize the installation. Fibers, whether naturally occurring or man-made, have inherent characteristics created by their individual chemistries. Yarn characteristics of **denier**, or thickness, degree of twist, number of plies, whether looped or cut, and other yarn characteristics will alter performance and appearance. There are a few different constructions that also affect design possibilities and performance characteristics.

Natural Fibers

Natural fibers come from animals (the protein fibers silk and wool) or plants (the cellulosic fibers). Although different fiber materials have varying performance characteristics, manufacturers work to make the aesthetic qualities of yarns used for carpet imitate wool.

Wool

You already know that wool fiber used for carpet is from sheep. Wool is a relatively expensive fiber compared to other fibers. It is the standard by which other fibers are measured. It is soft and resilient and can be easily bleached and dyed, in much smaller minimums than other fibers, to any color that your job requires. It is naturally stain resistant (not stain proof) and is naturally flame resistant. It ages gracefully. Wool is subject to static electricity and in some installations may require special treatment to combat this. If crushing of fibers is the most likely kind of abuse that the carpet will suffer in your client's installation (flattening from footfalls, relocation of furniture within the room, etc.) and price is not a restriction, then wool would be a good choice for the area.

> **Point of Emphasis 4.1**
> You should be able to find a carpet manufacturer who will dye wool carpet to your specification for a quantity as small as 30 square yards by selecting a carpet from custom-colorable offerings along with a color sample. The manufacturer will beaker-dye a small carpet pom for your approval. He or she may also produce a sample approximately two feet square to confirm style characteristics. If this is not offered free of charge as part of the process, it is a good idea to pay for it. The sample may cost $250 or more, but since custom-colored goods are not returnable it is a small price to pay to be sure the effect and color are to your client's liking before the entire order is produced.

Silk

Silk is a protein fiber, like wool. Silk found in broadloom is typically part of patterning in a wool carpet. While silk is a strong fiber, it is not resilient. The **luster** and fine denier are used decoratively as a contrast to the wool carpet field, or ground. It is an expensive fiber, more expensive than wool, so sometimes rayon is substituted as it shares many properties with silk in terms of hand, luster, and appearance but is less expensive than the silk fiber that it imitates. However, rayon does not resist flame as silk does.

The protein fibers, silk and wool, are naturally flame resistant; they shrink away from flame and are difficult to ignite. Of the two, wool is much more common in carpet manufacturing. Its flame resistance may indicate its use in commercial spaces but it is not as abrasion resistant as nylon (more later). Silk is not economical or durable enough for the commercial market although for light-traffic installations, wool carpet can be used commercially.

As you would expect, plant-based, cellulosic fibers like rayon are not flame resistant. They are also not as resilient as wool or as durable as synthetics, so you will find that floor coverings produced from cellulosic fiber are intended for the residential market. They cannot be cleaned with water-based methods, not even steam. Silk and rayon should be dry cleaned.

> Point of Emphasis 4.2
>
> Silk is not as typical a component in carpet yarns but is even more costly than wool.

Linen

Linen is used in limited quantity in broadloom carpet. It is often used in combination with wool. Linen is strong, has something of a luster, and dyes well. Cellulosic fibers like linen (and cotton) must be carefully cleaned because they can easily mat or flatten after being cleaned with methods that use water.

Cotton

Cotton is soft, dyeable, subject to wear, and will stain easily. It is not common in carpet because of wear and staining weaknesses, but it is available because it is irresistibly soft under bare feet. Any carpet will suffer if cleaned improperly, and cotton must be cleaned carefully and per the manufacturer's recommendations. When cleaned with water, cotton fibers clump together and it can be difficult to restore the carpet's original appearance.

> What Would You Do? 4.1
>
> When would you select silk fiber over rayon?

Synthetic Fibers

Man-made fiber begins life as plastic pellets that are melted into a solution. This solution is extruded into long, continuous filaments. These filaments might be spun into yarn or processed first to be bulked and crimped. These long, bulked, and crimped filaments are called bulk continuous fiber (BCF), meaning it is a long uncut strand of man-made fiber, **heat set** into a zigzag strand. It may be spun into yarn at that stage or cut to short staple lengths to imitate wool, and then finally spun into yarn. The carpet fiber that all other fibers are measured against is wool.

Nylon

Nylon is considered to be the most durable fiber in terms of abrasion resistance. It also resists mildew, moths, and mold. It is hydrophobic, that is, it does not easily absorb water or waterborne stains. Nylon has been around since the 1940s and has been such a successful fiber that manufacturers continue to invest in improving it since market demand is high. You may hear fibers described as first, second, third, fourth, fifth, and sixth generation. Interim fiber improvements, like the latest 6.6 nylon, are also distinguished to make specifiers aware that this nylon is improved from generation six. Nylon 6 and 6.6 are the ones currently used for carpet.

> A Cautionary Tale 4.1
>
> When more than one kind of fiber is part of the construction for a single carpet product, maintenance gets tricky. My client had his wool carpet, with a small linen vine design, steam-cleaned and the lustrous linen shrank and matted and nearly disappeared into the wool pile. He was a patient man, to say the least, and spent several evenings brushing the linen fibers with a fabric brush to "reorganize" them after their "bath." Clients should not have to get into such a Zen frame of mind just to maintain their surfaces, and for all his patience, the linen detail never fully recovered.

Point of Emphasis 4.3

Nylon is more abrasion resistant than wool but more likely to crush in traffic areas. In terms of appearance it is said to "ugly out" before it wears out, while wool attains a patina of age that many people find acceptable. Recognizing that the product is still serviceable but is eventually judged to be unattractive, carpet manufacturers will sometimes take back carpet and apply a printed pattern to the face to camouflage crushed traffic paths. The same carpet can then be reinstalled in the facility with its new, fresher look.

Nylon 6 and 6.6 makes the carpet more resilient and stronger with improved coloring. Carpet maintenance experts say the difference between the two is that the improvements of nylon 6 are even more pronounced in 6.6, which has a more elaborate dyeing process to make the color more durable. You will also hear claims that it resists stains better, but once it does stain, it is harder to clean.

Nylon is naturally subject to the accumulation of static electricity. Fiber engineering has produced carpets especially constructed to reduce buildup of static electricity. If you expect that high traffic will abrade fibers and wear the carpet out in traffic areas then nylon will be a good choice for your installation. Static dissipative carpet incorporates **metallic fiber** and special adhesives for environments that are especially sensitive to static buildup.

Polypropylene

Polypropylene is also called olefin. It has good stain resistance because of its hydrophobic properties and it is fade resistant because it is solution dyed. This is the fiber used for indoor/outdoor carpet. It is durable against abrasion, but it flattens in traffic areas (or under heavy furniture) and relies on construction to overcome this problem (low dense loop is typical). Olefin is an inexpensive carpet compared to other fibers. It is oleophilic, meaning that it has an affinity to oil-borne stains. It is blended with wool to lower the cost of wool carpet because, similar to wool, it is a springy fiber, texturally similar to wool.

What Would You Do? 4.2

When would you select a polypropylene carpet over a nylon one?

Acrylic

Acrylic fiber is soft and resilient. Its hand compares well to wool in many characteristics. It has low abrasion resistance and can sometimes pill. Acrylic is often a component in a blend. It can be solution dyed, making it resistant to fading.

Polyester

Polyester dyes well, resists fading, is soft and wear resistant, but has poor resilience and relies on high density to overcome this weakness. Because it is a bulky fiber that provides good coverage for little material in terms of weight, some manufacturers skimp on the density. Low-density carpets show crushing as the yarns "fall over," exposing their sides, so they do not retain their good appearance in traffic areas.

A snapshot comparison in Table 4.1 of the above fibers distinguishes their strengths.

Other fibers make an appearance in woven floor coverings even though they are not among the most commonly used materials. Silk and plant-based fibers are minor components of specialty carpets. Other fiber

Table 4.1
Comparison of the most common fiber types used for carpeting.

Fiber	Resilience	Abrasion Resistance	Flame Resistance	Fade Resistance	Other
Wool	Very good	Good	Burns slowly in direct flame, self-extinguishes	Vulnerable to degradation from UV rays	Good dyeability
Nylon	Good	Good	Melts in direct flame, self-extinguishes	Good resistance to sunlight	Hand variable with fiber shape
Polypropylene	Fair	Good	Has low melting point (266°F)	Fiber is degraded by UV rays, solution dyeing stabilizes color	Feels waxy
Acrylic	Fair to good	Fair to good	Acrylics burn, modacrylics self-extinguish	Fiber is degraded by UV rays, fade resistance varies	Hand imitates wool
Polyester	Fair	Good	Burns and melts unless treated to self-extinguish	Good resistance but prolonged exposure will degrade fiber	Fiber has loft so looks bulky

FIGURE 4.1A–C Plant-based fibers as floor covering:

(a) Sisal can be a scratchy fiber and a tight, flat weave like this one will minimize that quality.

(b) Abaca, made from banana leaves, presents a lot of natural variation in the fiber.

(c) Seagrass is sometimes called water hyacinth. The water hyacinth is a pest plant that clogs waterways in Asia but it is now being put to good use as it is harvested for floor covering.

Table 4.2
Comparison of the characteristics of natural plant fibers.

Fiber	Comes From	Characteristics
Sisal	Leaves of the agave plant	Tough, prickly fiber; flat or pile; most durable of plant-based fibers; often combined with wool; 13'-wide goods most common
Abaca	Leaves of banana plant	Coarse, dry hand; 13' wide
Seagrass	Leaves of underwater grasses	Smooth, slightly slippery; flat-woven; resists stains a little better than sisal or coir; hard wearing but not prickly or rough; difficult to dye so natural color is usually only option
Jute	Stem of the jute plant	Soft, crisp fibers; flat-woven; easy to dye; 13', 15', and 18' wide
Coir	Coconut shells	Prickly, stiff fiber; reacts to humidity by expanding and contracting; 13' wide; flat-woven for interior (although pile mats available for exterior)

is fashioned into floor covering as well. The following fibers are most suited to the residential market.

Plant Fibers

Sisal (Figure 4.1a), abaca (Figure 4.1b), seagrass (Figure 4.1c), jute, and coir are all plant-based fibers that are typically flat-woven (instead of having a pile that stands up) because they have poor resilience. They share many general characteristics. They can be dyed but are more frequently used in their natural colors, which range from khaki to straw. When exposed to sunlight, they change in color, becoming browner. They are subject to pests and are degraded and stained by waterborne solutions. They have slight differences in their appearance and hand. The three pictured in the close-up shots will allow you to see differences in the visual characteristics of the natural fiber and, in the instance of the sisal, notice how well they can take up dyes. Sisal tends to have little ends that poke out and make it feel a little prickly if the manufacturer doesn't remove them. Less expensive products will be pricklier than costlier products. Abaca has a softer, smoother hand and is less dense than seagrass, which is also smooth. If these products are installed wall-to-wall they should be glued down. A more costly alternative is to fit and bind them to conform to the perimeter of the room, staple or glue a slab urethane pad to the floor, and glue them to the pad. Table 4.2 defines general characteristics of these fibers.

Yarn

Whether natural and man-made, fiber goes through a number of processes before it is ready to be fashioned into floor covering. The diagram in Figure 4.2 orders the steps that might be undertaken to create yarn from natural and synthetic fibers.

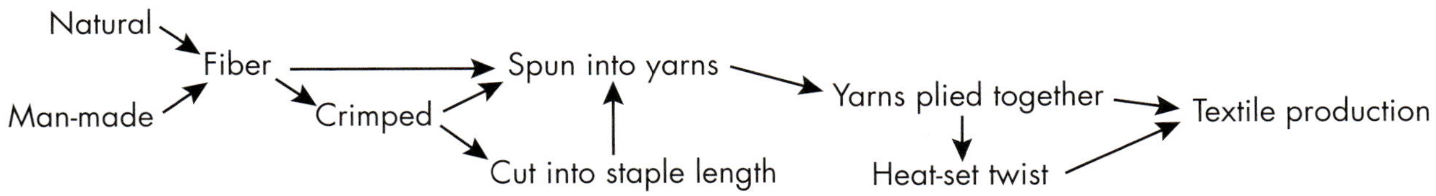

FIGURE 4.2 The production of yarn may involve several steps.

The acronym BCF stands for *bulked continuous filament* and refers to synthetic fibers in continuous form miles long. These long fibers are gathered into yarn bundles and texturized to increase bulk and coverage. Texturizing changes the straight filaments into kinked or curled configurations that are then heat set. Floor coverings made with BCF are less likely to pill or shed than those made from short, staple fiber.

Point of Emphasis 4.4

Bulking is processing yarn to provide more coverage without adding more material weight. Bulking and crimping add to fiber resiliency. Crimping creates "bulk" in individual filaments by creating a sawtooth, zigzag, or random curl relative to the fiber. These processes can make carpet with low density appear more thick and plush.

Staple fibers are short lengths that occur naturally in cotton or wool but synthetic fibers might also be chopped into staple lengths in addition to be being bulked and crimped. Staple yarns arrive at the carpet mill in bales (very large cubical bundles, similar to cotton bales). The bales are opened up and blended with other bales of staple to assure uniformity. The fibers are **carded**, spun, and twisted with other strands of yarn to make the final yarn.

Denier and Ply

In addition to fiber characteristics, carpet gets some of its features from the denier (thickness of the yarn) and the number of plies (number of yarns that are twisted together). Figure 4.3 diagrams the meaning of plies in yarn construction. The effect of increasing the number of plies is to produce a thicker yarn that has more resilience or memory. This improves the wear and appearance retention of the carpet. Yarns are twisted to varying degrees from a loose twist to a high twist. The combination of the denier, number of plies, and the amount of twist alter the appearance and performance of the final product.

Dense concentration of small denier, single-ply yarns, as used in velvet plush, will produce carpet having an elegant, formal aesthetic. Velvet plush will show every footfall, while thicker denier, multi-ply yarns will be grainier in appearance and less formal; they provide some camouflaging of footprints and will add to the resilience of the goods. The saxony plush will show fewer footprints than velvet plush and frieze will show

FIGURE 4.3 The number of yarns twisted together are referred to as ply:

(a) Single-ply yarn

(b) Double-ply yarn

(c) Four-ply yarn

Low twist (velvet)

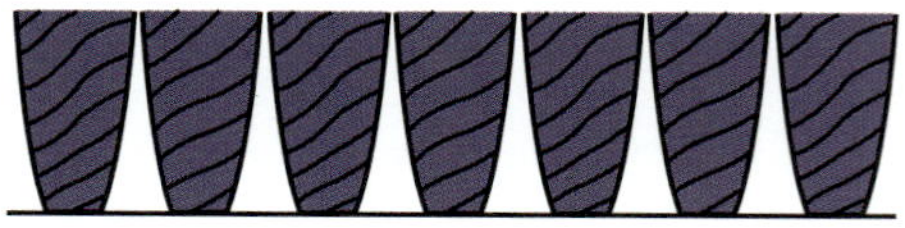

Medium twist (saxony)

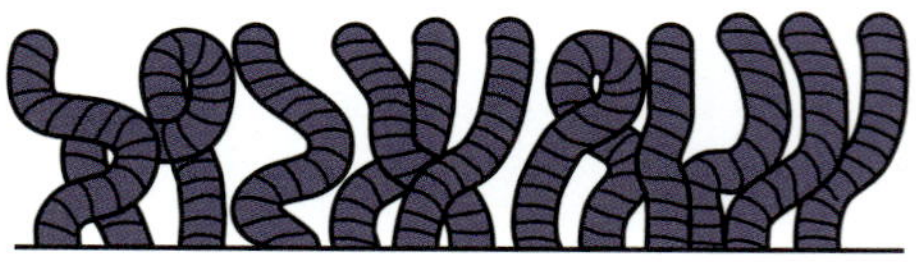

High twist (frieze)

FIGURE 4.4 The degree of twist affects the appearance and performance of carpet. Higher twist maintains an acceptable appearance more naturally.

A Cautionary Tale 4.2

I phoned a fellow designer at the end of the workday and asked him how his day had been. He told me that he'd spent most of it on his knees in his client's master bedroom suite. He wanted to photograph it for the company portfolio but it was impossible to make it look neat and lovely because they had installed velvet pile carpet. My friend used a fabric brush to organize the pile just right for the photo shoot. Even using a broom after vacuuming to order the pile left tracks. Velvet carpet leaves a record of all traffic that has trod across it.

the least of all due to the increased twist. Figure 4.4 illustrates this distinction.

CONSTRUCTION METHODS

Carpet is manufactured by various processes. Each process yields a product with different characteristics. The highest quality carpets are dense constructions in each category, meaning the yarns are positioned close together. Pile density, the number of carpet tufts both across (needles per inch or gauge for tufted carpet) and lengthwise (stitches per inch) of the carpet, is denoted by different measures that you will use as a comparison between different options when making selections for your client.

- Gauge is the distance between the needles. For example, one-eighth gauge simply means there is one-eighth of an inch between each needle, or there are eight needles per inch of width.
- Stitch rate (or stitches per inch) defines the number of times per inch a stitch occurs, just as gauge expresses the frequency of tufts across the width. Stitch rate is the number of times an individual needle inserts a tuft into the primary backing as the primary backing moves one inch through the tufting machine. This is sometimes abbreviated as SPI. Therefore, eight stitches per inch means that as the primary backing moved through the tufting machine, a single needle formed eight tufts or stitches per inch.
- Pile height is the length (expressed in decimal parts of one inch) of the tuft from the primary backing to the tip. All other factors being equal, a carpet with a higher pile height will possess more yarn on the wearing surface and will essentially be more durable.
- Pitch is the number of tufts or warp pile yarns per inch in the selvage-to-selvage direction. The gauge is responsible for the pitch

Tufting

Tufted carpet is produced in two elementary steps. Construction starts with the primary backing that is likely to be polypropylene mesh. The face yarns are poked down through the backing and then sealed in place with latex or some similar adhesive.

A looper forms the pile and determines the pile height. Loopers with a cutting knife attached are used to produce cut-pile or plush carpet. A loop-pile machine does not have knives, so it leaves the loops uncut or the structures are sheered after tufting is complete. Figure 4.5 shows a variety of loop and sheered options available as the tufted loops are cut after tufting. This material is not stable until a secondary backing is applied. The secondary backing is also likely to be polypropylene mesh, which is affixed with adhesive.

Weaving

Woven carpets are the most durable and expensive construction. Complex patterns are possible with woven carpets. For this reason, woven carpets are preferred for high-traffic locations, where there are extensive hours of operation, like hotels and casinos. The pattern conceals soiling and evidence of foot traffic in facilities that do not close for maintenance and the durability of this construction handles the constant traffic. The two most important weaving methods that you will encounter for carpet are Axminster and Wilton.

Axminster

An Axminster loom has control over each tuft of yarn making up the carpet. Axminster carpets are usually complicated designs and are always cut-pile. Spools of yarn that feed the loom can hold different colors and even different kinds of yarn. Axminster looms produce a stiffer product; sometimes it is difficult to bend the carpet over stair nosings. Installers will sometimes wet the back of the carpet to relax it temporarily in order to bend it. Axminster carpet may be wool or a blend of wool and nylon or all nylon.

FIGURE 4.5 The way the carpet is sheered, or not sheered, is defined by some general terms. Looped face is not sheered at all—the uncut loops create the surface. Random sheered is just what the name implies—loops are randomly cut. The upper left depicts loop-face carpet; the upper right shows random sheered; the lower left is loop and cut-pile; the lower right is a cut-pile velvet. *Samples courtesy of Watson Smith Carpets, Chicago, IL.*

Wilton

Wilton carpets are made of worsted wool, which is made from longer hair fibers that are tightly twisted. Yarns made of worsted wool tend to be made in finer deniers. Sculptured carpets have a varying pile height and are made on a Wilton loom by controlling pile height and by cutting, or leaving the face looped.

Flocking

Short fiber called flock is glued, usually using an electrostatic processes, to make the flock "stand up" in the glue, creating a very short pile material with a velour texture. A secondary backing adds body and dimensional stability. A few flocked carpets are made for bedrooms and bathrooms, but the majority is used in cars, planes, and buses. The short fiber and construction resist the appearance of crushing.

Fusion Bonding

Fusion-bonded carpet has yarns that are inserted into liquid vinyl, which hardens, locking the yarn in place. It is especially applicable to the production of carpet tiles.

Knitting

The knitting process represents a very small portion of the carpet market. The yarns are looped in a manner similar to hand knitting with loops that double back in direction, minimizing the possibility of unraveling, and then a coat of latex and secondary backing material gives the carpet dimensional stability. Variation in color, pattern, and texture is possible in knit carpet. It looks like tufted carpet.

Needle-Punched

Needle-punched carpet is made by barbed felting needles punching batting into a base fabric. This forms a flat, felted-looking carpet mainly used for indoor-outdoor carpeting and some carpet tiles. Needle-punched carpet can then be printed or embossed. A coating of weather-resistant latex or similar material is applied to the back.

A quick comparison of the different construction methods in Table 4.3 summarizes their differences.

MODULAR TILES

Modular tiles are cut from broadloom carpet, usually available in 18-inch to 36-inch square and rectangular tiles with PVC backings. Modular units are convenient over **access flooring** and allow for easy replacement in heavy traffic locations without disruption that would be caused by having to remove all the furniture in an area to replace broadloom. They may be installed with adhesives, peel-and-stick installation, loose-laid, or set with release adhesive for easier repositioning.

Tile backing systems can also offer moisture barriers from the base of the pile yarn to the floor, prevent-

Table 4.3
Comparison of the most prevalent construction techniques for carpet.

Method	Construction	Appearance and Characteristics	Uses
Tufting	Yarns are poked through primary backing, stabilized with a secondary backing	Pile construction looped or cut; depends on secondary backing for stability	Most common broadloom construction; many uses residentially and commercially
Woven	Simultaneous construction of face and backing	Pile construction for Axminster, Wilton, and velvet looms; very durable construction, complex patterns	Casinos, hotels, and other high-traffic locations
Knitted	Integral face and backing formed simultaneously	Loop pile construction stabilized by secondary backing	Commercial interiors
Fusion bonded	Yarns set in adhesive	Cut-pile	Commercial and carpet tiles
Flocked	Fibers set in adhesive	Velour appearance	Mats for vehicles and limited product availability for light-use areas
Needle-punched	Fibers matted/felted together and locked in place with adhesive spread on back	Felted appearance	Tiles and rugs

What Would You Do? 4.3

When would you select broadloom rather than carpet tile?

ing spills from penetrating and seeping down to the subfloor. In modular tiles, as well as with broadloom, a moisture barrier may be valuable in health-care environments where spills are inevitable and cleaning is frequent. The moisture barrier of the carpet itself and the sealing technique for the seams may lessen the potential for bacterial growth and provide lower long-term maintenance costs.

OTHER PROCESSES

After carpet is constructed, other finishing processes may be applied. Applying the secondary backing is considered a finishing process. If the carpet is to have an attached cushion, so that a separate pad is not required, it will be applied in finishing. Some fibers, like polyester, will expand in heat, so carpeting is "baked" to make the yarns plump up and give more coverage. Antistatic, antimicrobial, or stain-repellent finishes may be applied. Cut-pile may be sheared evenly, **tip sheared**, or **random sheared**. After tufting, carpet may be cut into tiles and have a **high-density foam** cushion attached.

COLORS AND PATTERNS

Color and pattern can be imparted in various ways. Remember that the patterns of the Axminster and Wilton carpets are woven in as the loom uses several yarn colors simultaneously. Yarn colors are either predyed or postdyed. Another way of giving carpet a multicolored pattern is to print the carpet after it is woven.

Predyed

Predyed methods account for all processes that occur prior to beginning the construction of carpet. They include the following:

- Solution dyeing—The "soup" that synthetic fibers are made from is colored before the material is extruded into fiber. The color is locked into the fiber making this the most resistant to fading.

Point of Emphasis 4.5

Solution dyed means that the color is introduced into the "soup" from which the yarns are spun. This locks the color into the fiber itself, making it fade resistant from sunlight and cleansers. Solution-dyed fiber can even be bleached without change to the color. This makes it a good choice when rigorous cleaning or indoor/outdoor conditions are part of your client's site requirements.

- Stock dyeing—The fiber is dumped into a vat and dyed before they are made into yarn.
- Skein dyeing—The yarns are dyed. This is a more expensive way of coloring carpets but is typical of custom carpets.
- Space dyeing—Produces a random color distribution as yarn is wound and printed with three colors in stripes (overlap of colors gives the effect of more colors). Warp yarns can also be space dyed but colors are less random. Space-dyed yarns are often found in loop style contract carpets having random-looking, multicolored visual textures.

Postdyed

Postdyed carpet is dyed after the goods are made into carpeting. The following are postdyed methods:

- Beck dyeing—Primarily for solid colors. Goods are dyed after tufting but before other finishing processes (such as attaching the secondary backing). Large rolls of uncolored carpet, called greige goods, are placed in a huge vat of dye solution called the dye beck. The vat is heated to high temperatures, and the tufted goods are agitated continually while they soak up the dye, making the color come out very even from end to end and side to side. The carpet (still without secondary backing) is then washed and dried. This is most commonly used for cut-pile carpet.
- Piece dyeing—Greige goods dyed after they are tufted and have had the secondary backing applied. This is common for residential carpet that is not as dense as commercial carpet and for which smaller quantities can be dyed as needed.

- Continuous dyeing—Greige goods are rinsed, and then passed under a dye applicator, which spreads or sprays dyes evenly across the entire width of the carpet. The carpet then enters a steam chamber, where the dyes are set into the fibers. This method is for longer runs of both solid and multicolor applications.
- Printing—As from an ink-jet printer, colors are sprayed from closely spaced jets. Pattern changes are made on computer.

> **Point of Emphasis 4.6**
> Printing is a poor man's woven product. It conceals soiling in places like 24-hour restaurants and budget hotels. The downside is that, unlike woven, where the color in the pattern is part of the yarn, the pattern is printed on these carpets, so it does not go all the way down to the bottom of the pile. These carpets will look "frosty" in traffic areas as the printed part of the fiber is worn away, exposing the unprinted fiber at the base.

- Differential dyeing—Tufted carpet with yarn either treated chemically or blended fibers that react to dye differently. When the yarn is placed in a dye bath where each yarn type reacts differently to the dye, it results in different shades of the same color.

BACKING

Tufted carpet will have two backings, the primary backing and the secondary backing. The primary backing, into which the tufts are inserted, may be made of jute, kraftcord (yarn made from twisted craft paper), cotton, and woven or nonwoven synthetics. The most common primary backing is polypropylene.

> **Point of Emphasis 4.7**
> Traditionally, carpet backing was made of jute. Because of jute's potential for browning and rotting, woven polypropylene became the preferred fiber for backings. Polypropylene is not sustainable, so manufacturers are now reconsidering the potential of jute as carpet backing. If biodegradable jute will not perform in accordance with your program goals, you should look into recycling programs available from the carpet manufacturers as you finalize your selection.

After tufting, a puddle of latex is poured, and then evenly spread across the back of the carpet, locking the yarn into the primary backing. A second coat of latex is applied to hold the secondary backing onto the primary backing. This gives the carpet its dimensional stability.

Dimensional stability, primarily imparted by the secondary backing, is the ability of carpet to retain its size and shape after installation.

Pads

Generally speaking, the firmer the pad, the less strain the carpet backing will have to endure; the softer the pad, the less crushing will occur on the face of the carpet. So a happy medium is often your goal when selecting the perfect pad for the carpet and for client preferences relative to the way it feels underfoot. For the life of the carpet, select the firmer pad when trying to decide between two options.

> **Helpful Hint 4.1**
> When a cheap pad is used, not only is the installation hard underfoot, but the tape used to seam the carpet can more readily telegraph through, highlighting every seam location. Always specify good padding or ask for a sample of the padding that the bidder intends to use.

Check for recommendations and restrictions from the manufacturer before finalizing your specification of a pad for your client's job.

Rebond

This type of padding is used most often by the floorcovering industry. It may be made from scraps of the high-density foams left over from furniture making, chopped and bonded together. Rebond padding comes in various thicknesses and densities (Figure 4.6a and b). The density is rated at so many pounds per cubic foot. For example, a five-pound rebond pad would weigh five pounds per cubic foot. The Carpet and Rug Institute (CRI) recommends a pad of at least five pounds and $^{3}/_{8}$-inch thickness for light residential traffic, and a pad of six pounds and $^{3}/_{8}$-inch for heavy residential traffic.

FIGURE 4.6A–B Rebond may be made from production waste foam and various densities are possible. It is often the standard offering if no pad is specified. *Sample courtesy of Watson Smith Carpets, Chicago, IL.*

FIGURE 4.7 The density of the waffle pad is variable with more air in some portions. The fibrous topping allows the carpet to slide over the surface as it is stretched into place. *Sample courtesy of Watson Smith Carpets, Chicago, IL.*

Waffle Rubber

The waffle part of the padding (Figure 4.7) gives it a thickness that is mostly air, and as a result, any of this type of padding rated less than 90 ounces is too soft for today's plastic-backed carpets. Also, the rubber used to make these pads may contain clay-type binders that break down with use. Rub your thumb over the surface of a rubber pad and make sure that it doesn't break down easily. A better pad will not crumble.

FIGURE 4.8 Dense urethane foam padding is considered to be an upgraded, premium pad. *Sample courtesy of Watson Smith Carpets, Chicago, IL.*

Slab Rubber

Unlike the waffle rubber padding, slab rubber does not contain big ripples of air (Figure 4.8). This pad feels similar to seven-pound rebond, but will resist furniture indentation and crushing for a much longer period of time.

Foam Padding

This type of padding is made from urethane foam and is available in different densities and thicknesses. Generally this type of pad is recommended for light traffic only (Figure 4.9). Urethane foam may be a homogenous foam or a composite of shredded foams bonded to a fiber "skin," which can be a fiber or a plastic that allows the carpet to slide as it is **stretched** over the padding. Density equals firmness. Dense pads provide good support for carpet backing; less dense pads feel more "cushiony" underfoot. Prime urethane cushion is distinguished in manufacturers' literature because it is new and not recycled.

FIGURE 4.9 The foam pad is an economy selection for light-traffic areas. *Sample courtesy of Watson Smith Carpets, Chicago, IL.*

Fiber

Fiber pads may be made from jute, hair mixed with jute, synthetic fiber, or recycled textile fiber. Thickness should be between 3/8 and 7/16 inch. Fiber is felted, which produces a firm-feeling pad. Originally made out of animal hair, they are now typically synthetic fibers, though sometimes are still referred to as hair or rubberized hair. This is a relatively expensive kind of pad and is also considered to be one of the lowest toxicity choices.

Frothed Foam

Super-dense urethane is approximately 5/16 inch thick and extremely durable. The pad shown in Figure 4.10 may be low VOC (off-gassing); look for the initials *CRI* (for the Carpet and Rug Institute) inside a house shape for padding tested to ensure a low off-gassing product. It costs about the same as a good slab rubber padding and should last as long.

FIGURE 4.10 This very firm, low-VOC pad addresses the increasing awareness of the damage done to living systems (like human bodies) by volatile organic compounds. The elderly and young children are the most vulnerable, so this is a pad that you may specify in spaces where children will spend time on the floor.

QUALIFYING INSTALLERS

Installers are not required to have any certification, but many elect to undergo training and testing to become a certified floor covering installer (CFI). In large markets, installers tend to specialize in a particular kind of flooring simply because there are enough installations to keep them busy with one kind of flooring. In smaller markets an installer might have to be more versatile to be busy all the time. CFI training pertains to carpet as well as to other flooring materials. Carpet installers, like many tradespeople, tend to learn on the job. According to the Bureau of Labor Statistics about 35 percent of carpet installers are self-employed.

You may hire installers directly or you may prefer to contract for installation through your supplier. When your vendor offers installation it is frequently via one such independent installer acting as a subcontractor. When your vendor includes subcontractor labor in the price they will undoubtedly put a markup on the labor. They are assuming the risks for the installation by reselling it and so they are entitled to the markup. There is a benefit to you and your client if the vendor takes responsibility for the entire installation, so I usually prefer it when the vendor offers this. Not all vendors do, however, so your local market may be organized such that designers resell the installer's labor and assume responsibility for the quality of the work, or you may have your client contract with the installer directly.

As always, part of qualifying any installer is to confirm, through pictures of completed jobs and references, that they have installed carpet that is similar to your client's carpet on a previous job. Some installation shops are small and therefore equipped for only small residential jobs, others have enough man power for big installations, so one consideration will be the size of the installation company. Some shops do a good job of installing wall-to-wall broadloom but have no capacity to bind edges or experience installing plant-based product like seagrass. Match your client's job with the shop's experience to find the best installer. Call references if you are interviewing a new installation company.

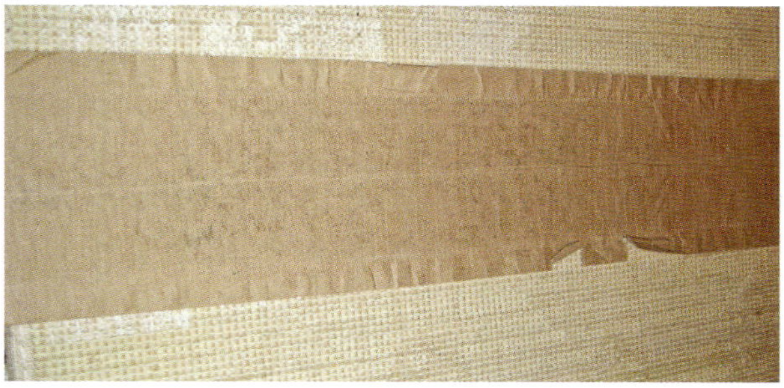

FIGURE 4.11A Hot melt tape is the common way of seaming carpet. The thickness of the tape with its glue can sometimes telegraph through and show on the face but it generally makes a fairly invisible seam.

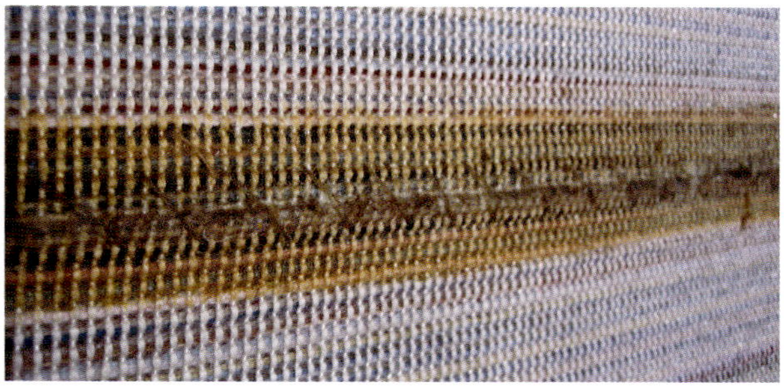

FIGURE 4.11B A sewn seam may be used on woven goods (uncommon on tufted). It will be slightly concave on the face of the goods. This one is "buttered" with adhesive for extra stability.

FIGURE 4.12 Some carpets seam more "invisibly" than others but you can almost always find the seams if you go looking for them. It is important to have an idea of what is possible when trying to minimize the appearance of a seam.

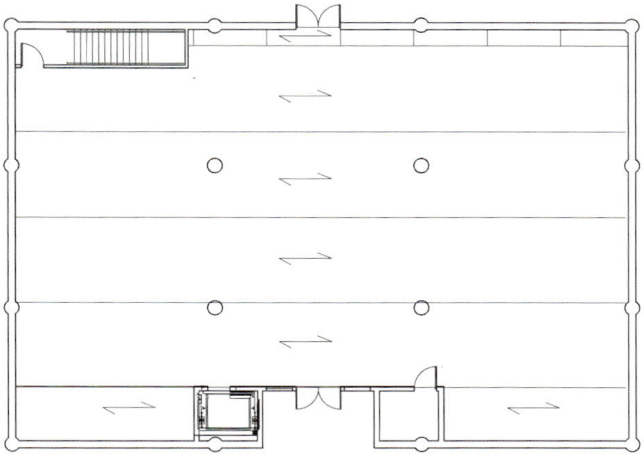

FIGURE 4.13 This simple seaming diagram shows the location and direction of the goods.

INSTALLATION

Wall-to-wall installation will include cutting and seaming the carpet before stretching or gluing it in place but your installation may also require that borders be attached (sewn or taped as shown in Figure 4.11a and b), or that binding be sewn on edges of stair runners or fitted pieces that will be assembled in a pattern or a logo. Before the installation proceeds you will confirm the details with the installer; the first thing to do is to check the seaming diagram.

Checking the Seaming Diagram

Carpet seams are **hot melt** taped or sewn and even though they are usually durably formed they are not invisible. See Figure 4.12 for a seam that is visible but considered acceptable. You will want the fewest number of seams that is practical. Seams should be in inconspicuous places (such as in closets, under areas planned for large pieces of furniture, away from bright light or windows and out of traffic areas). You want the seams in low-stress locations, away from doorways and other major traffic areas. If seams must fall within traffic areas they will be less vulnerable if they run parallel to traffic as opposed to across it. The goods should run parallel to traffic on stairs. You want to avoid seams in any location where traffic will change direction because this will stress the carpet and cause the seam to show up. You can imagine you will often have trouble meeting all of these conditions, so you must establish a hierarchy that is most appropriate to your client's installation and address the most important ones first. Figure 4.13 shows a simple seaming diagram depicting the location of the seams and the short symbol that indicates the direction the carpet should run. The symbol is typically included on all seaming diagrams, although it is redundant here because it is obvious which way it runs. However, in a smaller space, where it is not obvious, the arrow will be critical.

Tackless Installation

In the tackless method, thin strips of wood (usually plywood) with rows of small prongs are nailed or glued around the perimeter of the area to be carpeted. Padding is laid down within the area defined by the tack strips and the carpet is stretched into place by means of a power stretcher or knee kickers. It is the tension of the carpet pulled taut and held in place by these prongs that makes this glueless installation stable. The excess carpet is cut off and the cut edge is poked down in between the strip and the baseboard. Sometimes a baseboard is installed afterwards, but before specifying this kind of installation, consider the difficulties in replacing the carpet if the base must be removed to accomplish the replacement. The painters often have to come back to the site and touch up after the carpet installers are through. It is nearly impossible to maneuver large, stiff sheets of carpeting, and kick them into place, without damaging walls and trim. It is typical to omit the quarter-round when a floor is carpeted.

Glue-Down Installation

Carpet, with or without an integral padding, is glued directly to the floor. This is a good installation for gyms or areas where carts or equipment will be moved frequently. Double glue-down installations have a separate pad glued to the floor and the carpet is glued to the pad. Confirm that the pad selected is appropriate; some pads soak up too much glue. When installing glue down, confirm that the aggregate off-gassing of the pad plus the adhesive will not cause a problem. Chemically sensitive people cannot tolerate a lot of VOCs; neither can wine, so never glue down in a wine room.

> **What Would You Do? 4.4**
>
> Think of instances when you would specify a glue-down installation. When would a tackless installation be more appropriate?

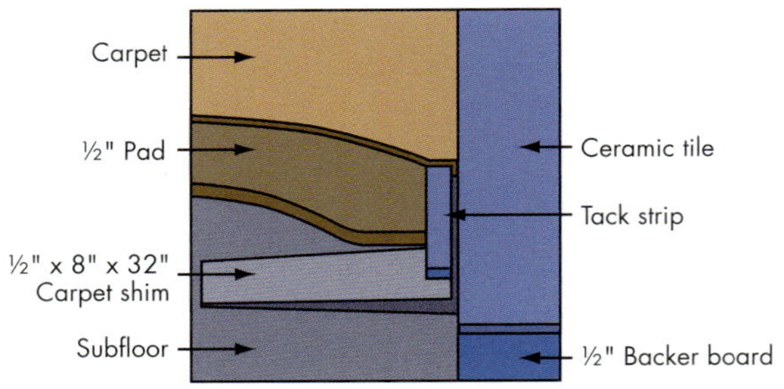

FIGURE 4.14 Carpet shims by Carpet Shims, Ltd., can ramp from a thin carpet to a thicker floor surfacing in a retrofit situation when the substrate cannot economically be altered. *Image courtesy of Carpet Shims, Ltd.*

Meeting Adjacent Flooring Materials

One common complication when remodeling an interior is that subfloors are already established, which makes adjoining materials of varying thicknesses a little more complicated. When a thin carpet must abut a thicker material surface, there are ways to "boost" the carpet up to have a better relationship with the companion floor. One way to handle the difference is to "float" the floor up with a cement-type product. Ideally the area under a thinner carpet will be floated so that it is still level throughout the space but "lifted" to bring the carpet level with the adjoining surface. A cement product could also be ramped up to the thicker material spanning a distance which would minimize perception of the change. Carpet shims may be purchased to ramp up to the thicker flooring adjacent to the carpet (Figure 4.14).

Installation on Stairs

Installation methods for stairs include waterfall, where the carpet is effectively one continuous run from top to bottom, tacked at the back of each tread at the bottom of each riser (Figure 4.15).

Installation on curved stairs might require that each riser-tread unit be cut independently of other riser-tread units, or that risers and treads are each cut independently and secured under the nosing, as well as at the bottom of each riser at the back of each tread. This method of installing carpet on stairs is called cap and band. Review Figure 4.16 for the way carpet must be cut to be installed on curved stairs.

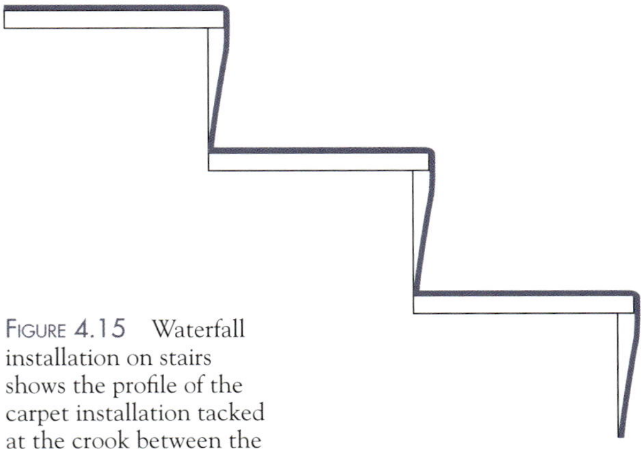

FIGURE 4.15 Waterfall installation on stairs shows the profile of the carpet installation tacked at the crook between the riser and the tread.

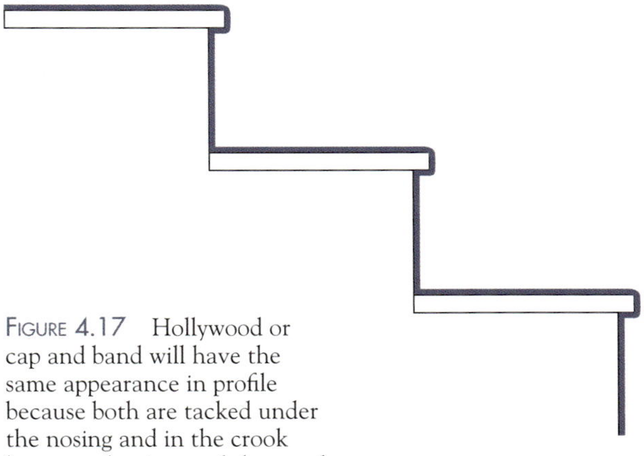

FIGURE 4.17 Hollywood or cap and band will have the same appearance in profile because both are tacked under the nosing and in the crook between the riser and the tread.

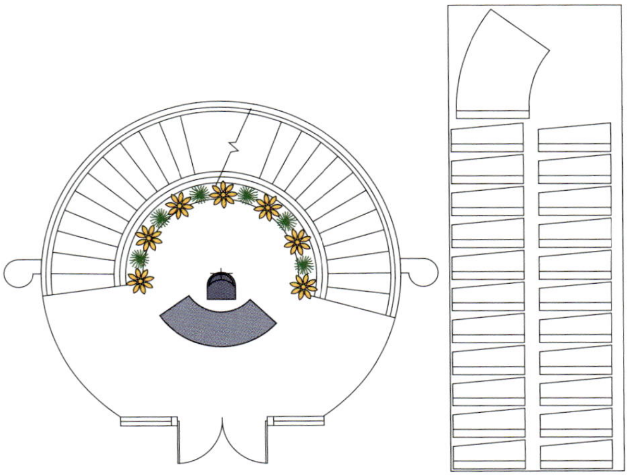

FIGURE 4.16 Cap and band installation is required for curved stairs to orient the carpet in a consistent direction relative to the treads.

Helpful Hint 4.2
Stairs take a beating and the carpet is likely to wear out before the rest of the installation. Fold extra carpet up under the top or bottom riser (so there are two layers of carpet there). When the treads start to show wear, but before they get wrinkles, unfold the extra riser and shift the carpet so the risers that have not been walked on become the treads. You can extend the life of the whole installation if you can preserve the stairs longer. However, note that wrinkles in older carpet mean that it has begun to delaminate and should be replaced.

An installation of a single continuous run that has the tailored appearance of cap and band is called hollywood (Figure 4.17). For a hollywood installation, carpet is tacked under the nosing and in the crook between the riser and the tread. Cap and band and hollywood are tacked in two places, creating a similar, tailored appearance.

Stair Rods

When carpet is installed on stairs as a runner (does not cover the full width of the stair but leaves the wood or stone exposed on both sides) you might specify a stair rod. It is decorative because the carpet has been glued or tacked in place.

Helpful Hint 4.3
When using patterned carpet on curving pie-shaped stairs, you are not always able to make the pattern match up just right (cap-and-band installation) and stair rods can distract the eye from the unmatched pattern parts between the tread of one step and the riser of the next.

Installation Sequence

Generally the process goes something like this: The carpet is selected and to-scale plans are sent to the suppliers from whom you are requesting a bid. These plans are used by the supplier for purposes of estimating yardage and labor charges if they will also install the goods. They will need to know what the goods are (including width, repeat, and match) and about any special conditions at the site, such as the following:

- If they must be prepared to move furniture.
- If the access to the space will make it difficult to move large rolls of carpet into the space, etc.
- If the floor contains a radiant heat system that must not be disrupted by fasteners, requiring that tackless strip be glued in place instead of tacked down.
- If adjacent flooring is thicker, thus necessitating ramping or carpet shims.
- If the floor must be patched, leveled, or sealed.
- If stair installation is wall-to-wall or runner with bound edges, and if floating treads or spindles must be wrapped.

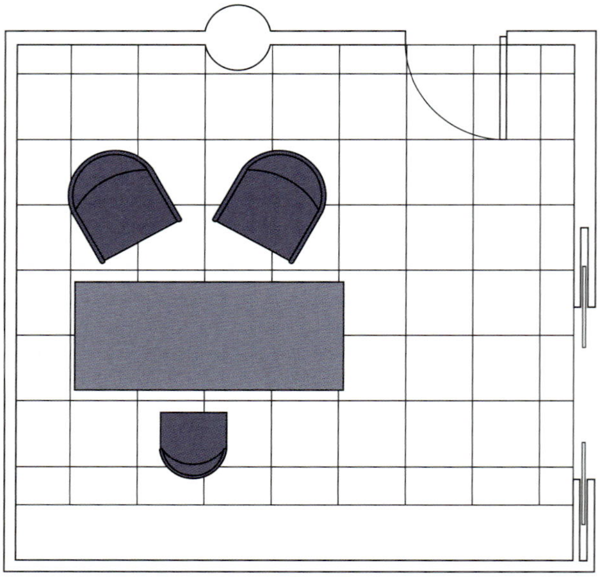

FIGURE 4.18 Carpet tiles will accentuate the deviation from square when one wall is not perfectly perpendicular to the other. Notice that the tile in the southeast corner is narrower than at the other end of that row in the northeast corner.

Installation of Carpet Tiles

Carpet tiles may be loose-laid or glued down. Regardless of whether or not they are glued in, you will want to specify the positioning and arrangement of the tiles.

Ideally your layout would utilize carpet tiles that are full size (full tiles throughout) but this is rarely possible so, just as with other tile products (stone, ceramic, resilient), plan the location of cut tiles as you position the product in your plan. It is common practice to begin the tile installation in the center of the space and work out toward the perimeter, but this is not a hard and fast rule and the conditions at the site may indicate a different starting point. Lay out the tiles to avoid skinny slivers of carpet tile at the perimeter of the room. When spaces are not strictly square, the diminishing width of the last row, where the room narrows, accentuates that fact. Notice in Figure 4.18 that the varying width of the last row of tiles on the right is eye-catching, calling attention to the fact that the room is out of square.

The manufacturer of carpet tiles is likely to recommend specific matches based on the pattern on the face of the tile. Orientation makes a difference for the appearance of a patterned carpet tile. Figure 4.19 diagrams the various options for the relationship between tiles. Figure 4.20a shows a detail where the monolithic installation presents a discontinuous pattern, however a quarter turn shown in Figure 4.20b is a checkerboard,

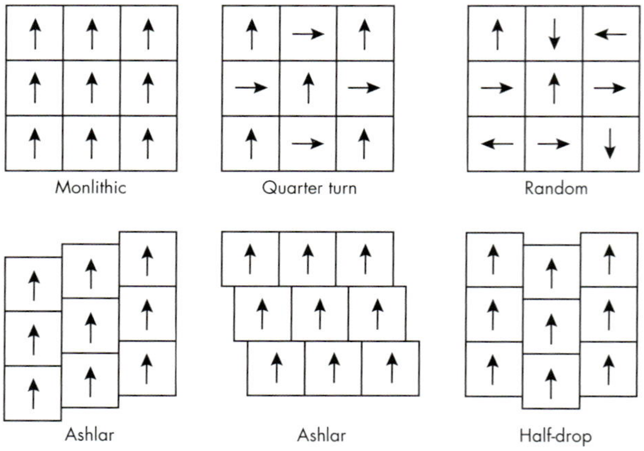

FIGURE 4.19 Carpet tiles offer not only the benefits of modularity for replacement and reconfiguration. Carpet tiles allow additional design flexibility as the individual units can be arranged with differing relationships between the tiles. In order of appearance: monolithic, quarter turn, random, ashlar, half-drop.

not a discontinuous pattern, so it may be considered more acceptable. Even though carpet tiles are cut from broadloom, it is often impossible to "put the puzzle back together" and have the pattern line up perfectly, so sometimes the best solution is to use a layout that intentionally disrupts the pattern.

(a) Monolithic

(b) Quarter turn

FIGURE 4.20A–B The same carpet tile can achieve a variety of looks. These two patterns were easily investigated by shooting a digital photo and using simple photo management software to try out these two options for arrangement.

PROTECTION AND MAINTENANCE

Carpet is degraded by grit and dirt, which is a special problem since it traps the grit that will eventually abrade the fibers and wear them out. Regular vacuuming is required for durability as much as for general cleanliness. In addition to vacuuming, carpet maintenance should include the following:

- Keeping outdoor areas clean so less soil is tracked into the carpeted area. Shovel to clear snow and ice rather than rely on chemicals or sand.
- Using mats, grates, or removable rugs in track-off areas. The rug should be big enough to require two or three steps to cross.
- Placing chair pads under desks to prevent dirt from being ground into carpet. Restricting food and beverage consumption (and spills) as well as smoking to specific areas.
- Maintaining the HVAC system, changing filters that will help remove particles from the air and prevent them from ending up in the carpet.

The life cycle of carpeting depends upon the kind of traffic an area is subjected to, on the carpet itself, and the regular maintenance that it receives. The cost of selecting carpet versus another floor surfacing encompasses not just the cost of new carpet (materials and installation); figure also the cost of maintenance and replacement. Because carpet can be maintained by unskilled labor using simple equipment, the cost of maintaining carpet is actually lower than the cost of maintaining most other floor coverings. Midtoned and multicolored carpets and patterned carpets show less soil and lint. Organic patterns show fewer spots than geometric patterns.

SAFETY

Carpet covers a lot of area, so the outgassing of VOCs from carpet can significantly affect the indoor air quality. Even after the building has been conditioned and the levels of VOCs being emitted have dropped significantly, people that have allergies to dust will still find carpet problematic. Carpet also cushions underfoot for people who spend a lot of time walking and standing. Items that are dropped are less likely to break, so some spaces for the elderly and children are safer if carpeted.

Allergens and Carpet

People with allergies are sometimes unable to tolerate carpeting for the simple reason that it traps a lot of dirt and becomes a veritable jungle of dust mites and microbes thriving on shed skin cells and other foods that are available to them even in the cleanest of environments. Generally, the denser the carpet is, the more soil resistant it will be, since dirt cannot fall down into the pile as easily. Some people are also allergic to wool. Synthetic fibers will be more hypoallergenic and resistant to consumption by moths or other pests.

Outgassing

Chemically sensitive people must contend with the outgassing of VOCs (volatile organic compounds) from the carpet and padding as well as the adhesives in glue-down installations. And don't forget about chemicals applied to carpet for stain, microbe, and static resistance. Carpet can also function as a "sink," accumulating VOCs that have been released from other sources. It also traps small particulates that might otherwise be airborne and find their way into people's lungs, so air is often cleaner in carpeted areas.

Nylon is unlikely to cause an allergic reaction and, after it has had a chance to outgas, is safe for use by most chemically sensitive people.

Bonded polyurethane carpet cushions contain a chemical, PentaBDE, that is harmful when the cushion deteriorates and the particles become airborne. Carpet cushion containing PentaBDE uses recycled urethane foam from the furniture industry and carpet cushion industry so, on one hand, the product diverts waste from landfills, but on the other hand, it introduces a toxin into the indoor environment, a classic sustainability quandary.

When carpet abuts a very thin flooring surface, like resilient flooring for instance, the thicker edge of the carpet where the two surfaces meet could pose a tripping hazard. A person using a cane or a walker or who is simply a shuffler could get hung up on the edge and take a tumble, so always devise flush conditions wherever two flooring surfaces meet.

SUSTAINABILITY

Carpet can be made of recycled plastic, and cradle-to-cradle programs, managed by carpet manufacturers, take back used carpet, separate the fibers, and recycle old carpet into new carpet material. Polyester carpet can be made from recycled plastic bottles, an example of recycling called up-cycling. Up-cycling turns used material into a product that has higher value than the original product. Modular carpet tiles can be shifted around to distribute the wear more evenly, lengthening the life of the material. Carpet that is installed with low-VOC padding and glue does not pollute indoor air the way some pads and adhesives can. Carpet that off-gasses at another location before coming to the job site does not pollute the job site but does emit chemicals into the air someplace, so it is better to avoid VOCs altogether when possible.

Too much carpeting ends up in landfills every year. Carpet restoration programs address the problem of carpet that looks worn before the end of its functional life. Carpet can be uninstalled and overprinted with a camouflaging pattern to conceal visible wear that is not affecting the performance or stability of the goods, and then reinstalled.

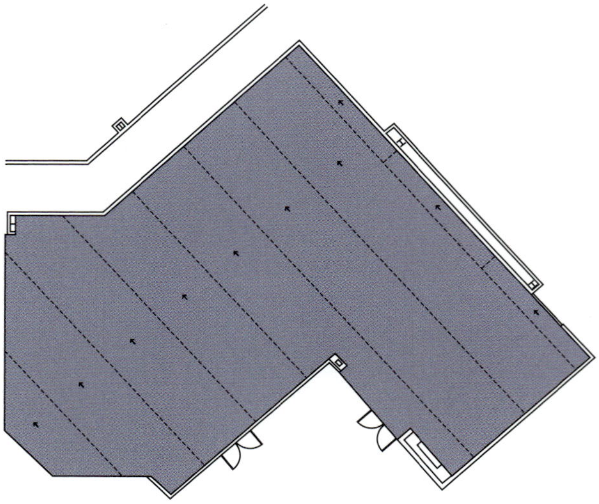

FIGURE 4.21 This seaming diagram shows how the installer can piece the good along the northeast wall so that a full-length piece can be avoided, and a shorter piece can be ordered and cut into sections.

MANAGING CLIENT BUDGETS

Carpet can be a very economical solution for your client's space. It is a material that offers low price for surface covered. It also solves problems with acoustics in an economical way, handling problems with airborne sound and impact from footfall without the need for additional materials or atypical constructions sometimes required for managing acoustics.

Confirming the Estimate

Estimating is most easily done on a to-scale plan. The following illustrates a method for accurately estimating broadloom:

> Draw the goods onto the plan in scale showing the correct width and the seam locations to derive the running feet of carpeting needed (as it comes off the roll). Remember, you have to buy the full carpet width even if you don't need it, so the required length of goods will be multiplied by the width of the goods not by the width of the room. In Figure 4.21 the carpet is drawn to scale to determine how many pieces of carpet it will take to cover the floor.

Then each piece can be measured for length at its longest section. Multiply the length times the width of the goods to determine how much carpet should be ordered. Notice on the east end of the room that the slender pieces required were cut from a shorter piece of goods.

There is a wide range of prices in this product category and that will have an effect on your budget. Installation will also vary as thinner widths require more seams (and therefore labor) and sewn seams will be more costly than taped seams. The carpet cushion will add to the price as well, whether it is integral to the product or a separate line item. If you fail to specify a particular pad, the installer will likely use a cheap pad to shave job costs and lower the price of the bid, but you may not get the serviceability that your client's installation requires and the more important life-cycle costs will go up if the installation fails.

ORGANIZATION OF THE INDUSTRY

The difference between commercial and residential traffic has divided the industry into two markets with several categories of product in each. Residential-grade carpet is for lower traffic situations, while it is generally understood that a commercial grade will be more durable. Light-, medium-, and heavy-traffic categories will depend on assessments you will have to make regarding the kind of use and abuse an area will receive. For instance, a light-use residential interior may include stairs. Stairs suffer more abuse in normal usage, so you may upgrade a light-use classification to medium or heavy to accommodate the stairs.

Another distinction between residential and commercial goods is the commercial match. Residential goods are held to a higher standard of perfection than commercial goods. A variance of 10 percent from standard is generally considered to be allowable, but if one piece is 10 percent lighter than standard and the neighboring piece is 10 percent heavier, that is a 20 percent difference and a negotiation with your vendor may ensue. This is more likely to be present in jobs that are purchasing very large quantities that straddle two dye lots from the manufacturer.

Large orders of full rolls are often discounted in price. Rolls vary from 30 to 100 feet long. The price that is printed in lists from the vendor are usually for cut price (meaning less than a full roll) but salespeople can quickly tell you the roll price if it is not posted.

You may take other precautions to protect the life cycle of the installation, perhaps ordering extra carpet for the stairs, folding one tread depth under the first riser and then shifting the risers to the treads at some point in the future, or ordering extra carpet called "attic stock" for your client to keep on hand for future repair. This is quite common for the jobs where you specify carpet tile. Ordering additional attic stock will make it more likely that the full benefits of modular carpet can be realized by your client.

Custom carpeting can be specified when your need is very specific. Minimum dollar or minimum quantity restrictions will often come into play. Typically, suppliers will have samples of different qualities that can be made up in custom-wool colors. Some manufacturers have minimums as low as 30 square yards. Commercial goods can often be ordered through custom programs in combinations of stock colors for larger minimums but the scale of commercial jobs will often permit you to meet these minimums and order custom goods.

There are to-the-trade vendors that do not sell carpet to end users. Their operations are wholesale and their accounting procedures are not set up to collect or pay sales tax, so they will sell only to architects and designers who resell the carpet to their clients and collect and pay the sales tax. There are also retail stores that sell carpet and installation to designers and architects at a discount as well as to end users at a higher price. Some of the carpet that they sell is developed specifically for that market and is not available to trade sources and vice versa. Large mills will have a commercial and trade branch producing different product lines for each. There are some products that are available through retail and trade sources, however.

SELECTION CRITERIA

There are several quality measurements that interior designers check when they are making their carpet selections. Some of the classifications you will check are required by law and others are a matter of conscientious practice. Flammability ratings and floor changes in height of less than ½ inch are requirements in all jurisdictions. Other standards are not required by law but should be understood to be just as mandatory for the professional interior designer. These additional requirements will pertain to your client's design program. Tested data defines some quality characteristics and you can use the numbered ratings as you compare one product to another. Table 4.4 lists characteristics that are measurable with standardized testing.

As always, your unique job requirements will help you assemble your selection criteria checklist. It is a good idea to organize your thoughts and you may decide to do so along the lines of the example in Table 4.5.

Table 4.4
Some of the tested properties of carpet samples address mandatory criteria.

Measures	Meaning
Pile face weight	Ounces of yarn weight above the backing. Commercial carpet is about 24 to 36 ounces per square yard. Pile carpet needs to be a denser than loop for appurtenance retention. Residential carpet will top out around 65 ounces per square yard.
Flammability pill test	Carpet must self-extinguish if something burning falls on it. Rug should also meet it or bear a label declaring that they do not and are not to be used near sources of ignition.
Flammability radiant panel	Flame is sustained and carpet burned under controlled conditions that supply heat. The more energy required to sustain the flame, the better the rating. Class I = .45 watts/square centimeter and Class II = .22 watts/square centimeter.
Smoke density	Smoldering carpet produces more smoke than burning carpet and test data should pertain to smoldering carpet and optical measure of 450.
Tuft bind	The amount of force required to pull a loop (FHA requires no less than 6.25 pounds) or cut-pile tuft (no less than 3) out of the backing. Commercial carpet should withstand up to 10 pounds or 8 pounds for modular.
Delamination	The amount of force needed to separate the primary backing from the secondary backing. FHA minimum is 2.5 pounds of force per inch of width and this is reasonable for commercial carpet as well.
Abrasion	Fuzzing (fiber slips out of yarn), pilling (entangling of fuzzing), and abrasion (fiber loss) tests are performed. The texture appearance retention rating (TARR) test numbers will range from 2.5 (moderate traffic) to 3.5 (heavy traffic).
Dry breaking strength	Pounds of pressure before a yarn ruptures. HUD minimum is 100.
Colorfastness	Measured for resistance to effects of light, color rubbing off wet and dry samples, ozone, cleaning agents, acids and gas fumes, so follow up on what exactly the colorfast rating listed in your carpet's specs pertains to. Carpet specified should receive an AATCC rating of 4 in any pertinent category.
Static electricity	Commercial carpet should not exceed 3 kilovolts and residential 5 kilovolts. Sensitive equipment may require a range around ⅕ to 2 kilovolts.
Green Label and Green Label Plus	Carpet and adhesives bearing Green Label certification has met voluntary standards for low emission of 70+ chemicals of concern.

Table 4.5
Selection criteria examples for carpet.

Condition	Program Implications
Is this a public space?	Fire codes and ADA guidelines must be satisfied.
Special needs space?	You may require antimicrobial or antistatic carpet.
Is the space in question connected very directly to the outdoors?	Select fabricated walk-off mats to coordinate with carpet selected.
Is the area exposed to a lot of sunlight or harsh cleaning chemicals?	Polypropylene is the most resistant to fading. If the area will be in bright sunlight make sure to review samples in bright sunlight as well as under artificial lighting.
What needs are there for visual organization and wayfinding?	Color selection or pieced patterns can help identify distinct areas. Find a series of goods that are visually compatible with each other.
What are the lighting conditions in the space?	Very dark colors soak up available light as well as show dust and lint-type soiling.
Will footfall tend to travel through structure to adjoining spaces beside or below the area?	Consider a carpet cushion.
Will you be trying to maximize daylighting?	Pale colors show soiling; recommended reflectance for floors is between 25 to 40%. Consider organic patterns if paler carpet is selected; it will hide more spotting than solid or geometric patterns.
How interested is your client in sustainability?	Select recycled material. Postconsumer recycled fiber is available.
Will this space be reconfigured often or do you expect uneven wear with distinct traffic paths?	Consider modular material that can be switched around or replaced without damaging the whole installation.
Are there stairs in the space?	Bend the carpet at a ninety-degree angle and see if the backing shows.
Will you be specifying a separate carpet cushion?	Match the cushion with the goods and the traffic and upgrade the cushion for stairs.
Will this be modular product?	Confirm the matching of the pattern and consult with your client about the amount of attic stock to order.
Will carpet abut other materials that are thicker or thinner?	Devise a detail that will avoid the shiny aluminum strip screwed down on top of the junction between the two.

SPECIFYING

Writing a spec requires knowledge of the site as well as the product. For this sample spec imagine that you have been hired to help with the reorganization of a not-for-profit agency and have selected a modular carpet tile product to be installed throughout the facility with the only exception being the staff kitchen and two restrooms. Carpet tiles were selected so they could be replaced in traffic areas, extending the life of the installation. You selected nylon fiber so that the tiles would be abrasion resistant. A midrange value was selected that would hide the most soiling so your not-for-profit client could maintain presentable appearances without excessive cleaning costs. An organic pattern was selected so spots from a dropped afternoon snack or drippy, slushy shoes would be harder to detect.

If you select the exact manufacturer's product prior to writing your spec, you can include the manufacturer's installation instructions in your spec. You can see that the following spec is reasonably complete in that regard, as would be the case if the manufacturer's instructions had been referenced.

SAMPLE SPEC 4.1

Part 1 General Information

1.1 Related Documents

A. Finish plan showing location of material and detail drawings showing terrazzo edging at transition to resilient product (by others) in kitchen and restrooms.

1.2 Summary

A. Install modular carpet tile with releasable adhesive and resilient base in areas specified.

1.3 References

A. All work and adhesives to comply with local fire and safety codes.
B. Finished surfaces to comply with ADA guidelines.

1.4 Contractor Submittals

A. Submit 2 samples of tile specified.
B. Submit one sample, minimum 4 inch length, of terrazzo edging demonstrating thickness and finish.
C. Manufacturer's specifications for carpet tile and adhesive.
D. Material safety data sheet for carpet and adhesive.
E. Maintenance recommendations from manufacturer.

1.5 Quality Assurance

A. Carpet tiles to be delivered to site in unopened wrappings bearing manufacturer's identification and the lot number.
B. Resilient base to be delivered in unopened wrappings bearing manufacturer's identification.
C. Terrazzo edging is to be delivered to site in sealed packaging accompanied by fabricator's label and identification.
D. Installation to be completed by firm specializing in the installation of commercial carpet tiles. It is recommended that the firm be a member of the Floor Covering Installation Contractors Association (FCICA) or certified by the Floor Covering Installation Board (FCIB).
E. Installer shall visit the site prior to delivery to confirm all conditions and quantity of material required.

1.6 Delivery, Storage, and Handling

A. All materials to be delivered to site 48 hours prior to commencing installation per manufacturer's instructions and stored flat in acclimatized, secured storage location at job site.

1.7 Maintenance of Installation

A. Do not begin work until all painting labor has been completed (except for touch-up installation) and all overhead work has been completed and approved.
B. Maintain minimum temperature of 65ºF.
C. During and for 72 hours after installation ventilate with fan system at full capacity.

Part 2 Products

2.1 General Information

A. Carpet tiles of sufficient quantity to complete the installation plus 25 percent attic stock to be provided (with leftover tiles and scraps of at least 50 percent of full tile size) stored at center director's instructions.
B. Releasable tile adhesive of sufficient quantity to complete job plus (1) 12-ounce unopened container of adhesive for future use stored at center director's instructions.
C. Resilient base selected to be provided and installed in areas indicated on finish plan.
D. Terrazzo edging cut to length for transition between carpeted areas and restrooms and kitchen.

2.2 Manufacturers

A. Best Choice Carpet Tiles, 1234 Industrial Drive, Anytown, ST 34567.
B. Metal Edge Accessories Inc., 9876 Industrial Drive, Anytown, ST 34567.

SAMPLE SPEC 4.1 (continued)

2.3 Products

A. Town Squares Series carpet tile 100 percent Ecosolution nylon fiber in color Autumn. 30-ounce tiles with attached cushion of 25 percent postindustrial recycled material.
B. Town Square Companion series straight rubber base in color Russet.
C. Set Me Free releasable adhesive for carpet tiles.
D. Set Me Free cement sizing primer for carpet adhesive.
E. ¼-inch terrazzo edging in oil rubbed bronze finish.

Part 3 Execution

3.1 Examination

A. Contractor to inspect floor prior to commencing work and confirm that conditions will permit acceptable installation of products specified. Failure to report unacceptable conditions will be determined to be acceptance of conditions.

3.2 Preparation

A. Sweep entire area and apply concrete primer according to manufacturers instructions.
B. Install tile adhesive with notched trowel of recommended size and following manufacturer's instructions for cutting and placing tile.

3.3 Installation

A. Adhere base to wall as instructed in manufacturer's literature. Use uncut pieces on all continuous wall spaces.
B. Begin installation of tile at junction of hallway and reception with full tile centered in width of hallway.
C. Work out from centerline of hallway into reception, all offices and conference room including closets.
D. Neat, straight cuts to leave no yarn "sprouts," snags, or cut loops.

3.4 Post Installation

A. Vacuum entire area.
B. Remove all base scrap and store reusable carpet tile scraps according to director's instructions.
C. Site to be ready for owner's acceptance upon completion of installation.

INSPECTION

Review the installation with your order and finish plans in hand to make sure you remember everything that you have asked (and paid) for. Confirm that:

- Floor was cleared of all debris prior to installation.
- Seaming diagram has been followed by installer and all goods are running in the same direction or tiles have been installed according to your instructions.
- Check for cleanliness of site—no glue, fasteners, or small carpet scraps have been left; carpeting has been vacuumed. Large scraps may be saved at client's direction for patching.
- Seaming is inconspicuous, there are no loose yarns or raised loops.
- Step on carpeting in doorways to confirm that Z-bar or glue secures the carpet there and that tack strips have not been used in doorways where there will be footfalls.
- No wrinkles, exposed cut edges, damaged or flattened fibers are discernible.
- When two or more pieces of the same carpet are seamed together, the pile is to run in the same direction.
- A properly constructed seam may not be invisible, but should be well made.
- Check all specified base and transition strips for correctness and neatness.
- Is binding neat and even (if applied)?

RELATED MATERIAL

Related material, in addition to accessory items that accompany your carpet installation, would be woven vinyl flooring.

AREA RUGS

Although area rugs have been assigned an official definition for delimits in fire code (less than 6 feet in any direction and under 24 square feet total), this definition does not align with the common understanding of an area rug or encompass all the sizes employed. Designers tend to think of an area rug as one that does not cover the whole floor, but rather defines an area within a space. Construction and options vary greatly among rugs in this category, from pile rugs to tapestries, canvas that is painted or stained, dyed or stenciled animal skins, rag rugs in all kinds of scrap cloth, leather, or suede, and felted rugs.

The major classifier in this area distinguishes between handmade and machine-made product. As a general rule, handmade product is considered the higher-quality option even though it usually lacks the "perfection" of a machine-made product. Handmade product generally starts out at a higher price point and retains more value over time.

Many custom options exist among handmade rugs, and artists working in the different techniques are often willing to work on commissions to create your designs, as well as to create or modify some standards among their own designs in alignment with the needs of your client's space. This process is more easily controlled when the designer works and communicates directly with the rug maker, but custom rug specifications can be communicated with success through your local vendor, who then communicates with weavers who are sometimes in other countries.

(a) Serging

(b) Tape binding

(c) Leather binding

FIGURE 4.22A–C Area rugs made from broadloom or other material cut to size, rather than made to size, must have their edges finished to prevent them from unraveling. Commonly requested edgings include these pictured above.

CATEGORIZING AREA RUGS

The area rug product is so varied that it nearly defies broad categories. Many rugs are one of a kind. Categorizing by production method may be the most succinct but it will not tell the whole story of rugs, which are often inspired, artistic reactions more akin to artwork than to floor covering.

Ready-Made Rugs

Ready-made rugs are produced by a wide variety of methods. Their characteristics are wide-ranging as well. At one end of this spectrum you will find machine-made rugs in utility fibers like polypropylene that are so sturdy they are used outdoors around pool decks to provide slip resistance. At the other end of the spectrum you will find a hand-knotted Persian silk that is a one-of-a-kind rug selected overseas by a vendor who bought it for stock in his or her shop, knowing that one day the right buyer would come in to buy it. These are ready-made because they are available for immediate purchase, but they have very little else in common to link them together. You will be able to find ready-made versions of all the rugs listed here in shops, at craft fairs, and online.

Semicustom Pile Rugs

Some manufacturers offer rugs that can be made up in set patterns that you can order in alternate sizes with colors selected from their standard color offerings. These rugs are available with a pile construction, **flat weaves**, as well as chain stitch, needlepoint, and other construction methods.

Pieced Rugs

A pieced rug is another type of custom area rug. Broadloom is cut and pasted with heat tape to form a custom pattern, and the edges are bound to create an area rug. Figure 4.22a through c show three options available. Often local installers can provide this kind of custom fabrication or they sub it out. Quite often with this approach, you will not receive a rendering from them, so you will have to create, on your own, all the tools required for checking the design composition and color relationships.

Helpful Hint 4.4

Ask your supplier if he or she does the work in-house or subs it out. If it is subbed out, you may be able to get a lower price by finding your own direct source and avoiding the markup. This legwork will take time, however, so if your client is purchasing your service on an hourly basis, you will not spend three hours to visit shops and inspecting work just to save your client $200 in production costs. But you may subcontract the work to your own resource if you already have a fabricator whose work is certain to be satisfactory.

Floor Cloths

Painted onto a textile, usually heavy canvas or sailcloth, floor cloths are often washable. Highly customized, one-of-a-kind designs result when these are "one-off" items, meaning each one is unique. Vintage floor cloths may be dry and a little stiff, but new floor cloths are pliable and can be rolled like a painting for transport because that is essentially what they are.

Rag Rugs

Manufactures may have semicustom rag rug offerings of various stock colors and set patterns that can be rearranged. A simple, woven rag rug, Figure 4.23, shows how rags are used in place of yarns on the loom to make these rugs. Individual craftspersons produce totally custom rag rugs, dyeing rags to match a color sample and laying them into the loom to create the pattern as directed. Unless the rug is pieced (two or more strips woven separately then sewn together), the width of the rugs will be limited to the size of the loom—the largest possible size being two times the width of the loom (a double weave technique can be used). Often a vendor will represent many weavers who have different abilities (including skills and loom size) and specialties. The rags form the weft interlaced in a string warp.

The rag strips may also be knotted in (like a pile rug) to create a "fluffy" versus flat surface; rags may be braided. These rugs are typically cotton rag on a cotton warp or wool rag on a wool warp.

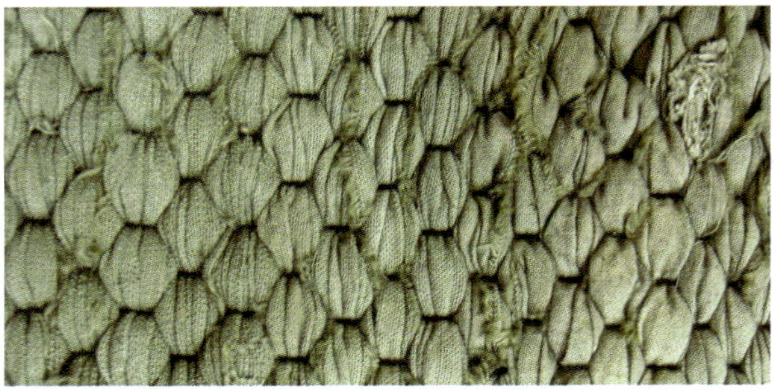

FIGURE 4.23 Rag rugs are still a craft tradition in the U.S. and small independent weavers still fill the demand for rag rugs. This simple construction entirely conceals the warp, but depending on the weave the warp may become part of the design.

FIGURE 4.24 Daring combinations of fiber are possible in the custom-rug market, like this wool and steel example.

Hand-Tufted

Hand-tufted rugs are produced by a hand-operated tufting gun that inserts a yarn into a backing similar to machine-tufted products, but instead of producing the appearance of tufted rows, the insertion is random and can follow an intricate pattern because tufting is entirely positioned by hand.

Woven Rugs—Other Materials

Plant fiber, leather, and metal are also used to weave rugs. The wool and steel rug in Figure 4.24 has fine steel wire woven with wool. Leather rugs are constructed on looms in a manner similar to the rag rugs described above, except leather strips are used in place of cotton rags.

What Would You Do? 4.5

Can you imagine a material that might otherwise be thrown away, which could instead be woven into an area rug?

Hooked Rugs

Hooked rugs are made by hand by hooking the yarn through a canvas backing. Rug hooking has long been a handcraft tradition in the U.S. and many vintage selections are available. Artisans are still producing reproductions and modern designs.

Braided Rugs

Braided rugs are made of braided rag or yarn and you will most commonly see them in round and oval designs. The braids are stitched together along their edges to hold the braids together. Custom colors will allow you to create designs that relate specifically to your client's space.

Felt Rugs

Felt rugs are made of wool fiber that has not been processed into yarn but is instead matted with heat, hot water, pressure, and controlled friction to lock the fibers together. This very hands-on (or feet-on, depending on the methods of the individual fabricator) method interlocks the fibers, perhaps incorporating felt strips or, as employed in Figure 4.25, felt sheets cut to shape. The felt fibers or pieces are dyed and distributed according to the design which is laid out on a mat or canvas. The whole assemblage is sprinkled with hot water and rolled up inside the mat or canvas. The matting or interlocking of fibers takes place as the rug is rolled back and forth inside the canvas to entangle the fibers and create the matted sheet. The finished rugs are rinsed and air dried. These nonwoven rugs will not unravel, so employing positive-negative (Figure 4.26) cutout designs will not compromise their structure.

FIGURE 4.25 This rug is made by traditional methods with lots of hands-on physical labor bringing the rug into being. Sheets of felt are matted together to create the pattern. *Image courtesy of Festive Fibers, Easthampton, MA.*

FIGURE 4.26 This felted rug has a laser-cut border, a notion never dreamed of by the original rug felters 8,000 years ago.

Tapestry Rugs

Flat-woven (having no pile) tapestry rugs with intricate patterns and multiple colors are used for floor coverings and wall hangings, a tradition said to have begun in the Middle Ages when tapestries were employed to insulate drafty castles. The pattern is woven into the body of the rug. When you flip a tapestry rug over, the back is also finished looking, although color distribution is different, a characteristic that could be exploited, with some planning, for a two-sided product.

What Would You Do? 4.6

Tapestry and needlepoint rugs are pretty flat. Can you think of a reason or two as to why you would specify a pad for under rugs like these if they were to be placed on a wood floor? What would be the characteristics of a pad that you might use under them?

FIGURE 4.27 Needlepoint rugs will have their "tails" remaining on the back side. *Image courtesy of S&H Rugs, Danbury, CT.*

Needlepoint Rugs

Needlepoint rugs are flat rugs whose pattern has been stitched onto a canvas back. When you flip them over, the "tails" of yarn (where the artist changed color) are left hanging, so a needlepoint rug is not a two-sided rug (Figure 4.27).

> Point of Emphasis 4.8
>
> Sometimes the name *tapestry* is applied to needlepoint rugs (there is some confusion about French and English understandings of the word *tapestry*) but generally the distinction seems to be that tapestries are a weave and needlepoint is in the embroidery family.

Orientals

There are many different kinds, styles, and weaves that are classified by age, origin, and sometimes furthermore by style, although the region of origin is often considered to define the style too. Because different regions have their own characteristic pattern organization and kind of knot, the region name is usually synonymous with the style name. For example, see Figure 4.28 for a map showing nearly 75 regions in Iran (Persia in the rug world) referenced to denote rug styles. Many of the place names are also the rug style names.

Helpful Hint 4.5
When purchasing a vintage needlepoint rug, the little tails on the back come in handy because they are the exact colors needed for any repairs and are readily available.

Years of study are required in order to be knowledgeable in this area and, unless you develop the specialty, you must find the best dealers and rely on them to evaluate the quality of the product that they resell. You must work with someone that you can trust to be your guide who can, over time, educate you.

The appraisal of Oriental rugs is a field unto itself, and many factors play into the value of a rug, some tangible and some intangible. Like the art market, the rug market is often influenced by factors that have nothing to do with physical attributes of a rug. Artistic qualities, as well as physical qualities, are tangibles for these products. Making an appropriate selection for your design is a little easier than evaluating the quality of a rug as an investment. The latter is something that most designers decline to evaluate and if your client is interested in the rug as an investment there are appraisers that can lend more accurate advice in this area.

FIGURE 4.28 Each tribal region produces characteristic patterns identified by the name of the region. The names of the different styles are actually locations. Rugs produced in a region, or sold in a region, will typically bear the name of that place.

ASSESSING PRODUCTS

You will encounter a lot of opinion about what constitutes a worthy rug and that is beyond the scope of this text, the aim of which is to get you through the requirements of your first jobs. You will develop your own opinions as your work experience continues and you are exposed to these materials. The following is the nuts and bolts of making sure the product fits and functions.

Size

In the initial planning stages, plan your space around a standard size, but as you shop be prepared to lightly sketch (take a pencil) alternative sizes on your plan that you see to confirm they fit. Variation in size deviating from strict standards is to be expected because even handmade rugs produced with the intention of adhering to a standard size will be a little off after final processes are complete. This is a good thing to remember if ordering a rug from a handmade rug program—the size cannot be strictly controlled down to the inch.

The following are standard area rug sizes: 2' × 3', 3' × 5', 4' × 6', 6' × 9', 8' × 10', 9' × 12', 10' × 14', 12' × 15', 12' × 18', 13' × 20'.

Material Quality

Material quality assessment includes not just the quality of the material in isolation but also the appropriateness of the material for the production process and your client's site. Although a wide variety of material is employed in producing products in this category, the more traditional materials are as follows.

Yarn

Wool yarn quality depends on the species, environment, and health of the animal used as the source of the fiber, if the fiber is animal hair. Wool should be in good condition, not dried out. After touching the yarn, you should be able to feel the lanolin on your fingertips. The yarn should feel springy not "crunchy" when you squeeze it. If an old rug sheds, don't buy it. New rugs may have sheared ends still in the pile, but after a rug is completed, it often goes through a series of washings so even new rugs will have very little loose fiber in them.

A visual inspection of the wool is not going to be enough because there are many postproduction treatments called washes that alter the luster. The fact that a rug has been treated or washed is not an indication of overall quality, as rugs of all quality ranges are treated or washed. Ideally the wool is lustrous before chemical treatments because chemical treatments can make the wool appear to be higher quality than it is.

Wool is not the only fiber in these rugs; silk is highly prized but expensive, so mercerized cotton has been used to create a silk look because it is soft and lustrous, as is silk, but it does not wash up the same. This substitution is acceptable if identified, but rugs change hands a few times en route to their destination and the information may be dropped from the description along the way. Your reputable dealer may have already confirmed the fiber prior to putting the rug on the selling floor. If cotton has been used, confirm cleaning instructions with the dealer, taking into consideration that cotton does not always wash up well.

A Cautionary Tale 4.3

My client wanted the ability to live with her house open to fresh air in the summer and to entertain casually with people moving in and out from the patio and pool to the living room. We ordered slipcovers and a "summer rug" with the intention of removing an important Oriental carpet in the warm months. I knew her wood floor would oxidize to a paler color under the rug so the two rugs would have to be the exact same size. Even though this was communicated and understood, the weaver cannot control the size of a hand-loomed rug with that kind of exactitude. When the rug was cut from the loom and washed, it became shorter in one direction. She tried to block (a finishing process that uses heat, moisture, and stretching to set dimensions and shape) the rug to size but it returned to the smaller dimension. Luckily, leftover yarn allowed her to weave two borders to band the sides in the short direction of the rug, making it match the size of the winter rug.

> **Helpful Hint 4.6**
>
> If you do not trust that the silk fiber in a rug is really silk, remove and burn a small piece of yarn (with the dealer's permission of course). If it smells like burning hair and fizzles, it is silk. If it smells like burning paper and is reduced to ash, it is cotton. Your reputable dealer will also not object to this test and, if you have doubts, will probably happily perform it for you if your interest is strong and your doubts are genuine.

Rags

Braided, hooked, and other "rag" rugs made of cut strips of cloth should be fairly high quality, usually cotton (for its ability to be dyed any color specified) but also wool. The rag should be cut on the bias so it is more pliable and, if cut ends are exposed as part of the design, it doesn't fray. The rag should feel soft, like a worn shirt that has been slightly felted with washing and time (not *felt*, but the surface of the rag cloth will be micromatted). You will be able to force your fingers through braided rag rugs but you should not see through them.

Leather

Leather is also used, like rags, to create the surface of an area rug. The thickest part of the hide is the back, generally the center of the skin. The thinnest part of the hide is where the legs and belly are. The legs and belly are less usable for upholstery and other items made of leather but they are perfect for working into rug surfaces because they are thin and pliable. Your design will indicate the best qualities for the leather thickness. Protection from soiling and moisture is very important for leather used in floor coverings. Leather cannot be cleaned with waterborne methods. Construction techniques vary and leather is frequently woven with heavy twine warps, or knotted like hooked rugs, into a backing.

> **What Would You Do? 4.7**
>
> What would you expect to be the difference between the supply chain of a braided-rug artisan in Vermont and a country rug cottage industry in Iran?

Plant Fibers

Abaca, sisal, seagrass, and other plant fibers discussed in the Carpeting section on page 117 are also popular for area rugs. These rugs are usually flat-woven patterns because plant fibers lack the resiliency required for pile rugs. Typically they are cut to fit from standard width products and their edges bound to prevent them from raveling.

Tufted Wool and Nylon

As is the case for the plant fibers mentioned above, tufted carpet is also used as an area rug when the edges are bound to prevent rugs from raveling or scratching (the edge of the backing is pretty sharp). The quality will be appraised by the same standards used to appraise the product for wall-to-wall installation.

DETERMINING VALUE

There are several aspects to consider when determining product value.

Age

When purchasing product that has been in use before, age is a significant qualifier in determining value. The longer a product survives, the more valuable it becomes, after an initial dip in value of a new, unused rug immediately after purchase. Similarly to the adage that your new car loses half its value when you drive it off the lot, products that have only been in use a few years are used, not aged, and can be purchased at bargain prices. The higher the quality of the rug initially, the better it will retain its value over time, even through the early "used product" years. The following list provides age classifications for area rugs.

> **Point of Emphasis 4.9**
>
> There is a very small market for vintage textiles, with especially fine examples of rugs in the rag, hooked, braided, and other categories. These products find their way to the used-goods market rather than the upscale markets where you will find Oriental rugs.

For the Connoisseur 4.1

Synthetic rugs do not retain value the way wool rugs do. They suffer the "new car dilemma," that is they lose value the minute you drive them off the lot.

Classification of rugs by age:

- 15 years or less = new
- 15 to 50 years = semi-antique or vintage
- 50 to 75 years = antique
- more than 75 years = classical antique

The issue of age is a significant consideration when you are shopping for an Oriental carpet for your client.

Wear

If the rug is not new, inspect the front and the back when evaluating whether it is in a condition that will hold up at the site. Check to see how much pile is left. Look at the back for evidence of water damage. Check places where one color transitions to another to see if any of the color has bled to surrounding areas. Reds, especially, like to move (Figure 4.29).

FIGURE 4.29 When this rug was washed, the red bled into the surrounding area. Reds enliven designs, to be sure, but they will often be the first to fade and bleed.

FIGURE 4.30 Abrash may be incidental or integral to the design. This modern rug relies on the abrash as a significant contribution to the design of the rug. *Image copyright 2005, Michaelian & Kohlberg, Inc.*

Design Aspects

Preferences for the nature of the design are highly personal but the quality of the design can be evaluated outside of personal design preferences. As an objective designer you are capable of assessing the elements and principles employed. You may have to educate yourself to attain an awareness of the general preferences among the different types. The naïveté preferred for traditional hooked rugs does not transfer to the category of Orientals, but the iconoclast who thoughtfully interprets the genre in a new way can also boost the value of his or her artistic creation.

There are some stock considerations when evaluating Oriental designs specifically. If there is a medallion, it should be centered. Lines that are intended to be straight should be so. If the design utilizes a repeated motif, it should be fairly uniform but they need not be slavishly so; small, charming variation revealed upon close inspection indicates the handmade process. The design should be well balanced. Lustrous colors are valued among connoisseurs but fashionably faded colors are widely acceptable. Nomadic rugs often have color changes along the weft. This is called abrash and it should be subtle and gradual (Figure 4.30). Abrash and small asymmetries are common but they must be attractive and not damaging to the design. If it isn't charming, it's a defect.

For the Connoisseur 4.2

Oriental rugs can be quite worn and still be functional. You will see rugs that have the pile nearly all worn away so they look like flat-weave rugs with traces of pile still visible in the small shreds of yarn still clinging to the warp. Rugs that are that "gone" are still interesting to fashionistas, but not to connoisseurs.

Point of Emphasis 4.10

The variation in color that is called abrash is a result of the way the yarn is dyed for rugs. The skeins are simmered in a dye bath and then laid out in the sun to dry. As the yarns are drying, the wet dye migrates to the bottom of the skein so the portions of the yarns that are on the bottom are deeper in color than the portions of the skein that are on top. Knowing the origin of the color change will allow you to recognize when the abrash has been faked, presenting abrupt color changes along the row.

Construction Issues

For woven and knotted constructions, look for warp yarns: you should see very little of them—in some weaves, not at all. The sides or selvages should be even. Leather, or other dimensionally stable material, may be sewn to the back along the edges to keep them flat. The rug should lie flat with fairly straight sides (especially if new). Appropriate density of the design should complement the pattern and the use of the rug.

Run your hand over the pile and feel for undulations indicating improper shearing or excessive, harsh washing.

Repairs

You may shop for vintage rugs for your clients. Look at the back of the rugs for repairs. Figure 4.31a and b show a discernible but acceptable repair. For Oriental carpets, it is sometimes impossible to find a well-done repair from the face. Repairs are common and acceptable in older rugs (especially if the alternative is a worn area in disrepair!). Poorly made repairs can be removed and re-repaired so a good-quality rug with a poor repair is not really a problem. Generally a repair implies that an area rug is important enough (quality of the construction and the pattern) to warrant the work.

FIGURE 4.31A–B Repairs are very common among the vintage and antique carpets that you will find and a good repair is usually not a deal-breaker. Poor repairs can be redone if the rug is worthy of the effort; the dealer will usually include the repair in the negotiated price, but confirm this as you are coming to agreement about the price of the rug. Example (a) shows a well-made repair on the left side of the image, seen here from the back, that stabilizes the rug without distortion. Example (b) shows the same repair from the front, now on the right side of the image. A color shift is slightly visible, plus the knot count is slightly higher in the repair than the surrounding area to compensate for the finer yarn used by the person making the repair. *Images courtesy of Minasian Carpets, Evanston, IL.*

FIGURE 4.32A–B A fine wool rug with an intricate pattern also benefits from a high knot count. The fine tracery in image is crisp and quite consistent, but if this rug were produced with a lower knot count the pattern would suffer for it. In the bottom image you can see the overall design is also very intricate. *Image courtesy of Minasian Rugs, Evanston, IL.*

FIGURE 4.33A–B This rug has a low knot count but the pattern is appropriate to the count and the design is well rendered at 100 knots per square inch. *Image courtesy Minasian Rugs, Evanston, IL.*

Knot Count

While a dense rug has greater durability and may have a quality appearance, knot count is no longer considered the critical indicator of good quality. Different desired looks are achieved by different knot counts but the count should support the fineness of the pattern. Figure 4.32a and b show an intricate pattern appropriately rendered by a fine knot count. A fine curve will disappear into "speckles" if the knot count is too low to hold the yarns in the correct location to support the pattern. A more robust pattern can be appropriately rendered by a lower knot count as shown in Figure 4.33a and b.

FABRICATION

If you are buying a rug that is already made, it is interesting to understand how the rug was produced, but if you are managing the commission of a custom rug, it is important to really understand all the steps. Surprisingly, the production process is similar for most of these product categories.

Step 1: Locate a close sample so you can make a contract with a fabricator and dealer who will be able to provide a final product that will be what you have in mind.

Step 2: Work with your representative (may or may not be the artist) on the design, color selections, and quality choices pertaining to material and methods. Either you or the artist (or their representative) may produce a drawing of what the finished rug will be like; color samples will be exchanged for communication.

Point of Emphasis 4.11

A minimum (if any) amount of design work will be performed by the artist or vendor before he or she has a contract and a deposit for the item. In the early stages of the process, the burden of communicating your expectations will fall to you. The designer typically produces drawings and color swatches for reference until an understanding and a price can be reached. After the order has been placed and a deposit paid, the burden for renderings and samples usually shifts to the artist or the vendor.

Step 3: Samples will be produced. If your color samples have been paint and fabric samples up to this point, now color samples in your selected materials will be produced for your approval. A corner sample might be produced as well. This is a small (24" × 24" is quite common) sample that demonstrates the material and method, the color relationships, and possibly the pattern.

Point of Emphasis 4.12

It is more important to see the quality and the juxtaposed colors than it is to see a portion of the pattern at this stage, so if the pattern is not represented on the sample, it is likely due to the desire to demonstrate how neighboring colors interact.

Step 4: The piece will be produced to specs and approved samples. Remember that an exact size is not usually controllable for handmade product. Rugs are typically washed and blocked before shipping. Variation of an inch or two per foot of rug is quite common.

From start to finish, this process may take several months. If your rug is large and produced overseas the entire process could take more than a year. To understand why this is, so you can manage client expectations, consider the production of a custom Turkish carpet.

FIGURE 4.34 Hand-knotted rugs have limitations imposed by the process that define the time required to produce them. Only so many weavers can physically fit side-by-side if a rug must be produced quickly.

The Turkish rugs that you find on the market are produced as follows: Nomadic tribes herd sheep into high mountain meadows in the summer. The low temperatures produce a lanolin-rich (oily) wool. The fleece is combed repeatedly during the winter, and then sheared in early spring. The wool is washed and sorted for length, and teased to separate and fluff the fibers. Then the wool is spun by hand into yarn. This much work can take place before you place your order but all of the following occurs after your design and negotiations have taken place (so you have likely invested one to two weeks in the process).

The wool yarn is often dyed with natural dyes (those derived from insects or from the earth, including madder root, indigo, milkweed, pomegranate, Osage, cutch, and cochineal). Samples for approval will be produced by the fabricator. Weaving is done on vertically oriented looms. A weaver can weave about the width of their body at a rate of four or five feet per month, so a rug can be woven at a rate of approximately five feet per month regardless of width because wider rugs permit more weavers to sit side-by-side (Figure 4.34). When complete, the rug is cut from the loom, stretched out on the ground, and sheared or given a **carved nap** by hand. It is the tradition of some fabrication techniques to work additional **overtufting** into completed rugs or work over a flat-woven rug with embroidery as part of the finishing process of some of these Oriental and nomadic rugs.

> **Point of Emphasis 4.13**
> It is sometimes the habit of the fabricator to dye all the yarn needed for the rug when the yarn for the sample is dyed but just as frequently the dyeing for the entire order happens after the pom is approved. It's a good idea to inquire about the process when finalizing the price because if the yarn is dyed before the sample is made, there may be additional cost if you change a color after review of the sample.

Transportation takes a significant amount of time. The completed rug will be transported to a port and may wait in the country of origin until a large shipping container can be filled with rugs headed to the next destination. That destination may be your country or a location where finishing processes are applied. These finishing processes may include one or a number of different washing formulas and the terminology you will encounter includes the broad distinctions in the following list. The exact chemistry varies and some of these processes seem to be similar but as they have been given different names, they are all included here as distinct.

- Chemical washing simulates age by mellowing the colors. Overuse of these chemicals can lend a glittery sheen to the yarn. This glittery sheen is overprocessed and will be less durable. If your client is not purchasing an investment quality rug, this may be a look they like for decades before the rug is ruined from normal wear.
- Gold washing mutes reds; rosy reds are diminished more than true reds.
- Tea washing lends an overall sienna cast to the colors, muting and blending them evenly.
- Sun washing and chemical bleaching both lighten colors throughout the rug. Sun washing and age will lighten fiber near the top of the pile more than the yarn deep in the pile. Bleaching is more consistent throughout the pile height.
- Luster washing increases the sheen of the yarn without improving or (if properly applied) diminishing the quality.
- Antique washing produces the appearance of age, lightening the colors, sometimes selectively as would happen with age. Dyes that are historically less durable are diminished more. Other formulas are counter to typical lightening from actual aging. For instance, reds tend to be fugitive and fade more quickly than other colors but some formulas for antique washes do just the opposite. Reds are left full intensity while the other colors are muted, with very attractive results. This implies that the chemical washing is not being applied to mimic the effect of age but as part of the artistic considerations in the production of the design.

After arrival in the U.S., the rug must go through customs, a lengthy process that requires more careful scrutiny of material being transported into the country.

FINDING A RUG

The best way to shop for a rug is to visit rug dealers that you trust with your floor plan fabric and finish samples in hand. Depending on the job, your client, and your usual working relationship, you may make arrangements for likely possibilities to come to the site for review. You may collect photos of the best possibilities to send to your client. Take any fabric samples with you and shoot a photo with the fabric lying on the rug so the color relationships can be represented to the client. Bring a tape measure to confirm that accurate sizes are listed on tags. Photos and sizes are required (1) as a comparison of rugs from different resources and (2) for an initial review by the client.

If you exhaust the resources in your area and still do not have the right rug, this is an item that is easy to buy from a more distant resource. Usually new rugs are more universal, and the new rugs found in one place are available in many places, but for semiantique and antique rugs it might even pay to extend your search to other cities at the same time that you are shopping locally.

Contact dealers with a description of the kind of rug you need, communicate with photographs to narrow your options, and have likely rugs shipped in for your client to see. If you have an ongoing relationship with the dealer, he or she may just box up the rugs and send them. If your relationship is new, the dealer may ask for credit card information as insurance. Dealers may or may not pay for shipping. If they pay shipping to you, you will still pay the return shipping if you do not keep the rug. Confirm all arrangements and get your client's approval for all charges.

CARE AND MAINTENANCE

The basic care and cleaning of the various rugs varies little among the different types of rugs. Most rugs are washed with water (leather or leather-bound rugs are not). Cleaning services for Oriental rugs will wash rugs. The rugs must then be spread in an area with a lot of air circulating within it, so that the rugs dry as quickly as possible, before they become musty smelling. For other rugs mentioned here it is a good idea to get instructions from the individual fabricator on how to care for the rug prior to finalizing your order (if the client cannot maintain the rug it is a poor choice). Processes and materials differ even within the same technique and the care of the rug will vary with the materials and construction.

Restoration

Rug dealers will usually restore vintage and antique rugs that they sell, and this is typically included in the price. They are also a resource for mending and restoring your client's own rug. If your client happened to purchase a vintage craft rug at a resale shop or an auction, you could probably find a cleaning and restoration service through a local dealer of similar items.

SAFETY

These products are typically safe to use. Not to minimize the hazards, their size as a proportion of the materials used in a space is small and so its effects will be diluted in the total area. Area rugs that conform to size limitations for fire ratings may be flammable if they bear a label declaring that they are flammable.

Many of these products come out of craft traditions and documentation of materials is not standard as for other parts of our industry. What has been a concern for designers is the safety and well-being of overseas craftspeople that weave and tuft these products, so it is important that you confirm working conditions and receive adequate assurance that child labor was not used. Child labor has been a fact of life in the rug industry for centuries, but it is no longer acceptable. An organization called Rugmark inspects production facilities to ensure that no child labor is being used before the product can bear their certification.

Another organization to inquire about is Arzu. This program has helped carpet weavers overseas by providing technical and financial assistance to women weavers, social assistance to their families, access to health care for mothers, and education and literacy programs. In addition to creating sustainable employment for the women, the program aims to establish expanded roles for women in the carpet production chain.

SUSTAINABILITY

Area rugs will vary with type when it comes to sustainability issues. There is low-embodied energy in hand-knotted area rugs but they are produced halfway around the world and require fuel to get to this part of the globe. Area rugs constructed of bound broadloom will likely have their production distributed as well, so transportation costs, as well as fiber production costs, will add to the environmental impact. At the other end of the spectrum, goods produced from an individual artisan sheering their own sheep for woven or felted product close to your job site will consume very little energy in the production of floor covering.

As an artistic expression, old rugs are being pieced together to make new area rugs. The sustainable origins of these rugs make their environmental costs especially low as rugs that normally would have been thrown away are put back into service as their stable portions are pieced into new floor coverings. See Figure 4.35 for the results of this recycling of old rugs.

MANAGING BUDGETS

There is not always direct relationship between quality and cost. Other factors that may affect cost are design, rarity, and beauty. Analysis of the value of a rug follows a similar path to analysis of a piece of art.

FIGURE 4.35 Rugs eventually wear out in traffic areas even when the rest of the rug is still sound. Oscar Isberian Rugs in Chicago carries a line of patchwork rugs made out of the sound portions of rugs that would otherwise be thrown away. *Image courtesy of Oscar Isberian Rugs, Chicago, IL.*

- *Patterns* Many kinds of Oriental rugs are meant to be symmetrical, though few are precisely and perfectly symmetrical. There is an old adage that imperfections and flaws were purposely woven in because of the belief that only God could create perfection. Flaws are flaws unless they are charming. If the flaws are not unattractive, they are not defects, but when in doubt, reject goods that do not charm you. This is an area where an accurate assessment will, to some extent, take a trained eye, but knowledge of elements and principles of design is a good basis from which to start.
- *Material quality* Some people still consider yarn count in an appraisal of value but quality is a more accurate word. A rug with 50 to 100 knots per inch will have a more primitive quality than a rug with 100 to 300 knots per inch. If you are viewing two rugs of the same style in two densities, the rug with the higher yarn count is likely to cost more but the appearance also changes. Very intricate and small patterns demand a high knot count to control the presentation. A large pattern may be well presented with a lower knot count, which furthermore has a pleasing texture for a more casual interior. So a direct comparison of knot count does not tell the whole story about quality. Individual rugs must be evaluated on all their characteristics. It is often the case that using more material in production will raise the cost but this is not always a direct effect.
- *Machine-made options in this category* Regardless of style, machine-made options will be less costly than handmade product.
- *Cost and quality of the materials used to produce the rug* These will affect production costs, purchase price, and value.
- *Production* The number of steps in the process from start to finish will increase the cost, as will the number of people involved.
- *Prestige and artist résumé* These products, when handmade, are considered to be fine craft and akin to works of art.
- *Appropriateness for your client's installation* This will affect the value and the long-term costs.

ORGANIZATION OF THE INDUSTRY

Let's use the Oriental rug market as one example of the organization of a part of this industry.

The rugs are produced within a cottage industry or as part of a small factory system with one, or at least very few weavers responsible for the production of a single rug. There are two categories of rugs broadly described as village rugs and city rugs.

Village Rugs

Village rugs are often smaller, having been woven on smaller looms that disassemble for transportation as shepherds move seasonally to care for their animals. Village rugs are produced in a shorter period of time to allow for seasonal changes in life patterns dictated by herding, shearing, and other activities of the business that defines the time available for weaving. They typically do not use a cartoon, a line drawing or diagram that guides the development of the pattern and colors during weaving, relying instead on tradition and memory.

City Rugs

City rugs are produced in a method called manufactory, meaning the rugs are factory-made by hand. These rugs are produced on permanent, large looms and allow for larger rugs and control over schedules that are not burdened by seasonal shifts. City rug manufacturing allows for more time, resulting in finer and more complex products.

Vendors

Perhaps your rug dealer in your home city will travel to the country of origin and meet with the cottage industry fabricators directly, but it is more likely that your dealer will meet with a representative who has either purchased or consigns rugs for the people who make them. Rugs are purchased directly to be shipped in large overseas containers and perhaps orders are placed for additional, custom-ordered rugs that your dealer feels will be popular enough to allow for sensible speculative purchasing.

Local Artisans

The local artisan-made rug will likely be produced by a craftsperson who may be credentialed by a fine-arts degree or has simply honed mastery of production as a hobby. The artist is likely to have an organized career path and may insist on more creative license. At the very least, you will be encouraged to work within the artist's preferred methods and materials to create a one-of-a-kind item. The designs created generally belong to the artist and you will probably not get an assurance of exclusivity, but artists generally don't like to retrace their steps so your client can probably rest assured that they will have the "only one" ever. But there may be no guarantee.

The master hobbyist will have equal technical skills but may be more willing to, or insistent on, implementing your design rather than performing design work on your project.

Dealer Services

Services vary with the kind of product sold. Shops that represent independent artisans will generally have a few samples hanging for immediate sale but will often coordinate between you and the artist in the fabrication of a custom piece for your client. In addition to hooking you up with an artisan or making a sale off the floor, dealers may offer cleaning and restoration service.

SELECTION CRITERIA

As usual, organize your design program to help you determine the proper hierarchy of goals that must be met for your client's area rug. You might organize your thoughts in a table with goals and characteristic implications side-by-side as in Table 4.6.

Table 4.6
Selection criteria examples for area rugs.

Condition	Program Implications
Is the space a public space?	Fire-rated material must be used or chemical fire retardants will have to be applied to the items. If addressing ADA guidelines, you may want to detail the flooring to provide a recess for the area rug to sit down into and avoid high-pile options.
Is the area exposed to a lot of sunlight?	These craftsman-tradition items are not typically as fade resistant as manufactured items, so care will have to be taken in the environment to shield the item. Some colors are more fugitive than others—red "loves" to fade.
What will the cleaning program be like?	Many of these items will be made of natural materials that should be dry-cleaned. Test proposed cleaning methods on a sample or confirm that your client site can follow the craftsperson's recommendation (if they have one—and sometimes you and the client's maintenance staff are on your own with this one).
Is this rug hanging on a wall instead of lying on a floor?	Large commercial spaces, like lobbies, with hard surfaces throughout get a little "boomy" acoustically speaking and so owners hang rugs as artwork. Not all products are stable for this kind of installation and may need special backing and must be sewn to stretchers.
Is a cushion required for longevity of the product or comfort?	Different cushions are available and often a cushion is part of the price, but you may not be able to purchase the one that you need from your dealer.
Will you be trying to maximize daylighting?	Reflectance for walls should be between 40 and 70% and for floors 25 to 40%.
How interested is your client in sustainability?	Rag rugs could be made of real, postconsumer rags, but more often they are made from new fabric. Leather rugs are often made of scraps.
Is this item an investment?	Oriental rugs are considered to be better investments than craftsman-tradition items but the rug market resembles the art market and the enduring value of such investments are not assured.
Will time allow for a custom option?	Custom rugs can take months to complete.

SPECIFYING

We cannot write a spec until we know exactly what we are ordering. For this spec sample, let's assume you are working on a hotel that requires three similar rugs that lend some identity to different areas of a large lobby. You have selected wool rugs because they are inherently flame resistant and the high-knot count you have specified will make them more stable for use by people using assistive-walking appliances and wheelchairs.

One rug defines an area near the door where you imagine people will wait for each other on their way in or out; one is near the corridor to banquet rooms and you imagine that people taking breaks from seminars (or wedding receptions) may sit here; and the other is near a lobby bar. It is this last rug that will be represented in this spec, but all the rugs are to share selected colors, so it will be necessary to reference the other two rugs here. The commonality is noted by the supplier, even though, for this example, the spec is for only one of the three rugs.

SAMPLE SPEC 4.2

Part 1 General Information

1.1 Related Documents

A. Refer to to-scale drawing of "Dragon Rug" indicating size of color areas and key to paint chip color representation (attached).

B. Refer to finish plan for location and details of recess in floor that will allow rug to be flush and level with hard-surface flooring (by others).

1.2 Summary

A. 150-knot rug to conform to drawing and approved samples to be woven with a 5-inch, plain border beyond patterned border to allow rug to be cut to fit and bound for loose-lay in recessed area of floor.

B. Rug woven in Tibet to be cut and adhered to secondary backing, serged, and installed by supplier.

1.3 References

A. Local fire and building codes.

B. ADA guidelines for flush and level flooring conditions.

1.4 Contractor Submittals

A. This rug is to meet Class-A fire rated requirements and certificate is to be provided for delivery to fire marshal.

B. Verification data must be provided to certify that the installation conforms to fire code and LEED requirements.

C. Color **poms** for approval.

D. 2' × 2' sample showing yarn and construction quality and demonstrating all colors and color adjacencies for approval.

1.5 Quality Assurance

A. Rug is to conform to approved samples and quality descriptors.

B. Rug to resemble two other rugs (specified separately but of this same order) in surface quality, pattern carving, density, motif color, and thickness.

C. Rug to bear the Rugmark label, which is to be transferred to the underside after adhering the secondary backing to be applied by installer.

1.6 Delivery, Storage, and Handling

A. Bound and backed rugs to be delivered blanket-wrapped to clean site at time of furniture delivery.

B. Rugs to be spread and smoothed by installers.

1.7 Maintenance of Installation

A. After installation, rug to be vacuumed by installer.

Part 2 Products

2.1 General Information

A. Custom rug to be fabricated as shown on drawings of 100 percent wool pile on wool warp with plain border woven as shown for allowance for adjusting size for perfect fit into recesses (by hard-surface contractor) for flush condition between hard and soft surface (this rug).

B. Nylon mesh to be adhered to back of rug with waterborne adhesive.

C. Rugmark label to be visible after secondary backing has been applied.

2.2 Manufacturers

A. Top of the World Rug Company,1234 Industrial Drive, Anytown, ST 45678.

B. Backpax Industrial Fabrics Corp., 5678 Industrial Drive, Anytown, ST 45678.

C. Stickystuff Ecoresins, Inc., 9876 Industrial Drive, Anytown, ST 45678.

2.3 Products

A. Dragon Rug from Tibetan series A; finished size to be per installer's template of recess, approximately 12' × 18'.

B. Backpax nylon mesh N38.

C. Tacktorrent waterborne adhesive.

Part 3 Execution

3.1 Examination

A. Installer to receive and inspect rug, trim, and bind edges to correct size, carefully remove and save Rugmark label, adhere nylon mesh to back of carpet, and reattach Rugmark label.

3.2 Preparation

A. Installer to measure and template, if necessary, recess constructed by others to receive area rug.

3.3 Installation

A. Installer to deliver and spread rug after site is clean and ready to receive furniture.

B. Rug is to fill entire recess evenly, touching terrazzo edging (by others) on all four sides.

3.4 Post Installation

A. Vacuum rug.

INSPECTION

These products may be custom but they should still conform to all the quality indicators mentioned above pertaining to hand, quality of materials, and the like. Take all color and quality samples with you to ensure all characteristics are as ordered. A long time interval between ordering and inspecting will make your memory less reliable, and your approved samples will make your inspection more thorough and accurate.

These rugs are typically laid in place. You may meet the installer and, using a tape measure and some blue painter's tape, mark the location on your client's floor of each corner to be sure it goes in the right spot (these rugs can be heavy to drag around by yourself after the installer leaves so you want to make sure it is in the right spot). Many of these rugs shade in one direction (have a light side and a dark side as the pile lays in one direction). Examine the rug from the primary vantage point to determine if you want to rotate the rug 180 degrees for the best color presentation.

RELATED PRODUCTS

You will often see hair-on cowhide used as an area rug. Occasionally these hides are printed to resemble zebra, tiger, and other exotic animals that cannot (or should not) be used for their hides. Kraftcord, which is a tenacious paper twine, and cord or wire of other products, such as vinyl and metal, also contribute similar product to the options available to interior designers.

SUMMARY

Interior designers specify a wide variety of textile floor coverings made up in a wide variety of materials. Two broad categories of carpeting and rugs are distinguished mostly by their installation. The implications for commercial and residential selection criteria also distinguish product types. While all categories covered have material production centered on textiles, other materials are also included. Ready-made, stock or standard offerings, semi custom, and custom options make a serviceable variety available for selection.

WEB SEARCH ACTIVITIES

1. Select a few names from a list of locations on a map of Iran or Iraq or use the map on page 138 and perform an image search. Pull up rug styles that were produced in those regions or that others are imitating, making rugs to resemble rugs from those areas. Notice that the regions have some stylistic distinctions. A Birjand rug does not look like a Kashan rug, for example.
2. Perform an image search for a picture of an area rug installed in an interior. What would your selection criteria have been for the installation?
3. Search for a specification guide for a custom area rug. Read it for comprehension.
4. Perform an image search for each of the mentioned constructions and select an installation of the product from the images you find. Search for images of manufacturers for each kind of construction (you may not be able to find knitted construction but the rest should yield some usable results).
5. Perform an image search for *low-twist yarn*, *high-twist yarn*, *short-staple yarn*, and *long-staple yarn*. You will probably come across yarn used for knitting but no matter—the characteristics will be visible just the same.

   Just by looking at the yarn you can probably imagine that the high-twist yarn will keep its shape better than a low-twist yarn, and you would be right about that. You will also notice that a long-staple yarn (one made of long fibers) is smoother than a short-staple yarn with all the little ends poking out making it fuzzy.

   Search for *master spec carpet* and read it for comprehension.

PERSONAL ACTIVITIES

1. Find a picture of an area showing a carpet installation. Imagine that the carpet has worn out and is starting to lose its stability. Where would you expect to see the most wear in the installation? What instructions would you have to relay to the installation company for the new carpet to complete the installation of your recommended replacement carpet (and cushion, stair rods, etc.)?

2. Consider an area in your own plan where you might use a carpeted surface or find a picture of an installation of carpet in an interior space. Write a spec for the item or surface.

3. Consider an area in your own plan where you might use a custom rug, or find a picture of an installation that has an area rug that might be custom. Using the spec template in Chapter 2, write a spec for the rug.

SUMMARY QUESTIONS

1. What are the characteristics of each of the fibers and when would you specify each? Organize your answer highlighting their differences.
2. Which fibers should be cleaned with dry-cleaning methods?
3. What are the two protein fibers? What fibers are cellulosic? Synthetic?
4. What does staple mean? BCF? What characteristic is improved by crimping the fiber?
5. What would be the performance and appearance difference between a low-twist yarn and a high-twist yarn?
6. What would be the performance and appearance difference between a small denier yarn and a thick denier yarn?
7. What is a performance difference between tufted and woven product?
8. When would you encounter product that was flocked? Needle-punched? Woven?
9. What benefits are available from modular carpet tiles? How are they made? How are they installed?
10. Which dyeing method produces the most durable color?
11. What are the unique outcomes of each individual dying method?
12. Which method of applying color can visually imitate woven patterns? What is the drawback of this imitation method of achieving pattern on carpet?
13. What method produces a random heathered effect that would be good at hiding spotting?
14. What characteristics of carpet are typically measured?
15. What are some of the different kinds of backings that you might specify?
16. What are the different carpet cushions made of and what is the strength of each? When would you specify each?
17. How would you qualify an appropriate installer for your job?
18. What are the different installation methods and when would you use each?
19. How can you specify to minimize soiling? The appearance of soiling? Visible spots from soiling on carpet?
20. What can be done to eliminate the appearance of traffic patterns on carpeting?
21. What is the difference between to-the-trade vendors and retail vendors?
22. What are the different installation methods for carpet? What methods are used on straight or curved stairs?
23. What kinds of health and safety issues pertain to carpet?
24. What characteristics of carpet and carpet installation are mandated by law?
25. How can you specify for sustainability?
26. What finishing processes might be applied to carpet?
27. What certification applies to indoor air quality?
28. What would you take into account when considering client budgets?
29. What factors can add to the cost of your installation?
30. When inspecting a completed job, what will likely be on your checklist for any carpet installation?
31. Describe the difference between custom and semi-custom rugs.
32. What do Oriental and tribal rug names signify?

33. What materials are used to make area rugs? What are the implications for cleaning them?
34. What production techniques are used to make area rugs?
35. What materials are substituted for silk in area rugs? Why?
36. What is the minimum age of an antique rug?
37. How is the Oriental market different from the other craft-tradition rugs when it comes to old rugs?
38. What are characteristics of good yarn? Good rags? Good leather (for rugs)?
39. What is the significance of knot count?
40. What are the steps in the production process that you must manage for your client's custom rug?
41. What finishing techniques apply to Oriental rugs?
42. What are indications of quality for Oriental rugs?
43. Why are repairs not necessarily a bad thing in old carpets?
44. How can you work with out-of-town rug dealers?
45. What services do dealers sometimes offer beyond sales?
46. Why might your sample for approval not demonstrate your precise pattern?
47. What are two organizations that aim to create a socially conscionable world rug market?
48. What characteristics in this product category pertain to sustainability? To safety?

Chapter 5

WOOD

Key Terms

Burls
Case goods
Distressed
Engineered wood
Figuring
Grain
Hand
Heartwood
Hollow core
Laminated
Mineral streak
Pecky
Plain-sliced
Quarter-sliced
Spalted
Veneer

Objectives

After reading this chapter, you should be able to:

- Understand why particular items are solid or veneer and what the common form is for items and surfaces that interior designers specify.
- Recognize the various characteristics of, and differences between, solid and wood veneer.
- Know how to select species and form of wood for surfaces and the implications of selecting solid or veneer.
- Understand basic fabrication processes and the way that the interior designer participates in those processes.
- Know the colorants and finishes that are most typically used for wood and when to specify them.

This chapter discusses the various characteristics of solid wood and wood veneer, its uses, and how to specify. Considerations for the differences between wood species and forms that you will specify will be discussed as well as the typical products that utilize wood and wood veneer. Fabrication processes and the way that the interior designer participates in those processes will be explained, as will the related items that factor into your selection decisions and the way you specify and manage your selections.

Wood is specified for use in interior design as solid, milled dimensional wood, as veneer, and as **engineered wood**. This chapter focuses on solid wood used for flooring, stairs, doors, millwork trims (dimensional wood components carved in a wood shop and cut to size for installation on-site), portions of **case goods**, and as veneer surfaces for case goods and interior surfacing. (Engineered wood substrates are discussed in Chapter 13, Laminated Materials.) You will be able to apply what you learn in this chapter to your furniture designs as well.

Wood contributes to sustainable design if specified properly and it sequesters CO_2, a greenhouse gas. This means that the CO_2 is bound up in the structure of the wood where it remains until the wood decomposes naturally or is burned. The tendency of trees to take in CO_2 and release oxygen is called the carbon cycle. Trees have a more efficient carbon cycle early in their lives and during periods of growth (like summer). Older trees are not as efficient as young trees at converting CO_2 to oxygen so the industry is organized to manage forests for this efficiency. It is okay to harvest old trees as long as you replace them with new trees in every instance. Preserving wood as well-maintained wooden surfaces keeps the CO_2 in the wood and not in the air.

Table 5.1
Nominal size indicates the lumber size before drying and planning to make them smooth.

Nominal	Actual	Actual
1" × 2"	¾" × 1½"	19 × 38 mm
1" × 3"	¾" × 2½"	19 × 64 mm
1" × 4"	¾" × 3½"	19 × 89 mm
1" × 5"	¾" × 4½"	19 × 114 mm
1" × 6"	¾" × 5½"	19 × 140 mm
1" × 7"	¾" × 6¼"	19 × 159 mm
1" × 8"	¾" × 7¼"	19 × 184 mm
1" × 10"	¾" × 9¼"	19 × 235 mm
1" × 12"	¾" × 11¼"	19 × 286 mm
1¼" × 4"	1" × 3½"	25 × 89 mm
1¼" × 6"	1" × 5½"	25 × 140 mm
1¼" × 8"	1" × 7¼"	25 × 184 mm
1¼" × 10"	1" × 9¼"	25 × 235 mm
1¼" × 12"	1" × 11¼"	25 × 286 mm
1½" × 4"	1¼" × 3½"	32 × 89 mm
1½" × 6"	1¼" × 5½"	32 × 140 mm
1½" × 8"	1¼" × 7¼"	32 × 184 mm
1½" × 10"	1¼" × 9¼"	32 × 235 mm
1½" × 12"	1¼" × 11¼"	32 × 286 mm
2" × 4"	1½" × 3½"	38 × 89 mm
2" × 6"	1½" × 5½"	38 × 140 mm
2" × 8"	1½" × 7¼"	38 × 184 mm
2" × 10"	1½" × 9¼"	38 × 235 mm
2" × 12"	1½" × 11¼"	38 × 286 mm
3" × 6"	2½" × 5½"	64 × 140 mm
4" × 4"	3½" × 3½"	89 × 89 mm
4" × 6"	3½" × 5½"	89 × 140 mm

SOLID WOOD

Solid wood has long been valued as a quality material in interior design and, because it is renewable, appreciation and use of wood continues. Solid wood architectural members that are properly specified and fashioned carefully into high-quality products can demonstrably last for hundreds of years if well maintained.

Material Makeup or Content

Whereas wood has characteristics that are shared by all types of wood, there is a lot of performance variety due to species and growing conditions. How the tree was cut to produce the lumber and even from where on the tree the wood was cut will affect performance. Table 5.1 shows standard lumber sizes you will need to know when you design surfaces and items made of wood.

Some species are generally harder than others but there will be variation within a single species too, because a windy environment causes the internal structure to develop differently. Conditions that slow growth produce differences in the properties of the wood harvested. If the tree was **plain-sliced** the wood will be different than if it is **quarter-sliced**. Wood taken from lower on the tree is more compact in its structure than wood taken from the upper part of the tree. **Heartwood** is stronger than sapwood. All of the above was mentioned so that you can understand that the information in this chapter is subject to nuance and variation.

You will select wood species for functional and aesthetic reasons when specifying components made of solid wood. The performance and appearance characteristics you will evaluate when making selections include the hardness, resilience, **grain**, color, ability to interact satisfactorily with the finishes, and other processes that you know will be required to meet your design program goals.

You will encounter two wood classification systems describing wood product qualities; one pertains to solid wood and the other to veneer. The classification system describing solid wood ranks wood from highest to lowest quality as Clear, Select, Number One Common, and Number Two Common. Figure 5.1a–d shows how these rankings translate to wood characteristics. Table 5.2 describes the characteristics that are acceptable for each grade. The sample images are intended to show all possible conditions and variation but in each case, you would hope to not see so much variation in such a small area. Rather, you would occasionally see a board that represents the color extremes in the images or a dark **mineral streak**, an unnatural color resulting from sap flow. Even though this is the preferred way of describing the degrees of "perfection" you may also find that Number One and Number Two are referred together as character grade.

What Would You Do? 5.1

Knowing that typical dimensional wood flooring is 2¼" × ¾", refer to the chart of nominal sizes for lumber and see if you can guess which standard size is milled into typical wood-strip flooring.

FIGURE 5.1A–D Reference standards for quality exist in several trades that you will specify to. The National Wood Flooring Association(NWFA), has established industry standards for quality distinctions between grades of wood flooring: Clear (a); Select (b); Number One Common (c); and Number Two Common (d).

Table 5.2
Comparison chart of characteristics indicating quality differences for different wood species.

Clear	Wood will be well matched for color and grain Sapwood in limited percentage Longer boards Only small (<⅛") sound knots No wormholes No mineral streaks (except minimally in maple, ash, and birch) No gum (except minimally in cherry) No bark pockets No pitch pockets
Select	Wood will have visual consistency for grain and color Sapwood limited to <10% Small (<¼") sound knots Fine, pale mineral streaks not affecting more than 25% of boards Wormholes smaller than 1/16" No bark pockets No pitch pockets
Common/ Character Grade	Wood will have most visual variation in lot of any grade Sapwood unlimited Bark pocket allowable up to ⅛" No pitch pockets allowed Sound knots up to ⅜" Mineral streaks permitted without limit

Depending on your preferences from a design and application standpoint, the lowest quality may be best for your purposes. Quality may be specified as a combination; Select and better is the most frequently specified quality.

Characteristics

Solid wood of any given species has characteristics that it shares with solid wood of any other species. To varying degrees, all solid wood will exhibit the following characteristics. Table 5.3 presents a quick comparison of wood species.

Shrinking and Swelling

Solid wood shrinks and swells in response to moisture. Even climate-controlled buildings are subject to these changes as humidity is lowered on purpose to keep condensation off of windows during cold weather. Plain-sawn boards shrink across their width, leaving gaps between boards in dry weather; quarter-sawn boards shrink in height so the floorboards may not all align in a smooth plane. If moisture is excessive, say from a leak, floors swell significantly and the boards can cup or the floor can buckle.

Shrinking and swelling happens as a percentage of area, so bigger pieces of wood will form larger cracks. When referring to this natural shrinkage, the cracks are called checking; the wood "checks" when it shrinks, as opposed to cracking. This also holds true for solid wood, patterned floors laid up in parquet blocks. The blocks behave like a bigger piece of wood and all the shrinkage within the block can be transferred to one or two gaps, making them quite large. This occasionally happens to wood plank or strip floors too; the floors "panelize," transferring shrinkage to one large gap location. Planks (boards wider than 3 inches) are more likely to develop gaps between boards or even cracks in the board face. Unless wood is maintained under perfect conditions, over time as it shrinks and swells, it will shrink a little more than it swells. That is why antique wood will be denser, finer, and harder than new wood of the same species.

Oxidation or Fading

Wood will oxidize, changing color over time; some species will change more than others. Cherry will darken noticeably over a very short time if left natural with a clear sealer (staining will lessen the appearance of change); others will bleach in the sun. This is in addition to the yellowing of some sealants or the tendency of soft wax and oil finishes to accumulate causing soiling and darkening. Wood that is covered by a rug will lighten in the area covered by the textile. This is temporary and the coloration will even out over the course of a few months after the textile is moved away.

Natural Color and Grain

Different species will have characteristic coloration as well as a tendency to exhibit visual variation in grain and color. Some woods will have a pronounced grain, like oak. Other wood will have a tight grain and more uniform texture, like maple. Some woods might be smooth to the touch but still have a pronounced visual grain because summer growth is different in color from winter growth, like fir. Wood might be naturally red in color, like mahogany, or brown, like pecan, or purple, like purpleheart, etc. Some woods will have even coloration, like beech, or wide variation, like walnut.

For the Connoisseur 5.1

Unusual wood examples are often prized by connoisseurs who will pay the higher price these woods will command on the marketplace. It is not usually the case that there is a performance-based improvement inherent in the unusual wood, and sometimes it is quite the opposite and these higher-priced woods are more difficult to work with or require special care or have longer lead times, etc. Please your connoisseur client by finding an unusual wood selection.

Figuring in Natural Grain

Trees will also succumb to influences that disturb the natural growth patterns and create unusual grain patterns in the wood that comes from that tree. These uncharacteristic grain patterns are called **figuring**. Figuring is highly prized and many figured woods are available only as veneer. These characteristics of grain, variation, and predominant color can be covered with finishes but are difficult to obliterate.

FIGURE 5.2 The grain presentation depends on how the wood was cut from the log. It is easier to understand the grain patterning on boards with this visual in mind.

Different Cuts Present Different Grain

The direction in which the wood is sliced creates variation in the appearance and performance of the wood strips. The dense, slow winter growth varies from the fast, less-dense summer growth, producing the alternating dark and light rings seen in a cross section of the wood (Figure 5.2).

Table 5.3
The different wood species.

Species (in order of general hardness)	Hardness	Grain	Color	Consider	Common Uses
Hickory	1,820 lbs	Moderately coarse, open grain	Yellow-tan-brown	Carved detail difficult	Furniture, cabinets, flooring
Maple	1,450 lbs	Fine and smooth	Yellow-pink/ creamy sapwood	Consistent color, smooth appearance, wood stains distribute unevenly	Flooring, cabinets
White oak	1,360 lbs	Fairly open, tighter than red oak	Khaki-tan-creamy	Consistent coloration	Furniture, flooring, cabinetry
White ash	1,320 lbs	Wide, open grain	Creamy-tan-brown	Similar to oak	Furniture, cabinetry, flooring
Beech	1,300 lbs	Moderately tight, fine grain	Pink-brown/ creamy sapwood	Bends well	Furniture
Red oak	1,290 lbs	Porous, coarse grain	Russet-red-tan	Plain-sliced has dramatic grain	Flooring, trim, doors
Yellow birch	1,260 lbs	Fine, smooth grain	Red-brown-pink	Some portions of grain figuring brittle	Cabinets, furniture, doors
Black walnut	1,010 lbs	Slightly open grain	Brown-purple/ creamy sapwood	Dramatic color shift, dark wood with pale sapwood	High-end furniture, laminated floors
Cherry	950 lbs	Fine, smooth grain	Russet-red	Oxidizes to dark color, wood stains distribute unevenly	Furniture, flooring
Mahogany	800 lbs	Fairly smooth, tight	Red-brown	Soaks up stain	Furniture, high-end cabinetry
Alder	590 lbs	Fine uniform, smooth	Golden-tan to brown	Easily carved	Furniture, especially with carving

FIGURE 5.3A–C The grain patterning on individual boards derives from the cuts of wood and no matter what the species, the grain characteristics will be similar within the cut category. Plain-sliced (a) will have more "cathedraling"; rift (b) will be the most linear and straight grained; and quarter-sawn (c) will also have a straight grain but will have flake running perpendicular to the grain.

Plain-Sawn Wood This wood presents more variation in the grain with some straight grain and some "flame-shaped," called cathedraling by the trade (Figure 5.3a).

Rift-Sawn Wood This wood presents a straighter grain than plain-sawn wood. Rift is the most stable cut but wastes material since it is cut with all boards radiating from the center (Figure 5.3b).

Quarter-Sawn Wood Quarter-sawn wood also has a straighter grain presentation but it is somewhat obscured by the cross-directional "flake" that is not present in rift-sawn (Figure 5.3c). Flake is a satiny marking that runs perpendicularly to the grain of the wood. This cut is nearly as stable as rift and is superior to plain-sliced.

PRODUCTS COMMONLY MADE FROM WOOD

Wood is a versatile material that is used structurally and decoratively. You will specify it in many interiors projects and will certainly use it in novel ways, but there are a number of instances where it has traditionally been employed, so you should be aware of the important considerations for these common uses of wood.

New Flooring

When people mention wood flooring generically, they typically mean ¾-inch-thick strips of solid wood that are 2¼ inches wide. Wood flooring comes in many other dimensions and in **laminated** constructions (thin layers of material bonded together) as well. Flooring that is wider than 3 inches is considered to be plank. Planks are easily available up 10 inches wide and occasionally can be wider. Planks are distinguished from wood strip by their wider width. Remember that when wood shrinks and swells as a percentage of its size this change will be more dramatic for planks.

The most common woods used for flooring are oak, walnut, pine, cherry, teak, and maple. Beyond the most common woods, your client can have virtually any kind of wood available (for a price). Specify exotic woods harvested only from sustainable plantations rather than from rain forests. Ask your vendor about sustainable forestry practices employed by the suppliers.

Wood for flooring is available as dimensional or laminated. Dimensional wood flooring typically refers to the aforementioned ¾-inch-thick strip flooring in variable widths. Dimensional wood-strip flooring can, reportedly, be sanded and refinished up to five times if carefully done.

Solid Wood Planks for Walls and Floors

Planks vary in width from 4 inches to 12 inches. They must be installed in a way that will allow them to move (expand and contract) in the installation without visually emphasizing the fact in dry weather, so details between planks and at junctions between planks and other materials should conceal movement. They might have beveled edges so that they always

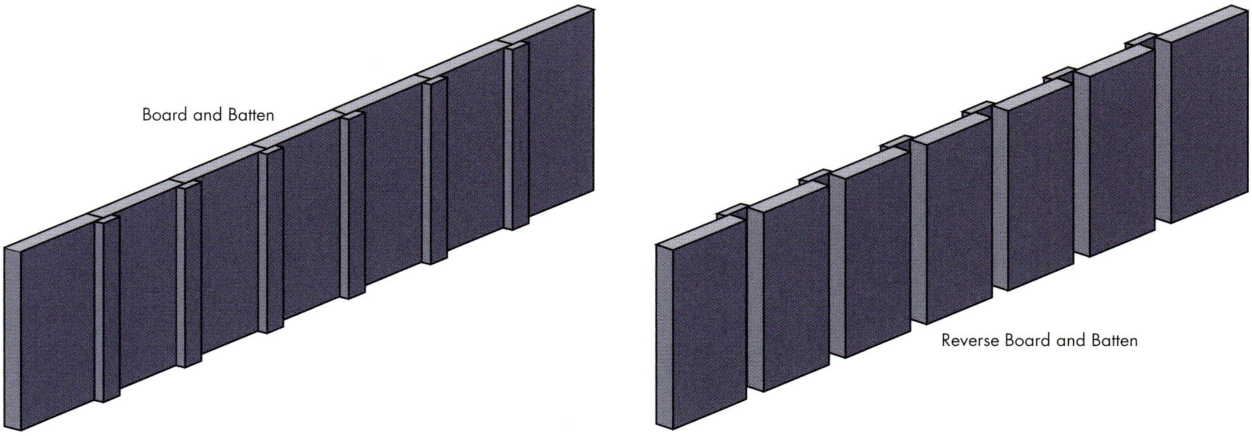

FIGURE 5.4 When you specify solid wood for large surfaces you will have to devise details that allow for expansion and contraction, like this board and batten or reverse board and batten.

present a visual gap between boards. On vertical surfaces they may be installed as a board and batten or reverse board and batten (Figure 5.4). The idea is to span the junction between the two boards so they can expand and contract.

Parquet Blocks

Parquet floors consist of shorter strips of dimensional wood-strip flooring arranged to form patterns. Standard pattern names include Brittany, Versailles, Bordeaux (shown in Figure 5.5a through c), and others.

Remember that shrinkage occurs as a percentage of the material, perhaps for the entire block if panelizing occurs.

Existing Wood Flooring

When you are working on an existing space, versus new construction, remember that the most sustainable flooring option available is likely to be the one that is already in place. There will be instances in your career when your specification pertains to an existing wood floor. Some existing wood floors that appear to be in bad shape may be easily salvageable. If the floor was previously waxed it will have to be sanded a little more aggressively to remove all traces of wax before it can be refinished with a synthetic sealer; if not, the new finish will not adhere or will blister after it cures. Sometimes, after having been waxed, a floor is unsuitable for any other finish and must continue to be waxed.

FIGURE 5.5A–C There are some generic names that you can refer to as you are planning and pricing parquet flooring. Different pattern names illustrated here are: Brittany (a), Versailles (b), and Bordeaux (c). *Images courtesy of Birger Juell, Ltd., Chicago, IL.*

> **Helpful Hint 5.1**
>
> When refinishing existing wood floors that have shrunk, it is tempting to fill gaps that have opened up. This is a mistake because the movement of wood, and expansion during warmer weather, will cause the filler to break, leaving what is often a jagged edge as the problem reappears. This jagged edge will be more eye-catching (in a bad way) than a nice straight line.

If damage or staining is severe in isolated areas and cannot be removed or covered up with new colorants and sealants, you may have to piece in new floorboards. It is sometimes difficult to achieve a good match. One option is to cannibalize a hidden area, such as a closet or secondary space, for wood to use in patching a prominent place. A closely matching wood would then be installed in the hidden space. If this is not possible, various processes could be selectively applied to new boards prior to staining and finishing by an experienced floor finisher.

> **Helpful Hint 5.2**
>
> Older floors that have shrunk a little will have a finer appearance than new wood. Thus, even if the original floor is plain-sliced, you may want to upgrade the new material to rift-sawn, which has a quieter grain so will blend better with the older floor.

Aside from design issues and matters of personal preferences, you should consider the following:

- The soundness of the floor: Is it generally secure, tight, and not squeaky, splintered, or damaged in too many places?
- The amount of damage: Is damage confined to the surface? If so, could it be sanded off? Could a limited number of boards be replaced if staining goes too deep? Can replacement boards needed for patching be taken from a closet or other isolated area so that a match in color and age can be made where original and replacement boards will be side-by-side? Has the cause of the damage been corrected (especially water damage)?
- The degree of staining: Could stains be camouflaged with a dark stain color in order to avoid having to rip up the floor?
- The remaining thickness of the floor: Is thickness sufficient to permit resurfacing and finishing? (Keep in mind that each sanding of the floor removes the top layer of wood, eventually weakening the strength of the top of the groove in a tongue-and-groove floor, as shown in Figure 5.6.)

Flooring Accessories

Part of your specification for wood flooring may include wooden vent covers or metal vent covers (that the painter may spray to match floor color), and transition strips between wood and other flooring materials. Ideally the two adjacent flooring surfaces will be flush when the installation is complete. Even when a flush condition can be created, the flush transition strip is still specified to lay across the ends of boards to cover the end grain there. The transition strip is not required if the adjacent material meets the side of the board instead of the end. When new wood floors are installed the shoe/quarter round is typically replaced as well.

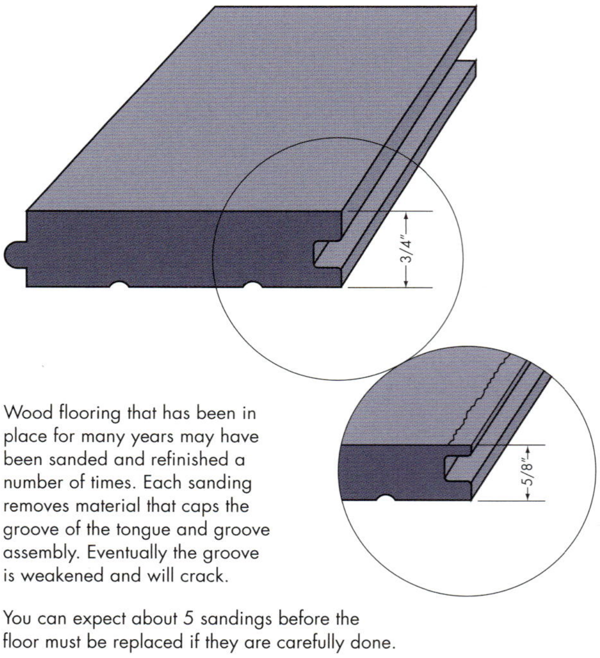
3/4"
5/8"
Wood flooring that has been in place for many years may have been sanded and refinished a number of times. Each sanding removes material that caps the groove of the tongue and groove assembly. Eventually the groove is weakened and will crack.
You can expect about 5 sandings before the floor must be replaced if they are carefully done.

FIGURE 5.6 A dimensional wood floor can be refinished three to five times with careful sanding but eventually the groove will be worn away to the point that it will split, revealing the tongue and fasteners.

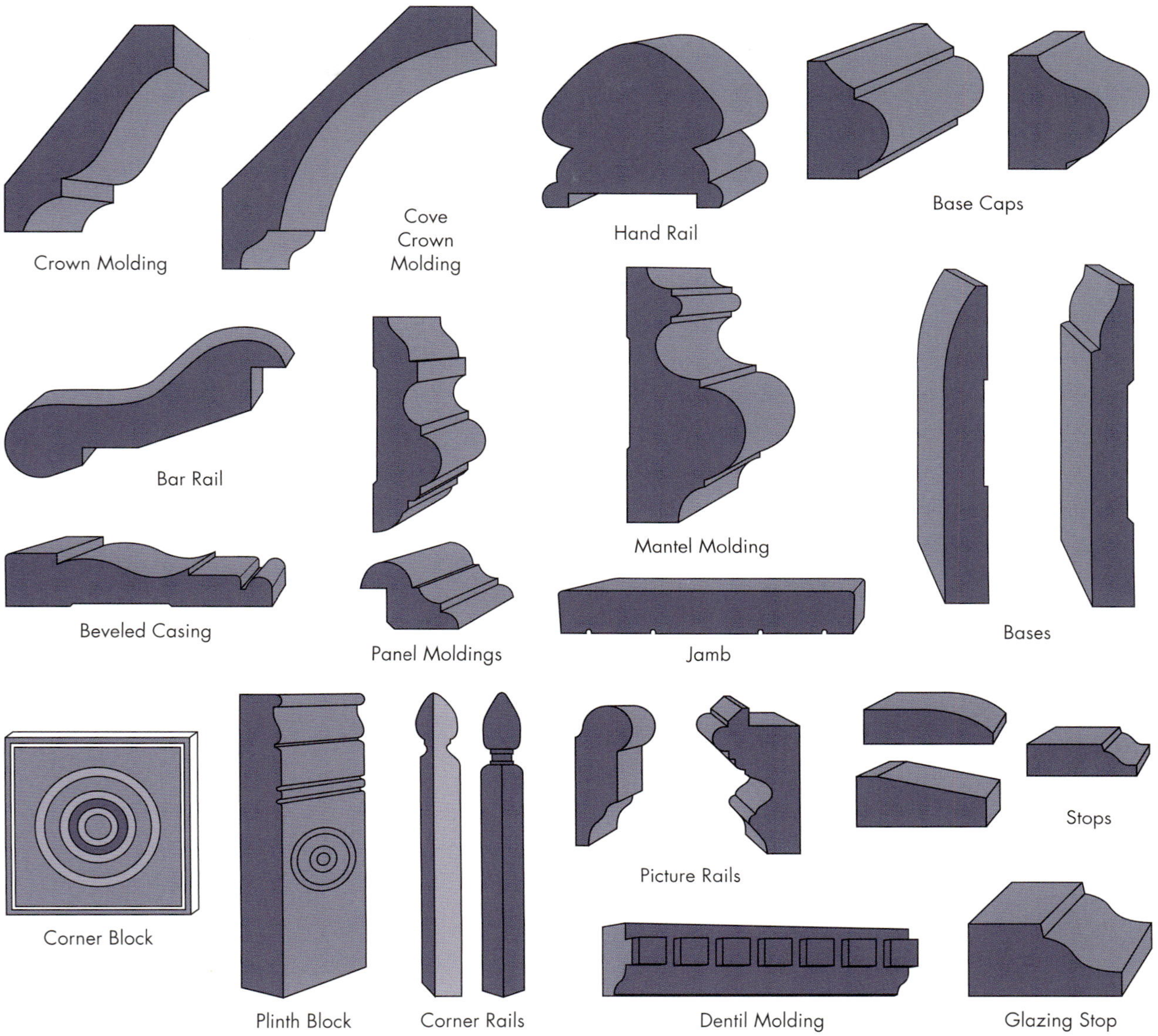

FIGURE 5.7 Traditional uses of these profiles give them their names, but you will use them where the profile suits your needs. *Images compiled by Ferche Millwork, Rice, MN.*

Architectural Trims

Architectural millwork generally conceals the junction between two materials or the transition between two planes. These are areas that could be expected to open up because of settling, that present cut lumber edges from construction, or that have some other feature that you would like to span or hide. You would span the distance between the jamb around a window or door and the wall surface next to it. You will hide the junction between the wall and the ceiling. While these instances could be considered to be functional as well as decorative, millwork trim is unabashedly used simply to decorate. It affects the visual proportion of space and articulates areas that might otherwise be too austere.

The various profiles originate in a specific function, but you may certainly employ them for any use that is suitable, whether functional or simply aesthetic (Figure 5.7).

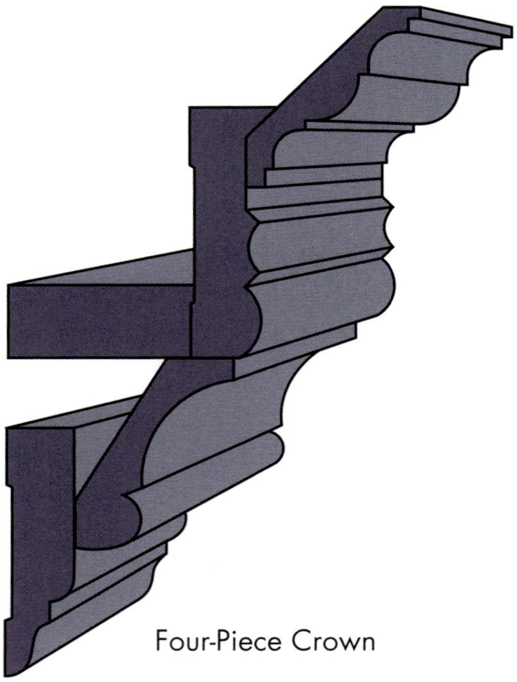

FIGURE 5.8 This four-piece crown is composed of a cove crown molding at the top, followed by a casing, followed by another cove crown molding finished at the bottom with a piece of upside-down base. *Image courtesy of Ferche Millwork, Rice, MN.*

- *Crown molding* spans the distance between the ceiling and the wall at an angle. It is not required that this trim project at an angle, but if it does it is indisputably crown.
- Similar to crown molding is *cove molding*, unique because of the concave section arcing outward.
- *Baseboards* create a transition between the wall and floor. *Base caps* extend the baseboards with an extra detail.
- *Bar rails* are the elbow rest at the edge of a bar.
- *Casings* trim the edges of openings like windows and doors.
- *Panel molds* are flat-backed profiles originally intended to conceal shrinkage between large panel sections.
- *Mantel moldings* are muscular moldings that frame the noncombustible surrounds of transitional and modern fireplaces.
- *Handrails* perform the obvious function of capping the railing.
- *Jambs* cover the many structural framing members in doorways with a single piece.
- *Corner blocks* provide a casing transition from vertical to horizontal.
- *Plinth blocks* terminate the casing at the floor creating a transition between casing and base.
- *Corner rails* protect out-corners.
- *Picture rail* is installed below the crown line (or below the ceiling if there is no crown). It was intended originally to avoid having to poke holes in plaster walls (and risk damaging the keys that hold the plaster on) to hang artwork. Art was instead hung from wire or cord hooked into the top of the picture rail.
- A *dentil* is a shamelessly decorative piece whose only function is to jazz things up a bit.
- A *stop*, as its name implies, is a narrow strip of wood that stops the door from swinging past center.
- *Glazing stops* hold glass and window screens in place on wooden frames.

All of the above are used in combinations to suit the needs of your job. Figure 5.8 shows casing, base, and coves combined to make an elaborate crown molding.

We have come to expect that these moldings are made of wood because that is the material historically used. Fine carved wood moldings may be imitated in resin and composition moldings that are at least, in part, medium density fiberboard. These may be combined with solid wood for trims that will be painted, because after painting, the fact that they are not solid wood is undetectable. Figure 5.9a–c shows a component that appears to be an elaborate architectural trim fashioned from wood but is in fact a pliable polymer foam, easily bent, to create a detail that would have been very expensive to carve from wood. The available profiles in such materials are limited, so select this material first if you intend to combine such a profile with solid wood used on straight runs. It is much easier to match the wood profile to the polymer than vice versa. In addition to pliable polymer options, composition material, usually shortened to *compo*, is made of sawdust and polymer and is easily formed into shapes that resemble intricately carved items that can be stained and finished like wood.

Reasons for switching to a nonwood option include price and labor-saving (which also boils down to price). For example: Primed MDF baseboard is a lower cost option than poplar base. It also saves on priming labor (but does not come pre-sanded, so that step in prepwork

B

FIGURE 5.9A–C You may supplement your solid wood trim installations with synthetic moldings likes this flexible crown that can be bent smoothly into curves or this composition appliqué that imitates carved wood but is a molded product of resin and sawdust. *Trim by White River, Fayetteville, AR.*

must still be budgeted). Flexible synthetic molding is specified for trimming arches and other circular forms. Special items like domes, niche shells, mantels, and other items imitating carved wood, produced at a lower cost, are also available. Companies that sell millwork trim will frequently also sell these and other decorative elements such as plaster ceiling medallions, and fireplace mantels (Figure 5.10a and b).

Designers are most often the project team member responsible for selecting the architectural millwork trim sizes and profiles. You will communicate your selection in specs and drawings and may forward your selections to the architect for inclusion into his or her material schedules if the team is collaborating on one document set, or forward them in your own material

FIGURE 5.10A–B If your architectural trim is to be painted you can avoid the expense of custom wood carving with cast synthetic pieces. Because molds have to be made, such pieces will not offer the flexibility of design available from carved wood so select these items first and then select the wood items that accompany them because you will have more options among wood choices. *Products for detailing by White River, Fayetteville, AR.*

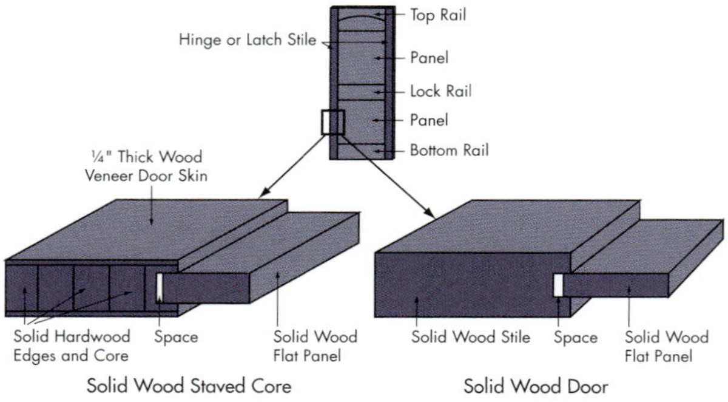

FIGURE 5.11 Doors may be made out of solid wood or they may have a staved core. Because wood expands and contracts, this panel in a panel door is "loose" in the joint. The space allows it to move as humidity changes without binding.

schedules. The exact sizes and profiles will be shown on your elevations, but if you have any compound moldings (such as the four-piece molding mentioned above), a dimensioned detail drawing should be included with your drawing set.

Doors

Doors may be solid wood or may be a combination of solid and veneer over an engineered core (more information about core materials will be in Chapter 13, Laminated Materials). Solid planks jointed together to form broad surfaces will have the vulnerability to checking and cracking for which solid wood is known. This is more of a problem for the exterior doors you will specify than for the interior doors. That is why exterior wood doors are typically an engineered base material covered with a thick (thicker than for interior doors) veneer skin. See Figure 5.11 for a diagram of door construction. Even if the aesthetics called for a plank door you might want to locate or design the look of a plank door that employs an engineered core for a stable substrate. A door with heavy allover carving may have to be solid wood planks.

Below are some of the characteristics of these solid doors.

- Better quality doors with curved pieces (oval or round windows in door, for instance) have raised molding ringing the curved cutout.
- The molding will often be in several pieces. This is an indication of better quality as the wood is oriented in the direction of greatest strength to prevent cracking.

FIGURE 5.12 You can imagine that if this junction between the panel and the rail were painted that the paint would crack and need a touch-up every few years. *Photograph by Alana Clark.*

- Solid wood doors are fairly good insulators and sound-blockers. Both of these inherent characteristics of wood are affected by the fit of the door and the condition of any weather stripping. Solid doors can be trimmed or shaved to fit if necessary.
- Solid wood construction (therefore vulnerable to shrinkage and swelling with changes in humidity).
- In some doors the center panel is constructed of planks (as described above). Because the panel is loose at the edges, any shrinkage is transferred there and should not crack the center panel (Figure 5.12).
- If the door is painted, seasonal shrinking and swelling is likely to crack the paint at the junctions.

Solid wood doors with the framework exposed consist of a top rail, lock rail, and bottom rail, with possible intermediate rails (mortise and tenon joint or doweled construction is typical). Occasionally the door will be glued in addition to jointed. The panels are typically loose to allow for expansion and contraction. High-quality exterior doors may have a split panel, which allows the interior and exterior faces to expand and contract independently of one another. For interior doors, the center panel may be louvers. If the center panel is solid (not louvers) the door will block sound well. Acoustic isolation can be improved further if the door is fitted with weather stripping.

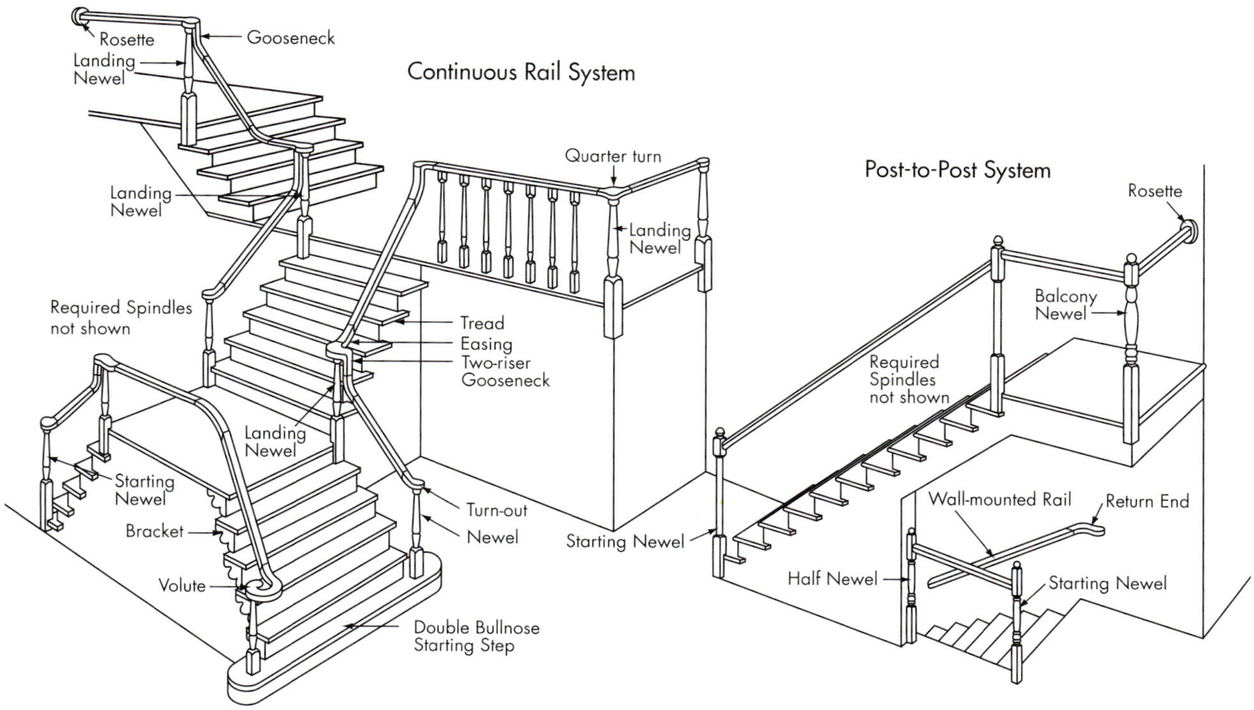

FIGURE 5.13 Stairs have many parts that you will want to be able to identify by name in your specs and on the job site.

Staircases

Staircases typically serve a sculptural function as well as a practical one and the aesthetics of a prominent staircase dominate the design of many environments, even as the elevator has become the primary means of conveyance between floors (Figure 5.13). Although many materials are employed to form them, solid wood often takes shape to create parts of stairs. Treads may be a single piece of solid wood but may also be composed of individual pieces, like a floor if you need to save money. Remember that the nosing must still be a bull-nosed piece of wood. Spindles, handrails, and newel posts are often turned and milled to form the parts assembled into a staircase.

FABRICATION

It will not come as a surprise to anyone that all the different wood items mentioned above are milled from trees into standard lumber sizes and then dried.

Wood must be dried because living trees are constantly transporting moisture and nutrients throughout their structure as part of their life processes. They will be variably moist at different times but will almost always hold more moisture than the air in buildings. If the lumber were not dried before being shaped, it would warp and shrink after installation in buildings, and stair spindles and door panels would become loose and wood floorboards would have side gaps between them. Wood is ideally kiln or air dried to the approximate moisture content for location of its final environment. If it is dried below that range, it will likely acquire the moisture out of the air anyway but wood should always be dried at least to ambient moisture, if not drier. An ideal moisture content for Las Vegas will be lower (at approximately 8 percent) than for Charleston (at about 14 percent). Because wood is rough-sawn to size then dried (which shrinks it because water volume is removed) and then planed smooth (which shrinks it again because material is removed), it is not the stated size; a two-by-four is not 2" × 4"; it is approximately 1½" × 3½". As you are designing custom wood products and their installation, you will want to account for the actual size and not the nominal size (the size by which wood is sold) of materials in your details and dimensions. Table 5.1

FIGURE 5.14 Dimensional wood floors have tongue-and-groove edges on two or four sides that allow for expansion and contraction without creating gaps clear through at their sides. This detail is used during installation to hide the nails that fasten the floors in place.

under Material Makeup or Content shows approximate sizes of the nominal lumber sizes. You will save money by designing your custom-milled parts out of standard sizes; even though nonstandard sizes can be accommodated by your custom mill, it will usually involve material waste and higher costs.

> **Helpful Hint 5.3**
>
> When you rely on specification guides for solid wood products that were prepared in other regions, the stipulated moisture content will be one of many things you adjust so that the moisture content of the wood is the average for air annually in your area.

Floors

Wood for floorboards are usually milled with tongue-and-groove edges on the two long sides and sometimes also on the ends of the boards. Figure 5.14 shows the tongue and groove in profile. The boards are successively nailed through the tongue into the substrate to secure them in place and the groove of the following board conceals the nail.

> **What Would You Do? 5.2**
>
> What grade would you specify if your client wanted an office in the character of the Oval Office at the White House? What would you specify for a "dressy-casual" clothing boutique? Your own family room? A ski lodge?

Traditionally floorboards were installed, sanded, stained, sealed, and finished on-site, and this process is still common today but, increasingly, floorboards are factory finished. Some durable sealant for floors cannot be applied in the field but even formulas used for field-finished floors can be applied in the factory. There are some benefits to factory finish even if the field finishes are applied there:

- More control over the application, temperature, and cleanliness of the area so ideal conditions can be maintained and there will be less likelihood that dust or other foreign matter ends up in the finish.
- The sides of the boards can be more easily stained so when they shrink a little in winter (which they will) the unstained sides do not show.
- Finishes that cannot be successfully applied in the field can be used.
- There will be less dust and fewer fumes if floors are not sanded, stained, and sealed on-site.
- Installation is quicker.

Architectural Wood Trims

Three-dimensional wood forms, like the moldings and casings that designers specify, are mechanically carved, sometimes in multiple steps, or passes through various cutting machines. These machines are equipped with knives that resemble keys for a door lock (Figure 5.15). They are spun at high velocity as a piece of wood is passed beneath them and they gradually chip away a

FIGURE 5.15 When you require a custom profile to match existing details or to suit your discerning client, you will have a custom knife cut to mill the profile. The shop will retain this knife in their collection. You may find that they have a knife that is close enough to the profile you need. This image shows knives that would be put on a rotating base, like a drill, and would be used to wear away a shaped profile.

profile that is the negative of their own shape. Wood shops usually have a variety of profiles on hand.

Custom profiles can be milled in wood for small orders because the cost of cutting a knife is small. When a custom profile is needed you may need to add a few hundred dollars to the budget for the knife, which is a small enough percentage for many jobs. A custom knife pays for itself, when matching existing profiles that are to remain, by avoiding the need to remove and destroy existing molding throughout to achieve a match.

Doors

Your door specification could be simplified by ordering a manufacturer's stock door if you do not have to match existing doors and do not require custom for any other reason. Standard door sizes are as follows:

- Width: 2', 2'4", 2'6", 2'8", 3', 3'4", 3'6", 3'8", and 4'
- Height: 6'8", 7', 7'2", 7'10", and 8'
- Thickness: 1³⁄₈" (typical for residential), 1³⁄₄" (typical for commercial), and 2"

Solid wood doors are assembled from solid wood or they have a staved core (pieces of wood assembled similarly to a butcher block countertop) with a thick veneer of wood that is the door skin. Staved core doors are typically used as exterior doors. Parts of a staved core door are likely to be solid wood as well. Solid wood interior doors will very likely be entirely solid wood, rail- and panel-style doors that can be easily made to your specifications by even small millworking shops. As with custom architectural trim, you may have to pay the charge for custom knives to produce specific profiles. The construction of standard, stock doors follows the same process as for custom doors; for this reason it is easy for some manufacturers to offer custom sizes of their stock door styles.

Loose-leaf, or slab, doors arrive as the door only. They can be ordered with hinges attached so the carpenter does not have to work on-site to mortise the hinges into the door, just into the frame. When ordering special hinges for loose-leaf doors, order the following number of hinges per door:

- 3 hinges for a standard interior door under 7'
- 4 hinges for 7' to 12' doors
- 5 hinges for 12' to 15' doors
- 6 hinges for taller doors

The general rule for positioning hinges is to place the top of the top hinge 5 to 7 inches below the top of the door and the bottom of the bottom hinge 10 or 11 inches above the floor, with equal spacing in between. The weight, as well as the height of the door, will also influence the number of hinges required. For instance a standard interior oak door could weigh about 7 pounds per square foot, whereas a hollow-core door is only 2 pounds per square foot. If a mirror will be affixed to the door, add 3.28 pounds per square foot and account for the additional thickness when selecting hardware.

Prehung versus Loose-Leaf Doors

Many doors that you will specify for new construction will be prehung. Both standard and custom doors can be installed prehung or loose leaf. The prehung door arrives in its jamb and will be set into the door bucks the rough carpenter has built to size. It may even have trim attached to one side; more frequently, however, the doors are trimmed out on-site.

Stairs

Wooden staircases may be solid wood or a combination of engineered wood substrates covered with a thick (¼ inch or more) wood veneer with spindles, handrails, and posts being solid wood. The risers and treads are supported by a stringer. This stringer may be open or closed; see Figure 5.16 for a simple illustration of the

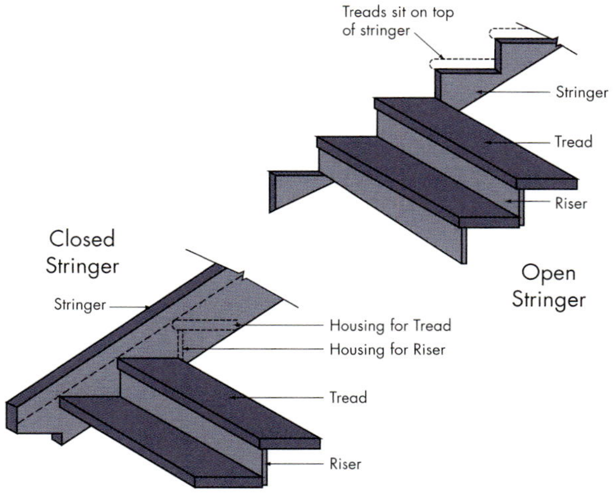

FIGURE 5.16 Open stringers, with their sawtooth shape, are less expensive than closed stringers because there is less labor involved. Closed stringers result in a more graceful form for freestanding staircases but are functionally equal to open stringers from a structural standpoint.

FIGURE 5.17 Special processes, like the hand-scraping shown here, add steps to your process (so extra time and money) but the versatility of wood to accept many kinds of processes allows you a lot of design flexibility.

difference. These flat-milled pieces may be solid or engineered wood. Turned spindles and newel posts will be cut with knives, as would the handrail if that is also solid wood.

FINISHING PROCESSES

The finishing of wood includes processes applied to the bare wood. It begins with the final sanding and includes creating the surface texture, whether smooth or **distressed** (texture that gives a timeworn look), applying the colorants, and sealing. These processes may all occur in the field after installation or in the factory or custom shop.

Special Processes

Special processes include imparting textures or adjusting the wood tone before coloring. Adjusting the color before staining may involve special chemicals like bleaching. Examples of special textures would be beveling edges, distressing, wire-brushing and hand-scraping the surface. The hand-scraped floor in Figure 5.17 imitates antique floors. Before mechanical sanders, floors were scraped by hand, leaving an undulating surface. This floor also has a beveled edge, which will minimize the apparent shrinkage that will occur during dry weather.

Colorants

Stains are used to color wood without greatly obscuring the grain. If a very dark color is desired, the item may be double-stained by applying the second coat while the first is still wet. The first coat opens up the pores allowing more stain to soak in. Wetting the wood with water will also open the grain allowing it to drink in more color.

If the finished color for a floor will vary significantly from the natural color of the wood, it is a good idea to stain the sides of the boards prior to installation. Then, when the boards shrink in dry weather, the contrast will not be so visible. If the wood species is more variable in coloration than your client would like, you might request that the job be bid as stained and then sealed with one coat of a tinted sealer and two coats of clear sealer.

Some acidic formulas alter the color of wood through a chemical reaction rather than by depositing a pigment. Other chemical formulas are used to imitate the patina of aged wood when only a portion of an installation must be refinished. Where this kind of finish is desired, the job should be awarded to a shop with a lot of experience in this kind of work.

Paint can be used as an opaque color or a translucent wash. If you are painting wood flooring, use paint specified as floor paint and seal the paint under a durable clear sealer coat.

Although bleach is more of an *un*colorant than a colorant, it can be used to alter the color of wood. In the process of removing color, bleach weakens the wood fibers. For this reason the process should be performed only once. Samples can be made on boards assembled for this purpose, but if you are bleaching installed material, test patches should be made in inconspicuous places. Bleach samples will not be as easily removable as stain samples.

Bleaching will lighten, but not remove, the inherent color of the wood, turning red oak pink, for example. If you require a very pale finish specify a wash in addition to bleaching.

Finishes and Sealants

Finishes and sealants are, essentially, a resin, a binder, and a vehicle. Categorized by formula, sealants have different characteristics summarized in Table 5.4. Generally speaking, sealants and finishes that dry as their vehicle evaporates are less durable than finishes that cure. Their inherent characteristics are often enhanced by additives

Table 5.4
Finishes applied to wood.

Finishes for Solid Wood	Characteristics
Polyurethane	Solvent-based; easy to apply; plastic finish; nonflexible; ambers with age
Water-based urethane	Resin, easy to apply; nonflexible; does not amber with age
Moisture-cure urethane	Very durable; very moisture resistant; some formulas yellow with age; odorous; difficult to apply
Acid-cure	Does not amber; difficult to apply; odorous until cured
Penetrating sealer	Soaks into the wood so offers little surface protection; topical sealer of the same formula or wax should be used with it
Tung oil	Penetrating sealer that imparts color or may be applied over a stain; buffing after applying creates a surface sealer; soft but repairable finish
Wax	Solvent-based surface sealer; may be applied over stain; buffing after applying wax forms a surface seal that is soft but repairable; often applied on top of other finishes as sacrificial sealer
Lacquer	Soft finish used only where abrasion resistance and durability are not required, such as for furniture or paneling
UV-cured	Resin; cured by ultraviolet light; factory applied; prefinished only
Acrylic-impregnated	Wood is soaked in acrylic resin; hard, durable; factory applied; prefinished only
Aluminum oxide	Very hard; abrasion resistant; factory applied; prefinished only

that improve UV protection, and provide slip resistance and other benefits in proprietary (manufacturers' secret) formulations. Sealants are available in several gloss levels described as a *percent sheen*. For example, a satin finish is described as a 35 percent sheen.

> **Point of Emphasis 5.1**
> Remember that solid wood shrinks and swells a percentage of its size in response to moisture in the air. Thin or slender items like the ¼" veneer of a door skin or a spindle can be successfully painted. Larger sizes of solid wood will not be as stable. Wide panels of panel doors, for instance, will need to "move" so painting doors that are truly solid wood (vs. staved core solid wood) may eventually show breaks in the painted finish at the junction between the panel and rail.

When it is your intention to paint wooden products at your client's site, remember that stock items produced in standard sizes can be specified unfinished or they may be primed for paint.

QUALIFYING INSTALLERS AND SUPPLIERS

If the wooden items that you select are stock items that are ordered by the general contractor or the client from lumber yards, they will be installed by carpenters hired separately for that work. If they are custom-made by a shop that is local to the client site, they may be installed by the fabricator, especially if they are part of a complex construction like stairs. Let's take a look at each point in the production of your wooden items where you must make a quality determination before finalizing your selection and hiring the work. They include:

- The manufacturer of standard-size stock items purchased from lumberyards
- Custom fabricators who only fabricate
- Custom fabricators who also install
- Carpenters hired independently to perform the installation of stock or custom items

Manufacturers

Stock items will be evaluated as people resources versus product characteristics, to the extent that you are verifying conscionable production from environmental and social standpoints. This is because it is the product quality that is of interest here. Review the specifications and make sure that the offerings meet your criteria for price, quality, material, finish (if applicable, many products are for site finish), and accessory parts. All the solid wood items covered in this chapter are available as stock items from distant manufacturers who will ship to the site for installation by others. Even staircases can be ordered from a catalog from a distant supplier by the general contractor and installed by local trades without requiring the designer to interact with the custom fabricator (although more frequently you will collaborate with custom fabricators for stairs). Review specifications for the manufacturer for wood species, grade, hardness, and preparation (drying process, milling practices, sustainable production, etc.).

Request to see samples. Sometimes you will only be able to see product in installations and other times there will be a rep within reasonable driving distance or examples can be sent to your studio.

Custom Fabricators

Your order for custom doors or custom architectural millwork trims may be delivered to the site and installed by finishing carpenters. The custom fabricators for these items may be local or they could be far away and ship your material via an over-road hauler. Shop drawings detailing the joinery, and finish samples for quality of the woodworking as well as the finish, may be sent for your approval. Fabricators working from a distance may not install, in which case you would hire local carpenters to install.

> **Point of Emphasis 5.2**
> Over-road haulers are also called common-carrier shippers. They are transportation for hire, moving items across state lines. They typically pick up and deliver to warehouses but will come to your job site with a delivery as long as there is access and someone to receive and off-load the order; they themselves do not unload. If there will be a responsible party (someone willing to take responsibility for inspecting the material) on-site when the truck shows up (not usually something that can be precisely scheduled in advance) and an appropriate, secure place to store the material, the common carrier will ship to the job site. If the material should not go to the job site for some reason, the common carrier could also deliver to a local warehouse that has a delivery service that can then take it to the site at a scheduled time.

Custom Fabricators Who Install

Some fabricators are very hands-on. For instance, it is common for custom floors and stairs to be ordered from local fabricators who will also install the product. Custom stair fabricators consult actively on the design of the stairs, making suggestions for details and components. Even if you select the component parts from the custom fabricator's selected offerings for spindles, handrails, and newel posts, these stairs are still a custom product and you will likely be requested to sign off on shop drawings that the fabricator will produce before proceeding with the work. In this instance of a local fabricator/installer, you will be qualifying the fabricator as well as the product. Evaluate their previous experience to determine if it is a match to your current job needs. Review evidence of their previous work in the form of pictures and references.

Many of these tradespeople will have learned on the job, either with or without a formalized training structure of apprentice to journeyman to master progression as skill level increases. You will usually accept the trades that have been hired by the fabrication company rather than qualifying the tradespeople individually; it is the company that you are hiring and the company is responsible for your satisfaction regardless of who is on the shop floor or job site.

Carpenters

The on-site carpenters who install product provided by others may have learned their trade on the job or in technical schools. They are likely to be independent subcontractors, hired by the general contractor. It is the general contractor who is responsible for their work. It may be the case that you have no control or responsibility for the quality of this crew and will trust that the general contractor has selected a carpentry firm to provide the finish (sometimes called finishing) carpenters qualified to install the products specified. The distinction may be made between rough carpenters, who install the studs for partitions, and the finishing carpenters who install doors and trims, but often you will see the same carpenters doing both levels of work.

INSTALLATION

It may not surprise you to hear that each of these products made from wood are installed differently from each other and by different trades.

Floors

Installation of dimensional and laminate flooring requires attention to pattern, color, and finish, among other details. The underlayment is also important since solid wood floors are usually nailed in and the subfloor must accept nails. Plywood is a typical substrate, installed before the solid wood flooring (or laminate flooring) that will be stapled or nailed in place.

If you are installing a simple wood strip or plank floor you can probably convey enough information in a written specification to order the installation. For a patterned floor or floor incorporating two materials, it will probably be a very good idea to draw a to-scale plan of the area showing not just the pattern, but how it will be located in the space and noting the significant alignments and relationships to the architecture. A full-scale sample of the pattern with the finish as specified should be provided for approval of a custom floor.

Often a custom color is mixed on-site and applied directly to the sanded floor. While the stain sample is still wet, it is a fairly good representation of the sealed color but once it has dried it cannot be referenced as a finish color unless wetted down with mineral spirits. All floor samples made on-site will be sanded off the floor before final staining takes place.

Helpful Hint 5.4

When you are working with a high-priced flooring contractor, you will have more amenities of service than with a low-priced contractor. They will make samples in advance and ship them to your office, prepare shop drawings, and perform other ancillary tasks that all clients want but not all can pay for. When a low-bidding shop has been selected it may fall on you to produce all the documentation. One example is in the finish sample for client records. There have been many times that I have had to stop by the construction Dumpster on my way to a floor finish meeting and grab some scrap board from the installation of the floor to bring to the meeting. When the final color has been approved I hand it to the contractor to put a sample of the approved stain on it. This sample is wet for hours afterward so I put it on a piece of paper in the trunk of my car. I have a can of clear sealer that I spray on after the stain dries so I have a record of the approved color. It is obviously not the sheen specified but I can confirm the color and refer to it as I make color selections in the office for fabric and furniture.

Inspect the flooring prior to staining and sealing and again when complete, but before it is covered, to protect it from other tradespeople working on the site. If the flooring installation is taking place at a point in the process when other trades are still working in the area, one coat of finish (perhaps gloss, regardless of your spec for sheen level) will be applied to the floors, which are then covered until the other trades move out of the area; then the flooring contractor will come back for the final coat or two.

All the above steps for installing site-finished floors, except for installation itself, will take place in the shop for the prefinished floors that you specify. Other steps or processes that may be performed on shop-finished floors include beveling, hand scraping, and wire brushing.

Architectural Millwork Trims

Molding and casing trims will be milled off-site but cut to fit and nailed in place by the finishing carpenters. Even though this work takes place when the space is nearly finished (often the next stage of production is the painting labor), saws will be set up in the area where the installation is occurring, frequently on top of the newly installed flooring. As you visit the job site for your weekly meetings, confirm that all protections are in place.

Point of Emphasis 5.3

You may feel that it is the contactor's responsibility to confirm that all installed materials are properly protected and that protection remains in place as long as needed. A more accurate stance is that it is as much your responsibility to police the protection of these surfaces as it is the responsibility of any other authority on the job site.

Construction crews will sometimes be so focused on their own task that the rest of the site is simply their work area. I have seen carpenters, handling punch list items after client move-in, set their toolboxes on antique furniture! When rosin paper protecting floors is ripped, gritty dirt can work its way underneath and scratch floors. Often contractors will put down two of three coats of finish specified in the event that there is some slight damage from an instance like this. Even though more finish will be applied, a deeper scratch from construction traffic may still be visible after the floor is coated for the third time. Whenever you see this kind of opportunity for damage, call it to the general contractor's attention and request that it be protected. Recoated floors should not have furniture placed on them for at least a couple of weeks and this could really disrupt the furniture delivery schedule.

Inspect millwork installations by confirming that the out-corners of the moldings and baseboards are miter cut, and the in-corners are coped. Right angles should be mitered. The nails will be pounded in just so far then a nail set (metal peg with an end only as big as the head of the finishing nails) will be used to tap the nail head below the surface. The small hole left by this operation will be filled with wood putty, leaving trims ready for finishing by others.

Doors

Prehung doors are slipped into the door bucks, built by rough carpenters, and shimmed to level them. The shims are nailed in place along with the door jamb and the nails set below the surface with the nail set, then they are puttied. Some time may pass before the casing is fastened in a separate operation.

Loose-leaf doors (slab doors) are installed into completed, site-built jambs. Typically, their hinges are mortised in and attached to the door and jambs by the carpenters on the site. They may also drill for cylinder locksets if this work was not done at the fabricators where the doors were made.

Stairs

The stairs are a precise system of component parts that arrive at the job site, unfinished or finished up to final coat. Most of the required pieces will already be cut to fit with just minor adjusting to be done on-site before the final coat of finish is applied.

PROTECTION AND MAINTENANCE

All wooden parts and surfaces need to be protected from other trades after they have been installed. Even hard dense wood can be dinged if other materials are moved carelessly through the area and surfaces can be scratched whether they have their final finish on or not.

Floors

Floors are especially vulnerable if people are still working in the area. If traffic is foot traffic only, perhaps rosin paper is sufficient. If wheeled traffic (such as hand trucks) is still present or sawhorses in use, you may prefer to see Masonite in those areas.

After client acceptance, regular cleaning maintenance will depend on the finish selected; most finishes can be damp mopped (mop wrung nearly dry) with or without any kind of soap. While it is recommended by some vendors that waxed floors are never damp mopped, if carefully done with a mop that has been wrung out very well, damp moping will get floors cleaner than dry mopping.

After some period of use, floors will require more maintenance than simply sweeping and mopping. Floors that are in good condition but have a finish that is hazy with numerous surface scratches can be screened, that is, buffed with a buffer fitted with a sanding screen instead of sandpaper to deep clean and roughen the floor for recoating, rather than refinishing. A sanding disk that looks like nylon window screening is used to remove only the very top layer of finish without breaking through to bare wood. The floors are then top-coated using the same formulation as the original sealant. Prefinished boards and flooring with a veneer or laminated flooring can sometimes be resurfaced this way as long as the formula for the original finish is known. Architectural trim, doors, and stairs will be kept clean in a manner similar to flooring maintenance and may, at some point, also require recoating.

SAFETY

There are codes and guidelines pertaining to these solid wood items and surfaces. Fire safety is a consideration because wood is, obviously, flammable. Different jurisdictions may have varying stipulations, and requirements for different occupancies will vary within those jurisdictions. Frequently it is required that wood either be limited in quantity to a maximum percentage of surface area of the total project or that it be chemically treated. If your designs exceed local surface maximums, you may chemically treat wood for flame resistance. Research and carefully compare chemicals and retain the material safety data sheet for your selection.

Slip resistance is required on all commercial floors and is sensible for environments with active children or elderly users. If you are not sure your combination of wood species and sheen level will provide a safe slip resistance, then you may want to look into special sealants that increase traction on the surface.

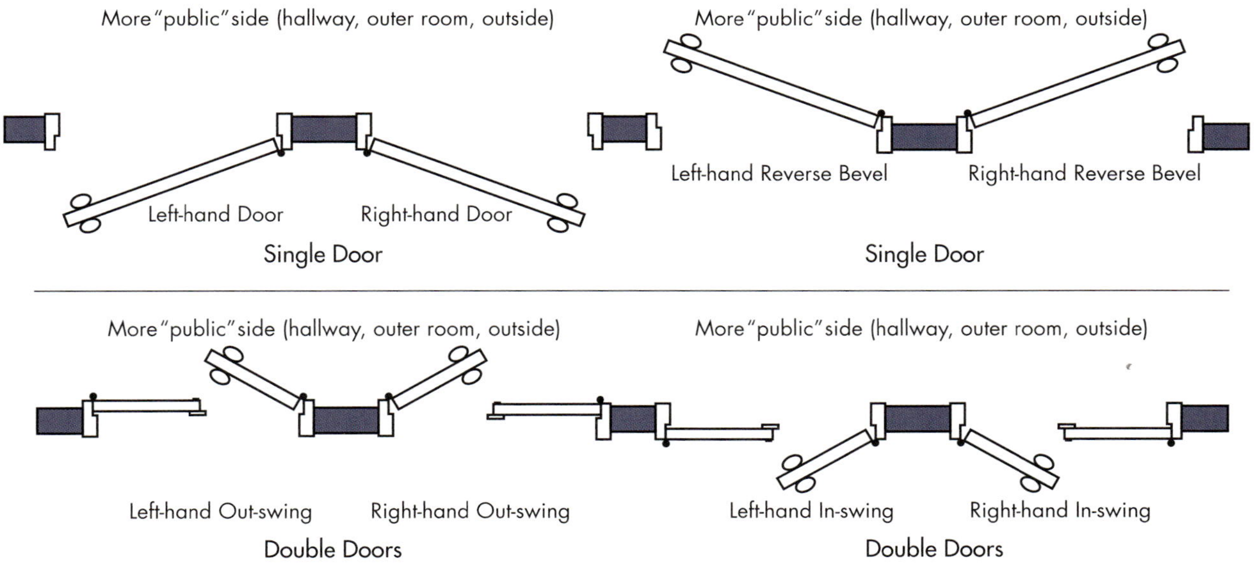

FIGURE 5.18 When you select the hardware for the doors you specify, you will have to identify the hand of the door. This is done by standing on the outside, or more public side, of the door.

Doors

Door safety pertains to hardware (operable without grasping, twisting, or more than 5 pounds of force) as well as to direction of swing. While it is customary for residential doors to swing into spaces, doors in an exit path in commercial installations are required to swing in the direction of travel toward the exit. You will ensure that this is met as you must identify the **hand** of each door that you specify (Figure 5.18).

Doors in commercial spaces must be fire rated. (Fire-rated doors are required to meet code, and standard mandates are 20, 60, or 90 minutes depending on the location of the door.) This will preclude the use of solid wood in those instances and you will select doors made of metal and glass. Even though this section is about solid products, not all doors are solid wood. When designing an area that will be used by children, solid wood is not the best option for doors because they are heavier than **hollow-core** doors. Hollow-core doors, which have air space or filler between door skins, are less likely to smash little fingers if children are opening and closing doors.

Stairs

Stair proportions must fall within a specified range to be safe. The general rule of 7/11 means that a tread is approximately 11 inches and a riser is approximately 7. Adjustments within the allowable range in your jurisdiction will accommodate any ceiling height. Banisters must support a static load of 250 pounds in most jurisdictions and the same slip resistance required of floor should be applied to stairs.

SUSTAINABILITY

Wood is a renewable resource, but it must be managed properly. When a tree is removed, it should be replaced by conscientious growers. It is currently felt that old growth forests should not be a source of wood products. This is debatable because the carbon cycle indicates that younger trees are more efficient at sequestering CO_2 than older trees.

Forest Stewardship Council

Managed forests, essentially "tree farms," are preferred sources of lumber. The Forest Stewardship Council (FSC) has organized a chain-of-supply system that allows conscientious harvesters and fabricators to document their sustainable path from harvesting through processing to installation. Sustainably harvested wood is processed by shops recovering the waste wood from production for recycling into other wood products. Wood products are then assembled using low-emitting adhesives and finished with low-emitting finishes.

Reclaimed Wood

Reclaimed and "antique" wood flooring is available, so rather than mimicking the effects and patina of aged wood you can specify old wood that has been removed from other places. Companies that supply this kind of product deviate from standards defining new wood in order to describe the characteristics specific to their particular products. The flooring may not have tongue-and-groove edges so would have to be face nailed with all fasteners counter-set and plugged or filled, or will have to be delivered to a wood shop that can mill the tongue-and-groove edges. Investigate characteristics like distress and wear, knots, and nail holes, and whether the wood has milled (tongue-and-groove) or square sides in order to select an appropriate product. New floorboards have an undercut back to compensate for any unevenness of the subfloor; antique or reclaimed flooring that was removed from its previous location may not have this undercutting. These details will influence installation costs and methods.

Some reclaimed floors are remilled; that is to say that they are cut to standard widths and lengths, and new tongue-and-groove edging is cut. If the structure that the wood is being reclaimed from is still standing, there will be fewer concerns about dampness and bugs than if the wood has been lying stacked on the ground. Depending on the size of the lot, it may be expected that the sale is for the lot. When this is the case, the quantity may be estimated in running feet of board or square feet of coverage. This rough estimate is for your convenience and is not to be relied upon as the seller is selling the lot and not board lengths. It is a good idea to inspect the lot and confirm availability of required lengths if your design requires long, unbroken lengths. The price may not include removing nails, bug bombing, or cleaning of any sort, so inquire about this so you include all required work in your budget.

Wood reclaimed from exteriors should be personally inspected before purchase. Wood claimed from interiors of people-serving spaces may be safely purchased via long distance after an evaluation of photos from a trustworthy seller. Wood reclaimed from industrial use sites will fall in between the two in terms of the need for a personal inspection.

MANAGING BUDGETS

Generally speaking, standard and stock products will be less costly due to economies of scale than custom, one-off products. Products produced in other countries can often be cheaper to buy, despite transportation costs. Even though these savings are significant and can make a difference to the budget, you will likely look into country of origin and confirm that working conditions there are socially conscionable with safe conditions and a living wage, and reject any selections that do not meet your standards. This is particularly important if your client is a prestigious commercial client with a public reputation to manage. Contributing to the oppression and abuse of workers in a poor country has, at the very least, been an embarrassment to public figures and, worse still, made them an unwitting party to exploitation.

Elaborate designs, with multiple materials combined or multiple processes applied, can contribute as much to costs as tricky site conditions. Whenever tolerances must be very exacting you will pay a premium.

ORGANIZATION OF THE INDUSTRY

Wood is an easily worked material that can be used to make the many things designers might specify, in addition to the items described in this chapter. For a partial list see Table 5.5. This makes describing the organization of the industry difficult because the immediate question is: *Which* industry? Many of the products in Table 5.5 are not things that you will specify but are included so you can see how important wood is to modern living and envision the necessity of reclaiming scrap during production of the things that you do specify.

Wood products obviously originate in forests or farms. Hopefully managed forestry practices are in place.

Trees are harvested by large forestry companies and by individuals with a few forested acres. Reclaimed wood is available from companies whose business is to seek out likely sources, even diving into rivers for logs that sank during transport over a hundred years ago; these companies have a wide, organized network. See

Table 5.5 There are many products made from wood or that use wood as a material component.

Solid Wood	Engineered Wood	As a Component in Products	Chemically Deconstructed
Lumber for studs and joists	Plywood	Shingles	Turpentine
Doors	I-joists	Putty-type wood filler	Cellulose nitrate (used in adhesives and lacquers)
Window frames and sills	LVL (laminated veneer lumber)	Rubber products	Rosin
Flooring	Parallel strand lumber	Insulation corkboard	Varnishes and lacquers
Kitchen cabinets	Glu-lam beams	Roofing paper	Fungicides
Medicine cabinets	Particleboard	Building insulation (loose and panel)	Concrete additives
Stair components	Medium density fiberboard (MDF)	Expansion joint filler	Epoxy additives
Moldings and baseboards	Hardboard	Cork products	Plasticizers
Paneling	Melamine paper-faced board		Metalworking chemicals
Veneer	Closet systems		Rosin-based adhesive products
Furniture case goods from altars to upholstered furniture frames	Garage doors		PVC stabilizers
Accessories	Toilet seats		Synthetic lubricants
Musical instruments	Wall tiles		Polyamides
Wooden sinks and tubs	Ceiling tiles		Corrosion inhibitors
Shutters			Cleaning compounds
Window blinds			Tannin (used in natural tanning process)
Countertops			Carnauba wax
Butcher blocks			Textiles
Lamp shades			
Garage doors			
Wallpaper			
Dowels (assembling wood furniture)			

Figure 5.19 for one example of the unique products that are available from such companies. Reclaimed wood is also available from the farmer who is pulling down an old barn.

Wood may then enter the manufacturing process to be made into product, either lumber or veneer or other depending on the quality and characteristics of the wood. It then moves to distributors who sell to craftspeople or lumberyards, perhaps changing hands and/or being refined or formed along the way.

The finished wood products that you specify will likely be milled in shops whether they are custom or stock items.

FIGURE 5.19 Reclaimed pecky cypress repurposed for a custom ceiling. *Installation by Goodwins.*

Table 5.6
You might organize your considerations in a manner that helps you compare your design program with project needs.

Condition	Program Implications
Is the space in question connected very directly to the outdoors?	Many wood finishes are not durable against abrasives, and moisture seeping between boards can cause dimensional changes in wood that could compromise the finish, which does not expand as much.
Is the area exposed to a lot of sunlight?	Wood is affected by UV and will change in color, deepening or lightening. Specify a sealant with UV protection. Wood stains lessen the visible changes.
Is this a walking surface?	Make sure slip resistance is addressed. Wood that has an open grain will provide more traction. Select a sealant that is formulated to provide additional slip resistance if necessary.
Are you maximizing the use of natural daylighting?	Light colors reflect more light than dark ones. Reflectance for walls should be between 40% and 70% and for floors 25% to 40%. In a related issue, the color of surfaces becomes a component in the light bounced off, so a strong color will be subtly cast throughout the space.
Are you actively managing acoustics in the space?	Finished wood is a reflective surface with a slight tendency to mellow the sound.
How much and what kind of traffic is anticipated?	Wood will deflect and crush; small pointed heels leave dimples. Finishes will abrade and have to be restored.
What are your sustainability priorities?	All wood shares some sustainability characteristics but not all sources are well managed from ecological or social standpoints.
What kind of installation window and conditions are desirable?	Wood can be installed as prefinished product or site finished. Prefinished minimizes time and fumes on-site but finishes may be damaged during installation and toning from piece to piece among components cannot be as easily done as for site-finished.
What aesthetic qualities are required?	Evaluate grain, color, hardness, and grade.

SELECTION CRITERIA

Your reasons for selecting wood products would certainly take into account the characteristics of wood that meet your project needs (Table 5.6). These reasons would include sustainability considerations of renewability, sequestering of CO_2, and low toxicity. Wood contributes to acoustics as a smooth material with good reflective ability; it can bounce sound. It is not as dense as other materials so some small part of the sound will travel into the wood, so sound will be mellower than if the surface was denser like stone or glass. One of the primary motivators for selecting wood is aesthetics; it lends a particular character to a space. Wood is agreeable to a number of processes, so it is a versatile product for the designer. Using your unique design program, organize a list of goals that can help you develop your own selection criteria for a particular installation.

SPECIFYING

Your specification will be carefully written to describe the desired material and installation completely and succinctly. It is difficult to write a spec before you know the exact material and installation details that you are writing about. For this specification let's presume we are working on the restoration of an old home that was recently purchased by a retired couple who intend to run a bed-and-breakfast there. Visitors will come and go throughout the day as they bike, hike, and antique in the area. Old, worn flooring must be removed.

The materials schedule tabulates the surfacing materials but does not cover items made of wood. While flooring will be described on the materials schedule, doors, millwork trims, and staircases will be recorded on the door schedule or millwork schedule.

SAMPLE SPEC 5.1

Part 1 General Information

1.1 Related Documents
A. Refer to finish plans for location and direction of flooring.

1.2 Summary
A. Remove existing linoleum, parquet, and tile flooring.
B. Remove all treads from front staircase.
C. Carefully remove existing baseboard, number and save for reinstallation. Deliver to stripper.
D. Remove and dispose of existing quarter round.
E. Patch pine subfloors with plywood only where necessary.
F. Install prefinished, reclaimed, remilled red oak planks.
G. Install new, prefinished oak treads on existing, front staircase.
H. Install new, flush, red oak threshold at kitchen doorway.

1.3 Contractor Submittals
A. Provide documentation confirming 100% recycled content of reclaimed floors in compliance with exempt status.
B. Provide material safety data sheet for finish.
C. Finish sample on boards from lot selected demonstrating range, finished to demonstrate color and finish for approval.

1.4 Quality Assurance
A. All workers milling, finishing, and installing flooring and treads to be experienced with such operations.

1.5 Delivery, Storage, and Handling
A. Deliver wood to site no sooner than 30 days after completion of patching of plaster walls.
B. Store wood in dining room for no less than 2 days to acclimate to site.
C. Care to be taken to ensure that no damaged boards or treads are installed.

1.6 Maintenance of Installation
A. Maintain site in safe clean condition for the duration of installation.
B. Leave site broom-clean upon completion of work each day.

Part 2 Products

2.1 General Information
A. Reclaimed and new wood product.
B. Low-VOC stains and sealants.

2.2 Fabricator and Installer
A. Mighty Nice Floors,1234 Industrial Drive, Anytown, ST 45678.

2.3 Products
A. Reclaimed red oak flooring provided by installer's resource to be from the lot inspected and tagged by designer. Product accepted has color matching consistent with Select and better grade; contains tight knots but no mineral streaks. Up to 4 knots per 4' length are acceptable. Boards containing more knots to be used in closet, center area of dining room, and for cuts required at perimeter of rooms.
B. Boards milled for tongue-and-groove edges all 4 sides and planed down to consistent ¾-inch thickness.
C. New solid wood treads of rift-sawn red oak.
D. New solid rift-sawn red oak threshold at kitchen door to span entire 10" thickness of door opening. $^1/_8$" bevel each, 36"-long edge.
E. Boards to be stained chestnut and sealed with 2 coats of gloss and 1 coat of matte, water-based urethane sealant selected. Finished boards to match approved sample.
F. New ¾-inch quarter round stained and sealed to match flooring.

Part 3 Execution

3.1 Examination
A. Flooring contractor to remove existing flooring and prepare substrate to receive reclaimed oak flooring. Patches required may be ¾"-thick plywood to match existing pine subfloor with no deviation.
B. Flooring contractor to remove existing stair treads from front stairs, inspect stair construction for stability, and patch or brace from underside if necessary.

3.2 Preparation
A. All nails and debris to be removed from substrate, including any material dropped by other trades.
B. Scrape and sand as necessary to bring substrate to flat, sound condition suitable for installation.
C. Install rosin paper over substrate.

3.3 Installation
A. Remilled, reclaimed red oak flooring to be blind-nailed into subfloor.
B. Install threshold.
C. Install treads into existing stringers.
D. Install quarter round with no seams in wall runs, cope seams at in-corners, miter seams at out-corners.
E. Reinstall (stripped by others) baseboard in their previous locations. Tops and bottoms to align. Leave ready for surface sanding and priming (by others).

3.4 Post Installation
A. Upon completion of installation, floors to be clean and dry.
B. Leave flooring exposed until acceptance by owner, then cover with paper throughout.

Key on Plan	Description	Hardware
1	Door Co. solid wood door for paint in Hanover style; 1³/₈"-thick interior door #FD/SI two-panel; flat astragal will be attached (on-site) to public corridor side, right-facing leaf of double doors; each leaf to be 36" wide × 80" tall (standard size) with standard depth interior double door jambs DBL DR/Interior; jamb to be mortised for hinges.	Solid brass lever and rose Hardware Co. brand #271 dummy set with roller catches. Hinges to be 3" heavy-duty solid brass ball bearing hinges.
2	Door Co. solid wood door for paint in Hanover style; 1³/₈"-thick interior door #FD/SI two-panel door 36" wide × 80" tall (standard size) with standard depth interior door jamb SGL DR/Interior; jamb to be mortised for hinges and bored for lockset. Right-hand door.	Hardware Co. brand solid brass lever #271 with rose interior privacy set for right-facing/east door; dead bolt with brass trim ring keyed on exterior with turnbuckle on interior. Both research rooms to be keyed alike. Hinges to be 3" heavy-duty solid brass ball bearing hinges.

FIGURE 5.20 Designers create a door and window schedule to document their selections

Figure 5.20 shows typical organization of information on the door schedule. This example is particularly comprehensive and was written as if the purchasing of the door and hardware would be by others and the schedule also served as specification.

INSPECTION

Solid wood must acclimate to the job site, that is, adjust to the environment in which it will be installed, before it can be installed. Prior to the installation the material or component parts will arrive at the site and you may elect to inspect before installation even begins.

Floors

If you are specifying a site-finished floor you will probably inspect the floors at a couple of points, once when the flooring is nearly all installed but not finished and once when the floors are complete.

Midpoint Flooring Inspection for New Floors

- Subfloor is free of damage, protruding nails, loose spots, soil, or wetness.
- All pieces are free of cracks and unacceptable defects.
- Strips are staggered so that no two adjacent joint ends are within 5 inches of each other.
- Shorter lengths and "off-tone" boards have been used in closets or other inconspicuous locations.
- If a pattern has been specified, the inspection takes place with drawing in hand to confirm that all architectural alignments and centers have been adhered to.
- A final inspection time has been established with the installer.

Midpoint Flooring Inspection

- All damaged, missing, worn and deeply stained boards have been replaced.
- All heating registers have been removed. If register covers are wood they should be taken out and refinished separately to match finished floor.
- The area is protected with plastic; this includes all openings into the HVAC ductwork.
- All small holes and chips are filled to match the finished floor.
- All problems that may have led to the need for refinishing (especially water leaks) have been repaired/caulked/modified.

Final Flooring Inspection

- Flooring conforms to sample and is installed as specified.
- Finish is clear of dust and "globs."
- The contractor is instructed to cover the floor to protect it from other trades who will be working in the area after the floors are finished.

Wood trim installation should also be inspected at a couple of points. The first inspection is to approve of the installation, and that is the one that pertains to this chapter. The second inspection is to approve of the painting labor, which is a different trade (see Chapter 2).

Inspection for Doors

- Installation has been checked, with drawing in hand for conformity to plan in type and location of trim specified.
- Doors hung properly. Check swing and clearance at frame. The door should stand in whatever position you place it without swinging open or closed on its own.

Inspection for Trims

- All trim is smooth, uncracked, and there is no oozing sap.
- All miters are smooth, even, and tight.
- All joints are sanded smooth. More sanding will be done by finishers so just check quality of material and of seams.
- All window trims are complete including skirts and returns.
- Closet interiors are trimmed.
- All bases installed; check details at cabinets, doorjambs, and stairs.
- Columns located correctly and are plumb and square.
- All material used on curves is clear of defects.
- All trims are tight to prevent need for excessive caulking.
- Mitered or coped corners occur at all out-corners and shaped in-corners, no butt joints.
- Finish nails only have been used; they are sunk, puttied, sanded smooth, and blending with finish.
- Joints and gaps are caulked and sanded smooth making joints indiscernible to touch or sight after painting.

Inspection for Staircases

Inspection of staircases will likely occur close to completion of the installation. Take any finish samples, your drawings, and other documentation of the design with you so you can use your own drawings and specs to check correctness of all details. Run your hand over turned spindles and posts to ensure they are sanded smooth and ready for finish.

RELATED MATERIAL

Some of the items that were used as examples of solid wood material are also available in synthetic materials and engineered materials. Combinations of wood and other materials will be discussed in Chapter 13, which pertains to laminated flooring products and engineered substrates, but you should also be aware of options that are not covered in this text. These options include synthetic architectural trims intended to receive paint and similar materials for doors, spindles, and posts for stairs, as well as engineered materials like medium density fiberboard.

Door Accessories

Door hinges will already be installed if your doors are ordered prehung (more to follow under Fabrication). The door hardware, meaning the door lockset, knob, or lever as well as any trims required, may come standard on prehung doors or ordered separately (Figure 5.21a–f). The various functions of the hardware that you will select to best fit

FIGURE 5.21A–F

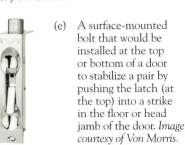

(a) A typical passage set—no locking mechanism. *Set from Baldwin.*

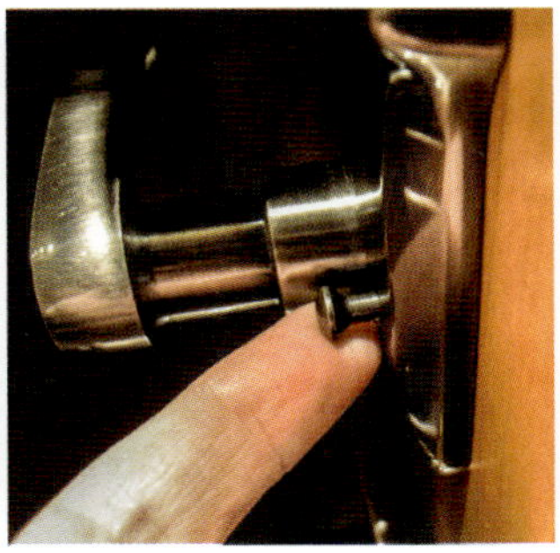

(b) A privacy set with a release button on the escutcheon. The level of security offered is not as great as the entrance set shown in (c). *Sets from Baldwin.*

(d) Panic hardware that allows the latch to be released by simply leaning on it. Fire code requires that doors be self-closing and -latching but easily released in an emergency when people may be panicked and not thinking clearly. *Image of Yale hardware courtesy of Assa Abloy.*

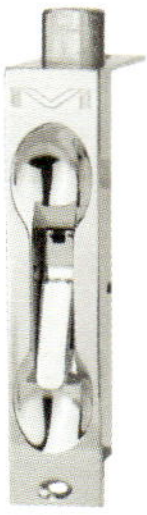

(e) A surface-mounted bolt that would be installed at the top or bottom of a door to stabilize a pair by pushing the latch (at the top) into a strike in the floor or head jamb of the door. *Image courtesy of Von Morris.*

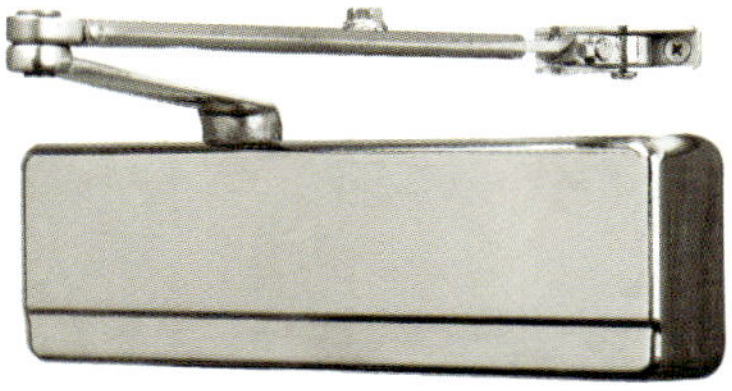

(f) A keyless lock. *Baldwin sets photographed with permission of Clark and Barlow Hardware.*

Table 5.7 The locking and latching function of the door that you specify is as important as the door.	
Latch, Catch, or Lock Type	**Function**
Roller catch and dummy pull hardware	Magnetic or roller catch holds closed door in place but no actual latching. "Dummy" set (knobs or lever) looks like a door hardware latch set but does not operate a latch.
Panic hardware	Allows for rapid egress from commercial buildings; latches operated by a push bar or rail. They are quite standard in commercial interiors.
Door closers	Mounted to door to control swing and close door; swing speed adjustable along path of travel, so closes slowly when reaching jamb so will not slam.
Passage set	The setup is the passage set. The passage set does not lock. It can always be operated by manipulating the lever or knob from either side.
Privacy set	Knob or lever will operate the latch from the inside. When locked from inside, latch is disabled; cannot be opened from the outside (emergency override).
Entrance set	When locked requires key from the outside, turn knob (single cylinder), or another key on the inside (called double cylinder) to unlock from inside. Double-cylinder use is restricted by code. When locked latch is disabled from outside, may still be functional from inside, or must be unlocked to operate from either side. Typically mortised in.
Electronic	Keyless locking function operated by keypad, card reader, fingerprint reader, or other; for security or convenience. Battery or current through electric hinges.
Bolt	Single locking function only, independent of latching. Door has cylinder bore for dead bolt and is mortised out at edge for surface bolts.

the security function of the door are described in Table 5.7. The finishes will have to be coordinated between the hinges that may come with the door, and the other hardware that you will likely order from another source. Slab or loose-leaf doors may ship with or without hinges.

Doors may come predrilled for the latch set. Interior doors are typically predrilled for cylinder-type hardware (Figure 5.22a) and exterior doors are typically prepared for mortise-type hardware (Figure 5.22b). You can see that the door will have to be hollowed out differently for one versus the other. Whether cylinder or mortise, the door will also have a backset. The backset is the distance from the outside edge of the lock stile to the center of the hole drilled through. Both cylinder and mortise sets have a hole drilled through (Figure 5.22c). Typical backsets for interior are 2³/₈" and for exterior doors 2³/₄" but this is not a hard and fast rule so you will need to confirm this before selecting the hardware for the door.

Helpful Hint 5.5
Prehung interior doors are likely to come routed for cylinder locksets, typically bored for a 2³/₈" backset and exterior doors with a mortise or cylinder bore (dead bolt will be a separate cylinder bore) usually having a 2³/₄" backset.

FIGURE 5.22A–C

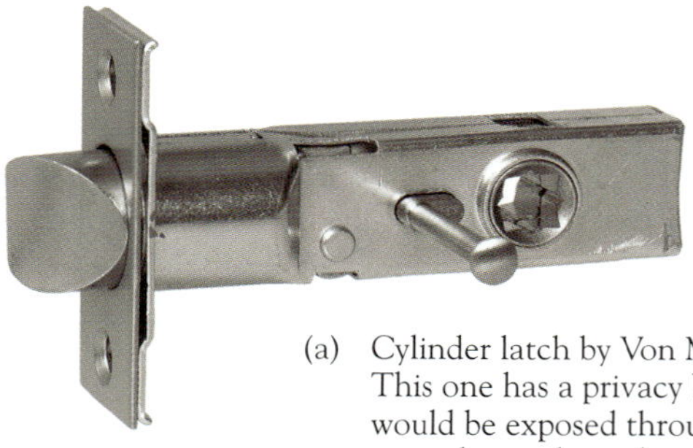

(a) Cylinder latch by Von Morris. This one has a privacy button that would be exposed through the escutcheon plate when assembled.

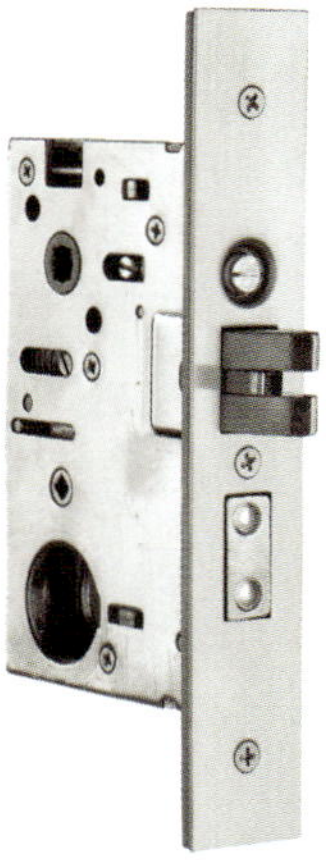

(b) Mortise latch by Von Morris.

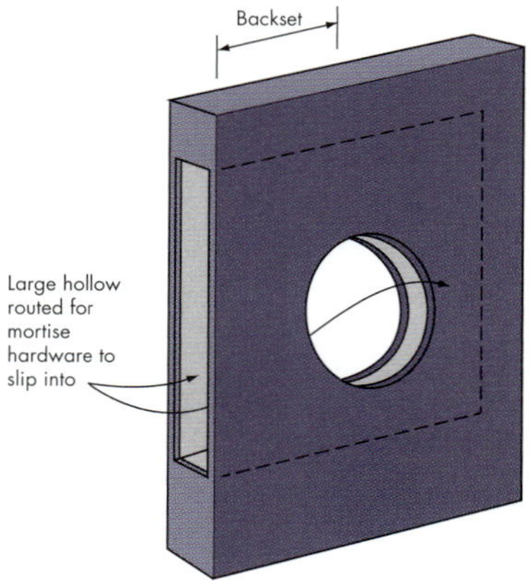

(c) Diagram of door routed for a mortise set showing how to measure for the backset.

Figure 5.23a–d

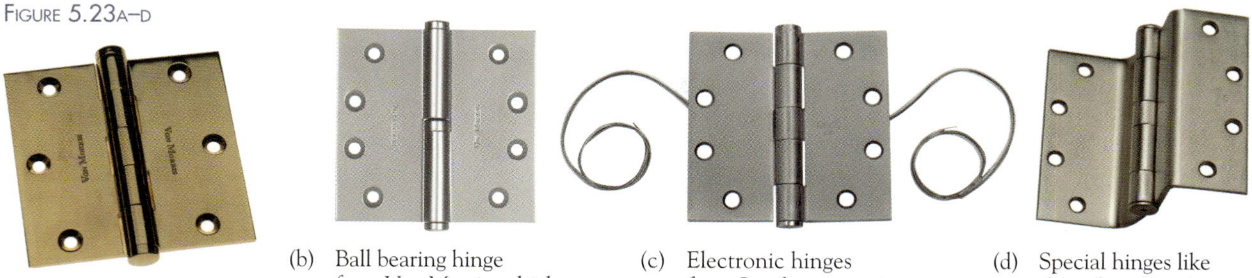

(a) Regular butt hinge from Von Morris.

(b) Ball bearing hinge from Von Morris, which has a different barrel than regular hinge.

(c) Electronic hinges from Stanley transmit electricity to the hinge or to the door leaf.

(d) Special hinges like these from Stanley swing clear and can solve special problems.

As with door locking and latching hardware, hinges may come as a standard on prehung or you may order for prehung or custom doors. The most common hinge style is the butt hinge (Figure 5.23a). A ball bearing (Figure 5.23b) will be specified if the door is heavy or will be consistently in use. Electronic hinges (Figure 5.23c) are a modification of a butt hinge. These hinges work with electronic locking or deliver electricity to something mounted on the door like a sign or motorized window coverings that might be mounted over a glass panel in the door. The mounting of the hinge is described by its relationship to the door.

- Full mortise—Mortised into door and jamb
- Half mortise—Mortised into door, surface on jamb
- Half surface—Mortised into jamb, surface on door
- Full surface—Surface mounted on both door and jamb

Special circumstances have developed the need for special hinges that you might need to specify. This "swing clear" hinge (Figure 5.23d) pushes the door entirely out of the opening even when the door can only open to 90 degrees.

Stair Accessories

It is not uncommon for stair designs to incorporate different kinds of materials. Your stairs may have metal or glass parts as well as wood. You will need to provide drawings showing where accessory parts, like step lights and contrasting materials, are to be positioned and what details will integrate them neatly into the design.

WOOD VENEERS

Wood veneer is so very different from solid wood that you might think of it as a separate material. This is because most of its performance characteristics come from the substrate to which it is adhered. It is typically adhered to plywood or particleboard and those dimensionally stable substrates make veneered surfaces largely decorative.

Wood veneers on engineered substrates solve your design problems with characteristics unique from solid wood so you will likely specify wood in this form as often, if not more than, you will specify solid wood.

MATERIAL MAKEUP OR CONTENT

Wood **veneer** is simply slices of wood, thinner than lumber, laminated to a substrate. Remember that as solid wood changes dimension in response to changes in humidity, it does so as a percentage of its size. This means that a bigger, thicker piece of wood will move more during these changes than a smaller, thinner piece of wood. This raises limitations for laminating because if you glue two dissimilar pieces of wood together, they will move at different rates and possibly break their glue bonds. If a piece of wood is adhered to a dimensionally stable, engineered substrate like plywood or particleboard, the same thing could happen—a veneer that is too thick could break away when it changes dimension with humidity changes. Even though the smallest, standard lumber size for solid wood is a nominal 1" × 2" (planed and sanded to an actual ¾" × 1½"), wood veneer thicknesses start at about ⅜ inch thick for hard-wearing surfaces like laminated floors and decrease in thickness to as thin as 0.007 inch; as a point of reference poster board is about 0.048 inch thick. Think of a piece of wood laminated to an engineered substrate as akin to braces holding your teeth in position.

Wood veneer is available to your fabricator as wood only or as wood backed with paper, pressure-sensitive tape, cloth, woven cellulose, melamine, or phenolic (plastic resin-infused paper). When veneer is laid up on a phenolic backing (the material on which plastic laminate is laid up), the phenolic backing will show at the cut edges. Be aware that a dark line under the veneer will be present at all exposed edges. If this will be objectionable, as in the case of a pale wood, you must note on drawings that this kind of backing is not to be used.

CHARACTERISTICS

Visual characteristics of wood can often be modified to a surprising extent by bleaching, staining, and dyeing. Stains color wood by laying down pigment particles, so stains obscure the wood surface a little. Using transparent dyes, wood can become a brilliant cerulean blue or any other natural or unnatural color. Similarly, an open grain can be filled or a tight-grained wood wire brushed so the grain of the finished surface appears more open. Many visual characteristics can be changed in the shop. Some characteristics, such as grain, figuring, and natural color will persist.

Grain

Grain refers to two characteristics of wood. One component of grain is the color variation between the fast summer growth and the slow winter growth of the tree. In some species these differences are pretty remarkable, like for ebony wood; in other species it is less pronounced, as for maple. The other component of grain refers to the physical texture. For some woods, like oak, parts of the grain are open (meaning you can feel the texture) and parts are smooth. This is a separate issue from the color difference. Ebony wood has a pronounced color difference in the grain pattern but it has a closed grain so it feels smooth.

Figuring

Figuring of wood describes the markings that are the result of outside influences that disturb the growth of the tree. Figure 5.24 shows some kinds of figuring that you can find among many species of wood. For example, *crotch veneer* refers to wood taken from the trunk at the point where a branch has grown out, leaving a V-shaped grain pattern. Stump veneer is taken

FIGURE 5.24 Figuring raises the value of wood, making some figuring available only in veneer.
SanFoot images courtesy of Jacaranda, Inc.

from the base of the tree where the grain is swirly like a burl and the pieces are small. Bird's-eyes are formed when the tree becomes diseased; **pecky** and **spalted** wood are the result of localized rot. **Burls** are the result of disease in the tree but are highly prized. Burls are typically small so burl veneers are small. They are also brittle, making them difficult to work with. Figuring marks occur in many species of wood in addition to those shown. Figuring should be selected, positioned, and oriented thoughtfully.

Color

The undertones of the natural wood color will usually linger, influencing the final color, even after bleaching, staining, and dyeing. Red undertones turn pink, khaki undertones turn green; the color becomes a pastel version of itself after bleaching but bleaching does not remove all the color.

Veneer is best laminated to a flat, smooth surface; applying it to a complicated form with lots of separate planes is expensive and for some forms, it is impossible. Therefore you would select, as an example, a solid wood for ogee fillets on a panel door even if the face of the panel were veneered.

Whenever you plan to use veneers and solids together to complete your design, take care to match their visual appearances between lot of veneer and lot of solid wood. It is a good idea to plan for a stain finish if possible to even out inevitable differences in the color and graining between the veneers and solid wood. Veneers and solids will age differently over time and, even if they match closely upon installation, they will appear a little different from each other as they age. Staining will also limit this change to some extent.

Veneer Grades

Veneer is assigned a quality grade of AA, A, B, C, or D, similar to the quality grade assigned to dimensional wood. It is unlikely that you will ever have reason to specify grade D quality for interiors work; it is a coarse grade allowing holes, knots, and worm bores. Grades A and B are the grades that you will be most likely to specify. If you veneer plywood for your projects, you must always balance the two faces to maintain an odd number of layers to prevent warping. You might decide that the visible portion should be A-grade veneer but the back, balancing side could be B or C grade if it will be completely hidden after installation. Keep in mind that the grading is distinct from the species and the cut.

A Cautionary Tale 5.1

My client required a large cabinet to conceal a bar in a room that had a pronounced curve on one end only, but was an otherwise symmetrical room. Creating a cabinet that curved with an identical sweeping curve to conceal the bar would also balance the room. The sliding tambour doors that pocketed to the left and right were constructed of solid maple slats; the remainder of the cabinet was bird's-eye maple veneer. Both solid and veneer were stained to match each other, a dyed color that I referred to as French gray.

A decade passed between the installation and a call from the client, who wanted to consult about another matter. When I arrived at the site I noticed that the tambour doors had a pronounced pink cast and the remainder of the cabinet had a pronounced gold cast. The client did not mention it. Possibly the change had been so gradual that they didn't really notice that it was taking place at all.

I phoned the cabinetmaker who had made it for some ideas to remedy the situation and was glad that I had not mentioned it to my client, because there was nothing that could be done but uninstall it, including unhooking all the plumbing, removing the stone counter concealed within, taking it back to the shop and stripping off the finish . . . and the list goes on.

Since my client had not expressed any dissatisfaction with the piece I thought it was best to let sleeping dogs lie and took on the problem for which I had been summoned and did not suggest that the cabinet be taken away and refinished.

What I learned from this was to create designs that call for contrasted finishes when I have to mix solids and veneers or specify a stain rather than a dye. Stains are pigments that cover the wood with color and dyes are transparent coloration that does not conceal as completely what is happening below the finish.

PARTS AND ACCESSORIES

It is an understatement to talk about the substrate as an accessory to the veneer when it is more accurate to say that the opposite is true, that the veneer is the surface for the substrate. Review the chapter discussing substrates to appreciate all of their characteristics and performance attributes. Because the veneer is a surface applied to a substrate, you will need to detail your designs to conceal edges. Imagine a wood veneered desk where you will see the edge of the top. You might sketch options, as was done in Figure 5.25, to picture ways of finishing the exposed edges of your panels. A common method of completing the edge is with a special tape, called edge banding, that is faced with the same veneer on its face as the one you have specified. This tape is heat activated or pressure sensitive. Once applied, it will be finished like the rest of the surface.

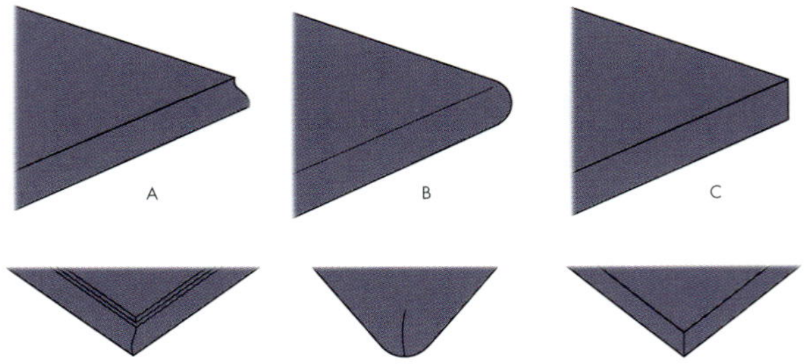

FIGURE 5.25 When a panel is veneered you will have to devise some way of concealing the fact that the thin veneer is adhered to a substrate of a different material. You might specify a solid wood edge that can be shaped or a simple edge that can be veneered or edge banded.

FABRICATION

Veneer fabrication itself is a simple matter; it is wood sliced thin (think of the thickness of poster board). After it is cut, the veneer must then be adhered to the substrate. Fabricators call this laying up the veneer and there are patterns that you will specify for the way the individual pieces are arranged.

Cuts

Veneer cuts (the way the log is sliced to produce the thin sheets of veneer) influence the visual characteristics of the veneer. See Figure 5.26 for an illustration of what this means for the log. Figure 5.27 compares plain-sliced (referred to here as flat cut or FC) to rift-sawn and quartered (QC). Plain slicing produces some areas with grain patterns having pointy "cathedrals" combined with areas of straight grain. Quarter slicing produces a straighter grain, in which flake running perpendicular to the grain is more apparent (the flake is more reflective of light relative to the general appearance of the surrounding wood). Rift slicing also produces a straight grain but without satiny flake. Rotary slicing produces the greatest amount of figuring and cathedrals.

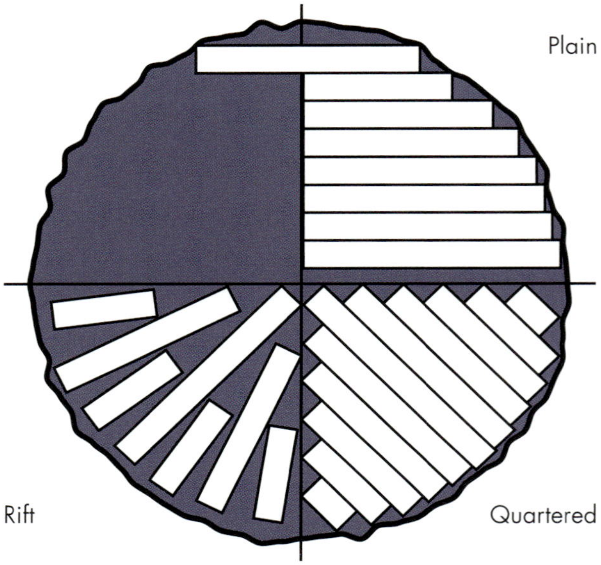

FIGURE 5.26 The cuts that are used for solid lumber also apply to veneers.

Patterns

Pieces of veneer will usually be smaller than the areas you would like to cover, so multiple pieces of veneer must be set up on a single piece of substrate. The way the veneer is applied to the face of the panels is called the veneer match. The kind of match specified will create the veneer pattern. These matches include diamond match, reverse diamond, end match, radial match, slip match, book match, and others. Figure 5.28a–f diagrams the arrangement of some popular matches. Patterns are only one of the kinds of matching that you will address with your specification.

FIGURE 5.27 The same wood species, even if cut from the same tree, can have a different appearance, depending on the cut. *Images courtesy of Jacaranda, Inc.*

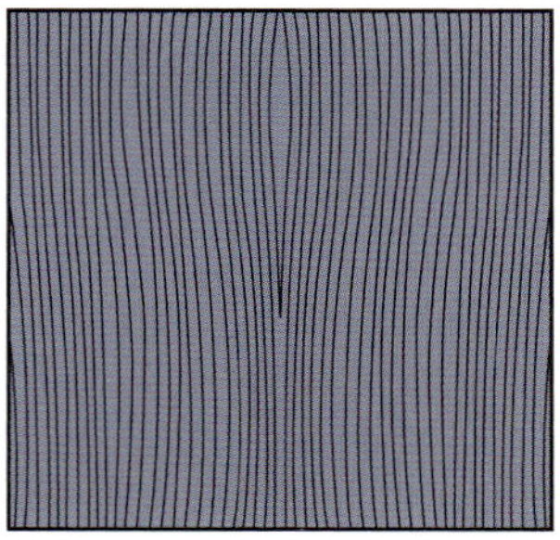

(a) Book match—Book match is the most common method of veneer matching. The effect is created by turning over every other piece of veneer so adjacent leaves are "opened" as facing pages in a book. Veneer joints match, creating a sequential pattern.

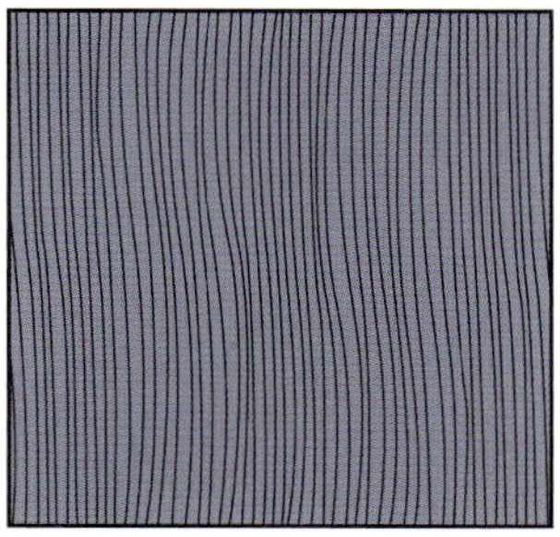

(b) Slip match—Grain figure repeats but joints do not show grain match. Color is uniform. Most commonly used with quartered and rift-cut veneers.

(c) Diamond match—Is like a concentric box tipped on an angle.

(d) Radial match—Veneer is matched around a center point. This example is a book matched radial match.

(e) Box match—Presents the grain like concentric boxes. It is like a diamond match but squared rather than angled.

(f) Reverse diamond match—Radiates out from a center point in quadrants (so fewer pieces than radial).

FIGURE 5.28A–F The names for different patterns created when the veneer is laid up on the panels.

> **Point of Emphasis 5.4**
> Slip-matched veneers can sometimes look like they are *running downhill.* Even though consecutive pieces of veneer in sequence look very similar, they do change slightly as you move through the log and this slight change becomes more noticeable as a direction when multiple pieces are laid up on sequence. Book matching tends to balance itself on the panel.

The relationship between the individual pieces of veneer will also be described in your specification. This relationship is often referred to as the veneer pattern or pattern match.

Pattern Matching

- Book match—Individual pieces are laid up to create mirror images of each other; every other one is "flipped over."
- Slip match—Individual pieces of veneer are laid up sequentially with the same side face up for every leaf.
- Random match—Purposely mismatched individual leaves of veneer.
- Radial match—Leaves of veneer are arranged in a starburst pattern radiating out from the center. The leaves will be cut into a triangular shape so the leaf as well as the grain radiates out.
- Diamond match—The leaves of veneer are oriented at an angle in a mirror image that forms a concentric diamond pattern.
- Reverse diamond match—The leaves of veneer are oriented at an angle in a mirror image moving out from the center. It is similar to the radial match but the individual pieces of veneer are not cut into triangles so it is only the grain figuring which radiates and not the shape of the veneer leaves.
- Box match—The veneers are arranged like a diamond match but instead of presenting the lines of the wood grain on an angle the graining is perpendicular to the sides of the panel.
- Butt match—The leaves in the preceding descriptions are matched side-by-side. Butt matched leaves are positioned top to bottom in an instance when the selected veneer is not long enough to cover the panel from top to bottom.

Matching describes the relationship of the veneer to the substrate; these include:

- Balance (need)—Pieces of veneer will be trimmed to fit the size of each panel, even though your panel sizes may vary. Panels look best if you use one of two options for balancing veneer on the face of a panel.
- Balance match—An even or odd number of leaves are trimmed to matching width. If two panels are required to be different widths the veneer leaves on one pane will be different than the leaves on the next.
- Balance and center match—An even number of veneer leaves from a sequential lot will be trimmed to matching widths positioning a seam in the center of the panel.

Figure 5.29a–d illustrates some of these matches.

Panel Matching

The third relationship that you will determine and specify describes the panels as they relate to the surface, such as to the walls or to the cabinet faces.

After the match of one piece of veneer to another has been specified (book match, slip match, etc.) and the relationship of the veneers to the substrate is identified (center, balance, etc.), the last piece of information identifies how the panels will relate to the wall surface. There are two primary options. One is to cut the substrate to fit the wall surfaces first and then apply the veneer to the perfectly sized substrates; this option is called blueprint matching. The other option is to apply the veneer to the substrate and then cut the pieces to fit the room. Sequence and warehouse matching fall into this second category.

FIGURE 5.29A–D

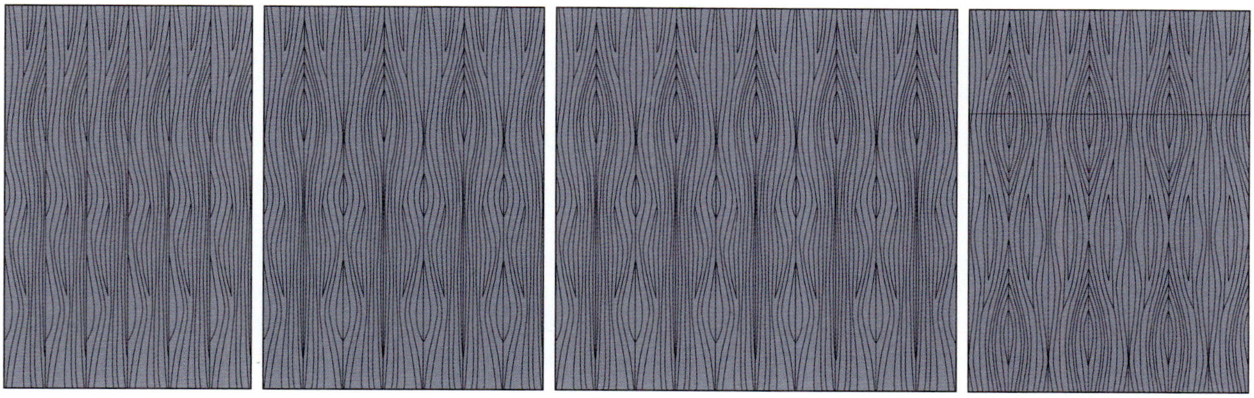

(a) Running match maximizes coverage with less waste. If part of a veneer sheet is left over, it is used on the adjacent panel. A small portion of grain pattern may be eliminated due to trimming.

(b) Balance match utilizes leaves of equal size; panel faces are made from equal width veneer sheets. Grain continuity may change when a different number of veneer sheets is used on adjacent panels.

(c) Center match will always use an even number of leaves of equal width veneer sheets. This produces the most symmetrical panel. Grain continuity may change between the left- and right-hand panel unless you specify that all widths must be equal as shown here. This is the most expensive type of matching.

(d) End match is required when the panel is longer than the strips of veneer.

Blueprint matching allows for the most continuous graining. All elevations are drawn up and matching is indicated (Figure 5.30a). All components are detailed and matched to adjoining members. If more than one flitch is required to fill the order, the additional flitches are carefully selected for matching. This kind of match is most easily done by the fabricator. The primary distinction is that the substrate panels are cut to fit the job, then veneered.

Sequence match requires that the panels be laid up as sheets are drawn from a single flitch or from matched flitches. Veneers are applied in the same sequence from which they were removed from the log so variation from one piece of veneer to the next is subtle and flows visually (Figure 5.30b). Some components will not be in sequence as the wall panels are laid up (doors, for instance, may be out of sequence because they will require a different substrate from the one required for walls) and corners may not match (because they are trimmed to fit the wall space remaining after the other panels have been installed). The panels are veneered one after another and then cut to fit the job, so portions of the sequence are missing and subtle discontinuity exists.

Warehouse match provides panels that are the same species in lots of 6 to 12 panels (Figure 5.30c). The next

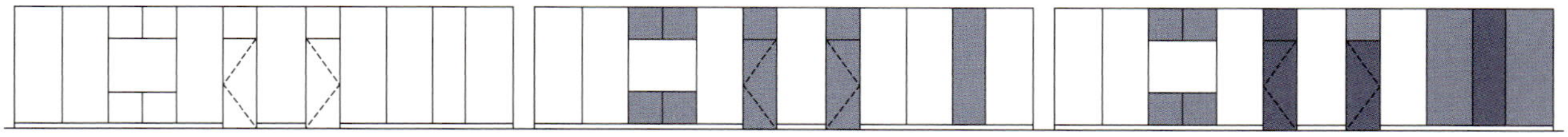

(a) Blueprint-matched panels are cut to size and then veneered so graining is continuous from one panel to the next with no ends sliced off to make the panels fit.

(b) Sequence-matched panels are veneered, then cut to fit, so some panels do not flow seamlessly to the next but all are installed in numerical sequence for more continuity.

(c) Warehouse match is also veneered then cut to fit and is the most economical and can be used without compromise when the lots are very similar in appearance.

FIGURE 5.30A–C Panels are planned for their relationship to one another when installed.

lot (if more panels are required) will not be in sequence. Doors will not be in sequence and corners will not match for the same reasons as apply to sequence matching. Warehouse matching is like sequence matching but there will be less visual continuity.

> **Point of Emphasis 5.5**
> As you might expect, there is a price difference between *blueprint*, *sequence*, and *warehouse* matches. If you anticipate that your client will not have the budget for a blueprint match, you should restrict your selection to wood species that generally have a lot of visual consistency. Ash, maple, and many other woods have more visual similarity from one lot to another than does walnut, cherry, or others that tend to exhibit more visual variety. You can still have a very presentable installation with sequence or warehouse-matched panels if you select a wood that does not range all over the spectrum.

Finishing Veneered Pieces

Wood must be sealed, at the very least, and there may be other finish processes that you would like to employ to achieve the results you envision. Finishes include:

- Colorants like stains, dyes, and paints
- Paste fillers to smooth out the surface texture of woods that have coarse grains when you do not want the actual grain texture on the finished piece
- Top coats and sealants

When multiple finish steps are required, all products must work together. For instance some oil-based paste fillers are incompatible with water-based finishes, so your experienced shop will recommend the best combination of finishes to fulfill on your performance specifications.

Broad categories of top coats include waxes, oils, varnishes, shellacs, lacquers, and water-based finishes. Waxes are not typically used alone but are often applied over other finishes to provide a surface that can be easily rubbed out if slight damage occurs with use. Generally speaking, finishes that cure versus harden through the evaporation of a solvent are more durable against water, chemicals, and scratching. Finishes that have *catalyzed* in their name and varnishes generally cure. Shellacs, lacquers, and many water-based finishes harden through the evaporation of solvents, so are generally less durable than finishes that cure. (See also Chapter 2, Paints, Coatings, and Wallcoverings.)

Special Techniques

Several finishing techniques may be employed on a surface, such as when you specify a distressed surface. If the piece is distressed, notice the realism of the distressing. Is it theatrically exaggerated or does it imitate the timeworn look of cabinetry that was carefully used for a century? Subtlety is essential to good-quality distressing. When you see good distressing it will have some of the following characteristics:

- Pattern of distressing: The distressing should occur in areas where use and handling would have been expected. For example, out-corners and raised edges would have dings and even small chips. These marks should not be crushed or crisp but should have been eased with hand sanding prior to finishing. Natural-looking distressing should also occur around the hardware and latches. There may be additional, random slight dents in other areas as well. Again, these areas should be sanded for smooth wear and not be severely deep or sharp. The concentration of wear will occur in the vulnerable areas, with only occasional and subtle distressing marks elsewhere.
- Wormholes: These should be small, neat, and clustered, not sprinkled all over. They are made with a slender tool about the size of a pin and may be darkened on their interior if the overall cabinet color is dark.
- Overglazing: Any glazing should provide moderate contrast to the overall color and its location should conform tightly to the grooves and corners where it is left on. The implication of glazing is that a piece was conscientiously cleaned over the course of its long life and some slight grime accumulated in expected places over many years. The effect of poorly wiped glazes is that the piece was left moldering in mud and then cleaned with a broom. Leave the latter for stage sets, not fine interiors.
- Ink spatters: Opinion is surprisingly contentious about such tiny marks. Some designers contend they are a dead giveaway to a fake. In a heavy-use space such as a kitchen, however, they provide a visual "break" in the surface, which is very practical. Use your own eye to evaluate the careful selection of ink for the cabinet color and the artistry exhibited in the amount and location of spatter.

QUALIFYING INSTALLERS

Millwork shops create your designs for furniture, architectural millwork, and paneling that you specify with wood veneer on engineered substrates. As is the case with many of the tradespeople who fabricate and install surfacing for your designs, millworkers often learn their trade on the job. You may find that some woodworkers attend a trade school to learn the basics that will allow them to compete for entry-level work in tight job markets but when the economy is rocking, woodworkers are simply trained on the job. When reviewing credentials of any individual woodworker you will likely find some acknowledgment of training through a woodworkers association like the Architectural Woodwork Institute or through a union. Workers who fashion wood with joints, in addition to using fasteners (such as nails and screws) that carpenters use, are sometimes referred to as joiners, so their work is often called joinery.

Your simple jobs may be produced by a small shop employing a joiner and a helper. Large jobs will obviously require more capacity. The reputation of the shop is the qualification that means the most to you, so review pictures of completed work, call references, and visit job sites in person if you get an opportunity. References are not always good judges of quality work—if they are end users rather than designers or architects they may have limited knowledge of what characteristics constitute good work. When you visit the shop's completed work, look closely at the veneered surfaces they created and check for the following:

- Finishes are smooth to the touch (run your hand over the surface and feel for dust in finish, bumps, and inconsistencies).
- The wood has no discernible wood filler.
- Finishes are clear and wood grain is visible, the grain is not obscured (unless it is a painted piece, of course).
- The finish is clear, not hazed or cloudy.
- All parts are securely adhered or well seated and there is no movement.
- Joints are tight and smooth with no gaps in veneer or substrate showing anywhere and no ragged-looking seams or edges.
- Panels align and match each other.
- The fabricator made good decisions when matching; wood colors and graining are well blended.
- Notice the match on the panels; individual pieces on any given panel should be nearly identical.

When you are inspecting jobs, you will be checking for more quality characteristics than will be presented by the veneer work alone. Every item or surface that is created has its own attendant list of quality distinguishers in addition to the quality of the veneer work and finishes.

For the Connoisseur 5.2

When large surfaces are to be covered, such as would be the case if you had specified a paneled room, you want to attend to quality details from the start. You might go to the veneer supplier and review the different lots that they had on hand for the species that you had in mind to use. The figuring, color tones, and expression of the grain will vary from lot to lot. If you need a quantity that exceeds the veneer contained by a single flitch (the wood taken from the same tree so it has a consistent appearance) you would want to confirm that the flitches could be combined in a way that works with your designs.

As the fabricator lays up the veneer (adheres it to the panels), every so often a piece of veneer is held off to the side in case there is some accidental damage to the surface (if a tool skipped or something fell against the surface damaging the veneer). How frequently a piece is held in reserve is determined by the fabricator, who hopefully notices when the pieces of veneer begin to exhibit enough change that it would be noticeable if a piece was later replaced. Wood that changes a lot, like walnut, requires more pieces held out in reserve than would a more consistent wood, like ash.

INSTALLATION

Veneered items are nearly always fabricated at the shop and transported and installed on-site. Construction requires vacuum presses to hold the veneer tight until the glue has set, high-quality lighting is required when wood is toned or stained, and the finishes need to be applied in a dust-free environment. For these and other reasons fabrication cannot take place outside the wood shop.

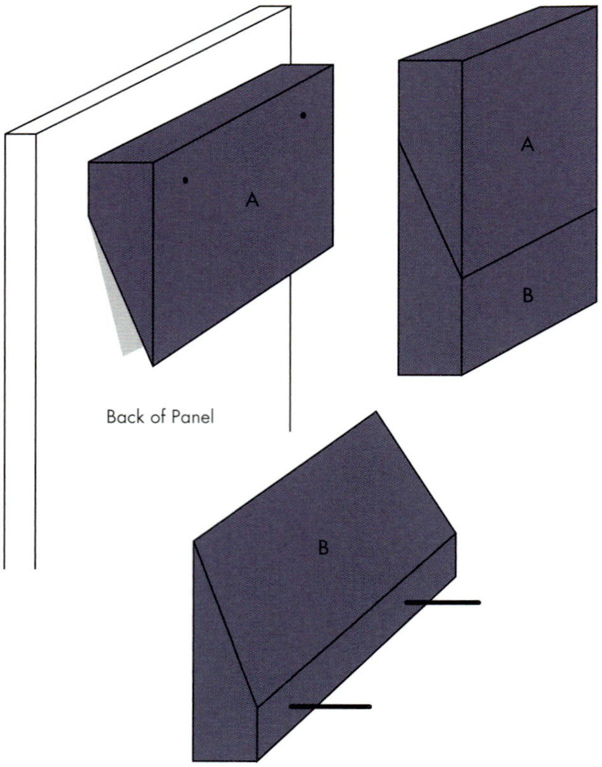

FIGURE 5.31 You might specify a cleat hanging system for you installation; your surfacing could then be demounted for possible reuse in another location.

Careful coordination between the built site and the veneered surfaces is critical if the pieces produced elsewhere are to fit perfectly. Veneered surfaces are installed with mechanical fasteners (nails and screws) and glue or they are hung on cleats; see Figure 5.31 for an illustration. Cleats are used for permanent installations as well as instances where you may want to demount the installation.

> **Point of Emphasis 5.6**
> Blocking is typically lumber or plywood fastened between studs or joists. This provides a stiffer material for the fastening of installed items, such as cabinets and wall hangings. Blocking is usually covered with Sheetrock by the time the installation takes place, so the installers will need to rely on your clear drawings and their own field check for the location of the blocking. Drywall is not sturdy enough to stabilize an installed item over time.

If your veneered item is a piece of furniture it may be simply set in place but if it needs additional stability, say a tall bookcase that could be top-heavy and fall forward, it might be fastened to the wall or ceiling at the job site. So at the very least, anything that must be installed as opposed to placed will require blocking in the wall or ceiling.

PROTECTION AND MAINTENANCE

The veneered substrate will be as impact resistant as the substrate but the surface veneer may also crush before any damage is done to the substrate. The hardness of the veneer often has little effect on durability of the assembly but the denser the wood veneer, the more durable the surface will be. Finishes also contribute to the surface's ability to resist soiling and damage.

Most of the sealants applied to veneered substrates are intended to be permanent and sufficient for the life of the product, so it is not usually the case that they must be replenished. If they are damaged, some formulas are easier to repair on-site than others. If you anticipate this need, you will account for it in your selection criteria and select an appropriate sealant.

SAFETY

Many of the finishes and glues used to make veneered items will outgas VOCs. Finishes tend to do so quickly ("wet" things outgas more quickly than "dry" things) and thus present less danger to occupants than do adhesives whose VOCs can continue to off-gas for some time. Worker safety is a concern as fabricators are exposed to finishes and adhesives on a daily basis. The EPA enforces mandates about filtration in spray booths (the portion of the shop where the finishes are sprayed on). You want to work with shops that care for workers in these less dramatic ways, as well as for the safety of their fingers, eyes, and lungs in other parts of the work performed. Of course there are saws and lathes and flying chips and dust during fabrication and all of these can be permanently harmful to workers. When you interview shops you might take a tour of their facilities so you can notice if workers are provided with (and encouraged to wear) goggles, masks, and respirators and if they demonstrate safe habits when using cutting machines. Safety is a culture-driven attitude. The culture in the shop is a top-down manifestation and it is management that creates the safe working environment with their attitude as much as with equipment. Ask if their saws have a device that automatically stops the motor if the blade encounters a hand or finger. The answer to that question alone will say a lot about how the shop cares for workers.

The substrates themselves are assembled with adhesives that become released as VOCs and as dust when pieces are sawn. Chemically sensitive individuals are likely to have problems with veneered products because of the adhesives used in the multiple layers and the formation of the substrates. Sealants often off-gas to tolerable levels quickly enough for the general public, but many adhesives continue to be bothersome to sensitive people. When installations are new, there may be a greater accumulation of VOCs so new installations are sometimes flushed with more fresh air than is typical for normal operation of the facility.

SUSTAINABILITY

Veneered surfaces conserve slow-growing hardwood and may have recycled wood waste in their engineered core material. You want to be sure that the wood that you specify is taken only from managed forests, where at least one tree is planted for every tree removed. The Forest Stewardship Council has organized a system for tracking the sustainability of wood products from harvesting through production of the final product, called the chain-of-custody. Salvaged dimensional wood is sometimes sliced into veneer.

MANAGING BUDGETS

It is economical to select a wood veneer that is closest to the desired final appearance. If you want a reddish-brown wood tone, start with a species that is naturally that color, such as cherry, mahogany, pommele, or anigre, and stain it the exact desired color. If you want a blond wood, start with woods that are natural blonds, such as maple, avodire, ash, or satinwood. For a brown wood consider walnut or pecan. Pearwood is naturally pink; purpleheart is naturally purple. Find the wood that most closely matches your desired color and figuring, and modify from there only as necessary. By limiting required modifications, you can more accurately predict the appearance of the final product and also control costs (because every additional process costs money).

If you require a special substrate for sustainability or toxicity reasons, you may pay a premium for them. Rare, figured veneers are more costly than more typical material. Complicated patterning, like marquetry, will increase time, and therefore dollars, required to complete the job.

ORGANIZATION OF THE INDUSTRY

When specifying custom millwork, detailed drawings must be made. The surface or item is drawn up in plan and elevation, to scale. All services that must be accommodated will be shown and detailed; these may include electrical, HVAC, and plumbing. The drawings that you submit will illustrate how the item will be constructed, how details will meet openings (windows and doors), and services (switch and outlet plates, HVAC grilles, etc.). The drawing should contain all specifications required to explain your intent. It is standard practice to leave the selection of joints, adhesives, and fasteners up to the fabricators, aside from a general note describing the desired results, such as "all fasteners to be concealed" (unless, of course, they are to be used decoratively as well as functionally) or "all adhesives to comply with LEED EQ 4.1 and 4.4," etc.

After a shop has been hired and paid a deposit, they will produce shop drawings. Typically produced by the fabricator, shop drawings will further illustrate construction as well as how the fastening method suggested will affect the details.

If the item is to be shop finished, the fabricator selected must have a spray booth complying with EPA mandates and a clean room that is a sealed area free of airborne dust, supplied and vented separately from the rest of the shop. Clean rooms must have a separate heating system and can function as a low-temperature oven to speed up drying time, further minimizing the risk of dust settling on a piece with tacky finish.

There are also stand-alone companies that specialize in finishing items and surface panels who can finish the piece. This work may be subcontracted by the fabricator. Figure 5.32 shows the air filters, mandated by the EPA, being changed in the spray booth. You can see that having such equipment is a big investment that not every fabricator can afford, so you may be working with multiple subcontractors as you complete the item that you have designed.

You may also make a second shop visit to view the components after they have been finished but before they are transported to the site. If there is any cosmetic blending or touch up required it can be more easily done at the shop than on-site.

WORKING WITH FABRICATORS

Your completed drawing is put out to bid with one to three shops (or more if necessary). For built-ins or paneling, a walk-through for an existing site or a plan review for a location not yet completed will give the bidder an opportunity to ask questions regarding your intention and requirements. If the item is large or fastened to the structure, the bidders may want to have an opportunity to check conditions with a walk-through. They will need to ensure that the pieces can be delivered to their location (size of access route, elevator interior dimensions, etc.).

FIGURE 5.32 Spray booths at the millwork shop have efficient exhaust systems that capture solvents and fumes. These spray booths are in "clean rooms" that have their own HVAC filtration so dust generated in the rest of the shop cannot find its way into this space and get stuck in the finish on your client's millwork.

Sometimes the bidders will estimate based on drawings alone and only want to view the site if hired. When soliciting bids, describe the samples, drawings, and mock-ups that you will require so that pricing includes them. The fabricator that is awarded the work will provide you with shop drawings and finish samples prior to beginning work after they are paid a deposit. You will review the shop drawings and mark any changes to the plans in red so that when the fabricator is building the item in the shop it is easy to see the changes that you have made. Sign and date the shops, return them to the fabricator with your approval, and the item can go into production. Figure 5.33 shows marked-up shop drawings indicating changes and corrections in red.

There can be a lot of variation among wood veneers even within the same species. If the exact coloration and markings must be controlled, you may want to go to the veneer supplier (where independent cabinet workshops purchase their veneer) to select the material to be purchased for your job. Not every job warrants a trip to the veneer supplier, but once there you will tag the veneer (the separate lots, called flitches, are groups of veneer sheets cut from the same tree having the same or similar markings and grain characteristics). Figure 5.34 shows the veneer display system at Bacon Veneer. A representative sampling of the veneer available in each flitch is housed in long wooden boxes that can be unstacked for review by the designer. After you have tagged your selection, your cabinetmaker will purchase that exact material to fill the order.

A shop visit will allow you to inspect the quality of the workmanship and the correctness of the detailing before the pieces go to the job site or into the finishing room. Timely approval of samples and drawings as well as of the work inspected during the shop visit will keep the job moving.

It is a good idea to plan a visit to the job site at the start of the installation (after materials have been unloaded) to answer any questions the installers might have regarding your intention. Visit the site again after the installation is largely completed to inspect the installation. Make sure there is no damage or soiling from the installation, that everything is aligned properly, etc.

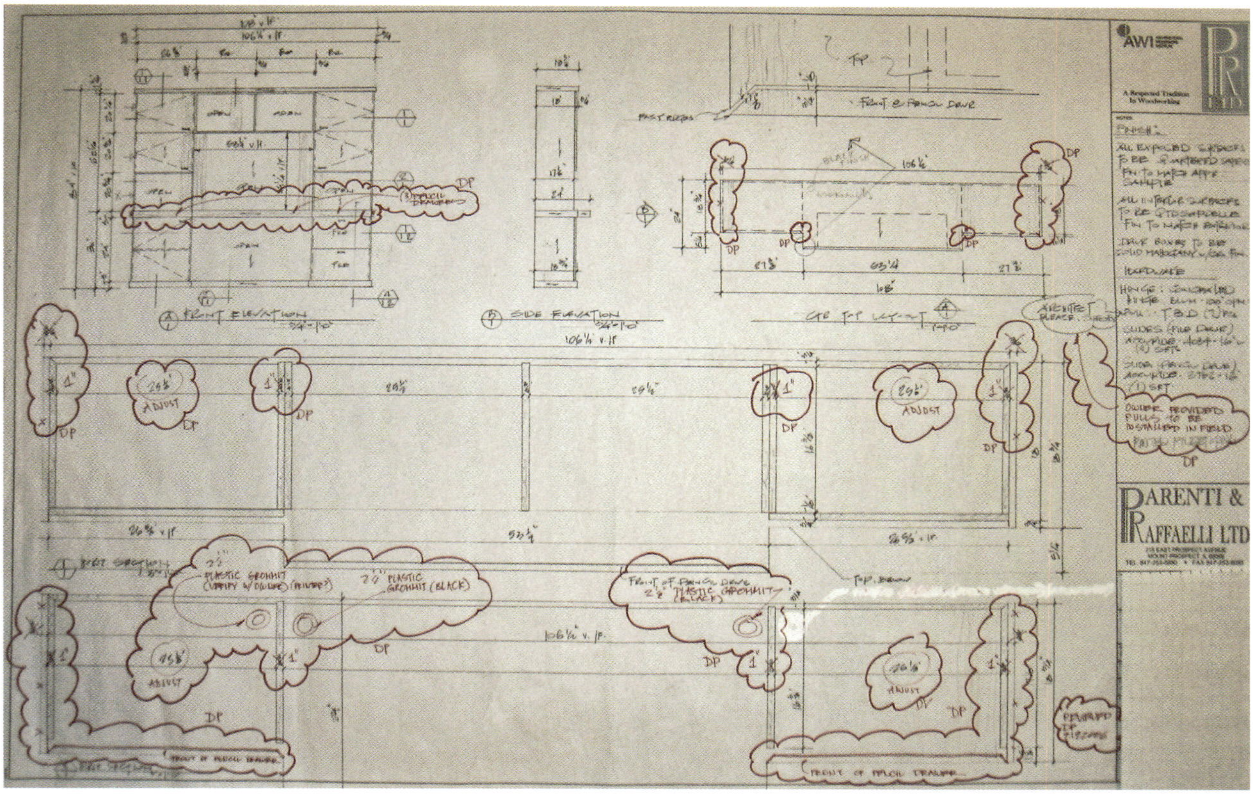

FIGURE 5.33 Shop drawings are prepared after a site measurement has been taken. Shop drawings are more detailed than the designer's drawings, which are for design intent. The shop drawings are for construction.

FIGURE 5.34 At the veneer supplier, representative leaves of veneer are viewed before a lot will be tagged by the designer for use by you or the fabricator. After you have tagged the veneer the fabricator will make a sample from that lot, with your specified finish. If the sample meets with your approval, the lot will be purchased for the job. *Image courtesy of Bacon Veneer.*

SELECTION CRITERIA

The performance characteristics of the wood species are less compelling than the appearance of wood veneer because the veneer is such a small part of the assembly. It is like a decorative coating. That said, you don't want to forget about the natural characteristics of wood that will carry over from solid to veneer selections. The color and the graining, the visual consistency, and the openness of the texture will be maintained in the veneered product. Select a wood that has visual characteristics that most closely match your vision, then address the program goals with the substrates and the sealants.

Remember that every process required not only adds time and cost to your job, but will alter the natural aging of the product. Sometimes that is a good thing, as when wood stains stabilize a color, but the interaction of a stain with glue may shift the color over time in an unexpected way. When you intermingle solid wood with veneer, they may not age the same way.

A Cautionary Tale 5.2

Figuring of wood is a visually dominant characteristic and the same species can produce wood that appears to be a different wood altogether if the grain pattern is markedly different. It is important to indicate the cut and figuring of the woods that you specify. An order was placed for a pair of chairs that were clearly intended to be a pair. They were ordered at the same time, for the same job, upholstered in the same fabric. I mistakenly thought that those circumstances alone were sufficient to cause the chairs to come in with matched wood grain but this was not to be. The chairs that arrived for my client not only exhibited different cuts of wood but different figuring as well. I was very surprised to receive one plain-sliced mahogany chair, as I expected, and one ribbon stripe mahogany chair (Figure 5.35). Ribbon stripe is prized for its uniqueness and you pay a small premium for it. I made no mention of cut or figuring on my order, so the manufacturer theoretically had the option to fill the order with any cut or figuring. Luckily my sales person at the showroom went to bat for me and had the ribbon stripe chair replaced with another plain-sliced mahogany chair such as the client anticipated.

FIGURE 5.35

Point of Emphasis 5.7

When the surfaces are veneered and before they are finished (with their stains and sealants) they should be partially assembled (as much as they can be without the structure of the site available) and positioned in the sequence that they will be in once they are installed. This usually takes place in a staging area at the shop, or on their dock—someplace with a large open area. This allows you to compare the units that will be side-by-side on-site and also to imagine the relationship of the panels to the space. A small pin knot in a corner is not as eye-catching as a small pin knot directly across from the entrance, framed by a pair of pilasters. This is the time to make any small, cosmetic adjustments to the surface before the parts go into the finishing room.

You will want to organize your own selection criteria around your project goals for your unique job. You might decide to set up a two-column table with goals and veneer characteristics paired for an organized review. Table 5.8 is a generic table of considerations; you will want to add site-specific considerations to your list of characteristics desired for your client's job.

When specifying, you may wonder whether solid or veneer is more important. The most important consideration is the need for stability. If you must have a stable wooden member, veneer is probably the best choice because it will be laid up on an engineered substrate that will be stable. Solid wood shrinks and swells as a percentage of its size, so the larger the surface, the more change in size there will be. If the surface will be subject to abuse (as is the case with kitchen door and drawer fronts and wood office furniture, for instance) then solid wood is a better idea, because a small ding in solid wood can become an unsightly scar on veneered product. If your client cannot tolerate

Table 5.8
Organize your selection criteria around the program requirements for your unique project. You may ask yourself questions like these to determine the most important characteristics for your selections.

Condition	Program Implications
Is this a commercial space that must meet fire rating?	Limit the use of plant-based substrates—they will only need fire-resistive treatment and that means chemicals. Special wallboard substrates provide additional fire-resistive properties beyond that of typical product.
Is toxicity a concern?	Traditional plaster installations are inert as long as you avoid admixture chemicals. Drywall is generally tolerable but the paper faces are recycled product so the content is not as controlled and chemically sensitive individuals cannot tolerate it. For plant-based products, look for options that contain no urea formaldehyde and offer evidence of low VOCs .
What are your sustainability goals?	The most sustainable product will endure on-site. Recycled material is a plus but weigh it against toxicity. Sulfur-containing compounds found in some recycled-product wallboard are under investigation for safety reasons. Plant-based substrates have recycled content options as well.
What kind of finish are you contemplating?	Different substrates are indicated for different finishes. Plaster products, tile, stone, paint, and wallcoverings are just a few examples of finish materials that have special wallboard substrates developed just for them. Wood veneers, plastic laminates, and resilient flooring are all installed on plant-based substrates.
What kind of sonic environment are you planning?	Dense materials contain sound, and plaster products in 1 to 3 layers all reduce noise transmission. Particleboard is naturally a reasonably good sound absorber for a hard surface. The way you install materials also contributes to their ability to absorb sound. To reflect sound, choose denser materials, including substrates.
Does your client need impact resistance?	Thicker materials for walls will be better at resisting impact. Select thicker and multiple layers of wallboard, skim-coated wallboard, and plaster. Move up to thicker options for plant-based substrates as well and, where there is the option, as for particleboard and fiberboard, select denser material.
Will moisture be a concern?	Wallboard products have been developed for wet areas so it is possible to specify those surfaces without worrying about biocides and other chemicals required for plant-based board, but such surfaces are not generally intended for coatings and require finish material that completely covers the material.
Are there existing surfaces that you could retain?	Patching in damage on existing surfaces that you can keep is a very sustainable option. If old plaster surfaces need repair, evaluate the extent of the damage and try to conserve material with plaster screws and plaster patching. You may also build up layers of varying thickness of drywall to duplicate plaster thicknesses for patching.
Will this facility need to be reconfigured to address "churn"?	Demountable and reconfigurable constructions will be preferred. If building items, use plywood substrates and smaller module sizes so they can be reconfigured in the future.

FIGURE 5.36A–B Notice that you can see the individual planks in the center panel of the solid wood cabinet door in photo (a) but that the veneer door in photo (b) has a more consistent appearance. If your client would prefer that kind of consistency, you should specify a veneered product rather than solid wood. *Photo (a) by Alana Clark.*

the difference in tone from one member to another (Figure 5.36a–b) then veneer is safer. Because a lot more veneer can be cut from any part of the log than boards, you will have more matching pieces in veneer than in solid lumber.

SPECIFYING

It is impossible to write a good spec until you have a product or surface and a specific site in mind. Imagine that you have designed a paneled wall in a stairway at a small commercial installation with medium traffic. To make the most of the natural daylight, you have selected rift-cut ash wood for its pale color and selected an abrasion-resistant sealant in a satin sheen. The job requires three matched flitches that you have inspected and tagged. Sample Spec 5.2 illustrates your instructions fot this item and scenario.

INSPECTION

When you inspect veneer you are inspecting more than the material itself, so lots of criteria outside of this subject will have to be considered. Cabinetry has a very different inspection emphasis than wall paneling, which is unlike a table. The inspection of the veneer will be the quality of the wood and matching, indiscernible fills, and the quality of the application of the colorant and sealer. There is something of an art to laying up veneer in a way that takes full advantage of beautiful grain, exuberant figuring, or conversely, the careful selection and positioning of material for austere restraint and quietude. Your aesthetic intent will be your guide in this judgment. Inspect for good craftsmanship as well. This means tight seams, neat cuts, and good relationships between the grain on two surfaces that abut or meet. The veneer used for table leaves should have grain that flows consistently from the table to the leaves.

Modern spray technologies possessed by most shops ensure that the quality of the sprayed finish is rarely defective. All the same, you should inspect for the quality of the finish coat and for work that precedes sealing. The finish should be clean, with no small debris caught under the finish. It should be consistent; if a touch-up was required you may notice a variation in the way the light glances off surface. It should be free of drips and sags. Good quality will have eased out-corners with the sharp out-corners sanded slightly to remove the sharp crease.

RELATED MATERIAL

The extensive focus on wood veneer is not to suggest that it is the only option for cladding substrates. Other popular choices are plastic and plastic laminates (see Chapter 7, Plastic Materials) and metal laminates (see Chapter 9, Metals). You could also adhere leather or cork to plant-based substrates. Wood veneer is a very popular option but not the only one.

An important related material, so important that it is covered in a separate chapter, is laminated flooring. It is frequently (though not always) a thick wood veneer on engineered substrates.

Reconstituted veneer is thin-sliced off of logs and then the sheets are glued together into a block that is again sliced thin into veneer sheets. These veneers are very consistent in appearance from one sheet to the next. They may look like natural wood or may have patterns and dyed colors that make no attempt to imitate natural wood. Other surfaces used in place of veneer may be chosen for cost savings, such as wood-look thermofoil discussed in Chapter 7. If durability of the surface is a priority, wood-look plastic laminates are specified.

Edge banding is veneer (or veneer replacement as described above) that is laminated to a paper or fabric backing with heat-set glue. It is "ironed" onto the edge of an exposed countertop or panel. This saves a little labor cost but precludes veneer matching on the edges. There are species limitations so it will not be available for every veneer that you might specify.

SUMMARY

This chapter discussed the various characteristics of solid and wood veneer, its uses, and how to specify. Considerations for the differences between wood species and forms that you will specify were discussed, as well as the typical products that utilize wood and wood veneer. Fabrication processes and the way the interior designer participates in those processes will be explained, as will the related items that factor into your selection decisions and the way you specify and manage your selections.

SAMPLE SPEC 5.2

Part 1 General Information

1.1 Related Documents

A. See elevations by designer for design intent and panel distribution.

B. Refer to approved shop drawings by fabricator for all dimensions.

C. Refer to shop drawings of staircase (staircase and handrail by others) for handrail height and mounting details to be accommodated by panel construction and installation.

1.2 Summary

A. Provide and install ash-veneered, rift-cut flat panel and rail paneling with rift-sawn ash veneers.

1.3 References

A. Installation to comply with local fire codes.

B. Quality to match AWI standards for Premium workmanship.

C. LEED credit EQ 4.1 adhesives and EQ 4.4 composite panels.

1.4 Contractor Submittals

A. Shop drawings showing sizes and dimensions, sequence numbers, grain direction, fasteners, furring, and blocking.

B. Material safety data sheets for panel products, adhesives, fire-retardant materials and finishes.

C. Veneer-faced panel minimum 18" × 18", veneered with ash from tagged lot, having at least one seam, treated with fire retardant and finished with finish specified.

D. Certificates for Sustainable Forestry Initiative, Forest Stewardship Council chain-of-custody certificate.

1.5 Quality Assurance

A. Shop to be certified participant in the Forest Stewardship Council program.

B. All fabricators employed by shop for this project to have a minimum 3 years' experience fabricating products similar to the paneling specified here.

C. Sequence-matched wood veneer to be from lots tagged by the designer.

D. Quality of workmanship to comply with AWI Premium grade.

E. Imprint indicating fire-rated material to be visible only on concealed surfaces.

F. Layout panels at shop, in sequence, for review by designer prior to finishing.

1.6 Delivery, Storage, and Handling

A. Deliver paneling to enclosed building after all wet work is complete and the HVAC system is operational, maintaining temperature and humidity levels as defined for occupancy.

B. Paneling to be stored at site, in vertical position for 24 hours prior to commencing installation.

1.7 Maintenance of Installation

A. Install paneling in conditioned site after material has acclimated sufficiently.

Part 2 Products

2.1 General information

A. Panels to be completed at shop as much as is practical, including assembly and finish. Disassemble for transport only as necessary for shipment.

B. Trial fit at shop assemblies that cannot be shipped assembled. Check dimensions against field measurements before disassembling.

2.2 Manufacturers

A. Panels Plus, 1234 Industrial Drive, Anytown, ST 45678.

2.3 Products

A. Flat panel and rail paneling per designer's elevations and shop drawings.

B. Rift-sawn, grade A, ash veneer, $^1/_{28}$" thick, for transparent finish. Assembled on blueprint-matched panels as balanced match, slip matched, with matching edge banding.

C. Core products to have a flame-spread index of 25 or less and smoke-developed index of 450 or less. Content as follows:

1. MDF made with 100% recycled wood fiber and urea formaldehyde–free binder.
2. Particleboard containing no urea formaldehyde in binder.

D. Adhesives to comply with LEED EQ 4.1 and 4.4.

E. Catalyzed lacquer finish, 35% sheen per approved sample.

Part 3 Execution

3.1 Examination

A. At field measure, prior to installation of drywall, confirm and locate for shop drawings all concealed framing, blocking, and reinforcements.

B. Where paneling is intended to fit to wallboard on lower level and second floor, verify dimensions of construction.

3.2 Preparation

A. Shop cut openings to the maximum extent possible for electrical outlets and sconce boxes using templates or diagrams to ensure that openings will be concealed by cover plates and back plates. Sand all openings and cut edges.

B. Fill or plug all fastener holes, blend with surrounding surface.

C. Inventory and inspect shop-fabricated work.

D. Shop finish all surfaces that will be visible in completed installation.

3.3 Installation

A. Install level, plumb, straight, and true with faces of panel rails aligned to within $^1/_{32}$".

B. Scribe to fit to adjoining surface, repair and blend finish at cuts.

3.4 Post Installation

A. Repair any damage from installation and blend with adjoining and surrounding surfaces.

B. Clean all panel surfaces and leave site broom clean.

WEB SEARCH ACTIVITIES

1. Perform an image search for *wood plank flooring* to see the variety of products and styles that you might specify.
2. Go to the Forest Stewardship Council's Web site (www.fsc.org) and select *Certification*. There are different kinds of certificates listed there; read the requirements pertaining to the certificates that wood product producers can be eligible for so you understand the meaning of the certificates that your vendors hold.
3. Perform an image search for *custom wood stairs*. Zoom in on a couple of images and notice the details that you would have to consider and define (in drawings and in written specs) if you had designed these staircases for a client. Looking at other people's designs and figuring them out is a great way to expand your repertoire.
4. Perform an image search for *prehung doors*. Find an image of a prehung door that is not yet installed. Next, search for *install prehung door* and compare that to the instructions that you find for *install slab door*. After reviewing the steps required to install a slab door compared to the steps required to install a prehung door, you will be able to understand why your client will pay more for the installation of the former.
5. Perform a search for *reclaimed wood* plus your zip code to see what sources of recycled wood are near you and what they offer.
6. Perform an image search for *domestic wood species* and then one for *imported wood species*. Find an image that has lots of different wood samples displayed in a single image, where you are able to do a visual comparison of a number of species.
7. Locate a master spec for solid wood flooring online. The American Institute of Architects (AIA) has authored a spec for a small project wooden floor. See if you can find that one—it is nice and straightforward (www.aia.org). Review it in its entirety for comprehension.
8. Perform an image search for *stave-core door* to see the different ways this core is employed in the manufacture of doors.
9. Search for the natural characteristics of wood listed in Table 5.3 on page 159 or search for the species listed to get an idea of what each of these descriptive terms mean. Perform an image search for the species, insert the word *floor* at the end of your search string so you will get a broader visual sampling to give you a better sense of the variation in the species.

   Construct a table placing the two images from row 1 next to each other, then row 2, etc., as a reference guide to these different characteristics.

PERSONAL ACTIVITIES

1. Find a picture of a solid wood product and describe it in terms of grain, texture, and color. Practice until you feel you are really seeing the characteristics of each kind of wood.
2. Consider an area in your own plan where you might use a solid wood surface or an assembly built of solid wood parts, or find a picture of an installation of solid wood in an interior space. Using the spec template in Chapter 2, write a spec for the item or surface.

SUMMARY QUESTIONS

1. What are characteristics that all natural, solid wood products share?
2. What are the quality standards defined by the grading system and how would you describe the wood that falls in each category?
3. Which will shrink more: a 2¼-inch-wide wood strip or a 10-inch-wide wood plank? Why?
4. What can make wood change color over time?
5. Describe the difference between open and closed grain. Consistent or varied color presentation? Prominent or subtle grain? Color undertones of wood?
6. What is the difference between grain and figuring?
7. How does the cut of a board change the way it looks? The way it performs?
8. What are the differences between strips of wood and planks of wood?

9. What is parquet flooring?
10. What are some examples of woods commonly used for solid wood floors? What are some less common woods that are also available?
11. What finish, traditionally used for wood floors, makes it difficult to apply a modern synthetic formula if you are reusing existing floors?
12. How can you deal with staining or discoloration on an existing floor?
13. What characteristics of old flooring are different from the same species as new wood?
14. What kinds of things would you consider if you were trying to decide whether to reuse or replace an existing floor?
15. When specifying a new or replacement wood floor, what other items might you order at the same time?
16. What are architectural millwork trims and what are they for? How do you specify them? How are they sold—units of measure? Finishes? Materials?
17. In what ways can wood's tendency to crack and shrink be overcome for doors?
18. What are characteristics of solid wood doors?
19. What are the differences between a prehung and loose-leaf door? What are the implications for hardware inherent in each?
20. What are options for stair treads?
21. Who typically makes the purchase for flooring material? Architectural wood trims? Doors? Stair parts? Who typically makes each? Who installs each?
22. What is the difference between nominal and actual size? Why are they different? In what circumstances will they matter?
23. Why would boards intended for a floor be given tongue-and-groove edges?
24. What are the benefits of prefinished floors over site-finished floors? What are the benefits of site-finished floors over prefinished floors?
25. What are the steps when installing a site-finished floor versus a prefinished floor? When would you inspect each?
26. What is the difference between staved core and solid wood doors?
27. What are common colorants for solid wood?
28. What are common sealants for solid wood?
29. What environmental issues pertain to sealants?
30. How does procurement and installation differ between floor installations and stair installations?
31. Who will typically finish a wood floor? Wood trim?
32. How can you tell if an installer is qualified?
33. What are the differences between stock and custom product?
34. What instructions should you give the installer about how to cut architectural millwork trims at installation?
35. How does the installation of prehung doors differ from loose-leaf doors?
36. How can the finish of a wood floor be restored?
37. What safety issues pertain to floors? Stairs? Trims? Doors?
38. What sustainability options can the designer exercise pertaining to solid wood?
39. What kind of choices will increase costs for wood selections?
40. At what point in construction would you inspect wood floors and what would you look for?
41. At what point in construction would you inspect wood millwork trims and what would you look for?
42. At what point in construction would you inspect wood doors and what would you look for?
43. At what point in construction would you inspect a wood staircase and what would you look for?
44. How and why is wood veneer on an engineered substrate different from solid wood?
45. What are the different backings that come on wood veneer?

46. What characteristics will wood veneer share with solid wood of the same species?
47. What processes can change the visual characteristics of veneer?
48. For what reason would you combine veneer and solid wood in the same project?
49. What are the different grades of veneer? How are they different from each other?
50. What does *figuring* mean? What causes it?
51. What substrates is veneer adhered to?
52. What is edge banding and what is it for? What alternatives are there to edge banding?
53. What are the different cuts used for veneer?
54. What are the different patterns utilized to lay veneer up on the substrate?
55. What is the difference between balance match and center match?
56. How are sequence and warehouse match similar? How are they different? What makes them different from blueprint matching?
57. What colorants and finishes are common to wood veneer?
58. What is a flitch and why is it significant?
59. When would you encounter phenolic and why would you want to address it?
60. What kind of fabricators make products with wood veneer? How can you vet the fabricators so you can figure out which one to hire?
61. What are some indicators of quality veneer work and finishing?
62. Why are veneered surfaces typically finished in the shop?
63. Why is the substrate significant for performance and durability of the veneered surface?
64. What kind of safety issues pertain to production of these surfaces? What kind of safety issues pertain to end users in the space?
65. What is the point of flushing a facility when an installation is new?
66. What does *chain-of-custody* mean and what organization defines its effectiveness?
67. What sustainability issues pertain to these surfaces?
68. What kinds of features will increase job costs?
69. What steps will take place as you manage your design from inception to installation?

Chapter 6

RESILIENT FLOORING

Key Terms

Full-spread adhesive
Glueless tile system
Grade level
Heat welding
Loose-laid
Patching compounds
Reducer strip
Wear layer
Welding rods

Objectives

After reading this chapter, you should be able to:

- Distinguish between the available product options in this category and make recommendations based on performance attributes.
- Understand product characteristics and be able to make site evaluations to guide your specifications for materials, prepwork, and labor.
- Consider the needs of different kinds of sites and understand the distinction between residential and commercial product.
- Understand the different installation techniques typical for different product types and how installation will progress.
- Know about the typical accessories that are part of a resilient floor installation and what alternative flooring meets some of the same goals as resilient product.

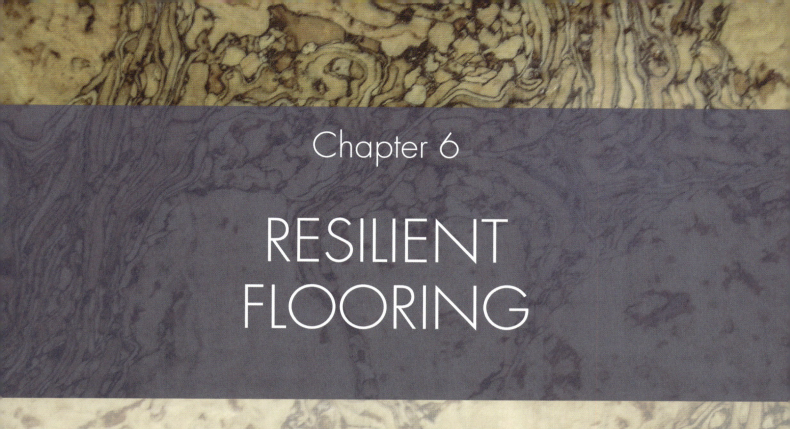

Resilient floor coverings are a product with broad appeal in many market segments spanning residential, hospitality, retail, institutional clients, and health care. Recent economic volatility has skewed annual quantities but it is safe to say that between 17 billion (yes—that's with a *b*) and 21 billion square feet of resilient floor covering were installed last year, so you will most certainly specify resilient product during your career.

MATERIAL

Resilient flooring is highly functional for areas where easy maintenance, low cost, and durability are required. It is impervious to water, resists stains, and can be easily disinfected. Resilient sheet goods can usually be used in seamless installations thanks to special seaming products available from the flooring's manufacturers. Products described as welded or fused have tighter seams than seams made with adhesives.

Material additives can build beneficial characteristics into the product to dissipate static electricity, protect against growth of microbes and mold, and self-seal the surface with buffing alone, eliminating the need to apply wax to protect it. Product offerings can have a high-tech or industrial appeal or imitate natural materials like wood or stone, allowing resilient flooring to express varied concepts. People with chemical and dust sensitivities can live with these floors because they can be easily cleaned and do not trap dust. Resilient floors may be color-through, meaning they look the same throughout their entire thickness and there is no surface to wear away. Other products have various functional layers topped with a decorative layer (patterns, geometrics, natural stone designs, and more) protected by a **wear layer**. The wear layer is critical to durability for this product category. For your heavy use, commercial installations look for wear layers of at least 0.05 inch and an overall thickness of 0.08 inch. Aesthetic choices will be driven by program goals but remember that patterned products can do a good job hiding soiling and scuff marks.

> **Helpful Hint 6.1**
>
> Organic patterns function better than very regular geometric patterns for camouflaging soiling. This is important when a high-traffic site must maintain its appearance but it is difficult to constantly clean the floor, such as in 24-hour facilities.

Resilient floors can become scratched, stained, or gouged, and they may develop bumps, bubbles, or curled edges, especially if not properly installed. Heavy foot traffic or the constant movement of furniture can cause wear patterns. They may fade in direct sun so exposure must be considered when specifying.

The product categories within the type are organized around their differing main ingredients. Cork is, of course, made of the bark of the cork tree and leather comes from cowhides. Vinyl floor products, sheet, tile, and wovens are made of polyvinyl chloride (PVC). Rubber may be made of natural rubber, tapped from rubber trees or, more likely, it will be a synthetic rubber styrene-butadiene rubber. Polyolefin flooring is a mixture of polyethylene and polypropylene, two ingredients that are environmentally preferable to the polyvinyl chloride products. Polyolefin products were developed to replace PVC, but it is taking some time to get specifiers to make the switch, partly due to up-front cost when compared to the vinyl that it was created to replace.

CHARACTERISTICS

The reason that this material category is called resilient is that it will conform to the substrate, so if the surface that the material is adhered to is not smooth the flooring will not compensate for that and the resilient surface will not be smooth. There are a number of material compositions available with some variation in performance and sustainability characteristics.

Linoleum

Linoleum is biodegradable, so subject to damage from excessive or standing water. It is composed of natural materials. It is manufactured by oxidizing linseed oil to form a thick mixture called linoleum cement that is mixed with pine resin and wood flour to form sheets on jute backing. It is hygienic; its inherent natural properties actually halt the breeding of many microorganisms. Naturally antistatic, it repels dust and dirt, making it easy to maintain a clean environment.

Linoleum is available in tiles ranging in size from 12" × 12" to 20" × 20" and sheets that are typically 78 inches wide and 65 to 100 feet long. Sheets can be cut and pieced to produce custom patterns. Linoleum's colors go all the way through. Linoleum is a green product because its components are manufactured from readily renewable, natural raw materials and it is recyclable.

Cork

Cork flooring is available in tiles ranging from 1/8 inch to 1/2 inch thick in varying sizes. Laminated cork "planks" are also available. They may have an engineered product backing them and sometimes have an additional cushioning layer. Laminated products typically have tongue-and-groove or click-and-lock edges. The characteristics of laminated cork options relate more to laminated product than to resilient flooring. The material that the cork is laminated to is often rigid, so review Chapter 13, Laminated Materials, to understand these cork products better. Cork is also a component in cork-vinyl tiles.

Cork shares some characteristics with wood: It comes from trees and expands and contracts with changes in humidity. It is susceptible to water absorption. It is sometimes used for its insulation properties and notable sound-deadening characteristics. It is available unfinished or prefinished with wax or polyurethane. In its natural (unfinished) state, cork is susceptible to staining, so it must be sealed, usually with the same formulas used for wood flooring. Finishes will alter the sheen and perhaps deepen the color a little as shown in Figure 6.1a and b.

Unfinished cork floors can be stained (like wood flooring) using a water-based stain. After the stain has dried completely, three coats of water-based urethane are applied following the manufacturer's instructions.

Cork flooring is antistatic, sound absorbing, insulating (against both heat and sound), and tolerable to people with allergies. It can withstand moderate traffic and weight and has a "memory," so it recovers well from compression. It is considered to be especially comfortable to stand on. Cork flooring product has a range of available visual characteristics (Figure 6.2a–c).

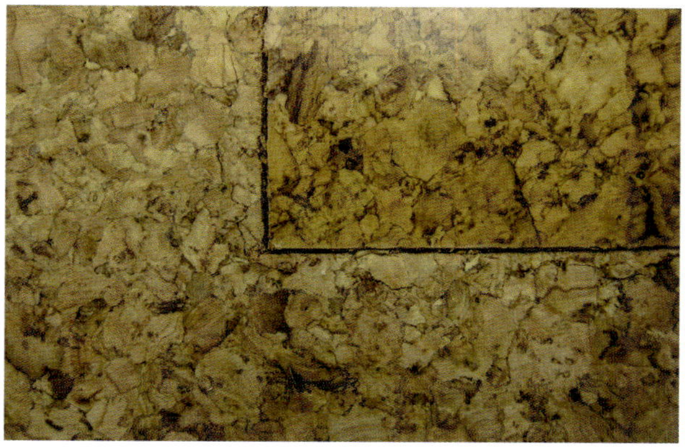

FIGURE 6.1A Cork flooring shown unfinished for finishing on-site and prefinished with a urethane top coat.

FIGURE 6.1B The softer sheen of wax compared to urethane. Wax satisfies a desire for naturalness but urethane is easier to maintain over time.

FIGURE 6.2A–C Cork is a natural product and strict control of visual characteristics is not possible, however variations within a range can be selected. It is a good idea to get current samples whenever possible.

FIGURE 6.3 Leather tiles are a luxury product for light-traffic situations.

Leather

Leather tiles are cut from the back area of very heavy weight skins. They are full thickness from unsplit hides because thicker skins are more stable and consistent. Tiles are available in different shapes and sizes (Figure 6.3) in both natural and dyed colors. Color and texture variation is present in both natural and dyed leather tiles. Leather tiles are sensitive to UV rays and quickly fade. Some people are charmed by this responsiveness to the environment. Make sure your educated client is one of them before you specify this product.

> **Point of Emphasis 6.1**
> Leather used for upholstery and apparel is made from split hides. This means that the hide was split to half of its thickness. Leather used for flooring is not split, but uses the entire thickness of the skin.

Leather tiles must be sealed to protect them from staining. In addition to any sealant applied at the factory, leather tiles should be waxed two or three times on-site (Figure 6.4). They will develop a patina of surface scratches over time when exposed to even light traffic. Explain to your client that these changes in the appearance of the material are normal and desirable characteristics as the material mellows with age. Leather tiles are considered to be comfortable underfoot and many people feel they become more beautiful over time as they wear in, but they are only for the client who appreciates the changes and patina that develops with age and are not for high-traffic installations.

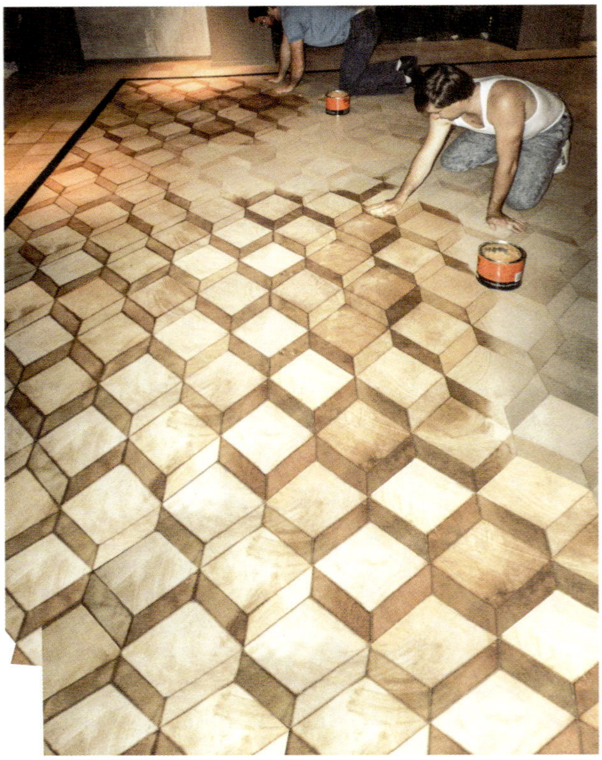

FIGURE 6.4 Leather floors are waxed at installation. Other than waxing, there is no recommended way of cleaning leather floors—they are similar to antique wood flooring in this respect. The wax acts as a top dressing and should be periodically cleaned and replenished to maintain the floor.

Vinyl

Vinyl flooring products contain varying degrees of vinyl, mineral aggregate (limestone is most typical), pigments, plasticizers, and stabilizers. Tile described as solid vinyl tile (SVT) is not composed solely of vinyl but is consistent all through its depth. Material that has other ingredients will be called vinyl composition tile (VCT). Only if the product is identified as pure vinyl will it be composed solely of vinyl. When you work on renovations, you will likely encounter vinyl asbestos tile (VAT). Asbestos is a hazardous material and you should avoid disturbing it if you can. A safe way of dealing with it is to cover it with another material. If it must be removed, this work must be done by trained experts.

There are various offerings of vinyl products addressing different program needs, so the organization of vinyl products is a little more complicated. Refer to Table 6.1 for a way to understand these vinyl products and how they differ from each other.

Point of Emphasis 6.2

Like VCT, VAT was only available as tile. You may encounter VAT on renovation work that you undertake. It is usually of a smaller dimension (8" × 8" or 9" × 9") and should never be sanded or be removed by regular demolition crews. Asbestos products require specialists to remove them.

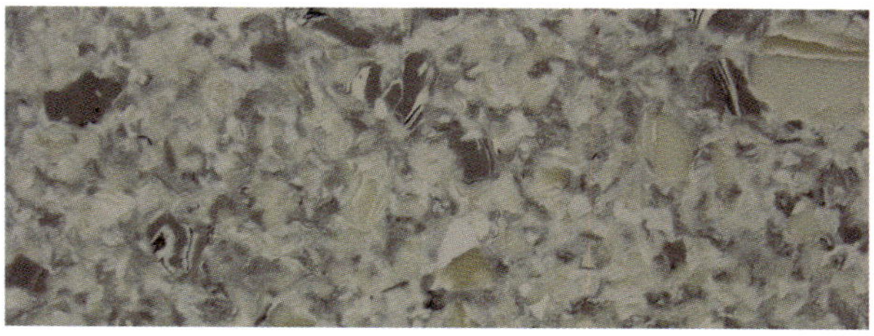

FIGURE 6.5A Solid vinyl tile imitating a terrazzo.

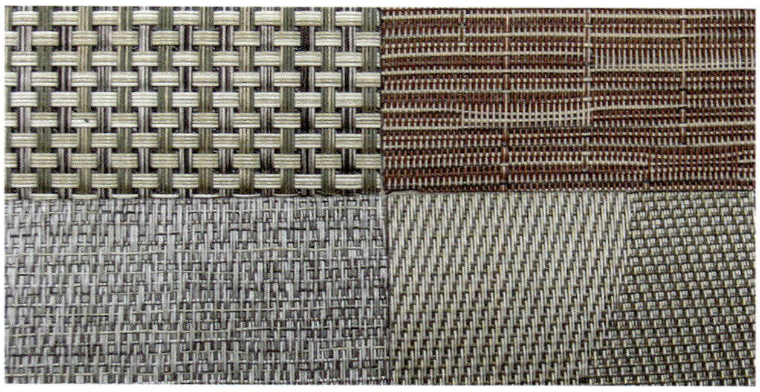

FIGURE 6.5B Woven vinyl product for floors has good slip resistance and easy maintenance with the moisture-resistance characteristics of solid vinyl.

Figure 6.5a and b show two vinyl materials: one is a smooth sheet and the other is woven on a loom. Woven vinyl is commercial-grade floor covering that is maintained like sheet vinyl and can be mopped. Vinyl is most commonly available as sheets or tiles but woven vinyl is also very serviceable.

Precision ground edges produce a floor that can have the appearance of a one-piece sheet vinyl floor. Other optional features that you will find among product offerings include products that disperse static electricity. These materials are installed as a system of specialty tile, grounding strips, and conductive adhesive. Other

Table 6.1
Vinyl product offerings are varied. Review this table to help you organize the types in your head between sheet and tile product types.

Type	Characteristics	Options
Inlaid vinyl sheet	Vinyl chips in a matrix usually attached to a backing Frequently with a protective top coat Color or pattern is an integral part of the wear layer	Backing may be felt, vinyl, or fiberglass
Homogeneous sheet flooring	Around 30% vinyl (PVC) with around 60% limestone Consistent in color and pattern throughout its full thickness; the whole thickness is the wear layer Not backed As much as 70% vinyl 3' or 6' wide × $^{3}/_{32}$" to $^{1}/_{8}$" thick	
Heterogeneous sheet flooring	Laminated product having minimally a felt fiberglass or plastic bottom layer May be cushioned to enhance sound absorption or underfoot comfort Must be at least 50% vinyl A decorative, printed, or patterned layer topped by a clear wear layer It may be smooth or embossed Typical width 6' or 6.5' × approximately .08" thick	Special backings have cushioning (for impact noise and comfort) Static dissipative, stain-resistant, and slip-retardant surfaces can be specified
Pure vinyl tile	100% vinyl Tile sizes up to 36" × 36"	Product offerings are very limited; often as electrostatic dissipative (ESD) product
Solid vinyl tile (SVT)	May actually be around 30% vinyl (PVC) with around 60% limestone Tiles up to 36" × 36"	The higher vinyl content allows for larger tiles than VCT
Vinyl composition tile (VCT)	VCT will have content similar to solid vinyl but will be 70% to 85% limestone Tile sizes up to 36" × 36"	Static dissipative product available
Luxury vinyl tile (LVT)	35% vinyl, 50% limestone; $^{1}/_{8}$" thick, 12' × 12' Tiles up to 18" × 18" or 3' long planks in 4" to 8" widths	
Enhanced vinyl tile (VET)	More vinyl than VCT Tiles up to 18" × 18"	No accepted definition among industry partners

products are designed to provide greater slip resistance or luminous strips for low-light or emergency situations.

Sheet vinyl that is popular for residential use is a slightly different product than commercial sheet vinyl. Residential grades have a surface that has been built up out of tiny granules fused together by heat and pressure, often over a cushioning layer of foam. It is usually available in 12-foot widths and continuous lengths up to 90 and even 100 feet. This sheet vinyl flooring derives its durability from its upper layer, or wear layer, which is a clear vinyl resin available in different thicknesses. The thicker the wear layer, the more expensive and longer lasting the product will be. The thickness of wear layers can range from .005 inch to .025 inch.

Many sheet vinyl floors have a very high gloss achieved by adding a urethane on top of the clear, vinyl wear layer. These urethanes are as durable as the urethanes that are used on hardwood flooring.

Sheet vinyls can be installed to be very impervious to water, especially when "welded" to coved base accessories. They emit very low volatile organic compounds (VOCs) after installation. They offer some cushioning with less maintenance than carpet. Patterns tend to have better appearance retention than solids and organic patterns stay clean-looking longer than geometric patterns. Even if you are more of an advocate of clean than of "clean-looking" you still must concede that there are high-traffic installations where it is unsafe or inconvenient to be continuously mopping the floor (24-hour environments like emergency rooms come to mind) so soil hiding is an important characteristic under some circumstances.

Two simple classification systems that you will encounter pertaining to vinyl tile refer to surface and product composition.

- Class I is monolithic (through materials).
- Class II is material with a surface decoration.
- Class III is material with a printed decorative surface.
- Type A has a smooth face.
- Type B has an embossed texture.

The way these two classification systems work together is that you may specify a tile that is Class I, Type A, which means it would be a single material through the entire tile body and a smooth face.

Rubber

Rubber tile may be natural rubber but more likely it will be synthetic styrene butadiene rubber (SBR) with very fine mineral aggregate, stabilizers, pigments, and wax. Manufacturers' literature is sometimes unclear about the composition of the rubber they use and if you are intent on locating rubber tapped from trees it may take some sleuthing. Natural rubber from trees does not age as well as synthetic rubber.

Rubber flooring is available as tiles or rolls. Tile is typically available in 12" × 12" up to 36" × 36" in 1/8 inch thickness. Rolls will likely be 1/12 inch to 1/8 inch thick and sold in rolls that are typically 3 to 6 feet wide and approximately 40 feet long, with heavier gauge material shipped in shorter lengths. It is often a homogenous product in solid colors, marbleized or with a design of small colored chips. Some products have a recycled rubber backing.

The material can be tightly butted. The seams can be "welded" for seamless installation. Heat welding is very common and requires that a groove be cut at the junction between two sheets; the heated "rod" is laid down in this groove. Some products allow for cold welding with proper caulks. Chemical welds are generally not as strong as heat welding and are too runny to use when the material is being applied to a vertical surface.

You will find that recycled product is readily available. Even though many recycled materials have only darker or desaturated colors, there is a wide range of colors available for recycled rubber flooring (Figure 6.6). Various thicknesses and configurations for lock-in-place allow modular units to be repositioned, and many goods are available with integral cushioning for sports and work environments (Figures 6.7 and 6.8). Custom installations can be cut and assembled from solid material. Laminated product or compound product can provide alternative characteristics to meet your program goals, like extra cushioning for work environments where people spend a lot of time on their feet, as shown in Figure 6.9. Sheet goods, including rubber, can provide opportunities for custom designs like logos, directional motifs for wayfinding, or as shown in Figure 6.10, a map of a region that is instructional, engaging, and aesthetically appropriate as it breaks up a large expanse of floor that would be blank and uninteresting.

Figure 6.6 Recycled rubber flooring. *Burke Mercer.*

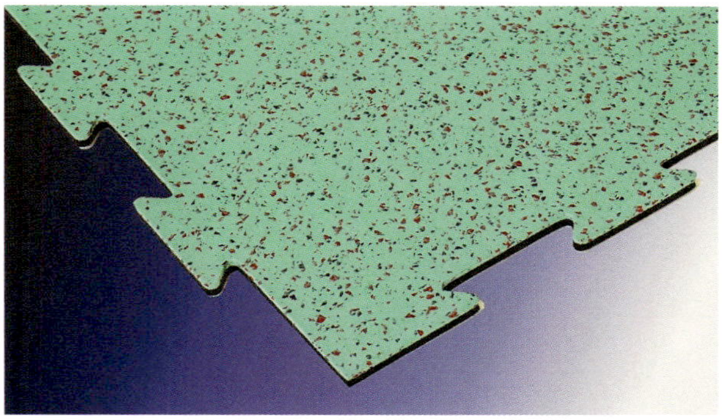

Figure 6.8 Interlocking modular tiles allow for moving or replacing individual tiles. *Burke Mercer.*

Rubber and synthetic rubber are both degraded by oil but are otherwise durable flooring. They require regular buffing to maintain appearance because they tend to show scuffs. Rubber flooring is naturally slip resistant and many rubber flooring products have a textured face to increase slip resistance (Figure 6.11). Most rubber flooring offers a coefficient of friction of .8 or higher, exceeding the ADA mandate of .6 or greater. Some products have a granular nonslip feature or strip to provide even more traction. Of all the products in this category, rubber tends to provide the best slip resistance and best comfort underfoot. Naturally elastic, rubber also reduces impact noise.

Polyolefin

Polyolefin products are a very minor player in this category but worthy of a mention because of their potential to replace vinyl. Common ingredients are polyethylene, chalk, and clay. They were developed in an effort to diminish the market for the environmentally unfriendly PVC required for vinyl products. In comparison to VCT, which it attempts to replace, it is reportedly easier to clean and, according to research by the Health Care Research

Figure 6.7 Ecostone. *Burke Mercer.*

Figure 6.9 Rubber tile with integral cushioning for sports locations and other areas where slip resistance and a softer surface are required.

Figure 6.10 The custom capabilities of rubber flooring is appealing for large spaces where a meaningful pattern, such as this map in a schoolroom, could contribute to the design program with a very serviceable surface.

Figure 6.11 Standard rubber-tile surface textures.

Collaborative, nursing staff reported that it was more comfortable underfoot. One area where it as yet requires development is in its resiliency. These floors show evidence of wheeled traffic. Adhesives have not been developed that form long-term, reliable bonds to some common substrates. Like the VCT tiles they are being developed to replace, this product cannot be installed seamlessly.

Available as tiles in 12" × 12" and 18" × 18", they have thicknesses of 3/32 inch and 1/8 inch, as are available in other resilient materials. Polyolefin floors are also available as laminate product in tile and plank formats.

PARTS AND ACCESSORIES

Resilient flooring is typically easy for the professional installer to install because it is simply glued in place. The tricky part is applying the correct adhesive for the substrate that is also compatible with the resilient product and will stand up to site conditions during use. Absorbent substrates to which the tile might be glued will require different adhesives than nonabsorbent substrates.

The condition of the substrate is very important for this material because any divot or dimple in the subfloor will telegraph through to the face. Concrete leveling products or engineered panels like plywood or particleboard may be specified as substrates for this material.

These materials are thin. If they are abutting an equally thin material you could specify a butt seam. If resilient material is abutting a thicker material a transition of some sort will have to be provided. If the difference is greater than ½ inch it will be a good idea to raise the resilient material up with the substrate specified.

If you have stairs in your installation, look for product that has coordinating treads. These products often have textured surfaces and curved nosing edges, coordinating with your flooring and providing a nice finish to the stair surfacing without necessitating extra labor and edging materials. Coordinating baseboards are also readily available.

A typical finish detail for the edge of the resilient material when it transitions to another is a metal edge. A variety of metal transition strips are manufactured for this precise purpose; they range from a very minimal "terrazzo"-type edging (Figure 6.12a) to broader strips that bridge more pronounced differences in material thickness (Figure 6.12b).

Another transition area to be specified is the transition between the floor and the wall. In addition to more

FIGURE 6.12A–B Transitions between the usually thinner resilient product and adjoining surfaces must be detailed carefully to meet code in commercial installation and provide an attractive transition in any installation. A variety of products are available.

(a) Generally a minimal transition is preferred and if flooring substrates can be specified to make the finished installation flush with adjoining flooring then a very minimal terrazzo edging can be specified.
(b) If a minimal transition is not possible, you may have to specify a transition strip that provides more of a "bridge" from one material to the next.

FIGURE 6.13 In commercial installations it is quite common to specify a vinyl base for resilient material and for carpeted areas. Manufacturers tend to color coordinate across the industry so coordinating base and stair accessories can be companionable when paired with resilient flooring material.

traditional products, resilient product accessory items, such as base strips, are available to accompany the resilient flooring that you specify (Figure 6.13). These bases can be chemically welded to the flooring for seamless surfaces that are easy to clean. They are also often simply adhered to the perimeter wall surface. Stair treads, with or without abrasive feature strips for additional traction, coordinate with tiles and sheet goods.

SITE CONSIDERATIONS

The fabrication of the materials themselves is less critical for you to understand than the installed assembly. Some issues specific to this kind of flooring pertain to the prepwork for the installation.

Moisture Control

Rooms with floors at or below **grade level** sometimes have moisture migrating up through construction materials that can cause the flooring to loosen, especially around the edges of the room. In these cases, the moisture problem must be solved before installing or repairing an earlier installation for installation of new resilient flooring. If there is a risk of moisture migration from below-grade concrete slab floors, a moisture barrier (often 6 millimeter film of polyethylene) is required. A plywood subfloor is installed on top of this barrier and the flooring is glued to the subfloor.

Subflooring

Resilient flooring is a thin, flexible material so any unevenness in the subfloor will telegraph through to the surface in a very short amount of time. A 35-pound particleboard with square edges is often used as a subfloor for cushioned product. Particleboard will absorb water; this is a limiting factor in the total assembly. Many resilient flooring materials can stand up to water but if water should leak down to the subfloor the installation will be ruined. Sometimes particleboard is covered over with MDF board for a really hard, smooth surface. Plywood subfloor is often specified as A-C with the higher quality face (A) "up" so resilient flooring material is adhered to the smooth, better quality surface.

If heavy water spills are anticipated, the perimeter of the room should be caulked prior to installing molding or baseboards. You may specify cementitious backer board with properly prepared seams for some products installed where excessive water is a concern.

If the floor is uneven or if the thin resilient material must be brought to a flush relationship with a thicker adjacent floor you might decide to "float" the floor with a self-leveling compound to bring finished flooring surfaces into flush alignment with each other. Sometimes, rather than float a large area, material may be ramped from the resilient flooring area up to the finished height of the adjacent flooring. If the compound used to create the ramp is feathered out sufficiently, it is likely that the slight incline will go unnoticed. The material typically used to accomplish these changes in surface and level often contains cement that may have to cure before resilient flooring can be glued to it. Curing some of these compounds takes about four weeks, so confirm that the schedule allows for this or select other options.

Helpful Hint 6.2

A simple test for presence of moisture in concrete subfloors is to tape a piece of plastic to the floor and leave it there for a day. If there is a damp square when you check back you will have to specify an appropriate moisture barrier.

A Cautionary Tale 6.1

Resilient flooring made perfect sense for this high-traffic installation in a school but the budget did not allow for thorough prepwork to be performed on the cement substrate prior to installation. Because the substrate was "not that bad" it was presumed that the less-than-perfect cement surface could just be covered over with resilient product. It was not long before the installation began to show the underlying stresses on the surface of the material. There was some slight movement and further cracking of the subfloor. While it was not structural, it was significant enough to telegraph through the finished flooring in several places (Figure 6.14).

FIGURE 6.14 Improper subfloor preparation has allowed defects to telegraph through to the surface.

Existing Floor as Substrate

If you are specifying resilient flooring as a replacement material, you might use the existing flooring as the substrate for the new resilient product. The previous floor surface would have to be flat and smooth (or made so by floating the floor) and tightly adhered throughout. If the previous floor is coming loose in places, those places will have to be secured or broken out and the surface patched to a flat, flush condition in order to use it as a substrate. When you encounter asbestos tile, the preferred way to address it is to cover it with safe flooring. You could glue new resilient flooring over sound asbestos material and avoid costly, expert removal.

What Would You Do? 6.1

Imagine that you were using resilient flooring to lend identity to different areas of a hospital to help with wayfinding and to appeal to patients and visitors. What kind of installation do you imagine when you think of a ward for childhood diseases? For the obstetrics department? Would you use tile or sheet goods to implement the designs that came to mind? What kind of product would you specify?

QUALIFYING INSTALLERS

Installers of this kind of product will often learn on the job and improve their skills working first as a helper or apprentice and, as they prove ready to be responsible for more details of the job, move into an installer position. Manufacturers will frequently offer training courses for a fee and it is quite typical that a valued employee of the installation company will be sponsored by their employer to travel and participate in a training course.

When you hire an installation company to perform this kind of work, you are hiring the company and not the individual installers, so the qualifications that you will look for will pertain to the overall experience and reputation of the company providing the individual workers. The installation company selected should have experience with the product that you specified. They should probably demonstrate their professional commitment through a membership in an appropriate organization such as the Floor Covering Installation Board (FCIB) and perhaps with a training certificate from Certified Floorcovering Installers (CFI).

If any part of the system (flooring, substrate, or adhesive) that you are specifying is a new system you may ask the product manufacturer for the names of installers who have installed the product in your area. If you encountered the product through a dealer, they will likely install it or they know who in the area is trained to install it.

INSTALLATION

Although you will be relying on a professional installer, you need to know enough about the installation of the flooring material you have specified to be able to evaluate the installer's work. Remember that evaluation of the substrate is important because this product will conform to that surface. If your client's site requires repair of the substrate, make sure that products are compatible with each other and that lead times allow for patches to fully cure. **Patching compounds** have variable properties to solve specific problems and not all are compatible with recommended installation. Read manufacturer information about patching and subfloor recommendations carefully before completing your spec for prepwork.

After proper preparation of the subfloor (see Site Considerations above) sheet goods will either be fully adhered with a **full-spread adhesive**, perimeter-adhered (just glued down at the edges), or **loose-laid**. Unless tile is designed to be part of a **glueless tile system** it will always be glued down. Glueless systems have shaped edges that slide or nestle together or use an adhesive system of tabs that stick the tile down. These systems are usually intended for areas where you may want to remove the flooring for repositioning or reuse elsewhere.

The manufacturer will typically recommend the proper adhesive from their product line and it is generally a good idea to use what they recommend. Peel-and-stick tiles are generally for DYI installations and if your residential consulting client plans to install their own flooring that might be an instance when such a product is the best choice.

What Would You Do? 6.2

Rolls of resilient sheet goods are not unlimited in length. If you have a long corridor at an airport or hospital you may need longer runs than can be gotten from one roll. What kinds of details have you seen that would help you hide a seam in this kind of material?

Seams in sheet goods will be either chemically welded or have a heat-activated material laid into a V-groove between the sheets, which melts and bonds, forming a moisture-proof seam.

The flooring material may be coved up onto the walls as well so there is no seam between the floor and the wall base. This installation requires a special detail that omits the right angle crease at the junction between wall and floor. Figure 6.15 diagrams the difference between an applied vinyl base and coved flooring base. After the flooring is glued down it will likely be rolled with a 100-pound roller periodically and according to the manufacturer's instructions.

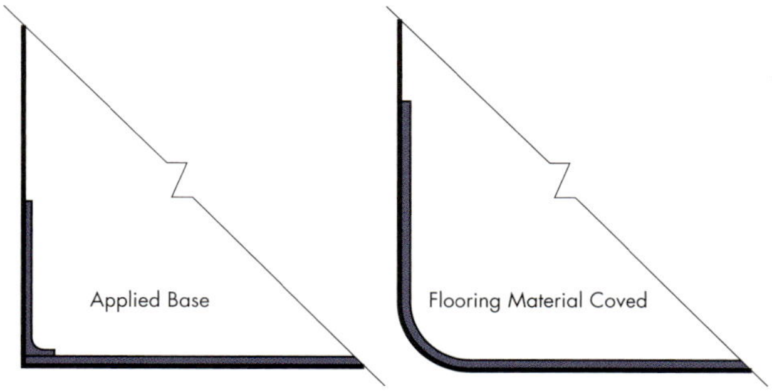

FIGURE 6.15 Diagrams of two options for finishing the perimeter where floor meets walls. An applied base is quite typical but wherever sanitary conditions are needed a coved detail is easier to clean.

PROTECTION AND MAINTENANCE

Resilient flooring is soft compared to other surfaces that you will specify, so it must be protected until the owner takes possession of the site after construction is complete. Traffic should be kept off the floor, except for resilient flooring installers who will periodically reroll the floor until the adhesive has set sufficiently. Try to keep all construction traffic off the floor or cover the floor with the appropriate protection, either paper or Masonite. If using Masonite you may have to have the whole floor covered because corners pressing into the material from above may mar it.

Resilient flooring is relatively easy for your client to maintain. Rubber may require special equipment to buff it, but other options can be damp mopped, or dry mopped followed by damp mopping. They can be maintained with nontoxic cleansers. Some, but not all, will required periodic rewaxing.

SAFETY

Vinyl flooring is under the most intense scrutiny for content, production, and disposal reasons. It is such a practical option for so many situations that we are loath to give it up even though it is currently one of the least sustainable options. Complaints about vinyl include the presence of phthalates that are suspected of leaching out PVC into the environment and causing damage to reproductive organs of aquatic wildlife. Dioxin is produced as a by-product of PVC production and is also released when vinyl is incinerated.

Rubber products are flameproofed with products that can contain PTBs, which are known carcinogens and endocrine disruptors. The vulcanization process in the production of rubber can release VOCs. Polyolefin products will emit small amounts of VOCs.

Many environments where resilient flooring is an appropriate selection will be subject to mandatory slip-resistance measurements. You will meet or exceed mandatory slip resistance as required for your project goals. A coefficient of friction of 0.6 or greater is required for many environments. You will want to specify material that inherently provides this rather than rely on coatings because coatings could unintentionally be replaced with a noncompliant formula in the future.

This material is thin relative to other materials. You will want to detail your installation in a way that brings all finished surfaces to a flush condition. When you are renovating it is not always feasible to adjust the substrate to boost this thin material up so it is flush with thicker material adjacent to it. In such an instance you may legally use a **reducer strip** if the difference between the two surfaces is less than ½ inch; however, if your facility will be used by the handicapped or elderly this is not ideal, even though it meets mandates. Individuals who shuffle when they walk or use canes can be tripped up by even this little change in height.

SUSTAINABILITY

Some resilient products that you can specify come from renewable resources such as cork and linoleum. Vulcanized rubber cannot be recycled into material that resembles new rubber. As with many materials that are a mixture of multiple ingredients, it is hard to separate the constituents for recycling. It is instead down-cycled as filler or as backing for new rubber-faced products and much of it ends up in landfills.

Recycled rubber content must be carefully considered because it may contain toxic traces from its previous life "on the road." Emissions of VOCs and formaldehydes have been identified in relation to resilient flooring products. The measurable amounts of these emissions will vary with the specific product that you are considering.

Polyolefin presents relatively few environmental concerns other than that; despite the fact that it is technically recyclable, most waste ends up in landfills.

Even linoleum, one of the sustainability stars in this product category, presents the possibility of contributing to eutrophication of water because of its high bio content. Fertilizers used to grow crop plants end up in waterways where they cause an imbalance of growth that can deplete the water's oxygen levels. Waste from production and postproduction scrap is biodegradable but most postconsumer linoleum products end up in landfills. Linoleum, like cork, comes largely from renewable resources. Polyolefin products are less toxic than vinyl products.

MANAGING BUDGETS

This category of flooring is sold by the square foot. As with carpet, lay this material out, in the width of your selected product, to calculate an accurate quantity. Prices vary with product and installation requirements. If extensive surface preparation is required or the installation requires special systems and accessories, the price will go up.

Within the category, rubber has the highest upfront costs, but the lowest life-cycle cost. Polyolefin is considered to be an expensive floor but only because it is compared to VCT. It is more expensive than VCT but less costly than other products in this category.

What Would You Do? 6.3

How would you present to your client an argument in favor of a sustainable option when budget is a client concern that is making them lean toward a vinyl product?

ORGANIZATION OF THE INDUSTRY

The resilient flooring industry is organized with manufacturers who make the products, reps who educate specifiers and scout out sales leads, distributors who sell the product to installers or resellers, and resellers who

Table 6.2
You may organize your selection criteria for your own job scenario in a table like this to address goals with your resilient product selections.

Condition	Program Implications
Will this floor be wet in use (such as in a 24-hour institution or near to an exterior door)?	Wet shoes and dripping umbrellas can increase slipperiness of resilient floors; might need a special top sealer.
Must this area be sanitized?	Select a sheet product with fused/welded seams. Consider rubber and linoleum for infection control (they are naturally antimicrobial). Consider base details for easy maintenance.
What needs are there for visual organization and wayfinding?	Color selection and distribution can be used to create meaningful contrasts to organize the space and indicate direction.
Is cost a significant consideration?	Vinyl products are still the best for up-front cost but if the installation will be used for a couple of decades, the life-cycle cost of rubber flooring will be very low. Polyolefin also drops in price as you factor it out over the length of its life.
Is antistatic important?	Cork and linoleum are naturally antistatic and selected vinyl products are manufactured to be dissipative too.
Will you be trying to maximize daylighting?	Reflectance for walls should be between 40% and 70% and for floors 25% to 40%.
How interested is your client in sustainability?	Cork, linoleum, and recycled product will be worth your first consideration.
Is comfort underfoot important?	Cork and linoleum are considered to be the most cushioning. Also look for products with integral cushions.
Do you need to minimize downtime?	Consider rubber and polyolefin.
Is this surface above or below grade?	Extra precautions will be required related to moisture migration for installations below ground level.

sell the product to clients. Two or more of these functions may be combined, such as the manufacturer who has their own representatives or the reseller who buys large quantities from the manufacturer instead of from a distributor. This variable organization can make it difficult to determine who you should contact for what. The best way to understand a person's role in the supply chain is simply to ask them to tell you about their business and if you happen to try to purchase from a rep who does not sell product, they will gladly direct you to the right person. It is a very symbiotic network.

SELECTION CRITERIA

Your design program will, as always, be the place to start formulating your own selection criteria. You might organize your thinking in a manner similar to Table 6.2.

SPECIFYING

In order to write a proper spec you will need to have a clear idea of what material you intend to install and where the material is going. Let's imagine that you are the lead designer on a new medical facility that houses a cancer care center for radiation, ambulatory care, imaging, blood donation, and several medical offices.

Your specification will be carefully written to describe the desired material and installation completely and succinctly. It is difficult to write a spec before you know the exact material and installation details that you are writing about. If you select the exact manufacturer's product you want to use before you begin to write your spec, you will have the benefit of the manufacturer's research and instructions and you can transfer that information into your spec.

SAMPLE SPEC 6.1

Part 1 General Information

1.1 Related Documents

A. Refer to finish plan for location and details.

1.2 Summary

A. Linoleum flooring and coved rubber base to be installed in MRI labs and patient rooms of new cancer care building on Hospital North Campus.

B. Fourteen patient rooms and MRI suite including three MRI offices.

1.3 References

A. Local fire code.

B. ASTM E648 Critical Radiant Flux of 0.45 watts per sq. ft. or greater, Class 1.

C. ASTM E662 Smoke Generation Maximum Specific Optical Density of 450 or less.

1.4 Contractor Submittals

A. Submit shop drawings, seaming plan, cove base details and manufacturer's technical data, installation, and maintenance instructions for flooring and accessories.

B. Manufacturer's standard samples showing the flooring specified, **welding rods**, and coved rubber base.

C. Material safety data sheet for all products.

1.5 Quality Assurance

A. Installer to be competent in the installation of Linofloor Granitmitite sheet flooring using heat-welded seams.

B. All materials required for installation to be provided by one manufacturer and delivered to the job site in the original, unopened containers. This includes patching and leveling compounds, adhesives, seaming rods.

C. All materials submitted to meet requirements for SCAQMD Rule 1168 490 and Green Seal Standard GC-36 requirements for low-emitting adhesives.

1.6 Delivery, Storage, and Handling

A. Deliver materials in good condition to the job site in manufacturer's original unopened containers that bear the name and brand of the manufacturer, project identification.

B. Store materials in clean, dry, enclosed space, off the ground and protected from weather and extreme cold and heat.

C. Move all products to acclimatized site 48 hours prior to installation.

D. Maintain temperature between 65ºF and 100ºF.

1.7 Maintenance of Installation

A. Work area to be kept free of debris and trash. All scraps to be removed to recycling at the end of the shift and area to be broom-clean.

Part 2 Products

2.1 General Information

A. Provide and install linoleum sheet flooring including all compounds, sealants, adhesives.

B. Provide and install cove base including all required adhesives.

2.2 Manufacturers

A. Linofloor Flooring Products, 1234 Industrial Drive, Anytown, ST 45678.

2.3 Products

A. Linofloor Granitmitite linoleum sheet flooring in color: Everest, 6.5 feet wide × 0.10 inches thick with wear surface of polyurethane-coated homogeneous mixture of linoleum cement, wood flour, cork, pigments and filler complying with ASTM F 2034 Type 1 Standard Sheet Linoleum Floor Covering.

B. Solid color weld rod in color Trail coordinating with field color of flooring.

C. Top-set wall base to be Linofloor rubber base in color Brown Bear.

D. Recommended adhesives.

Part 3 Execution

3.1 Examination

A. Confirm that the concrete subflooring maintains recommended moisture according to ASTM F 1869 and pH. All test results to be documented and retained.

B. Visually inspect for alkaline salts, carbonation, dust, mildew, and mold.

C. Ensure that surface is free of cracks, holes, ridges, and other defects that might prevent adhesive bond or impair durability or appearance of the flooring material.

D. Failure to report defects will be construed as acceptance and approval of the subfloor at time of installation.

3.2 Preparation

A. Smooth and patch rough surfaces and fill low spots with fast-setting cement-based underlayment as recommended by flooring manufacturer.

B. Vacuum or broom-clean surfaces to be covered immediately before application of flooring to make floor free of all dust, dirt, and foreign materials.

SAMPLE SPEC 6.1 (continued)

3.3 Installation

A. Install flooring wall-to-wall before the installation of base cabinets and furniture, extending flooring into toe kicks, closets, and door recesses as shown on plans.

B. Adhere flooring to subfloor without cracks or voids. Roll with 100-pound roller, hand roll at perimeter.

C. Weld with **heat welding** rods specified.

D. Install base on walls, in toe kick of casework, on columns and other permanent fixtures. Bond tightly to vertical substrate with continuous contact in strips as long as practicable.

3.4 Post Installation

A. Clean according to manufacturer's installation tips sheet.

B. Dispose of all scraps and debris.

C. Protect flooring from construction traffic.

INSPECTION

Upon completion the flooring should be installed as directed with straight cuts and details as described in your spec. At all transitions to other materials, including other flooring types, floor registers, outlets, and pipes, cuts should be completely covered by flanges or escutcheons. Material should be flat and secure throughout; seams should be fully adhered and in many cases invisible. There should be no deviation in the surface.

RELATED MATERIAL

Soft surfaces, such as carpet, are often used in some areas of installations that have resilient flooring products. These soft surfaces must coordinate with resilient surfaces (and hard surfaces too, if present, of course) in color, pattern, and thickness. There are also poured floor products that have similar seamlessness.

Resilient flooring is also laminated to rigid material and cushioning material. When laminated to rigid material, it will not be subject to defects in the substrate affecting the surface. It may also be installed without adhesives if the substrate panels have click-and-lock edges. Such flooring may even be removable so it can be taken up and reinstalled at another location. Cushioned product may have enhanced durability against puncture damage.

Polymeric poured floors are seamless when the installation is complete. These floors are applied as a liquid, sometimes alone or in combination with plastic aggregates or other fillers.

SUMMARY

In this chapter you looked at how to distinguish between the available product options in this category and make recommendations based on performance attributes. Product characteristics and site evaluation considerations were reviewed to guide your specifications for materials, prepwork, and labor. Different kinds of sites and the distinction between residential and commercial product were discussed. Installation techniques typical for the different product types and the installation process were discussed as well as typical accessories and alternative flooring.

WEB SEARCH ACTIVITIES

1. Search for *rubber flooring*, *natural rubber flooring*, and *natural rubber flooring from rubber trees*. Notice how the choices differ. Read the information provided by the manufacturers and see how many products are natural rubbers tapped from rubber trees.

2. Search for each of the flooring types listed and locate a manufacturer for each type of product. You may find that a manufacturer produces more than one of the products but try to find a different manufacturer for each so that you broaden your knowledge of available resources. After you have located manufacturers, search for a dealer who represents that manufacturer. Review their Web site. Will they install as well as sell the product?

3. Perform a video search for *how to install vinyl floor* or *DIY rubber floor installation* or some other similar search string. You may find amateur videos of DIY demonstrations or excerpts from TV shows demonstrating the installation of the product. Most of these products are installed in a similar way, so you need only watch the installation of one material to get the gist of it.

4. Find a manufacturer's specification guide for their own resilient flooring product. Refer to a plan that you have from another class or one that you found in a design magazine. Read the guide for comprehension, understanding how you would need to modify it if you were going to use it for your installation. Cruise the Web site for accessory items that accompany resilient flooring specs, such as resilient base and trims where the material transitions to another kind of material.

PERSONAL ACTIVITIES

1. Consider an area in your own plan where you might use a resilient surface or find a picture of an installation of resilient flooring in an interior space. Using Sample Spec 6.1 in this chapter as an example, write a spec for the item or surface.

SUMMARY QUESTIONS

1. What are the general characteristics of resilient flooring, shared by all resilient products? Include strengths and weaknesses in your answer.
2. What characteristics are unique to linoleum? Cork? Leather? Vinyl? Rubber? Polyolefin?
3. What sizes does each product category come in?
4. What is the difference between homogeneous, heterogeneous, and inlaid flooring?
5. Where would you use static control and slip-resistant flooring?
6. What is the difference between residential and commercial sheet flooring?
7. What is the difference between welded and adhered seams?
8. Which products are made from renewable resources? Which can be made of recycled material?
9. How is cork flooring site-finished?
10. What does it mean that cork has a "memory"?
11. How are leather tiles installed and sealed?
12. What kinds of accessories should be considered as part of your specification?
13. What options does the designer have for bringing thin resilient flooring to a flush condition with thicker adjacent material?
14. How can the designer specify in order to create a water-resistant seam between flooring and wall base?
15. When should the designer anticipate moisture problems and how can you specify to avoid them?
16. What are typical subfloors for resilient flooring?
17. What conditions must be present in order for existing flooring to serve as the subfloor for new resilient flooring?
18. How can the designer qualify appropriate installers?
19. What steps in the installation should the designer address in their spec?
20. When the designer is inspecting the completed installation of resilient flooring, what kinds of things should be confirmed before signing off on the installation?

Chapter 7

PLASTIC MATERIALS

Key Terms

Chemical bond
Mechanically bonded
Phenolic
Plastic
Polymers
Quartz
Thermoplastic
Thermoset

Objectives

After reading this chapter, you should be able to:

- Recognize the most typical plastics that designers specify and their properties.
- Understand how these materials are used and how to select the best type and form for your projects.
- Complete typical assemblies for items using this type of surface.
- Understand how the industry is organized for the production and installation of these materials.
- Evaluate and specify material.
- Understand the most prominent environmental and safety issues pertaining to plastics.
- Recognize other materials that are used in conjunction with and in place of plastics.

PLASTIC

Items made of **plastic** can imitate natural materials so effectively that they are replacing other building materials. Plastics are often referred to as synthetic materials. To some people this has come to mean that they are fake, but plastics are also used quite frankly as plastic, without compunction to appear to be anything but what they are—plastic. So think of *synthetic* as meaning the materials are synthesized from oil, starch, or sugar.

This chapter covers plastics that you will likely encounter in your career as an interior designer.

MATERIAL MAKEUP OR CONTENT

The chemistry of plastics is certainly fascinating but interior designers need not be chemists to comprehend the material. Ingredients that make good plastics form long chains of **polymers** and variations on these chains give each plastic its distinctive characteristics, and these characteristics indicate the best uses for each type. Some plastics are more common to textile and wallcovering production and resilient flooring (such as nylon, polypropylene, vinyl, etc.) so those plastic products are covered in those other sections.

Most plastics use petroleum as their source but rising fuel costs are making bio-based plastics from plant sources, previously a costly proposition, more economically viable. You will hear the term *bioplastics* used to mean resins that are derived from plant sources like cashew shells, sugarcane, pea starch, and corn. It is also used for the kinds of plastics that can replace biomaterial, as in synthetic body parts.

In addition to issues of recyclability and recycled content or biodegradability, designers are interested in performance attributes. One of the most significant for product designers, or interior designers working on product solutions for their clients, is whether the material can be shaped after manufacture. Two basic broad distinctions of types of plastics are **thermoset** plastics that cannot have their shape altered after production and **thermoplastic** plastics that can be softened and formed with heat. One such thermoplastic material that is in common use is acrylic.

> **Helpful Hint 7.1**
>
> Even though it takes higher heat than water to reshape plastic, hot water can "etch" the surface of thermoplastic formulations. Over time the surface becomes dull. It can be buffed back to nearly original condition.

Acrylic

Acrylic is often used in its solid, clear form. It is a chemically clear, colorless resin, but it can have color introduced into the material before forming. Because it is thermoplastic it can be heat formed at about 350°F.

It is available as sheets and rods (round and square) that can be bonded together and used to build forms. It can also be cast into molds and heat formed. Thicknesses range from ⅛ inch to 1 inch. Special formulations offer UV protection. You might consider acrylic for locations where glass would be too heavy or breakage too dangerous. Well-known brand names are Lucite, Lexan, and Plexiglas. Acrylic is also a component in solid surfacing materials.

Solid Surfacing and Engineered Stone

Solid surfacing products are nonporous, thermoplastic or thermoset materials. Common sheet thicknesses are ¼ inch, ½ inch, ¾ inch, and 1¼ inches. This material can often be worked with the same kinds of tools used to cut and shape wood. It is often used to make sinks, soap holders, and other molded objects, which can be adhered to the material. Its most common use is for countertops (Figure 7.1).

Custom work is possible because many plastic formulations are thermoplastic, so they can be softened with heat and bent to order without necessitating expensive molds (Figure 7.2a and b). Acrylic is one of the resins used for this kind of product and polyester is another.

Figure 7.3 shows the typical components of solid surfacing material.

FIGURE 7.1 Corian can be worked like wood. This countertop, in the color willow, was worked with the same tools and methods used to shape wood. *Photo courtesy of DuPont Corian.*

Helpful Hint 7.2

A practical example of the kind of consideration to be given to chemical resistance would be the use of acrylic formulas in medical offices. Acrylic material may bond with the acrylic molds used in dental offices so this is one location where acrylic would not be a good idea. In this case you may want to consider polyester. Acrylic materials used in nail salons could also pose problems for your solid surfacing spec.

When natural **quartz** is combined with polyester resins, the material may be referred to as engineered stone. Engineered stone slabs are typically available in 4-foot widths and 10-foot lengths. They are resistant to (although not impervious to) scratching, burning, and staining. Engineered stones are nonporous so they can be used where natural stone is prohibited, such as for food service and health care applications.

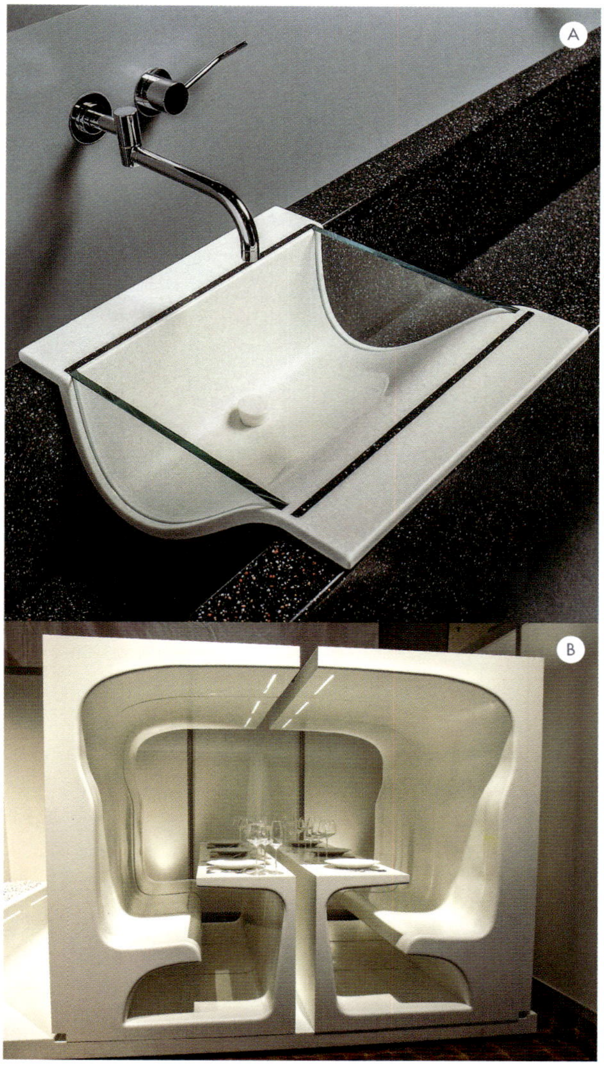

FIGURE 7.2A–B Solid surfacing (a) is water resistant and dimensionally stable. Unique custom designs have been created out of Corian as designers compete for recognition in contests and contribute to fundraising efforts such as this DIFFA Dining by Design installation (b). *Photo courtesy of DuPont Corian.*

Acrylic
or
Polyester + Natural Minerals + Pigments
or
Acrylic/Polyester Blend

FIGURE 7.3 Basic ingredients in plastics.

Table 7.1 Comparison of natural stone to engineered stone.			
Material Characteristics	**Quartz-Based Engineered Stone**	**Granite**	**Marble**
Hardness*	7	5 to 6	4 to 4.5
Abrasion resistance as measured by ASTM C501 for relative resistance on an SI scale	175 to 250	100 to 250	15 to 90
Flexural strength	4,500 to 7,000 psi	1,200 to 4,300 psi	800 to 2,300 psi

* Measured on a 10-point Mohs' scale.

The nonporous surface does not require sealing, as does natural stone. Table 7.1 compares resinous material with natural stones known for durability.

Polyester resists some chemicals better than acrylic. Some fabricators prefer the ease of fabrication that acrylic offers over polyester because polyester is more brittle so it is harder to fabricate. It is cheaper and more chemically resistant than acrylic.

Plastic Laminates

Plastic laminate is essentially layers of paper bonded together with resins to produce a surfacing veneer with properties that vary only slightly among multiple product offerings. This product category is divided into high-pressure and low-pressure laminate. High-pressure laminate is kraft paper saturated with **phenolic** resin. These layers are pressed between 1,000 and 1,200 pounds per square inch for one hour at over 280ºF to produce a durable surfacing material. Low-pressure laminate is also referred to by the name of the kind of plastic used to make it: melamine. Low-pressure laminate is a melamine resin–saturated paper with either a color or a gravure print decorative surface.

Thermally Fused Foils

Do not be misled by the name—these materials do not contain metal. Foils are essentially a cellulosic "paper" impregnated with melamine, acrylic, and urea resins. The precise blend of plastics depends on the end use. For instance, if a foil must be very bendable it will have more acrylic in it and acrylic is softer than melamine. If it must be hard for horizontal surfaces the plastic blend will have more melamine. After the foil is cured it may be printed (photographic wood grain is very common) and embossed (various sheen levels are created with texture). Thermofoils can be applied to surfaces that are not flat (as would be required for a plastic laminate). Surface textures can be embossed to imitate the texture of materials represented by the decorative layer, so a wood-grain or stone-vein image can also imitate the texture of those materials. Figure 7.4 shows embossed thermofoil imitating a wood grain. Thermofoil layers will delaminate when exposed to heat. Some formulations will yellow from exposure to heat, which is unfortunate because a popular use for this surface is in low-priced kitchen cabinetry.

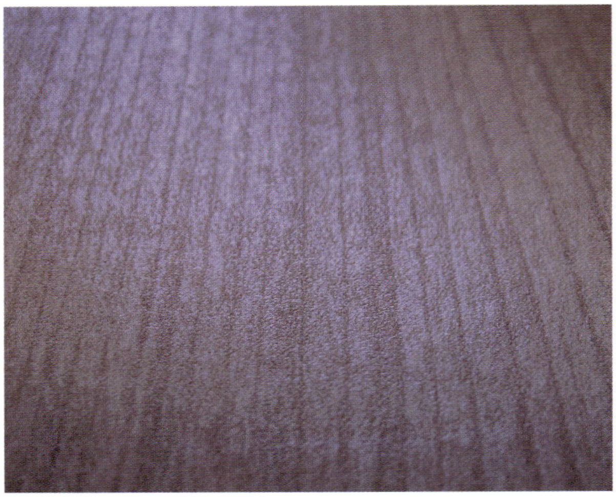

FIGURE 7.4 Thermofoil is printed and embossed to imitate wood grain.

Helpful Hint 7.3

If you are trying to save money and decide to specify a thermofoil cabinet system for a kitchen, detail around the cooking appliances to separate them somewhat from the cabinetry to prevent discoloration in your client's installation. A narrow cabinet with tall tray slots made from a contrasting material or a high-pressure laminate color matched to your thermofoil that is just a few inches wide will be more than enough separation.

Decorative and 2D Foils

Solid-colored, patternless thermofoil is referred to as 2D foil, low-pressure laminate, or simply called melamine. It has been considered an economy material and used when cost is a primary consideration. Recent advances in resins, printing, and processes have improved performance and appearance but sensitivity to heat remains an issue.

Rigid Thermofoils

These foils are typically applied to MDF substrates that have deep contours, raised panels, compound curves, and intricately shaped edges. They are called 3D thermofoils because they conform to complicated shapes, and do not require edgebanding to finish panel ends. They fully encapsulate the substrate and create a seamless surface for environments where meticulous maintenance is important, such as health care, childcare, or education environments. They can wrap "soft" corner shapes in environments where sharp corners and crisp edges are a safety concern.

CHARACTERISTICS

The various plastics have different performance characteristics indicating different uses. They are visually versatile, so you will select the kind of plastic to use according to the performance characteristics that you require.

Acrylic

Acrylic is a soft material and can be scratched by abrasives; shallow scratches can be buffed out. It will deform under pressure or weight; thicker material is stronger. Like bulletproof glass, it is good at resisting impact when it is thick. It is vulnerable to some chemicals, like ammonia, which is present in many glass-cleaning products. Because acrylic looks like glass, surfaces made of pure acrylic are often mistaken for glass and ruined by glass cleansers. Ammonia will make the acrylic surface cloudy, so your client must be informed of this so that the material will not be improperly cleaned with ammonia-containing glass cleanser.

Acrylic is also a component of solid surfacing materials. Polyester is the other. Of the two, acrylic is considered to be the easiest to work with.

Solid Surfacing

These materials come in thicknesses ranging from $^{1}/_{8}$ inch to 1 inch. Sheet sizes are typically 30 inches to 36 inches with some products having a 48-inch width and lengths up to 10 and 12 feet. Formulations are proprietary (unique to the specific manufacturer's products), and performance characteristics vary slightly from one product to another. Polyester material is less expensive, but the seams are **mechanically bonded** rather than chemically bonded, as with acrylic seams. These materials can be used to build items as well as for surfacing. Different resins have different characteristics, so they are individually suited for different functions. Table 7.2 distinguishes between the different formulas.

Color-Through

All products in this category are color-through, meaning the material is consistent throughout its entire thickness. Because of this, stains and burns may be removable by light sanding and buffing.

Typically this material should not be bonded (with adhesives) to substrates; rather, the details should employ "floating" constructions (such as a counter that sits on top of cabinetry) or use mechanical fasteners such

Table 7.2
Comparison of resins from surfacing materials in health care facilities by DuPont.

Comparison of Resins	Acrylic	Acrylic/ Polyester Blend	Polyester
Abrasion resistance: Resists erosion of material from abrasion	Very good	Very good	Very good
Elongation: How much it stretches before breaking	0.9%	0.6%	0.1%
Flexural modulus: Flexibility vs. stiffness	1.4 × 106	1.3 × 106	1.2 × 106
Tensile strength: Strength required to pull the sample in half	6,200 pounds/ square inch	5,000 pounds/ square inch	4,300 pounds/ square inch
Flexural strength: Ability to resist deforming under pressure	10,500 pounds/ square inch	8,700 pounds/ square inch	8,300 pounds/ square inch
Gardner impact resistant: Impact weight required to create visible rupture in surface	100 to 120 inch-pounds	65 to 70 inch-pounds	20 to 25 inch-pounds
Thermoformable: Can be bent after heating	Yes	No	No

as clamps or screws. These requirements will affect the details of your custom constructions so refer to your specific product's literature before finalizing the construction details.

Seams

It is a good idea to avoid seams in your design wherever possible as the nature of the material makes it hard to minimize seams. It is important to include the seam locations in your drawings for a couple of reasons (which are the same across all of these materials). One reason is that simply drawing the seams on your plans or elevations will force you to consider their effect on your designs. The other reason is to communicate your intent to the bidders and fabricators. Balance seams left and right and keep them away from cut-outs and away from any feature in the design. Avoid small pieces and irregular rhythms whenever possible. Just as with carpet and other materials that come in set sizes, you may have to create a hierarchy of importance as you review these guidelines for seaming related to your designs because it is not always possible to address all suggestions in your seam plan.

High-Pressure Laminate

There are two basic types of laminate: Nonforming is rigid and will want to remain as a straight sheet in your application. Forming has been adjusted in the curing process to be more flexible so it can be bent under heat. This postproduction adjustment is called post-forming. The difference is the kind of resin used. Melamine and polyester are two thermoset resins; they are cured with heat. Melamine is hard and scratch resistant. Polyester is stain and chemical resistant.

Thickness

Thickness varies and has a direct relationship to serviceability for vertical and horizontal grades. Horizontal grade has a more durable wear layer to handle the extra abrasion that you could expect on horizontal surfaces. There is variation among different manufacturers' products, but approximate thickness for vertical grade is .030 inch, and horizontal grade is .050 inch thick. Post-forming grade is generally in between.

Surfaces

The visual characteristics of plastic laminate pertain mostly to the color and pattern on the decorative layer, and to the gloss level. There are numerous papers offered as the decorative layer from several manufacturers, and this is before custom options even come into play. Available surfaces are typically gloss or textured. Manufacturers have similar, proprietary matte surface textures; not all product offerings will be available in all texture options so you'll want to confirm the available textures once you have made the initial color or pattern selection.

Specialty backings and surfacing formulations that address special use situations are available from manufacturers. There are specialty laminates and adhesives to address fire resistance, high abrasion, chemical resistance, ability to use as a dry-marker surface, and rigorous indoor air quality needs. Also available are nondecorative sheets that do not have the colored paper top layer; they are the backing only, for use as liners for other materials or finishes or for balancing layers for multiple-ply constructions.

> **Point of Emphasis 7.1**
> When you are using a plywood construction with a surfacing material, you need to maintain an odd number of layers. If you were building a cube of plywood substrate and intended to use a sheet of plastic laminate on the finished surface, you would have to specify a balancing layer on the other side of the plywood so that it would not warp.

Sheet Sizes

Sheet sizes vary slightly among manufacturers. Generally sheets can be found in widths from 30 to 60 inches and in lengths of 8 to 12 feet.

> **What Would You Do? 7.1**
>
> For what reasons would an interior designer find out the sheet size while still in the design phase of the process?

Custom Laminates

Manufacturers can place your custom artwork on the decorative layer of a laminate product that you can special order (Figure 7.5). Contact the manufacturer for instructions on file size (for artwork) and file type (TIFF, JPG, and Bitmap are common) and the recommended laminate for your application.

Color-through laminates are similar to high-pressure laminates except that colored sheets are used for all layers, so there will be no brown backer layers showing at cut edges.

Low-Pressure Laminate

Low-pressure laminate is also called melamine for the predominate kind of plastic used. Unlike high-pressure laminates that are sold as thin sheets to be adhered to a substrate, low-pressure laminates are typically already applied to a particleboard substrate that is cut to size and fashioned into a surface or item.

PARTS AND ACCESSORIES

These materials are not used alone; they are always adhered to a substrate. Because these surfaces are made of layers of two or more materials, whenever there is an exposed edge, it must be covered if the layered composition is not to be exposed.

Substrates

Solid surfacing material may rest on rigid substrates but require no edge banding or other accessories to complete the installation. In fact, solid surfacing materials are often used for their own accessories. For instance, it is common to have a solid surface backsplash or shower enclosure with molded accessories, like a soap dish, of the same material affixed to the solid surface material.

Laminates should be bonded to substrates. The substrates that are most commonly used for this are wood products, so you can learn more about them in the section pertaining to wood veneer. Tile backer board is further discussed in the section about wallboard. These substrates are:

- Particleboard
- Medium density fiberboard (MDF)
- Plywood having one A face to which the laminate will be applied
- Tile backer board

FIGURE 7.5 Custom laminate work executed by Wilsonart.

FIGURE 7.6 Plexicor Karran sinks are undermounted in laminate tops by a special process that protects the substrate from damage by moisture.

The characteristics of the substrate are important because this material is never used alone; it is always adhered to the substrate and is, furthermore, part of an assembly. As an example, laminate is a popular material for countertops. Countertops in kitchens, obviously, contain sinks. Water is not a problem for laminate—it is water resistant. It is a problem for many wood-based substrates, and for this reason, the substrate must be protected from water penetration. If water reaches most substrates they will swell up—breaking the adhesive bonds between the laminate and substrate. It is common practice to use only overmounted sinks in laminate and seal the cut edge of the substrate against water drawn in by capillary action. (Review the other characteristics of engineered substrates in Chapter 13.) It is possible to install an undermounted sink into a laminated countertop. A special multistep process and a sink of a companionable material is required to make this possible. Figure 7.6 shows an inset sink being installed, effectively seamlessly, into a plastic laminate-clad top.

Your quality fabricator will follow all the manufacturer's recommendations for proper adhesives and techniques, including handling, cutting, and drilling of their material. Many laminate manufacturers recommend their own adhesives, and unless there is a good reason to use something else, you should have your fabricator use the proprietary adhesives to further ensure a trouble-free installation.

What Would You Do? 7.2

For what locations would you use water-resistant substrate? When would you prefer plywood over cement board?

Edging

Laminate details for an exposed edge may require some attention because this thin material is just a surface and the side of the sheet will show. This is less of a problem if the material is color-through, but if the decorative face is different from the phenolic backing, the brown line will be visible. Designers frequently devise an edge band to conceal this edge or specify another material to conceal this edge.

FABRICATION

Composing these surfaces and items is variable, depending on the material being used. Laminate surfaces are glued to substrate solid surfaces and are simply put in place and held down by gravity, if being used as a horizontal surface like a countertop. Such surfaces may also be mechanically fastened (i.e., held in place with hardware rather than adhesives) with screws or cleats. These materials may also be bonded to a substrate or support structure.

Bonding

The materials are constructed as described above, but what is of interest to the interior designer will be how the materials are detailed for installation. Since these products come in limited sheet or panel sizes and frequently your designs will call for larger sizes, these materials need to be joined. They are bonded to each other and to the substrate.

What Would You Do? 7.3

When would you prefer a fused seam over one formed with adhesion?

Mechanical Fasteners

Screws or a combination of screws and other mounting hardware may be used to hold thicker surfaces in place. There may be instances when you would like to be able to demount these materials to access services beneath them or to change the surface without damage to the structure, in which case you will detail a cleat of some kind.

Chemical Bonds

Glues that are specified may fuse the surfaces together by interacting chemically with the material. Not all glues form a **chemical bond**. Some glues produce a mechanical adhesion.

Material-Specific Considerations

These materials have characteristics that indicate their use for specific performance attributes. Each material tends to be used in particular forms and these forms are produced and installed in different ways.

Acrylic

Solid acrylic items that you might design for your jobs could be self-supporting because, in addition to panels as part of an assembly, you will be able to make free-standing items out of it. If you are designing an item that will be produced in large quantities, you might design an item that will be cast into a mold. If your design will be produced only a few times you may design your item so that it can be assembled from stock sheets and rods. The seams can be chemically welded or fused, but will still be visible. Don't forget that thermoplastic acrylic can be bent to your desired radius by your acrylic tradespeople, so seams may be avoidable in some instances. This material will deflect if weighted down, and thicker material will be more resistant to sagging, so pair your weight bearing and long spans with the correct thickness. Work with your experienced fabricator to make the final determination.

Solid Surfacing Material

Although most typically used for countertops where no deflection is desired, thermoplastic versions have been used by designers to create some really inventive shapes for their custom products.

> Point of Emphasis 7.2
> DuPont regularly hosts a competition for innovative uses for thermoplastic material like their Corian. Winners are featured on DuPont's Web site, if you want to see innovative, one-off custom designs.

When edges are exposed you will specify a profile for the edge. Your selected aesthetic will contribute to your decision, but so will the thickness of the material; some thicknesses look better with some profiles than with others. Any edge that you would specify for a wood top can be cut into the edge of solid surfacing.

When you are specifying a solid surfacing material, the material can support itself over short distances but it does deflect. So if your design is going to span more than a couple of feet, you will detail a supporting sub-top. Solid surfacing material may be epoxied or fused with a chemical bond at seam locations. Chemical bonds are more durable than adhesive bonds, so if you need to join two sheets for an environment that must be scrupulously clean, you may want to consider acrylic formula options first since they are fused.

When installing on vertical surfaces, the material will be adhered to a substrate like marine-grade plywood or green board/water-resistant gypsum board, using the appropriate adhesive recommended by the manufacturer of the product you have specified.

High-Pressure Plastic Laminate

This is only a surfacing material, so the structure that you have designed will be built from a different material and covered with laminate sheets. Don't forget that this material comes in set sheet sizes and remember to locate the seams in your drawings so they are well planned for durability (away from heat and moisture) as well as appearance. Your substrate will likely be a wood-based product like plywood, particleboard, or MDF.

Thermofoil

The most popular substrate for decorative foils is particleboard or MDF, but they are occasionally laminated to plywood. The foil manufacturers usually apply one of two kinds of adhesive to the paper before shipping it to laminators: hot-melt EVA (ethylene-vinyl acetate) or wet-line PVA (polyvinyl acetate). Wet-line adhesive is used for large production runs. Hot melt is appropriate for smaller-scale operations or where the added moisture resistance of the adhesive system is called for. This material is used for large-scale production.

QUALIFYING INSTALLERS

These products are often installed by their fabricators; the local millwork shop that makes the countertop will typically also install it. If the shop is far away, a carpenter will install it. Many fabricators and installers will have learned their trade on the job. They may have a certificate issued at the end of a training session. These training programs may be provided by manufacturers of particular products or they may be classes that were organized by experienced fabricators and installers who are willing to share what they know and train newcomers to the field.

There is no credential more reliable than past experience when it comes to these products. Some fabricators will have large shops and high-capacity operations, with computer-guided cutting machinery, and at the other end of the spectrum will be small shops that are limited in capacity but may complete simple jobs for a low price. This is not to say that the large sophisticated shop is an inappropriate choice for a small job because many large shops will happily handle small jobs in this industry.

Acrylic

Fabrication of acrylic pieces and surfaces tends to be handled by acrylic specialists. They will use many of the same tools that woodworkers use, but this work is not typically performed by woodworkers. They will have varying capabilities, and not all shops will be equipped to cast custom items, only being able to construct them from standard sheets and rods.

Solid Surfacing and Laminate

Solid surfacing and laminate-clad items and countertops are frequently provided by woodworking shops. There are shops that specialize in solid surfacing material too, but laminate work is typically done by the millwork shop that makes items of wood.

INSTALLATION

Installation of items that are constructed of acrylic may be handled by the fabricator or may be completed by carpenters. The fasteners that they would use to install acrylic items would be similar to those for wood or glass items. Clear acrylic would need a little more attention to detail because the fasteners would show more than for opaque materials. Plastics do change their dimension (albeit slightly) with changes in temperature, but climate-controlled building interiors change very little, so these materials are also successfully installed with adhesives. If temperature does cause a change in the dimensions, the material may break its bond or may fracture.

PROTECTION AND MAINTENANCE

These relatively soft surfaces require care in handling. Many of these surfaces are repairable, but that does not minimize the importance of careful handling. Because they shrink and grow with temperature, they should be fully acclimated to site conditions before installing. After installation, the material should be protected if other trades are working in the area. These products are easily maintained with commonly available products. Acrylic is damaged by window cleaners containing ammonia and unwitting maintenance providers may accidentally clean them with the wrong cleanser, so you will need to emphasize this to your client. Acrylic also tends to attract and show dust, so it will need to be dusted frequently with a soft cloth. All plastic surfaces need to be protected from scratching; they are abrasion resistant but only up to a point. Even high-pressure laminate can scratch.

If solid surfaces are damaged, they can sometimes be restored. These surfaces are consistent all the way through, so the damage can be abraded out and the surface buffed to a sheen similar to the original. Obviously if the damage goes deep a "dip" in the surface may be discernible since the damaged material is removed to restore the surface. Acrylic can also be buffed out if small surface scratches show up over time. Damage to plastic laminate is usually permanent.

SAFETY

Many of these products will burn. They may be categorized as slow burning but they will burn, as will the adhesives used to install them. These products may off-gas but tend to do so quickly, so they are tolerable upon installation. They can be cleaned with nontoxic cleansers.

Worker safety is a concern because these materials emit fumes when heated (as happens during their fabrication) and dust from cutting the material can injure people's eyes. If cutting or processing dust is inhaled, it can also hurt workers. Review the material safety data sheet for any products that you have under consideration.

In the event of a fire, plastics will burn and will also generate smoke. When making selections for your projects, you will compare flammability and smoke-

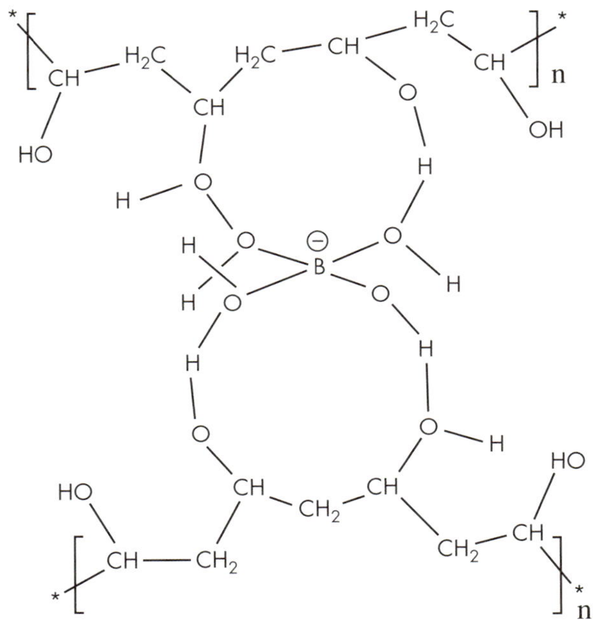

FIGURE 7.7 Plastic chemistry is not sufficient for understanding performance, so designers rely on testing data from physical tests on plastic samples.

generation data. Some kinds of thermoplastic formulas have a higher tendency to generate smoke. Plastics that have oxygen as part of their chemistry have less propensity to generate smoke and plastics that have aromatic compounds, like phenolics, have more tendency to produce smoke. Polymer chemistry is complex. Figure 7.7 is included here, not because you should be able to understand it, but as an illustration of why interior designers rely on the testing data of others to determine the characteristics of plastics. You would have to be a chemist to deduce the meaning of this diagram and even a chemist cannot predict the properties of this plastic without testing a sample. That is why tests are performed, not just on samples but on constructions as well. If you are going to adhere your specified plastic to a particleboard substrate, you will want to find testing data from a test performed on that assembly.

When these materials are fabricated they are typically cut to size. The dust generated is problematic and your conscientious shop will have vacuum and filtration systems, as well as a policy about eye protection, face masks, and respirators, that will keep workers safe.

SUSTAINABILITY

Thermoset plastics are not currently recyclable. Thermoplastic resins are recyclable but the industry generally lacks infrastructure to recycle them. Most of the plastic products that designers specify are recycling code 7, the miscellaneous category. When product components cannot be easily separated from each other for recycling they will land in category 7 (Figure 7.8). Many plastics require toxic chemicals in their production that must be handled carefully and disposed of properly.

Recycling is one way of achieving sustainable materials. Another way is to use bio-based plastics. Bio-based plastics are under development, but not widely represented in building products. Characteristics of bio-based plastics that make them attractive are that they come from renewable resources and some can biodegrade under the right conditions. Petro-free resin is one example of a bio-based plastic used in the making of a solid surface, countertop material that also incorporates recycled paper.

There are currently more recycled options than biomaterial options. The biomaterial designation includes not only plant-based starch sources for plastic but also plastics that will biodegrade. There are a number of promising technologies including plastic made from scrap wood from paper that is durable enough for furniture.

FIGURE 7.8 Many of the surfaces that you specify will be recycling category 7.

The Sustainable Biomaterials Collaborative (SBC) defines biomaterials as those that:

1. Are sourced from sustainably grown and harvested cropland or forests,
2. Are manufactured without hazardous inputs and impacts,
3. Are healthy and safe for the environment during use,
4. Are designed to be reutilized at the end of their intended use, such as via recycling or composting, and
5. Provide living wages and do not exploit workers or communities throughout the product lifecycle.

You might also add to the list a stipulation about the preferred source of the bio-based plastic. Some are derived from cellulose and others from foodstuff. Food crops that are diverted to plastic production could potentially have an effect on the food supply, possibly driving up prices as demand for bio-based plastic increases, which is likely to happen given the broadening interest in sustainability and an increasing demand for new products.

What Would You Do? 7.4

Think of all the potential environmental effects of food production, from fertilization to transportation. Which ones apply to bio-based plastic too? What else happens to bio-based plastic that might take energy?

MANAGING BUDGETS

Laminates are one of the most economical surfacing materials available and if a laminate meets your program needs in functional and aesthetic areas, it will be easy on the budget. These materials are not expensive, so the bulk of the cost will come from fabrication and installation. Custom-cast plastics, as with any custom casting, will be more expensive than if you fashion the item from premanufactured parts. Custom casting will be subject to a setup charge to build the mold and organize production. This option will likely only be economically feasible if you need multiple instances of the item you have designed. This would also hold true if you were going to heat-slump a sheet into a precise form and needed a mold or form to control the outcome; the cost of making such a thing could also rise. An established shop with sophisticated machinery will be able to easily bend material to a defined radius, but eccentric shapes could be more costly. You can imagine that if your design is complicated, unique, and requires setup, it will be costly, and if it is simple and typical, it will be less costly.

Point of Emphasis 7.3

The thing about typical versus unique is that if a job is a lot like other jobs the fabricator has done, it will be easy to estimate costs because it will be a very predictable process. It could be that your design is simple enough but that there are some required processes that are not typical; these become "unknowns." Estimators tend to put a little extra cost onto a job to cover unknowns.

ORGANIZATION OF THE INDUSTRY

The industry is organized with manufacturers selling to distributors or dealers and dealers selling to trades. It is uncommon, and in some supply chains prohibited, for end users to purchase the material. Just as the millwork shop includes the cost of the wood used in the fabrication into the cost of the job, the fabricator will include the material costs in their work. An itemized bid may break material costs out, or if two options are under consideration (such as two different thicknesses) then a material comparison will be drawn up for you or your client.

Surfaces of engineered stone are often fabricated by stone fabricators. This material is usually made with a high percentage of its total weight coming from natural stone. It is too hard to work the material with woodworking tools, as is possible for other products in this section.

The fabricators will be varied in the scale of their production with some shops being large with sophisticated, computer-driven cutting equipment (CNC) and others being small millwork shops (remember that most of these materials are fabricated with the same tools as wooden items).

Table 7.3
Organize your program points into selection criteria for products.

Program Characteristic	Implications
Will surface be subject to abrasion or staining?	Select solid surfacing material for its repairability.
Is the budget very limited?	Plastic laminate applied over an engineered substrate will be the most cost-effective for simple forms.
Will chemicals be used in the area?	Confirm compatibility with all products to make sure surfaces cannot be damaged by them.
Is a seamless look desired?	Solid surfacing seams the best.
Must the material assume a 3D form?	Thermoplastic formulas and post-forming material are indicated.
Must material match between horizontal and vertical surfaces?	Be mindful of thickness and plan details to allow for dimensions.
Will material span a space?	Material must be supported by a stiffer material.
Do you envision an elaborate edge?	Material must have sufficient thickness or be able to be built-up or receive a companion material.
Is a custom pattern desirable?	Laminates have the potential for custom patterns if setup charges can be budgeted or quantity is large enough.
Must construction be fire rated?	Not all of these products are fire rated although product offerings in all categories can be found with fire-resistive properties.

SELECTION CRITERIA

Your selection criteria should be founded in your unique design program. Consider both the site and use conditions to organize your requirements. You might organize a set of considerations and implications as shown in Table 7.3.

> **Helpful Hint 7.4**
>
> You will match your job to the shop's current capability. What this means is that a small shop may be tempted by your large order but as a responsible designer you must carefully evaluate when it is appropriate to give a small shop its first big break and when you will reserve contracting with the small shop for small jobs, that will frequently produce "one-off" custom work for a reasonable price compared to large shops with more overhead.

SPECIFYING

This material forms a surface on a construction. The use will help you determine the best material and the details. The following spec is an example of how a spec for one of the materials in this chapter might shape up. It is drawn up using the spec format used by designers and architects and it presumes that we are responsible for the selections at a health club and have selected a solid surfacing material for the walls of the showers in the locker rooms.

After you have selected your material, you will likely find guidance for completing your spec on that manufacturer's Web site. Many of the recommendations that can be found in the manufacturer's specs for a given product will guide you as you assemble your own specification. You will be referencing information from manufacturers; that is the way professionals ensure correct information on their specs.

SAMPLE SPEC 7.1

Part 1 General Information

1.1 Related Documents

A. Refer to finish plan for locations.
B. Refer to sections and approved shop drawings for installation details.
C. Refer to manufacturer's recommended installation instructions.
D. Refer to plumbing fitting templates for size of cutouts.

1.2 Summary

A. Solid surfacing material to be installed on walls of 6 shower stalls in each of men's and women's locker rooms in conjunction with precast terrazzo bases by others.
B. All seams to be watertight, and flexible, with silicone sealant approved by manufacturer in color to match panels for seamless look.

1.3 References

A. ASTM D570 Water Absorption.
B. ASTM E84 Burning Characteristics.

SAMPLE SPEC 7.1 (continued)

1.4 Vendor and Contractor Submittals

A. Vendor to submit documentation confirming 25% preconsumer recycled content and 10% rapidly renewable content.
B. Vendor to submit documentation of compliance with LEED credit EQ 4.1 Indoor Air Quality.
C. Vendor to submit instructions and shop details regarding recommended installation.
D. Vendor to submit material safety data sheet for panels, adhesives, and seam sealants.
E. Contractor to submit training certification for contractors installing product confirming completion of manufacturer's training course on use of adhesives.
F. Contractor to submit two samples showing material specified, set up on board with silicone sealant to be used on job applied between them to demonstrate material and sealant.

1.5 Quality Assurance

A. To be fabricated and installed by tradespeople possessing a minimum of 5 years' experience constructing and installing product specified.
B. All work to be performed in accordance with approved shop drawings and manufacturer's recommended methods for clearances and adhesives.

1.6 Delivery, Storage, and Handling

A. Deliver fabricated sheets to job site 24 hours prior to installation and store flat on clean drop cloths until installation.
B. Materials to be fully acclimated to site prior to installation.

1.7 Maintenance of Installation

A. Panels to be stored flat at the job site on clean drop cloths with material staged for minimal handling of material and minimal distance to surfaces to receive material.
B. Keep job site clear of all debris and deliver pieces removed to the recycling area upon completion of the installation, leaving the area broom-clean.
C. Leave protective sheets on faces except where removed to finish edges.

Part 2 Products

2.1 General Information

A. Provide and install panels cut to fit per plans and fabricator's own field measure. Installer to provide all tools, shims, blocking, and bracing recommended by manufacturer's instructions required to complete job.
B. Full-height panels to be adhered to tile backer board substrate (installed by others).

2.2 Manufacturers

A. Panels, adhesives, and seam sealer from: Solid Surface Supply, 1234 Industrial Drive, Anytown, ST 45678.

2.3 Products

A. ½"-thick solid surface Series Fire and Water in Storm for men's locker room and Aurora for women's locker room shower walls.
B. ½"-thick material for bullnose-edged facing pieces of matching material as indicated in drawings.
C. Installation kit for each, kits containing recommended adhesive and silicone seam sealant to match panels.

Part 3 Execution

3.1 Examination

A. Prior to installation, inspect installation of substrate; confirm that recommended clearance above top of shower pan (provided and installed by others) is complete and in condition that will allow for acceptable installation of wall panels.
B. Confirm that terrazzo shower pans are level and securely seated.

3.2 Preparation

A. Panels to be cut to fit per fabricator's own field measure.
B. Panels to be seamed slightly at corner locations.
C. Facing pieces to receive half bullnose as shown in designer's details.

3.3 Installation

A. Mark and neatly cut ½"-diameter openings for plumbing. All cutouts for plumbing fittings to be completely covered by plumbing fitting escutcheon plates.
B. Install with adhesive onto backer board leaving a $^{3}/_{32}$" gap in corners, caulk gap with silicone caulk from installation kit.

3.4 Post Installation

A. Upon completion of installation, area should be ready for acceptance by owner or owner's representative.

INSPECTION

Inspection will depend on the item or surface that has been installed. Of course you will inspect with your approved plans in hand because there will likely be too many details to remember, especially because designers sometimes make plans a year or more in advance of the installation on large projects like new construction jobs.

If your installation is a simple surface, like a wall cladding or countertop, the task is a little simpler. You should make sure all cuts are neat and polished or edged as specified and that all seams are tight. All electrical covers, air grilles, and other service devices should be straight and even and conceal all cut edges. Adjacent pieces should be flush and align. Three-dimensional constructions will be inspected with fully dimensioned drawings in hand to confirm all details, especially if this work must fit portions of the design that will be constructed by others.

Plastic material usually ships to the fabricator with a protective plastic film adhered and this film is frequently left in place until the end of construction when it is removed by the crew hired to clean the construction site prior to turning it over to the owner or the owner's representative. You will want to carefully inspect any areas where the protective film was torn during handling; this in itself is not a problem but make sure that there are no abrasions or the material will have to be buffed prior to your signing off on it.

RELATED MATERIAL

Veneers of other materials besides plastic are similar in the details that you will devise although the other materials would (of course) vary in performance and visual characteristics. For flat surfaces, wood, metal, glass, and stone products may also serve for surfaces where you consider these plastic products. All of these materials can be laminated to substrates for dimensional stability. For 3D items or surfaces with a high relief, plastics work well and can be economical if you are doing a high quantity. They are more expensive if you are only doing a few.

Plastics are used in the production of textiles. Nylon is a common textile fiber; if you review textile chemistry properties in Chapter 3 you will see that it is abrasion resistant. Knowing that, you will not be surprised when you are evaluating the specs for a cabinet someday and see that the drawer glides are made of nylon. This chapter covered the most commonly specified interior surfacing material in the most typical forms but the topic of plastics is vast and could easily be a book on its own.

You will notice that building products, like plumbing parts and plastic lumber, are part of the projects that you work on. While you are less likely to be involved in specifying components like these, if you are able to wield any influence, push your team to specify products that contain recycled content, are biodegradable, and that avoid PVC.

Plastic for prototyping is used for investigating form of small items and a number of formulas are used for hand-molding, casting, and 3D printing. These items are typically not for use in interiors but are used during the exploration phase of the design of objects or possibly surfaces that will be later produced in other materials.

SUMMARY

In this chapter we reviewed the most typical plastics that designers specify and their properties. How these materials are used and how to select the best type and form for your projects was discussed. You gained insight into the assembly for these surfaces when they are not complete on their own. We covered how the industry is organized for the production and installation of these materials and you encountered some criteria for evaluating and specifying these materials. Sustainability was addressed with a review of the toxicity and safety issues pertaining to plastics. Other materials that are used in conjunction and in place of plastics were discussed.

WEB SEARCH ACTIVITIES

1. Perform an image search for each of the following common uses for and types of plastics: *plastic laminate*, *solid surfacing*, *acrylic*, and *thermofoil*.
2. Perform an image search for *laminate edge banding* to see the kind of products that interior designers will specify to finish exposed edges. Perform a second search for *laminate edge detail* to see other options for finishing the edge. They will range from post-formed curves to contrasting materials.

3. Search for *solid surfacing material* and click on one of the manufacturers that you find there. Search the site for their material safety data sheet (MSDS). Perform a similar search for *high pressure laminate MSDS* and *low pressure laminate MSDS* and again for *acrylic MSDS*. Browse an example of each for a sense of the safety issues associated with this category of products.
4. Search for *petro-free resins* and *bioplastics* for an idea of the current state of this segment of the industry.
5. Locate a manufacturer of solid surfacing, high-pressure laminate or acrylic and search their site for a master spec template. Or, alternatively, search for one of the products with a search string similar to *high-pressure laminate specification*. When you find a master spec or a master spec intended for use as a guide for writing a unique spec, review it for comprehension.

PERSONAL ACTIVITIES

1. Locate a picture of an installation featuring plastic. Draw up a list of all of the things that you would mention in your spec if this was your design and you needed to communicate it to a fabricator.
2. Consider an area in your own plan where you might use a plastic surface or an item containing plastic, or find a picture of an installation of a plastic surface in an interior space. Using Sample Spec 7.1 in this chapter as an example, write a spec for the item or surface.

SUMMARY QUESTIONS

1. What are some common plastics used in interiors and what are sources of raw materials for making them?
2. What is the difference between solid surfacing plastic materials and engineered stone materials?
3. What are the differences between high-pressure and low-pressure laminates?
4. What is the difference between thermofoil and plastic laminate?
5. What does *thermoset* mean and when would you specify it?
6. What does *thermoplastic* mean and when would you specify it?
7. What are the general characteristics of engineered stone? Solid surfacing plastic panels? High-pressure laminate sheets? Acrylic materials?
8. What is a nondecorative laminate sheet and what is it used for?
9. What are common substrates for plastic laminate?
10. What is the complication related to an undermount sink in plastic laminate counters? Can they be overcome?
11. Which products covered in this chapter can be acceptably restored on-site if they are damaged?
12. How are installers credentialed?
13. What tradespeople fabricate acrylic items? What kinds of trades fabricate plastic laminate and solid surfacing? What kinds of trades fabricate engineered stone?

Chapter 8

GLASS

Key Terms

Annealing
Chemically strengthened glass
Electrochromic
Float glass
Frit
Heat-strengthened glass
Laminated glass
Reflective glass
Suspended particle
Tempered glass

Objectives

After reading this chapter, you should be able to:

- Understand how different forms of glass are made and what their properties are.
- Recognize new glass technologies that could add to products available to interior designers in the near future.
- Select and specify glass products.
- Understand how the industry is organized.
- Understand sustainability and safety issues pertaining to glass.

GLASS

Glass is used as a surfacing material and as part of free-standing assemblies (like partition walls and staircases). Various kinds of glass are preferred for different circumstances. Even though glass is a simple material compared to many, there are a few processes that are applied to glass to change its performance and appearance.

MATERIAL

The main ingredient in glass is quartz sand, fused with heat. The presence of other minerals, in the formulas commonly specified by interior designers, alters its properties very slightly. The sand is fused by heating it to temperatures of about 2,000ºF. Simple glass is altered to improve its properties for specific uses and combined with other technologies for functional and decorative products.

CHARACTERISTICS

Glass is chemically a noncrystalline solid that gives glass (and plastics) transparency. Glass is quite impervious to staining and is durable against scratching. Its tendency to break into sharp shards is well known. Glass that is **tempered** or **laminated** improves its usefulness as a safety glazing. The simplest glass construction is **float glass**. Processes are applied to float glass to change its properties. Glass products can receive more than one of the processes listed in Table 8.1.

> Point of Emphasis 8.1
>
> You will hear the term *plate glass* as frequently as you encounter the term *float glass*. They are functionally the same thing, but were produced by different means. Plate glass is an older technology whereby large sheets of glass were formed by rolling molten glass between two rollers to create a consistent thickness. The process left surface imperfections that had to be polished flat so the view through the glass was not distorted. Float glass also produces big sheets of glass but molten glass is poured onto a pool of molten metal, which is of course perfectly flat, so the face of the glass that was in contact with the metal needs no polishing—only the "air side" must be polished on float glass.

The introduction of various minerals into the basic recipe for glass will alter its properties. Soda-lime glass is the most common. You may notice that glass tends to have a green cast, especially when it is thick, due to naturally occurring iron in the minerals that were used to produce it. Low-iron glass is a special formula that is clear, lacking this green cast. Other refined formulations are typically for optical use but low-iron glass is one special formula that you will likely encounter.

Properties

Among the properties that you will consider when selecting glass for an installation are the:

- Degree of light transmittance
- Strength
- Energy efficiency
- Fire resistance

Light Transmittance

Regular float glass allows 75 to 92 percent of light to be transmitted through it (it varies with thickness of the glass). Measurement of this transparency is referred to as light transmittance. When glass is treated to reduce light transmittance, to limit fading from UV and reduce heat gain, color rendition in the space is usually altered too. Transmittance is controllable all the way down to zero when glass is enameled with **frit**. Frit is made of glass particulates that are fused to a sheet of glass; it can render the glass entirely opaque.

> Helpful Hint 8.1
>
> If you are requested to consult on the selection of tinted glass, be sure to review samples of the tint options in the glass thickness which will be used. Tint is not a film that sits on the surface so the tint will be intensified if the glass is thick. If you saw a sample of ¼-inch-thick glass but were going to specify ⅜ inch, they would not look the same.

Strength

The controlled cooling process that glass undergoes as it travels away from the oven is called **annealing**. This cooling rate influences the strength of the glass. Glass that is cooled at a faster rate than is typically produced by the annealing ovens at the factory becomes stronger.

Table 8.1
The different kinds of glass that you might specify for various functions.

Type of Glass	Techniques	Characteristics	Uses
Float	Molten glass is poured onto a pool of molten tin (perfectly flat surface)	The tin side of the pane is perfectly flat; the air side may be polished to make it more perfectly flat	Most flat glass sheets are produced this way
Rolled	Semi-molten glass is squeezed between rollers; the top roller is a smooth cylinder and the bottom has a negative of the relief pattern carved into it	Textures and patterns pressed into one face of glass; thickness is controlled by the distance between the rollers	Where light transmittance and a suggestion of the scene beyond is desired along with a diffusion of light or view
Cast	Sheets of glass are laid upon carved beds and heated until softened so that the sheet sags into the patterned surface of the mold	The thickness of the original glass sheet determines the thickness of the final product; while one side may be the "front" it will not be flat on its back	Same as rolled glass but this product need not be flat; technique allows for more 3D form
Tinted	Minerals are mixed in with the standard glass ingredients, producing specific colors	Lower solar penetration reduces heat gain; glass color affects color perception	Energy conservation or where a color is desirable for aesthetics
Low iron	The basic ingredients are altered for low iron	Clear glass without the green tinge	Where color rendition or utter transparency is important
X-ray protective	Lead is mixed in with the standard glass ingredients	Blocks X-rays in medical or industrial facilities; glass may have an amber color	Select for specific function of blocking X-rays
Bent	Sheets of glass are heated while in contact with a form that the glass relaxes onto as it softens	Curved sheets of glass are typically clear; standard radius curves available from manufacturers as well as custom-order shapes	Curved windows for buildings and cabinetry
Tempered	Sheets of glass are reheated and cooled at a faster rate than for regular glass production; fully tempered glass is cooled the fastest	Heat-tempered glass is stronger than regular glass; it breaks into oblique beads (fully tempered) or thin fingers and is more likely to stay in frame if broken; strain marks may be visible in finished glass	Specify tempered glass wherever broken glass is a foreseeable possibility and would pose a safety concern; code requires tempered glass in specific situations; cannot be cut or worked after tempering
	A second method (less common): glass is immersed in a chemical bath	Stronger than heat-tempered glass; complex forms can be tempered as glass is not softened in process	Less common than heat-tempered, can be cut after strengthening but loses some strength near the cut
Laminated	Two or more layers of glass with one or more sheet(s) of polyvinyl butyral resin (PVB) between them or resin is poured in between two closely spaced sheets of glass	The material sandwiched between the glass sheets varies for specific functions such as noise reduction, security, UV, and energy control	May be selected for functional or decorative reasons; the characteristics of the internal layer lend specific properties
Holographic	Laminated with multiple layers of plastic film	Produces visual effects that are 3D and frequently colorful	Primarily an aesthetic choice although there is potential for functional light-transmittance improvements
Fire resistive	May be achieved with a special coating or ceramic glass	Varying characteristics depend on the technique and materials used so review manufacturer's claims about thermal shock, smoke, flame, and heat resistance	Specify products to meet code and safety considerations
Acid-etched	Float glass is chemically etched to achieve a uniform matte surface that obscures views	Views obscured and light diffused via even "frosted" appearance	Specify where obscured views desired or where light should be diffused and clear vision is not important

(continued)

Table 8.1 (continued)
The different kinds of glass that you might specify for various functions.

Type of Glass	Techniques	Characteristics	Uses
Sand-blasted	Areas that are to remain clear are masked and the exposed portion of the glass is blasted to varying degrees	Clear glass combined with a variety of "frosted" pattern area used for decorative or functional effect	Where patterns, logos, or images are desired or privacy and view are simultaneously desired (frosting lower portion of shower door for instance)
Reflective	Reflective material applied to glass while it is still hot (during annealing)	Reflective in one direction so views are still available to those in the "dark" environment (inside during the day)	Obscure the darker environment (interior during the day) and create reflective surface on the brighter side of the glass
	Vacuum-applied coatings	Vacuum-applied finish is delicate	Used for the inside face of insulated glass units
Low-E	Microscopically thin layer of metal oxide may be baked on while glass is still hot from production	Allows light to penetrate but blocks longer, infrared wavelengths so light moves through but not heat	More durable surface, can be tempered or laminated like regular glass
	Metal oxide layer applied via special technique (called sputtering)	Also blocks long wavelengths but produces a more delicate surface	Used only on the inside (protected) faces of insulated window units
Mirror	Reflective metal (usually silver) coats the back of the glass, usually protected by another layer of metal or paint	Reflective surface on clear or tinted glass	Where reflection is desirable for aesthetic or functional reasons
Enamel or screen printed	Mineral pigments are used to make enamel that is applied to glass and heat fused to the surface	Patterns are created for sun control and aesthetics	Heat fusing of enamel also strengthens glass so enameled glass is used for exterior and interior glazing
Anti-reflective	A coating applied to float glass maximizes transmittance, reducing reflectance of the glass	Glass is exceptionally clear, invisible from some angles but a dichroic reflectance is visible from oblique viewing angles	Specify where clarity and control of reflectance is critical—like for shop windows or artwork displays
Self-cleaning	A microscopically thin photocatalytic film loosens dirt's grip on the window while the hydrophilic nature of the film causes rainwater to flow in sheets instead of drops	Glass stays cleaner without maintenance for longer periods of time; water does not bead up on surface	Specify wherever water spotting or soiling is inconvenient to remove frequently
Wire	Metal mesh is sandwiched between 2 layers of semi-molten glass then passed through rollers that squeeze them into a single sheet	The mesh is visible in both clear and patterned wire glass; when it breaks the glass clings to the mesh retaining something of a barrier	Usually selected to serve a practical function rather than selected for aesthetic reasons
Electro-chromic	A microscopically thin film on glass turns from clear to a color or from clear to frosted when a low-voltage electric charge runs across it	Solar heat gain is reduced when electricity is supplied manually (flip a switch) or automatically (sensors)	Primarily used for reducing heat gain through exterior windows
Liquid crystal/ electronic glass	A liquid crystal film sandwiched between 2 layers of glass is translucent when the crystals are not aligned but turns clear when electricity induces the crystals to align	Is frosted in the absence of electrical current but turns clear when electricity aligns the crystals	Used for interior glazing to change from privacy to clear glass
Insulating	2 or more panes of glass separated by a dehydrated vacuum or gas-filled space	Blocks transmittance of cold through glass	Exterior glazing is the most common use
Lead glass (crystal)	Chemical composition contains lead	Sparkles because of light refractance	Art glass and also popular for light fixtures

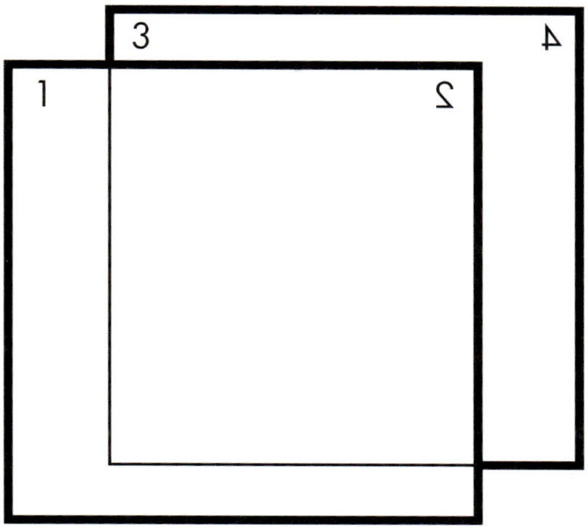

FIGURE 8.1 When specifying coatings for the faces in an insulated unit, describe them according to the numerical order that industry uses.

Heat-strengthened glass is approximately two times stronger than regular annealed glass and is used where regular glass (nontempered) is allowed but increased strength is desired. Fully tempered glass, which is cooled even faster than **heat-strengthened glass**, is four times as strong as regular annealed glass.

Energy Efficiency

Tinted, reflective, **electrochromic**, **suspended particle**, and insulated assemblies address energy efficiency. Some products are a combination of the above.

Insulated glass is actually two independent panes of glass, not a special kind of glass. Manufacturers of insulated glass units refer to the characteristics of the four faces of glass used. The exterior panel facing out is surface number 1, the exterior pane facing the inside is 2, the interior pane facing the center of the assembly (facing the vacuum) is 3, and the interior pane facing the interior space is 4. **Reflective glass** coatings, metallic coatings to reduce solar heat gain, applied to the faces of the glass in the assembly improve performance of the window. See Figure 8.1 for the location of the faces described. The appearance of the assembly is altered by the reflective, tinted, and patterned panes used and by where in the assembly they occur. For instance, if a reflective finish is used on surface number 1, the exterior of the building will be reflective. If it is used on the other side of the same pane—surface number 2—the glass will appear to be tinted.

Glass selected for its contribution to energy savings will be rated for its U-value (heat loss or gain through the glass) and its R-value (resistance to heat transfer). The higher the R number, the better the performance in each measurement system. The opposite is true for U-value—a lower number is better.

Fire Resistance

Fire resistance is enhanced when glass is produced and then held at a high temperature until crystals begin to form in the glass. The resulting glass, called ceramic glass, is very heat resistant, because the crystal formation stabilizes the glass against thermal expansion. It can be fire rated for up to three hours. It is still transparent.

Dimensions

Many standard thicknesses are available. Common thicknesses are $3/32$ inch, $1/8$ inch, $3/16$ inch, $7/32$ inch, $1/4$ inch, $3/8$ inch, $7/16$ inch, $1/2$ inch, and $3/4$ inch. Sheet size varies with thickness, thinner material generally coming in smaller sheet sizes, up to a point, then weight becomes a limiting factor and thicker material is smaller in length and width.

PARTS AND ACCESSORIES

Glass is frequently held in a channel, a U-shaped piece of metal because it expands when subjected to heat and a channel installation can be configured to leave a little room for the glass to move so it will not crack as it tries to "grow" in high temperatures. Another reason for a channel installation is that glass is brittle and it may be a good idea to separate large sheets from a structure that might move or settle. If you look closely at a window frame you will notice that the frame forms a channel that the glass sits in. The amount of expansion and contraction of a material is usually as a percentage of its size, so a large piece will need more room to move.

Small sheets of glass can usually be adhered to a substrate without fear of cracking. You will devise your details to accommodate the needs you anticipate. If a structure is new or built to flex a little (like high-rise constructions) you will probably take extra precautions when you specify fastening glass to the structure. If the sheet size is small, the building is established and settled or rigidly built, you may decide to adhere the glass to the substrate with mastic.

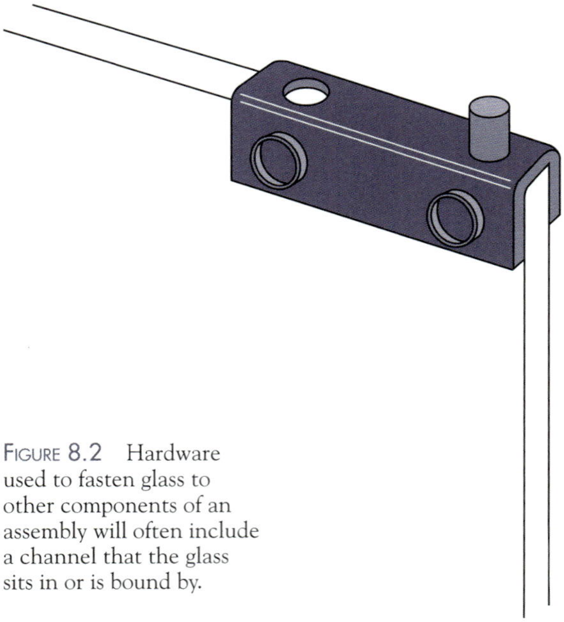

FIGURE 8.2 Hardware used to fasten glass to other components of an assembly will often include a channel that the glass sits in or is bound by.

Other parts and accessories will be required for the things that the glass is part of. If you are designing a glass partition for a conference room, you might want clear plastic gaskets between the panels for sound blocking. The door will be hinged, perhaps with a glass-on-glass hinge or with a pivot hinge that has a small channel as part of its construction, as shown in Figure 8.2. You will notice that some hinges will require that the door be drilled to allow screws to pass through, but other hinges have small set screws that use pressure to hold the glass. Door pulls are also an accessory part for this use of glass (although you can well imagine that a latch set is not an option for a glass door unless the glass is installed in some other kind of frame).

In addition to hardware and channels, glaziers use mastic, putty, gaskets, glazing compound, bolts, clips, and moldings to hold glass in position.

Films and decals are another part of some installations. Decorative or functional, they are adhered to the glass, rather than an integral part of it.

FABRICATION

Many kinds of glass actually start out as float glass and are subject to further processing to become other types of glass. Even though cast glass is formed this way some of the time, it can also be cast from a molten state into a form; these processes are not restricted to methods that reheat float glass.

Float Glass

Float glass is the current technology for producing large sheets of glass that may be manipulated with other processes to alter its characteristics. Laminating and tempering are the two common processes that designers specify to make glass safer.

Cast Glass

Like float glass, cast glass can be tempered and used architecturally (for doors, partitions, railings, etc.) (Figure 8.3a and b) and for furniture, light fixture diffusers, and surfacing. Cast glass may be produced by casting molten glass onto a form or by laying float glass onto a carved ceramic form and resoftening it so it slumps into the relief of the mold's surface. It is then slowly cooled so it

FIGURE 8.3A Custom installation of architectural cast glass engineered to meet aesthetic and code requirements. This entirely custom job can fulfill program requirements for pattern and signage. *Glass by Architectural Glass Art, Louisville, KY.*

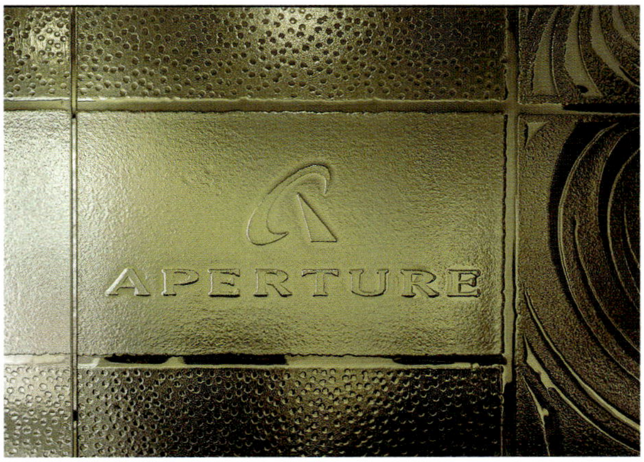

FIGURE 8.3B Cast glass detail showing the fine textures that can be achieved.

does not shatter. Large sheets with fine textural details can be produced but carving the molds requires a large budget or economies of scale (multiples so the cost can be distributed among many panels).

Laminated Glass

Laminated glass is just as its name implies; two pieces of glass are laminated together, sandwiching a layer of something (usually plastic) in between. This plastic is especially formulated to perform different specific tasks such as buffering sound; blocking light, heat gain, or view; or adding color or other performance or aesthetic function.

> Point of Emphasis 8.2
> The windshield of your car is laminated glass. That is why when a windshield breaks, pieces of glass cling to the plastic sandwiched in between and sag like a hammock in the car frame.

Tempered Glass

Tempered glass is glass that was held at a high temperature after its production then quickly cooled in order to improve its strength and safety characteristics. It qualifies as safety glazing because it breaks into small cubic "beads" upon impact instead of sharp shards. Tempered glass is identified by a permanent label in the corner of each piece tempered. This label, called a bug, cannot be removed (because tempered glass cannot be cut or worked after tempering). Tempered glass that does not include this bug must be requested as a special order.

There is no such thing as a grandfather clause when it comes to required tempered glass. You can only retain existing glass after a renovation if it is safe and legal to do so but must upgrade to approved glass as part of your project.

> **Helpful Hint 8.2**
>
> If you are not sure if a piece of glass on your job site is safety glass you can check without instruments. If the glass is laminated, hold your fingertip against the glass as if pointing at it but touching it. You will see a reflection off both surfaces if there are two pieces of glass in the assembly. If you are wondering if the glass is tempered, look at it through a pair of polarized sunglasses; you will be able to see streaks or stress marks left from the tempering process that are invisible to the naked eye.

Tempered glass cannot be worked after tempering. That means it cannot be cut or drilled; the glass will shatter if the glazier attempts to work the glass after tempering. Glass can be untempered (as it must be for it to be recycled) but it is best to make all design decisions, and complete all work, requiring cutting and drilling before the glass is tempered.

Tempered glass is a little stronger than regular annealed glass because it will deflect (bend) to a greater degree before breaking.

Chemically Strengthened Glass

Glass that is immersed in a chemical bath is currently not typical for interiors but material technologies and economies change quickly, so it is easy to imagine that the advantages of **chemically strengthened glass**, coupled with potential economies of scale, should demand increase, and would bring this product onto the readily available market. This process allows for thinner panes of glass because the stresses accompanying the strengthening process are lower than for heat-strengthened product. Another benefit is that heat strengthening causes slight distortion because the glass is softened during the process and its shape is alterable in this softened state. Because glass is cheap and plentiful there is little demand for superthin panes, but if weight or thickness were problematic for your design program, you might seek out this option among specialty or optical glass resources.

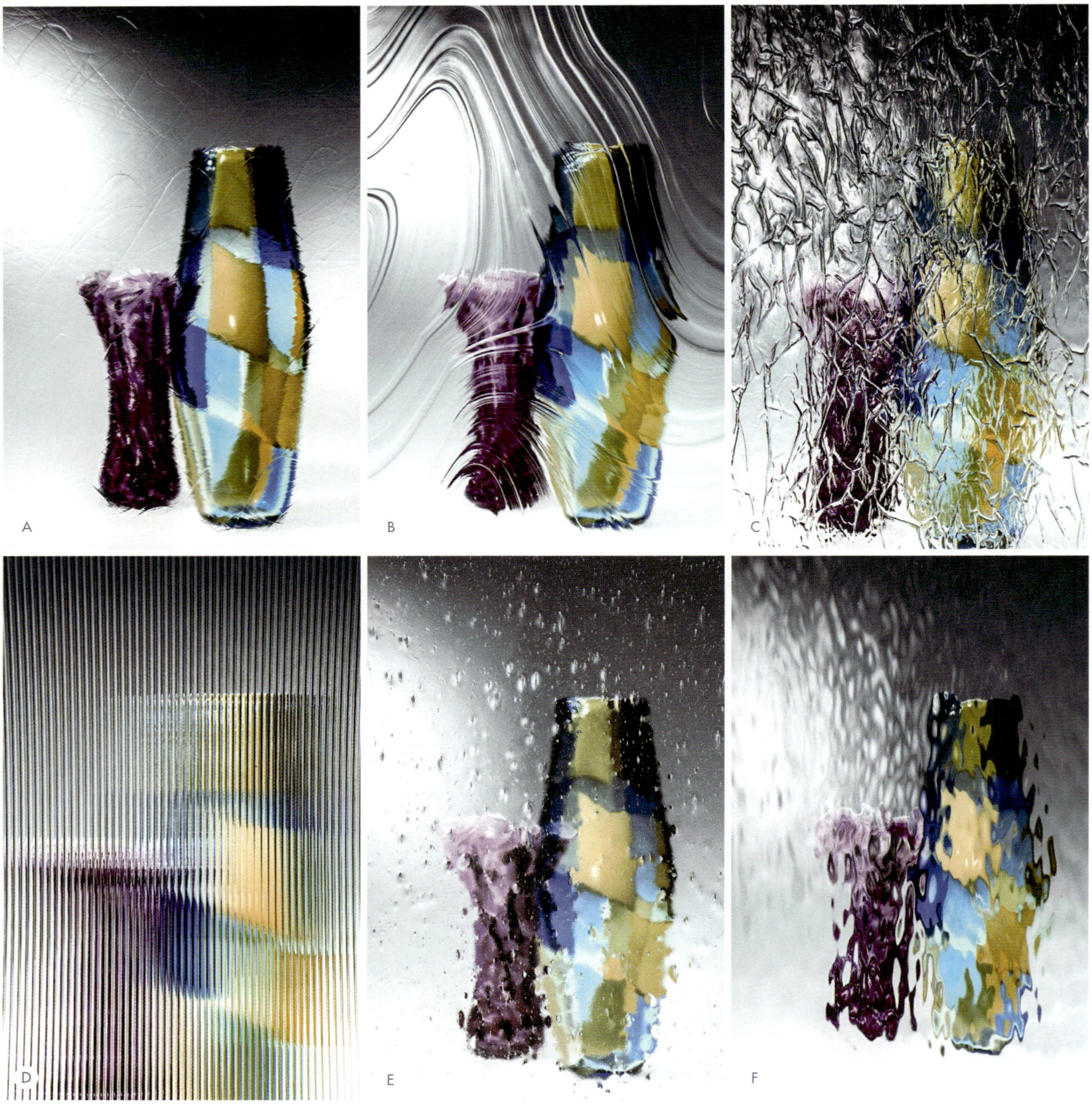

FIGURE 8.4A–F Patterned glass is available for specification on your jobs. Many patterns that you see on the market are proprietary (only one source) but others are classics that are carried by more than one source. These patterns are all proprietary: (a) is called Antique; (b) is Baroque, which is also a generic name; (c) is Krinkle; (d) is Reeded, which is also a generic name; (e) is Seedy, a generic name; (f) is Water. *The named patterns from Spectrum Glass, Woodinville, WA.*

Patterned Glass

Patterned glass is passed through rollers that press a texture into one or both sides. Figure 8.4a–f shows some of the available patterns that obscure views to varying degrees. Most patterns can be tempered and large sizes are available for use as interior partitions where the safety of tempered glass is required by law or desired for your design program.

Wire Glass

Wire glass has wire mesh embedded in it. Traditionally it was used for fire-rated partitions because the wire kept the glass in place even if broken by thermal stress. Even though it was not whole, it still provided something of a barrier to smoke and sparks because the broken glass clung to the wire instead of exploding into the room. It was also used where vandalism was a concern because the wire mesh in the pane was one more barrier against intruders. It is losing popularity to ceramic glass, which is also fire rated, and to polycarbonate plastics, which are clear and withstand impact better than wire glass. The wire actually compromises the integrity of the glass that encapsulates it, making the glass less stable.

Point of Emphasis 8.3

The wire in the glass actually compromises the integrity of the glass itself and there is some speculation that the glass is weakened a little because of the wire. You should know about this material because it is still available and you may decide to keep wire glass in an installation that you are designing for sustainability or budget reasons, but there is less reason to specify it now that there are superior glass technologies available. You may consider it if budget constraints do not allow for newer, more effective materials.

What Would You Do? 8.1

Think back to the last place you saw wire glass. Imagine that you are the lead designer on a project to remodel that space and have the option of retaining the wire glass for reasons of sustainable design. Evaluating the situation, would you keep the wire glass or replace it with a different kind of glass or other material?

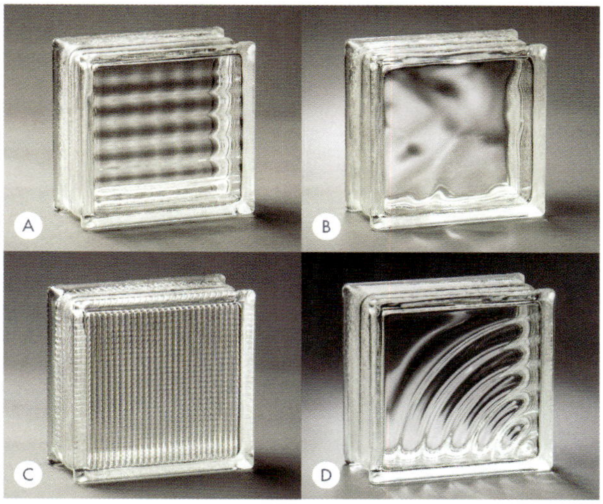

FIGURE 8.5A–D Glass block is a self-supporting transparent or translucent product. The proprietary patterns here are: (a) Argus; (b) Decora; (c) Essex; and (d) Spyra.
Patterns by Pittsburg Corning.

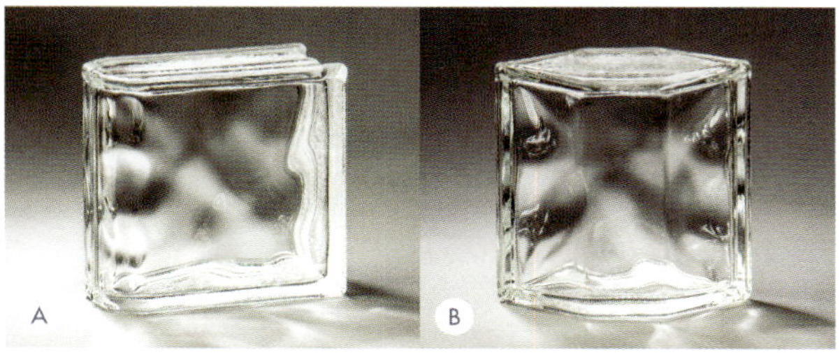

FIGURE 8.6A–B To finish the ends and edges of a glass block construction, special trims are required. These proprietary trims are: (a) End Block (shown to coordinate with Decora), (b) Hedron (shown to coordinate with Decora).
Patterns by Pittsburg Corning.

Glass Block

Glass is available as blocks in certain standard sizes, 4 inches thick or 3 1/8 inches thick, both with a hollow vacuum center, or as a solid piece of glass that is as thick as 3 inches with no hollow center. Figure 8.5a–d shows glass block units with various surface patterning that obscures views through to varying degrees. It is also available in pavers 1 inch or 1½ inches thick. Individual blocks are set in mortar, or preassembled panels are installed with a mortar or silicone sealant. Accessory shapes, two of which are shown in Figure 8.6a and b, are available for corner and end pieces to cap the ends and edges of your designs. Glass block walls are self-supporting but are not load-bearing walls, so they

FIGURE 8.7 Back-painted glass is an art form that creates a beautiful and highly serviceable kitchen backsplash. *Created by Bruce Jackson of Goldreverre.*

need no support to hold themselves in vertical position but they cannot bear any added structural weight. Specially shaped pieces are available to terminate glass block structures, because the edges of a glass block are otherwise not intended to show.

Surfaces

Glass can be colored or tinted via a couple of methods. The glass can be colored in its molten state with the addition of minerals, usually metals, introduced as powder. This is the method used for making stained glass. Glass can also be colored with the application of a frit, which is composed of glass chips that are applied to the surface of the glass and then heat fused to import color and make transparent, translucent, or opaque glass. Glass can be decorated by postproduction methods (after it has cooled). It may be sandblasted, back-painted (shown in Figure 8.7), mirrored (the back silvered), or carved.

One-way mirrored glass is popular for concealing monitors and TVs when not in use. The surface is a mirror when the device is off and a window when the device is on. One-way mirror depends on two components. The first is glass with a very thin layer of silver, thinner than that used for a regular mirror. The second part of the equation is the light in the area. The surface in the area with the highest light level will appear mirrored and the dark side will be a window. So if you are on the bright side you will see a mirror but anyone on the dark side can see through.

What Would You Do? 8.2

Where have you seen one-way/mirrored glass used? What reasons can you think of for using it in those locations? Where else might this kind of glass be used for functional or aesthetic reasons?

Edges

Almost any edge profile that can be applied to stone can be applied to the exposed edge of glass, limited by the thickness of the glass, which is typically thinner than stone. Figure 8.8 shows some of the profiles that can be applied to thick exposed edges as might exist on the edges of countertops, tabletops, stair treads, etc. As with stone edges, interior right angles (Figure 8.9) are more difficult to grind into a special profile since the in-corners must be ground by hand, matching the machine-made edge on the straight runs. Wherever the edges of glass will be exposed you must specify an edge treatment because the cut edge will be very sharp. At the very least you will specify that the edges must be seamed, which means grinding off the sharp edge that could easily cut someone.

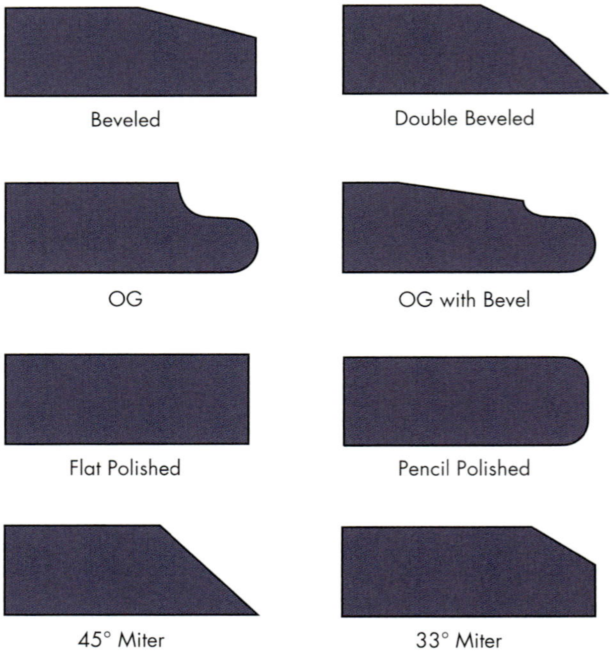

FIGURE 8.8 Glass edges can be ground into shaped profiles.

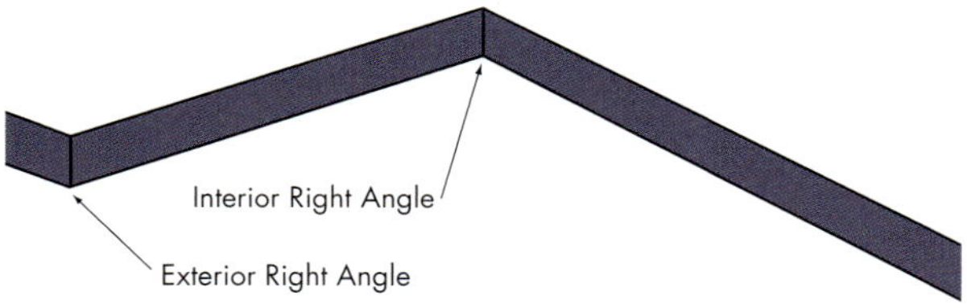

FIGURE 8.9 Interior right angles are hard to grind so take expertise and cost a little more than grinding a profile onto a straight edge.

QUALIFYING INSTALLERS

Not all glaziers have had formal training. A common means of learning this skill is on-the-job training starting out as an apprentice or helper and advancing as they prove competent. Aside from informational sessions offered by manufacturers, there are not a lot of formal learning opportunities, so you will likely find skilled glaziers with no more credential evidence than possessed by unskilled glaziers. For this reason it is very important to investigate the skill and reputation of glassworkers.

A Cautionary Tale 8.1

I specified a custom-made door with eight individual panes of glass that coordinated with custom cabinetry between a butler's pantry and a dining room for a client's new home. Two lessons were learned thanks to this custom door. One was that tempered glass (required for a door like this) comes with a "bug," which is a little etched symbol confirming that the glass was tempered. We were able (for a fee) to reorder it without the bug, but unless you specify that way, you will find a little symbol in the corner of every pane of glass.

The second lesson was that some glaziers define their job quite narrowly. The panes of glass are held in place within window muttons that are complete on one side but lack a small strip of wood on the other. This strip of wood is the "stop" because it stops the glass from falling out after it has been installed. The glazier hired for the job was willing to hold the glass in with putty but felt that the carpenter was responsible for installing the stops. Luckily the carpenters were still on the job site so it was not a problem, but they did not have the work in their contract, so my client got an unexpected up-charge on the carpenter's bill.

The first thing to do when selecting a glazier is to find one that is an expert in the kind of work that you need to have done. The industry is organized around specialties. Review their portfolio of past jobs and, if possible, go see some of their work and talk to their references. If your job is unique with a lot of custom details, ask them how they would approach the work, how long it should take, what kind of preparatory work would be included in their contract, and what required work you must find another tradesperson to perform.

INSTALLATION

Glass is used as a surfacing material, or part of an assembly, like doors and windows, or as objects like furniture, so the way the glass interfaces with the other components is often critical to your specification. If it must be drilled for hardware this must be done before tempering. You will specify the other components of the installation as well. Determining what these other required parts will be entails thinking through the entire installation.

Glass will not endure the stress of settling and a large surface must be very stable. If there is any question about movement of the surface, precautions must be taken. For example, when installing a large sheet of mirrored glass in a gym or commercial lobby, the mirror can be backed with a very dimensionally stable material such as plywood to be hung on a cleat rather than gluing the mirror directly to the wall surface.

When glass is part of a functional assembly like a door or glass partition, hardware will be specified as well as the kind of glass to be used. The installation usually depends on the hardware that grips and holds the glass. It is rarely glued into place for an assembly the way it sometimes is when used as a surfacing material (although it may be caulked for acoustics or cushioning).

Helpful Hint 8.3

While you can always order a metal U-channel to hold the glass, consider the possibility of incorporating a channel into the receiving material. I have had the stone fabricator route a channel in the back of stone countertop to receive the mirror. We laid a bead of clear silicone caulk in the bottom so the back of the mirror would be sealed against moisture (oxidation of the silvering turns the mirror black, so protect it from water).

PROTECTION AND MAINTENANCE

You are undoubtedly familiar with the vulnerabilities of glass. It is a brittle material and in addition to protecting the safety of the people in the environment where glass is used, the glass itself should be protected with good design details. You should be reluctant to use glass where there is likelihood that it will be struck with enough force to break it. You might not want to use it at the bottom of a staircase where an object could be loosed and pick up speed on the way to the glass, increasing impact and the likelihood of breakage. Glass that is handled and must move is also vulnerable and even though you often see glass doors (and of course windows) these items must be carefully designed to withstand the stresses of normal use.

A quality glass installation is very easy to maintain with nontoxic cleansers, although it does need maintenance. You don't need a textbook to tell you that glass that is touched will show fingerprints. Etched surfaces will show oily fingerprints more pronouncedly than polished glass will. That is why many designers will specify laminated glass for frosted glass doors that will receive handprints. The outside faces are polished on both sides of the door but the laminated sheet in between them provides the frosted privacy they need.

Some safety coatings provide actual texture and, like etched surfaces of a frosted pane of glass, textures will be a little harder to clean.

SAFETY

The obvious safety concerns pertaining to glass are breakage and slipperiness when used for walking surfaces. Specify tempered glass whenever demanded by code or when the glass is installed as part of a freestanding assembly (doors, partitions, stairs, etc.). If used as a walking surface, specify a nonslip abrasive frit that can be fused to the surface and a texture in addition to that for greater safety allowable by the material.

Another consideration pertains as much to your design as it does to the material. When quality glass is very clean and the light sources are shielded (as is the case in a well-done lighting installation) glass is invisible. If the space you are designing will be used by people unfamiliar with it, such as a public or commercial space, evaluate the safety of glass. A person with good eyesight can still walk forcefully into a pane of glass if they are in a hurry, preoccupied with their own thoughts and unfamiliar with the environment. Glass is a hard surface, so even if it is tempered and laminated and remains unharmed by the encounter, people have split open their foreheads thanks to events similar to the one just described. If glass is indicated by your design program to share natural light or allow people to see when a conference room is occupied or available, consider etching a portion of the pane so that it is obvious that there is a piece of glass there.

Glaziers' work can be hazardous. You can well imagine that they are vulnerable to cuts on the job. They also frequently work in high places and must often lift heavy panes of glass into position. As you are working out the details of your design imagine yourself as the glazier; picture how you would accomplish the installation that must be performed to complete your design. This ability to envision the process will help you design details that can be more safely accomplished.

SUSTAINABILITY

Glass is recyclable and can contain recycled materials; it is quite common for preconsumer glass scrap to be incorporated into glass production. Glass tiles may utilize recycled glass. Glass aggregate for terrazzo for floors and countertops can be recycled material. There are many companies producing surfacing materials from recycled glass. Glass is inert, so nontoxic, and is an impervious surface requiring no harsh chemicals to maintain it. Exterior glazing makes an important contribution to energy conservation with window films and other technology to inhibit heat gain from the sun and heat loss during cold weather.

MANAGING BUDGETS

Glass is not an expensive material on its own but it is frequently patterned, textured, coated, back painted, or subjected to some other process to alter performance or visual characteristics. This additional processing adds to the cost of the surface. Other factors contributing to

Table 8.2
You might organize your selection criteria for your unique job something like this.

Program Considerations	Implications
Will the glass have to support weight?	The longer the span, the thicker the sheet must be to support the same load.
Will this glass be used as a walking surface?	Select an abrasive frit and possibly a textured surface too.
Is this a partition?	Temper the glass and, if privacy is desired, select a textured or etched surface or electronic glass.
Is glass being used as a surfacing material?	Evaluate building conditions for possible movement or settling and devise a separation from the structure.
Is this glass part of an assembly—like stairs or a partition wall?	Select the glass in conjunction with the whole system; some systems include glass so make your selection from their offerings.
Is the glass mirrored?	Protect the silver backing from moisture so it doesn't oxidize.
Will the green cast be objectionable?	Select low-iron glass.
Will large expanses of glass be used?	Evaluate the acoustics in the space and consider how to deal with reflection and reverberation.
Will the glass be touched regularly?	Texture the glass; if frosted texture is desired consider laminating.
Is this a window selection for the building facade?	Investigate problems with heat gain and glare.

cost are formulation (low-iron glass is more expensive) and thickness of the panel. Standard glass having simple details can be inexpensively produced.

ORGANIZATION OF THE INDUSTRY

The glass industry is divided in specialties. Shops will possibly specialize in interior work, exterior work, commercial storefronts, curtain wall construction, and highly specialized "boutique" work. Shops will have varying production capabilities and capacities. Some shops will fabricate units, others will only install units they have sold to general contractors, designers, or clients. When multiple processes are required, some will be performed by the glass supplier, such as tinting, texturing, tempering, and laminating. Other secondary processes will likely be performed by another party under a separate contract, such as back painting, graphic transferring, or assembling into a structure like stairs or partitions. You can imagine that it is critical for all parties to be in communication as details are finalized and contracts drawn up for the work, and all design details discussed should be depicted in your drawings and specifications.

SELECTION CRITERIA

As always, the selection criteria will be organized based on your design program. Table 8.2 is a starting point for your considerations and you will build upon this as your unique job requires.

SPECIFYING

Glass may simply be used as a surfacing material but it is just as common to see it as part of an assembly. For the sample spec let's imagine that you have decided to use a glass partition to separate a conference room from the general open office area for an insurance company. To write this kind of spec it is a good idea to find a likely system and write a closed specification. There would be drawings attendant to the spec for an assembly like this and all dimensions would have to be precise because the glass will be tempered and cannot be field cut to fit.

SAMPLE SPEC 8.1

Part 1 General Information

1.1 Related Documents

A. Refer to designer's drawings and specifications for location and interface with structure.
B. Refer to approved shop drawings for details of the system.
C. Refer to electrical drawings for location of power and hookups (to be completed by electrician).
D. Refer to specifications and manufacturer's parts list for components.

1.2 Summary

A. Install partition system to enclose main conference room space 104.
B. System consists of tempered, laminated, electrified privacy glass for stationary partition and for doors.

1.3 References

A. ANSI Z97.1 Safety Performance Specifications for glazing material used in buildings.
B. ASTM C1048 Heat-treated flat glass.
C. ASTM C1172 Laminated glass.

1.4 Vendor Submittals

A. Vendor to provide product data for electrified privacy glass.
B. Vendor to provide shop drawings detailing glazing setting methods, sheet sizes, tolerances, wiring diagram.
C. Samples of glass specified minimum 4" × 6".
D. Manufacturers certificates confirming performance of assembly.
E. Installation and maintenance instructions.
F. Copies of warranties.
G. Contractor to provide certificates confirming completion of manufacturer's training course for all installers assigned.

1.5 Quality Assurance

A. Install electrified privacy glass in accordance with National Electric Code requirements for the building and local building codes.
B. Use only trained, certified installers.
C. Inspect conditions and electrical work by others and confirm it is in accordance with plans and will permit installation as planned prior to commencing work. Alert designer immediately regarding any discrepancies.

1.6 Delivery, Storage, and Handling

A. Transport glass only in conditions permitted by the manufacturer.
B. Deliver and store glass in manufacturer's cases.

1.7 Maintenance of Installation

A. Remove panels from front of crates as described by manufacturer.
B. Do not rest panels on uncushioned surface.
C. Install according to manufacturer's instructions and as defined by designer's drawings.

Part 2 Products

2.1 General Information

A. Specialty glass and metal framing to be installed per manufacturer's instructions and approved shop drawings in order to not void warranties.
B. Installer to provide all tools required for installation including but not limited to shims, blocks, ladders, wiping cloths, and recommended cleaner to install and clean all evidence of installation handling of glass and frame components.

2.2 Manufacturers

A. Elektrik Glass Co., 1234 Industrial Drive, Anytown, ST 34567.

2.3 Products

A. Privacy Film Glass 0.169 mm thick with liquid crystal inner layer encased by conductive polyester coating, laminated in clear annealed tempered glass.
B. Spark Series polished aluminum channels top and bottom and electric glass-on-glass hinge in polished aluminum.
C. Install all connections to be fastened to the system and leave ready for hookup by electrician.

Part 3 Execution

3.1 Examination

A. Verify proper supply location for conduit and boxes, and number of connectors, and confirm GFCI connectors.
B. Verify that all parts of assembly are clean and in good condition.

3.2 Preparation

A. Drill holes in frame to receive electrical wiring. Clean all burrs and remove metal filings from channel.

3.3 Installation

A. Install according to manufacturer's instructions.
B. Install all gaskets provided, without voids to ensure unbroken bond to glass.

3.4 Post Installation

A. Upon completion of electrical hookup (by others) test system according to manufacturer's instructions, verify performance, and test control switching.
B. Clean all glazing and framing and prepare for approval by owner's representative.
C. Demonstrate operation to owner's representative.

INSPECTION

Inspection will depend on the item or surface that has been installed. Of course you will inspect with your approved plans in hand because there will likely be too many details to remember, especially because designers often make plans a year or more in advance of the installation.

If your installation is a simple surface, like a mirror mounted to a wall, the task is a little simpler. You should make sure all cuts are neat and polished or edged as specified and that all seams are tight. All electrical covers and grilles should be straight and even and conceal all cut edges. Adjacent panes of glass should be flush and aligned so that the reflection is continuous from one pane to the next. Alignments should be level. The glass should be free of scratches and defects.

RELATED MATERIAL

Ceramic glass cooktops, glass incorporated in computer displays, and other combinations of technologies can inspire the designer hoping to create functional surfaces.

Switchable glass turns from frosted to clear when electricity is run through it. It uses the same technology to deepen the color of tinted glass.

> **What Would You Do? 8.3**
>
> Imagine walls as touch screens—where would you use them for entertainment and information? Glass floors allow for interactive technology as well. Can you imagine how a system of wayfinding could be facilitated with glass flooring? What would it look like? How could it work?

Super-thin liquid glass coatings are being developed for stain resistance for textiles, and other new glass technologies are in the developmental stage.

SUMMARY

In this chapter we reviewed how different forms of glass are made and what their properties are. New glass technologies that may add to products available to interior designers in the near future were discussed. Considerations that will affect your decision-making as you select and specify glass products were suggested. We looked at how the industry is organized and considered sustainability and safety issues pertaining to glass.

WEB SEARCH ACTIVITIES

1. Perform an image search for pictures of items that are made of glass and notice the construction details that require additional parts to hold the glass in place. Find pictures of:

    Glass partition
    Glass floor
    Glass stairs
    Glass canopy
    Glass furniture

2. Search for *new glass technologies* or start your search at www.glassonweb.com for a new glass technology you would like to incorporate into a project.
3. Perform an image search for *glass door hinges*. Look at the pictures you find and envision how the hinges function.
4. Perform an image search for *patterned glass* to see a seemingly unlimited offering of patterns to accommodate your job's aesthetic.
5. Search for some of the decorative processes mentioned such as *glass frit*, *back-painted glass*, *colored glass*, *etched glass*, etc., to get a sense of product offerings. Perform an image search for corresponding pictures.
6. Locate the Web site for a manufacturer of glass staircases, doors, partition walls, or surfaces. Search the site until you find a sample specification for use by interior designers or architects. Read it for comprehension, looking up any references to testing or codes.

PERSONAL ACTIVITIES

1. Locate the bug on tempered glass used in a public place.
2. Sketching to scale, determine how thick a piece of glass should be before it can support a shaped edge like an ogee. A bevel? A bullnose?
3. Consider an area in your own plan where you might use a glass surface or an assembly containing glass, or find a picture of an installation of glass in an interior space. Using Sample Spec 8.1 in this chapter as an example, write a spec for the item or surface. If you intend to use an assembly, such as a staircase or partition wall, it might be helpful to find a product online to reference.

SUMMARY QUESTIONS

1. What is soda-lime glass? What is low-iron glass?
2. What is annealing? Heat strengthening? Tempering? Laminating?
3. What are insulated panels and why is it important to identify the faces in the assembly when you place your order?
4. For energy-efficient glass, is a high R-value a good thing or a bad thing? What about a high U-value?
5. What is ceramic glass?
6. When and why would you separate a large sheet of glass from the structure when installing it on walls, ceilings, or floors as a surfacing material?
7. How are functional hardware items, like hinges and door pulls, attached to glass?
8. What are some functions of films?
9. What are the properties of cast glass? Laminated glass? Tempered? Wire glass? Patterned glass? Glass block?
10. In what ways can the appearance of glass be altered?
11. What are some options for exposed glass edges?
12. What tasks do glaziers perform?
13. What makes glass nontoxic?
14. What kind of problem can occur if people handle frosted/etched glass?
15. What safety considerations should the designer evaluate before specifying glass?
16. What characteristics make glass sustainable?
17. What characteristics of an installation can raise the price?

Chapter 9

METALS

Key Terms

Alloy
Anodized
Cold rolled
Galvanized
Malleable
Mock-up
Oxidize
Tensile strength

Objectives

After reading this chapter, you should be able to:

- Distinguish between the different metals that are used in surfaces and items that interior designers typically specify and know their general characteristics.
- Understand the different forms that metal comes in and how they are made.
- Understand how metal surfaces and items are fashioned.
- Understand the finishes and textures used for metal.
- Qualify fabricators and manage the fabrication of custom surfaces and items.
- Select metal for your project and know how to specify it.
- Understand sustainability and safety issues pertaining to metal.
- Inspect for quality.

The characteristics affecting the performance of metals are due to the characteristics of the metals themselves and the new characteristics that emerge when metals are combined in an **alloy**. Unlike other composite materials where you can assume the characteristics of the composite based on its ingredients, metals interact with each other on a molecular level and often new characteristics emerge out of the union. Luckily, you will not need in-depth knowledge of metallurgy, because interior designers tend to specify metals that are widely available and well understood. Many of the metals that you encounter as you search for materials for your projects will be part of an assembly (metal-clad cabinetry for instance) or a unit in a construction (metal spindles in a staircase) and you will focus on the performance specifications for the whole assembly. You just need enough information about metal to evaluate its appropriateness for your use.

MATERIAL MAKEUP OR CONTENT

Many metals share characteristics. Some will **oxidize** if they are exposed to air and humidity or moisture. This means that a copper-faced laminate will have characteristics of laminate (require adhesives to install, will have a dark edge where the phenolic backing shows, etc.) as well as characteristics of the metal, meaning that the face may oxidize if it is not protected by a lacquer. Iron, copper, brass, bronze, zinc, and silver will all oxidize. Aluminum, chrome, stainless steel, and **galvanized** steel will not oxidize.

Sometimes the fact that metals oxidize is used to decorative advantage—for example, copper may be allowed to oxidize to a particular duskiness or be oxidized by the use of an acid. Then it will be stabilized and sealed to present a brown metal finish with a copper "glow" discernible underneath.

CHARACTERISTICS OF VARIOUS METALS

Not all metals are common in interiors, so the following focuses only on the metals that you will most commonly encounter as you select and specify metal surfacing and items for your projects.

Ferrous Metal

Ferrous metals contain iron. Iron is easily worked, oxidizes rapidly, and is susceptible to acids. Iron is seldom used alone for products that you will specify; it is often a component in alloys, meaning it is combined with other ingredients.

Cast iron (cast meaning that the molten metal is poured into a mold) is relatively brittle, with a very high compression strength, and is ideal for stair components and grating. Cast iron with an enamel coating is used for bathtubs and sinks. Wrought iron is relatively soft, and is corrosion and fatigue resistant. It is machinable and easily worked. It is often cast into bars or pipes that are, in turn, welded and formed into 3D shapes of furniture or architectural ornamentation.

Iron is the main ingredient in steel. Steel is iron with carbon and is stronger and more corrosion resistant than iron. Other metals can be added to the iron and carbon product to produce stainless steel. The most commonly used metal is nickel but there are many types of stainless steel utilizing a number of metals in combination with iron and carbon. As one example, type 304 stainless, which is used for stainless steel sinks, has 8 percent nickel and 18 percent chromium. The properties of this type are unique to the actual content of the alloy and include formability, weldability, and a luster or sheen; it is nonmagnetic. A corrosion-resistant coating arises naturally on the surface of this steel; if this is damaged, the corrosion resistance of this kind of stainless steel is reduced.

Nonferrous Metal

Nonferrous metals do not contain iron.

Aluminum

- soft
- highly corrosion resistant
- lacks strength
- lightweight
- often used as one component in an alloy, increasing its strength
- difficult to weld

Zinc

- bright silver-colored metal
- more corrosion resistant than steel
- used as a plating to prevent corrosion in steel
- can corrode in water
- attracts minerals out of water and forms a surface scale protecting the zinc underneath from corrosion, so it is used in some plumbing fittings
- often specified as sheeting for a surfacing material

Copper

- resistant to corrosion
- will oxidize
- resists impact and fatigue
- used on exterior building components (roof sheathing, gutters, and downspouts)
- used for interior accessories and lighting and some plumbing fixtures and fittings
- good **tensile strength**

Brass

- alloy of copper and usually zinc
- frequently used in interiors
- cannot be formed with extrusion method
- some types of brass alloy are called bronze
- some nonbronze brass alloys are commercial bronze and architectural bronze

Bronze

- bronze is an alloy of copper and aluminum or silicon
- can be extruded
- will oxidize in the air to a color often referred to as verdigris

Chromium

- used as an alloy to alter the characteristics of other metals (in steel, for instance)
- used for plating because it can achieve a high shine and because of its ability to resist corrosion
- the metal object is frequently plated first with nickel and then chrome

German Silver

- alloy of copper, nickel, and zinc
- corrosion resistant
- hard but not brittle

Nickel

- corrosion resistant
- can achieve a high polish, so it is used for plating
- found in the composition of alloys such as steel and German silver

Pewter

- tin-based alloy
- soft and **malleable**

Titanium

- corrosion resistant
- lightweight
- strong
- frequently used in alloys for added corrosion resistance

Zinc

- corrosion resistant
- somewhat brittle
- commonly used in alloys with other metals to enhance corrosion resistance

What Would You Do? 9.1

Think of all the metal surfaces and components specified by interior designers. Review the list of metals, both ferrous and nonferrous, and see which characteristics you would match up with some of the instances of the use of metal in the interior. Which metals would you think would be best suited for each instance?

PARTS AND ACCESSORIES

Depending on the application, the parts and accessories you should know about might include fasteners and decorative attachments and hardware made of metal.

FORMING METAL

Metal and metal alloys are formed in a number of different ways into the surfacing materials and objects that designers specify. Not all metals are compatible with all methods but there are numerous options available in each of the following forms.

Sheets

Metal sheets are often used to cover surfaces (nonstructural, not self-supporting). Metal laminates have a thin sheet of metal laminated to the same phenolic backing that plastic laminates are backed with or they may be solid metal sheets. Some metals can be **cold rolled** and so are easier to bring to uniform thickness.

The thickness of the sheet metal is described as the gauge. Smaller numbers refer to thicker sheets of metal: 11 gauge is about 1/8 inch thick, 20 gauge is about 1/32 inch thick. Metal thicker than 3 gauge (which is just under 1/4 inch) is usually described as plate metal rather than sheet metal. Sheets can be formed over a substrate with corners welded to make structures like countertops and wall panels. Sheets can be fastened to other substrates with adhesives or mechanical fasteners (screws, for instance) to clad many kinds of surfaces. Examples of sheet metal products that you might specify are flat sheets and stamped sheets:

- *Flat sheets:* Whether contemporary or embossed sheets imitating vintage tin ceilings, they may be prefinished or field finished with paint or special techniques (Figures 9.1a and b and 9.2). Panels may hang in a suspended grid system or be fastened directly to the substrate with nails or glue. Depending on the system, the fasteners may remain exposed or be covered over with a concealing strip that may be held in place with mastic. Prefabricated panels come in set modular units and are purchased as a complete system. Custom wall panel installations may be formed to your specifications and installed per your drawings.
- *Stamped sheets:* Another fabrication technology is stamped metal (Figure 9.3). Sheet metal is shaped against a dye using heavy pressure. Embossed reproduction ceiling tiles have been stamped, so have stainless steel sinks, which are stamped in a succession of increasingly deep dies (sturdy forms that are more durable than the material being stamped) until the full depth of the bowl is achieved.

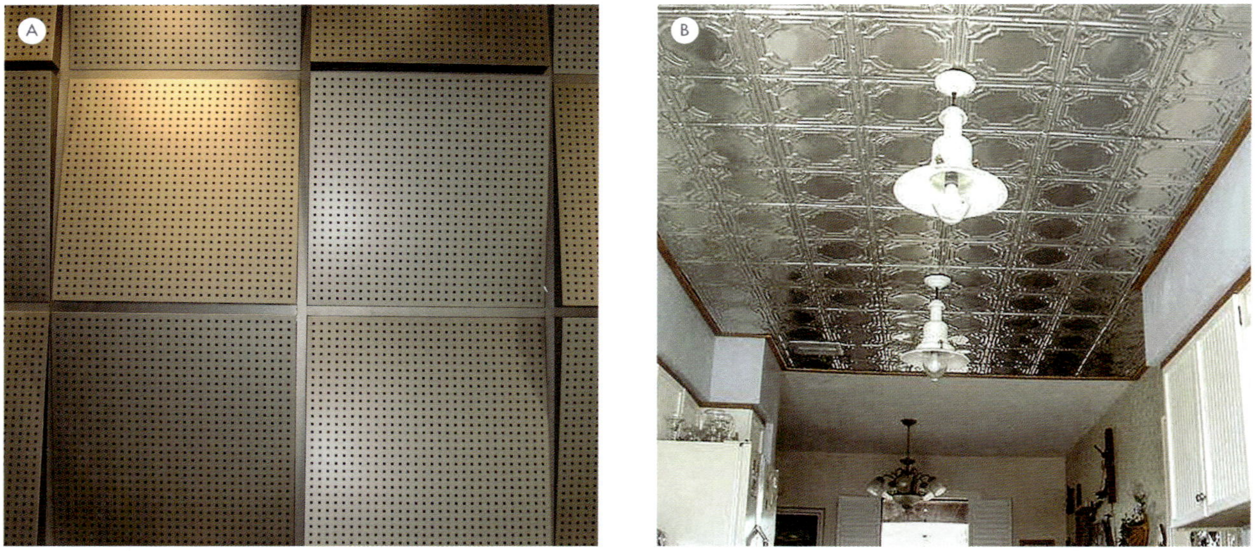

FIGURE 9.1A–B Metal sheet products: Perforated product available from *United States Gypsum* may be combined with acoustical product (a); embossed tin ceiling from *M-Boss* (b).

FIGURE 9.2 Wall cladding: Custom metal wall panels by *Tesko Enterprises.*

FIGURE 9.3 A very common stamped form. *Image by Alana Clark with permission from K&B Galleries in Chicago, IL.*

FIGURE 9.4 Cast metal fixture.

Plate

Plate is a designator used to describe sheets that are very thick and can be used structurally. While the thickness of the metal sheet is described by the term *gauge*, metal plate is described in thickness stated in inches. For instance, 3/16-inch stainless steel plate up to 1½-inch stainless steel plate is a range typical of plate.

You might specify plate as support for shelving (angle iron is stamped plate) or as self-supporting tops for counters or tables or furniture bases. You might build shelves into a surface or construct stair parts from it.

What Would You Do? 9.2

When would you choose plate over sheet metal?

Cast Forms

Casting metal means pouring molten metal into a mold. Like plate, cast metal parts can be self-supporting members of assemblies. After removal from the mold it may be "cleaned up" (removing extra metal built up at the seam between the two halves of the mold and filing any burrs smooth). The cast metal may additionally be forged, which means it is worked further by a metalsmith, who reheats the metal to soften it and shape it by delivering successive blows that squeeze the metal into an altered form.

Metal can also be cast into complex forms such as grilles, screens, gates, and so on (Figure 9.4). Often, custom casting has an initial cost to produce a mold, but after that cost has been incurred, the cost of additional castings is not high, especially if you are casting multiples and the cost of forms can be distributed among each one. If a piece is being duplicated from an existing item, the original may have to be destroyed in the making of a new mold; however, you save the cost of the **mock-up**. Casting is also used to create metal bar stock, which is welded and shaped into custom items.

Pipes and Tubes

Pipes (round profile) and tubes (square profile) of various standard sizes are used to fabricate metal components for your designs. Pipe dimensions refer to the inside clear diameter and the gauge (thickness) of the pipe wall must be added to that number to describe the outside dimension. The outside diameter is the pipe size plus the thickness

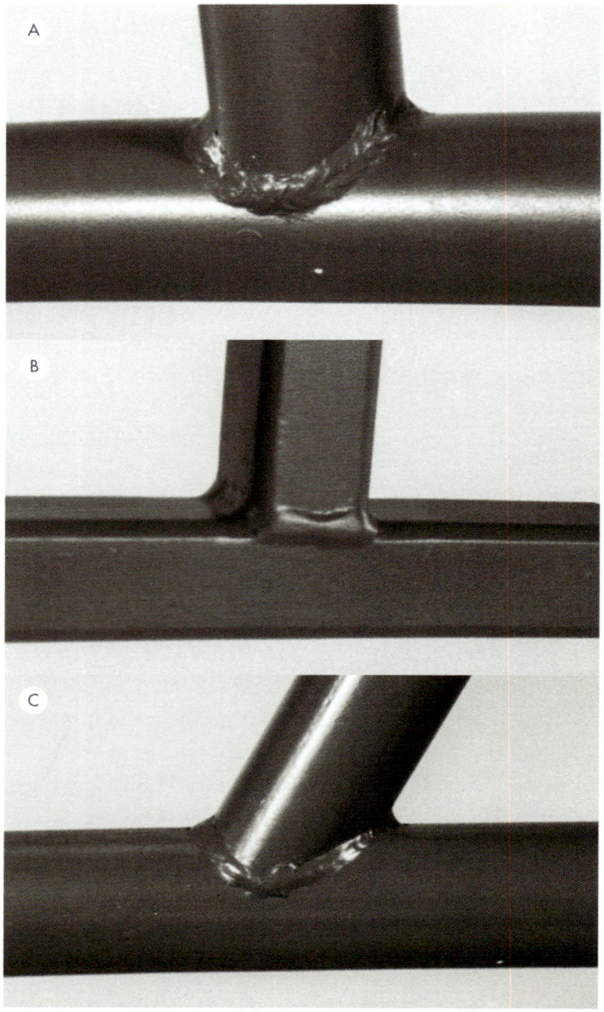

FIGURE 9.5A–C Tubes are hollow metal profiles that may be square, oval, or rectangular and are described in terms of their wall thickness and outside dimensions. Pipe (a) is round hollow stock, (b) is tube stock, and raked pipe is shown in image (c). National Ornamental and Miscellaneous Metals Association (NOMMA) uses these standard descriptors for metal pieces and constructions.

times two. Tube dimensions refer to the exterior size, and the thickness of the tube wall (gauge) is included in the size listed. The gauge of the metal may be listed along with the outside diameter. The gauge will be a figure like 0.035 (20 gauge) to 0.120 (11 gauge). The size may be actual (measured with calipers or other instrument) or approximate (tape measure). (See Figure 9.5a–c.)

Tubing and pipe can be cut and welded (Figure 9.6) into complex forms such as railings, furniture bases, fixture parts, etc. Widely available stock profiles include square, rectangular, round, and flat.

FIGURE 9.6 Metal fabricators such as *Tesko Enterprises* weld these tubes and pipes into complex constructions for furniture and architectural details. *Stock at Tesko Enterprises.*

Quality designations for cast metal that indicate the degree of finish also have implications for cost. Foundry grade is the least costly and architectural grade the most costly.

- *Foundry grade* will have more surface pitting/textural variations and there may be some variation from piece to piece among "identical" items. This grade is quite coarse and not for items that would be seen up close or be handled.
- *Commercial grade* items will be more uniform and smoother. The largest variations will be cleaned up but the casting seam will still be present.
- *Architectural grade* is smoothed and sandblasted to further minimize surface variations.

What Would You Do? 9.3

When would you specify foundry grade? Architectural grade? Commercial grade?

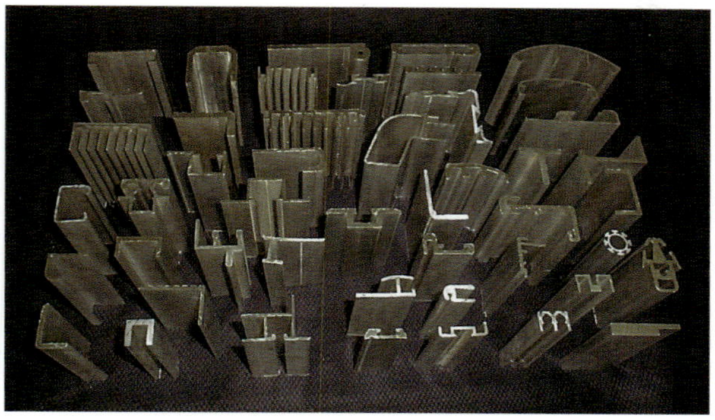

FIGURE 9.7 Extruded metal from *Allied Metal Products* fabricates extruded metal for industry.

Extruded

Extruded metal process works something like a spritz cookie cutter; metal is extruded in shapes specifically designed to perform a function. Extruded metal parts are stronger than stamped metal. Extruded metal is used to form channels, frames, and other working members of various assemblies (Figure 9.7).

FIGURE 9.8 Spun metal such as these forms from *Franjo* are used as stand-alone objects such as accessories or as components of furniture.

Spun

Spinning metal means to turn it on a lathe (similar to shaping a piece of wood). Decorative, accessory items and cabinet hardware are the most likely examples that you encounter. See Figure 9.8 for examples of spun metal.

Welding and Soldering

Welding occurs when two pieces of metal are fused together without the aid of a metal filler. Soldering (pronounced: *sod-dering*) uses another metal as an adhesive to fasten two metal members together. Soldering is also called brazing. The National Ornamental and Miscellaneous Metals Association (NOMMA) has a reference standard for the quality of metal welds. Figure 9.9a–d has examples of different quality welds.

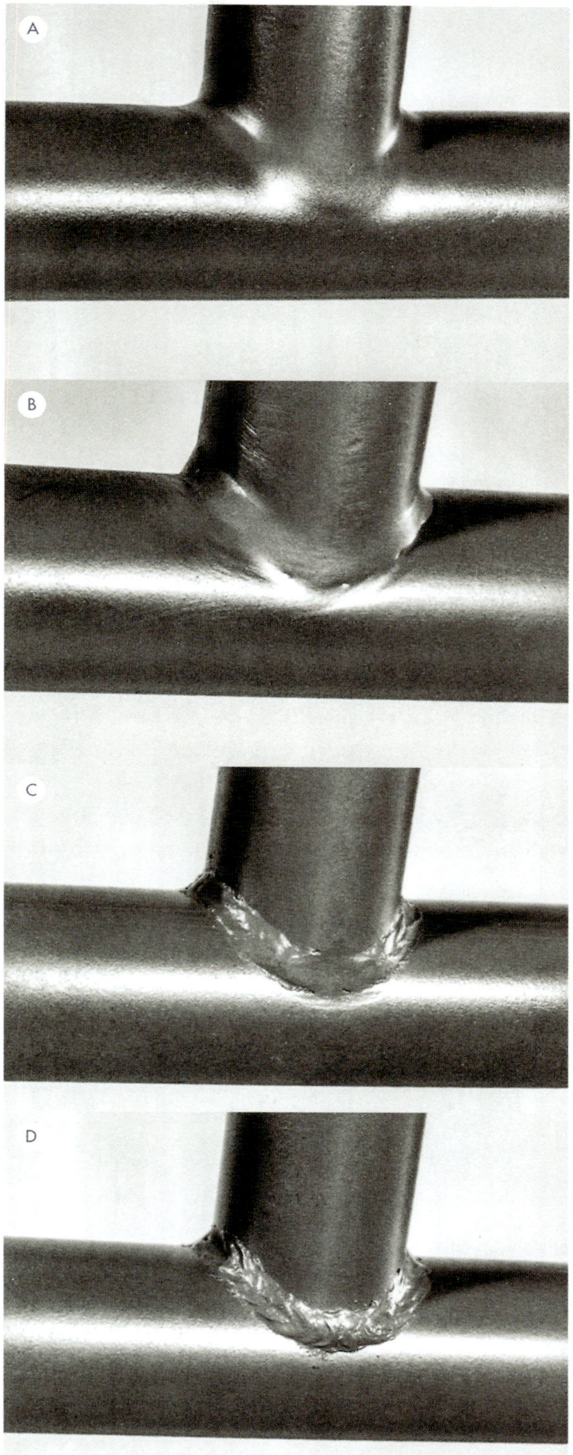

FIGURE 9.9A–D Various descriptors established by National Ornamental and Miscellaneous Metals Association (NOMMA) as reference standards for weld quality range from the most cleaned up example (top) to the coarsest for utility and hidden parts (bottom).

FIGURE 9.10A–B Metal wire can be woven on looms like fabric looms, producing a variety of weave patterns. *Woven metal from Cambridge Architectural.*

If your job requires a lower level of finish for purposes of aesthetics or economy, you may decide to allow for a less labor-intensive weld. Standard 1 welds (Figure 9.9a) shown on the previous page are "cleaned up," and other standards are progressively rougher (Figure 9.9b–d) as may be required by your particular job. You may allow Standard 4 welds if the metal is a substructure and the weld will not show.

Weaving

Metal weaving produces a surfacing or screening material (it is not structural). It uses metal wire in place of fiber but the construction is very similar to woven textiles. Figure 9.10a and b shows a durable mesh suitable for a partition and a fine metal mesh used to clad the front of a reception desk.

FINISHES

Finishes refer to surface textures. The shininess of the surface of metal can vary. (Figure 9.11 shows metal being polished.) Bright is the highest shine. It is achieved by dipping the metal in an acid. Buffed finishes are produced by successive polishing and buffing using increasingly fine abrasives. Brushed textures are directional with a satiny sheen produced by making tiny parallel scratches on the surface with a belt or wheel and fine abrasives or by rubbing with steel wool. Matte is a nondirectional texture produced by blasting the metal with sand, glass beads, or metal shot. Etched metal has a matte or frosted surface from treating the face with acids or alkaline solutions. Figure 9.12a–c show three textures.

FIGURE 9.11 Surface quality is achieved by a number of processes. Polished metal is ground to a smooth reflective surface in a hand-done method here at *Tesko Enterprises*.

FIGURE 9.12A–C *Chemetal* in Easthampton, MA, produces metal surfacing product in wide-ranging variety. This image shows three of the most common textures for metal surfaces: brushed (a); polished (b); satin (c).

QUALIFYING CUSTOM FABRICATORS

When you are looking for a fabricator for custom metalwork for your project, you will need to discover the following in order to make a good selection:

- Have they done work similar to that required by your job?
- Have they received recognition for their work?
- Do they have at their disposal the technologies required to complete the work or can they access the required equipment?
- Will they sub out portions of the work to others and if so, who will be responsible for the quality of the product if this is the way it will proceed?
- Do they produce their own shop drawings for your review?
- What is the sampling procedure like—will they make samples for your approval prior to commencing the work?

INSTALLATION

Depending on the metal item or surface planned, installation will proceed in various ways. Obviously, if your installation is a system, like a staircase or a ceiling system, the parts will be delivered to the job site and assembled using all the requisite hardware, fasteners, etc., that will undoubtedly arrive with the other parts. If you are adhering a sheet of metal to a surface, the substrate is likely to be delivered to the shop and the metal affixed off-site at the fabricator's shop and delivered to the site, to be hung on cleats or affixed with adhesive. If your metal specification is for an item such as an exhaust hood or a light or plumbing fixture, it will be completely fabricated elsewhere and attached with hardware. It is uncommon for any part of metal fabrication to occur on-site, so even your custom fabrications will be designed to be installed rather than fabricated on-site.

PROTECTION AND MAINTENANCE

Metal is vulnerable to oxidation as well as abuse during use. Some metals will receive only a polish but metal that must be protected during use will receive plating, coating, or anodizing.

Plating

Plating means applying one metal to another by electrolysis, hot dipping, or electroplating. Materials commonly used for plating include the following:

- *Brass* is a durable, long-lasting metal alloy that holds up to heavy use. It is costly initially because it is a costly material and requires complicated manufacturing processes. Brass may be a solid brass fitting or a brass coat applied over a base metal. Brass is a common base for other plated finishes. Brass can be made tarnish free in the air by an electroplating of a titanium alloy.
- *Chrome* is extremely hard and does not oxidize. Chrome is electrochemically deposited over nickel-plated base metal.
- *Copper* is softer than brass and is prone to corrosion and scratching. Copper may be an undercoat or cover in a multistep plating process. For instance, it is sometimes deposited on base metal parts that are to be chromed or put over the back of the silvering on a mirror to protect the silver.
- *Gold* is used only for plating. When specifying gold-plated fixtures in a bathroom never allow gold flash or gold wash (which can wear out in a matter of months). Never expose gold plate to abrasives or acids.
- *Nickel* is frequently used for plating because of its resistance to oxidation and deep rich luster.
- *Pewter* is an alloy of tin with brass, copper, or lead added. It is very soft and is a term that refers to the appearance of pewter rather than the actual metal. "Pewter" finishes are usually chrome or nickel with a darkening overglaze of tinted lacquer.

Helpful Hint 9.1

If you have need of an item in a metal finish that seems to be unavailable, say you wanted a particular faucet in copper but it doesn't come that way, order it in brass. Brass is very amenable to accept a variety of plated finishes. Order the item unlacquered if available (saves you the time and expense of stripping the lacquer off). The item can be plated with the metal finish you require, typically by dipping it in a tank. This, of course, points to a size restriction. Not all platers have large tanks so if your item is large (like a chair or table base) you will need to confirm that the plater has a tank that can hold the whole item.

Coatings

Coatings are surfaces applied to metal that bond to varying degrees with the metal. They are unlike plating because they sit on the surface and do not become integrated into the metal body.

Metal Coatings

Liquid copper, brass, and bronze are composed of an acrylic binder and powdered metal, creating a flexible coating over the metal substrate. These coatings will oxidize to a lesser extent than would the natural metal. Heavily oxidized effects (such as verdigris) must be encouraged with an acid or applied as a faux finish, where paint imitates oxidation.

Patinas

True patinas are created from actual oxidation of the metal coating, which can naturally occur over time or be encouraged by acids. Formulations can be hot or cold. Hot patinas are often waxed as a last step in the process before the metal is allowed to cool down. Patinas are sometimes combined with dyes to enhance colors.

Patinas and coatings are both used to achieve similar effects, but one difference between the two is that the coating will be an opaque coat while the patina will be a change to the actual metal surface; it does not obscure the surface—it is the surface.

Baked Enamel and Porcelain

A baked enamel finish is usually attracted to the metal part electrostatically (less waste in overspray), then baked on so it really clings to the surface. The final finish is around 0.7 to 1.1 millimeters when dry. Porcelain is also baked on. Air-dry formulas are available for touch-up but they are brittle and may crack if the underlying metal is deformed.

Powder-Coated Finish

Powder-coated finish is a more durable abrasion-resistant coating than paint with better weather resistance. It is applied in a multistep process beginning with the preparation of the surface to be painted, then the paint, which is a dry resin powder, is sprayed on. Electrostatic process prevents overspray. The particles sail around the piece coating the back with varying degrees of success, depending on the exact process. The finish is then baked at 320°F to 410°F (160°C to 210°C). Some are thermoplastic (can be heated and softened); other formulas are thermoset (more like a curing process from which the material cannot return to its original characteristics).

Anodizing

Anodizing is specific to aluminum products; it is an oxide coating. It is transparent and weld marks are not concealed by **anodized** coatings. Anodizing is not as precise as you might expect in producing a consistent finish. If you specify sheets and extruded members in the same finish they are difficult to match exactly.

Many colors are available ranging from finishes that imitate other metals such as bronze, pewter, or copper to brilliant colors such as red and cobalt blue. The anodizing process also improves the durability of the surface.

Wax

Wax is brushed onto the heated item and rubbed and buffed by hand to a smooth matte finish. It is fairly durable and easy to maintain.

Problems with Coatings

Coatings are similar to paint. When problems occur, they can be described with terminology that also applies to paint. These problems typically show up immediately upon curing or drying. Problems may include:

- Alligatoring, wrinkling, orange peeling, crazing, and cracking distinguish between different unwanted surface texturing.
- Cratering and pinholing describe pockmarking of the finish after an even application.
- Runs, sags, and drips are degrees of excess coating that went on the move before setting up.
- Lapmarks and framing are the result of inexpert coating labor that layered subsequent coats unevenly.

Finishes that are common in the building industries are described using numbers in Table 9.1. The United States and Canada share a similar system for designating what kind of metal finish is being specified.

Finishes have visual characteristics that will be as important to your selection process as their performance characteristics. Some are silver in color, some yellow, etc. The slight differences between brass and bronze are highlighted in Figure 9.13, showing satin brass and bronze. The differences between stainless

Table 9.1
The metal industry has determined number designations for various metal surfaces.

U.S.	Canada	Finish Description
USP	CP	Primed for painting
US2	C2	Zinc plated
US3	C3	Bright brass, clear coated
US4	C4	Satin brass, clear coated
US 7	C7	Brass, nickel, oxidized
US9	C9	Bright bronze, clear coated
US10	C10	Satin bronze, clear coated
US10A	C10A	Antique bronze, oxidized
US10B	C10B	Oxidized satin bronze, oil rubbed
US14	C14	Bright nickel plated, clear coated
US15	C15	Satin nickel plated, clear coated
US 19	C19	Flat black coated
US20A	C20A	Dark oxidized, statuary bronze, clear coated
US26	C26	Bright chromium plated
US26D	C26D	Satin chromium plated
US27	C27	Satin aluminum, clear coated
US28	C28C	Satin aluminum, clear anodized
US32	C32	Bright stainless steel
US32D	C32D	Satin stainless steel
US55	C55	Dull brass, oxidized

FIGURE 9.13 Satin brass (bottom) versus satin bronze (top) exaggerates their differences; bronze is slightly browner than brass.

steel, chrome, and nickel are highlighted in Figure 9.14, showing brushed steel, chrome, and nickel.

FIGURE 9.14 Brushed nickel (left) versus brushed chrome (center) versus brushed steel (right) side-by-side to highlight their different appearances.

Properly protected, metal requires very little maintenance and regular maintenance will include buffing with a cloth to remove dust and fingerprints or occasionally cleaning with, typically, nontoxic cleansers. Many metal items are cleaned with glass cleaner.

If you are able to reuse existing metal items in your new designs, more aggressive restoration may be called for. Metals that will oxidize may have been lacquered and the lacquer may be damaged. If this is the case the item will be removed from the site and typically taken to a metal plating shop to be stripped, buffed to acceptable condition, and relacquered.

Occasionally metal will need to have oxidation removed and for this a light abrasive is frequently applied in a paste and the surface buffed. Light scratches can also be removed this way on-site. Plated metal items that have been in use for some years may need to be replated if the base metal starts to show through. In this case, the item will be uninstalled and delivered to a plater who may strip the plating off and start from scratch applying the plate as if the piece were new. It is valuable to understand what is involved in the plating of new pieces if you are going to order this kind of work.

SAFETY

Metals are generally inert. Occasionally a process, such as plating, lacquering, or coating, will require the use of chemicals that can be harmful and for this reason you want to work with suppliers that can provide assurance that the work will be performed in a safe manner to protect workers.

The usual caveats apply to metal used for walking surfaces; these surfaces must meet safety codes and disability guidelines for slip resistance. Obviously the installation must be secure to protect those using the space; pieces cannot unexpectedly come loose and all hookups must be tightly made.

SUSTAINABILITY

Metal recycling is a mature industry in the U.S. and recycled content in metal products includes postconsumer content. Alloys are a little more difficult to recycle than pure metal and plating and coatings may have to be removed in order to recycle the products that you specify when they reach the end of their useful life. While efforts are being made to reuse metal, it is initially expensive, in terms of dollars and environmental impact, to extract and process. For this reason, try to source your products from those suppliers with waste metal in their material stream. Plating and the patination of finishes often require caustic chemicals that must be handled and disposed of properly.

To keep embodied energy low, specify metals that do not require plating or coating to protect them. Platings are generally more durable than coatings. Replating metal is more sustainable than replacing metal surfaces but the energy and cost involved is higher than the initial plating.

Salvaged Metal

Salvaged material most frequently used is cast metal. It is available in a surprising abundance from salvage companies, and sometimes reworking an existing piece is less costly and more interesting than purchasing or commissioning new material. This can be true even when some modifications are necessary to fit the salvaged material to the new situation. Having some history accompanying a piece is appealing to many people. Sometimes the composition of old metal is an alloy containing two or more metals. This makes refabrication a little tricky, because you cannot easily predict the metals' properties. Consult the fabricator who will do the modification before making a purchase. Develop details that rely on fasteners rather than welding.

MANAGING BUDGETS

Custom work will typically cost more than stock items. It is also likely that you will have options within a manufacturer's standard offerings for finish, sizes, and details and these semicustom options will fall somewhere between the cost of custom and stock options.

The more steps involved in completing the installation, the higher the cost is likely to be. If multiple trades are involved, you will need to assemble pricing from all parties to have an accurate idea of costs. For example, it is simple enough to do a material comparison between two shower systems, but one may require more work to configure the plumbing supply, so both options should be reviewed by your plumber.

Some fabrication techniques will cost more than others. If your design can be produced by bending sheet metal, it will be less costly than if it must be extruded or cast. If your design must be extruded or cast, production cost may be prohibitive for one-off items (if you are only going to produce one) and you may have to reserve those options for multiples. There will be setup charges for making molds or gearing up production with custom dies that will be distributed among all the pieces produced, and if you are only making one, these setup charges can be significant. If you are working on a restoration job or trying to use an existing item that you will need more of, then the savings that you realize for the material that does not have to be replaced may offset some of these costs and bring prices in alignment with budgets.

Organization of the Industry

A variety of manufacturers will be making metal items that you might specify. The plumbing industry, lighting manufacturers, and cabinetmakers are obvious examples of industries whose product is partly metal. Each industry has its own configuration but typically they will include manufacturers, distributors or dealers, and vendors who may sell directly to the trades (architects, designers, installers) and sometimes to retailers. If you are purchasing a system that requires assembly, the contractors who assemble the items are often trained by manufacturers and are certified to assemble and install the product.

When you are having a custom product fabricated to your specifications, you or your client or your client's contractor will be responsible for finding the right kind of installer for the job and you will need to vet the installer by interviewing them, visiting other similar installations, and otherwise checking their credentials.

Selection Criteria

As always, refer to your design program to assemble selection criteria that pertains to your unique job. Assess the safety of your proposal by looking into slip resistance of surfaces, and grounding options (if electrical work is part of the assembly) because metal is a very good conductor. Evaluate the site for moisture, which speeds oxidation of metal surfaces, and abuse because many metal surfaces can easily scratch. If you like, you could organize your program considerations as shown in Table 9.2.

Table 9.2
You might organize your own evaluation of ideal characteristics in a table like this to help determine critical considerations for your unique project.

Considerations	Implications
Will the metal serve as a walking surface?	Slip and abrasion resistance will need to be addressed.
Will the structure have to support significant weight of this metal object?	The structure may have to be reinforced and a material that will allow fasteners to hang on with tenacity may have to be installed.
Are building systems like plumbing and electricity required to complete the installation?	Safe and secure coupling of the item to the system required will have to be determined.
Will the metal be vulnerable to oxidation by moisture in the course of its use?	The metal item will have to be protected.
Will the item be handled?	Fingerprints may be hard to keep up with in some installations so the texture of the finish will be important.
Must the item be movable, as in the case of furniture?	Metal is a heavy material; chairs are a common metal item that must be moved by end users. You will need to find a way of making the item lightweight.
Is the metal item designed to support something that is heavy?	The stiffness of the metal under consideration must be evaluated. Soft metals may not be up to the task and you may require a strong base metal and use your preferred metal as plating.
Will the tendency of metal to conduct heat be important?	If the interior-use item is in contact with the exterior select a metal with low thermal conductivity.
Do you have access to the trades required to complete the installation?	If you have to use resources long distance, this can add to time and money required.

SPECIFYING

Your specific metal item will define the description included in your specification and you will need to comprehend the item being specified as well as the conditions of the site to write a clear and complete specification. The manufacturer of an item may provide you with a specification after you have made your selection and you may alter the spec to address your unique conditions, basing your description of the product on the manufacturer's description. The following example is a mock specification for a semicustom metal staircase. It will often be the case that the fabrication of the product and installation are each completed by different parties. For the purposes of illustration, the following spec was constructed as if the purchasing and installation of the staircase were to be the responsibility of a general contractor, so product and installation instructions are both included in the spec. The ASTM and other references in the following spec would be identified by the manufacturer and transferred to your spec.

INSPECTING FOR QUALITY

As with all work performed to produce an item or surface, there are quality differences that will affect the price. We are all familiar with reproductions of modern icons such as the chrome-plated Barcelona or popular Mart Stam chair that can be found in a mind-boggling array of prices. How do you account for the large cost difference? The accounting will be distributed between quality of materials and quality of workmanship.

As an example of these differences, consider the production of the above-mentioned chairs. The decorative chrome plating utilized by furniture and fixture industries involves several steps and other plating metals in addition to chrome. The base metal parts will be varying gauge tube or solid stock that has been machined, polished, and joined with welds. This seam will then be ground and polished. Good-quality chrome plating will then involve a minimum of two layers of nickel, first semibright nickel and then bright nickel. The actual chrome plating is very thin (measured in thousandths of an inch), and the quality of the polished surface depends on the quality of the work that precedes the actual chroming. Each step and material mentioned is subject to possible differences in quality.

When you are confronted with a price discrepancy such as the one we notice with reproductions of chairs, evaluate the weight (heavy gauge metal). Closely inspect the welds for smooth, "seamless" transition between arms and back or at the crisscross joints. If the piece is a polished finish, check the (hopefully) mirror quality of the reflection by holding a tape measure perpendicular to the surface and see how "high up" you can still read the numbers. Plating with the numbers going hazy by 3 or 4 could indicate a quality that will not be enduring—requiring regular application of car wax just to keep it from pitting! You certainly want to be able to clearly read to number 10 and beyond if you are looking for quality chrome.

This kind of inspection will hold true for most metal items—plated or polished. If a finish is etched, brushed, satin, etc., you cannot rely on reflection but you can still notice the quality differences between the surfaces of two different items under consideration. Look for consistency across the entire surface—is the brushing/etching/satin surface the same all over? Directional light will help while you make this determination.

Items made of metal often will have their own standards as well. One example would be light fixtures. Quality of light fixtures are organized as builder grade, architectural grade, and specification grade and a single manufacturer may offer all quality levels in order to hit required price points while bidding. Because metal is usually part of a system, inspection is a little more complicated than if you were just inspecting a surface.

RELATED MATERIAL

Any item made of metal would be a valid consideration here. This includes furnishings, fixtures like plumbing fixtures or light fixtures, plumbing fittings, or door hardware. All such items will have unique fabrication and distribution methods.

> **Point of Emphasis 9.1**
> You will encounter chromed plastic in plumbing fittings. This is sometimes an indication of an economy model of moderate quality but can be found on high-quality items as well. If the fitting must be held by the users, like a pull-out spray on a faucet for instance, plastic is more comfortable to hold because it insulates against heat. Hot water running through a metal holder would grow too hot to touch so plastic may be used for that portion of a quality fixture. In such an instance it is not an indication of a low-end product.

SAMPLE SPEC 9.1

Part 1 General Information

1.1 Related Documents
A. Refer to designer's plans for location of staircase.
B. Refer to manufacturer's installation instructions for installation procedures.
C. Refer to approved shop drawings for all dimensions and fasteners to be used.

1.2 Summary
A. Provide and install metal staircase, provided by others as detailed in designer's drawings and manufacturer's instructions.
B. Completed installation to meet all local codes and ADA guidelines.

1.3 References
A. Components to comply with standard testing meeting the following:
   1. ASTM A36/M-04 Structural steel.
   2. ASTM A53-04 Pipe, steel, black and zinc-coated welded and seamless.
   3. ASTM A307-04 Carbon steel bolts and studs.
   4. ASTM 786M-00 Cold rolled low alloy steel plates.
   5. AWS D1.1-00 Structural welding for steel.
   6. AWS D1.3-90 Structural welding sheet steel.

1.4 Contractor Submittals
A. Shop drawings of staircase including all parts, connectors, and sizes.
B. Samples of all finishes.
C. Documentation of recycled content.

1.5 Quality Assurance
A. Product to be fabricated according to approved manufacturer's specifications.
   1. Design to support live load of 1,000 pounds per square foot.
   2. Design to be in strict accordance with approved shop drawings.

B. Installers to have completed manufacturer's training course and have experience installing similar product.

1.6 Delivery, Storage, and Handling
A. Product to be delivered to the site by the manufacturer's own truck.
B. Product to be stored flat in acclimatized site until installed.
C. Care to be exercised to avoid damaging the product or finishes while uncrating, assembling, and installing staircase.

1.7 Maintenance of Installation
A. Maintain clean work site.
B. Check all packaging for fasteners prior to disposal; stairs come complete with all required parts. Inventory all components before commencing installation. Alert designer immediately if parts are discovered to be missing. Parts accounted for during inventory but missing upon installation are the responsibility of the installer.

Part 2 Products

2.1 General Information
A. Steel treads, support brackets, pipe rail, and all fasteners required for installation are to be included with staircase components.
B. Copy of installation instructions to be included with items shipped.

2.2 Manufacturers
A. All components to be provided by: Stair People, 1234 Industrial Drive, Anytown, ST 78945.

2.3 Products
A. Soaring Stair series in matte steel finish.
B. Sound guard matting cut to fit base.

Part 3 Execution

3.1 Examination
A. Work to take place only in acclimatized site.
B. Installer to confirm readiness of site to receive staircase including completed installation and preliminary finishing for floor surfaces on first and second floor.
C. No other trades are to be working in the area during installation.
D. Inventory all components shipped from the manufacturer.

3.2 Preparation
A. Inspect all pieces shipped for good condition, having no burrs or rough places.
   1. All welds to be Finish Level 121.
   2. All textures and finishes to be visually identical on all visible parts.

B. Layout parts on clean drop cloths to stage installation in phases recommended by manufacturer.

3.3 Installation
A. Install according to designer's drawings and approved shop drawings detailing installation.
B. Completed stair to comply with all codes and guidelines as required.

3.4 Post Installation
A. Clean staircase as recommended by manufacturer in instructions included with materials shipped. Upon completion stairs to be in condition for owner acceptance.
B. Installer's representative to be present when owner's representative inspects completed installation.

Materials that can be used in place of metal are also likely considerations. Some items are intended to look like metal, such as plastic parts of fixtures that are plated with metal finishes or surfaces imitating the appearance of metal such as pressed "tin" ceilings. These items will imitate the appearance of metal but not necessarily the performance; however, as you draw up your own selection criteria you may determine that some forms of rigid plastic meet all of your criteria and that the cost and weight of metal indicate that a different material is better.

SUMMARY

In this chapter we discussed the different metals that are used in surfaces and items that interior designers typically specify and their general characteristics. The different forms that metal come in and how they are made as well as the various textures and finishes used for metal were covered. You learned some of the considerations for qualifying fabricators and managing the fabrication of custom surfaces and items. You considered criteria for selecting and specifying metal for function, appearance, and safety. You reviewed a checklist for inspecting metal items and surfaces.

WEB SEARCH ACTIVITIES

1. Perform an image search for *metal stairs*. Select (and zoom in on) various images and see if you can tell which parts were probably cast. Look for varying volume in the form. If parts of a form are thick in two dimensions rather than just one, you are probably looking at a cast form. If the form is thick in only one dimension, you may be looking at a forged form.
2. Perform an image search for *architectural salvage* to see the kind of components that are being reclaimed from old buildings.
3. Perform an image search for *installation of metal ceilings*. Notice that images that come up range from vintage-looking "tin" ceilings fastened to the (usually gypsum) substrate with adhesives to ceiling systems that are suspended in metal frames hung from wires from the ceiling structure.
4. Search for a manufactured item made of metal and search the manufacturer's site for a master specification or specification guidelines. Alternatively, perform a general search for an item like *metal ceiling specification* or *recessed light fixture specification*. When you find a maser spec for such an item, read it for comprehension.

PERSONAL ACTIVITIES

1. Sketch a design for an item that you would use sheet metal to make, or imagine a surface clad in sheet metal. What processes would the item or surface have to go through to form it to match your vision?
2. Consider your own plan and determine a place where you could use an item made of metal, or find a picture of an installation that you could use as your guide while considering what characteristics would be important when you are finalizing your selection of a metal item for a specific job. You might organize your evaluation like the selection criteria sample table.
3. Consider your own plan and determine a place where you could use an item made of metal, or find a picture of an installation that you could use as your guide while considering descriptions that you should include in your specification of a metal item. You may want to select an item from a manufacturer (such as a plumbing fixture or a decorative light fixture, like a chandelier or sconces) before tackling a custom item.
4. Imagine a metal item or construction that you might create for your client's job or search online for items that you might design for your jobs in the future, such as *metal stairs*, *metal stove hood*, *metal bathtub*, etc. Imagine how you would make it. What kind of work would be required? How would you assemble and stabilize it for use? How would it be supported? Designers are often called upon to design unique forms never before built. The way to start the design process is to conceive of a form then deconstruct it in your mind (assisted by sketching) so you can imagine a way to fabricate it.

SUMMARY QUESTIONS

1. What does it mean if a metal is an alloy?
2. What are the general characteristics of all metals?
3. What is a ferrous metal versus a nonferrous metal and what are examples of each?
4. How does performance vary among the different metals?
5. What are the common forms for metal?
6. What are typical textures for metal surfaces?
7. How would you select appropriate installers for your metal item?
8. What are the typical protections applied to metal items?
9. What safety issues can you think of pertaining to metal surfaces?
10. What characteristics will increase the cost of your installation?
11. What links would you expect in the supply chain for a custom or semicustom item?
12. What finish and construction details indicate good quality?

Chapter 10

TILE AND BRICK

Key Terms

Anchors
Bicottura
Bonds
Bond coat
Cement grout
Courses
Feathered (edge)
Lippage
Monocottura

Objectives

After reading this chapter, you should be able to:

- Understand the basic properties of clay products.
- Recognize alternatives to clay product in this product category.
- Understand some of the variations in material and form among different tile and brick products.
- Understand the tile industry from production through installation.
- Evaluate circumstances and products to make good selections for your program goals.
- Evaluate the sustainability of the products that you select.
- Understand some of the things that will affect your budget in this product category.
- Specify these products for your interior design projects.

TILE

You are certainly well aware that tile has a long history and you are probably already familiar with many of the properties of tile, such as its rigidity and its general degree of imperviousness. If you run your hand over unglazed terra-cotta tile and then over a glazed clay tile or a glass tile, you might guess that the unglazed terra-cotta tile would have a greater tendency to soil and stain—and you would be right. Many characteristics important to your selection process are made apparent by your senses.

When considering a tile surface for your project, you will address all the components of the installation, including the material that the tile is made of, how it is formed, the surface quality, the finish on the body of the tile, the size of the tile, the installation method, the grout, and sealants. In most cases you will also be selecting the substrate to which the tile will be applied.

MATERIAL MAKEUP OR CONTENT

Tiles are made from a variety of materials. The most common tile body is clay of all kinds, from soft terra-cotta to durable porcelain. Glass, stone, concrete, metal, brick, and composite are other materials made into tiles.

Clay

Since clay is mined from the earth, the characteristics of natural clay vary. Some white clay bodies are only suitable for wall tile, while porcelain clay, and gray, tan, and terra-cotta clay bodies can be used on walls or floors. The color of the clay tile body, the mineral content of the clay that lends many performance characteristics, and its coarseness are inherent properties of the clay.

Clay tiles that are handmade have slightly irregular shapes and surfaces. The term *handmade* may mean that the tiles were formed by hand or that they were machine-made (often with an intentional variation in surfaces, edges, and size to look like they were made by hand instead of machines) but glazed by hand.

FIGURE 10.1 Unglazed terra-cotta is porous and should be protected with grout release during grouting.

Clay tiles are fired in kilns at high temperature causing a molecular change in the material. After firing the clay is forever modified and can no longer return to a plastic condition. Tiles that are fired once are referred to as **monocottura**; those that are fired twice are more impervious and are referred to as **bicottura**.

Clay tiles are generally ¼ inch to ⅜ inch thick. Terra-cotta tiles (Figure 10.1) are usually thicker—sometimes 1 inch or more. If an exact dimension is required, as when different tiles are being used side-by-side in a pattern, the thickness of a sample should be measured rather than relying on manufacturer's literature. If tiles are glazed past the edge of their faces (so no unfinished clay is visible on the edge), the change in thickness may make an interesting design detail, but you cannot typically count on glaze trailing onto the sides of field tile. Only trim tiles designed for an exposed edge will certainly have glaze covering their sides as well as their faces.

The various kinds of clay tile are often distinguished by their absorption rates, which are a measurement of the porosity of the tile.

- Non-vitreous = 13% or more
- Semi-vitreous = 3% to 13%
- Vitreous = 0.5% to 3%
- Impervious = 0.5% or less

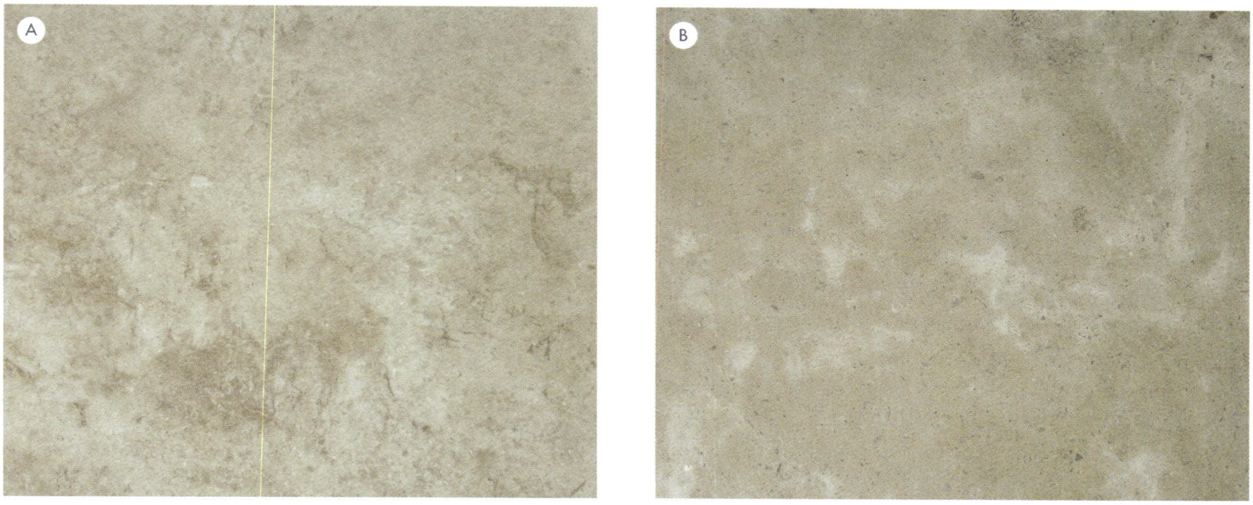

Figure 10.2a–b When a stone look is desired but more durability is required, stone-look porcelains with random variegation and color-through bodies are hard to distinguish from stone tiles. *Photographed by permission of the Tile Gallery, Chicago, IL.*

Porcelain

Porcelain tiles are in a category of their own, having an absorption of less than 0.5 percent, meaning they are very impervious to staining. They are usually formed by pressing very dry clay into a mold. They are made of fine-grained porcelain clay that is about 50 percent feldspar, which measures in at 6 on Mohs' hardness scale (a standard measurement of hardness). As a point of reference, quartz, which is one of the hardest materials we specify, measures 13 on the Mohs' hardness scale. Porcelain tile is formed with very little water and then fired at very high temperatures, creating a very uniform, impervious, molded product. Porcelain tiles may also be rectified, meaning that they are ground to uniform size with grinding wheels. These tiles will have nearly perfectly square, flat edges and consistent sizes that allow for much tighter grout joints, as small as 1/16 of an inch wide.

Porcelain is very durable and serviceable. Porcelain tiles (Figure 10.2a) are often designed to imitate more vulnerable stone tiles (Figure 10.2b) for areas where a stone look is desired but more durability is required.

Porcelain tiles may be glazed or through-body, meaning that the pigment that colors the tile goes all the way through the clay; there is no glaze to wear away from heavy abrasive traffic. Porcelain tiles are available with a variety of surface qualities:

Figure 10.3 This porcelain series is available in three surface qualities. The gloss version is not an applied glaze, rather, it is a ground surface rubbed to mirror hardness. *Series by Crossville.*

- *Polished surfaces* are not the result of a glaze or applied surface treatment. Instead, they are mechanically produced (ground like polished stone) to a hard, smooth, shiny surface.
- *Matte surfaces* provide good slip resistance. They have a flat, even, fine stipple-like texture.
- *Textured surfaces* create excellent slip resistance. The texture may be random and "natural," similar to the cleft of a stone or consistent such as the raised pattern of a geometric relief or a grainy additive that rises up above the surface of the tile. Figure 10.3 shows the same tile available in polished, matte, and textured surfaces.

Very large tiles can be produced from durable porcelain clays. When the installer installs very large tile (or very uneven tile) the backs should be buttered (spread with the mastic that the tile is laid in immediately before the tile is placed) to eliminate any voids. Voids left under the material are apt to allow the tile to crack under pressure.

Super-thin porcelain tile is differentiated from regular porcelain. These tiles are less than ⅛ inch thick, typically very large format, 20 inches square and larger (anything over 8 inches square is considered to be large format). They are designed to be installed over existing, sound finished surfaces.

Quarry Tiles

Quarry tiles are slightly thicker than usual clay tiles; ½ inch is typical. They are made of coarse clay material and are glazed or left unglazed providing good slip resistance for high-traffic commercial environments. Unglazed tile may exhibit color variation if fired in an oxygen-reduction atmosphere (flashed); they may be sealed against staining, but may also be unglazed, similar to porcelain tile.

Stoneware

Stoneware tiles have low absorption but are less resistant to breakage than porcelain. Tiles referred to as porcelain stoneware resemble porcelain properties.

Glass

Glass tiles are formed by casting glass into molds. Glass tiles might have integral color, or color enamel that is baked on. The enamel creates opacity as well as color in the tile. Tiles can also be clear glass or translucent glass with polished or matte surfaces. If you are specifying clear glass tiles, request that the installer make up a sample board with a few pieces set up and grouted for approval. The mastic must be evenly applied so the surface visible through the tile is smooth (Figure 10.4). Trowels used to spread mastic have serrated edges that measure the amount of mastic applied but can create a "striped" mastic bed that could be seen through the tile after it is pressed into position. You may want to instruct the installer to "knock the notches down" (smooth out these ridges) or to "butter the backs" of the tile.

Glass tiles are impervious to many chemicals and can withstand cleaning by commonly used cleaning

FIGURE 10.4 This clear glass mosaic must be expertly installed because the mastic will not be hidden as it would if this tile were opaque. The installer must knock down the notches left in the mastic by the serrated trowel so there is no striped mastic showing through the installation when it is complete. *Photographed by permission of the Tile Gallery, Chicago, IL, courtesy of Boyce & Bean Natural Glass and Clay Co.*

agents. Glass tile changes in dimension in response to changes in temperature. Since they are more sensitive to drastic temperature changes, use around fireplaces (especially hotter, wood-burning fireplaces) and on countertops should be carefully evaluated. This is not an amount that you can discern but it does stress the grout joints (this micro change is the reason for leaving grout joints). Though properties vary by product, glass tiles are generally a little more brittle than other tile bodies, so a flat, rigid substrate, such as a cement-based substrate, is especially important.

Translucent tiles set into thinset sometimes exhibit "picture framing" during curing. The appearance of the installation changes as the setting bed cures. This might cause unnecessary concerns for your client during the time it takes the mastic to cure so you may want to schedule the installation a month or so earlier to allow the appearance to even out before your client must use the space. Modified thinsets sandwiched between an impervious substrate and impervious glass tile may have an extended curing time, and the larger the tile is, the more likely it is that your client will notice this uneven color during curing. If you are having the tile set up on a membrane or other impervious surface, moisture may also be visible behind clear glass tile.

Recycled glass tiles are readily available. Some have an iridescent surface, which is not a glaze but is integral to the material.

Glass tiles are available in a variety of sizes. Mosaic tiles (Figure 10.5) may be smaller than ¼ inch square and are available with flat or irregular surfaces. Irregular surfaces can be ground flat after installation if desired or left with the variation of the surface texture. Mosaic tiles are sold mounted in approximately 12" × 12" squares. They may be mesh-backed (mounted faceup to fiber mesh applied to their backs) or paper-faced (mounted facedown on paper). It is important for the installer to maintain the grout spacing predetermined by the mounted tiles for a seamless installation that does not highlight the 12" × 12" squares. This is trickier with paper-faced tiles because the installer cannot see relationship as easily as with mesh-backed tile.

FIGURE 10.5 Glass tile is a versatile product and need not always be sleek and modern. This rusticated glass tile has a natural irregularity but still displays the translucency of glass as light penetrates the material. *Photographed by permission of the Tile Gallery, Chicago, IL, courtesy of Oceanside Glass Tile.*

Stone

Stone tiles are distinguished from stone slab by length, width, and thickness; stone tiles will typically be ¼ inch to ⅜ inch thick. Stones with uneven surfaces, like cleft-face slate (Figure 10.6), will present the same installation requirements as uneven tiles such as terra-cotta, possibly necessitating a thicker setting bed to level the material.

Stone tiles are typically designed for tight joints; 1/16 inch is common. This allows the installer to use unsanded grout. Sanded grout could scratch the polished surface of soft stones like marble; even in the instance of harder stone material, unsanded grout should be preferred.

Distressed stone tiles, popular at the time this book was written, often require wider grout joints because of irregularity along the tile edges. Wider joints should have sanded grout (to prevent cracking). Care must be used in grouting to avoid scratching the face of the tile; even distressed tile with irregular edges can be finished with a slight sheen to reflect small scratches. Distressed tiles may have small pits in their faces where soft material was worn away. It would be hard to clean grout off the face of such tiles so you may want to specify that the installer use grout release before grouting.

FIGURE 10.6 Many varieties of stone are available as tile. Stone tile is cut thinner than stone slab. *Photographed by permission of the Tile Gallery, Chicago, IL.*

Concrete

Concrete tiles for interior use (Figure 10.7) are available in many sizes and colors. They have characteristics of concrete (see Chapter 12, Terrazzo,

FIGURE 10.7 Concrete tile may be tinted to imitate other material. This tile imitates terra-cotta tile. *Photograph by Alana Clark.*

FIGURE 10.8 Stainless steel tile by *Crossville*.

FIGURE 10.9 Because tile made from clay starts out very plastic a limitless variety of surface relief patterns and textures is possible. *Photographed by permission of the Tile Gallery, Chicago, IL, courtesy of Quemere International.*

Composites, and Concrete). They should be sealed against staining, and concrete tiles can be finished with polyurethane or acrylic to prevent some kinds of staining. They can be used for exterior surfaces and, if thick enough, resist damage from freezing. When used outdoors they are sealed but not top-dressed with polyurethane or acrylic because the topdressing is less durable out in the weather than inside. Concrete tiles cure to harden (chemical reaction) rather than being fired in tile kilns at high temperatures, so a variety of materials can be embedded in the tile body. Examples of unusual materials that can be embedded include golf tees or chips of semiprecious stones. Often containing recycled or reclaimed material, these composite tiles can increase the "green" quotient of an installation.

Metal

Solid metal tiles (Figure 10.8) have characteristics inherent in the metal selected (see Chapter 9, Metals). Tile may be solid metal or may be metal fused to a porcelain body. Clay-body tiles with metallic glazes are sometimes used instead of metal tiles. Metallic glazes on clay tiles abrade more easily than other glazes and are not always suitable for floors.

Composite

Composite tiles are a combination of two or more materials, often including glass, plastic, or natural stone and resin or cement. (Composite materials are covered in Chapter 12.) The size and material combinations vary. Tiles can be composed of small chips or larger pieces of stone. The color often derives from a pigmented matrix and the color of the companion material.

CHARACTERISTICS

All of the materials used for tile bodies have their unique characteristic such as surface quality, absorption, hardness, and brittleness. Table 10.1 compares the characteristics of different tile materials. Their surfaces also lend performance attributes, creating variety within each type. When the tile body is exposed, as with unglazed tile, surface characteristics, including texture, are derived from the clay. Both glazed and unglazed tiles can have surface texture from relief patterning (Figure 10.9) or granules added to the face of the tile for slip resistance.

Table 10.1
The varying tile bodies present differing characteristics.

Material	Forms or Composition	Characteristics	Common Uses
Clay	Ceramic body typically 1" × 1" to 12" × 12"; ¼" to ⅜" thick	Lots of variation based on qualities of clay	Light-traffic situations, some suitable for wall tile only
	Porcelain typically mosaic to large format 22" × 48"; ¼" thick	Hard, durable, impervious	When tile must be impervious to staining and durable in traffic
	Quarry tile typically 3" × 6" to 12" × 12"; ½" thick	Hard, durable	High-traffic, commercial settings
	Bisque up to 6" × 6"; ¼" thick	Fired once, unglazed	When specifying custom-glazed tile for vertical surfaces
	Super-thin, large format (some 18" × 18" and larger) less than ⅛" thick	Designed to go over any sound substrate	Tiling over existing surfaces or managing weight of materials
Glass	Cast glass ⅛" square up to 6" × 6" and larger	Thick body tile may have smooth or textured surface; impervious tile with variety of characteristics stemming from thickness and surface manipulation	Horizontal or vertical surface; treatments must be added to provide required slip resistance for commercial interiors
	Rolled glass ½"±	Thin tile relies on color and characteristics of glass itself	Horizontal or vertical surface
	Mosaic ⅛" to ¼" with thickness frequently matching length/width	Potential for complex pattern and slip resistance provided by numerous grout joints	Horizontal or vertical surface; decorative option
Metal	Cast	Depends on characteristics of metal used; soft metal will dent	Accent tile—expensive option for field tile
	Fused to porcelain body	Still depends on metal for surface but body will have characteristics of porcelain	Where large area is to be covered and expense of metal tiles is prohibitive
Stone	Mosaic to 12" × 12" and larger thickness varies with stability of stone	Varies with species of stone; potential for staining must be considered and stone sealed as required	Horizontal and vertical; slip resistance varies with texture for commercial installation
Concrete	Typically 4" × 4" and larger tend to be thicker ½" or ⅝"	Surface varies from coarse to fine; smooth surface may be ground flat; seal to protect from staining	Horizontal and vertical surfaces
Brick pavers	Similar face sizes and materials as brick but ¾" thick	Durable surface not impervious (requires sealing against stains)	Serviceable for horizontal surfaces; also used vertically decoratively
Composite material	Varying sizes and thicknesses	Combination of resin or cement plus aggregate with characteristics varying with components	Horizontal and vertical surface; evaluate component materials for appropriateness

FIGURE 10.10 Hundreds of glaze formulations are available and many are proprietary secrets. Crackle glaze is purposely distressed to imitate aged tiles. *Photographed by permission of the Tile Gallery, Chicago, IL.*

Unglazed Tiles

Unglazed tiles rely on the quality of the tile body for their color and other characteristics. Terra-cotta tiles shown in Figure 10.1 are porous with a natural matte texture, which is difficult to clean. This difficulty extends to the cleaning of grout from the face. When specifying to your installer, add to your instructions: "Windowpane-ing of grout on face of tile is unacceptable; use grout release, all grout to be cleaned from face of tiles," or words to that effect. For tiles with a coarse face you may specify a temporary paraffin wax sealer for protecting the surface from grout during the installation. While unglazed terra-cotta tiles are vulnerable to staining because of their porosity, other unglazed tile with denser clay bodies fired at higher temperatures, like porcelain and quarry tiles, are less porous even though they may also be unglazed.

Glazed Tiles

Glazed tiles have surface characteristics similar to glass; they are usually impervious to water and staining but have some of the same vulnerabilities as glass (chipping, scratching). Glazes installed in traffic areas show wear over time, especially if they have glossy finishes. Glossy finishes are generally considered to be unsuitable for floors because they show scratches and are slippery, but they can be installed in light-use areas as an accent.

Crackle glazes are less impervious to staining. The intentional cracks in the glaze are decorative, imitating vintage or antique tile. The cracks are sometimes inked to enhance them (Figure 10.10). If you can feel the crackle on the surface, the glazed surface has been compromised and the tiles are vulnerable to infiltration of moisture. They are not advisable for high-moisture environments like steam showers or saunas but are okay for regular showers and, of course, for dry areas. Some crackle-glazed tiles have a second glaze coat, sealing the tile face, and these crackle tiles are more durable than those that are crackled entirely through the glaze.

Glaze is not typically discussed in terms of its formula, but rather by its appearance. Terms that you will encounter are pretty straightforward:

A Cautionary Tale 10.1

I specified an unglazed terra-cotta tile for a client's vacation home. Because this was a second residence, I was on a very tight budget and kept squeezing the pricing I was getting from all the installers, trying to keep the materials that I had sold the client on in the project. I had really worked the tile installer over on the price of the installation because the terra-cotta was being installed throughout the entire cottage.

I finally got the installation price down to where it needed to be but at some point in my negotiation with the installer the grout release that I was expecting "went away." This is no surprise in retrospect; installers need to make the work profitable for their companies too, so if they are going to really squeeze the pricing down, something has to give.

When I got to the residence, just a couple of hours ahead of the furniture truck, I was stunned to see the picture framing of grout adhering to the coarse tile face around the perimeter of every tile. The only remedy was to hold off on the furniture installation and hire the tile setter to come back and grout the whole face of every tile—so they would be uniform across their surfaces.

I phoned my client with the bad news and she said "No way!" She was already on her way, with her children, and they had all been looking forward to their summer at the beach and she decided to leave the floors that way—forever a testament to that dangerous combination of squeezing installers too much and writing sloppy specs.

- *Bright glaze* means a high-gloss coating with or without color.
- *Clear glaze* is transparent with or without color.
- *Crystalline glaze* contains microscopic crystals.
- *Matte glaze* is a low-gloss glaze with or without color.
- *Opaque glaze* means a nontransparent coating with or without color.
- *Semi-matte glaze* is a medium-gloss finish with or without color.
- *Speckled glaze* features granules of oxides or ceramic stains of contrasting colors.

Visual Character

Some tiles are intended to be visually consistent within the lot and other designs rely on variation. The industry uses a system to define the amount of variation; V-1 is very consistent from tile to tile in the lot and V-4 is inconsistent, as you would hope if you were specifying a stone-look porcelain tile (Figure 10.11).

When you are specifying a tile that is V-3 or V-4, one sample is not enough to comprehend what the tile will be like. Ask for a range of tile and a photo of a completed installation so you can get an accurate idea of the colors that will be present and how the installation will look when completed.

Spacing

Tiles that are 4" × 4" or smaller are often mounted, on mesh backing in 12" × 12" units, establishing a grout joint width. Some tiles are self-spacing with lug spacers or protuberances on the sides of the tile that automatically space the tile for grout joints. Independent spacers are used by installers setting wall tile, that hold the tile at a consistent distance until they have set up, then the spacers are removed and the tile grouted.

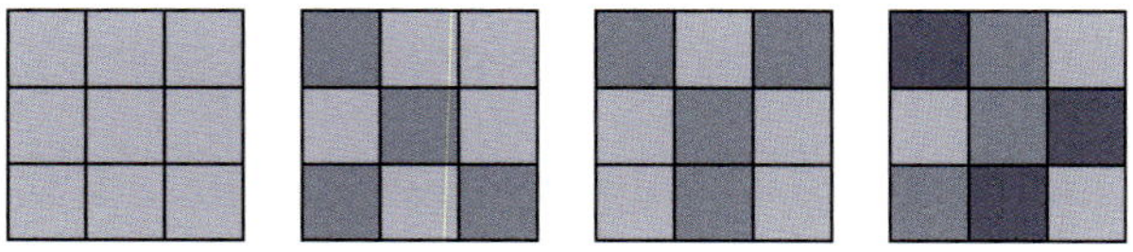

FIGURE 10.11 Standards for describing variation in the tile designed for random effects are required for specification purposes. The various trims required to finish off the edges of the installation must be ordered separately. Most trim pieces are sold by the tile.

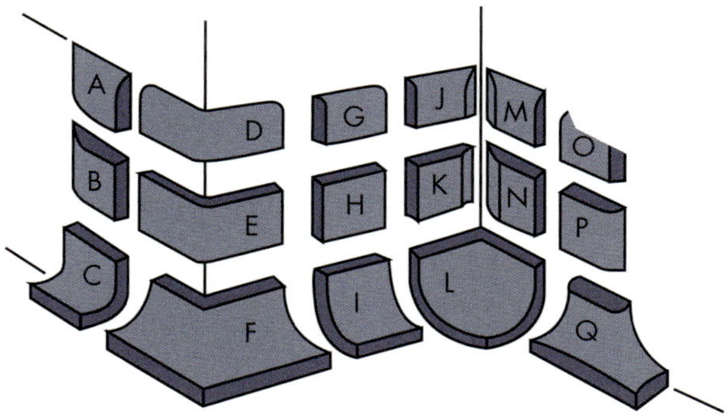

A. Bullnose, B. Bullnose, C. Cove, D. Bullnose out-corner, E. Field out-corner, F Cove out-corner, G. Bullnose, H. Field tile, I. Cove, J. Bullnose in-corner mitered, K. Field mitered, L Cove in-corner, M. Bullnose mitered, N. Field mitered, O. Bullnose corner, P. Bullnose, Q. Cove end

FIGURE 10.12 Trim tiles are specified (when available) to finish your job.

PARTS AND ACCESSORIES

When tile covers a whole flat surface, an entire wall or entire floor, you may have no need of trim tile, only field tile, but as soon as you need to transition to another material or bend around a surface, trim tiles will be required. Figure 10.12 shows these trim tiles and their typical uses. Some trims are functional, bending or terminating a tile surface, and some are decorative, used to create patterns. These trim tiles are sold individually as opposed to being priced by the square foot as are field tiles. If you require bullnose trim and the tile you want to use does not have a companion bullnose, it is possible to have the tile finish imitated on bisque, but it is much better to restrict your selection to tile that has matching trim.

> **Point of Emphasis 10.1**
> The custom bullnose tiles that you have made to finish your job when they are not available from the tile manufacturer will be glazed by a third party so you may not be able to get an exact match if your tile is a through-body porcelain. So your tile installer may be able to grind the edge to finish it. Confirm that you can get an acceptable match before your financial commitment extends beyond producing samples.

As an alternate to bullnose trim, providing a professional-looking finish to a tiled area, there are a number of trims made of metal or plastic that can conceal the unglazed edge of a field tile that may have no trims available.

Fabrication

Tile is typically formed in molds, although some glass tiles are formed in sheets and cut into tile sizes/shapes and stone tiles are obviously cut from thin slabs of stone.

Manufacturers who wish to imitate handmade tile, with slight irregularities, may have a series of similar molds that they use to produce tile lots that have such slight variation that they are still easily assembled in a single installation but the tiles are not identical to each other.

> **Helpful Hint 10.1**
>
> Inexpensive offerings of tile that was cut from sheets of glass or slabs of stone may have poorly made edges at the cut sides. Well-cut stone and glass tile will have edges that are "seamed," meaning the edge is ground to remove the crisp right angle created by the cut. As you are congratulating yourself on finding an especially low price be sure to check the edges. If they are sharp, you may need to instruct the installer to float the grout up to the very top of the tile so the sharp edge is not exposed.
>
> If the tile in question is glass, the manufacturer may recommend epoxy grout. Epoxy grout tends to "slump" into the joint, so it is not easy to get the grout floated all the way up to the top of the grout joint. These sharp edges are discernable by bare feet and hands.

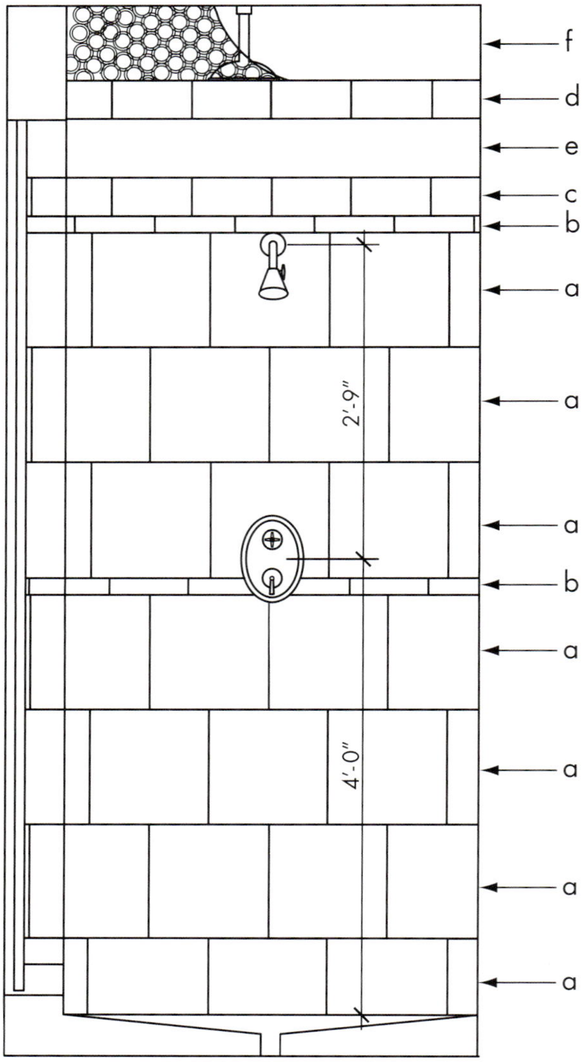

(a) 12 × 12 Jerusalem gold limestone
(b) 1.5 × 8 branch
(c) 4 × 8 alternate bear tile
(d) 4 × 8 pinecone tile
(e) Jerusalem gold field cut limestone to align with top of door opening
(f) Meridian glass octagon

FIGURE 10.13 You will draw your tile installation to scale to confirm details and trims, and to communicate with the installer.

Layout

The other part of fabrication of tile surfaces is the installation. Given the fact that structures are not usually square and plumb, it is sensible to design details that allow for imperfection. Do not design an installation with a lot of critical dimensions requiring strict horizontals and verticals that must be adhered to.

A drawing will clarify instructions regarding acceptable placement of cut tiles versus full tiles as well as alignments (Figure 10.13). For example, should wall grout lines align with floor grout lines or be purposely offset? A drawing of the tile layout not only tells the installer the location of the tile, it describes the pattern (if there is one); the relationship of the pattern, tiles, or joints to any features in the architecture; and how to deal with services (switches, junction boxes, electrical outlets, or vents for HVAC). It also identifies the trims that are required and where to use trims such as those shown in Figure 10.12. Trim tiles finish the installation at the "edges" where tile meets another material or where two surfaces come together.

QUALIFYING INSTALLERS

Tile contractors may belong to an organization that fosters an apprentice to journeyman to master structure that is the result of an organized training program or they may be an independent craftsperson and qualified for the work with a patchwork of certificates representing training in specific areas. Your qualified tile contractor will be someone who has experience doing the kind of work you require and can demonstrate that experience with pictures of their installations, references, and a tour of some completed work that is similar to your client's job, whether or not they have any formal training at all. Tile setters may have attained their skills on the job or they may have attended a community college that educates them to the apprentice level, but eventually they must do the work in order to advance.

> Point of Emphasis 10.2
> For a small-scale, highly specialized job such as an artistic mural on a low-stress surface like a residential kitchen backsplash, you may be looking for someone who is "two-parts artist and one-part tile setter." Some jobs allow for someone who falls outside the normal definitions of a tile setter who still does a perfectly acceptable job. The trick is to match the right craftsperson with your client's job.

INSTALLATION

You will design the tile layout, producing drawings. A simple drawing may be a finish plan indicating the horizontal or vertical surface that is to receive tile if your project simply calls for surfaces to be clad in the same field tile throughout. If you require a pattern, your drawings will indicate this and you must give an indication of the size of each pattern area. It is very common for designers to make very exact, to-scale drawings showing every piece of tile for patterns that incorporate trim tiles or different kinds of tile completing their pattern. Even though these drawings are very exact, it is still common practice to meet with the installer at the outset of the installation to review conditions and dimensions, or see a dry fit of large randomly patterned tiles or stone tiles prior to their commencing work. When you make your large-scale drawings to communicate with the installer, you will find that they are also an aid to you in thinking about the installation. For instance, an out-corner in an installation that does not have a bullnose trim tile may have to be **feathered** and mitered. Your large-scale drawing will help you discover this detail so your specification can clearly describe your expectations.

Prior to Setting

The layout should be dry fitted if necessary to ensure that there are no tiny slivers of tile along the perimeter and yet the installation is "balanced" on any important feature. A general rule is that the layout should present no tile that is less than half of the full width. A slight change in the width of the grout line can sometimes make the difference between a logical, beautiful installation and one that calls attention to itself for all the wrong reasons.

> Point of Emphasis 10.3
> A dry fit is a good idea in a couple of instances. If the tile is large (8" × 8" or larger) it is used to confirm whether to start with a tile or a seam in the center of the room. At the dry fit, the installer will lay out a row of tile north–south and east–west. The grout joint will be confirmed (sometimes just adjusting the grout joint will avoid a little sliver of tile at the perimeter).
>
> Another instance when the dry fit is very valuable is when there is a lot of variation in the tile. If it is a natural stone or a stone-look porcelain, you will want to make decisions about how to deal with the randomness. If the material has a grain or vein, do you want to orient them in the same direction or mix them up like a checkerboard? These decisions are easier to make when you lay the material out at the job site.

If the selected tile has a lot of variation (Figure 10.11) in it, a dry fit is advisable. At the very least, you will want to open a few boxes and look at the actual material, especially if it comes set up on a mesh backing. The contractor will most likely lay the tile as it is set up on the mesh but if material in one box is very different from material in another, the contractor may have to remove the mesh, mix the batches up, and set the tiles individually to evenly disperse the visual variety shipped in your order. At the very least, the tile setter should open several boxes and mix them up as they are laid to avoid a patchy installation.

Setting the Tile

Setting means to affix the tile to the substrate. This is accomplished by the **bond coat**. Common bond coats, or setting methods, that are used include:

- *Wetset* is used on a cement substrate or mortar bed that has not hardened or is at least still not cured. A thin mortar is mixed using cement, water, and sometimes sand and effectively bonds the tile to the cement that is already in place.
- *Thinset* refers to a portland cement mortar made of cement, sand, and methylcellulose, which holds water, allowing the installer to set dry tile. This layer would be ¼ inch to ⅜ inch thick. The various formulations available from different manufacturers offer different characteristics such as higher bonding properties, faster drying times, higher water resistance, or reduced shrinkage. White is usually used for walls and counters; gray thinset is used for floors.
- *Medium set* is a portland cement–based mortar in a thickness between thinset and thickset. If your tile is heavier or uneven but not so much so that thickset is advisable, the tile setter may use medium set.
- *Thickset* material consists of 1¼-inch-thick portland cement; in some cases, reinforcing wire or galvanized lath is incorporated. Thickset should be considered if you want to level out unevenness in the substrate, incorporate slope in the tile layer if needed (e.g., slope to a drain), reinforce the substrate for complete rigidity (for wood framing), or create sufficient thickness for burying radiant heating or other tubing.
- *Neat* is a portland cement that is used to bond tile to a cement setting bed that has not hardened yet. Dry set can also be used to bond tile to a still-plastic cement bed.
- *Latex portland cement* can be used to bond tile to a bed that has hardened for 24 hours but is not cured. Dry set can also be used for this kind of installation.
- *Dry set* is portland cement and resins. Preferred for absorptive tiles.
- *Organic adhesive* can be used on floors and walls. Organic adhesives come premixed in watertight containers. Type 1 mastic is used for walls and floors; type 2 is used for walls. They are not suitable for high-moisture installations but form a more flexible bond.
- *Epoxy mortar* is a two-part system used when chemical resistance is needed. It is "stickier" and can be used for setting tile on metal or plywood, or installing tile on top of a previous tile installation.
- *Additives* are not a bond coat, they are used to modify the characteristics of setting beds to make them "stickier," more flexible.

The different mortar systems that you might use are simplified in Table 10.2 by general type of mastic.

If you intend to use two tiles of different thicknesses next to each other, and differences in thickness are minor, a setting bed could even up the difference. If differences are greater, you may have to instruct the installer to "back butter" (slather more mastic on the back before positioning) the thinner tiles to "boost" their surfaces into flush alignment with the thicker tiles.

The setting bed material will ooze up between the tiles. This must be monitored by the installer as the tile is set so that there is enough depth for the installation of the grout. This is a greater concern when tiles are very thin; the setting material should allow for at least a 1⁄16-inch-deep joint for the grout. If tiles are very thin, the joints may have to be scraped back to the substrate to allow sufficient depth for grout. This added step could affect installation costs. (See Chapter 12 for more information about mortar.)

Substrate

The substrate for tile must be appropriate to the tile selection and the use. It must be entirely rigid. Any give or springiness will lead to cracked or loose tiles. Sheets comprising the substrate should be flush with one another. If tile is bonded directly to the substrate any movement in the substrate will cause cracking of the tile or the grout. Tile can be bonded to the concrete in a building constructed of concrete. In other construction methods a material will be affixed to the frame to receive the tile.

Table 10.2
In simplest terms, there are two basic mortar types.

Type	Composition	Uses
Cement based	Wetset: a slurry of cement sand and water is applied to wet cement	When the cement substrate is still plastic or not entirely cured
	Dry set: mortar applied to a substrate that cannot bond with the tile on its own	When the substrate cannot bond to the tile directly
	Thinset: cement, sand, and methylcellulose	Tile and substrate are flat and sound, and movement is not anticipated
	Medium set: like thinset but thicker than 3/16"	When tile thickness needs adjustment by pressing it into the setting bed, such as for uneven tile
	Thickset: thick mortar bed may bond directly to tile or be separated by a fracture membrane (like thinset installation over mortar substrate)	Even out substrate; when installing radiant heat system; creating a sloped surface
	Polymer-modified	Thousands of proprietary formulations alter properties of mortar
Adhesive	Tile glue that is not cement based; also called epoxy system	For impervious tile; most simply: type 1 is for floors and walls, type 2 is for walls only

Helpful Hint 10.2

If the installation will be exposed to water, it is a good idea to have a waterproofing sealant applied to the substrate, no matter how water resistive the substrate material is.

Several substrate products are available:

- *Water-resistant "green board"* or blue board should be used if any water will be used during the installation. Both have a gypsum core laminated with a paperlike covering that is water resistant. The gypsum core will disintegrate if water reaches it. Blue board is designed as a substrate for plaster coatings, so it also resists moisture while providing a good bond. This is one of the two most commonly used substrates for tile.
- *Regular gypsum board "drywall"* should be used as a tile substrate only if the area will remain dry during use and tile is to be installed with a waterless adhesive and grouted with an epoxy or other waterless grout.
- *Cementitious backer board* (cement board) is available in fiber-reinforced or glass-mesh faced sheets. These substrates contain no gypsum and are water impervious. This is the most common substrate for wet areas like showers.

Helpful Hint 10.3

Use cement board wherever water will be present even if only when a mishap occurs—like a laundry room or bathroom floor. If a tub or washing machine overflows, a plywood substrate (typical for floors) could delaminate. Plywood with cement board on top, properly waterproofed, could keep the temporary water mishap from turning into a construction project.

- *Plywood* of exterior grade is designed to resist delaminating in the presence of moisture and can be used as a backing for tile.
- *Existing surfaces* may be suitable as a substrate for new tile work "as is" or after being leveled with a gypsum, self-leveling compound. Remember that these compounds must cure, as all cement products must cure, for 28 days. New super-thin porcelain tiles (1/8 inch or less) are designed to be installed right over existing finish surfaces that are in sound condition. These thin tiles are more likely to crack if the substrate is not in excellent condition.

Grout

Tile is very dimensionally stable, even so it will change due to temperature changes, so space is left between tiles—this is the grout joint. The function of grout in a tile installation is to fill the space between the tiles. It seems to be a relatively simple task, so you may wonder why there are so many options for grout formulas. Differences in grout formulas accommodate different substrates and different tile materials. Unique conditions—like tiled surfaces that will be immersed in water or experience extreme temperature changes—will require different characteristics as well. (Review the Grout section in Chapter 12 for more information.)

Point of Emphasis 10.4

When small tiles are set up on 12" × 12" sheets, the distance between the tiles on the sheet determines the rout joint width. When tiles are loose, you will specify, or determine with your installer, the best width for grout joints. Generally speaking—the more uniform the tile is and the crisper the edges are, the narrower the grout joint can be. The inverse is true for tiles with irregular sizes and edges.

Use unsanded grout for joints up to 1/6 inch; use sanded grout for joints up to 3/8 inch; and use a wide joint mix for joints wider than 3/8 inch. Wide joint mix is generally the same formula as sanded grout but has more sand in it so your installer may tell you that he or she will just add more sand and this will probably be acceptable.

Sometimes the largest tile in a box can be as much as 3/32 inch larger than the smallest tile in the box, so we don't split hairs over grout joint width because there will be slight, unnoticeable differences in the installation. You might prefer to specify the width as tight, small, medium, or wide.

Joints that are planned to handle building movement will not be grouted. The setting bed will be scraped back to the substrate and a flexible silicone sealant (caulk) will be used in place of grout. Review the structure and/or the plans to locate these joints as you plan your design and call attention to them when you review the job with the installer. Caulk should also be specified wherever two surfaces come together. Examples of these joints occur where two walls meet, or where the wall meets the floor, countertop, or tub deck. Also seal around plumbing fittings to prevent water from traveling into the wall cavity.

PROTECTION AND MAINTENANCE

Some of the tiles that you specify will need to be protected during the installation if your client's site is still under construction. If the tile is porous, textured, or unglazed it may need to have a protective coat of grout release (material used to prevent bonding of the cement to a surface) applied so grout can be wiped completely off the face of the tile. All horizontal installations and even vertical installation in high-traffic areas should be protected during construction, not because tile is delicate—it is typically a durable surface. It is very difficult to, later, replace any tiles that might be damaged without being able to spot the repair in the grout and you will want to turn the job over to your client in perfect condition, so always protect materials that have been installed.

Most tiles do not need to be sealed, but terra-cotta tiles that are not glazed should receive a penetrating sealer prior to installation. If you specified a grout that has the grout sealer built in, you will not have to seal the grout, but if you specified a portland **cement grout**, it will cure for 28 days and then can be sealed. If the site has been in use during the duration, have the grout cleaned first and then sealed.

Tile can be cleaned with simple, nontoxic cleaning products. Grout should be periodically cleaned and resealed. If you selected a tile that must be sealed, your client should maintain it with compatible cleaning products, otherwise the cleaning products could remove the sealant.

SAFETY

Tile is nontoxic and does not require the use of any product that will off-gas. Select sealants that are low or no VOC solutions so you do not introduce VOCs into your client's environment every time the surface must be resealed.

You are probably well aware that tile is a hard surface and if the tile has a glossy finish, it can be slippery when wet. Many tiles are so impervious that the option of top-dressing the tile, the way you would top-dress stone, is not advisable. If slip resistance is a requirement of your project, select a tile that is designed to be slip resistant.

Helpful Hint 10.4

Grout lines provide some additional traction and you can enhance the slip resistance of tile flooring by using a smaller tile that will have more grout lines.

SUSTAINABILITY

Tile is durable, so proper installation is especially important. The wrong substrate or improper adhesion is a shame because these mistakes can cause the surface to break down long before the tile has stopped being serviceable. One only has to travel to some archeological sites where there are intact tiles that are several hundred years old to comprehend how durable tile can be. A tile surface can outlast the building it is installed into! For this reason it is important that your design decisions have longevity. Designs based on what is currently fashionable rather than what is congruent with the general building design will be short-lived because fashion moves on and the designs based on changing fashion can waste otherwise long-lived materials.

Some tile bodies contain recycled material. It is easy to find glass, concrete, and composite tiles that list some recycled content. Tile is a material that is produced all around the country. Tile that is made within a 500-mile radius of your project site is considered to be "local" and therefore would contribute to your client's points for LEED certification.

If you scrutinize the individual material types you will find pros and cons pertaining to sustainability. Concrete may contain fly ash (diverted from the waste stream) but production of portland cement itself uses fuel and generates greenhouse gasses. Glass contains silica and ceramic tile contains clay; both are abundant but must be removed from the earth to make tile. Stone tiles are also in limited supply; some quarries have already been exhausted and certain stones have already "gone extinct" so to speak.

MANAGING BUDGETS

Materials can vary dramatically in cost and can be the biggest cost variable in the job. Installation costs can rise with the complexity of the job. Any preparation required prior to installation will, of course, contribute to the cost. For example, if the existing substrate is inadequate it must be improved before installing tile, so the cost will be higher.

If the tile setter is simply laying down pregrouted sheets on a large flat area, the square-foot cost will be lower than if there are many different trim pieces to install, complicated architecture, or a complex design or pattern. The per-hour charge for a highly skilled installer will be higher than for

A Cautionary Tale 10.2

I ordered stone tile from a very reputable supplier who was quite "high-end" (dealt in expensive product) with whom I did little business. The client was on a tight budget and I was frankly surprised that the material I found at this expensive shop was in her budget. Because it was a simple installation of 15" × 15" stone tile on a floor I allowed my client to hire the cheapest tile setter she could find (we were also trying to limit my own involvement since I charge by the hour, so she sourced all the labor).

What I did not realize, even when I went to see the installation prior to grouting, was that the grout joints were a little wider than specified and it was not until the installation was complete that we could see that the tiles were not cut squarely (see Figure 10.14) and the room seemed to "list." The wider grout joint required more sand in the grout, so the grout proved to be difficult to clean.

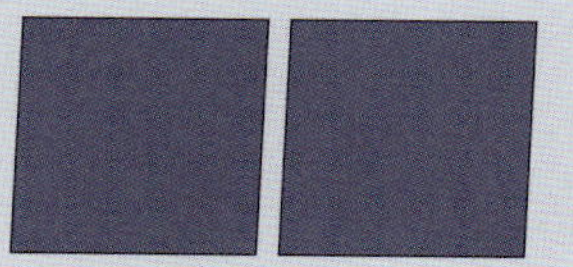

FIGURE 10.14 Tiles that are not cut squarely.

Because "installation constitutes acceptance" in our industry, we were not entitled to any remedy from the supplier, and since I infrequently gave business to that shop I did not have an ongoing relationship as leverage, even if my client could have afforded to remedy the problem—which she could not.

The earnest inexperienced installer that was hired didn't know to alert us to the fact that the tiles were not square and had completed the installation.

Things to take away:

(1) If the deal seems to be too good to be true—it probably is.
(2) Don't take on work that you cannot afford to do well. The budget for the job was too small for a designer to be involved and for expensive material like stone tile. I should have structured my contract for design consultation only and not participated in actual material selection or management since I was only performing part of the managing of it anyway.
(3) A low-priced, inexperienced installer can cost you more money than they save.

someone whose expertise does not stretch beyond the simplest installations. Do not underbuy or overbuy expertise.

The method of setting also factors into the price. The care required to install uneven tiles or tiles with variegated coloration is time-consuming. Uneven tiles must be pressed into place in a thick bed to create the most even surface possible. This not only requires careful judgment (and possibly a more skilled, therefore more costly, installer) but also time. Even low-quality tiles are generally very serviceable and your client's economical installation can be very durable and long-lived.

> Point of Emphasis 10.5
> Variegated color also requires skill in placing and orienting tiles to achieve a nicely uniform mottled appearance versus a blotchy installation. Your expectation with respect to these two items in particular must be communicated to the installer. To confirm your intention for the installation is fully understood, meet your installer for a dry fit before the installation begins.

ORGANIZATION OF THE INDUSTRY

Tile is available from a wide variety of resources. They range from large companies who own their own production facilities to the individual artist creating tiled murals for a specific client. Tile production takes place all around the world and tiles range in quality. Some tiles are like commodity items and you will find versions of them from many manufacturers. Others are highly unique relief tiles with custom patterns and secret-formula glazes. Exclusivity increases price, while a commodity tile is frequently produced to be competitively priced.

Tile distributors may represent several manufacturers. Some distributors will sell directly to the public and some will sell only to resellers. Big resellers, like big box stores, may have direct relationships to manufacturers, eliminating the distributor from the supply chain. This is one means of securing the low prices they are famous for.

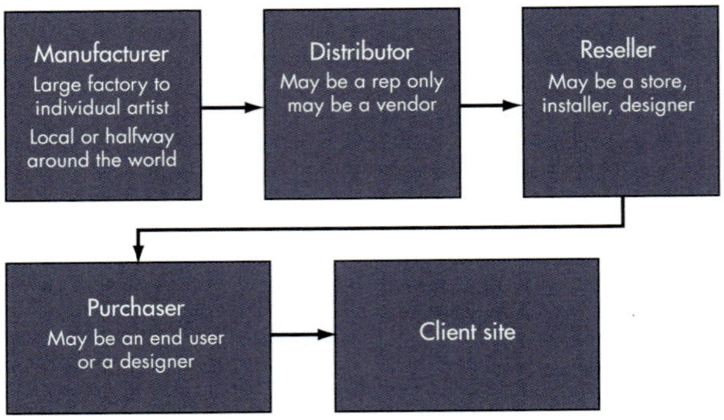

FIGURE 10.15 Links in the supply chain; bear in mind that not all these links will be present in the supply chain of every tile. Your client's tile will pass through at least two links in the supply chain before it arrives at the job site.

Figure 10.15 shows the links in the supply chain, but you can understand that not all of these links will be present in the supply chain of every tile.

> Point of Emphasis 10.6
> An artist that I know produced a custom mural on tile using watercolors. She used Velcro dots to fasten the unglazed bisque tile to the wall of her studio like a canvas in order to paint on it. The bisque tile had been fired once, but since the tiles were unglazed they had a velvety "tooth" that accepted the watercolor.
>
> After the paint had dried, she covered the tile with clear glaze and fired it in the kiln. If you have ever glazed pottery you will not be surprised that the clear glaze was the color green before it was fired. That is the reason she decided to use watercolor instead of glazes; she did not like not knowing what color she was going to get as she painted, but that is the nature of glazes.
>
> She fired the tiles in small batches in the kiln of a local potter whom she knew. The batches had very slight variation that she pointed out to me but you really had to look for it. She made duplicate tiles for each tile that had to be nipped to allow plumbing fixtures to poke through. We did not need them but I still think it was a good idea.

Table 10.3
Consider logical program points you would identify for an installation and explore the implications of those characteristics for your specification.

Consideration	Implications
Is there a direct connection to the outdoors?	Walking surfaces could become slippery or soiled, so selection must provide a wet coefficient of friction of 0.6 or better and must be impervious to staining.
Is toxicity an issue?	Minimize grout joints and select grout that does not need to have a sealant applied periodically.
Is there steam in the environment?	Do not specify a crackle glaze since it is a compromised surface and mildew can grow in the cracks.
Is your site a high-traffic location?	Select color-through porcelain tiles—they will retain their appearance even as the surface wears away.
Can your site be maintained vigilantly?	You may need to select a soil-hiding color and pattern if maintenance will be spotty due to constant use.
Do you require trim tiles to finish your installation?	Not all tiles come with trims. If your selections do not have trim tiles you will need to use metal or plastic accessories or perhaps thresholds of other materials like stone.
Are you planning a pattern that combines multiple tiles?	If so, you may need to find companion tiles that are the same actual (not nominal) size and thickness.
Is your tile an absorbent stone or unglazed clay tile?	You may want to seal the tile prior to installing , especially if you are using a contrasting grout.
Are you working on a project with a sustainable emphasis?	Search for locally produced tile with recycled content; install with cementitious mastic and grout.

As a designer you are potentially a reseller; many designers make a significant share of their income reselling items and materials with a markup. You may discover that some of the installers you work with prefer to purchase the tile and include the price of the material in their bid. There are a couple of reasons for this, the first being that they also like to make money on the sale of the tile. The second reason is that they have more control over quantity and they don't want to come up short—especially if the order is semicustom and it will be difficult to match a new order to an existing lot. They also do not have to rely on the information provided by a middleman as they will work directly with the supplier.

SELECTION CRITERIA

Your selection criteria will account for site conditions as well as material characteristics. Slip resistance is defined by many codes as a coefficient of friction of 0.6 or better. If wet conditions are likely, you may need to do better than that. Soiling of grout is a common complaint and many people feel that the least amount of grout is the best way to combat this. Some grouts need to be sealed and this will introduce chemicals into the environment, so you may consider a resinous grout instead of a cement grout if you are designing for vulnerable populations. You may want to organize a table like Table 10.3 based on your own design program.

SPECIFYING

Writing a good spec takes knowledge of site conditions at the time of installation and while in use, as well as product knowledge. Imagine that you are going to install recycled glass tile on the walls of a locker room at a high-end health club. Your spec might contain information similar to the following.

SAMPLE SPEC 10.1

Part 1 General Information

1.1 Related Documents
A. Refer to finish plan for location of material.
B. Refer to elevations for pattern and distribution of colors specified.

1.2 Summary
A. Provide and install tile specified on walls of men's locker room at Hilltop Health Club. Cementitious wallboard to be installed in showers (by others) prior to commencing work.
B. Green board to be installed in all dry areas (by others) prior to commencing work.
C. Rough plumbing work to be completed (by others) prior to tile installation.

1.3 References
A. American National Standards Institute (ANSI) national standard for tile.
B. Tile Council of America handbook for tile installation.

1.4 Contractor Submittals
A. Provide grouted sample of portion of pattern indicated on drawings, 24" × 24", grouted, for approval.
B. Provide documentation certifying recycled material content.
C. Material safety data sheet for all materials, mastics, and grouts specified.

1.5 Quality Assurance
A. Installers to be certified by the Ceramic Tile Education Council and have minimum 3 years' work experience installing glass tile.
B. All material to be delivered in manufacturer's original, unopened containers.

1.6 Delivery, Storage, and Handling
A. Material to be transported only under conditions specified by the manufacturers and delivered to acclimatized site 48 hours prior to commencing installation.

1.7 Maintenance of Installation
A. Temperatures to be maintained between 50ºF and 90ºF.

Part 2 Products

2.1 General information
A. Installer to provide all material required to complete installation, including but not limited to mortar, tile, grout, tools, protective clothing, and masks.

2.2 Manufacturers
A. Manufacturer of tile to be Glass Tile Jungle, 123 Industrial Drive, Anytown, ST 12345.
B. Manufacturer of mortar, grout, and joint sealer from Mortar & Grout Connection 456 Industrial Drive, Someplace, ST 98365.
C. Waterproof membrane by Super Seal, 1389 Industrial Drive, Hereswhere, ST 51389.

2.3 Products
A. Tile to be glass tile from Circuitous Series, 1" × 1" tile mesh-mounted in sheets $11^{15}/_{16}$" × $11^{15}/_{16}$" in colors as follows:
   1. Steel for general wall color
   2. Stormy Green for accent band 131
   3. Vermillion for accent band 132
B. Thinset epoxy adhesive type ANSI A118.3 as recommended by manufacturer.
C. Epoxy grout ANSI A118.3 as recommended by manufacturer.
D. Liquid weatherproofing, cold-applied with fabric reinforcing, compatible with setting materials.
E. Silicone joint sealers.

Part 3 Execution

3.1 Examination
A. Surfaces to be tiled to be free of foreign matter, ridges, and projections.
B. Voids to be filled with setting materials.
C. Allowable tolerance to be $^1/_8$" in 8'.
D. **Lippage** of $^3/_{32}$" or greater is not acceptable.
E. If area is not in suitable condition, and cannot be brought to suitable condition by tile installer, installer must notify designer immediately.

3.2 Preparation
A. Install waterproofing and allow to cure for 13 days as required by manufacturer's warranties.

3.3 Installation
A. Install tile in accordance with ANSI 108.6 thinset epoxy adhesive per manufacturer's recommendations.
B. Grout joint to match width established by mesh-mounted sheets.
C. Follow tile manufacturer's instructions to the letter.
D. Tile to set for a minimum of 48 hours prior to grouting.
E. Make all joints watertight without excess mortar or excess grout.

3.4 Post Installation
A. Remove all grout from face of tiles.
B. Area to be cordoned off by contractor to protect from other trades upon acceptance of tile work.
C. Installation to be ready for owner acceptance upon completion of work.

INSPECTION

After your dry-fit consultation with the installer, the tile will be set (adhered). When the tile has been set, but before it is grouted, confirm the following:

- The intent of the pattern has been satisfied.
- The layout is according to plan with joints positioned so as to avoid awkward alignments.
- Tile joints should be evenly spaced, smooth, parallel, and perpendicular to each other and walls, where applicable.
- There should be no defects, damage, or irregularities present in material installed.
- All cuts should be even and smooth.
- Trims should be used as specified.
- All tiles in a single surface should be flush and level with each other (relief trim tiles excepted).

When the installation is complete it will be inspected and accepted (or not) by you. Check the following:

- Grout should be floated up to flush with tile, or slightly recessed; it should be consistent in color across each surface.
- If desired, extra material should be left at the site, marked and stored as directed.
- If tiles are sealed, confirm that the sealer was evenly applied with no thin spots or runs.

RELATED MATERIAL

Material that you may also consider at this time would include any surface that could perform in such a way that it would meet your program requirements. Solid surfacing, brick, tempered glass, and even some kinds of oily woods could meet the criteria for water imperviousness that is provided by tile. Other materials you might consider in relation to your selection would be those that are used in conjunction with tile, such as edging systems that finish off the installation when the tile selected lacks trim pieces. Separation membranes that decouple the installation from the structure prevent cracking due to building movement.

BRICK

Brick is both an exterior and interior material. Interior designers are often called upon to make decisions about "decorative surfacing" for exteriors of buildings, so this is one topic where some exterior issues will be sprinkled in among interior considerations.

Brick is sometimes referred to as burned mud; *burned* because it is fired in a kiln and *mud* because it is found in the soil layer of the earth and the brick we specify is, in a sense, a special kind of fine mud that contains other minerals, often including shale. Other brick materials include sand-lime, adobe, and cement, but sand-lime is not common and adobe is less common in interior design, and cement is covered in another chapter, so we will narrow our focus here to typical brick.

Brick has been a valuable surfacing material across a far-reaching history and is used for interiors as flooring and for vertical surfacing for walls. It is frequently used for accent walls and, because it is noncombustible, for fireplace surrounds. The popularity of urban loft living has created an entire genre in design and brick walls are essential to achieving the look in both home and hospitality design.

Composition

The brick that you will likely specify is clay. Clay is quarried out of the earth in open pits. Clay is refined and mixed with water to the preferred consistency for making brick. Even after the clay has dried out, its plasticity can still be reconstituted with water, until it has been fired. In firing, the properties of the clay change and it cannot be returned to a plastic state after it has been fired. Clay also contains organic material and other components, but these components lend little to the structure of clay bricks.

> **Point of Emphasis 10.7**
> Clay is very fine-grained soil with the mineral shale. Bricks are made of mud and shale.

Characteristics

You undoubtedly have some familiarity with brick and are aware of its hardness and density and have probably encountered a number of different surfaces common to brick. Because the clay used to form brick is mined from the earth, the chemical composition varies with geographic location and with the depth from which it was gathered. The color of brick depends on its composition and the firing environment. For example: clay with iron oxides (common to clay) will burn to a red color in an oxidizing atmosphere and to purple in a reducing atmosphere (oxygen intake limited). Some bricks are glazed but generally they are left with the body of the brick clay showing.

Brick as a surfacing material for interior spaces takes a little advance planning because of its dimensions. It is thicker than most other interior surfacing that you will specify. When you are specifying for new construction, details can be devised to allow for the thickness, so you can easily specify dimensional brick (full brick). If the site will not allow for dimensional brick, you may substitute veneer brick that looks like dimensional brick but is thinner and can be applied in a manner similar to a tile installation.

Dimensional Brick

Bricks are also available in nominal sizes (approximate facial sizes or thickness of tile expressed in inches or fractions of an inch). Sizes vary somewhat from one supplier to another. The following sizes in Table 10.4 could be the basis for initial designs but if you are working on a small-scale design (like a fireplace surround) make your selection as early in the process as possible so you can design with precision. Just as with lumber, tile, and other materials, if an exact size must be known it is best to refer to samples rather than manufacturer's literature.

You will encounter terms and descriptors that indicate specific kinds of dimensional brick.

- Acid-resistant brick—Brick suitable for use in contact with chemicals, usually in conjunction with acid-resistant mortars.
- Adobe brick—Large, roughly molded, sun-dried clay brick of varying sizes.
- Angle brick—Any brick shaped to an oblique angle to fit a corner.
- Arch brick—Wedge-shaped brick for special use in an arch; extremely hard-burned brick.

Table 10.4
Example of standard brick sizes.

Name	Approx. Depth	Approx. Height	Approx. Length
Modular brick	$3\frac{5}{8}$"	$2\frac{1}{4}$"	$7\frac{5}{8}$"
Standard brick	$3\frac{3}{4}$"	$2\frac{1}{4}$"	8"
Jumbo brick	$3\frac{5}{8}$"	$2\frac{3}{4}$"	8"
King brick	$3\frac{5}{8}$"	$2\frac{3}{4}$"	$9\frac{5}{8}$"
Roman brick*	$3\frac{5}{8}$"	$1\frac{5}{8}$"	$11\frac{5}{8}$"
Norman brick	$3\frac{5}{8}$"	$2\frac{1}{4}$"	$11\frac{5}{8}$"
Jumbo Norman brick	$3\frac{5}{8}$"	$2\frac{3}{4}$"	$11\frac{5}{8}$"
Economy brick	$3\frac{5}{8}$"	$3\frac{5}{8}$"	8"
Utility brick	$3\frac{5}{8}$"	$3\frac{5}{8}$"	$11\frac{5}{8}$"

* Notable variation in sizes available from different manufacturers, all others are slight.

- Building brick—Brick for building purposes not especially treated for texture or color. Formerly called common brick.
- Clinker brick—A very hard-burned brick whose shape is distorted or bloated due to nearly complete vitrification.
- Dry-press brick—Brick formed in molds under high pressures from relatively dry clay (5 to 7 percent moisture content).
- Facing brick—Brick made especially for facing purposes, often treated to produce surface texture. They are made of selected clays, or treated, to produce desired color.
- Fire brick—Brick made of refractory ceramic material that will resist high temperatures.
- Floor brick—Smooth, dense brick, highly resistant to abrasion, used as finished floor surfaces.
- Gauged brick—Brick that has been ground or otherwise produced to accurate dimensions. Also a tapered arch brick.
- Hollow brick—A masonry unit of clay or shale whose net cross-sectional area in any plane parallel to the bearing surface is not less than 60 percent of its gross cross-sectional area measured in the same plane. (See ASTM Specification C 652.)
- Paving brick—Vitrified brick especially suitable for use in pavements where resistance to abrasion is important.

- Salmon brick—Generic term for under-burned brick, which is more porous, slightly larger, and lighter colored than hard-burned brick. Usually pinkish-orange color.
- Soft-mud brick—Brick produced by molding relatively wet clay (20 to 30 percent moisture). Often a hand process. When insides of molds are sanded to prevent clay from sticking, the product is sand-struck brick. When molds are wetted to prevent sticking, the product is water-struck brick.
- Stiff-mud brick—Brick produced by extruding a stiff but plastic clay (12 to 15 percent moisture) through a die.
- Brick and brick—A method of laying brick so that units touch each other with only enough mortar to fill surface irregularities.

Brick Pavers

Brick pavers are often used on floors. They are specially designed for horizontal applications. Pavers are thinner than the bricks used to build walls. They range in size from 1⅛" × 3⅛" × 7⅝" to 2¼" × 4" × 8". Brick tiles range from approximately ½-inch to nearly an inch in thickness ranging from 2" × 4" to 4" × 8".

Helpful Hint 10.5

It is not always easy (or accurate) to imagine the appearance of a large expanse of any particular kind of brick by looking at individual samples or even pictures online. Before you finalize your selection it is a good idea to travel to places that have used the brick you have in mind. The manufacturer will be happy to compile a list of places for you to visit to make sure you have made the selection that is most appropriate.

Brick Veneers

Brick veneers give the appearance of brick with a fraction of the depth and weight required for dimensional brick. Brick veneer is usually the thickness of tile (½ inch to ⅜ inch is common). Salvaged bricks are sometimes sliced into tile. Exterior faces of sliced, reclaimed brick will have a different appearance than interior slices. If your job demands only weathered exterior brick faces, you will pay a premium.

Advantages of Thin Brick Veneer

Thin brick veneer is most appropriate for many interior surfacing situations.

- Interior thin brick veneer finishes can be applied by moderately skilled craftspeople.
- Thin brick veneer is very durable and longer lasting than other wallcoverings.
- Prefabrication with thin brick veneer is easily and economically done compared to brickwork.
- Better sound- and fire-resistance properties may be obtained using thin brick veneer than with some nonmasonry surfaces.
- Thin brick units are more durable than imitation brick units made from gypsum, cement, or plastics.
- Walls built with thin brick units are lighter in weight than conventional masonry veneer.
- Thin brick veneer may be used where structural support for conventional brick veneer is not available.

Disadvantages of Thin Brick Veneer

- The durability and overall quality of thin brick veneer systems may not be equivalent to that of brick (but for most interior surfacing applications there should be little concern).
- Thin brick veneer cannot be used structurally.
- Sound- and fire-resistance properties are less than those of conventional brick masonry veneer.
- Thin brick veneer does not provide the thermal mass of brick, so it does not make a contribution to regulating interior temperature.
- Sound blocking from brick veneer is not as effective as for actual masonry. Acoustically, dimensional brick is one of the most efficient materials for reflecting all sound, even the more tenacious bass notes.

PARTS AND ACCESSORIES

The monolithic appearance of a brick surface makes it easy to forget that you have probably seen bricks in nonrectangular shapes as well. These shapes are decorative as well as functional: angled brick shapes will allow the material to shed water and snow to slide off edges.

In addition to specially shaped brick, you will investigate, on an as needed basis, other items that will be required for some of your installations. These might include angle iron to hold a brick course (that is the term used for a horizontal row of bricks) above an opening or ties that are used to hold bricks against a vertical surface.

FABRICATION

Brick is formed by soft mud, stiff mud, and dry-press processes. What makes these production methods different from each other is that the aesthetic characteristics of the final product are somewhat affected by the amount of water and the kind of clay. Soft-mud bricks are irregular in shape and not as dense as other formulas, partly because of the amount of water used in their production (Figure 10.16). A very precise, tailored, uniform brick results from the low-water process, dry press, and a more irregular result when more water is present in the clay, as with soft mud. Table 10.5 compares the different production methods. These terms indicate both production processes and stiffness of the brick during production.

In addition to the production described above, bricks may be handmade. Soft mud is used because it requires the least force to form it into bricks. If a handmade look is desired but price is a concern, some manufacturers will drop an extruded brick into a sand-lined form and "shake it up" a bit to work sand into the surface and soften the edges like a handmade brick. Because reclaimed brick is prized but, ironically, more expensive than new brick, the look of old brick is imitated by tumbling new brick.

What Would You Do? 10.1

What kind of brick would you like to use for a ski lodge hotel lounge in Snowmass, Colorado? A library lobby in Los Angeles? The floor of a shopping center in Massachusetts?

Finishes

Ceramic glazes may be applied either before the bricks are fired or after one firing, and then the bricks are refired. Some sealants may be thought of as finishes because they are film-formers altering the surface characteristics. Brick is sometimes painted, although it cannot be ordered from the manufacturer that way; paint would be applied after installation and all the considerations pertaining to film-forming sealants apply to paint as well. Brick likes to breathe and special paint formulas are imperative to avoid deterioration of the brick.

FIGURE 10.16 Soft-mud brick is more irregular than brick made with stiffer, cleaner clay. *Photograph by Alana Clark.*

Table 10.5 The amount of water in the mix influences the characteristics of the brick.

Brick Fabrication	How It's Formed	Amount of Water Used	Resulting Characteristics
Soft mud	Pounded into forms that have a release agent inside	20% to 30% of weight	Least consistent forms with irregular surface and "rusticated" faces.
	Sand-struck—release agent is sand		
	Water-struck—release agent is water		
Stiff mud	Clay and water mixed then a vacuum "de-airs" the clay and it is extruded into a column and cut to size	12% to 15% of weight	More consistent form and sizes. The column is sometimes run through a slurry to alter the surface appearance.
Damp or dry press	Tremendous force (500 to 1,500 psi) is used to pound the very stiff clay into molds	10% of weight	This is the most precise and consistent brick.

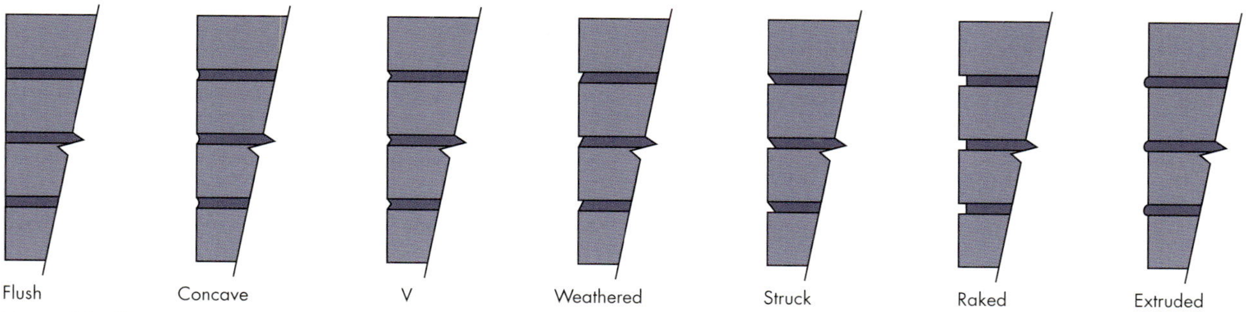

FIGURE 10.17 Various mortar joints that you will specify.

QUALIFYING INSTALLERS

Masons and bricklayers with experience in the kind of work your job requires would be the place to begin your search for a qualified craftsperson. An experienced company is essential for large jobs or structural work but a meticulous single craftsman can be hired to build a small project such as a fireplace surround or a planter, so you should not dismiss the "handyman" who claims to be able to build a small project like that, even if they are not associated exclusively with the brick industry. You would need to more actively vet such a craftsman by seeing their work and talking to references but a perfectionist who is not necessarily a mason could be the answer for a small simple job.

> **Helpful Hint 10.6**
>
> It is a fact of life that we sometimes make perfectly suitable selections of tradespeople based on little information, but a safer approach is to let personality be the first word instead of the last, meaning that you must be able to work with any trade expert in an easy collaboration, so once you have determined you can work easily with a tradesperson, then invest the time to perform the rest of the investigation. If you find the relationship difficult during the interview process the best qualifications will not make up for a poor working relationship.

Like many other trades, bricklayers will be certified in particular areas of expertise and this certification will, quite possibly, come from a number of sources. A mortar manufacturer may offer a training seminar and provide participants with a certificate upon completion, or if the craftsman is a member of a union, there will likely be a path for advancement established there with apprentices learning the trade on the job as well as in formalized instruction available through the organization. Some bricklayers will attend community colleges to learn the trade in a saturated job market where those lacking experience have difficulty getting started in the field. Because there is no set path to expertise, you will want to see samples of work produced for other clients, discuss their experience, ask them how they would approach your job and if they anticipate any complications with the work. Ask them what training they have had and see if you feel it is pertinent to your client's needs.

INSTALLATION

For vertical surfaces, bricks are set into mortar. The mortar joints can be flush with the surface of the brick or concave (below the surface of the brick) or convex. Different formulations have different characteristics. Non-load-bearing mortar type O is sufficient for interior applications of surfacing material.

If vertical surfaces that you will select material for will not be load bearing they may have to be anchored to another wall surface behind them just to stand up. These **anchors** or ties are fastened to the wall periodically and concealed in the mortar joint.

Horizontal surfaces can be set in mortar with mortar between them (so all but the face that shows is in contact with mortar), or tightly fitted and laid loose on roofing felt or another membrane with no mortar used, or set on a bed of mortar with no mortar between the bricks. Roofing felt is often asphalt-impregnated, and there are odors and toxins associated with these products.

Mortar Joints

Joints are tooled to different profiles (Figure 10.17). (Tooling means compressing and shaping the face of a mortar joint with a special tool other than a trowel.)

Considerations related to exterior performance issues are included because interior designers frequently consult on exterior surfacing options for continuity of design. As a specifier of interior surfacing material your motivations for selecting one of these types would be visual.

- *Concave joints* and *V-shaped joints* are normally kept quite small. These joints are very effective in resisting rain penetration and are originally intended for use in areas subject to heavy rains and high winds.
- *Weathered joint* imitates erosion; the working of this joint requires care as it must be worked from below.
- *Struck joint* is a common joint in ordinary brickwork. As masons often work from the inside of the wall, this is an easy joint to strike with a trowel. Some compaction occurs, but the small ledge does not shed water readily, resulting in a less watertight joint than other joints—a consideration if you are specifying for an installation subject to water.
- *Flush joint* is the simplest joint for the mason, since it is made by holding the edge of the trowel flat against the brick and cutting in any direction. This produces an uncompacted joint with a small hairline crack where the mortar is pulled away from the brick by the cutting action. This joint is not always watertight.
- *Raked joint* is produced by removing the surface of the mortar while it is still soft. While the joint may be compacted, it is difficult to make weathertight and is not recommended where heavy rain, high wind, or freezing is likely to occur. This joint produces marked shadows and darkens the overall appearance of the wall.
- *Extruded joint* allows mortar to flow beyond the face of the brick as the brick is seated into position.

Horizontal Installations

Horizontal applications do not require mortar. The subfloor can be depressed (or a detail devised to safely elevate the area adjacent to the brick) and the brick can be laid on top of building felt (1415 or 1430) that has been spread on top of rigid base. A mortar bed may also be detailed if it is not advisable to loose lay the brick (for example, if reclaimed bricks are irregular and you want to level and fill gaps). Here the subfloor must be depressed (or the surrounding area raised) to accommodate the brick plus the setting bed thickness. A bond coat of cement and extra water (or a latex additive) may be added to the top of the mortar as the bricks are being laid and leveled (it all happens at once, not in stages) to improve the strength of the bond. This bonding coat will not factor into the calculated depth because it is so thin (no more than 1/16 inch is recommended). When bricks are set in mortar this way it is typical to use mortar between them. The same mortar that is used to set the brick will be used to fill the joints. Sand may also be used between bricks for exterior applications but this is impractical for interiors where floors will be vacuumed as part of normal maintenance unless the entire installation is to be coated (for easier maintenance and to lock in sand).

An alternate to mortar between bricks would be to grout between them. The texture of the brick faces will want to hold onto the grout that is smeared across the surface when grouting is taking place. This grout is impossible to remove, so unless you want this as an effect, you will want to order brick with a paraffin coating, which protects the brick face from being stained during grouting and is then steam-cleaned away (obvious complications related to this step must be planned for).

Brick Orientations

Bricks are oriented in to expose their different-sized faces to create patterns, some of which are shown in Figure 10.19; these patterns depend on orienting the brick in different directions so require the added depth to allow brick to be oriented as required. The names for the different faces of bricks described in Figure 10.18 are oriented to form various **bonds** when **courses** are installed.

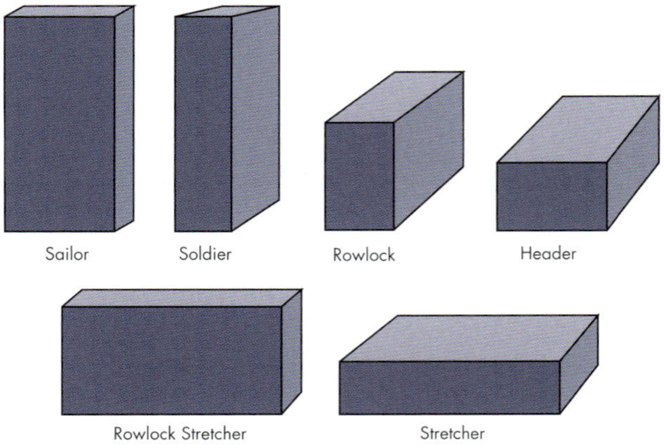

FIGURE 10.18 The names for the brick faces

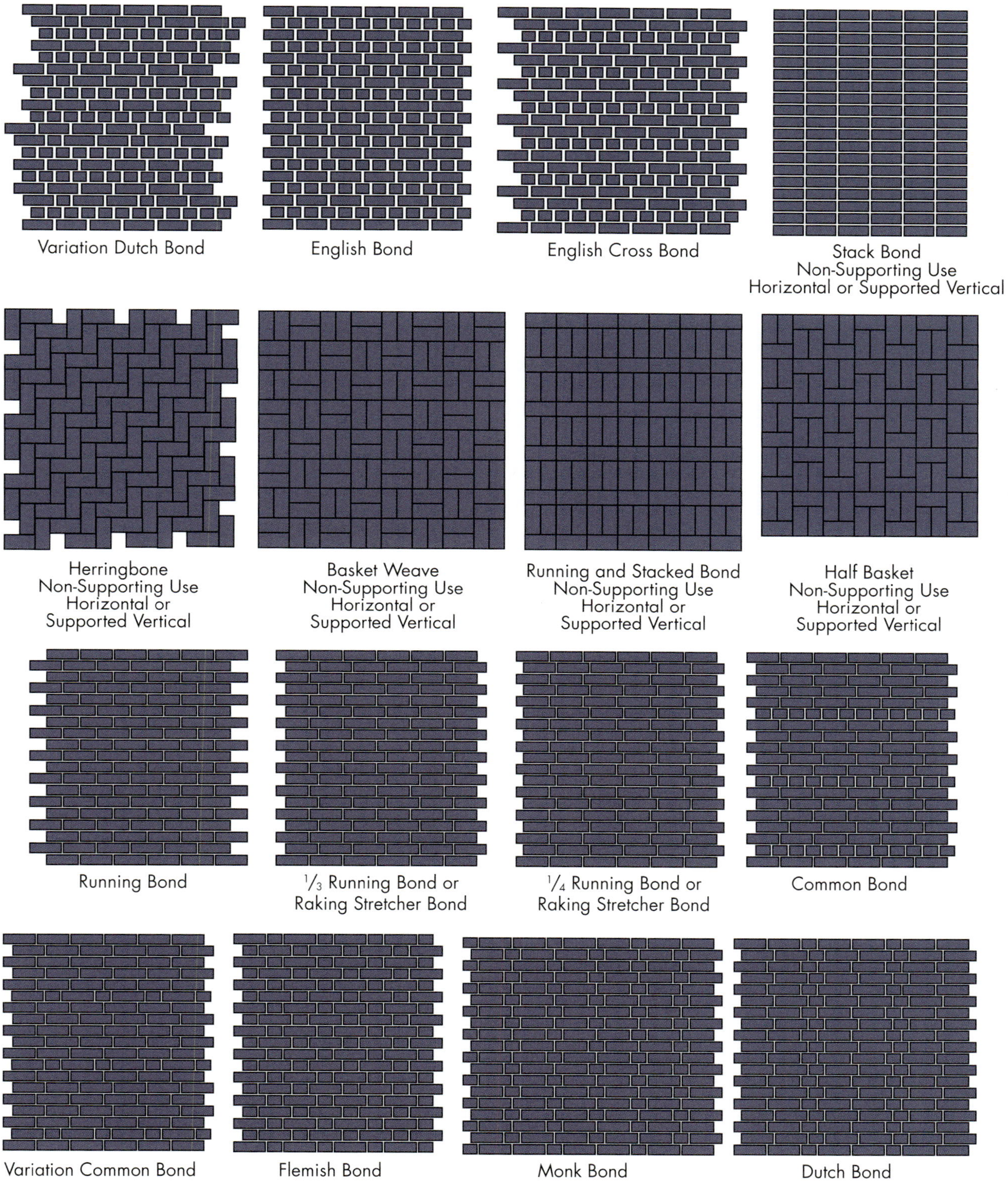

FIGURE 10.19 Orienting the various brick faces in the courses creates patterns called bonds.

As the mason builds the surface, the rows are called courses. The patterns that display the wide faces only (such as stack bond) are not used structurally and must be supported. Interior designers do not supervise structural components, but we do specify cladding for them. You may consult on the brickwork patterns to render a decision based on aesthetics and it is a good idea to understand that some patterns are independently secure only as horizontal patterns. They can be used vertically but they will require ties to hold them to the structural substrate.

PROTECTION AND MAINTENANCE

Brick is a porous material made of quite impervious stuff, so while clay is impervious to most waterborne staining, capillary action could draw discoloration into the porous surface of brick. Bricks can be finished with any approved clear, masonry sealer to enhance their already impervious surfaces and to impart sheen.

Coatings may be considered for brick to improve some performance characteristics, such as the ability to clean away soiling or graffiti or to repel rainwater. Coatings may also be specified to enhance the gloss or color of the brick. They may be considered after sandblasting brick, which makes it more vulnerable to soiling.

Both penetrating and topical coatings are available. Film-forming or topical sealants are more frequently specified for interior surfacing materials than penetrating types because film-forming coatings solve soiling problems and enhance color.

Some coatings are designed to be "sacrificial," meaning they are cleaned away, with the soiling or graffiti, and must be reapplied. Test for ease of removal when considering a product like this. Acrylics and urethanes work well for graffiti protection in interior spaces.

Film-forming coatings can prevent the migration of moisture by sealing the surface, but they can also trap moisture trying to leave the brick and cause a cloudy appearance. They decrease slip resistance of brick somewhat. They may need to be replenished more frequently than penetrating sealers. The correct formulation must be used, or maintenance will become a nuisance. Topical coatings should be replenished by a professional stone and masonry maintenance company as part of normal maintenance and "grocery store" products should not be applied by end users or their maintenance staff.

Helpful Hint 10.7

Specify a vapor barrier behind brick if you think moisture will migrate from behind it.

Film formers will bridge the micro-gaps in a porous material like brick. Penetrating sealers work by coating rather than bridging these capillaries, so they allow the brick to breathe. This prevents trapping of damaging salts within the brick. Trapped salts can deteriorate brick, so penetrating sealants are preferred for exterior walls.

What Would You Do? 10.2

When would you be inclined to use a penetrating sealer and when would you prefer a film-forming coating?

SAFETY

Brick is a relatively safe material to specify as it typically has no VOCs, unless a sealant is problematic in this regard and then it is often temporary, becoming tolerable after it has dried. Worker safety is one area of concern because dust from cutting brick can harm eyes and lungs, so safety goggles and face masks should be used when dust is created during installation.

What Would You Do? 10.3

What would you do if you visited a job site and discovered that workers were cutting brick and generating dust but were not wearing masks or goggles?

In use, brick is a very hard surface, so dropped items will be more likely to break and falls will be more damaging and painful. It sometimes has a coarse surface, so brushing against it can scuff the finish on items or even scuff skin. As a walking surface it should provide good slip resistance but in order to keep the walking surface easy to cross for wheelchair users or those who use assistive appliances like walkers and canes, you will want to specify uniform brick with flush grout or dry-lay uniform brick without mortar joints at all.

SUSTAINABILITY

According to the Brick Industry Association, brick is produced in 38 of the 50 states, so it is fairly local. Its high thermal mass makes it a good choice for passive solar construction. Because of its small unit dimension, waste is minimized. Brick is one of the most salvaged materials, thanks to its durability. Brick structures hundreds of years old are still in use today. Some bricks have recycled components, such as incinerator ash and waste glass, in their makeup. Petroleum-contaminated soil can be used in making brick.

Brick is inert and is generally tolerable for people with notable toxicity sensitivities. Brick typically has a low embodied energy. The durability of brick exceeds the needs of most interior applications and when compared to other exterior paving materials the relatively high initial cost is paid back in about a decade and its long life and easy maintenance make it much more economical in the long run.

Brick conserves heating and cooling energy. Brick is superior to many other materials in providing thermal mass, reducing heating loads in buildings that can utilize solar radiation.

Salvaged or reclaimed brick is commonly an option driven by a desire for sustainability and perhaps a rugged appearance. The material is often salvaged from buildings that were solid masonry construction with low-fired salmon brick in the interior and better quality burned bricks on the exterior. Reclaimed brick lots often have both of these types of brick all mixed in together. In low-stress environments (interior surfacing applications would usually qualify), this randomized variation may be used to decorative effect; problems occur when using this material for exterior or rigorous environments because low-fired brick does not withstand the elements as well.

Because brick is so durable, even salvaged brick may not have the beautiful patina of age that the design program suggests, so new distressed brick (Figure 10.20) may be specified to achieve this appearance of age when required.

Salvaged brick presents some risks when reused for structural or exterior paving applications, but these risks are not usually significant factors for consideration when specifying interior surfacing. Vertical applications requiring mortar demand good bonds, so bricks must be sufficiently cleaned to allow for good absorption and good bonds. However, because the most significant characteristics influencing brick selection for interiors surfacing are aesthetic, salvaged brick can usually be safely specified.

FIGURE 10.20 Antique brick duplicated in new product is often less costly than reclaimed brick but does not have the sustainability advantage of reclaimed brick. *Old Hampton distressed brick by Pine Hall, Winston-Salem, NC.*

MANAGING BUDGETS

Bricks are sold by the 1,000 but shipped in smaller quantities. Brick tiles are sold by the square foot, just like ceramic tiles.

Estimating for quantity of brick pavers for purposes of budgeting material costs is a simple square-foot takeoff with one extra step to come up with a count. The square-foot takeoff is performed just as it would be for tile or resilient material, by multiplying the length of the area by the width. To convert the square footage to paver quantity, multiply by a factor, which varies with the size of the paver.

If you are using	Multiply by
4" × 8" pavers	4.5
3⅝" × 7⅝"	5.2
3½" × 7¾"	5.1

For example, let's say you are performing a cost-comparison of materials for your client's solarium, which is 15' × 20'. You are considering using 4" × 8" pavers. Multiply 15' × 20' for the square footage of 300 square feet and then multiply that by 4.5 to discover that you need to budget for 1,350 pavers. As with any material, there will be waste during the installation. Brick quantities should be rounded up (similarly to tile quantities) by 10 percent, so add 135 pavers for waste and multiply paver price by 1,485 pavers to have enough material minimally to complete the job. If you are using salvaged material or material that has a lot of variation that you may want to control for, you will add more waste to your estimate.

The same method can be used for all brick sizes. To estimate other brick sizes to quantity of bricks, use the conversion rates below to multiply the square footage by bricks required per square foot.

King size = 4.8
Builder's special = 5.33
Modular = 6.85
Colonial = 4.9
Queen size = 5.2

A mason plus one helper can lay about 700 bricks a day if you are trying to estimate installation costs, as trades often calculate costs based on a day or half-day per "man" required.

Small jobs tend to be priced a little higher relative to big jobs, so your small decorative fireplace in the hotel lounge will seem to have more expensive labor than the large floor area in the lobby if you ask the brick contractor to price them individually. Complexity will also influence the price as will the exact brick selected because the price can be twice as high, or more, for some kinds of specialty brick.

ORGANIZATION OF THE INDUSTRY

The industry tends to divide itself according to the scale of the job. Some firms are set up for economical production of large jobs and other companies will take on small jobs. On a large-scale job you will likely have more than one skill level. There will be laborers who haul and carry material. They are sometimes apprentices and sometimes they are simply laborers who will work in any industry providing manual labor but are not intent on learning a particular skill. Bricklayers will assemble the surfaces or structures and supervisors will oversee the job, and it is likely that most of your interaction will be with the job supervisor who then orchestrates the other work. On a small job the craftsman will fill all those roles.

Table 10.6
Example of how to organize your selection criteria around your design program.

Condition	Program Implications
Is the surface a walking surface?	The installation should be level and flat if it is serving the public so users who shuffle can walk safely.
Should sound be contained in the area or is a thermal mass desired to reduce night-time heating load?	Select dimensional brick rather than veneer to keep sound in and to absorb heat from the sun during the day that can be radiated back into the space at night.
Is this a retrofit situation?	Brick veneer with its thinner dimension will be easier to accommodate within existing allowances.
What are the lighting conditions in the space?	If glare will be a possibility you may want to specify a low-sheen polish, matte topdressings, and avoid very dark colors that will present sharp contrasts. Select for surface reflectance no greater than 40% on floors.
Is this a surface that will be touched or is graffiti a possibility?	Specify to minimize potential for soiling to show, seal the brick so it can be more easily cleaned.
Is an intricate profile desired?	Select material that has accompanying special shapes.
How interested is your client in sustainability?	Consider salvaged brick and low-VOC sealants.

SELECTION CRITERIA

Your design program should be the basis for forming your selection criteria in order to address the unique conditions of your client's job. Table 10.6 is a suggested format for organizing your criteria with some suggestions that will pertain to common program goals.

SPECIFYING

Let's assume that you have a client who owns a small business hotel in Montana and they approached you for help in attracting more customers. You noticed that there was little need for a business hotel but that the area was a vacation destination for families, so you suggest remodeling the public spaces for a more rustic, western atmosphere. You suggest removing a wall between the lobby and the dining room and installing a brick fireplace mass, floor to ceiling, open to both spaces. A spec that you write for cladding the fireplace mass with brick might be something like the following.

SAMPLE SPEC 10.2

Part 1 General Information

1.1 Related Documents

A. Refer to plans and elevations for location and design details.
B. Refer to section details of fireplace surround for location of special brick shapes.
C. Refer to electrical plans for location of uplights recessed in raised hearth.
D. ASTM standards for facing brick C216.

1.2 Summary

A. Fireplace wall to be clad with thin brick veneer with immediate surround of firebox opening having a special profile as shown on elevations, plans, sections, and described in this document. Partition containing prefab fireplace unit to be constructed, by others, of concrete masonry units (CMU).
B. Related work specified elsewhere
   1. Construction of fireplace mass.
   2. Electrical work for convenience outlets and uplights.
C. This contract pertains to the cladding for the CMU fireplace mass and building a decorative surround at the firebox.

1.3 References

A. All work to comply with local fire codes and guidelines from manufacturer of prefab firebox.

1.4 Contractor Submittals

A. Shop drawings for approval showing all special shapes, location of thin brick veneer, and accessory brick veneer pieces creating the illusion of dimensional brick at veneer edges.
B. Material safety data sheet for veneer panels, mastic, and mortar.
C. Mortar samples for approval on single panel of veneer demonstrating material and finish to be used. Sample may be used in completed work if it is indistinguishable from other panels upon completion.
D. Sample of dimensional brick and special shapes to be used at firebox opening.

1.5 Quality Assurance

A. All products specified to be purchased from a single manufacturer and to match control samples submitted.
B. Installation to be performed by experienced journeyman bricklayers, certified by manufacturer of veneer panels to install the product, and by the International Union of Bricklayers and Allied Crafts Union.

1.6 Delivery, Storage, and Handling

A. Material to be transported to arrive in clean, dry condition. Mortar and mastic to arrive in original manufacturers' unopened containers. Protect material so it remains clean and dry until installation.

1.7 Maintenance of Installation

A. Upon completion construction to remain undisturbed until mortar and mastics have cured sufficiently to withstand movement. Temperature between 40ºF and 100ºF is an acceptable range for fresh mortar.

Part 2 Products

2.1 General Information

A. Brick veneer, special shapes, and dimensional brick as shown on drawings to be provided and installed in accordance with specs, drawings, and manufacturer recommendations.

2.2 Manufacturers

A. All brick, veneer, and dimensional and special shapes to be purchased from Best Brick, 1234 Industrial Drive, Anywhere, ST 12345.
B. Mybest Mortar and Grout 5678, Industrial Drive, Anywhere, ST 12345.

2.3 Products

A. Wild West thin brick veneer panels.
B. Wild West thin brick corners.
C. Western Sunset Queen Size $2\frac{5}{8}" \times 2\frac{5}{8}" \times 7\frac{5}{8}"$.
D. Watertable Rowlock.
E. Watertable Rowlock Internal Corners.
F. Clubcar Mortar.

Part 3 Execution

3.1 Examination

A. Confirm that fireplace mass construction is in acceptable condition to ensure that quality installation can be completed, plumb and square with openings as defined in dimensioned elevations. Written dimensions precede scale.
B. Notify designer regarding any unsatisfactory prepwork performed by others.

3.2 Preparation

A. Clean surface prior to commencing work.
B. Corrugated ties to be fastened to CMUs at recommended intervals.
C. Dampen substrate surface to form proper masonry bond.
D. Protect surrounding surfaces from mortar spatter.

3.3 Installation

A. Construct firebox surround in accordance with approved shop drawings.
B. Masonry courses to be of uniform dimension having mortar joints of uniform thickness.
C. Install thin brick veneer modular units to produce consistent width for all mortar joints.
D. Remove excess mortar and mortar smears as work progresses.
E. Rake mortar joints to not less than $\frac{3}{8}"$.

3.4 Post Installation

A. Clean all defective or inconsistent mortar joints and repoint with new mortar.
B. Work to be ready for inspection by owner upon final completion.

RELATED MATERIAL

Brick is not the only material made from clay that you will specify. Tile is also made from clay and as is the case in many instances where materials have a lot in common, you will find there are some products that span the distance between brick and tile. Glazed terra-cotta cladding seen on the exterior of buildings is rather like brick and somewhat like tile. Thicker tile material that is suitable for exterior as well as interior application, whether it be made of clay, concrete, or other material, will be somewhat akin to brick. Although it is convenient to divide material into distinct categories, this does not always serve you; as a designer it is expected that you will come up with novel uses of materials beyond what is typical. You will be well served if you consider the characteristics of each material rather than assigning it to a category of expected use.

SUMMARY

In this chapter we reviewed the basic properties of clay products as well as some alternatives to clay products. Variations between the various tile and brick products were discussed. Criteria used to evaluate circumstances and products to make good selections for your program goals including materiality, sustainability, and installation were noted for your consideration. Budget considerations and how to specify these products for your interior design project goals were discussed. An overview of the tile industry from production through installation gave you a sense of how to manage your tile and brick installations.

WEB SEARCH ACTIVITIES

1. Search for *large format, super-thin tile* to see how far tile technology is pushing limits for size and thinness.
2. Search for rigid tile products that contain more than one material. These tiles may be concrete-type products that contain semiprecious stones. They may resemble terrazzo to the extent that you decide they *are* terrazzo, even though they are not identified as such. Many will contain recycled material. These products will be unique and some of them may only be available from one manufacturer.
3. Perform an image search for each of the tile bodies (*glass tile*, *ceramic tile*, etc.) listed in Table 10.1 and compare them visually.
4. Perform an image search for *tile trim*, *trim tile*, and *decorative tile trim* to get clear on the distinction between:

    Tile trim, made of tile, that performs a function like terminating the tile area or bending around a corner.

    Tile trim, made of tile, that performs a decorative function, creating a pattern.

    Trim made of metal or plastic that provides a concealed ending point to your field tile installation.

5. Search for the various substrates listed in Table 10.2, and notice the characteristics, sizes, and thicknesses described.
6. Search for a *tile MSDS* (*material safety data sheet*) and read through to get an idea of the safety of tile. Perform a search for *grout sealant MSDS* and read about the potential hazards for these products. There will likely be some variation due to different formulas.
7. Search for a spec guide or master spec for a tile product. The Tile Council of North America (TCNA; www.tileusa.com) has links to their members' Web sites and some of them will have spec guides for their products, but you should be able to find what you are looking for by doing a general search for *tile master specifications*.
8. Perform an image search for pictures of a *clay quarry*. Perform the same kind of search for images of a *lime quarry*. It is difficult to make the case that sand-lime bricks are more sustainable, except that they do use ash that is left over from burning coal for electricity in their formulation.
9. Perform an image search for *brick shapes* and review the different shapes that various manufacturers offer.
10. Go to a brick manufacturer's Web site and search their product line for different surfaces they offer. The Brick Industry Association's Web site is a good place to start: www.gobrick.com. Recently it was possible to perform a search by state; if that is still an option, select your state to see how many brick manufacturers are close to your location.

11. Review the names for the different orientations of brick (*stretcher*, *rowlock*, etc.) then revisit the images of brick shapes you found above. Review their names. Do the profiles make sense in light of their orientations when you envision how you might use them in a design?

12. Search for a spec guide for a brick installation. You may perform a general search or go to the site of an organization associated with brick, like the Brick Industry Association, www.gobrick.com. The spec guide will be found under tabs labeled "Technical Notes" or "Architects." You may have to hunt around a little.

PERSONAL ACTIVITIES

1. Look at pictures in a kitchen and bath magazine or perform an image search online and find pictures of tile installations for *tub surrounds* or *shower surrounds*. Notice the various uses of trim tiles both decorative and functional.

2. Study the plan for one of your projects or find a plan in a trade magazine showing the kind of work you would like to do. Consider the conditions that you would anticipate for that design program once the client has started using it. Select an area where you would use a tile. In a manner similar to Table 10.3, make a list of conditions at the site and the material under consideration. Draw up a list of implications for your design.

3. Using the plan and selection criteria for your project, or a plan found in a trade magazine and your imagined selection criteria, select a tile product for a specific area. Using Sample Spec 10.1 in this chapter as an example, write a specification for the tile and the installation.

4. Select a location in your own project where you could specify brick. Imagine the details that you would use or locate an image that shows a brick installation with details that you like. Decide what information should be shown in a drawing and what information is best conveyed in a spec. Using Sample Spec 10.2 in this chapter as an example, write a spec for the brick and the installation.

SUMMARY QUESTIONS

1. How do the properties of the different tile bodies differ?

2. Which tiles can receive a penetrating sealer? Which tiles cannot?

3. What does *through-body color* mean and which tiles will have this feature? What benefit does it offer?

4. What special instructions might you give the tile installer who is adhering transparent glass tile to the substrate?

5. What does it mean if a glass tile is *picture-framing*? What does it mean if an unglazed terra-cotta tile is picture-framed?

6. What grout joint width is common for stone tile? Would that width apply to distressed stone—why or why not?

7. Which tile bodies can more easily contain recycled material?

8. Which unglazed tiles are impervious to staining? Which are not?

9. Sketch the profile of each trim tile and note what each is used for.

10. What alternates are there for trim tiles?

11. What are the different setting methods and when would you use each?

12. Under what circumstances would you approve of a dry fit? When would a dry fit not be necessary?

13. When would you fill a space with grout? When would you caulk a space or use some other flexible joint?

14. When would you seal tile? Which grouts must be sealed? Which grouts do not require sealants?

15. What specific kinds of options are available for your client with an interest in sustainability?

16. What material and installation characteristics will raise the cost of your project?

17. Which parties in the supply chain will sell to designers, architects, and shops but not to end users?

18. What is the distinction between top soil and clay?
19. What are the characteristics of brick?
20. What are the functional differences between dimensional brick and brick veneers?
21. What are the different methods of producing brick and how do they affect the brick product?
22. What sealants and finishes pertain to brick?
23. What is mortar for?
24. What are the common finishes for mortar joints?
25. Which mortar joints are likely to darken the overall appearance of the brick surface?
26. Must vertical dimensional brick surfaces have mortar? Horizontal?
27. What are the names of the different faces of a brick (the different orientations)?
28. What are special cautions pertaining to film-formers when you are specifying sealants?
29. What safety issues pertain to brick?
30. What characteristics make brick sustainable? Is there anything about brick that damages the environment?
31. What factors can increase the cost of your installation?
32. What kind of certifications can a brick installer acquire?
33. What pieces of information are essential when specifying the product in order to ensure that the correct brick arrives at your job site?

Chapter 11

STONE

Key Terms

Book-matched
Calcite-based stones
Gauged
Gneiss
Honed
Limestone
Lippage
Marble
Metamorphic stones
Mud veins
Onyx
Penetrating sealant
Polished
Quartzite
Running match
Sedimentary stone
Serpentine
Slabs
Slate
Soapstone
Spall
Tolerance
Topdressing
Travertine

Objectives

After reading this chapter, you should be able to:

- Identify the various stone types that interior designers typically specify.
- Describe the differences between the different stone types and suggest appropriate uses for them.
- Understand what, in addition to the stone type, you need to select or specify to complete your installation.
- Understand what surface textures are typical for stone that you will specify and what those textures are like.
- Understand the concept of matching and sequenced lots.
- Make decisions pertaining to sealing and maintaining stone surfaces.
- Inspect stone installations for quality and qualify tradespeople appropriate for your jobs.
- Understand safety and sustainability issues pertaining to stone.
- Form a general idea of how the industry is organized.
- Identify what kinds of tradespeople participate in stone fabrication and installation and what services are available.
- Understand what kind of information must go into your stone spec.
- Work with resources.

Stone is generally a tough, durable material although characteristics vary greatly from one stone to another. When a stone is described as soft in this chapter, it is meant to refer to its hardness in relation to other stones. It might be said that stone has personality; some stones are flamboyant, others restrained. They can seem formal or casual or rustic. The appearance of some stones is austere and others nearly baroque. Their functional characteristics vary just as widely and understanding the characteristics of the different types of stone can give you a head start in comprehending the characteristic of a particular stone that you might have in mind for your client's job. The stone discussed in this chapter is stone that is referred to as *veneer*, meaning it is not structural or self-supporting but is fastened to the structure. An example would be the stone mantel that is fastened to the wall around a firebox opening or stone slabs adhered to walls or floors.

FIGURE 11.1 Stone will vary considerably from one lot to the next within the same species. This material not only ranges from lot to lot but there is great variation within the slab so multiple pieces cut from the same slab could display very different markings. This Louise Blue quartzite is a typical example. *Quartzite from Marble and Granite Supply International, Evanston, IL.*

CHARACTERISTICS

Within each type of stone there is a range of hardness, resistance, grain, and color to be found. Individual **slabs** of stone (stone pieces usually 1¾ inches [2 centimeters] or 2¼ inches [3 centimeters] thick and approximately 5' × 8' size) can present unexpected variation in coloration and markings. Stone may vary from one area of the quarry to another so occasionally material taken from different parts of the same quarry looks different.

When you visit stone yards to preview options for your jobs, it is important to view slabs with your drawings in hand so that you can visualize how the material will look when it is cut to size and installed. As an example, the variation in the slab in Figure 11.1 could cause the material cut from it to appear to be two different materials if a small piece from the upper left were used on a small section of counter and a small section of the upper right was used on an adjacent section. If you were the designer on a job that required several small pieces of stone, you might decide that the **limestone** in Figure 11.2 would allow for more visual consistency from one area of the stone to another area. (Limestone is a calcite-based stone, generally softer than **marble**.)

FIGURE 11.2 Limestone is generally a more visually consistent stone with very different performance properties than quartzite, so this is not intended to suggest that one could be substituted for the other. Multiple pieces cut from this slab would be visually similar to one another.

Point of Emphasis 11.1

Stone is often named after the quarry that it comes from and it simplifies sourcing a stone if you know the name the quarry uses. Sometimes a quarry will have more than one name for the material it delivers. Because stone is a natural product, its characteristics may vary from one end of a quarry to another. As they work the quarry, they may encounter material that looks so dissimilar to material from another part of the quarry that they give it a new name to avoid confusion.

Another reason that stone may not be referred to by its quarry name is that vendors want to avoid price comparisons and want the material they hold to seem to be exclusive to their stone yard. They will rename the stone so you cannot "shop it" by searching by name.

If you intend to use tile and slab of the same stone on your job site, you can imagine that this variation throughout the quarry would result in tile material appearing different from slab for the same reason. It is not always easy to get material that is visually similar. If you select tile and slab from the same vendor, it may be a little easier to confirm that you have a companionable match. It is rare to get permission to open multiple boxes of tile to view coloration and graining the way you can when viewing slabs.

Identifying Stone Characteristics

Within the general categories of stones, visual characteristics such as graining or visual texture can be predicted. **Granite** (a hard, crystalline rock composed of feldspar, quartz, and other minerals) often has a pronounced speckled texture, marble has veins, limestones are generally visually smoother, and so on. General categories can also be used as a guide to porosity, abrasion resistance, resistance to etching by acids, and other physical properties even though there will be variations within each kind of stone.

Visual and Functional Characteristics

Both the mineral composition and the way it was formed create the stone and this results in different visual characteristics that you can use to identify the stone types as you make selections for your client. **Sedimentary stone** is stone built up over time by disintegration of animal, vegetable, and mineral sources, and its stratified composition shows the resulting veining; **metamorphic stones** are minerals that have undergone a chemical alteration due to heat and pressure of being buried under the earth, etc. Performance characteristics of metamorphic stones cannot be deduced from the classification in the way that they can be from the subcategories (marble, slate, granite, etc.). Marble and granite are both metamorphic stones. Granite is a kind of metamorphic stone called **gneiss**, which is a common sort of stone whose formation generally leaves it with a "granular" distribution of minerals and colors. Marble and limestone are chemically very similar but have different characteristics because marble has metamorphosed.

Point of Emphasis 11.2

Because marble has similar chemistry when compared to limestone, it shares characteristics that depend on chemical makeup with limestone, the most significant of which is that they are both etched by acids. Because it has metamorphosed, it is more durable in other ways. It is denser and more impervious to staining; it can be polished to a higher sheen.

The ingredients that lend color to the stone may be from organic material, in which case colors could fade in direct sunlight. For instance, the color black results from the presence of tar or petroleum, both organic, so black-colored marble will fade in intense sunlight. Mineral colorants do not fade although some iron-based colors can "rust." It has been said that dark-colored stones that have a **polished** surface will scratch easily. This is functionally true because they will show scratching more easily. A dark stone that is as hard and abrasion resistant as a light stone may become hazy because small surface scratches show up better on dark stone (light scratches on dark surfaces rather than light scratches on light surfaces). Unlike fading, scratched stone can be restored by polishing or touched up with a **topdressing**, which is a surface coating applied to stone.

> **Helpful Hint 11.1**
>
> Some stones fade in sunlight. If sun angles limit exposure, only a restricted portion of the floor will fade. There will be instances when you will want to model the sun angles to confirm that the floor will not fade so unevenly that it will cause it to be removed before the end of its useful life.

Lime or **calcite-based stones** such as marble, travertine, and limestone are susceptible to being etched by acids. Marble and travertine are denser than limestone so they can be polished to a more reflective sheen than limestone. Hard, dense materials can be polished to a high reflectivity, but porous materials can never achieve a high shine from polishing and will need to be topdressed if gloss is desired.

> **Helpful Hint 11.2**
>
> A high-sheen topdressing on a porous stone like limestone or a rough stone like slate will look unnatural and a little "plastic-looking." Always evaluate samples of the material with and without the sealants to make sure the stone you specify will look and perform to your expectations.

Tests of Physical Characteristics

As is the case with most materials, interior designers perform very few tests on materials, relying instead on information provided by experts in the material itself. There are, however, some simple tests that designers can do in the interest of due diligence and you should review the results with your client when you make your material recommendations. For absorbency, put a drop of lemon juice on the stone and see how quickly it soaks in. If oil will be present, test with oil; if abrasion is expected, test with emery cloth. You should request sealed and unsealed samples to understand the product's natural characteristics, and its characteristics after it has been sealed. This is especially important for field-applied sealants that are to be reapplied as part of maintenance. You will have no control over the diligence of the maintenance schedule but you are responsible for the soundness of your selection (even if it is not maintained as directed) so select a stone that is serviceable in its natural state whenever possible.

> **Helpful Hint 11.3**
>
> You will need to determine which will be more likely in the interior that you are specifying—scratches or stains. Light or dark, polished or honed, material with comparable hardness will scratch and absorb stains equally but scratches will show up more on dark and polished stones. Stains will show up more on light stones. You may have to select harder material if you are selecting a dark stone in order to minimize the appearance of scratches.

STONE SPECIES

Stones that you may consider specifying in your interior design projects include granite, soapstone, marble, serpentine, travertine, slate, limestone, quartzite, and **onyx**.

Granite

A very hard, dense stone, granite has a crystalline, quartz structure and is often relatively uniform in visual texture as shown in Figure 11.3 (grains range from small to medium). Some granites are very consistent with very little visual "movement." Other granites present their granular texture in swirls and streams, like the Milky Way, as seen in

FIGURE 11.3 Granite in these samples demonstrates the variety of markings within the species. Granite is a very durable stone but is often considered to be too "modern" for some installations.

Figure 11.4. Granite is hard and dense, so it can be polished to a high gloss as well as several degrees of reflectivity. It is strong enough to withstand the abuse of flaming (the surface is alternately heated and cooled, so small chips flake off leaving pocked-texture, slip-resistant surface). The most impervious surface treatment is polished with a subsurface sealant.

Granite is generally preferred where resistance to acids and abrasion is important because it is generally not etched by common household acids the way marble and limestone can be etched by orange juice, or the citric acid in shaving cream. While this is generally true it may vary in specific instances because granite is a natural product and not grown in a lab, and some granites also contain calcite material, so those portions of the stone can be etched with acids.

FIGURE 11.4 When tradition is required, a granite with more movement seems less modern in appearance.

Soapstone

Soapstone, a variety known for its stain-proof qualities, is a tough and durable stone with a talc and quartz component (very strong mineral). It does not react to heat, so there is no danger in setting hot pots directly on a soapstone surface. It is fairly impervious, but it is traditional to seal it with mineral oil. (See Figure 11.5.)

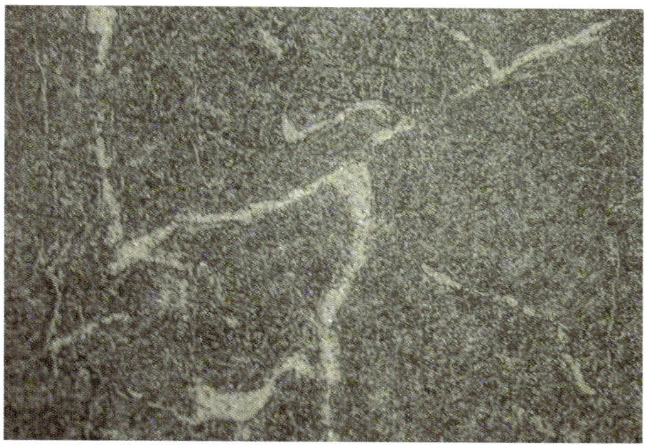

FIGURE 11.5 This soapstone is not yet sealed. As it is oiled over the life of an installation it continues to darken and old soapstone installations look almost black.

Application of mineral oil darkens the soapstone over time, and eventually it darkens into a deep charcoal color. After installation, mineral oil is reapplied every week for a couple of months, then periodically as part of normal maintenance. People do not always elect to seal it if installed where detergents will be used. Undressed soapstone (no mineral oil applied) will still darken with use but will not match any oiled soapstone in the same vicinity.

Slab sizes are often smaller than for some other stones, but with effort, soapstone can be located in large slab sizes and 9-foot sections without seams might be possible.

Marble

Marble, a crystalline, metamorphic stone, is typically recognized by its veined appearance as in Figure 11.6. Marble is recrystallized limestone (sedimentary rock). This is why it is called metamorphic, which means that it has undergone a chemical change. It is softer than granite, and sensitive to acid and will soak up oil. The most common textures are polished and **honed** (having a smooth, matte finish). Small scratches are likely to occur on polished surfaces. Honed surfaces will not show scratches as readily, so they will maintain their

FIGURE 11.6 As is true for all stones, there is a wide range of visual characteristics among marble with color and markings unique to each individual lot on top of the variations from one kind of marble to another. *Negro Protoro marble from Marble and Granite Supply International, Evanston, IL.*

FIGURE 11.7 This white Carrara slab has the cuts marked in painter's tape so the fabricator knows where to cut the pieces required for the job. *Carrara marble from Marble and Granite Supply International, Evanston, IL.*

appearance better, although honed surfaces are more vulnerable than polished surfaces to absorbing stains.

It is very important to hand-select the actual slabs to be used; you may want to mark off the exact area of stone to be used as some veining can be visually strong and placement is important. Figure 11.7 shows a slab with the cuts marked. Vendors may ask that you mark the cuts with soap or chalk rather than tape because some adhesives do not come off without solvents, which can etch marble. If a change should occur after you have taped the surface, you may have to repolish the slab surface. The reflection off a polished surface will highlight veins that contain softer material so do not take polish to the same degree as the surrounding surface. Very soft mineral veins are sometimes called **mud veins**. Your experienced fabricator might be consulted to evaluate them for stability before you finalize your selection because marble likes to crack along mud veins.

Helpful Hint 11.4

You can test the relative hardness of a marble tile by ear. Balance a marble tile on your fingertips and rap on it with your knuckles. Hard marbles will ring like a bell and soft marbles will produce a soft thud. This does not work with other kinds of stone but provides a quick comparison when shopping for marble.

Marble has variety in visual and performance characteristics within the species. Some marbles are quite soft; you may find hard limestones (like French limestone), typically a softer species than marble, that equal the density of softer marbles (like Greek Thassos).

Serpentine

Serpentine is an igneous metamorphic rock named for the prominent mineral that defines it—serpentinite. Often referred to as green marble, it is actually a different kind of stone altogether. It is about as hard as, or slightly harder than, marble. Some serpentines, like some marbles, have been reported to have warped in wet areas, so make sure you use material that is thick enough not to soak through in the presence of standing water if this will be likely in your installation. Installers often set this material with dry adhesives instead of portland cement adhesives for this reason. It is dense and homogenous in structure, with a fine grain and no cleavage lines. Colors normally range from olive green to greenish black, but the presence of impurities in the rock may give it other colors. The most common textures are polished and honed.

Some types of serpentine are subject to deterioration due to weathering and are useful only for interior work. Black serpentine is highly resistant to chemical attack and is useful in situations where it is likely to come in contact with moisture-borne chemicals.

Travertine

Travertine (Figures 11.8 and 11.9), which is a dense limestone formed by materials deposited as hot springs bubbled up, is often characterized as a marble because it can take a polish. Cross-cut travertine has holes in its face that are often filled with a resin, or material similar to grout, especially if the stone is to be used on horizontal surfaces. Vein-cut travertine does not exhibit the voids that cross-cut does and often presents a very linear grain. The most common textures are polished and honed.

The fill used to plug the natural voids in cross-cut travertine does not polish to the same high sheen that the stone does. The stone acquires a sheen from polishing while the fill remains dull, so even filled it will retain the visual interest created by the holes. Harder travertines have characteristics similar to marble.

FIGURE 11.8 Travertine has holes in the slabs formed when it was percolated into existence. These holes can be left unfilled in vertical applications.

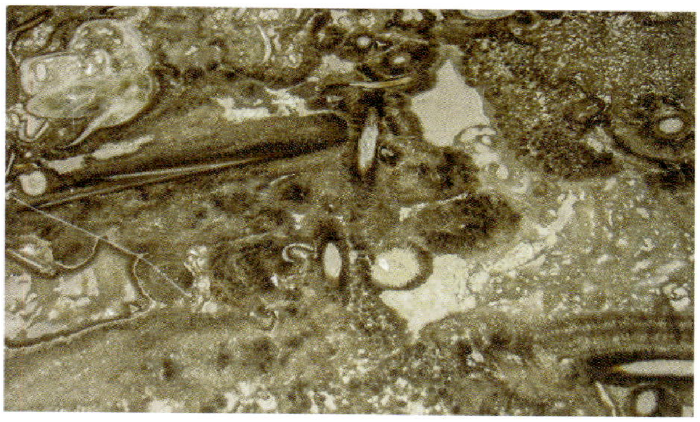

FIGURE 11.9 Travertine is filled for horizontal applications. This travertine has been filled with a light fill for contrast.

FIGURE 11.10 Classic cleft face that slate is known for.

FIGURE 11.11 Limestone sample. *Marble and Granite Supply International, Evanston, IL.*

Slate

Most slates will naturally have a cleft face as in Figure 11.10. Occasionally a **slate** will be stable enough to maintain a flat surface after the cleft face has been abraded off. Even then, the surface may **spall** (thin, waferlike chips may leave the surface) over time. While some slates are prone to spall and have cleft textures on their faces, other slates are very smooth and even. These slates may be **gauged**, meaning they are ground to a consistent thickness throughout. Slate comes in a wide range of colors from yellows through pinks, reds, greens, and grays with some kinds of slate exhibiting a wide range within each slab, while other slates are consistent in color throughout.

Some slates have no cleft at all. They are so consistent and flat that they are used under the felt of pool tables for an indisputably flat surface. Slates from Vermont are smooth and consistent when gauged.

Even though the components of slate are quite hard, the matrix may be soft so slate may soak up stains or scratch easily. In addition to penetrating sealers (which should be used on all stones) slate may be top-dressed with wax or acrylic to enhance the color and provide a slight sheen. Slate is not described as polished or honed because the cleft face does not allow for this variety.

Limestone

Generally, limestone is a soft stone, although some French limestones are hard enough to take a low polish, similar to a hone on marble (Figure 11.11). They are a calcite-based stone, sometimes formed from the disintegration of shells. Occasionally, when the shells are still visible and not crushed beyond recognition, the stone is referred to as shell stone. Shell stone is often more porous than other limestones. Because they are calcite-based like marble and travertine, limestones are also susceptible to etching by acids. Most common surfaces range from a "flamed"-looking surface to a high hone.

FIGURE 11.12 Quartzite is a very hard natural stone with dramatic variation among the different types.

FIGURE 11.13 Louise Blue quartzite displays many colors in one stone.

Quartzite

Quartzite is made up of grains of quartz sand cemented together with silica and is usually distinguishable by its coarse, crystalline appearance. This natural stone is not to be mistaken for man-made quartzite which is a composite containing quartz and is also referred to as quartzite. The quartzite discussed here is natural stone quarried from the earth, not the man-made stone that contains natural quartzite and a resin (a material discussed in Chapter 7, Plastic Materials). Colors typically include red, brown, gray, tan, and ivory, often with several colors being found in one slab (Figures 11.12 and 11.13). Even though quartzite is very hard and dense, it is not always available in the large sizes you might expect for dense stones. Some lots of quartzite are available only in smaller slab sizes so confirm size before finalizing your design. If fabricators will have to piece more pieces together to cover the surface because slabs are small, or sharpen their cutting tools because of the density of the material, they will charge more for fabrication.

Onyx

Onyx is a term applied to translucent varieties of many different kinds of stones. It is most accurately a microcrystalline quartz, but there are calcite-based stones containing quartz that are also referred to as onyx. It is so translucent light shines through it (Figures 11.14 and 11.15). Designers often exploit this characteristic by backlighting the material. Table 11.1 summarizes relative characteristics of various stones.

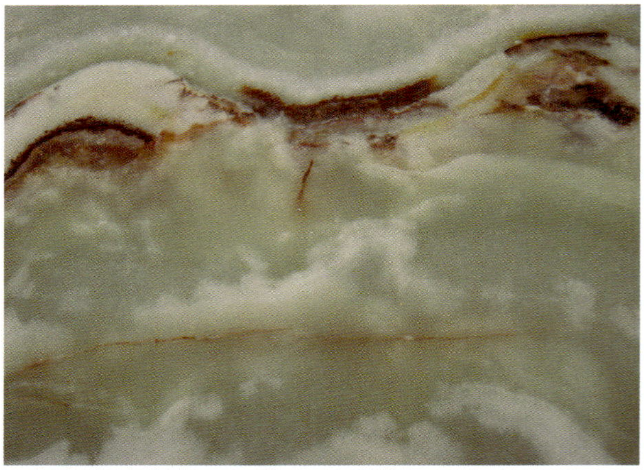

FIGURE 11.14 Onyx is prized for its translucency. Onyx tiles are sometimes used as lighting diffusers as they transmit so much light.

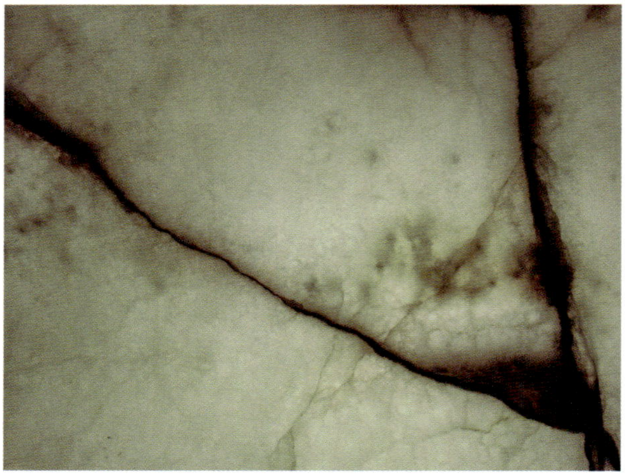

FIGURE 11.15 Onyx is translucent so light will pass through it when it is back-lit.

Table 11.1
Comparison of the general characteristics of stone types.

Stones (in order of general hardness)	Characteristics	Typical Finishes	Considerations
Quartzite	Very hard stone Coarse, crystalline appearance Metamorphosed sandstone (but much harder) Many colors	High polish achievable as well as full range of sheen levels Penetrating sealer	Hardest category of stone; good stain- and abrasion-resistant surface
Granite	Crystalline, quartz structure Hard, abrasion resistant Low absorption so good stain resistance Many colors	Any finish from high polish through honed as well as textures such as flamed Penetrating sealer	Appearance may be uniform or have movement
Serpentine	Limited colors: pale gray through green to black Sometimes mistaken for green marble or for jade More abrasion resistant and acid resistant than marble	Polished finish is typical Penetrating sealer	With marblelike appearance but lacking vulnerability to acid, it is often substituted for countertops
Marble	Calcite-based stone Veined appearance Multiple colors Metamorphosed limestone (much harder)	Polished and honed with degree of polish limited by hardness Penetrating sealer and possible topdressing	Calcite-based stones can be etched by mild acids (like orange juice)
Travertine	Calcite-based stone Colors generally tan and brown through red and orange Cross-cut travertine has holes that may be filled	Polished and honed Filled or unfilled holes Penetrating sealer and possible topdressing	Calcite-based stones can be etched by mild acids (like orange juice)
Limestone	Calcite-based stone Colors generally gray and tan through pink and brown Softer stone, absorbent	Honed (too soft for polish) Penetrating sealer	Calcite-based stones can be etched by mild acids (like orange juice)
Slate	Face cleft to smooth Hard, durable surface Many colors; some slates present multiple colors, some are consistent	Honed (will not polish) Penetrating sealer and possible topdressing	Cleft faces may continue to spall over life of installation
Soapstone	Tough, durable stone Does not react to heat Typically given a mineral oil finish	Honed, natural texture does not achieve a high polish Mineral oil sealer	Finished with repeated applications of oil that eventually darken it to nearly black
Onyx	Translucent, veined appearance Softer stone, not abrasion resistant	Polished finish typical, enhances translucency Penetrating sealer	Can be etched by food acids if containing calcite

OPTIONS TO SPECIFY

When you are writing your specification you will include a number of descriptors besides the location of the surface and the species of the stone. This will vary with the job as appropriate but most of your stone specs will include the following.

Surface Textures

You will designate a surface texture (Figure 11.16) for the stone that you specify. Remember that soft stones cannot achieve a high shine. Stone is frequently brought into your vendor's warehouse with its face already ground to a sheen level that will be called polished or honed. If the finished face is not the sheen you require, you will have to budget to have it reground. High polish can be achieved with dense stones while low polish is the extent of sheen achievable by softer stones. Honed finishes may be applied to hard or soft stones and also range from high to low in the degree of sheen, a high hone or low hone.

Designers may find what they are looking for in the stone yard but occasionally you will have the option of designating the surface or you may decide that the surface should be reground to a different sheen. If you find material that has the properties that you are looking for but it does not have the sheen level that you need, you may decide to have the material reground to a different texture at an additional charge.

FIGURE 11.16 The appearance (and slip resistance) of stone surfacing is partly dependent on the surface texture. This granite is visually quite different in its flamed (left) and polished (right) forms. The color of the flamed sample could be enhanced to the color of the polished but the gloss would not be duplicated without a topdressing (which would then interfere with slip resistance—the primary reason that granite is specified to be flamed). *Samples produced by Marble and Granite Supply International, Evanston, IL.*

Texture affects not only the way the surface feels, it alters the apparent color of the stone as well. Higher polishes look darker than other textures. This is a trick of the light and not a change in the material. If a deep color is required of a textured surface you might want to specify a special, color-enhancing sealer.

General descriptions for surface texture are:

- *Polished* produces a surface as nearly like a mirror as the stone will achieve (soft stones are not capable of a mirror polish). This treatment applies to marble, granite, serpentine, limestone, and travertine.

> **Helpful Hint 11.5**
>
> The harder the stone is, the higher a polish it can achieve. This means that you have lots of options for sheen level if your selected stone is hard but will be restricted to softer sheens if your selection is soft. The higher sheen levels will be more impervious to staining.

- *Honed* produces a duller surface than polishing with no markings; often described in terms of degrees (high hone, medium hone, low hone); the degrees are due partly to the amount of polishing the surface receives and partly to the hardness of the stone. A polished limestone (a relatively soft stone) can have the appearance of a honed or high-hone marble. This treatment applies to all stones except sandstone and slate.
- *Flamed*, also called thermal, uses controlled heating and cooling of the surface to produce the texture as chips spall off leaving a dimpled surface. This treatment applies to granite and limestone.
- *Sandblasted* surfaces have fine stippling from blasting by an abrasive. This treatment applies to all stones.
- *Shot-blasted* surfaces are achieved in a manner similar to sandblasting but instead of sand, steel balls are used.
- *Bush-hammered* surfaces are hit with a multipointed tool that dislodges material to dimple the surface with irregular dimples.
- *Brushed-face* surfaces are mechanically distressed with a dimpled surface resulting from a process similar to wire brushing.

- *Tumbling* is restricted to tiles. Marble tiles are tumbled in a drum to simulate centuries of use and exposure to the elements. The resulting tiles have a hazy surface covered with small scratches, chipped corners, and some inconsistency in size and thickness. Your client may prefer a waxed finish to keep the dark colors from looking quite so dusty, or you might specify a color-enhancing sealer to restore the color while still retaining the rustic quality of the tumbled tile. Slabs are mechanically distressed (beaten) to approximate tumbling.

Helpful Hint 11.6

Tumbled or distressed stone tiles have irregular edges and so require wider grout joints and sometimes more expert setting of tile. When tile has been mechanically distressed or tumbled, surface irregularities along edges may hold grout. Just as would be the case for porous tile, distressed tile should be sealed with grout release prior to grouting.

- *Sawn-face* treatment produces a surface in which arcing saw marks are visible. This relatively rusticated treatment can be given to any stone.
- *Leather finish* is a wire brush process that acts on the softer minerals in the slab, wearing them away, creating a surface that undulates.

Helpful Hint 11.7

In areas susceptible to abrasion, a honed finish will better retain its appearance than a polished one. Flamed and sandblasted surfaces provide better traction but are harder to clean than polished or honed surfaces.

Profiles

Slab materials that will have an exposed edge when installed (as on a countertop, for instance) require an edge profile designation. They should be specified as flat polished or as receiving a profile. The cost of the job will be increased according to the length of the exposed edge because polishing and shaping are additional steps and the work is priced by the lineal foot. Individual shops will often have knives set up to produce edges they have ground in the past. The shop may also include the cost of a new profile in its bid if you cannot use one of the profiles for the knives on hand. Often the shop will charge only the cost to purchase the new knife so the cost of a custom edge is not usually prohibitive, but it makes economical sense to try to use a profile that the shop is already equipped to produce.

> **Point of Emphasis 11.3**
> Straight runs of a countertop are often ground into profile shapes by machine, but curves must often be ground by hand, so it is difficult to make, say, an ogee edge, look exactly the same in shape and sheen along a straight run as on a curve.

These profiles (Figure 11.17) can be combined to create more complex profiles and, in the case where two layers of stone are laminated together to present a thicker edge, they can conceal the seam. The characteristics of the stone must be considered when selecting an edge and deciding whether to build up the edge by laminating. When considering the profile, remember that dense, fine stones can have finer details and more complex profiles than more porous stones. When building up stone edges make sure the resulting thickness does not interfere with the finished height of surfaces or overhang on the face of the cabinet. The mitered angle

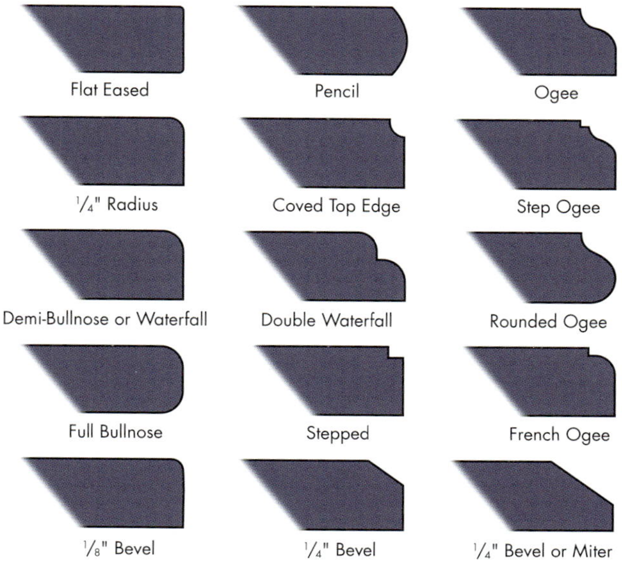

FIGURE 11.17 The exposed edges of stone slab can be detailed with profiles that are ground by machine and finished by hand.

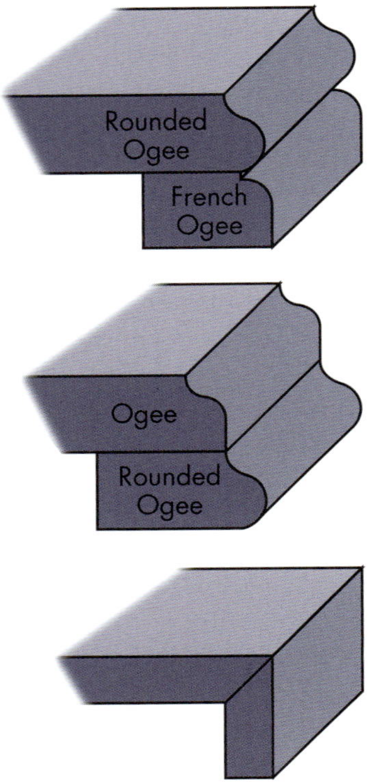

FIGURE 11.18 Built-up edges give the appearance of a thicker slab. Designers plan details to conceal the seam.

on the right in Figure 11.18 could interfere with doors and drawers opening if it extends too far downward. It is difficult, and therefore expensive, to match the markings on the piece added to a built-up edge. The markings on the top slab will not always continue onto the facing piece added, so this is something to discuss with your client before finalizing the selection of a built-up edge and profile. Exposed edges of cutouts for sinks will have to be built up too, if you are to avoid giving away the fact that the material was built up. Few clients will insist on this difficult detail but you can tell that the top was built up if you do not do this, so make sure your client is okay with that before you allow a single layer at the cutouts paired with a built-up edge.

What Would You Do? 11.1

Consider the built-up stone edge profiles shown here.

Of the profiles shown, which would you be least likely to use as the edge of a kitchen countertop for a busy family with children?

Why?

Shaped profiles are extremely difficult on cutouts and typically a square edge will be specified for cutouts even if more elaborate profiles are specified for other edges.

Match

Stone slabs are cut from a stone block the way slices of bread are cut from a loaf. There are obviously two faces to every slab. One will be the finished face and one the back. If stone faces are finished for **running match** and your job requires mirror-image **book-matched** slabs (Figure 11.19) the backs of alternating slabs will have to be polished at an additional expense. Just as if your job requires a honed surface and the material was brought in only polished, the slabs will have to be reground at additional expense.

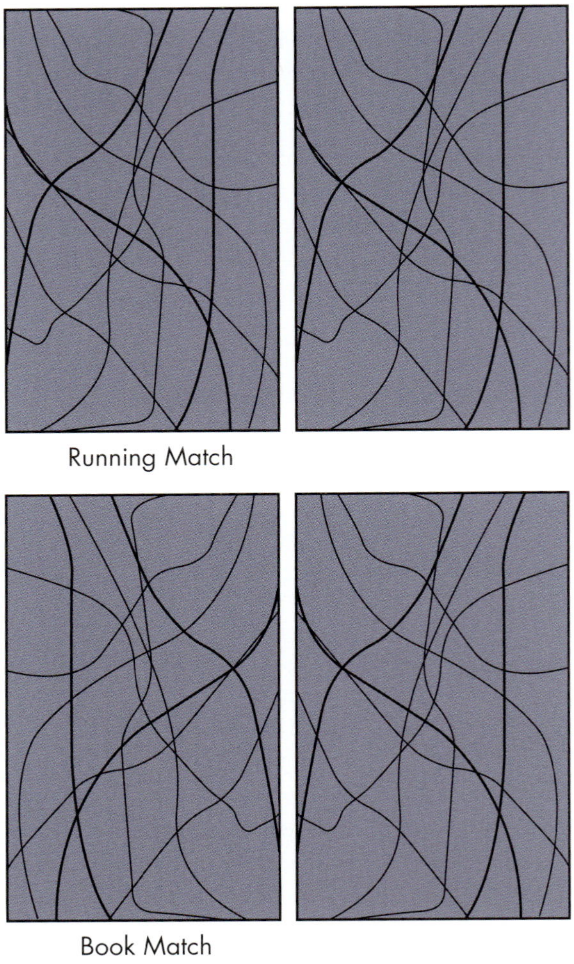

FIGURE 11.19 Slab matches must be specified for stone in the same way that wood veneers must be matched. The two most common matches available on stone imported to the U.S. are running match and book match.

Helpful Hint 11.8

Sometimes the existing sheen is hard to duplicate exactly, so you may find when polishing the backs to achieve the match you require that, in order to use the slabs side-by-side, you need to repolish all the faces to make the sheen level match exactly the same.

Table 11.2
Quality distinctions between stone slabs.

First Choice	Structurally sound Visual consistency Subjective appearance is considered especially attractive
Standard Grade	Structurally sound Visual inconsistencies render material visually variable Subjective appearance considered average
Commercial or Second Quality	Reparable defects Visual inconsistencies "blotchy"; material may need to be culled Generally reserved for large-scale commercial jobs where costs are central to decision making

Grade

Stones are evaluated for quality and categorized as belonging to one of three general grades. This grading system is not universally applied but the concepts are valid and could be understood by a supplier even if they do not grade their own inventory that way; they will still know what you mean as you source material defining it by descriptors like those in Table 11.2.

SEALANTS

All stones should be sealed. There are basically two types of sealants: penetrating sealants and topdressings. There are various formulations available for each of the two types, some with additional characteristics like color enhancement or UV protection.

Penetrating Sealant

Penetrating sealant, a protective formula applied to the stone, soaks into the material, and topdressings form a protective skin on top. All stones should be sealed with penetrating sealants and many stones are brought into the stone yard with a penetrating sealant already applied. If the stone has not received a penetrating sealant, you should specify one on your order. Figure 11.20 shows a stone at the vendor that already received a penetrating sealer. You can see on the cut edge how the sealant has soaked in to a certain depth (and also where the sealer has dripped along the edge).

If the stone already has the sealant applied, you should find out what was used so you can identify compatible maintenance products for your client. Some formulas of stone cleansers are incompatible with formulas of some sealants. If the wrong cleansers are used they may remove the sealant.

Topdressings

Topdressings, also called sacrificial coatings, are akin to a wax that can be removed when they become soiled or damaged. They protect the stone surface underneath and are more easily repaired than the stone itself because they can be dissolved and stripped and reapplied more easily

FIGURE 11.20 Stone should have a penetrating sealer applied. Many stones have the sealant applied before the stone arrives in the warehouse. You can see how it has penetrated (and dripped) at the edge of the slab.

than if you had to regrind the stone on-site. Topdressings are softer than stone, however, so you will have to weigh the potential for light abrasion or staining against the need for more maintenance required by a topdressing.

> **What Would You Do? 11.2**
>
> When would you use a topdressing in addition to a penetrating sealer?

Enhanced sealant formulations are available to improve performance in a particular way. UV protection and color-enhancing properties are two common enhancements that are often available with special formulas.

Sealants, both penetrating and topdressings, must be periodically reapplied. The schedule for this maintenance will vary depending on the stone and where it is used. Stone that is frequently (or improperly) cleaned will have to be resealed more often. A simple test for determining if it is time to reseal the stone is to apply a drop of water to the surface and see if it soaks in. If the water droplet sits like a bead on the surface the sealant is still working. If it soaks in, it is time to reseal.

Some maintenance product systems seal the stone when the cleaning products are used. It is important to instruct your client, or their cleaning staff, regarding the correct maintenance of the stone you specify so it performs satisfactorily over time (your reputation may depend on it). The cleanser must be compatible with the sealant because the wrong cleanser will remove sealants, leaving the stone vulnerable to staining.

Remember that stone is a natural product and, unlike man-made product, there is no control over the exact mineral composition. The varying ingredients in different types of stones create the differences between stone varieties that are visible to the eye. The ingredients of any given lot of stone within a single species is not exactly and completely known. It would be impractical to chemically analyze every stone lot. This discussion is presented to underscore the importance of applying the correct sealer to the stone you have specified. A dense stone requires a more viscous vehicle to deliver the "active ingredients" into the pores and crevices. A sealant that forms more of a "coat" can prohibit the migration of moisture, even water vapor, out of a stone, causing it to effloresce and spall. Numerous other considerations must be assessed to select the best sealer.

> **A Cautionary Tale 11.1**
>
> A client's new granite countertop developed dark patches during the first week after installation. Water was used to cool the blades when the stone was cut and the top had been sealed before all of the water had evaporated. Water, attempting to migrate up out of the top, was trapped by the sealant. The sealant had to be removed, the top allowed to dry, and then the countertop was resealed.

MANAGING BUDGETS

While there is a wide variation in slab costs, the biggest factor in job cost is typically the labor involved. A complex job with lots of cutting and fitting, cutouts, and profiles or site complications will raise the cost of the job. That said, some stones are known to be expensive, like granite and quartzite, and are significantly more expensive than any other stones. The differences in the cost of the stones themselves contribute to the cost. A stone that is rare or difficult to get will be more costly. The most costly granites, currently those with blue coloration, are as much as eight times the cost of the cheapest granites on the market.

Harder stones tend to price out higher than softer stones. Stones that are commonly available introduce cost competitiveness that keeps the price of some kinds of material relatively low within their category.

> **What Would You Do? 11.3**
>
> Look at the profiles in this text or find more options online. Which profiles would you expect to cost more than others? Remember that profiles that are composed of built-up edges have an addition labor step.

In the long run, the most economical stone is the one best matched to its purpose. The softness and absorbency of the stone are the primary limiting factors in selection. Softer stones are more susceptible to staining, wear, and etching. Marble, limestone, and travertine are susceptible to etching by acid and to absorption of oil, characteristics that would indicate that they are not the best selection for a residential kitchen. They can be used successfully in kitchens with the proper sealant, but will require more maintenance.

The complexity of the installation and the fabrication required also contribute to the cost. The complexity may be the result of site conditions, such as lots of prepwork or a very articulated space that requires lots of cutting and fitting. There may be a pattern under consideration that will be very time consuming; edge profiles may require a complicated fabrication effort. Laminating material to create a thicker edge also contributes to the cost of the installation.

> **Point of Emphasis 11.4**
> Natural stone does not meet standards for commercial kitchens because it cannot be sanitized. Knives are quickly dulled if stone is used as a cutting surface.

Many restoration options are available for stones that have suffered staining or abuse, but if these problems can be avoided by the selection of the stone, the total cost over the life of the installation will be reduced.

PROTECTION AND MAINTENANCE

In addition to the maintenance that your client will perform on a regular schedule, there may be occasions when special maintenance, employing stone maintenance professionals, is required. If a natural stone acquires a stain, a poultice may be used to draw the stain up out of a stone. Scratches can be ground out but usually you cannot grind out only the area with scratches, the entire surface must be ground out because it may not be possible to make the sheen level of the repaired area match the rest of the surface.

> **A Cautionary Tale 11.2**
>
> A client purchased a home with a white marble tile foyer floor. There were faint rust-colored stains here and there throughout the foyer so I contacted three restoration companies to bid on using a poultice to draw the stains up out of the stone. The first two bid on the job as requested, but the third pointed out that the rust stains were rust, probably from rebar too close to the surface in the concrete substrate. If a poultice was used to draw rust up through the stone, the rusty marks would grow worse.

QUALIFYING TRADESPEOPLE

Shops vary in their capacity, ability, and expertise. Some shops have a large equipment investment with the latest technology such as water-jet cutting equipment and water filtration that allows them to reuse water that cools blades as they cut stone. Ideally the shop you hire has such updated features but the reality is that tight client budgets create a market for the less-endowed shops. Stone fabrication was successfully done long before these technologies existed so, obviously, the work can be done by small shops without the capital investment in sophisticated equipment. If your client's project is small, kitchen countertops for a residential client for instance, then large capacity and sophisticated capability is not required. The best shop for your client's job will be one that has experience in the kind of work your project requires, demonstrated ability to produce the quality that you require in your time frame, and will provide careful installation. Your task in assessing the appropriateness of a particular shop is to pair your project needs with the shop that can provide it for the lowest cost. The shop with simple tools, occupying 1,000 square feet, may be all that you need for your small job, but large-scale production or complex designs would be out of their league. The best way to ensure that the shop you are interviewing is qualified is to see installations of work similar to your designs that the shop has installed. You should talk to references but understand that end users may not know how to judge the quality of an installation. It is important that you inspect actual work. Photographs can demonstrate experience but not quality. When you inspect actual work look for:

- Neat cuts with no chips
- Members are plumb and square and flush; there is no noticeable **lippage**
- Tight joints
- Adjoining surfaces that are in perfect alignment
- Consistent appearance in reflection (indicating expert polishing and careful application of sealer); check for consistency between horizontal and vertical members too
- Neat, consistent grout joints
- Invisible seams on laminated pieces (you will be able to see a change in the natural markings of the stone but the seam should be hard to notice barring grain changes)
- Consistent overhangs and tight junctions between stone and adjoining material

Recall that there is a lot of variation in stone, not just from one kind to another but also subtle variation from one lot to another of the same kind of stone, and a vendor/fabricator who possesses extensive knowledge of stone properties, beyond fabrication experience, is sometimes extremely valuable. Occasionally something goes wrong on a job and often when you least expect it. It is in those instances when you hope that your fabricator is something of a "stone geek" who can ferret out the problem and suggest remedies.

SAFETY

Safety considerations are not restricted to your client site; mining stone requires safety equipment that is not always made available to workers quarrying stone in countries that do not impose safety standards the way OSHA does in the U.S. Dust generated by many mining techniques affects workers' skin, eyes, and lungs. Conscientious mining practice protects work safety and minimizes waste. Best practices include such things as using saws instead of blasting to remove stone from the quarry. Mills can minimize dust with updated equipment.

When the stone is in use, it should be maintained with low-VOC products that are nontoxic. If the stone is on the floor, it may be slippery when wet, in which case a sealer that additionally provides some slip resistance is a good idea. If your interior is for a vulnerable population you may want to confirm that the stone selected does not emit radon. The danger present from radon in granite is still a subject of debate in the industry, but for vulnerable people (elderly, compromised immune systems, etc.) it is better to err on the side of caution until we know for sure. You may want to do some research for your project but meanwhile black granites may be safer than those containing more quartz.

SUSTAINABILITY

Stone is a very durable surface. Stone can have sustainable characteristics such as durability and the ability to be maintained without toxic chemicals. Stone is a limited natural resource. Although it is very durable and lasts literally hundreds of years in some installations, fashions and functions change and stone is often disposed of out of buildings before it has reached the end of its serviceability. Stones are not renewable; they can be recycled (downcycled) as aggregate. Most stones are inert although some granites have detectable radon. All stone must be sealed and the sealant replenished periodically so specify a low-VOC sealant. Stone can be cleaned without poisonous chemicals. If you specify stone that comes from within a 500-mile radius of your job site it is considered a local material and saves fuel.

Quarry waste is another problem with the stone industry. Turning stone mass buried in the ground into the tidy rectangles required for building surfaces has its material inefficiencies and many quarries use the scraps for backfill in the open mines. Some quarries grind the scraps for industrial or agricultural uses. It has been estimated that for every 1,000 tons of stone quarried, only 70 tons will be used in building and that as much as 50 percent of stone that enters the fabrication process may end up as waste for trimming, grinding, rejection of material, and the like.

Production waste can be minimized with the help of computerized production. Even using thinner saw blades can reduce the amount of stone turned into dust. Stone scrap can be used as a component in other materials. Crushed stone can be used for landscaping, and unsound blocks have potential for the production of tile. Sustainability efforts are quite variable and this list is not to imply that all these options are commonly exercised, rather it is here to create awareness that fabrication is part of sustainability, just as the materials' characteristics are important to green building.

ORGANIZATION OF THE INDUSTRY

The stone industry is truly a global market. Despite your efforts to source stone for your project from a local quarry, it is highly likely that you will be specifying stone imported from around the globe. Stone from Europe, China, and South America are commonly found in your local stone suppliers' warehouses.

Stone is brought into the country by various stone dealers who travel to all parts of the world and purchase it by the block or by the slab. These dealers may also be fabricators. They buy big blocks of stone that are sliced and finished and sell it to fabricators. Fabricators use the slabs, which are roughly rectangular in shape (but are not usually neat rectangles), to fill the job orders that come in from end users and designers. They will cut it to size, give it a specified edge profile, and cut out required openings (sinks for instance). They will also install the material at the job site.

Point of Emphasis 11.5

When a fabricator brings in an unusual material, one that cannot be easily sourced elsewhere, any competitive bidders for the fabrication will have to purchase the material from the fabricator bringing it into the country. The fabricator who is also selling the stone will know who their competitors are when the other fabricators call them for the price of the material. This is a common practice and usually they are willing to sell the material and make their profit on the stone even if they do not win the fabrication order.

Helpful Hint 11.9

If your job requires only a small stone slab surface you might find the cost prohibitive because your client may have to purchase an entire slab even though they don't need all of the material. There are options such as changing to a stone-look man-made material or using tile instead of slab but the best option is to make a selection from the leftover pieces your fabricator probably has on hand from completed jobs that did not use the entire slab. In such an instance you would not shop at the stone vendor but rather at the stone fabricator.

The designer will begin searching for the right stone in the vendor's showroom (Figure 11.21). Actual slabs may be reviewed in the warehouse to confirm that the current stock is as expected. The slabs in the warehouse will be arranged sequentially, just as they were cut from the block. Figure 11.22 shows a lot identified as "Lot 8" with all slabs (except 16, which likely broke into unusable pieces in transport). Variation in markings will be subtly different as you move from one slab to the next but the difference will be clearly noticeable between the first and last slab in the lot.

You may make your selection from the front or back of the lot but you will not be permitted to cherry-pick the lot because an uninterrupted sequence is more usable. The missing slab 16 in Figure 11.22 may be problematic for the vendor because slab 15 may be visually similar to 14 but not to 17 so a smooth transition may be lost there. That is why you will find that many slabs have a fiberglass backing (Figure 11.23). This backing may keep all the pieces together if the slab breaks during transport or fabrication, so it can be repaired.

FIGURE 11.21 Small samples of stones are displayed in the showroom so you can narrow your search before proceeding back to the warehouse to view actual slabs. *Samples from Marble and Granite Supply International, Evanston, IL.*

FIGURE 11.22 When you tag stone at the fabricator you will select sequential slabs so that the material will be most visually similar and the slabs can be matched. These slabs of marble, which are numbered on their edges for lot and sequence, have already been sealed once. *Slabs from Marble and Granite Supply International, Evanston, IL.*

FIGURE 11.23 Many stone slabs have mesh reinforcing on their backs to stabilize the material in case of breakage.

Point of Emphasis 11.6

When you review slabs at the stone vendor, you will often notice crystal-clear veins in various slabs. These veins are, quite likely, repairs. These repairs are not a defect, they are sturdy and attractive.

You will quickly discover that as the grain varies from one lot to the next within the same species that you prefer some kinds of markings for your job over other kinds of markings, so you may find yourself reaching beyond local markets for stone slabs for your job.

Helpful Hint 11.10

If you find stone that you prefer for your client's job in another market area, there will likely be additional costs associated with bringing stone into your locale. Typically, your local fabricator has bid to provide, fabricate, and install but may not be willing to cover shipping charges.

SELECTION CRITERIA

For your design program, identifying the characteristics that the material must possess is the starting point of your selection. For a tough, durable material like stone, the aesthetic properties are a matter of function because you don't want your design to become dated. The performance characteristics must be carefully evaluated in light of the site conditions that you must work to anticipate. Table 11.3 has a few characteristics to get you started in your evaluation and suggests a format for organizing your thinking.

No material is perfect; they all have pros and cons and stone is no exception. Some drawbacks are more important to your program than others, so the presence of a characteristic that could be considered a weakness may or may not matter to your client. You will notice on the list below that some of the characteristics mentioned are desirable characteristics, but must be accommodated with special treatment such as stabilizing mesh, sealants, filler, etc.

What Would You Do? 11.4

What contribution could stone lend to acoustical properties in a space?

Table 11.3
Select specific stone properties for client sites based on the kind of abuse the stone will have to endure there.

Site Characteristic	Examples of Abuse	Select
Abrasion	Traffic on floors, stairs, ramps; items that will be dragged (briefcases, grocery bags, center pieces) or may slide against the surface (keys, and pocket contents)	Abrasion-resistant stones, dense stones; honed vs. polished surfaces
Impact resistance	Moving parts (like café tables) or surfaces where things are set down	Stable stones with a fine grain vs. veined stone; stone that is dense; avoid stones known to be brittle or to spall
Soiling	Food, makeup, items carried in from other places (foot traffic, things people set on transaction counters)	Polished surfaces; coloration similar to expected soiling
Staining	Food, dyes, oils, rust	Dense stone; polished surfaces
Heat	Cooking, candles, hearths	Durable, stable stone with interlocking structure
Acoustics	Lots of people and conversation as in the lobby of an opera house or places like train stations	Uneven surface that bumps in and out; shaped profiles and companion materials that soak up sound

The stones listed as examples below are not the only instances of the characteristics listed. Such characteristics included:

- Porosity (like limestone)
- Holes (like travertine) that require filling
- Veins (like marble) that may be less sturdy
- Spall (like slate)
- Warp (like serpentine)
- Efflorescence (like limestone) that requires sealing
- Fading (like black marble)
- Rusting (like some orange stones)

A designer performing due diligence in advance of finalizing a specification may perform the following tasks:

- Confirm that the site is or will be made suitable for the stone installation. This often requires inspection of the substrate for flatness and rigidity.
- Visit a number of stone yards and view slabs in person or cast a wider net via an Internet search for the perfect color and markings. Request high-quality photos of several slabs in the lot so you can zoom in, accompanied by physical samples.

Helpful Hint 11.11

When you must work with distant vendors they will e-mail pictures and samples demonstrating color range. Some vendors will break samples off the corner of a slab, others have a library of small samples. Ask that included in the pictures sent they have a couple of pictures that show the physical samples they will send you against the center of the slabs they have on hand. You will have a better idea of the accuracy of the physical samples that they send.

- Request samples both sealed and unsealed to check the selection's performance in the face of the abuse you anticipate on the site when in use. See what happens when you stain or abrade the material duplicating conditions anticipated for the client's site.
- Confirm that the sheen level is as desired.
- Confirm that the material is available in the desired thickness, polished for the desired match.
- Investigate the general characteristics of the stone to see if it varies from other stones of the general type (is it unique as a granite or marble in some way?).
- Look into the kind of sealants and adhesives that will be used, request material safety data sheets for all.
- Confirm that the material is within the budget.
- Educate the client about the properties and maintenance of the material. Make sure the recommended maintenance is acceptable to the client.

SPECIFYING

You might specify stone for a variety of uses for interiors, and for exteriors too, as designers are often expected to make all the material selections for a project inside and out. Table 11.4 lists some common uses for stone and special considerations for each use.

Some code considerations that pertain to stone would address the slip resistance of walking surfaces and ramps and the need to sanitize surfaces; for instance, you could specify stone for a residential kitchen but it will not satisfy the criteria established for commercial kitchens in most jurisdictions because none of the types is impervious enough.

Table 11.4
Common uses for stone and special considerations for each use.

Use	Consideration
Floors	Durability of material for withstanding scratches and stains. Appearance retention—honed surfaces show fewer scratches but will stain more easily. Slip-resistant finishes or sealants that improve coefficient of friction ratings. Potential for glare if the stone is pale and polished.
Walls	Sheen levels pertaining to light reflectivity for using natural daylight in buildings (also consider potential for glare). Difficulty making changes to available services if needs for electrical outlets shift.
Ceilings	In steam room it is a good idea to have more impervious surfaces than in other rooms. Use thinner material and detail for added support.
Fireplace mantels and hearths	Stone can withstand the heat of well-managed fires and will not support combustion so is one obvious choice. Remember that prefab fireplaces are more like appliances than architecture and may need to eventually be replaced. Detail for as little destruction of surround as possible if the unit must be removed.
Countertops	Considerations similar to those for floors. If the counter will be used for food prep or service specify food-grade sealers.
Stair treads and risers	Any stone, no matter how dense and durable, should be fully supported from below. Also detail all exposed surfaces.
Tub decks, shower surrounds, and vanity tops	Standing water is common in these areas. If it is allowed to dry on the surface, it will leave pale mineral deposits. Darker stones will require more upkeep and more periodic buffing maintenance to remove them. Porous stones will also soak up soap scum and may need to be scraped and stripped periodically. Dense polished surfaces are very slippery when wet.

Your specification will be carefully written to describe the desired material and installation completely and succinctly. It is difficult to write a spec before you know the exact material and installation details that you are writing about. If you had in mind to write a spec for stone slabs for the shower walls in a health club locker room, your specifications might develop along the lines of the following example.

SAMPLE SPEC 11.1

Part 1 General Information

1.1 Related Documents

A. Refer to plans for material location.
B. Refer to elevations for location of seams and plumbing fittings.
C. Refer to details for junction between shower walls and pan.
D. Refer to plumbing specs for cutout size, number, and spacing.

1.2 Summary

A. Provide and install stone panels as described (following) on shower walls in the women's locker room. Stone fabricator is to take all required measurements and alert designer immediately to any discrepancy between drawings and as-built measurements. Failure to measure does not alleviate fabricator's responsibility for providing and installing material as described here. Do not perform measure until plumbing roughs have been stubbed out.
B. Partitions and cement board cladding by others, custom cement shower pans and tile cladding by others.

1.3 References

A. Material Specifications ASTM C166 Quartz-based dimensional stone.
B. Test Standards ASTM C97 test method for absorption.
C. Other Application Standards ASTM C110 portland cement, ASTM C1186 cement backer board, ASTM 920 joint sealers.

1.4 Contractor Submittals

A. Provide shop drawings showing all joints, cutouts, and details.
B. Provide material safety data sheet for all mortars, grouts, and adhesives used.
C. Maintenance information.

1.5 Quality Assurance

A. Contractors producing and installing work to have a minimum of 5 years' experience fabricating and installing stone slab surfaces.

1.6 Delivery, Storage, and Handling

A. Material to be cut and finished off-site, delivered to site wrapped to protect from weather and flying debris during transport. Material to acclimate on-site for 48 hours prior to installation.

1.7 Maintenance of Installation

A. Upon completion of installation material to receive final coat of sealant.

Part 2 Products

2.1 General Information

A. Quartzite slabs of sufficient quantity to produce slabs as required for shower stall interiors and partition faces.
B. Material has been tagged by designer at Stone City, 1234 Industrial Drive, Anywhere, ST 12345.

2.2 Manufacturers

A. Fabricator: Stone Miracles, 1234 Industrial Drive, Anywhere, ST 12345.

2.3 Products

A. Brazilian Pink Quartzite, 2-cm-thick faces polished for running match.
B. Separation membrane: Premier System brand Devine Divider membrane.
C. Grout: Acme brand Tuflex unsanded in color 123 Rose.
D. Mallard brand Monsoon sealer.

Part 3 Execution

3.1 Examination

A. Partitions to receive stone are to be plumb and square with right angles. Do not proceed with work until partitions are in acceptable condition. Installed material to be free of all damage and defect and fully acclimated to site prior to installation. All cuts to be neat and allow for no chipped edges where edges are exposed. Exposed edges to be polished to match faces. Cuts around plumbing openings to be neat and fully concealed by escutcheon plates delivered with plumbing fittings.

3.2 Preparation

A. Shower walls to be waterproofed prior to installation of separation membranes.

3.3 Installation

A. Install wall panels as shown on drawings with recommended adhesive. Upon completion material is to be demonstrably plumb and level by testing with a bubble level placed in the center of the installed unit, and plumb line dropped in corners.
B. Maximum **tolerance** (allowable deviation from specs) not to exceed $^3/_{32}$" lippage between adjoining members.

3.4 Post Installation

A. Upon completion, remove all grout haze from face of slabs without scratching surface.
B. Leave area broom-clean.
C. Apply final coat of sealer according to manufacturer's recommendations.
D. Protect from other trades until installation is stable.

INSPECTION

In the list of inspection checkpoints that you read in the Qualifying Tradespeople section on page 315, there are a number of attributes that should be present on your job as well. In addition to this list would be all the specific design details unique to your job. You may inspect parts prior to completion of the whole job. For example, let's say you were working on a fireplace surround for a ski resort. After tagging the material at the vendor, you might go to the fabricator's shop and lay the cuts out to ensure that the way the material will be cut would present the color and graining the way that you wanted. You might also visit the shop after the pieces of the surround and hearth were completed to confirm that the cuts were neat and tight. Finally you would visit the completed installation to make sure that all the checklist items that pertain to your installation were correctly and neatly done.

WORKING WITH RESOURCES

It is common practice for designers to design the details of their idea and send the drawings out to bid to three or more contractors for pricing. If your job is large, the details of the stone installation will be included in the bid package for the entire job. The more complete the information is, the more accurate the estimate will be. It is possible to get usable numbers for managing the budget by identifying the material as "marble" or "slate," etc., but unless you select the particular material within the generalized type, you run the risk of being limited to just a few common types of that stone and will not have allocated enough money if you later select something that is more unusual. After you receive the estimates, a contractor will be selected who will receive a deposit. The warehouse is likely to require the fabricator's name in order to allow you to put material on hold. They will tag it with the fabricator's name (not your firm's name) because the fabricator will be purchasing and picking it up.

> Point of Emphasis 11.7
>
> After you have tagged material at the warehouse, follow up with the fabricator. There is often a time limit on the hold and if they do not pick it up on time it may be released to another buyer and you will have to find more material. This is especially difficult if you have shown the material to your client and gotten their approval on the lot. Repeating the process is bad enough (because no one will be compensating you for your time) but in the client's mind, the replacement material will never seem as good as the initial selection.

SUMMARY

This chapter discussed the many different characteristics of nonstructural stone—stone fastened to a structure to form a veneer. That includes:

- Additional characteristics the designer must specify
- Selection criteria such as maintenance
- The organization of the stone industry
- Safety and sustainable characteristics
- Specification and inspection of stone installations
- How to work with resources

WEB SEARCH ACTIVITIES

1. Perform an image search for pictures of *stone slab*. See how many stones (granite, marble, etc.) you can identify by sight.
2. Perform an image search for pictures of each of the stone textures listed below:
    - Sandblasted
    - Shot-blasted
    - Bush-hammered
    - Brushed-face
    - Tumbling
    - Sawn
    - Leather finish
3. Perform an image search for pictures of stone edge profiles.

4. Perform an image search for *marble slab* or *granite slab*. Find pictures of full slabs. Find an example of a slab that would:
   - Be dramatic for book match
   - Make a nice rhythm for running match
   - Work well as full slabs
   - Also work if cut into smaller pieces as would be the case for countertops or tiles
   - Seam well and hide the seam if you wanted to build up the edge for a thicker appearance
5. Perform an image search for a picture of a stone slab with dramatic markings. Right-click on it and Save it to open in a graphical software program that will allow you to crop and rotate it.
   a. Crop the slab image into a rectangle that your fabricator might make from the slab to use on your client's job. Copy and Paste several times.
   b. Flip or rotate the slabs to depict book match, running match, and butt-matched relationships.
6. Search for a master spec for *marble veneer*. Read it for comprehension.

PERSONAL ACTIVITIES

1. Find a stone installation that you can visit in person. Perform an inspection as if you were inspecting completed work for your client's job or as if you were inspecting work while selecting a fabricator. List the characteristics that you feel are significant indicators of quality. Supplement with images as appropriate if you compile a report, as might be required if you were working on a design team.
2. Find a picture of an installation using a stone slab, or imagine the material and details that you would like to use on one of your projects. Write a specification for your selected installation. You will have to determine which portions of your description should be words and which you could convey more succinctly with a drawing, referenced in your spec so that the contractors know to look for it in the drawing set.

SUMMARY QUESTIONS

1. Why might two different lots of the same kind of stone from the same quarry bear two different names?
2. Why is it a good idea to plan the cuts before finalizing your selection and tagging material?
3. What accounts for the different characteristics among the various stone types?
4. Which stones can be etched by mild acids?
5. What test can you perform to see if it is time for your client to reseal their stone?
6. What characteristics are unique to each kind of stone? Fill in the following chart.
7. List surface textures applied to stone and note how to identify them.
8. What does it mean when you specify a *built-up edge*?
9. Briefly describe the kind of job where you would use each of the different quality grades of stone.
10. What are the two general types of sealants? How are they different? When would you use each kind? Include enhanced and special sealants in your answer.
11. Why must the sealant and cleaning products be coordinated?
12. Why might limestone require a different sealant than granite?
13. What factors contribute to the cost of a stone installation?
14. For what kind of client would you feel comfortable using a small one-man fabrication shop? What kind of client requires a large show with advanced equipment?
15. What characteristics of an installation indicate acceptable quality?
16. What kind of issues pertain to worker safety in stone fabrication? What kinds of issues pertain to user safety in the installation?

Table 11.5
Fill in this blank table to organize stone types according to their characteristics.
You will want to know the strengths and weaknesses of each type to make good selections for your clients.

Stones (in order of general hardness)	**Characteristics**
Quartzite	
Granite	
Serpentine	
Marble	
Travertine	
Limestone	
Slate	
Soapstone	
Onyx	

17. What characteristics of material or production contribute to sustainability?
18. List the steps that a stone in the ground goes through to become a top for a conference table? How efficient is the process?
19. What does it mean that stone comes in sequenced lots?
20. What are some common weaknesses in stone, as a surfacing material, which must be accommodated if certain kinds of stone are to be specified?
21. What tasks might you perform as you are signing off on the stone installation at your client's job site?

Chapter 12

TERRAZZO, COMPOSITES, AND CONCRETE

Key Terms

Admixtures	Pervious	Thermal mass
Cementitious	Portland cement	Topping

Objectives

After reading this chapter, you should be able to:

- Understand the similarities and differences between terrazzo and concrete.
- Know the material components of each.
- Understand the characteristics of and uses for these materials.
- Know in what forms these materials are used.
- Anticipate potential problems and be able to specify to avoid them.
- Know what trades install these materials and how to interact with them for installation and the production of custom work.
- Know how the industry is organized for each of these materials.
- Select from accessory items and products.
- Understand related materials that also contain cement.

TERRAZZO AND SIMILAR COMPOSITES

Terrazzo has been a surfacing material for hundreds of years. Initially a stone and clay surface, it was developed into a stone and cement surface and today is available as a stone and cement surface as well as a modified version of the same or with an epoxy matrix. Because of its potential for recycled content, it is increasingly popular as a durable, sustainable material. Other similar composite materials have a lot in common with terrazzo but are categorically distinct from it.

MATERIAL

Composite stone flooring has two basic components: (1) aggregate (stone or glass chips); and (2) the matrix or binder that holds the aggregate together (cement or epoxy). The basic recipe has few ingredients but, like concrete, additives tailor performance to your job's requirements and the selection of aggregate allows for many different options that may be specified. Terrazzo can be poured in place or purchased precast in custom or standard units.

Traditional terrazzo, marble chips in cement, has some properties in common with concrete. Like concrete, which has no "give," terrazzo with a cement matrix is a rigid material. When buildings move due to settling, wind, or movement of people or objects within the building, rigid material may crack. New formulations for terrazzo, with additives in the cement or epoxy matrix, are a little more resilient. Another tactic for preventing cracking would be to separate the terrazzo installation from the structure with a membrane or a layer of sand. With these types of installations, the rigid material is not bonded to the building, so it can slip a little (imperceptibly) instead of cracking when the building moves.

Aggregate

Stone aggregate in Figure 12.1 shows typical samples of marble chips of various sizes at a terrazzo showroom. You would review such samples to make selections for the composition of your custom terrazzo installation. The aggregate sizes are defined in Table 12.1.

The aggregate is a primary factor in the visual appearance of the finished surface. Figure 12.2a–e shows the variety achieved simply through the selection of aggregate sizes. The large pieces of stone slab in image (e), palladiana, are 4 inches or more across.

Terrazzo cures without drastic temperature or dimensional changes so nontraditional aggregate can be used, as was the case in Figure 12.3, that incorporates pieces of mirror. Plastic, wood, and other less traditional aggregate can be considered as long as it will meet your criteria for durability. Glass is a popular aggregate. Figure 12.4 shows recycled glass aggregates; even the sand for the matrix can be custom specified. Figure 12.5 shows glass sand for terrazzo. Recycled glass will cost more if there is litter in the mix (as is often the case).

FIGURE 12.1 Aggregate chips are graded by size.

Table 12.1
Aggregate sizes that you specify in your terrazzo order are designated by number.

Size	Min.	Max.
#0	1/16"	1/8"
#1	1/8"	1/4"
#2	1/4"	3/8"
#3	3/8"	1/2"
#4	1/2"	5/8"
#5	5/8"	3/4"
#6	3/4"	7/8"
#7	7/8"	1"
#8	1"	1 1/8"

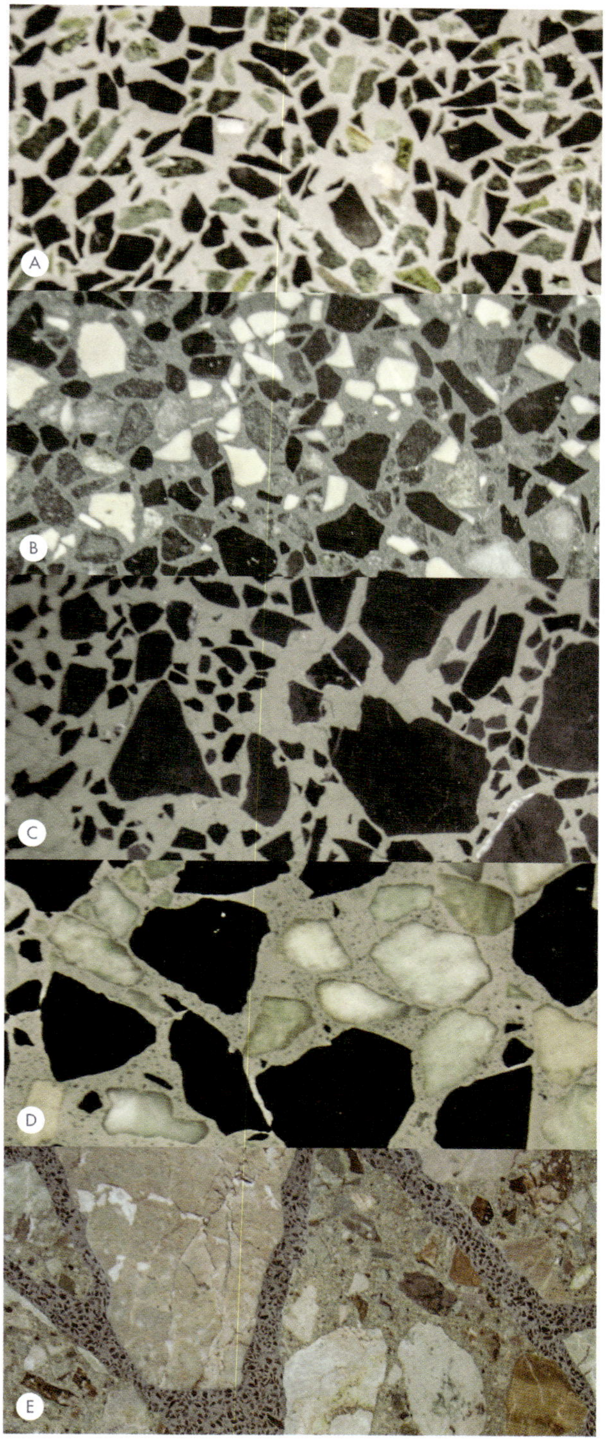

FIGURE 12.2A–E These samples demonstrate the range possible in the selection of aggregate size alone. The largest aggregate is shown in sample (e), which is called palladiana terrazzo. It is the most labor-intensive terrazzo to cast because the slabs are often broken and hand-fitted on-site. *Samples produced by Caretti Terrazzo, Morton Grove, IL.*

FIGURE 12.3 This exotic combo uses mirrored glass aggregate and metal shavings in the aggregate mix. *Combo produced by Caretti Terrazzo, Morton Grove, IL.*

FIGURE 12.4 Glass aggregate allows for more intense color. Recycled glass is readily available for use as terrazzo aggregate.

FIGURE 12.5 Very fine glass aggregate, as fine as sand.

What Would You Do? 12.1

What materials can you imagine that could be used for aggregate?

After the terrazzo is cast, it is typically ground flat. Successively finer and finer grit is used until the floor reaches the sheen level that you have specified. The exception to this is in the case of rustic terrazzo. Rustic terrazzo is cast and then as it begins to set up (harden) the top of the cement matrix is flushed away with water and the specially selected aggregate is exposed to produce a coarse surface. The aggregate cannot be the chipped stone or glass because that would be too sharp and dangerous. Figure 12.6 shows rustic terrazzo with its rounder aggregate.

FIGURE 12.6 Rustic terrazzo shares some similarities with exposed aggregate concrete in that the aggregate selected must be rounded, not chipped and sharp. Rustic terrazzo is not ground flat. *Sample produced by Caretti Terrazzo, Morton Grove, IL.*

Matrix/Binder

Three basic types of binder or matrices are common: (1) **cementitious**, portland cement and water; (2) modified cementitious, polyacrylate modified cement is a composition resinous material as the binder in thinset terrazzo; and (3) resinous epoxy, a two-component, thermal setting resinous material. The matrix can be pigmented with powdered coloring agents. Some matrix plus aggregate combinations are more successful than others; for instance, glass aggregate typically requires an epoxy matrix. A cement matrix is not "sticky" enough to hold impervious glass aggregate.

Various terrazzo systems using the above matrix types have different characteristics for you to consider when selecting the most suitable system for your job. As you review Table 12.2, consider what site and program conditions would make each of the different system types preferable.

CHARACTERISTICS

Terrazzo will have characteristics of the materials that it contains. If the matrix that holds the stone chips together is cement, it will have the characteristics of cement. The most important consideration here being its rigidity (cracking) and porosity (staining). A modified cementitious polyacrylate will have a little more flexibility, less tendency to crack, and it can hold glass ("sticky" enough, unlike a cement matrix). Composites tend to have the characteristics of their component parts so once you have identified what is in the composite you will be able to predict its properties.

What Would You Do? 12.2

Which formulation, cementitious, polyacrylate modified or epoxy, would you expect to be the most inert/nontoxic? Why?

You can understand from reviewing Table 12.2 that the different systems require different thicknesses. For new installations, thicker systems will require that the floor structure in the areas to receive a sand-cushioned system must be depressed if the completed terrazzo floor is to be flush and level with adjacent flooring, which is not as thick, if you are to meet codes and ADA requirements.

An epoxy matrix with glass aggregate will be more impervious to staining because the materials in it resist absorbing stains, but a cement matrix with marble aggregate will have the same tendencies to stain as concrete and marble. You can understand from this difference that the various terrazzo products

Table 12.2
Several different terrazzo systems suit different site conditions and program goals.

System Type	Installed	Characteristics	Distinctions	Considerations
Sand-cushioned • Cement based • Not bonded to slab	• Portland-cement based • Wire reinforced • On isolation sheet • Placed over sand layer	• Maximum undivided field size approximately 5' × 5' • 2" to 2.5" thick plus .5" thick terrazzo topping • 25–30 pounds/square foot	• Stable • Inert • Easy to pigment • Good crack resistance • Does not bond well with glass aggregate	• Design with divider strips every 5' or so
Bonded • Cement based • Bonded directly to slab	• Portland-cement based underbed • Placed on slab • Terrazzo topping	• Bonded directly to slab • Maximum undivided field size approximately 5' × 5' • 2" thick • Weighs up to 20 pounds/square foot	• Moderate crack resistance	• Less reliance on condition of slab because of underbed
Polyacrylate • Cement based (modified by additives) • Bonded indirectly to slab	• Slab is primed and a membrane adhered • Terrazzo placed on top of fixed membrane	• Nominal ⅜" thick • Weighs 3 to 5 pounds/square foot • Undivided field size approximately 12' × 12'	• Can hold glass aggregate • Colors are stable • Moderate crack resistance	• Does not "float" on cushion so stability of slab important
Epoxy • Resin matrix • Bonds indirectly to slab	• Slab is primed • Membrane adhered to slab upon which the terrazzo is placed	• ⅜" thick • Weighs up to 5 pounds/square foot • Maximum undivided field size 20' × 20'	• Cures quickly for grinding • Typically best choice for glass aggregate • Excellent crack resistance	• Does not "float" on cushion so stability of slab important
Rustic (similar to bonded) • Cement based • Bonded directly to slab	• Portland-cement based underbed • Topped with terrazzo topping that is not ground flat	• Maximum undivided field size approximately 5' × 5' • 2" thick • Weighs up to 20 pounds/square foot	• Moderate crack resistance • Rough nonslip texture may be maintenance consideration	• Less reliance on condition of slab because of underbed
Monolithic • Cement based • Bonds to slab	• Portland-cement based • Terrazzo topping bonds with concrete slab	• ½" thick • weighs about 8 pounds/square foot • Maximum undivided field size approximately 12' × 12'	• Poor crack resistance	• Relies on condition of slab
Tile • Epoxy based • Bonds to slab	• Epoxy matrix • Slab is prepared, leveled or ground flat • Cured and/or cleaned	• Tile thickness and adhesive thickness only	• This product is comparable to tile products; grout minimizes stress on tiles	• Relies on condition of slab
Precast (cement or epoxy)	• Varies with item type	• Varies with composition	• Item may be adhered to support structure or freestanding	• Relies on stability of structure if adhered

require different care and maintenance. Care for cement-plus-stone systems as you would for each of those materials. Both require penetrating sealants and possibly topdressings and must be cleaned with cleansers that will not remove the sealants. Epoxy-plus-glass systems are more impervious to stains but will still scratch. Both cement and epoxy systems will occasionally require more maintenance than simple washing.

Periodically the floors will have to be stripped of their sealants, the surfaces ground to remove scratches; pits and spalls may have to be filled with grout or replacement aggregate. Then the floors are reground to the desired sheen and resealed.

Table 12.3
The most commonly specified types of terrazzo are indicated by letter in specifications.

S	*Standard terrazzo:* Marble chip sizes #1 (¼") and #2 (⅜") equal parts combined with portland cement, gray or white, with or without pigments
TS	*Thinset terrazzo:* Marble chip sizes #1 (¼") and smaller in combination with resin or cement binders, with or without pigments
V	*Venetian terrazzo:* Marble chip sizes #1 (¼") through #8 (1⅛") with portland cement, gray or white, with or without pigments
R	*Rustic terrazzo:* Uniformly textured terrazzo that uses marble chips, granite, riverbed stone, or other aggregates in combination with portland cement, gray or white, with or without pigments (Note: This system requires that the matrix be depressed to expose more of the aggregate; it is not ground flat during finishing)
C	*Conductive-type terrazzo:* Density of 60 percent or less of marble chips size #1 or smaller in combination with carbon black matrix (Note: This system is specially designed to conduct electricity, eliminating the buildup of static electricity)
P	*Palladiana:* Thin, random, fractured slabs of marble with joints standard-type terrazzo between each piece of marble

Your terrazzo specification can be customized to suit unique site requirements. Some specialty installations are common enough to have been given their own designation in the industry. Table 12.3 lists some of these special kinds of terrazzo.

PARTS AND ACCESSORIES

Terrazzo surfaces are often finished with trim details, such as coved baseboards, thresholds, and other transitional pieces also made of terrazzo that finish your terrazzo installation. These pieces may be shaped and ground on-site, but many contractors will form these extra pieces in a shop and then cut, fit, and adhere them on-site. Divider strips are another accessory item that is likely to be part of your installation.

What Would You Do? 12.3

If you were going to install a custom terrazzo floor in the lobby of an institutional building, like a government building, what alternative materials would you consider for thresholds, baseboards, and the like if you wanted to introduce variety in the scheme?

Precast Items

Wherever two surfaces meet or two materials come together, the designer must detail that junction. Your terrazzo installation will require materials and details to finish it off. Precast units such as stair treads, wall base, sill, or countertops and other custom or customizable items may be specified to finish your installation. Precast units may be described simply as precast, meaning they are standard sizes that you cut to fit, or custom precast, meaning they are made to your specifications. Some of these items will be entirely freestanding, such as planters or benches. Other precast items are fastened to the building, such as wall base or stair treads.

What Would You Do? 12.4

What advantage can you imagine for custom-forming a baseboard on-site versus having it precast or custom precast off-site and installed as an accessory part?

Vendors who provide terrazzo surfaces frequently provide these precast units as well and when you contract for the terrazzo surface these items will be ordered from the same provider to match or coordinate with the rest of your job. Some are stock items, meaning the profiles and sizes are determined and you will only specify the color of the matrix and the aggregate, with the rest of the material matching the remainder of your job. For your custom work, forms would be built and material cast and polished to spec.

Divider Strips

Divider strips minimize cracking in cement-based systems and separate color areas; they form the edges of your pattern colors. Divider strips often are an alloy of zinc, brass, or plastic. The divider strips are as tall

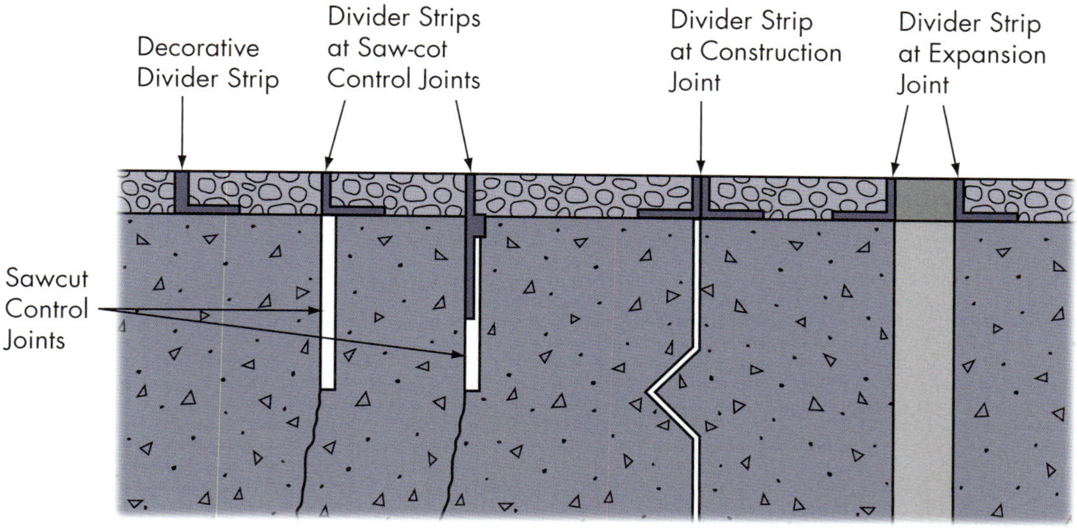

FIGURE 12.7 The various divider strip profiles serve different functions.

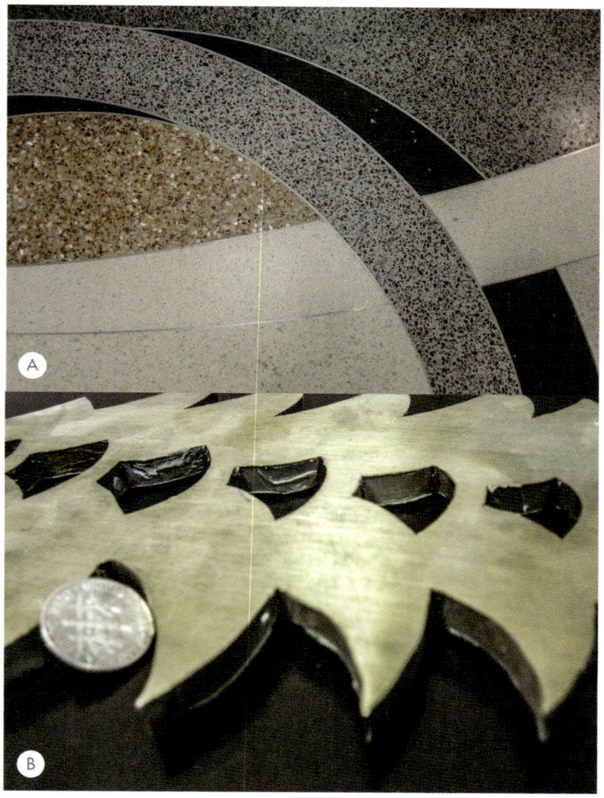

FIGURE 12.8A–B Divider strips were traditionally employed to control cracking. They contribute to the decorative quality of the terrazzo whether they are functional as shown here or purely decorative as in image (a). Metal inserts are traditional in terrazzo installations. They are very frequently metal strips but occasionally decorative metal inserts are used as in image (b). *Samples produced by Caretti Terrazzo, Morton Grove, IL.*

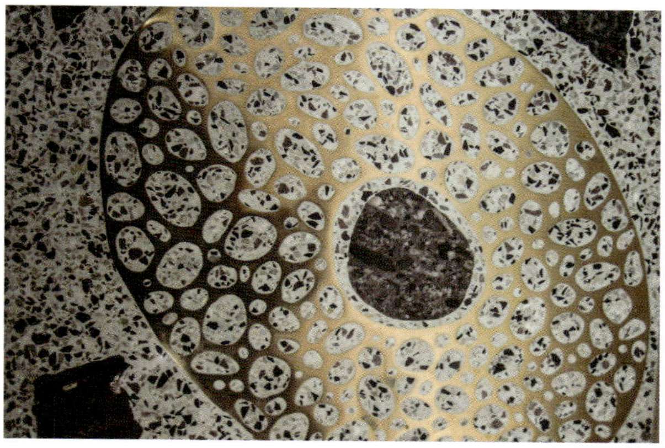

FIGURE 12.9 Dividers are not always strips. Custom-cut plate becomes an important part of the design, not just for separating the colors but as a unique element in the design. When metal is used for decoration in this manner, it will be laser-cut plate. *Decorative metal by Caretti Terrazzo, Morton Grove, IL.*

as the finished terrazzo surface is thick. Different profiles will be used for specific reasons, some of which are shown in Figure 12.7. Brass and plastic divider strips may have a reaction with some resinous materials and should be specified only if proven compatible with the binder specified. You can tell from Figure 12.7 that the divider strips are as thick as the terrazzo installation itself. Figure 12.8a–b gives you an idea of the heft of these metal accessory parts. More elaborate metal inserts can be custom made to replace simple, straight divider strips in some locations on your job, fulfilling a function that is mostly decorative, such as the laser-cut metal plate shown in Figure 12.9.

FABRICATION CONSIDERATIONS

The thickness of the terrazzo is not the whole story. You can see from the above descriptions and diagrams that some systems can be installed directly on the structure, but some systems require additional material in the underbed (the cementitious materials to support divider strips and terrazzo topping), and can increase the thickness significantly. Precast, small chips in polyester resin matrix can be as thin as ¼ inch thick, while monolithic (poured in place) will be about ½ inch thick, and Venetian will be about 2¾ inches thick. Obviously, the thicker the installation is, the more it will weigh. Some systems require a 3-inch slab depression with an additional dead load structural capacity of 30 to 35 pounds per square foot.

Substrates

Sand-cushioned systems work to separate the terrazzo from the building with a layer of sand that can shift with movement of the building while protecting the terrazzo from that movement. Sand-cushioned systems have much better resistance to substrate movement because they are separated from the structural slab, but do not work in every instance, especially for renovations. The level change must often be accommodated with design changes if thinner material has been removed to be replaced by terrazzo. Sand-cushioned is normally the most expensive and time-consuming terrazzo installation.

Curing and Finishing

Other trades must be kept off of the terrazzo until it has been ground and polished. After this surfacing has been completed, which involves grinding, grouting, and polishing that occurs after the terrazzo has cured sufficiently, it will be sealed and protected with Masonite. Terrazzo containing **portland cement** must cure for approximately one month before it can be sealed. Natural stone aggregate and concrete binders will both benefit from being sealed. Penetrating sealers and topical sealers (also called topdressing) are applicable to this material. Remember that topical sealers are softer than the surface they protect, so require more maintenance, but the maintenance is easier to perform than would be for stone restoration.

QUALIFYING INSTALLERS

Qualifying terrazzo companies is similar to qualifying other kinds of contractors: investigate their experience, credentials, and references.

Experience

Qualified installers have experience with the kind of work that you require. They will demonstrate this with pictures of their completed work and references for you to contact. If your job is large or if they are very interested in winning the bid, they may offer to take you to some of their similar, local installations. Even if they do not offer a tour, you may want to request access to a couple of sites to see in person. This is obviously easier for their commercial clients to accommodate but home owners are often also willing to allow an inspection, so you might ask for an on-site review of their completed projects even if it is not offered.

Beyond experience there is passion; while not required, it is always desirable to find the "geek" who gets excited about what they do and constantly consumes information related to their field. The passionate, experienced installer will be a member of trade organizations such as the National Terrazzo and Mosaic Association (NTMA). They will be able to recall the latest training seminar they attended. They will be able to recall instances where they had to do some tricky problem solving by suggesting particular materials or approaching the job in a unique way. They will have acquired knowledge of structure and will be able to discuss the kind of prepwork required for cracks in substrate and have good solutions for the particulars of your job.

Credentials and Training

It is typical in the terrazzo industry for the certification of trades to be done by manufacturers who train tradespeople to use their proprietary products. Rather than holding a certificate from an institution, like a school, terrazzo installers will be certified by individual companies as trained in the installation of their formula. Terrazzo contractors also take training courses through trade organizations and receive a certificate of completion of a specific course of study pertaining to some part of the installation. Qualified installers may have attained a patchwork of individual certificates in various aspects of the required work.

References

If you visit an installation, notice if it has remained sound or if there is evidence of building movement showing in the material. Notice overall craftsmanship and the evenness and flatness of the final polishing. Design and client attention to maintenance are out of the control of the installer but see if the surface is intact throughout and ask the installer (who will likely accompany you) about their explanation for any damage that you see.

INSTALLATION

Terrazzo as a material cannot be divorced from its form. Obviously a precast planter may be simply placed at your client's site. At the other end of the spectrum a sand-cushioned, cement-matrix installation is much more involved. When a bonded method is selected, preparation of the substrate is important because the terrazzo is adhered to the substrate. The condition of the underbed is important and you must detail to avoid cracking at control joints, which are seams positioned in structure to allow for movement that would otherwise crack the surfacing material.

The steps required may include grinding, patching, leveling, filling, priming, or sealing. After the preparation of the substrate is complete, the divider strips will be fastened to the floor. The terrazzo product that you specified will then be mixed in batches and placed in the areas created by the dividers per your drawings.

After the terrazzo sets up, but before it is ground, it will not look like the floor you specified. The aggregate will have settled into the binder. As the floor is then ground with successively finer and finer grit, the cement is polished off the surface and the aggregate will reappear. Successively finer grit will be used until the floor achieves the desired sheen: 80 grit is a standard "supermarket" sheen and grit can get into the thousands for a mirror polish, just to give some points of reference. As you attain higher and higher sheens, the floor may be filled with grout paste, a mixture to plug any small holes left as aggregate is flipped out during polishing or air bubbles beneath the surface are exposed. The floor then will receive a final polishing and then may be sealed.

Terrazzo tiles are laid into a special bed of sand and cement that is allowed to set up for 24 hours or so. Then the surface is flooded with watery grout that must be pushed into the seams between the tiles as it settles and shrinks into the seams. The grout is left on the face of the tiles after this process but will be ground off during finishing in a few days.

PROTECTION AND MAINTENANCE

Cement-matrix floors must be sealed with a penetrating sealer. Resinous or epoxy matrix systems will not absorb a penetrating sealer but if you would like to alter surface characteristics there are topical sealers available to do so. Floors should be resealed annually or more often if the environment calls for it. Once properly sealed, terrazzo is a very low-maintenance surface and can be easily cleaned without chemicals. Often rinsing with water is enough; sometimes mild detergent is required for soiling that must be dissolved to remove it.

What Would You Do? 12.5

Under what conditions would you specify a top-dressing/topical sealer?

Terrazzo surfaces can be repaired on-site by qualified restoration people. Common repairs include cleaning, polishing, sealing, restoring pitted surfaces, patching, and repairing failed expansion joints. Vacuum grinders allow for dry grinding. Obviously restoring the existing surface is a sustainable, money-saving option that should be considered over replacement whenever possible.

Helpful Hint 12.1

When you are attempting to come up with a close ballpark estimate, you will get a more accurate number if you reference a job that the estimator did in the recent past. When you are considering a new contractor you will often visit jobs that they completed as part of your due diligence before recommending them. As you travel to a few job sites with them, notice which location resembles your vision the closest. When you request the ballpark figure for your preliminary budget, you can reference that job and get a more accurate square-foot price.

SAFETY

Terrazzo floors are hard surfaces and a possible danger to those who fall. Because of their durability they are considered for public buildings and often for circulation spaces so you would want to carefully evaluate your specifications when you use terrazzo near entrances so you manage slip resistance with the right level of polish and best sealant. If there is a very direct connection between your terrazzo floor and the outdoors, you may even specify that the surface be grooved to provide additional traction but evaluate the practicality of the maintenance implications of a floor that is not flat and smooth.

Residential environments have few code stipulations governing slip resistance but you will always specify for safe environments. Commercial installations require a coefficient of friction of 0.6 or greater. Ideally your specification for the material will ensure a compliant floor without the use of transitory topical sealants but if a sealer is relied upon to provide slip resistance, compliance with slip resistance should be confirmed by third-party testing data of the topical sealants formula. These products have potential for introducing chemicals into the environment, so check the material safety data sheet as well. Many terrazzo tile products are available with nonslip surfaces integral to the product, such as metal grit as part of the surface. Tiles with nonslip sealants are visually so similar to those without that it is not easy to tell the difference. They are cleaned and maintained similarly as well. Make sure the maintenance instructions that you pass along to the client are emphatic about using the proper sealant; you wouldn't want code compliance to be compromised in the future because the wrong product was used to maintain the floor.

If toxicity is a concern, remember that VOCs can be introduced into the environment by the product and the sealer. While the traditional, cementitious terrazzo is inert, it must be sealed, so search for low-VOC product. Resinous products require no sealants but they may outgas during curing. Both cement-based and epoxy-based terrazzo systems are nontoxic after they have cured.

What Would You Do? 12.6

What is the potential danger in relying on the sealant to provide slip resistance, rather than the texture of the terrazzo?

Aggregate selection can contribute to safety. Rustic terrazzo, which is not ground flat but allows the specially selected, rounded stone (instead of sharp chipped stone) to rise above the surface, will provide more slip resistance. Specialty aggregates that glow in the dark for several hours could indicate the directions to exit or locations of steps during power outage or in environments that are dark in the normal course of their use, like nightclubs.

SUSTAINABILITY

The production of cement uses a lot of energy and is responsible for significant contribution to greenhouse gas emissions, and epoxy is a petroleum product, so this product is not without its drawbacks. However, different terrazzo systems will present different sustainable characteristics.

Cement matrix with stone aggregate, and without admixtures, is likely to be inert and can be cleaned without harsh chemicals, but it should be sealed with a low-VOC sealant. Cement matrix can be recycled after removal and could also use waste stone chips. An epoxy matrix does not have to be sealed, it can use recycled glass chips for aggregate (inert), and can be cleaned without harsh chemicals.

Terrazzo aggregate may be recycled porcelain from plumbing fixtures or recycled glass, plastic, or concrete. A well-made installation will be durable, another characteristic of green products.

What Would You Do? 12.7

What postconsumer items can you think of that would be thrown away, but could be cast into terrazzo? It would have to be something that could be ground down with the rest of the material in the composition.

MANAGING BUDGETS

Although the ingredients comprising a terrazzo surface are sold by weight or volume, the cost of your installation will be quoted for the job and the material is typically included in the job cost. Estimates that you request early in the process as you research alternate companies will be ballpark figures, probably based on surface area estimated in square feet. When you are ready to select a contractor for the work, a more comprehensive bid will likely be produced with all details accounted for.

The exact materials and complexity of the job will make a difference in the price of the work. Brass divider strips are more expensive than white metals, as are divider strips wider than 1/8 inch. Designs with small areas and lots of color changes, curved shapes, or diagonal patterns; chip sizes larger than 162 (3/8 inch); and exotic aggregates are also more costly than other choices. A custom divider will be more costly than if your design can be produced with stock divider strips, which are straight. A portland cement matrix is more labor intensive and therefore more expensive than other matrices. Thicker systems will be more expensive than thinner systems.

Terrazzo is one of the most expensive floor surfaces in terms of initial cost but when life-cycle costs are calculated this is entirely inverted and terrazzo becomes one of the least costly surfaces over the length of its life. It lasts much longer than other surfaces and is easily and inexpensively maintained.

ORGANIZATION OF THE INDUSTRY

Some terrazzo installers specialize in large jobs only and others do not have the capacity for large-scale work, so that is one determinant to consider during your initial selection. There are many manufacturers who have developed proprietary systems with slight changes to the basic recipe for both traditional and epoxy terrazzo. These products start with the same basic ingredients; however, different installers are likely to specialize in select manufactured products and may not have direct experience with every brand that you encounter on the Internet. Remember that certification programs are often centered around a particular manufacturer's product. While one product may very well be quite like another, you don't want a nuance to compromise your results, so the combination of the contractor with the right experience and capability and the best formula is your goal in approaching potential installers.

FIGURE 12.10 Your vendor may have a showroom where you can view samples and plan your specification. This is the *Caretti Terrazzo* showroom in Morton Grove, IL. *Caretti Terrazzo is a member of the Krez Group.*

You will work with a terrazzo installer that is local to your job site or is able to orchestrate the job at a distance as required. They may have a showroom where you can view samples, similar to the showroom shown in Figure 12.10, or you may communicate with them through photographs.

SELECTION CRITERIA

As implied in the previous section, the selection of a unique system is inextricably linked to the installer as they tend to have experience with a limited number of systems and products. Your design program should be the starting point of your selection criteria because it is there that you define your performance goals for the installation. You will consider the use, the aesthetic, and the site as you draw up your list of requirements. Some questions that you might ask yourself pertaining to your terrazzo installation are organized in Table 12.4.

Helpful Hint 12.2

Before finalizing your spec, request samples of different sealers applied to material similar to your spec so you can see how they alter the appearance of the product. You may want to alter your spec slightly to accommodate the changes that occur after the application of your preferred sealer.

SPECIFYING

The following spec presumes that you have a client whose job requires an epoxy terrazzo floor for a small commercial building with suites leased to medical practitioners. This will be a renovation that calls for the removal of carpet that has been glued to a concrete floor.

RELATED MATERIAL

There are a number of composite materials on the market that have a lot in common with terrazzo as they are composed of aggregate materials, often natural quartz stone, and a binder. These materials come in a variety of sizes and thicknesses and resemble precast terrazzo in that they are formed and installed with mastic or adhesive.

Artificial Stone

These products are often composed primarily of natural stone or silica, held together by a polymeric resin of some kind. They often look like natural stone but are capable of a broad variety of appearance in graining and color, matched by a variety of characteristics depending on the exact, proprietary composition. Some products are thermoplastic, meaning that sheets of material can be heated and bent and will retain the new shape after cooling. Most products will off-gas VOCs during manufacture but not after they have cured. Many are extremely stain resistant and quite scratch resistant, although all can be damaged from excessive abrasion.

Table 12.4
You may find it beneficial to organize your selection criteria in a table like this when you are finalizing your selection.

Condition	Program Implications
Is the space in question connected very directly to the outdoors?	Wet shoes and dripping umbrellas can increase slipperiness of terrazzo floors, necessitating more traction, so you might specify a lower sheen in the final grinding or a special top sealer.
Is the area exposed to a lot of sunlight?	UV rays, even through tinted windows, can alter the appearance of materials like sealers. Possibly select a UV-resistant sealer to prevent yellowing of the sealer or the material itself.
What needs are there for visual organization and wayfinding?	Color selection and distribution can be used to create meaningful contrasts to organize the space and indicate direction.
What are the lighting conditions in the space?	If glare will be a possibility you may want to specify a low-sheen polish, matte topdressings, and avoid very dark colors that will present sharp contrasts. Select for surface reflectance no greater than 40% on floors.
What kind of noise will be generated in the space?	Impact noise will easily travel through terrazzo. You may want to look into options for a buffering layer between the terrazzo and the subfloor.
Will you be trying to maximize daylighting?	Reflectance for walls should be between 40% and 70% and for floors 25% to 40%.
How interested is your client in sustainability?	You may want to select binder and aggregate for their recycled content.
Is this an institutional building or space?	A building, or area of a building that is expected to serve for decades, will indicate the most durable of materials, so avoid specialty aggregates that are less abrasion resistant and stick to glass and stone.

SAMPLE SPEC 12.1

Part 1 General Information

1.1 Related Documents

A. See designer's plans for location of terrazzo showing colors and details.
B. Refer to designer's selected sample chip selections.

1.2 Summary

A. Prepare concrete surface for epoxy terrazzo specified. Install according to plans and specifications. Seal and protect from other trades.
B. Lobby area of 400 square feet with medallion centered and oriented as shown on drawings to be provided under terrazzo installer's contract.
C. Provide and install precast terrazzo thresholds to match field color identified, at doorways into offices, and transition to corridors to be carpeted (carpet by others).
D. Provide and install precast terrazzo coved base specified to match field color identified, at entire perimeter of lobby as well as down the full length of both north and south corridors.
E. This work excludes corridors except for area immediately abutting new terrazzo floor, which is to be sloped and feathered to provide flush transition from carpeted corridor to lobby. Adjust terrazzo bases for level tops. This work also excludes the elevators.
F. Maintain flush transition to existing metal transition strip at new exterior doors (by others).

1.3 References

A. All work to comply with local codes pertaining to slip resistance and flush conditions.

1.4 Contractor Submittals

A. Provide detailed shop drawings of laser-cut aluminum plate dividers for center medallion showing all thicknesses and measurements.
B. Provide shop drawings based on contractor's own measurements from site for layout and distribution of colors.
C. Create and provide control sample 6" × 6" for approval of all terrazzo colors specified. Samples are to accurately represent finish as well as color.
D. Provide documentation of reported recycled content for glass aggregates.
E. Provide material safety data sheet for nonslip topdressing specified.
F. Provide maintenance instructions and product recommendations.

1.5 Quality Assurance

A. All contractors performing work to have a minimum of 3 years' experience and certification verifying training with terrazzo system to be used.
B. Contractor to submit a list of completed projects of similar magnitude and complexity.
C. Contractor to be a member of NTMA and to perform all work in accordance with NTMA standards.

1.6 Delivery, Storage, and Handling

A. Deliver materials in original manufacturer's unopened containers. Materials to be mixed and handled in accordance with manufacturer's recommendations. Materials to be protected from moisture and freezing. Material to acclimate to site conditions prior to installation.

1.7 Maintenance of Installation

A. Install in accordance with manufacturer's instructions for preparing surface by shot-blasting, and priming prior to installation of terrazzo. Installed material to be protected from damage after installation until owner takes possession of it. Clean floor of all grit and cover with plastic, taping sheets together to form continuous coverage. Cut Masonite to fit and lay in traffic patterns taping sheets together.

Part 2 Products

2.1 General Information

A. Epoxilicious terrazzo system in colors and aggregate specified here.
B. Color area defined on drawings to be filled as indicated in construction documents.

2.2 Manufacturers and Suppliers

A. Contractor to be Terrazzo Technique, 1234 Industrial Drive, Anywhere, ST 12345.
B. Epoxy system from Expoxilicious.

2.3 Products

A. Install according to plans:
   1. 'A' for field to be a mixture of aggregate 4 parts crushed recycled porcelain plumbing fixtures, chip size 162, 1 part green recycled bottle glass chip size 161and 1 part amber recycled bottle glass chip size 161 in epoxy color 321 selected.
   2. 'B' for borders as defined on plans and sections of medallion indicated to be 100% amber recycled bottle glass chip size 161 in epoxy color 321 selected.
   3. 'C' for sections of medallion indicated to be 100% green recycled bottle glass chip size 161 in epoxy color 321 selected.
B. Custom aluminum plate, $^3/_8$" × 36" × 36" laser cut with logo as shown in approved shop drawings.
C. 16 gauge × $^3/_8$" dividers.
D. All surfaces to be prepared for installation prior to commencing work.

SAMPLE SPEC 12.1 (continued)

Part 3 Execution

3.1 Examination

A. Carpeting to be removed and carpet scraps scraped off, adhesive removed by others, and area broom-clean.

3.2 Preparation

A. Remove existing metal thresholds. Threshold at exterior door to be wrapped and saved for reuse. Remaining thresholds to be disposed of for recycling.
B. High spot near west wall to be ground down and entire surface to be shot-blasted.
C. Cracks to be patched, taped, and sealed. Any defects that will affect the stability or appearance of the installation are to be corrected.
D. Entire area primed with manufacturer-recommended primer.

3.3 Installation

A. Install divider strips and place medallion logo as shown on approved shop drawings.
B. Place terrazzo as shown on approved shop drawings, toweling to top of divider strips.
C. Rough grind with 24 or finer grit stones followed by initial grind with 80 grit stones.
D. Rinse with clean water twice, dry and grout with color matched to matrix.
E. Grind with 120 grit stones.
F. Install precast thresholds and bases neatly, aligning all faces within $\frac{1}{32}$" deviance, using low-VOC adhesive.

3.4 Post Installation

A. Wash all surfaces with neutral cleaner, rinse, and allow to dry.
B. Apply low-VOC sealer.
C. Upon completion work shall be ready for final inspection and acceptance by owner.

These products are most often used as countertops and vertical surfaces and some are designated as floor surfacing. Typically they require no special products to maintain them beyond soap and water and manufacturers do not recommend sealing them. If existing surfaces are dull, scratched, or chipped many can be repaired by trained, experienced restoration companies that are easily found.

> Point of Emphasis 12.1
> Many of these "engineered" stone materials are more durable and more repairable than natural stone.

CONCRETE

Concrete is considered a versatile, sustainable material and for that reason (and for reasons of current fashion) it has become a very common material in many kinds of interiors, no longer relegated to utility spaces. It is a chameleon of sorts because it is capable of such a visual variety. Although there are proprietary formulations that alter its characteristics, it is typically a rigid, hard surface that shares many characteristics with stone (think of it as having a lot in common with limestone).

> Point of Emphasis 12.2
> You can find polished concrete flooring in big box stores as well as high-end restaurants. There are few materials that are as versatile as that!

MATERIAL

The simplest recipe for concrete is:

1. Water
2. Aggregate (sand and rocks)
3. Portland cement (mixture of calcium, silicon, aluminum, and iron with small amounts of other materials)

Manufacturers and fabricators often have proprietary formulas that produce varying characteristics in the finished concrete. These formulas vary the proportion of ingredients used to make the cement, and the ingredients themselves as additional compounds, called **admixtures**, are introduced to alter the properties of the finished material. These admixtures include:

1. *Fly ash*, a by-product of burning coal recycled in concrete production, which improves workability and makes finishing the material easier.
2. *Air-entraining* compounds introduce air and improve durability in freezing weather.
3. *Accelerants* are additives that decrease setting time and speed up curing time.
4. *Retardants* are admixtures that increase the setting time by slowing down hydration or curing time.

5. *Glass fiber reinforced concrete (GFRC)* reduces small surface cracks that are common to portland cement–based products.

CHARACTERISTICS

You are probably already familiar with concrete and understand that it is a rigid material. It is crucial that you keep this in mind when specifying it because it has no "give." This means that when the building moves (as all buildings move due to settling, movement of people and things inside, or because of wind or other environmental reasons) the concrete has no flexibility, so it will crack in response to movement of the substrate. Thus, substrates for concrete surfaces must be entirely rigid and separation membranes are often required between the concrete surface and the structure that supports it. Structural concrete flatwork (a floor surface, for instance) requires expansion joints to control cracking. These control joints will be located by the structural engineer. Any concrete **topping** that you specify cannot span this joint.

> **What Would You Do? 12.8**
>
> What would be some instances when concrete's sound-reflective quality would be a benefit and you might elect to leave it exposed?
>
> Imagining an instance when you might leave it exposed, what kind of surface finish would you specify for that interior space and what should the concrete look like?
>
> As you read the rest of this chapter, be alert for processes that you might specify to create the surface you just imagined.

Concrete has good compression strength (can bear weight) but not good tensile strength (cannot span long distances unsupported). Concrete is a porous material and is similar to limestone in tactile quality and absorption. Because it is porous there are more options for coloring and sealing the concrete since color and sealer can penetrate or be applied as a top coat. Sealing is required for any concrete product that you specify. Concrete, when used to define spaces (such as poured as walls), is a dense material that would contain sound in any space that used concrete to create a dense perimeter. You can also imagine that concrete is a sound-reflective material that would bounce sound back into a space. On vertical surfaces you could add a texture that would muddle the sound but noise will not be effectively soaked up by concrete.

FIGURE 12.11 Stock concrete tiles.

FORMS

Whether the concrete that you have in mind for your job is a surface or a form, a stock item or custom, precast or cast-in-place, will affect how you approach the job and find a fabricator to do the work. Plumbing fixtures (sinks and tubs but not toilets, which must be impervious), fireplace surrounds, countertops, surfaces, and furniture are commonly specified in concrete. Shops tend to specialize in the kinds of items that they produce so, for instance, if you have a custom sink in mind, look for a company that is experienced in making sinks. Fabricators usually know what concrete mixes and finishes work best for which applications and you want to take advantage of their expertise in specific areas.

Precast

Available in precast units such as shower pans and floor tiles, custom items, or cast-in-place surfaces and overlays, concrete can be specified by designers to solve a variety of design problems. Figure 12.11 shows precast tiles that

Figure 12.12 This custom fireplace surround was cast and finished off-site, then delivered and adhered. *Fireplace surround by Flying Turtle Cast Concrete in Modesto, CA. Photo by Alana Clark.*

Figure 12.13 Concrete is such a plastic medium that it will retain the texture of the form that holds it as it hardens.

Figure 12.14 The heat emitted by concrete as it cures is so low that it will not damage special aggregates, like this composition that contains shark teeth. *Created by Tom Ralston Studios, Santa Cruz, CA.*

demonstrate the versatility of this product. These tiles call to mind soft clay terra-cotta tiles but they are a little more durable. These tiles are a stock item but custom items can be precast for installation at your client's job site. The fireplace shown in Figure 12.12 was custom made and cast off-site, then delivered and fastened in place.

Surfaces

Concrete is used to produce structural members. As an interior designer you will not have responsibility for engineering any structural members, but you may be called upon to suggest finishes for them. You may also specify non-load-bearing components.

In order to create a vertical surface, concrete is poured (cast) down into a form. These forms can be lined with material that imparts a texture to the surface of the concrete because concrete, in its plastic state before it cures, will pick up even the most subtle textures. Figure 12.13 shows concrete that picked up the fine texture from the plywood form it was cast onto.

Concrete does not "dry" to harden, it *cures*, meaning a chemical reaction takes place. Because the chemistry of the concrete is changing as it cures, many applications that you might specify for coloring and sealing must be precisely timed. For some applications concrete must cure completely, which may take about 28 days. Other applications must be employed before the concrete cures completely. This curing time is also crucial when you specify a concrete leveling product to repair a floor for resilient or other flooring surface. Since the concrete is undergoing a chemical reaction for the 28 days needed for it to cure, adhesives cannot be trusted to adhere properly, finishes might not come out right, and sealants might not be stable. Different formulations may have different properties in this regard but the basic recipe for concrete will need to cure before most subsequent processes can be used.

Concrete cures with an exothermic chemical reaction (emits heat during curing) but it is not so hot that you cannot touch it while it cures. This means that there are many materials that could be embedded in the plastic surface. Figure 12.14 shows a composition that includes

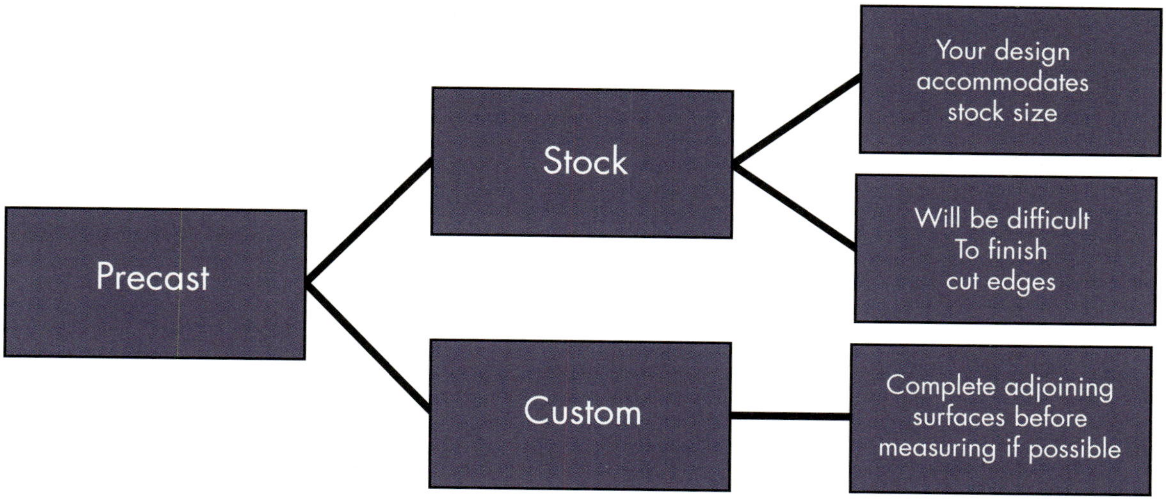

FIGURE 12.15 The work will proceed somewhat differently depending on which option you select.

sharks' teeth and colored stones. It would not be possible to bake sharks' teeth in the body of a tile, but the low heat produced by curing will not damage heat-sensitive materials. The ability to construct custom forms and surfaces without high heat has allowed designers to embed recycled items in blocks of concrete that are then cut into tiles and slabs revealing everything from recycled golf tees to semiprecious stones.

If you are reusing your fabricator's known formula, you can probably safely work off of the existing shop samples to understand what the results of various processes will be. Each shop's proprietary admixtures (compounds that are added to concrete to alter its properties, such as weight or curing time) must be apportioned exactly or it might cause unexpected results, so a finish sample from one fabricator may not be a good guide for a different fabricator whose concrete is possibly a different formula.

Stock or Custom

It is important to understand the implications of the characteristics and form of concrete that you are specifying (Figure 12.15) so you can not only oversee the project properly, but design it in the best way. Just using one form option—a precast item—you can see that it will make a difference during your design planning and specification management whether you are specifying an item in stock sizes or a custom-size precast unit.

Custom work is easily available; Figure 12.16 shows a custom sink designed especially for this space.

FIGURE 12.16 When custom concrete must interface with building systems or contain manufactured parts, as is the case with this sink, you will request that the fabricator produce shop drawings that show the interfaces.

Producing a custom item like this is a collaborative process as you work with your concrete specialist to determine what is possible and sensible. Drawings that you have made may be supplemented by shop drawings produced by the fabricator, especially in this instance where you will want to confirm that purchased plumbing connectors will fit exactly and align with plumbing pipe. A simple form like a countertop may not require shop drawings, but fabricators should see the site and take their own measurements, before the work begins. Special processes and admixtures might be specified to finish the concrete.

Helpful Hint 12.3

Specialty work is part craft and part art. It is not always possible to anticipate all the junctions in a process that require a design decision, and even though your specification will be as complete as you can make it, and will reference examples and samples, there will still be instances when the fabricator must make decisions. Even the subtlest details have an effect on the finished work and you must find a fabricator who shares your vision and is competent to produce the work in an artistic, as well as a functional, manner.

What Would You Do? 12.9

Imagine that you are planning to install a custom concrete sink. In a specific installation (find a picture of an installation or imagine one), make a list of questions you would like to have answered and who you might be able to turn to for answers. What trades would you be collaborating with?

Toppings

Concrete overlays are a mixture of resin, sand, and cement with additional proprietary admixtures. They are used as a surfacing material and are applied over a supporting substrate. They include self-leveling concrete products that are the consistency of a milkshake when applied. They are poured on top of the substrate that could be a new surface or a previously installed surface, like tile or even a resilient floor or wood floor. The thickness of these overlays varies from ⅛ inch for a skim coat on stable rigid substrate to ¾ inch for textures, or thicker to even out the substrate surface. The installation will vary depending on the substrate. Some suggestions from the Concrete Network are described in Table 12.5.

Table 12.5
Concrete overlays can be installed over a number of surfaces, which may suit your job conditions.

Supportive Substrate	Prepwork for Substrate	Installing Overlay
Concrete	Clean and possibly scuff or shot-blast the surface	Pour directly onto prepared floor
Tile	Clean and possibly scuff surface; seal grout, possibly with several layers so grout joints won't ghost through	Pour directly onto prepared floor
Wood for dry location	Install ¾" plywood then a roofing paper slip sheet	Screw galvanized metal lath to plywood, pour overlay onto surface
Wood for wet location	Install ¾" marine-grade plywood and anti-fracture membrane	Screw galvanized metal lath to plywood, dipping screws into latex before using; pour overlay onto surface

Think of concrete overlays as a thin topping of concrete, and even though formulas will vary slightly, they will still have a lot of properties in common with the concrete used to make items like sinks and furniture. Since overlays are all about their surface you will want to be aware of common options for finishing and decorating. The colors and textures that you specify will meet functional or aesthetic program goals.

What Would You Do? 12.10

Overlays are nonstructural. If you wanted to use an overlay on the floor of the room where you are right now, could you do so? What about this floor makes you think so (or think not)?

FINISHES

After the concrete is laid, possibly before it has even set up, there may be additional procedures that you should specify to meet your client's performance or aesthetic requirements.

Textures

Concrete is such a plastic material when it is first laid that it can be imprinted with even finely detailed and intricate textures. The desired outcome and the production process will indicate the best method of achieving your results. See Table 12.6 for some commonly available options.

Table 12.6
Forms and textures for concrete installations can be manipulated in a number of ways.

Method	How It Works	Process	Results	Considerations
Polishing	Surface ground with abrasives to desired sheen	Multistep grinding process: successively finer grit Dust controlled with water or vacuuming	Smooth surface with sheen	May be top-dressed with penetrating hardeners or solutions that require periodic reapplication a) polishing compound for added sheen b) anti-slip conditioners
Seeding	Decorative aggregates or other materials are embedded in wet concrete	Aggregate tamped into wet concrete May be ground flat after curing for 14 days ±	Materials on surface or throughout	Tamping is frequently done by hand so labor intensive with good control New concrete work only Lots of water in finishing
Exposed aggregate	Aggregate that has sunk into body of concrete is re-exposed during curing process	Concrete is placed and the top layer of paste is removed	Texture of aggregate become surface	Select smooth, rounded aggregate New concrete work only Lots of water in finishing
Salt	Plastic concrete is seeded with rock salt	Concrete is placed and rock salt tamped into surface then melted away after curing	Fairly smooth face with small hollows	Small depressions could collect dirt in horizontal surfaces New concrete work only Lots of water in finishing
Broomed or brushed	Surface is brushed with broom while concrete is still plastic	After concrete is placed, surface is brushed	Directional textural striaé	New concrete work only
Stamped	Freshly poured concrete is embossed with forms imparting specific texture	After concrete is placed large rubber mats with texture are tamped onto surface before it cures	Variety of textures often imitating stone and brick	New concrete work only Lots of water in finishing Powdered releasing agents help remove mats without sticking; these agents are washed away
Formed edges	Molds are held against edges of newly poured concrete	Forms lined with molds that shape edges of cast unit	Edges that appear to be carved	New concrete work only
Sandblasting	The hardened surface is subjected to sand or "shot" to remove portions of the surface	High-powered "guns" spray the sand or shot onto the surface	Surface is abraded to matte condition, the texture depends on the size and type of abrasive used	Utter control is not possible but even effects are achievable; sometimes stencils are combined with sandblasting to create patterns

What Would You Do? 12.11

What textures have you seen recently that could be transferred to concrete for horizontal or vertical surfaces? Concrete will conform to fine details. What would happen if you cast it onto dried leaves, rolled tire treads across it, pressed handprints into it, etc.? What other textures could you have imparted and how would the process go?

Pigment

Pigment can be added to new concrete as it is being mixed or it can be sprinkled (broadcast) onto the surface just after the concrete has been placed but before it hardens. Remember, new concrete may need to cure for 28 days before applying most coloring agents but these colorants are obviously designed to be applied prior to curing. You might combine multiple processes for control over more of the surface properties. Chemical compatibility should be confirmed with actual samples before finalizing specifications. Don't forget to leave time in your production schedule to produce samples that must also cure prior to subsequent processes. Begin the sampling process early in case you don't nail it the first try and need a second 28-day curing time to come up with the finish that best serves your program goals.

Decorative options include penetrating stains and dyes, manipulating the surface with seeding, polishing, or applying surface coatings like paints and tinted sealers. Multiple options may be combined in one installation. Color is employed decoratively, or functionally to satisfy program goals, such as the creation of a pathway directing traffic to your client's door as the one in Figure 12.17, leading to the door of the coffee shop. Table 12.7 describes some of these options.

Sealants

Concrete is vulnerable to staining and bleaching by common substances such as foods and cleansers; it should be sealed with a penetrating sealant, coated with a topdressing, or both. When combining compounds such as colorants, sealants, and topdressings, confirm chemical compatibility as some compounds react with each other and produce unexpected or non-durable results.

Penetrating Sealants

Penetrating sealants tend to leave the appearance nearly unaltered. Remember, if you are sealing a surface that will be used for food preparation or consumption, use a food-grade sealer. Even when protected, this is a surface that will change visually over time, and you should educate your client so that the patina is anticipated and appreciated.

Film-Formers

Topdressings are also referred to as top coats or film-formers. Film-formers are better at resisting stains, and they are sometimes selected to enhance the color. They can also impart a gloss. Paste wax sealers are a popular film-former and can be used to increase the depth of color in concrete. Film-formers must be replenished more frequently than penetrating sealers. Table 12.8 lists some common sealants.

Helpful Hint 12.4

Whenever you specify a topdressing kind of sealant remember that some of the properties of the surface will then depend on the topdressing—not on the concrete (or whatever material is used) beneath it. Impact resistance and weight-bearing ability are dependent upon the concrete but staining, slip and stain resistance, and scuffing will be dependent upon the topical sealant selected.

FIGURE 12.17 This pigmented, custom installation leads the customers of this coffee shop right to the door. *Created by Tom Ralston Concrete, Santa Cruz, CA.*

Table 12.7
Options for finishing your concrete surface.

Method	How It Works	Process	Result	Considerations
Pigment mixed in	Powdered pigment is put into concrete before it cures	Pigment may be mixed into the batch before it is placed or sprinkled on the surface and worked into the concrete	Consistent color throughout batch	Color throughout component
Pigment broadcast	Powdered pigment is sprinkled onto concrete and bonds with concrete	Pigment is broadcast onto the surface before it sets up	Variegated color and opacity	Pigment penetrates approximately ¼"
Reactive stains	Chemical reaction between acid solutions and metallic salts in stain and lime in concrete	Stain applied to cured concrete surface	Translucent variegated color	Permanent bond with concrete material
	Solvent or water based			More difficult to control than other options
				Limited color palette
				May require sealer
Nonreactive stains	Pigment particles soak into open pores	Surface opened to allow penetration	Even, opaque, uniform color	May require acid wash prior to use to open pores
	Solvent or water based	Stain applied to surface		May require sealer
				Broad color palette
Dyes	Pigment particles soak into open pores	Surface may have to be opened up to allow penetration	Translucent variegated color	When dying a stained surface allow stain color to fully develop before applying dyes
	Concentrated pigments blended or thinned for custom color	Stain applied to surface		Broad color palette highly customizable
	Solvent or water based			Require a sealer
Paint	Epoxy coating forms a skin on the concrete	Seal and prime; paint with appropriate paint; seal again	Solid color or paint techniques and faux finishes	Coating sits on surface and may peel without proper preparation or abrade if not sealed at end of painting job
Tinted sealant	Pigments tint sealant	After curing concrete is sealed with tinted sealer	Consistent, translucent color	Curing compounds should not be used
				Confirm compatibility with other finish processes

Table 12.8
Sealant options and requirements for concrete.

Sealer	Properties	Install	Maintain
Silicone	Penetrating, not permissible in some states	Easy to apply	Easy to replenish
Acrylic: water based	Relatively soft	Easy to apply	Easy to replenish
Acrylic: solvent based	Softer than water-based acrylic High-sheen surface	Easy to apply	Easy to replenish
Epoxy: water based	Hard Water impervious	Not as easy to apply as acrylic sealers	Reapplication not as easy as for acrylic
Urethane	Most durable	Install over water-based epoxy	Reapplication more difficult
Hybrid sealers	Penetrate and form thin film	Easy to apply, repeated soaking process	Maintain with wax
Waxes: beeswax	Soft, smudgy surface, never really dries	Easy to apply and reapply	Must be frequently buffed and reapplied
Waxes: carnauba	Harder than beeswax, maintains sheen with little smudging	Easy to apply but must be buffed to desired sheen before drying	Must be reapplied periodically

Seaweed in the ocean was the starting point for the custom installation. Concrete is such a plastic medium that it will settle into the fine details of the leaves, but Tom Ralston had to devise a way that would transfer the form without embedding seaweed into the concrete.

Actual seaweed was harvested from the water for use as a model for making molds. The fabricators had a couple of ideas for imprinting the concrete.

The first idea was to use clay to make molds. It is easy to understand the price of custom work when you see that 3–4 men work several hours to figure out the best way to transfer the texture to concrete. At the time of this writing, trades bill out around $75/hr × 3 men × 4 or 5 hours = over $1000 just to investigate this option.

The clay molds are further smoothed and worked

Naturalistic configurations had to be devised. This obviously takes more than technical skill, it requires an artistic eye. Your search for the right shop becomes complicated when you must find a craftsman/artisan to collaborate with you on such unique custom jobs as this one.

A resin was eventually used to create a model of seaweed. This process formed an accurate "negative" of the seaweed form, like the mold that a jewelry designer would use to cast metal, but instead of a wax carving for the initial form, seaweed created the negative in the resin mold.

The seaweed models were pressed into the newly laid concrete to transfer their relief pattern to the plastic concrete. The plank paths are necessary because the concrete was a soft paste at this point. The surface had to be smoothed to a finished surface and the molds carefully applied and rolled so as to not scar the soft concrete around them and yet completely transfer the form with no voids from air gaps.

After the concrete set up, the surface was prepared for a highly custom stain application. Remember that concrete is still undergoing a chemical change for about a month after it has been laid, so the chemistry to control the color must be exacting. You can see that this was a finished space complete with cabinets! This client did not want the process to stop completely for the duration of that month required for curing. The work had to proceed.

The results suggested the depth of water and seaweed forms. The final custom product retained the delicateness of seaweed, transferred completely to the concrete.

FIGURE 12.18 When your design program has several requirements, as is the case for the sealant of this sink, your search for appropriate product becomes quite narrow. *Installation by Two Stones Design, Port Byron, IL.*

When your installation has special needs, such as a surface that must be sanitized or that should not have a toxic sealant because food will be prepared on it, your selection becomes narrowly focused. Consider the sink in Figure 12.18. The drain board is a good place to let vegetables sit after you have rinsed them, so you would like a food-grade sealant. Dishes may sit here on their way to be cleaned in the sink or may sit here to dry after being cleaned. This sealant will be exposed to dish soap as the area is cleaned up, so the sealant cannot be dissolved by dish soap. The drain board has metal slides inserted into the concrete. When the sealant is replenished it may get on the slides, so it should not react to them chemically, or even bond with them, as the bond may not be very strong and your client will not want to watch it chip and blister as it removes itself due to an improper bond.

INSTALLATION

Obviously the installation will vary depending on what form the concrete has taken. You can imagine that if you have had concrete cast into a fireplace surround (Figure 12.19) in one or more parts, the installation may resemble the installation of stone members and a mason would be hired to assemble and adhere the pieces to the

FIGURE 12.19 Syndecrete precast concrete fireplace is made of a special, sustainable concrete. *Fireplace by Syndesis, Santa Monica, CA. Photo by Sandy Wiener.*

FIGURE 12.20 Several different surface characteristics require different products within one installation for this swimming pool and bar. *Installation by Tom Ralston Concrete, Santa Cruz, CA.*

structure. Several kinds of surfaces, each having different performance characteristics, are required to complete the installation shown in Figure 12.20, where a pool interior must be painted and the deck must be slip resistant. The bar surface must be smooth for easy cleaning and everything must be resistant to UV and chlorine.

If the installation that you have designed is an overlay on a floor, then concrete contractors will be hired to perform the pouring and texturing of the surface. Sometimes a single shop will prepare, install, and finish the surface but it could also be the case that one contractor will prepare the surface while a second installs (pours) the concrete, and a third finishes it with artistic painting, acid staining, or another decorative treatment per your specification.

MANAGING BUDGETS

While concrete is sold by the cubic yard to contractors building roads and buildings, custom concrete work that is typically specified by interior designers is sold by the job with the cost of material and labor factored together as the fabricator typically supplies both. As a precast material, the units vary from "each" (shower pans for instance) to "lots" of varying sizes and as square feet (as for tiles).

QUALIFYING INSTALLERS

As mentioned previously, shops specialize in particular kinds of concrete work. If you request that a shop perform work outside their experience you run the risk of disappointing results, but with such a versatile material it is likely that you will envision something that is so unique that nobody has tried it before. It is important to understand the material well enough to anticipate potential risks in such instances and try to anticipate everything required to realize your vision. A list of things that could go wrong becomes your checklist as you follow up on details of the production. The qualified installer will have experience with work that is very similar to your client's job. They will be financially responsible, have positive references, etc., as would be expected with any contractor performing work for your jobs.

Concrete is frequently used for structural or load-bearing work and the contractors who specialize in that kind of work may not be experienced in the production of items and surfaces for interiors. It is important to realize that a countertop is not a "sidewalk" on top of cabinetry. You need to differentiate between those contractors who simply pour a lot of footings and those who understand the issues particular to interior work, so make sure your bidders have experience with the kind of job you are doing and ask to see samples and photos.

Interview your prequalified contractors:

- Think about how they will achieve the results you want and what work they have done that can demonstrate their ability to do so.
- Go over your to-scale plans with them and show them any pictures that you have to define your vision.
- Ask how they would approach the job and what work must be provided by others.
- Ask how long the job should take and what steps will be performed to complete it.
- If your job is large and you require large capacity make sure the shop has the resources to stage and produce the work.
- If your job necessitates that a number of people work to fill the order, ask what kind of training and experience the workers have.
- Ask for references and call them; visit the site of completed work if that can be arranged.
- If you would like the contractor to produce information to pass along to your client, such as how to maintain the product, how to repair it, what, if any, repair services are available through the fabricator, guarantees of stability or performance, or anything else you will require, make sure they can provide it.

SAFETY

Concrete is a hard surface. Breakable items that fall onto it are more likely to break than if they had fallen onto softer surfaces (like carpet or resilient flooring). If a person were to fall on concrete it will do nothing to cushion their fall. Concrete will vary in slipperiness depending on the surface texture and the kind of sealant used; some topical sealants increase friction. Concrete in its simplest form is inert, emitting no volatile organic compounds (VOCs). Most commercial compounds are nontoxic. Water-based colorants and sealants used are less noxious than solvent-based.

Concrete does not burn and is considered an appropriate fire barrier in the construction of fire separation walls. Concrete may contain recycled material. Some of the chemicals used in finishing and coloring concrete contain toxic ingredients, so review the material safety data sheet (MSDS), which describes potential hazards related to a material or its installation and how to guard against them.

SUSTAINABILITY

To make portland cement, ingredients must be heated to more than 1,400°C; this uses a lot of fuel and releases carbon dioxide into the atmosphere, contributing to greenhouse gasses. Some of the recipes for concrete contain ingredients that would normally end up in landfill sites, such as fly ash (a by-product of burning coal), ground slag (a by-product of the iron and steel industries), and silica fume (a by-product of silicon production). Old concrete can be broken up and reused as aggregate for new concrete. New formulations of concrete that may not require portland cement are under investigation.

Concrete is a durable material if used and installed properly. It contributes to the **thermal mass** (dense material that can absorb radiant heat from the sun during the day and release it at night) of buildings, helping to regulate energy use during heating and air-conditioning seasons.

For horizontal, exterior application, pervious concrete can be specified. **Pervious** concrete has a lower percentage of fine aggregate. The lack of fine aggregate allows storm water to percolate through its mass, filtering rainwater and reducing runoff. This keeps water on the site to feed plants or replenish the water table and reduces stress on the sewer system trying to funnel water diverted by the pavement, away from the site. It can be a high-albedo material, meaning it reflects sunlight, reducing heat-island effect outdoors.

ORGANIZATION OF THE INDUSTRY

Because the concrete industry is compartmentalized it is fairly easy to narrow your search for a contractor because flatwork and precast items are usually produced by different firms. Some shops will specialize in artistic finishes and others will stick to tinted products that require no hand work. Remember to select a contractor that has a specialty that is similar to your design.

Helpful Hint 12.5

If you do not have an idea of who to contact, then it is okay to contact a shop that you know is inappropriate for the job to ask for a lead to the right kind of shop. In my experience many tradespeople know who is working in a similar field in your geographic area and they are often willing to help you out. If you feel funny about it you can even start your conversation with "I know this isn't the kind of work you usually do, but I'm looking for someone to . . ." Contractors are very used to helping each other out with referrals.

SELECTION CRITERIA

Before you finalize your plans to use concrete as a surface, you will try to anticipate all conditions that should be addressed in your specification. Your particular design job will present some conditions that are unique and anticipating these conditions is the responsibility of the working designer. The list below is very generic but should get you started as you develop your own list of requirements. The design program for your job will help you complete the list of conditions the material must meet before it is a serious contender for your client.

Table 12.9
You may want to structure your thought process this way with requirements and options as you finalize your selection.

Condition	Program Implications
What visual and textural qualities can be produced?	A sample, or series of samples, may be required to develop a technique that can create the look you require.
What is the life expectancy of this interior?	Concrete is very durable and can be difficult to break out and remove. It is a good substrate for other materials if it is smooth and flat.
Will site conditions permit installation?	Thinner applications require a substrate that is more rigid. Thicker applications require a substrate that can bear more weight.
Concrete must be sealed.	Sealants vary and you will want to test the sealant on a concrete sample by subjecting it to the kind of staining that will be typical at the site. Sealants will alter the appearance of the surface too. If there is any testing data available you might review that in lieu of performing your own tests.
How closely will the installation resemble the samples produced?	Some processes are prone to visual variety due to differences in exact chemistry, precision of application of colorants, the "signature" of the installer(s) imparting the texture, etc.
Does the concrete surface abut another material?	A detail must be devised that protects the edges of the materials and seals the junction.
Concrete is a reflective material.	Acoustics may need to be managed with absorbency on other surfaces.
Is the surface inside or outside?	Colorants may vary in fade resistance; some sealants are more suitable to one or the other environments.
Concrete must cure before use.	Many subsequent processes cannot be applied until after the concrete has cured.
What kind of traffic is anticipated?	This affects sealants selected; if they "walk off" and need to be reapplied will they required stripping first? Be odorous? Is slip resistance dependent on the sealant? If so, how can you be sure the right formula will always be used?

Helpful Hint 12.6

When testing the concrete sample prior to finalizing your spec, test it sealed and unsealed to see if the sealer is one that might "walk off" or "wash off," so you can demonstrate to your client the importance of maintaining the surface and to understand how repairable the surface will be. Even though clients have the best of intentions for meticulous maintenance, the surface wears so gradually that it is often not noticed until it is too late, so you want to make sure that if this happens, the soiling or abrasion can be remedied.

Considerations for concrete selection and details form the basis for the program goals that your specification must satisfy. You may organize your selection criteria in a table format like Table 12.9.

SPECIFYING

As you would imagine, specifications for a concrete surface are quite different from specifications for a concrete item. A specification for a concrete countertop for a kitchen might be worded something like this:

SAMPLE SPEC 12.2

Part 1 General Information

1.1 Related Documents

A. Refer to millwork drawings for cabinet sizes.
B. Refer to partition plan for plumbing locations.
C. Refer to plumbing specifications for size of cutouts for sinks and faucets.

1.2 Summary

A. Provide and install concrete countertops and subtops required for support. Do not proceed with work until plumbing and electrical roughs are complete. Confirm all locations for plumbing and electrical supplies in the field prior of fabricating tops. Wire-reinforced concrete countertops for manager's apartment kitchen cabinets.

1.3 References

A. ASTM 134-91
B. ASTM C 1611
C. ASTM 4263 83
D. ASTM 4260 88
E. ASTM 607-96

1.4 Contractor Submittals

A. Scope of work describing all phases of production and installation.
B. Shop drawings referencing all plumbing fixtures and fittings by number.
C. Maintenance information.
D. Sealed and unsealed samples 12" × 12" × 2" for color and texture.
E. Statement of percentage of recycled material.
F. Material safety data sheet for all admixtures, colorants, and sealants.

1.5 Quality Assurance

A. Fabricator to have minimum 5 years' experience and to have passed the certification test of the Concrete Countertop Institute.

1.6 Delivery, Storage, and Handling

A. Countertops adhered to marine-grade subtops to be transported blanket-wrapped. Upon arrival at site countertops to be stored flat in conditioned site and allowed to acclimate for 12 hours prior to affixing to cabinetry. Tops to be protected from soiling and scratches.

1.7 Maintenance of Installation

A. Countertops to be fastened to cabinet cases with Mr. Sprocket SWS6/BRK-SSS stainless steel "L" brackets and countersunk flat-head wood screws. Upon completion of installation all tops are to be covered with pink rosin paper.

1.8 Related Work

A. Cabinets to be assembled, installed, and leveled prior to constructing templates.
B. Rough plumbing and electrical to be installed prior to constructing template.

Part 2 Products

2.1 General Information

A. Countertops to conform to configurations and dimensions as listed on millwork drawings and per contractor site measure. Material to be per approved, signed, and dated sample. Grade A-C marine-grade plywood subtop and angled steel "L" brackets to be provided and installed as part of this order.

2.2 Manufacturers

A. Custom Concrete Counters, 1234 Industrial Drive, Anywhere, ST 28263.

2.3 Products

A. Site measure is to supersede millwork drawings for increments of ½" or less. For disparity between shops and site measure exceeding ½" fabricator is to notify designer prior to commencing work. Rigid templates are to be constructed by the concrete fabricator and all plumbing and electrical cutouts required are to be marked on templates. Countertops to be wire reinforced with reinforcing throughout, including location of stainless steel runner for built-in trivet but excluding wire reinforcement at all cutout locations.
B. Food-grade penetrating sealant to be applied in shop, dried completely before delivery to site.
C. All exposed surfaces to be polished including edges of cutouts and sides of tops.
D. Food-grade topical sealant.

Part 3 Execution

3.1 Examination

A. Material must be free of defect, delivered to the site after the heating plant has been up and running for a minimum of 2 weeks prior to installing. Material to be fully acclimated to site prior to commencing installation.

3.2 Preparation

A. Prior to installation, cabinets and rough electrical and plumbing are to be installed.

3.3 Installation

A. Install countertops as shown on drawings, with angle brackets specified. Upon completion countertops are to be demonstrably level by testing with a bubble level placed in the center of each cabinet run.

3.4 Post Installation

A. Apply final coat of food-grade sealant, or topdressing to be applied and buffed to approved sheen; cover countertops with pink rosin paper.
B. Site to be free of dust and debris upon completion of work.
C. Contact designer with 3 days' notice for final inspection.

INSPECTION

As is the case when specifying, inspection checklists will vary with the kind of work produced. The following list is not exhaustive but meant to be a starting point for your inspection. You would add other, logical characteristics to the following list.

- Does the item or surface conform to your specifications and expectations?
- Are multiple pieces well fitted with smooth junctions that are as seamless as you expected?
- Are surface characteristics (like texture and color) consistent across each piece and from piece to piece?
- Are all exposed edges finished like faces (are countertops flat on the bottom and the top)?
- Are members consistent in size and thickness as required?
- Is the item entirely free of even small cracks?
- Has sealant specified been applied evenly, is it of the proper sheen, and does it contain no pinholes to allow penetration?

RELATED MATERIAL

Other cement products that you will specify include mortars and grouts. These products are also mentioned in Chapter 10, Tile and Brick, and Chapter 11, Stone, as they are so integral to the installation of those materials and you will find more information there.

Grouts and Mortars

Concrete has traditionally been an ingredient in grouts and mortars, so this is the logical place to learn about these "accessories" to your stone, tile, or brick installation. The cement product is acting like glue. Substrate and material being adhered both must have some porosity if concrete is to reach into the surfaces and hold everything together. Today not all grouts and mortars are cement based but cement-based mortars and grouts are still in widespread use.

Mortars

Mortars hold tile to the substrate and grouts fill the space that must be left between tiles to handle minor expansion and contraction of the tile material.

Table 12.10
This is a simple way of looking at options for bonding surfaces with mortar, cement-based or organic adhesives.

Type	Composition	Uses
Cement based	Wetset: a slurry of cement sand and water is applied to wet cement	When the cement substrate is still plastic or not entirely cured
	Thinset: cement, sand, and methylcellulose	Tile and substrate are flat and sound and movement is not anticipated
	Medium set: like thinset but thicker than $\frac{3}{16}$"	When tile thickness needs adjustment by pressing it into the setting bed, such as for uneven tile
	Thickset: thick mortar bed may bond directly to tile or be separated by a fracture membrane (like thinset installation over mortar substrate)	Even out substrate, when installing radiant heat system, creating a sloped surface
	Dry set: mortar applied to a substrate that cannot bond with the tile on its own	When the substrate cannot bond to the tile directly
	Polymer modified	Thousands of proprietary formulations alter properties of mortar
Adhesive	Tile glue that is not cement based; also called epoxy system	For impervious tile; most simply: type 1 is for floors and walls, type 2 is for walls only

Traditional cement mortars have been improved over centuries of use. Recently mortar additives and other formulations have been developed to address new tile bodies that have low porosity. Other additives alter the mortar's working properties (how it behaves as it is being applied) and functional characteristics (how it performs on the job). These additives are identified by letters, or letters and numbers, so you may see a tile manufacturer's recommendation for additive P2 for installing on plywood, or S2 for mortar for thin, large-format tiles that require a deformable (flexible) adhesive. Table 12.10 may help you organize the mortar types for your specifications.

Grout

Grout formulations also use cement although there are some grouts that use none. Grout that contains cement will have characteristics in common with portland cement mortars and with concrete. Four basic types of grout are available:

- Portland cement–based grouts are the most common. They are naturally gray or white depending on the color of the cement used. They are available pigmented in many colors and they may be sanded or unsanded. Sanded grout is used for most installations. It cleans up easily, making it good for porous surfaces. The sand in sanded grout limits the amount of shrinkage, so sanded grout is less likely to crack. Care must be taken on polished tiles as the sand may scratch polished surfaces. Unsanded grout is used for close-butt joints and should not be used on joints wider than ⅛ inch because shrinkage will cause cracks in the grout joint.
- Epoxy grouts are available as two- or three-part systems. This type of grout must be used immediately after it's mixed up. It is nonporous, chemically resistant, and easy to clean. Epoxy grouts are more expensive to buy and install but in some circumstances (restaurants and other sterile places) the extra cost is considered to be worth it for the ease of maintenance. They may be "sanded" for wider grout joints, but the sand will probably be a specially selected mineral filler. Modified epoxy grout is composed of epoxy and portland cement. Its characteristics are similar to those of portland cement grout, but it is harder and forms better bonds.
- Silicone rubber grout cures rapidly and is resistant to hot oil, steam, humidity, and prolonged temperature extremes. It should not be used on food preparation surfaces.
- Furan resin grout is highly resistant to certain chemicals, especially acids. It cures within minutes because furan is a very volatile chemical. The installer should follow the manufacturer's directions, and tiles should be pre-waxed to prevent grout from adhering to tile faces. Grout residue is removed from the tile faces by steam-cleaning. This type of grout is most typically available in black. Furan is toxic and the toxins are bioaccumulative, meaning that they build up in organisms' bodies.
- Polymer-modified grouts have additives incorporated into the grout for better adhesion and application of the grout; properties that you can select for when choosing modified grouts are:
  - Stain resistance
  - Reduced water absorption
  - Grout for very narrow joints
  - Grout for wide joints
  - Grout that contains sealer
  - Grout that maintains color consistency

Color Grout is available in a range of colors. The tile setter should be instructed to make up a test sample on a board with the tile from the lot ordered and the grout mixed up from the grout ordered for the job. Keep in mind that each time grout is mixed, even if from the same bag, the color will vary slightly. There is no way to control this precisely, so be very practical about accepting or rejecting a color sample. Even if it is not an exact match, but still works with the other colors, it will be sensible to accept it.

> **Point of Emphasis 12.3**
> Grout changes color over time, not just because of soiling—it actually changes color. Black grout will fade to "charcoal" in a short period of time. This color shift also includes grout samples; when your actual grout samples are three or four years old, it is time to request new samples, even if the colors are still current. The paper samples in brochures are often more accurate than old grout samples are. This is one reason that you will always want to see a sample board with four of your tiles grouted with grout from the bag(s) ordered for the job.

A Cautionary Tale 12.1

I specified a green slate tile for my client's loft conversion shower surround. She had wanted to use slate slab, but the cost was prohibitive, so we settled on 12" × 12" tile, and I suggested that we match the grout color to the tile precisely to give it a more monolithic look.

I found the perfect color and formula, but the only supplier was far away, and the grout had to be shipped in on a truck, causing some short delay. I always request that a grout sample be made from the bag of grout purchased for the job by grouting four tiles set up on a piece of scrap board. Because of the delay caused by waiting for the grout, I waived the sample. I could hear the aggravation in my client's voice when she called and commanded that I come to the job site to see the *gray* grout, and when I got there she was not wrong.

I found the bag of grout that was nearly empty and it was quite green in the bag. Here is what happened: The pigment that made the grout the perfect shade of green had settled to the bottom of the bag during all the jiggling it endured during shipping, so when the grout was poured out of the bag to grout her shower, only the unpigmented gray portland cement grout made it into the bucket. Little (if any) green pigment was in the grout mixed with water for the job, so the grout on the wall was gray instead of green. My client was so disappointed and angry that she refused to pay thousands of dollars of my design fees. It was a big price to pay for waiving a sample.

Sealants

All exposed concrete, including portland cement–based grouts, should be sealed as soon after installation as the manufacturer will allow. This typically takes 28 or more days. The best possible situation is one in which all traffic will stay away from the surface until the sealant has been applied and dried. Since cement must cure for such a long time, this is not always possible. If an area must be used during curing, the surface must be cleaned and allowed to dry thoroughly prior to sealing.

SUMMARY

In this chapter you looked into the similarities and differences between terrazzo and concrete and learned about the material components of each. You reviewed the characteristics of and uses for these materials and the forms that are typical for them. You learned about some of the potential problems and how to specify to avoid them. You reviewed the organization of fabricators, installers, and finishers of these materials and learned how to interact with them for installation and the production of custom work. You looked at related accessory items and products as well as other materials that contain cement.

WEB SEARCH ACTIVITIES

1. Perform an image search for *Venetian* and *palladiana terrazzo*. Notice the consistency of Venetian from one supplier to the next and then the variety of products that are called palladiana. It will probably occur to you that when a material is open to interpretation, you want the results to conform to your interpretation. What would be one way of communicating your intention to the fabricator?

2. Search for *precast terrazzo* and notice the options that are available. If you are working on a computer that has CAD installed on it, click on the *CAD details* that you find on the sites you visit to get a sense of how these items are constructed and installed.

3. Intricate custom dividers are sometimes laser cut from metal plates (thick metal sheets, not metal plating). Search for one of the common metals used as divider strips such as brass, aluminum, or zinc. Use a search string, such as *brass sheet plate*. Pull up one of the manufacturers that you find there and notice the thicknesses available. Remember that the dividers must be as "deep" (thick) as your terrazzo topping.

4. Perform an image search for *decorative dividers terrazzo*. Look for pictures of installations. Notice the intricacy that is possible for overall designs. Search for close-up views. Notice the different metal types used and also the various thicknesses of the metal dividers. The divider strips that you see are as thick as the terrazzo. The width of the divider strip that shows on the face of the finished product will be determined by you. It is clear from the photos that the face width of the divider strip is a decorative element in your design so you would specify it and request samples.

   You might want to make a digital "collage" by right-clicking images and Copying and Pasting them into a document as a quick reference for the variety of possible dividers to refer to when you are designing your projects.

5. Search for *terrazzo floor installation*. Perform a video search to locate and watch a couple of videos showing terrazzo installations.

6. Search for *sealants for terrazzo* that have special characteristics, such as nonslip. See if you can locate a material safety data sheet for the product you are investigating.

7. Search for a master specification for a terrazzo installation. The National Terrazzo and Marble Association (www.ntma.com) may have spec templates like this. Review for comprehension all the items stipulated on the spec that you find.

8. Search for *quartz surface* and select one of the manufacturers you find. Look up the specifications (you may need to find a tab that says *Technical Information, Architects, Professionals* or something similar).

9. Search for a couple of custom concrete fabricators sites or sites that discuss custom concrete formulas. See what other possibilities people have devised for concrete for interiors. You may want to start a file for techniques or local fabricators.

10. Search for a material safety data sheet for concrete. Individual companies producing concrete will often post such information about their products. Review the information to get an idea of the implications for human beings when you order and install concrete products.

11. There are a number of underlayments and surface preparations that contain concrete and others that prepare the surface for concrete. Imagine that you are designing a client's site and, for reasons of aesthetics, want to use concrete flooring where there is currently a particleboard subfloor. What products would you seek out and what steps would you take? Use the Internet to locate specific, proprietary products and processes to compete this task.

12. Perform an image search for items typically specified by the interior designer that are made of concrete, such as furniture, light fixtures, sinks, etc.

PERSONAL ACTIVITIES

1. Look at images of completed terrazzo installations and make a list of things that you would expect to see in a quality installation. Include considerations for the design, installation, and maintenance.

2. Using your selected plan or looking at a picture of a location where terrazzo might be an appropriate selection, draw up a list of program goals for the flooring that could be the basis for your selection criteria. Start with the items in Table 12.4 and then expand into the considerations that are more unique to your site.

3. Imagine installing terrazzo on your plan or find a picture of a terrazzo installation. What terrazzo specification would be best for that installation if it were new construction? What would be best if it were a renovation?

   Using Sample Spec 12.1 as an example, write a specification for the installation as you imagine you would design it.

4. Imagine that you want to duplicate an intricate logo in your design and require a laser-cut metal divider. How thick could your terrazzo be if you were to create the logo this way? How much would the piece of metal cost your fabricator, who would likely include this metalwork in their estimate?

5. Review the composition of the material for terrazzo. Find a material safety data sheet (MSDS). See if the product has any sustainability features and review them for "green washing" or confirm that they are truly legitimate claims the working designer can trust as valid. (Green washing is the tactic of making a product appear to be sustainable when it is not. A green-washed product may advertise as "environmentally friendly" or "green" with no substantiation for this claim.)

6. Recall all the uses of concrete you have encountered in design magazines and in person (or search the Internet for examples). In which instances would you expect the concrete to require support beneath it to handle its poor tensile strength?

   Sketch a detail for one of these instances that would conceal the support or make a design feature of it.

7. Find a picture of an installation of concrete or imagine an installation of concrete in the plans that you have made for another class. Using Sample Spec 12.2 as an example, write a spec for your installation.

SUMMARY QUESTIONS

1. What is the function of the matrix?
2. How is terrazzo similar to concrete?
3. How is terrazzo different from concrete?
4. Which systems would be less likely to crack from building movement? Why?
5. What are the common aggregates?
6. What is the difference between a cementitious and a modified cementitious matrix?
7. What advantages does an epoxy matrix have over a cement matrix?
8. What advantages does a cement matrix have over an epoxy matrix?
9. Which installation system is the thickest? Which is the thinnest?
10. What is the difference between precast and custom precast?
11. What options are there for dividers?
12. How long must a cement matrix cure before it can be sealed with many types of sealers?
13. After laying terrazzo, how long must installers wait to grind the terrazzo? What other processes might take place during grinding?
14. What are the two basic types of sealants? How are they different from each other? How do they work? What is the reason for each?
15. If you were contemplating a complicated renovation, say removing tile flooring and installing poured-in-place terrazzo, what characteristics would you look for in an ideal installer?
16. What steps would you take to confirm that a particular installer is qualified to work on your client's project?
17. What is one third-party organization that you can turn to for general information about terrazzo?
18. When terrazzo installers get certified, what possible meanings are there for the term?
19. If you wanted a mirror finish on the terrazzo wall panels in the lobby of a spa, what grit would you specify for the final grind? If you wanted good traction in a supermarket, what grit would you specify for the final grind?
20. How is terrazzo maintained?
21. What restoration options are available?
22. What safety issues will your terrazzo installation present and how can you specify to minimize any potential damage to users or to the terrazzo?

23. What are some options for recycled aggregate?
24. What characteristics would a sustainable terrazzo installation have?
25. What kind of considerations come into play when you must adhere to the confines of a slim budget, for a facility that will occupy the space for decades to come, when selecting for a terrazzo floor?
26. What are some benefits of terrazzo surfaces over other options that you might have for floors and walls?
27. What characteristics do man-made surfacing materials containing quartz or silicates have in common with terrazzo? How do these composite materials differ?
28. What is the basic recipe for concrete and what kinds of admixtures have been developed to improve it?
29. What are some restrictions in concrete as a material and what approaches can the designer take to overcome them?
30. How does concrete transform from a paste into a solid? How long does this take? What implications does this have for other processes that must occur?
31. Why is it risky to ask one fabricator to match a sample that you borrowed from another fabricator?
32. What kinds of things would you think about if you were trying to select the best fabricator for a unique custom job?
33. List the common ways of altering the color and texture of concrete.
34. What are the two common ways of sealing concrete and when would you use each?
35. How is concrete priced out?
36. What considerations would come to mind if you were trying to select the best fabricator for your client's job?
37. What safety issues come to mind when you are thinking of specifying a concrete item? What is a MSDS? What safety issues pertain to concrete floors?
38. How is concrete typically priced out to the designer or client?
39. What sustainability considerations pertain to concrete?
40. When you are inspecting concrete in order to hire a contractor or looking over your own specification, what kind of things would you look for? It might help you formulate your answer if you imagine or look at an installation.
41. What is mortar and how does portland cement mortar adhere two surfaces together?
42. Why are there different formulations of cement mortars?
43. What are the most commonly used grouts and what are their properties?
44. What additives are used to improve the characteristics of portland cement grouts?

Chapter 13

LAMINATED MATERIALS

Key Terms

Plies
Site-finishing
Subfloor
Tongue and groove
Underlayments
Wear layer

Objectives

After reading this chapter, you should be able to:

- Understand the reason for laminating materials together and how to evaluate laminated material for your use.
- Know what kinds of products are common to the market and what options are available when you need a material that is not available "off the shelf."
- Understand how these products are installed and maintained.
- Understand what sustainability and safety issues pertain to these products.
- Know how to select and specify a laminate product.

LAMINATED MATERIALS

The term *laminated* means that two (or more) layers are adhered together; they may be multiple layers of the same material, like plywood with a veneer face, or they may be different kinds of materials, like natural stone laminated to a porcelain tile substrate. The characteristics, of this product category vary significantly because all kinds of products, with their own inherent characteristics, are part of this category. The thing they all have in common is that they are adhered in layers, usually to provide a performance or aesthetic improvement over any of the materials used singularly. Sometimes there is a price reduction over the single material option, but this is not always the case since these materials are often more labor intensive to produce and their components may include sophisticated, expensive materials.

Typically the substrate of the laminated assembly will be superior to the facing material in some way that improves upon the material. Stone veneer on a porcelain backer can offer more stability to the material and the same stone on a composite backing can be lighter in weight than natural stone. High-rise buildings and transportation require lightweight materials, so laminating heavy material to lighter substrates lightens dead loads. Dimensionally stable materials (those that retain original dimensions during the service life of the product) bonded to less stable materials, such as wood bonded to a more stable substrate, improve performance over the life of the installation.

When you understand the properties of the materials that are used on the face and the back of these laminated products you will be able to comprehend how the facing material benefits from the backing material. All the materials that are discussed in this book are available as components in laminated product. We could even legitimately include materials such as carpet (primary and secondary backing laminated together) and plastic laminate! (Obviously layers of craft paper laminated together are *laminated*.) Laminated or engineered products may well become the norm. The main drivers of laminated products are stability and sustainability.

MATERIAL MAKEUP OR CONTENT

In the simplest manifestation of these materials, there will be a substrate and a facing material. Typically the substrate is selected for performance and the facing material is selected for appearance. Sometimes it is the case that there is a performance layer on top of the material selected for appearance, as is the case for some laminated flooring products. These products will have a performance substrate that is a dimensionally stable, engineered product faced with a wood veneer selected for its appearance and may be topped with a coating film that is laminated over the aesthetic material, which lends durability to the surface.

Substrates for Laminated Products

Substrate simply means the material that is under or behind the facing material. For laminated products you will encounter substrates that are cellulosic products, like engineered wood sheets; there will also be porcelain, metal, plastic, paper, and glass substrates. You will also encounter these materials in unusual forms such as honeycomb paper and foamed metal.

> Point of Emphasis 13.1
> You know how cardboard is made especially rigid by layering bent cardboard between two smooth layers, making a box much stronger than if it was made of three flat layers of cardboard? The same principles apply to other materials as well; honeycomb aluminum and plastic are similar in that bent material lends rigidity to a panel that is mostly air so it is rigid, yet light.

Cellulosic

Besides plywood, particleboard, and medium density fiberboard (described in Chapters 5 and 7), there is an additional engineered wood material called high-density fiberboard (HDF). HDF is common in laminated products but is not commonly used under the finishes that interior designers specify. High-density fiberboard is similar to medium-density fiberboard (MDF) but it ranges between 50 and 80 pounds per cubic foot. It is available as standard in 4' × 8' or 5' × 8' sheets that are ½ inch, ¾ inch, and 1 inch in thickness. Figure 13.1a–c shows the appearance of these familiar materials.

When you are designing a custom surface that uses plywood as a base layer, you must always maintain an odd number of **plies** to prevent warping. This means that if you add a material to the face of a

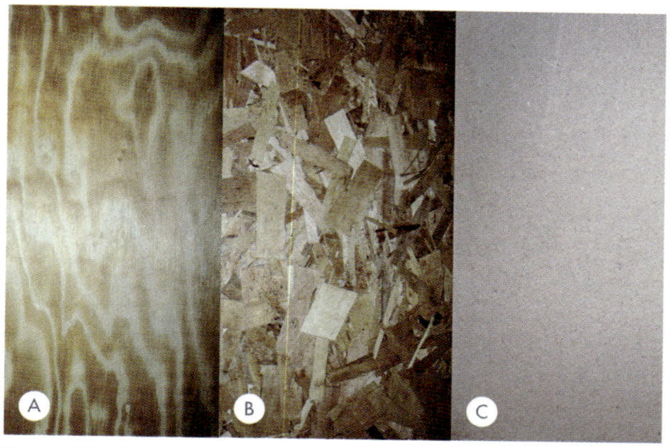

FIGURE 13.1A–C Substrates for flooring include (a) plywood, which is superior at holding mechanical fasteners like nails; (b) particleboard, which is the most common substrate; (c) MDF, which is seldom used for flooring substrate, but is a common substrate for other wood constructions.

FIGURE 13.2 Engineered wood product as the core of this laminated panel.

plywood core, you must add a balancing layer to the back. Plywood constructions with an even number of layers will warp.

Engineered wood substrates have some benefits over natural wood. They are:

- Stable so they do not expand and contract with changes in moisture.
- As impact resistant as the substrate, which may be denser than the wood species on its face.
- Able to cover larger areas so big, undivided panels are possible.
- More sustainable because such a thin layer of wood is used that it conserves slow-growing hardwood.

Other less common wood-based substrates are also used. A product called finger-core or finger-jointed core has thin strips of wood laid parallel to each other forming the sheet. End-grain slats or pickets are sheets made from pieces of wood sliced crosswise on the tree. Wood sliced this way is very good at bearing weight. This product is similar to staved-core—which is like butcher block and is used for the substrate in exterior doors that are covered with veneer—also a laminated product. Figure 13.2 shows an engineered wood product as the core of this laminated panel.

Softwood is used in solid form. A piece of a faster-growing, less costly solid wood can form the core or underlayer of a laminated product.

Plastic Substrates

Plastic substrates you will encounter may be foamed plastic incorporated for sound abatement in certain products. Honeycomb structures made of plastic will lend rigidity to the panel. Different plastic formulations have different strengths. All are moisture resistant, and they exhibit varying degrees of chemical and heat resistance depending on the formula. Some have better strength and stiffness than others. They are generally not high performers when exposed to flame, as you would probably intuit.

Manufacturers offer a variety of plastics to solve different problems; the best plastic for bearing weight is made of a different formula than the best plastic for resisting impact. When evaluating items made of plastic or designing a custom plastic solution for a client, you will rank your program needs in a hierarchy so that the plastic selected addresses your most important needs. You may not be able to find a formula that solves every single problem presented by that item. For example, if you wanted an impact-resistant item and your design theme called for the item to also be white, you would have to choose between the best plastic that contains carbon fiber and the white-colored choice, because plastic cannot contain carbon fiber and also be white. Cost is often an issue, and if you can use a plastic that is considered a commodity (available as pellets or sheets purchased by your fabricator) the item will be less costly than if you had to hire an engineer to develop a special plastic for your job. It is often the case that a commodity will be significantly less expensive than a specially engineered one.

Metal Substrates

Metal honeycomb panels have good strength, stiffness, and fire resistance but have a "medium" level moisture resistance. The two common metals used are aluminum and stainless steel. In addition to honeycomb there is also foamed metal, and in some instances you may decide you should use solid metal, although weight and expense will both increase if you do.

Textile Substrates

Aramid is a high-performance material that has excellent flame resistance and better moisture resistance than metal honeycomb panels. It is often spun into a fiber. Textile substrates have the advantage of being very flexible.

Other textiles that are laminated to materials include woven, nonwoven, and knitted textiles that are laminated to textiles, wallcoverings, and wood veneers. When these materials are laminated to fabrics they are usually adhered to reduce seam slippage, improve the hand, or lend stability to the fabric. When applied to wallcoverings they may improve acoustical characteristics, minimize problems with the wall surface beneath, or lend durability. When they are applied to wood veneers they lend stability.

Glass and porcelain are also used as substrates for products, most typically natural stone veneer and composites containing natural stone components.

Facing Materials

The facing material is usually selected for its aesthetic properties. The look of stone slab may be preferable for your design program, but the weight of actual stone slab is inappropriate for the elevator cab, so you specify laminated stone. A thin layer of stone may be laminated to honeycomb aluminum. The characteristics of the facing materials that you will select are described in the individual material chapters but other characteristics, such as stability or, in this case the weight, will likely come from the substrate. Because of their potential to solve a variety of weight, stability, sustainability, impact resistance, and other problems, laminates are being developed to replace many materials. Thinner material is possible with resin infusion and new bonding technologies have made more laminate combinations possible than ever before.

PRODUCTS

The facing material adhered to substrates is usually selected for its appearance. Some of these laminate products are more familiar than others that will likely be very familiar before the edition of this textbook is out in print. Even laminated products that offer opportunities for new surface imagery, attempting to imitate natural wood or stone, have a lot of room yet to exploit all the potential for these surfaces. Laminated flooring is one such material.

Laminate and Engineered Flooring

Once thought of as interchangeable, the terms *laminate floor* and *engineered floor* have come to mean two distinctly different flooring products. *Laminate* is understood to refer to products with a photographic representation of material under a protective melamine **wear layer**, the top surface of the laminated product that withstands abrasion, while *engineered* has come to mean a layer of real wood bonded to a substrate, protected by one of a variety of possible top-coating formulas.

Laminated Wood

These panels are used for surfacing walls and ceilings and also for cabinetry and furniture. Wood veneers and plastic laminate are the two most popular surfaces but metal laminate also plays a role. Remember that these two-component systems will create products that are unlike the solid versions in some ways but retain other characteristics. These products may be specified as a material that must be fashioned into custom surfacing or may be specified as a product. Figure 13.3 shows a wood-paneling system using wood veneer on an engineered substrate integrated in a mounting system that is also part of the product, so the details of the system are already devised. You would select your preferred product system before drafting the details so you represent sizes and installation correctly.

Engineered Wood

Wood veneer used on such systems as these will obviously require a lesser amount of high-quality wood than solid wood, to cover the same surface. They will be as dimensionally stable as their engineered substrate. The

FIGURE 13.3 Wood panels from *Marlite* are modular laminated products that are stable and demountable.

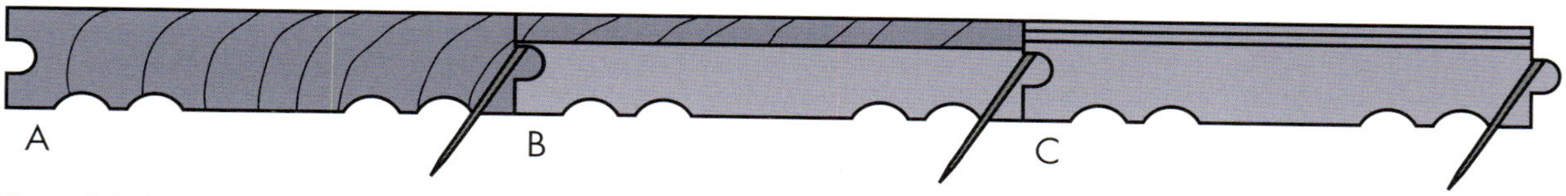

FIGURE 13.4 The difference between solid (a), engineered (b), and laminated (c) flooring.

face veneer will still respond to changes in moisture and be subject to soiling like solid wood so should be sealed and protected, similarly to solid wood. The thickness of the veneer layer may allow for sanding and refinishing the floor. Figure 13.4 diagrams the difference between solid, engineered, and laminated flooring. Notice that if you refinished the solid wood floor, you could not sand it beyond the **tongue-and-groove** profile anyway, so the engineered floor can give you the same refinishing options as solid wood. The laminated floor is not suitable for your client if he or she will one day want to refinish the floor.

Many laminated and engineered floors are factory finished with finishes that are much more durable than field applied finishing systems. With proper maintenance, your client should not have to refinish the floor because the finish failed (unless your spec was improper to begin with). Make good functional and aesthetic choices at the outset so refinishing is not required.

Laminated Stone

Super-thin stone panels with a variety of backings not only decrease weight but allow for characteristics unavailable in stone slab. Resin-impregnated stone can be easily bent into curves, something impossible for stone slab. Backings for these materials include fiberglass mesh, metal and plastic honeycomb panels, glass, ceramic, and cement. Each kind of backing is suited to a different application:

- For exploiting the translucency of these super-thin stone surfaces you would select glass.
- For rugged product that can withstand traffic, select porcelain or possibly some plastics or metals.
- For thin, flexible composite products, fiberglass would be a good backing.
- For lightweight moisture-resistant products look for plastic honeycomb.
- For lightweight products with superior strength, look for metal honeycomb.

Table 13.1 Flooring products commonly available on the market: laminated, engineered, cork, and other products.			
Product	**What It Is**	**Possible Options**	**Install**
Laminate flooring	Photographic representation of material surface	Wear layer hard and durable like laminate countertops	Floating floor: glue-down or edges profiled so it can snap together
Engineered flooring	Wood layer on top of plywood	Special processes like hand scraping and distressing possible	⅜" product typically nailed in place; ½" product glued or nailed; ⅝" nail, glue, or install as floating floor
Wood-veneered substrates	Thin wood veneer glued to an engineered substrate, plywood, particleboard, or MDF	Characteristics vary with substrate; many more veneer options than exist for solid wood	For wall, panels may be fastened with screws or hung on cleats; furniture will be assembled with fasteners or biscuits
Cork planks	Layer of cork laminated over engineered substrate, typically fiberboard	May be backed with built-in sound abatement like cork layer	Very frequently click and lock, or glue as floating floor
Leather, rubber, vinyl laminated flooring	Leather or recycled leather (shredded leather and binders like rubber) over fiberboard; other resilient material over HDF or combination substrate	May be backed with built-in sound abatement like cork layer	Typically click and lock, for glue-down or nail/staple
Laminated stone flooring	Thin sheets of stone (or composite) laminated to another material—most commonly porcelain (floors) or aluminum (vertical application)	Has the same durability as thicker stone material; ability to repair surface with grinding varies with product; has potential to delaminate	Install as called for by backing material, which may be porcelain, aluminum, plastic, or other; critical to keep water out of the installed material to avoid delaminating

Laminated Cork, Leather, and Other Products

These products, or composites containing them, also benefit from being laminated to an engineered substrate. Leather and cork are resilient products but with a rigid underlayer, they are not so dependent on the condition of the substrate. As with all of these products, their faces will still retain the characteristics of the material but even this is altered when the cork or leather is used as an ingredient. Recycled leather is mixed with rubber and adhered to substrates for flooring that is more impervious to staining and fading than the solid leather it imitates. Table 13.1 shows some of the products that are commonly available on the market.

Laminated Metal

What is meant by that is that a metal laminate applied to an engineered wood substrate will be lighter in weight than solid metal, but the face will still be characteristically a metal, so it will oxidize and scratch just like solid metal forms. All the considerations and precautions you enlist in your specification of a solid metal will apply to these surfaces as well. With no indication of thickness, the fact that it is laminated will not be visually apparent as you can see in Figure 13.5a–c.

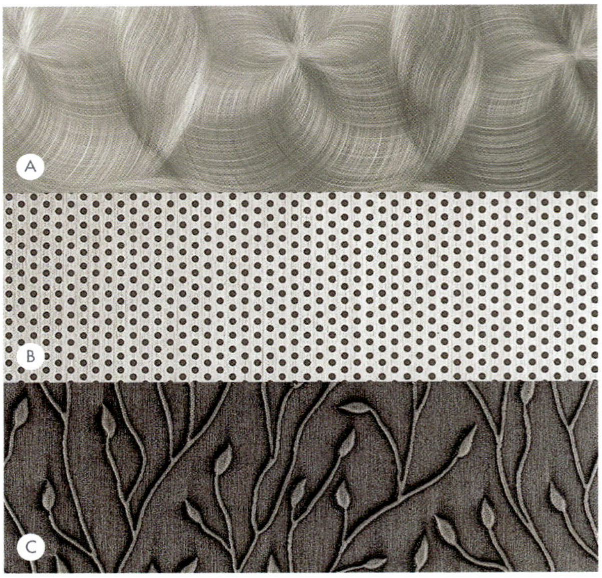

FIGURE 13.5A–C Thin metal sheet is laminated to substrates for metal surfaces lighter in weight and lower in cost but still stable and impact resistant as required for most of your projects. Solid aluminum (a) is polished with a special router to create the controlled surface scratches that give this laminate its texture. Solid aluminum (b) is perforated to create this product. The pewter vine pattern (c) is a high-pressure relief with a thin layer of metal foil pressed onto phenolic backer. The material is then polished to brighten up the raised leaf pattern. *All images courtesy of Chemetal.*

Laminated Glass

This material is also discussed in the Chapter 8, Glass, so please review that information as well. Laminating glass increases strength and safety and laminating glass to another material can lend strength without increasing opacity.

CHARACTERISTICS

Laminated and engineered wood, cork, leather, and resilient flooring options are all adhered to engineered wood substrates. It will likely be the case for every laminated material you select that it is more stable and lighter in weight than solid versions of the same material.

Wood Products

Engineered wood flooring has a thin wood face (1/8 inch is typical, 1/4 inch is available) bonded to a substrate (often plywood). The combined thickness of the layers is often 1/2 inch to 3/8 inch, 5/8 inch or 3/4 inch. Many products conform to the 3/4-inch thickness that has long been established for solid wood flooring. They may be factory or field finished. Factory-applied finish (also called prefinished) on prefinished engineered wood floors may be the same formulations that are applied in the field or they may be catalyzed or UV-cured formulas that can only be factory applied (see Table 5.4 for description of theses finishes). The finishes that can be field applied can also be repaired in the field.

> Point of Emphasis 13.2
>
> Just because a field repair is possible that does not mean it will necessarily be easy to do. Review the finish information in Chapter 5, Wood, and Chapter 2, Paint, Coatings, and Wallcoverings, to see which finishes are considered easy to repair, because not all sealants are equal in this regard. It is still an advantage to have a field-repairable finish but the work will typically have to be done by professionals.

When selecting a prefinished floor consider the ease with which tradespeople can make repairs in the field if a portion of the finish is damaged (for example, burned or a small area scraped off). Not all finishes can be repaired and blended successfully in situ. Site-finished floors with a 1/4-inch- to 3/8-inch-thick veneer top layer can be sanded and refinished, at least once, the same way you could sand and refinish a solid wood floor for your client. Engineered floors can also be purchased for site finishing but site-finished floors are less and less the norm (even for solid product).

> Point of Emphasis 13.3
>
> There will be many instances when you will have to weigh the pros and cons of solid wood versus engineered wood products to make a selection for your client. One of the biggest hurdles that you will have to overcome may be client perceptions that solid wood is better quality. One misconception is that the selections for color and finish for an engineered floor are limited. This is not true, the same versatility available for solid wood is available for engineered floor, you just have to contract with a company offering such a product and process combination. Another misconception is that you can refinish solid wood more often than you can refinish engineered floors. This is also untrue for many products. When you select an engineered floor that has a 1/4-inch-thick solid wood veneer on the engineered substrate you will realize that if it were solid wood, you would not be able to sand it past the tongue anyway. The solid product can only be sanded as often as the engineered product can.

Laminating wood to an engineered substrate lends stability to the wood; it reacts to changes in humidity to a much smaller degree than solid wood. The thicker the veneer face, the more it will react but the change in dimension is much less than it would be for solid wood. Engineered floors look and sound like solid wood underfoot but because they don't shrink and swell in reaction to humidity, their finishes are not as stressed. They also don't exhibit the gaps between boards that you may notice with solid wood. The durability of the finish and the stability of the substrate help them to retain their appearance longer.

It is possible to specify many of the same processes for engineered floors that are available for solid wood products, if the facing veneer layer is thick enough. You can specify wire brushing or hand scraping (popular if an antique or distressed look is desired). Other details popular for solid wood, such as beveled edges (when the designer feels that a "plank" look should be accentuated) and distressing (when the floor will be installed in a high-traffic area where you want to "pre-patinate" the surface so the light damage that you anticipate will not be as noticeable) are also available for your high-end engineered floor. These floors should not be refinished because the mechanical sanders will remove all the textures that have been applied.

There are quality differences between various manufacturers' offerings in this category. A very thin veneer face on a substandard substrate will still be, categorically, an engineered floor, but it will not perform like a quality engineered floor so you must still pay close attention to each product's specifications and not lump them all together, assuming that *engineered* automatically means good quality.

Laminate Floors

Laminate floors have a photograph of a material surface in place of a material. They are quite abrasion resistant. They consist of a high-pressure decorative laminate top surface bonded to a core that is often MDF. The assembly is backed by another laminate layer for stability and strength. Close inspection of some of these products may reveal their "photographic" (versus actual material) surface and the wood-grained patterns sometimes lack the surface texture of real wood. These floors are thin, as thin as ¼ inch and ½ inch thick is very common, allowing for a flush installation where abutting thinner material. They are also more economical for a small area than dimensional wood.

> **Point of Emphasis 13.4**
>
> Resin surfaces applied to laminated products can be embossed with a texture so it is possible, with a combination of embossed resins and a huge repeat, to produce a very realistic-looking imitation surface. I was at a condo with a potential client once and could not be sure if the kitchen cabinetry there was a real wood veneer or laminate. I had to look very carefully before I finally found the pattern repeat "way down the row" before I was certain it was a photograph in laminate. I scanned about 10 feet of cabinet run before I found it.

Laminate flooring can be installed over many kinds of substrates, including an existing finished floor. Laminated flooring is usually not fastened to the floor with glue or nails. Instead, it is installed "loose" over a layer of thin foam. This installation, with the pieces of flooring fastened to each other but not to the structure, is referred to as a "floating floor," as it does not need to be nailed or glued to the subfloor and can be installed over most existing floors. It leaves the assembly feeling a bit "spongy" and footfalls sound more hollow than they do against dimensional strip flooring. Laminate flooring can also be glued to the subfloor to mitigate the bouncy hollowness of a floating installation. There are proprietary **underlayments** designed to minimize these characteristics as well.

As with engineered floors, laminate floors also come in an array of quality levels, so you will evaluate each unique product offering. Generally the perception is that laminate floors are inferior to engineered floors and it is true that anything that a laminate floor can do, an engineered floor can do too. You will likely consider using laminate floors to meet budget and thickness restrictions and an engineered floor to imitate solid, dimensional wood installations.

> **Helpful Hint 13.1**
>
> When using laminate products with a photograph rather than a natural material, take care to avoid placement that allows the repeat to be visible if you are using laminates with multiple pieces preset in panels. You can more easily create a convincing look in a space that will have a lot of furniture covering the floor, or it is such a small space (foyer, powder room) that the repeat will not show.

Stone Veneer

Super-thin stone veneer is a laminated product too. Thinly sliced stone, composite stone, which looks like natural stone, or reconstituted stone, is laminated to porcelain tile for use on floors. This material presents a stone face so the characteristics of the stone are an important consideration when selecting for the surface qualities. Remember, stone will retain its characteristic porosity and appearance. The stability of the stone is usually improved by the porcelain underbody. Stone that may have had a tendency to crack may be more durable because it has been bonded to porcelain. It may

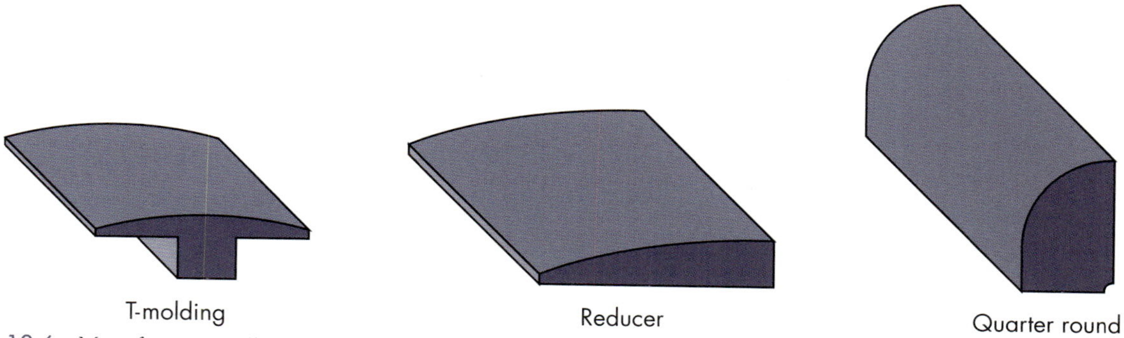

FIGURE 13.6 Manufacturers will generally offer a few special pieces to complete typical installations. These are typically: T-molding, reducer, and quarter round.

not be able to be ground down like a thicker stone if the installation has too much lippage (uneven installation so adjacent tiles are not flush and level) or if it suffers some damage during use. The stability of porcelain should avoid lippage in the first place. Super-thin stone veneer may also be laminated to honeycomb aluminum for large, lightweight panels.

Resilient Products

Product covered in the resilient flooring category is also laminated to similar substrates for the same reasons.

Cork and leather floors are available in solid form but are frequently found in laminated flooring options. They may have fiberboard substrates and click-and-lock profiles for glueless installation. Both are frequently found in prefinished products but are also available unfinished for **site finishing**, whereby the material is stained and sealed at the installation site.

Leather may be whole skin or a leatherlike product reconstituted from leather scrap that has been ground into fiber and mixed with a binder like rubber and pressed into sheets or adhered to a textile core to create sheets or recycled leather. These products are more durable than leather; when you touch them they feel a little rubbery but they even smell like leather.

Other Surfaces

You are probably able to recall other materials that you have seen laminated, or can imagine the benefits of laminating materials that you are already familiar with.

ACCESSORIES

Manufacturers will generally offer a few special pieces to complete typical installations; these are usually terrazzo edges, T-moldings, reducers, and quarter round. Additional accessories will be available from some of the manufacturers but they will all have these three (Figure 13.6) included. When laminated floors are sold for a floating installation there will typically be a thin foam sheet specified to eliminate some of the hollow sound produced when walking on it. Stock-manufactured engineered floors will have the same kinds of accessories as laminate flooring but if you are specifying a custom-engineered floor you will be able to specify the accessory pieces you need and they will be made to order.

FABRICATION

This product category is being rapidly developed and new product combinations are frequently introduced to solve design problems. Manufacturers of laminated products may not even be the producers of any of the components used; they may purchase the individual materials from others. The complexity of these materials requires expertise that a collaborative effort can provide. Two materials bonded together require careful selection for their individual properties, plus an adhesive that suits both as well as the environmental conditions. A number of processes may be applied to material that is mechanically shaped (like cutting and sanding) or molded (cast, extruded). Material may then be coated, impregnated with resins or densifiers, and bonded to another material. It may be additionally sealed or encapsulated.

If material that you specify requires custom fabrication, a local shop may perform other work of fitting and shaping the material before it is installed at your client's site. It is likely that you will have to devise an edge detail to conceal the layered construction at all cut edges.

QUALIFYING INSTALLERS

Among installers for many of the materials in this book you will find specialists who may have acquired their skills on the job or may have a combination of on-the-job training and have taken classes, frequently offered by the manufacturers of the products they install. These classes are usually not free, so they demonstrate a level of commitment in any installer who has taken installation courses. Another avenue for training would come through organizations like the Certified Floorcovering Installers (CFI), who also offer classes for a charge in the same way. At the end of the course the installer who successfully completes the training is declared by the manufacturer or the organization to be a *certified* or qualified installer. While the terminology can have a variety of meanings, belonging to an organization or participating in formalized training is an indication of professionalism that should be taken into account as you evaluate bidders.

You may find installers through the vendor of the product that you are specifying. This is usually a good route to a qualified installer because vendors don't want to have any problems with an installation that might drag them into a remedy, so they are likely to recommend installers that have proven to be capable of installing their products. Because veneered stone products are new (at the time of this writing) you will likely have the best luck finding an installer by asking your vendor who has experience with their product.

INSTALLATION

When determining the best installation for laminated products you will consider the material, particularly the one on the back of the assembly, the substrate that it will be affixed to or adhered to, and the method of attaching the material, either mechanical, like fasteners and cleat systems, or by use of adhesives.

Laminated Floor Products

Laminated materials are often installed on floors in a floating installation, meaning that the units are fastened to each other but not necessarily to the structure underneath. The individual pieces might be snapped together, glued together, or stapled or nailed to the structure below. The manufacturers of these products are usually very exacting about how they should be installed, and of course their recommendations should be followed to the letter. If you have unusual circumstances they do not describe in their recommendations, you would get in touch with them so they instruct you per your job site conditions. Manufactured product often comes with some warranty of serviceability and it is quite common that installing in a manner not explicitly recommended by the manufacturer will void warranties. That having been said, here is what you might expect to find in their instructions:

- Suggested underlayment as part of the requirements listed in the installation instructions: Floating floors are often specified to be installed over a sound-dampening foam sheet to eliminate some of that hollow-footstep sound people have objected to, especially with laminated product. If the product is being installed below grade or a concrete construction does not pass a moisture test, a vapor barrier (plastic film used to prevent moisture damage from concrete subfloors) may also be required in the installation instructions. If you require sound abatement, you will have to check with the building for their requirements and then review the restrictions that may be listed in the manufacturer's instructions so a system compatible with the flooring and approved by the building can be selected.
- Product to be adhered to the substrate: Engineered floors with a plywood substrate can be nailed or glued to the **subfloor**. Flooring with particleboard or MDF in their composition may also be intended to be glued to the substrate.
- Product designed for a floating installation: The edges of the engineered substrate may be shaped like puzzle pieces that snap together without glue or they may have traditional tongue-and-groove edges that are intended to be fitted together with glue.

Point of Emphasis 13.5

A simple moisture test is to tape a piece of plastic to a concrete floor and check the next day to see if it is moist under the plastic. If it is, you know that moisture is migrating through the surface into your client's space.

Underlayments

Floating floors are usually installed over a sheet of material referred to as underlayment. The manufacturer of the flooring will recommend the correct underlayment. Flooring manufacturers sometimes produce their own proprietary material for underlayment, and unless the cost difference between it and similar product is significant, it is a good idea to consider using it. In these instances, the manufacturer will stand behind the performance of the assembly, not just the flooring product (provided all instructions are followed to the letter by your installer). If underlayment is required (as it is with most floating floor installations) see if the manufacturer recommends something specific to your project's needs.

Helpful Hint 13.2

It is a good idea to use the underlayment designed by the flooring manufacturer for the product selected, even if it seems to be identical to a slightly less costly product that you find elsewhere. The more people included in the installation chain, the greater the risk that the pieces in the process or assembly will not seamlessly mesh, and every additional tradesperson and supplier gives those involved more places to point fingers when something does not perform as expected. It is a false economy to start mixing and matching product from different resources to complete your job; when too many people are involved nobody considers themselves to be responsible.

The sound-abatement underlayments likely to be suggested are cork, foam, or engineered materials. Cork underlayment is used under floating and glued-in laminate floors and is sometimes used under dimensional wood flooring installations when sound abatement is needed. In the case of a floating floor, it will be dry-laid into the space. For other installation methods, it may be glued down. It is typically just under ½ inch thick. Many multitenant buildings (both commercial and residential) require a sound mat of some sort under any hard-surface flooring. Because of its generic character, cork is often specified.

Foam underlayment is about ⅛ inch thick and your installer can buy it in 100-square-foot rolls (sometimes larger). It is for above-grade applications where a sound barrier is not critical. If it is to be installed below grade, you could still use this underlayment as long as you also specified a moisture barrier.

Moisture-resistant foam or foam and film combination consists of foam underlayment, as described above, with the addition of a moisture barrier. It is about ⅛ inch thick, and your installer will purchase it in 100-square-foot (or larger) rolls. Install this kind of underlayment below grade or over unfinished crawl spaces.

Engineered sound-abatement products have been developed for use as underlayment. They include high-density foam, closed-cell foam, fiber pads, and rubber pads. A number of manufacturers have tweaked these premium products for special performance characteristics. Some focus on limiting transmission through the assembly; others address the hollow sound of floating floor installations to create an experience more in line with a nailed-in, dimensional wood floor installation. When multitenant buildings specify sound abatement as a performance specification, you will need to carefully compare the statistics of your selected assembly to the stated requirements. The test methods that produce the performance numbers should be similar to your required installation method if you need to end up with the same performance to meet association rules or the landlord's requirements for sound abatement.

Stone Veneer Products

The substrate will be as much a part of your considerations as the product as you select a method of installation. A cement mortar would be a typical mastic for solid stone and stone tiles and is likely to be the recommended mastic for stone veneers and composite veneers laminated to porcelain or cement. The installation method for other backings may be similar but the adhesive will be different. These products can be adhered to gypsum board and some can be installed over other finished surfaces. Panels will be held in place with clips or adhesive. Installation systems often include the use of double-stick foam tape until the adhesive can set up.

When these products are being used on floors in high-rise buildings they will also be subject to sound-abatement requirements mandated by the building, condo association, or whoever has the authority in the property. Hard surfaces transmit impact noise through the structure, potentially disturbing other parties in the building.

Modular Systems

Modular systems usually include a means of hanging or affixing the material as part of the product. The hanging system for the modular panels shown in Figure 13.7 is part of the product purchase.

FIGURE 13.7 There are many surfacing options for laminated materials because the face is primarily decorative and most of the performance comes from the substrate, as with these plastic modular panels. *Image courtesy of Marlite.*

Custom Installations

When devising a custom surface using a laminated product, meaning it will be locally fitted or shaped for your unique site, you will seek installation advice from the manufacturer of the product. It is not uncommon to forward your drawings and specifications to the manufacturer for confirmation that the installation as planned is advisable for your site conditions.

PROTECTION AND MAINTENANCE

The products on the face of these laminated assemblies will retain their surface characteristics so they should be cared for as your client would care for the solid versions of the material. For example, dimensional stone and wood should be sealed, as should veneered stone and wood. Regular maintenance of these laminated products with natural materials as their face will likely be very similar to the care required for the natural materials in solid form. Methods of repairing damage that are typical for the solid version of these materials may not be available for these products. Wood is resurfaced by sanding the damage away and stone is resurfaced by grinding the damage away. The thinness of these materials will probably prohibit those kinds of repairs. It will probably be a good idea to order "attic stock" for your client to store safely in case some of the units you specify have to be replaced. If you are trying to sustainably restore a client site and it has such materials installed, but in damaged condition, hopefully there will be some material still on hand. If not, you will still be able to make a cosmetic repair. Stains and resins can be used by expert restoration professionals to make cosmetic repairs. This work taken at face value will seem expensive, but when compared to the monetary and environmental cost of replacing a surface, it is a low-cost, sustainable option to be sure.

SAFETY

A common concern with engineered substrates is the presence of formaldehydes, which are common in a lot of glues and resins. If the material was fireproofed with chemicals, then toxins might be present. The material types that are laminated together may modify one another's properties slightly but you can still rely on logic to help you sort through the safety issues presented by the material. Flammability is a consideration when plastics are part of the assembly because many plastics are flammable. Glass is brittle and sharp impact can break it. Materials respond to heat differently so you will need to pay attention to temperature ranges in manufacturers' specs because one of the materials could break its bond with another if they are expanding at different rates. Durability is often the motivation behind laminating materials together and durability contributes to safety when materials resist breaking.

SUSTAINABILITY

Laminated materials are available with recycled material content, either in the substrate or the finish face. Because the tight grain and mellowness of old wood is prized, some salvaged lumber is sliced into veneer. Many laminated leather floors are made of recycled leather laminated to hardboard that contains post-production waste wood. Sustainability is variably addressed by the products in this topic. For instance, bamboo has been the poster child for sustainability but designers are now realizing that if the bamboo product is adhered with urea formaldehyde, produced in a manner that wastes energy, pollutes the environment, neglects human rights, and is sealed with acrylic that does not hold up against the rigors of many environments, it is not enough that it is rapidly renewable. Designers should look at the characteristics of the facing material, the composition of substrates and adhesives, the production and packaging, and life-cycle analysis to determine the sustainability of these products.

Glueless systems do not introduce the VOCs common in adhesives into your client's space. Click-and-lock systems have shaped tongue-and-groove profiles that fasten together with enough tenacity that no other fastening is required. This kind of system is said to make it possible to remove and relocate the flooring without damage to the material because floating installations are not fastened to the building. Different products accomplish this with varying degrees of success.

MANAGING BUDGETS

Laminated products vary in quality and exclusivity. This affects the cost of any given product. Here are a couple of scenarios pertaining to engineered floor to illustrate the costs, but if you change the material names the concept applies to any of these materials. The specifications in Table 13.2 are actual specifications comparing two products currently available on the market. Product option B is two and a half times the cost of option A, but for good reason.

Table 13.2
Actual specification comparing two products currently available on the market; notice the quality differences that you can discern from the specifications.

Characteristic	Engineered Option A	Engineered Option B
Wood species	Maple	Maple
Thickness	9/16"	3/4"
Other species available?	Maple or birch	Numerous species available
Thickness of face veneer	0.08"	0.375"
Substrate	7-layer birch ply	11-layer birch ply
Width and length	5"W × 24" to 40"	Specified width up to 72" to 96"L
Colors	Natural or light brown	Stain to spec
Finish	3-layer satin urethane	Select from several options
Grade	Mix of A, B, and C veneer grades in every shipment	Per your order, exclusively grade ordered, no B or C in grade A order
Wood matched for color and grain	No	Yes, from selected flitches
Knots	Up to 1/2" allowed	Pin knots in some species
Wormholes	Filled, up to 2 mm (3/32")	Filled up to 3/32"
Defects	Limited to 5% of small manufacturer defects	Free of manufacturer defects
Cracks and other defects	Not allowed	Not allowed
Formaldehyde free?	No	Yes
Installation available?	No	Yes

Point of Emphasis 13.6

Different flooring products have different characteristics. For instance:

- *Click-and-lock* systems have specially shaped tongue-and-groove joints that snap the individual planks together.
- *Floating floor* does not need to be nailed or glued to the subfloor and can be installed over most existing floors.
- *Glued laminate flooring* requires a specially formulated glue to be applied to the tongue-and-groove areas for each plank. Once the glue is dried the planks are almost impossible to pull apart.

The features that are part of laminated material are:

- Quality of face and backing material
- Available sizes
- Matching between units
- Options for finish

The features that are *not* part of the material are:

- Variation outside of product offering
- Control over product with exact specs
- Installation

Obviously the first place to look when trying to control costs for this example and for these products in general is thoughtful selection of the product itself. Situations that can add to job costs include the complexity of the job (such as a lot of cutting and piecing in small complicated spaces) or that significant prepwork is required before installation. You will have less control over these factors than you do over the product selection.

There will be many instances when the selection of the veneered product saves money versus the solid-material product; if not for cost savings you may turn to these products for improved performance or sustainability reasons.

ORGANIZATION OF THE INDUSTRY

These products are all manufactured, unlike the opportunity to compose an open spec as for the solid versions of natural materials. Many laminated products are currently produced overseas. You will likely limit your search to product that is represented locally unless you are planning to order a large quantity, then you may decide that working directly with an overseas provider is worth the investment of time and the complication of orchestrating the shipping and importation. Wood-laminated products have wide representation in the U.S. and Canada. Supply chains may be long with manufacturers represented by reps who direct business to distributors who then sell to resellers who will then sell to end users. Or the chain could be very short with manufacturers performing all steps in the process plus installation. Custom product tends to have the shortest supply chain.

SELECTION CRITERIA

Table 13.3 will help you start thinking of some of the criteria you might consider for your clients' jobs. Your thorough design program will assist you in compiling a hierarchy of characteristics to be met as you compare these laminated options, not only to each other but also to the solid versions of the same materials. The variety in this category means you will be required to perform a more comprehensive analysis if you are inventing a new use for a material. You can expect materials that are available off the shelf to have compatible components, since the substrate, the adhesive, and the facing material are likely to have been selected for tested properties (flame impact, moisture and abrasion resistance, etc.). Data should be available for the assembly, if not for the material in use.

SPECIFYING

Your firm has been hired to design the offices of a start-up marketing company. They have leased space in the basement of a 1920s-era building. As they are just starting up, the budget is tight. You have selected a laminated floor for reasons of budget and because the offices are below grade and the laminate flooring selected is very moisture resistant. Your specification for the flooring and installation would likely look something like Sample Spec 13.1.

Table 13.3
Selection criteria that you might consider for your clients' jobs.

Condition	Program Implications
What surface will this material cover?	Substrate and facing material are often paired to meet very specific functional needs. All the facing materials common to these products can be used on ceilings, walls, or floors and the substrate and finishes are selected to address the special needs of each type of surface.
Is the surface below grade?	Moisture is always a consideration when spaces are below ground level. Some products are not appropriate and other products can be installed below grade if you specify a vapor barrier between the structure and the material being installed. Metal substrates are not as moisture resistant as plastic.
Is this a floor in a multitenant occupancy?	These surfaces are hard and if they are in contact with the structure, sound can telegraph through the material to adjoining spaces. You will need to include sound abatement in your assembly.
Is weight an issue in this installation?	Some substrates are specifically designed to be lightweight, so select for honeycomb metal or plastic as appropriate.
Will you need to meet fire code?	Flammable substrates and finish layers will have to be fire treated. Often a flammable finish layer that is less than 1/28" is not accounted for in material calculations (but confirm this with local code) so select a noncombustible substrate and very thin decorative finish layer to avoid fireproofing chemicals.
How are you addressing sustainability in this project?	A thoughtful selection that pairs site conditions and client needs with material will lead you to a durable selection. Because these products often limit the use of nonrenewable resources to the minimum, they conserve material. Many substrates can utilize recycled material, although recyclability of these products is complicated by the different material layers.

SAMPLE SPEC 13.1

Part 1 General

1.1 Related Documents

A. Refer to finish plan for location and direction of flooring.

B. Refer to manufacturer's installation instructions.

1.2 Summary

A. Install per plans and instructions; laminate flooring on stairs to lower level, lower vestibule, and throughout offices of Bedazzle Marketing Group office suite with the exception of washroom.

1. High pressure decorative laminate flooring.
2. Stairs and steps.
3. Underlayment and vapor barrier.
4. Trims and moldings.
5. Sound mat and vapor barrier.

1.3 References

A. ASTM E1333 and California state code for emissions.

B. ADA guidelines.

1.4 Contractor Submittal

A. Material safety data sheet for all products installed.

B. Manufacturer's recommendations for product handling, storage, acclimation, installation, protection, and maintenance.

C. Shop drawings: Submit installation details showing layout and location of each product type and accessory component including design(s) and finish texture(s).

D. Samples: Submit selection and verification samples for design(s) and finish texture.

1.5 Quality Assurance

A. Installation shall be performed by a firm experienced in the application of systems similar in complexity to those required for this project. Additionally, installers shall be in possession of the manufacturer's installation manual and adhere to the instructions.

B. Manufacturer to have not less than 10 years' experience in the laminate flooring industry and a record of successful commercial applications.

C. Obtain all products and materials from one source.

1.6 Delivery, Storage, and Handling

A. Deliver materials in manufacturer's original, unopened, undamaged cartons.

B. Store horizontally on pallets.

1.7 Maintenance of Installation

A. Maintain air temperature between 55ºF and 80ºF and humidity levels between 25% and 60% for 48 hours before, during, and after installation.

B. Install decorative laminate flooring after other finishing operations have been completed.

SAMPLE SPEC 13.1 (continued)

Part 2 Products

2.1 General Information

A. High-pressure decorative laminate plank flooring with mechanical locking system and attached underlayment applied over a moisture barrier and concrete slab.
B. High-pressure decorative laminate plank flooring with mechanical locking system and attached underlayment applied over a wood substrate.
C. Flooring system of "floating floor" construction type allowing for expansion and contraction due to changes in humidity.
D. Vapor barrier as required over concrete based subfloors.

2.2 Manufacturers

A. Fast Floors, 1234 Industrial Drive, Anytown, ST 45678.

2.3 Products

A. High-pressure series floor product, style Highway laminate flooring with click-and-lock system for glueless installation.
B. High-pressure series treads and trims.
C. Soft Step underlayment.
D. Vapor Loc barrier.
E. Reducer at restroom floor, quarter round to match flooring throughout.

Part 3 Execution

3.1 Examination

A. Examine substrate conditions, application areas, and confirm job site conditions are acceptable for product installation.
B. Verify concrete slab subfloors have cured. Do not install flooring if alkaline content is high.

3.2 Preparation

A. Remove carpeting, scrape adhesive from surface, clean and prepare floor for laminate flooring installation.
B. Condition flooring materials in unopened cartons for at least 48 hours prior to commencing installation.

3.3 Installation

A. Install polyethylene vapor barrier sheet on concrete subfloors.
B. Install sound-abatement foam on floors.
C. Install laminate flooring as a floating floor connecting the planks via click-and-lock mechanism D. Stagger the planks' end joints a minimum of 12".
D. Provide a minimum of ½" expansion space between flooring planks and perimeter walls, columns, and other fixed objects.
E. Install reducer at washroom door.
F. Floor-recessed strike for door lock at entry to remain functional.
G. Install quarter round at floor perimeter and at vertical obstructions.

3.4 Stairs and Steps

A. Install stairs and steps in compliance with manufacturer's installation instructions.
B. Use laminate flooring planks for treads combined with stair nose moldings.

3.5 Post Installation

A. Clean entire floor with Quick Clean included in the installation kit.
B. Cover installed flooring to protect it from damage during the remainder of construction. Use heavy kraft paper or other suitable material.

INSPECTION

Your inspection of these materials will vary a little with the specifics of your job but generally the one thing you will need to confirm is that the faces of the units are aligned, since they are intended to cover surfaces in a flush manner. This is especially important for high-light situations when the material has a high sheen. Reflections exaggerate any surface anomalies. These products often require accessories to transition from one material to another because they cannot be cut to fit in the way their solid-material counterparts can. These transitions are another point of scrutiny; they should cover all substrate so there is no evidence that these are laminated products. Only the finish surface should show.

Hopefully the installation has left all units entirely undamaged. These products are typically only capable of cosmetic repairs. If you notice damage on any part of the installation, you should request that the unit be replaced with an undamaged one.

RELATED MATERIAL

Bamboo is technically a grass, so it grows quickly, making it very renewable and sustainable. The large stalks of grass are sliced into thin strips that are laminated together with glue, with the wide part of the strip facing out or the narrow edge of the strip facing out. When the wide face of the strip faces out it is referred to as horizontal and is visually distinguishable because you can see the "knuckles" of the bamboo joints on the face of the product. Alternatively, when the narrow edges are presented on the face of the vertical grade, it has a fine, linear grain. A third kind of bamboo is strand woven. The trimmings of the stalks that are left over when the individual slats are trimmed to consistent size are glued together and sliced into boards that may present a fine smooth grain that resembles birch or maple, or present a randomized grain resembling particleboard flakes in contrasting colors. Bamboo may be a light "natural" color or caramelized. Caramelized is a medium-brown color produced by heating the bamboo. This softens the material a little so it will be less durable against crushing than the natural-colored bamboo.

Like bamboo, butcher block is a single material laminated to itself, as is reconstituted wood veneer. There is a very wide range of quality characteristics on the market and you cannot rely on information pertaining to one product to predict the performance of another. Products may be sourced from overseas companies that do not have the same investment in reputation you are used to from U.S. companies. These price-competitive companies sometimes value-engineer their product into lower performance characteristics so you cannot even count on past performance of the product as a predictor of how the product will perform on your client's job. The adage "you get what you pay for" holds true for this and all products. For one example of the potential differences in quality, review the finishes described in Chapter 5, Wood.

Laminated glass is discussed in Chapter 8 but, as is obvious from its name, it is a laminated product too, with a sheet of plastic sandwiched between two sheets of glass.

SUMMARY

In this chapter you considered the concept of laminating materials together and how to evaluate laminated material for your use. A variety of substrates and facing materials are available in off-the-shelf and custom surfacing. Installation and maintenance vary with the types of materials used and combinations will require that you investigate all component materials before finalizing your selection. While many of these products have been developed specifically to address sustainability, some performance-driven options may warrant closer scrutiny because of one of their component layers.

WEB SEARCH ACTIVITIES

1. Perform an image search for a short series of properties that you can imagine would be desirable for a laminated construction, such as *clear rigid thermoplastic*. What uses would require the properties that you searched for?
2. If there are any substrates that you are unfamiliar with, perform an image search for what they look like—to see if you are familiar with them, if not by name. These include plywood, MDF, HDF, particleboard, and jointed or staved core). The softwood core will just be pine or fir as solid wood.
3. Search for *honeycomb aluminum* and *honeycomb plastic* to see what is available for backing the products you might specify. Also search for *marble veneer* and *composite stone veneer* to see what's new.

PERSONAL ACTIVITIES

1. Review the materials covered in this text and consider the properties of varying combinations. You could randomly consider them: For instance, what would be the characteristics of glass fused to porcelain or rubber fused to an engineered substrate? Alternatively, you could select a kind of space, such as a commercial kitchen. Define characteristics that would be desirable in such an environment and consider what two products might be laminated together to solve surfacing problems.

SUMMARY QUESTIONS

1. Why are laminated products being developed at this time?
2. What characteristics do these products have that make them especially pertinent to design goals for high-rise installations?
3. What characteristics address sustainability?
4. What are the different substrates in use and what are the strengths/performance characteristics of each that make it different from the others? What kinds of situations can each address?
5. What is the difference between engineered and laminated flooring products?
6. What characteristics are an indication of quality for laminated and engineered flooring?
7. What is the difference between a substrate and an underlayment? What kinds of problems or functions does each solve or perform?
8. What is a floating floor? What about the installation could give away the fact that it is not a dimensional product? How can this be minimized?
9. How can a glueless installation be achieved?
10. Why are typical remedies for damage to the solid versions of these materials not available to thin veneer facings?
11. How are these products installed?
12. What kinds of accessories are typical and why are they required for these materials but not for solid versions of the same?
13. How would these various materials be maintained?
14. What is your best recourse, relative to these materials, when working with restricted budgets?
15. What is the connection between the length of the supply chain and possible customization of the product?

Chapter 14

ACOUSTICS

Key Terms

Ambient sound	Dead	Reverberation
Bright	Live (liveliness)	Structure-borne sound

Objectives

After reading this chapter, you should be able to:

- Understand basic acoustical concepts and how noise affects interior environments.
- Distinguish between the different characteristics of sound that you will control.
- Know the approaches to managing the acoustic environment.
- Be aware of materials and products that you can specify to manage specific sound characteristics.
- Understand how materials and assemblies are configured to manage sound.

ACOUSTIC CONCEPTS

The U.S. Department of Health and Human Services has mandated that health care providers offer confidentiality to patients who must discuss their health and other private issues with professionals in health care providers' offices or spaces. A health care provider must "employ reasonable privacy safeguards to ensure that conversations about a patient are not overheard." However, the term *reasonable privacy safeguards* is not further defined by the document. So interior designers are beholden, by law, to provide reasonable acoustical privacy in situations where people are verbally relaying personal information. This consideration would also apply to banks, counseling or advising offices, any place where billing is discussed, and in many other circumstances. Exact definitions have not been established but designers must plan for acoustic privacy. Designers also plan for an appropriate acoustical environment. A restaurant owner may want to allow for a convivial murmur of conversation and the clink of glassware in one restaurant and wish to create a hushed elegance in another, so you will need to "tune" the sonic environment to match the brand or aesthetic created with the materials in your design.

While all materials are acoustic materials, because they interact with sound waves and thereby alter the sonic environment, the most common understanding of a material that is "acoustical" is one that will absorb sound. This is an oversimplification. A minimal understanding of sound and related issues will help you solve simple problems and communicate with acousticians.

Familiarity with some measurement standards is a good place to start as we work to address the needs identified by the Department of Health and Human Services, as well as the needs identified by your individual design programs.

CHARACTERISTICS OF SOUND

The characteristics of sound are what it is we control for when we manage the acoustics of spaces. In the acoustics portion of your design program you will identify the desired quality of the **ambient sound** and sometimes quantify (state a testable range of acceptable numbers) pertaining to specific characteristics. You may anticipate some problems with sound when you evaluate the configuration of the space you are designing. Common problems include echo and flutter echo, amplifying noise by focusing sound generated in the space, and **reverberation**, which is sound having no identifiable location.

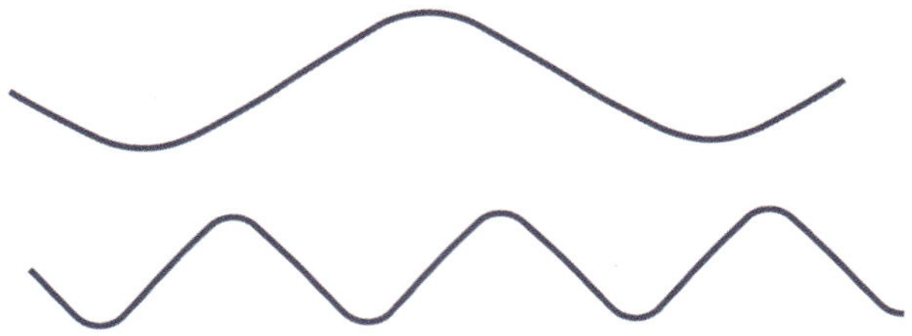

FIGURE 14.1 Low notes have long, loose waves that can wend their way out of spaces that would trap short waves of higher pitched sounds.

Echo

An echo is a reflected sound sufficiently delayed from the original sound that it is perceived as a separate entity. The typical culprit is a wall that bounces sound. Use a material that will absorb or break up the sound.

Flutter Echo

Flutter echoes are echoes that occur in rapid succession—usually between two parallel walls. Handle flutter with sound-absorptive material on wall panels, or with baffles, or banners on the ceiling to absorb and/or diffuse sound. Use multifaceted, curved, or slotted materials.

Frequency of Airborne Sound

Frequency in sound can be thought of in terms of pitch, such as a high-pitched sound or a low-pitched sound. High-frequency (high-pitch) waves are short and are easier to contain than low-frequency waves, which are sometimes long enough to "bend around" objects in their path. Figure 14.1 diagrams an abstraction of a low-pitched sound and a high-pitched sound. The low-pitch rumble of equipment or a motor has a very long wavelength that can escape the methods used to corral the short wave lengths.

Different materials will absorb different frequencies more effectively than others. Cork can be very effective generally in absorbing sound as can acoustical tiles. For specialty applications (studios, performance spaces), materials that have been specifically engineered for the sounds that will be produced are a better choice for acoustical panels, if required. Don't forget that there will be a wider range of frequencies for music than for speech.

Reverberation

Reverberations are sound reflections as sound bounces around in a space, lengthening the duration of the sound. The sound endures in the space even after it is no longer being emitted by the source. Hard surfaces increase reverberation time (meaning the sound will keep bouncing around in the space instead of disappearing). Soft and uneven surfaces cause the sound to decay—a term indicating the rate at which a sound dies down, usually referring to the steady decline in the loudness of the reverberation—and decrease reverberation time.

Focused Sound

Large concave surfaces will focus sound and distort it so that sounds occurring near the focal point will be perceived as too loud relative to other sounds. Unless such areas are intended to focus sound, the sound must be managed with absorptive materials or acoustically transparent coverings that allow the sound to travel through to an area where it can be managed. This configuration can contain sound better. An example would be a domed area over a seating grouping in an open-plan lobby.

RATING AND MEASURING SOUND

As you are managing the acoustics in your project with surfaces and barriers, you will encounter various ratings pertaining to materials under consideration. Even though managing acoustics in a space requires both moving and blocking sound, our industry does not tend to focus on material that promotes the movement of sound, but a hard, smooth surface will bounce sound effectively. Absorbing, diffusing, and blocking characteristics are measured, and numeral comparisons can be drawn between materials. This is a little simplistic but it is a workable method. Measurements that are of interest to designers comparing characteristics of materials are privacy index, sound transmission class, impact isolation class, noise reduction coefficient, speech range absorption, ceiling attenuation class, and sound absorption coefficient.

Privacy Index

Privacy index (PI) measures speech intelligibility. A PI measurement of less than 60 percent offers no speech privacy and is considered "poor." A 60 to 80 percent PI indicates that speech is readily understood; this is considered "marginally effective." It could also be understood to not interfere with comprehension in spaces where privacy is not a goal. An 80 percent to 95 percent PI rating means that speech is distracting but requires effort to be understood and is considered "normal" or "nonintrusive." A PI of 95 percent and better indicates that confidentiality is possible.

Sound Transmission Class

Sound transmission class (STC) measures sound moving through partitions or barriers. The number rises as efficiency increases because the measure is of how much sound is lost as it moves through the barrier. It is easier to remember it as sound "trapping" class because more effective construction prevents transmission. Sound transmission is affected by:

- The mass (and stiffness) of the materials used in the partition.
- The thickness of the assembly.
- Control of flanking and structure-borne paths ("airtight" construction).

Some useful numbers to clarify value of the ratings follow:

- STC of 25 to 30 means speech can be fairly readily understood.
- STC of 35 to 45 indicates that speech is audible but not intelligible, and perceived volume falls so that at the upper end, loud speech becomes a murmur.
- STC of 50 renders loud speech inaudible.

Impact Isolation Class

Impact isolation class or *impact insulation class* are two terms you will encounter that mean the same thing. They both describe a measure of the amount of impact noise blocked by the surface. A measurement of 50 is adequate, and this can almost always be achieved for floors simply by carpeting. This is a little simplistic because it does not account for varying kinds of impact. The tapping of stiletto heels is noise of a different nature from that of heavy footfall on a floor assembly, so the efficiency of the assembly cannot be considered to be equal across all kinds of impact noise. To mitigate impact noise, cushion the surface. You might specify a cushion that can be installed underneath a hard surface if you expect sound to telegraph through. For example, a layer of cork under cement board with a stone tile on top would keep footfall from telegraphing through the floor assembly.

Noise Reduction Coefficient

Noise reduction coefficient (NRC) measures the ability of materials to absorb sound. Select high NRC to eliminate echoes by limiting reverberation.

- A rating of 0 means that no sound is absorbed.
- A rating of 1 means that all sound waves striking the material are absorbed.
- A standard acoustical ceiling will have a rating of about 0.55.

Speech Range Absorption

Speech range absorption (SRA) measures the absorption of sounds that come specifically from speech. (*Absorption* here means that when the sound wave strikes a fibrous surface, it does not slow down due to the friction but keeps its same speed and gets quieter.) This will often be a different number from the NRC rating for the same product because NRC averages all sound. Our ears are "tuned" to hear human voice, so we are most distracted by 1000 hertz more readily than by 100 hertz, so materials to control speech transmission will absorb more vigorously in the range of speech; 300 to 400 hertz is considered to be the critical hertz range of speech intelligibility.

Ceiling Attenuation Class

Attenuation is a weakening of sound over distance or from absorption. Ceiling attenuation class (CAC) indicates the ability of a ceiling system to block sound transmission. A CAC of 35 is considered to be a good performance rating and means the construction reduces sound by 35 decibels.

Sound Absorption Coefficient

This rating is a percentage of sound that will be absorbed by an assembly. It is nicely straightforward; if it is rated at 75 percent that means that it will absorb 75 percent of the sound, reflecting only 25 percent back into the space.

MANAGING SOUND

Noise (unwanted sound) interferes with activities, reduces productivity, and causes stress. When you are intent on controlling sound and creating a sonic environment in line with the design program, we have a small "tool kit" we can employ. Materials can absorb, isolate, insulate, block, mask, and zone in our projects to diminish noise. They can bounce and aim to control, and can focus and amplify to enhance. Because the tools employed for managing sound work in combination with each other, it is not realistic to consider just one isolated material or configuration—everything works together.

Designers create a sonic environment, just as they create a visual environment, with planning and goals in the design program. All materials are acoustic materials because they all reflect, fracture, absorb, and transmit sound. All of your client's senses relay information about the environment and you should be no more willing to design an environment with poor sound quality than poor lighting, an inappropriate color scheme, or poor circulation. It may likely be part of your design program that you want the sound from the dining room to carry into the reception lobby but you don't want the sound from the washrooms or the kitchen to travel there. You will design and specify to manage that sound.

Too many **live** surfaces can create sonic chaos and too much **dead** surface area can be disconcerting—actually causing people to talk louder as they subconsciously

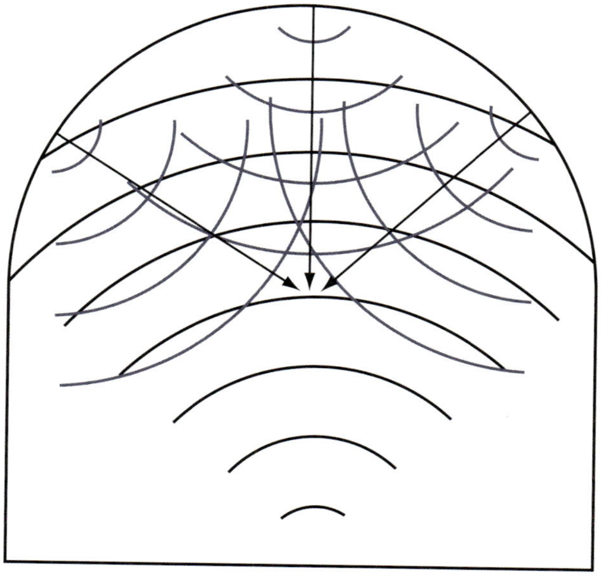

FIGURE 14.2 Sound radiates and bounces. The shape of the space works with materials in the space to control sound.

try to normalize the environment and produce some of the expected echo that is usually present. It is very important to remember that managing the presentation of sound in spaces is not just about "mopping up all the loose sound." Managing acoustics means intentionally creating an environment where sound is useful, pleasant, and congruent with the whole experience of the space.

Live and Dead

The simplest way to begin your planning is to consider where to position live and dead surfaces. Live surfaces bounce the sound off; they enliven, adding sparkle. Dead surfaces soak up and trap sound. Some bounce is desirable to create enlivened, natural-sounding environments. The live, concave surface in the diagram shown in Figure 14.2 illustrates the effect of a live surface positioned to bounce the sound generated into the center—rounding out the sonic experience in the space. It creates "surround sound."

If the space in question is deep, you will need dead surfaces too. There is a very primitive rule of thumb called the 30-millisecond rule, which conveniently translates into the 30-foot rule. If a sound sails past you and then bounces back to you, traveling 30 feet on its trip, that is enough travel time to cause a perceptible delay between arrival of the original sound and its echo; the delay will be distinct enough to muddle the sound. It will be harder to comprehend its meaning. So you will try to position live surfaces along the side walls to bounce the sound to the center, and dead surfaces at the back wall of the space diagrammed in Figure 14.3 to stop the echo from the back wall on the right from muddling speech generated on the left.

Decibel Reduction

A decibel, or dB, is a measure of the loudness of sound: 30 dB is a whisper; 60 dB is normal conversation; an alarm clock may be about 70 dB, which is the upper end of sound that people usually accept as a normal range. Perception of sound is dependent on personal sensitivity, content, duration, time of occurrence, and psychological factors such as emotional state and expectations. A sound level of 110 dB may be preferred at a rock concert but be entirely unreasonable in a building lobby.

A change in decibel level of 1 dB is not discernable; 3 dB seems to be the threshold of perception for noticing a change in decibel level. A change of 6 dB is clearly noticeable. A reduction of 10 dB is functionally "half as loud," and 25 dB is perceived as "one-fourth as loud" according to people who were surveyed about their perceptions.

Attenuation

Every sound has a discrete wavelength, so it makes sense to control for the length of the wave when you set out to absorb a sound. A double-stud wall construction that

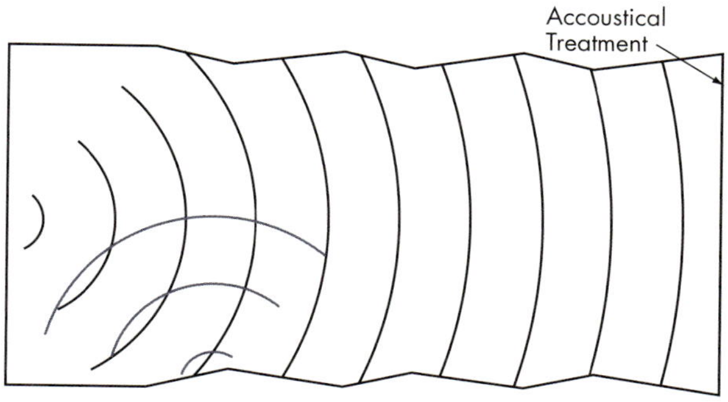

FIGURE 14.3 Sound waves in this long room could be reflected off the back wall, causing an interfering echo because of a time delay. The acoustician may suggest angling the side walls to lend dimension to the sound and adding a sound-absorbing material on the back wall to stop interfering echoes from bouncing back into the room.

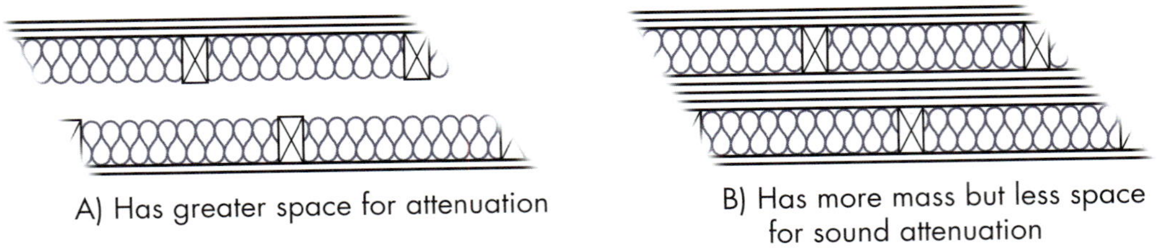

A) Has greater space for attenuation
B) Has more mass but less space for sound attenuation

FIGURE 14.4A–B Drawing (a) has room for better sound attenuation and will do a better job than (b) at stopping higher frequency sounds.

provides a greater distance between each side of the construction may control the migration of speech better than increasing the amount of material in the construction. For example, drawing (a) in Figure 14.4 may be a more effective partition because the space between the two surfaces muffles the sound of a particular length better than if the cavity were packed full of insulation (b).

All components of an assembly contribute to the sound transmission and sound absorption of the assembly in some way. Construction materials that have been specifically developed for stopping, baffling, and absorbing sound can be specified in your drawings and material specs. These can be combined with surfacing materials that reflect as well. Construction technique should also be specified (Figure 14.5). For example, in order to contain sound in an area all air gaps must be sealed or closed, and this must be carefully managed with other building systems since air gaps are required to deliver air (and spaces are of no use without air!). Instructions to caulk all gaps with an approved caulk are noted in construction specs and instructions to the installer. The HVAC ductwork that is shared by the two spaces is another opportunity for noise to bother people. We can't seal off the air ducts so we specify a dampening mat or baffle to muddle sound but still allow airflow.

Point of Emphasis 14.1

Configuration also contributes to managing sound. A domed ceiling will focus sound downward and direct it to the area below rather than bouncing it away into other areas. When doors line a corridor, offset the door locations so sound cannot travel easily right across the hall into another space. Analyze your layout and see where it will be easy for sound to travel or bounce into other areas and employ sound-absorbing or sound-deadening materials to control this movement.

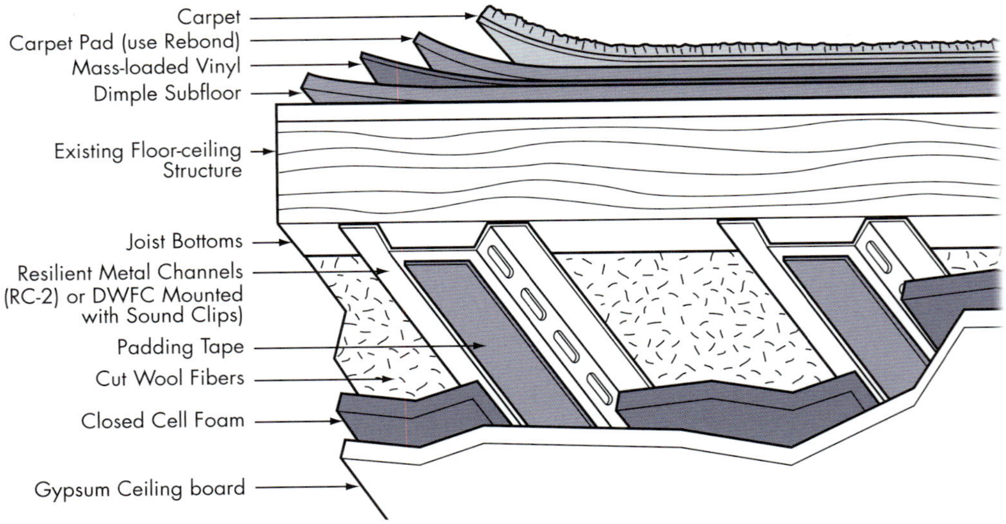

FIGURE 14.5 Design for sound containment. *Drawing courtesy of Super Soundproofing Co., San Marcos, CA.*

PRODUCTS

All materials have acoustic properties and the subtleties of acoustics are often subsumed in other considerations. Table 14.1 lists NRC ratings of some common materials. Even as you are positioning materials for reasons of aesthetics or physical performance, keep in mind that these materials will also affect the sound. For example, a hard, smooth glass surface will be sonically **bright**, bouncing sound with a crisper or harsher quality than will a wood surface. A small space with hard surfaces will be enlivened whereas a large space with the same surfacing will be boomy, that is, reverberating, especially in lower frequencies.

Materials are applied to constructions, and the structure plus the surfacing material is referred to as the assembly. Assemblies alter the acoustical properties of materials in the assembly. The products listed here are not the whole story. Remember that spaces can trap sound and that shapes of spaces can focus sound. If you detail partitions up to the deck above your client's space rather than stopping them at the height of the dropped ceiling you will block sound more effectively.

Manufacturers often control the testing of their own product, so testing conditions of two similar products may not be identical. For instance, a material installed over a fiberglass substrate will test at a higher NRC than the very same material installed over gypsum board. The number alone is not enough to tell the whole story. When comparing two materials, review the description of the assembly that was tested to ensure that a comparison based on NRC will be valid, and also consider whether the tested assembly is close enough to your project conditions to permit you to draw conclusions about your project from the assembly tested.

Table 14.1
All materials are acoustic materials in that they all reflect, absorb, or fracture sound waves.

Noise Reduction Coefficient (NRC) Ratings for Some Common Materials	
Brick painted	0–0.2
Brick unpainted	0–0.05
Concrete painted	0–0.05
Concrete unpainted	0–0.2
Marble and terrazzo	0
Linoleum on concrete	0–0.05
Rubber on concrete	0–0.05
Plaster	0–0.05
Fabric on gypsum	0–0.05
Steel	0–0.1
Glass	0.05–0.1
Plywood	0.1–0.15
Concrete block painted	0–0.05
Concrete block unpainted	0.05–0.35
Wood	0.05–0.13
10 oz. drapery	0.05–0.15
14 oz. drapery	0.55
18 oz. drapery	0.6
Carpet on concrete	0.2–0.3
Carpet on foam pad	0.30–0.55
Cork floor tiles ¾" thick	0.1–0.15
Cork wall tiles 1" thick	0.3–0.7
Polyurethane foam 1" thick	0.3

Ceiling Systems

These products are typically specified as a system of panels that fit into a suspended framework. This suspended framework conceals ductwork and sprinkler pipe and sometimes electrical conduit, as well as creates an attenuation space that also helps to control sound in the habitable space below. Sometimes designers will specify additional sound control, such as insulation that serves to further muffle sound that may travel through this plenum space into another space.

These products are made of a variety of materials. Some examples include mineral fiber faced with materials that are designed to maximize light reflectance, and vinyl-faced fiberglass panels to resist moisture and inhibit mold. Some products have recycled content, wood, and wood products as well as perforated metal products that are designed to absorb and/or trap sound.

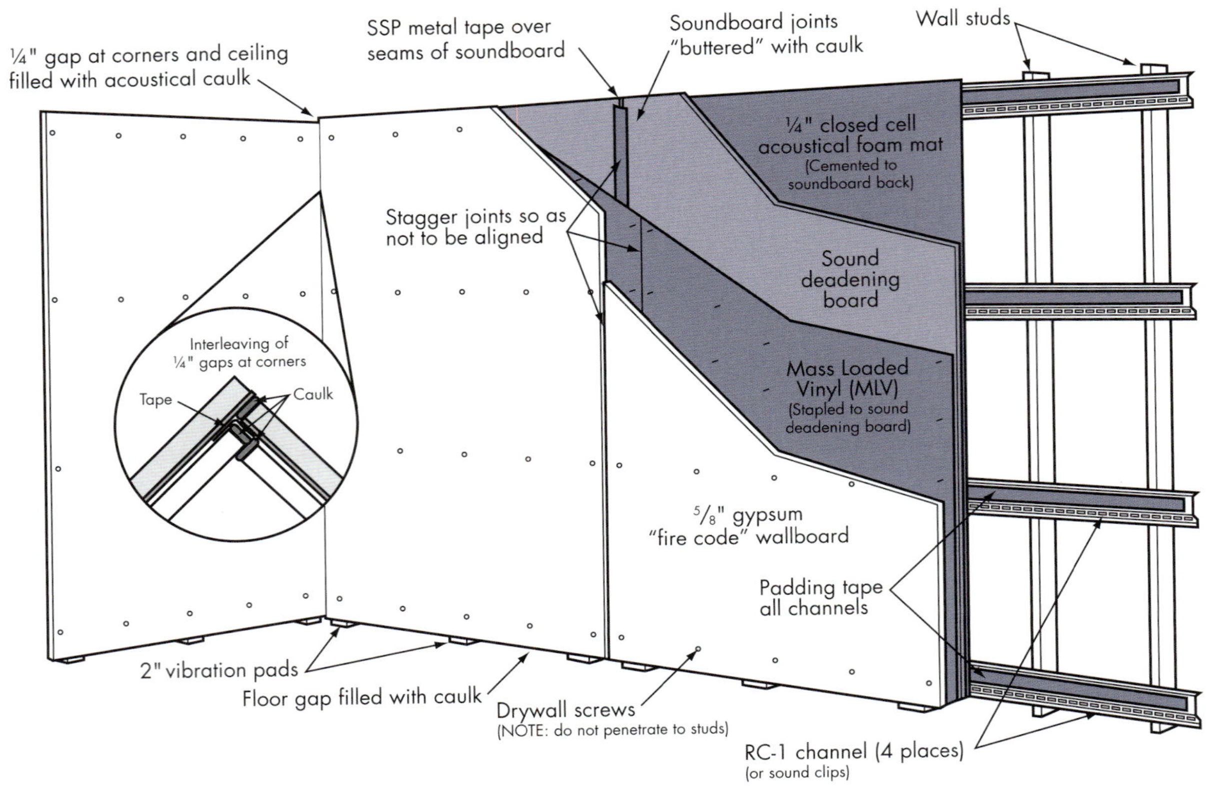

FIGURE 14.6 You might specify special construction accessories to build sound barriers for special installations. *Drawing courtesy of Super Soundproofing Co., San Marcos, CA.*

Wall Systems

These products are also sold as systems with customizable frameworks that hold fabric and conceal sound-absorbing materials.

Resilient Channels

This product is essentially a special fastening system that separates the wall surface from the wall structure (Figure 14.6). It is a flexible connection between the wallboard and the studs. These channels can add up to five more points to your STC rating. This solution is effective at mitigating **structure-borne sound**.

Acoustically Transparent Surfaces

Don't forget that you will not always want to block, absorb, or break up sound. There will be instances where you want to transmit sound. If you need to visually and physically enclose a space or visually conceal sound equipment, there are acoustically transparent fabrics that can be stretched on frames and divide spaces or conceal an array of speaker equipment. You may specify such fabric if you have special sound-absorbing foam surfacing affixed to your partitions beyond and want to make sure that *all* of the sound gets through to the special foam surfaces concealed beyond the special fabric and none is bounced back into the space.

Sound Abatement Mats

Proprietary materials have been developed to absorb airborne sound and cushion impact sound. These materials may variably address other needs as some are more rigid or water or flame resistant than others. You might specify a generic solution, such as a half-inch layer of cork under a hard surface or piece of vibrating equipment.

Other Material Solutions

Materials that you may not think of as acoustical materials can be very effective at managing the sonic environment. You must first plan for the sonic function of a surface; it must bounce the sound (hard and smooth), contain the sound (dense), absorb the sound (spongy), or muffle the sound (bumpy).

Plaster and Skim Coats

There are special acoustical plasters, like the "popcorn" ceilings, that you are likely familiar with, but regular skim coating of walls and ceilings will also contain sound and stop it from traveling through partitions into other spaces. Acoustical plasters utilize a foamy structure and a textured finish surface to keep a space from becoming too acoustically boomy.

Carpeting

Although we don't think of carpeting as an acoustical material, you can often meet your sound goals for dampening impact noise from walking and absorption of some airborne sound by simply carpeting the floor. Carpet also significantly reduces the ability of the floor to bounce sound back into the space.

Recycled Denim Insulation

While your initial decision to use recycled blue jeans insulation may be motivated by a desire for low toxicity and sustainability, this product delivers better sound-absorption ratings than fiberglass insulation.

SPECIFYING

Your specification will be carefully written to describe the desired material and installation completely and succinctly. It is difficult to write a spec before you know the exact material and installation details that you are writing about. If you had in mind to write a spec for an acoustical ceiling system you might organize your spec something like this.

SAMPLE SPEC 14.1

Part 1 General Information

1.1 Related Documents

A. See manufacturer's installation instructions.
B. Refer to finish plan for location and details.

1.2 Summary

A. This work includes the installation of the suspension system and panels, coordinated with lighting and sprinkler equipment by others.

1.3 Contractor Submittals

A. Vendor to submit sample of each material specified representing finish type and quality.
B. Manufacturer to submit installation and maintenance instructions.
C. Manufacturer to submit confirmation of recycled content.

1.4 Quality Assurance

A. All materials to be delivered to acclimatized site in manufacturer's unopened packages.
B. System to be installed by certified installers having at least two years' experience installing such systems.

1.5 Delivery, Storage, and Handling

A. Material to acclimate to site for 24 hours prior to installation.

1.6 Maintenance of Installation

Part 2 Products

2.1 General Information

A. This section includes all materials including acoustical panels, anchors, and complete suspension system.

2.2 Manufacturers

A. Super-Silent Ceilings, 123 Industrial Drive, Anytown, ST 12345.

2.3 Products

A. Cloud Nine 2' × 2' acoustical panels.
B. Enameled aluminum concealed spline grid.

Part 3 Execution

3.1 Examination

A. Inspect material and install only material in undamaged condition.

3.2 Preparation

A. Site to be fully acclimatized. All ductwork, sprinkler equipment, and recessed lighting to be in place prior to commencing work.

3.3 Installation

A. Install per manufacturer's recommendations.

3.4 Post Installation

A. Install per Reflected Ceiling Plan; center tile or spline in each space, having no less than half-tile width at perimeter.
B. Scraps and waste are to be disposed of by installers prior to leaving job site.

INSTALLATION

Many of these products are installed by carpenters. Systems, as opposed to products, are best installed by experienced carpenters because the configuration must be installed exactly right or the system can be compromised and will not deliver the ratings suggested by the manufacturer.

Most painters have experience installing acoustical plaster, and your soft goods workroom, which installs upholstered wall surfaces for you, is likely to be able to install these acoustically rated, specialty wall systems. If you do not know of a tradesperson or company to install a product, ask the vendor or manufacturer for a reference to an experienced tradesperson in your area. Some manufacturers have training programs and will certify installers who have successfully completed the training. If such is available, hire a certified installer.

INSPECTION

As part of your investigation of the product before you specify, you will likely review installation information so you will be somewhat familiar with the methods and materials.

However, for complicated systems it is a good idea to have your vendor inspect the installation; even your general contractor may not have the familiarity with specialty systems to know if it has been properly installed.

SUMMARY

In this chapter we reviewed basic acoustical concepts and how noise affects interior environments. You learned about the distinctions between the different characteristics of sound that you will control. You considered different approaches to managing the acoustic environment and the materials and products that you can specify to manage specific sound characteristics. You reviewed materials and assemblies and how they are configured and installed to manage sound.

WEB SEARCH ACTIVITIES

1. Search for the products that were listed in this chapter that you are not familiar with. Notice the variety from one manufacturer to another.

2. Perform an image search for photos of interiors where sound is especially important, such as *opera house interior* or *theater interior*. See if you can determine techniques used by the designer to manage the sonic environment, including live and dead surfaces, uneven surfaces, special acoustical materials, or other methods.

PERSONAL ACTIVITIES

1. Review plans for a variety of spaces having a variety of uses and imagine that you are charged with creating a pleasant sonic environment. Where would you bounce sound? Contain it? Absorb it? What would you use to accomplish those tasks?

SUMMARY QUESTIONS

1. How are acoustics addressed by law?

2. What characteristics of sound are measurable? How are they measured? What measurements are generally acceptable?

3. How does the kind of sound generated and required in an environment indicate the need for certain configurations and surfaces?

4. How would you deal with impact sound? Echoes? Transmission of airborne noise between spaces? Speech intelligibility? Speech privacy?

5. Why is it important to know not just the sound rating of a rated material but also the way it was tested?

GLOSSARY

A

Access flooring Portable flooring systems with a walking surface elevated above the structural surface. Support posts hold up tiles that comprise the walking surface, creating a space below for running electrical and low-voltage cabling as well as for heat conveyance. Individual tiles can be lifted to access this space, when furniture is reconfigured, to move the services housed below without necessitating construction costs. These systems require modular flooring, like carpet tiles, to take advantage of this versatility. (Chapter 4)

Admixtures Material other than water, aggregates, or cement used as an ingredient of concrete or mortar to adjust the curing process, workability, or to impart additional properties. (Chapter 12)

Air changes per hour (ACH) Movement of a volume of air in a given period of time; if a house has one air change per hour, it means that all the air in the house will be replaced in a one-hour period. (Chapter 1)

Alkali burn When alkalinity of fresh cement, concrete, or plaster causes the breakdown of a paint's binder, causing the paint to deteriorate. (Chapter 2)

Alkyd A synthetic resin used in oil-based paints. (Chapter 2)

Alligatoring A pattern of small surface cracks or checking that may result from incompatibility of paint and base coat. This also refers to a decorative effect imitating this kind of damaged surface. (Chapter 2)

Alloy Combination of two or more metals to enhance performance or appearance. (Chapter 9)

Ambient sound Sound in a location at a given time, composed of all the sound within the environment. (Chapter 14)

Anchors Pieces or assemblages, usually metal ties, used to attach materials to building structure. (Chapter 10)

Annealing Controlled cooling, which is done in a lehr (a temperature-controlled kiln) to prevent residual stresses in the glass. (Chapter 8)

Anodized Electrolytic action to provide a hard noncorrosive oxide film on the surface of aluminum; the anodized surface can take up colorants and the aluminum can imitate the appearance of other metals or achieve a brilliant hue. (Chapter 9)

B

Best practices Any method or standard that will produce superior results when compared to other methods or standards. (Chapter 1)

Bicottura Method for producing tile by firing twice. Usually has two glazes on the tile, the first a nontransparent on the body and a second transparent glaze on the surface. (Chapter 10)

Biocide Additive that tries to kill anything that wants to live on the surface (bacteria, mold, etc.). (Chapter 2)

Biodiversity Diversity in plant and animals species in an ecosystem. (Chapter 3)

Bleed Pigment spreading beyond the design outline or one color overlapping another. (Chapter 2)

Bleeding The migration of color from the substrate, causing discoloration of the paint. Wood resins and inks are often the source of color migrating into the paint from below. (Chapter 2)

Block fillers A thick, paintlike material used to smooth out very rough masonry surfaces like cinder block. It is generally brush applied, then painted. (Chapter 2)

Blooming Hazy or raggedy pattern because of formula incompatibility of the inks and the coating. (Chapter 2)

Bond coat A material used between the back of the tile and the prepared surface. Suitable bond coats include pure portland cement, dry set portland cement mortar, latex-type portland cement mortar, organic adhesive, and the like. (Chapter 10)

Bonds
(1) Tying various parts of a masonry wall by lapping units one over another or by connecting with metal ties. (Chapter 10)
(2) Patterns formed by exposed faces of units. (Chapter 10)
(3) Adhesion between mortar or grout and masonry units or reinforcement. (Chapter 10)

Book-matched Stone slabs or wood boards or veneers that are sequential in the lot and finished so that side-by-side they create a mirror image. (Chapter 11)

Bright Quality of the sonic environment in which there is an abundance of treble range reflections giving the feeling of "brightness" or "liveliness" to the sound. Sound in a tile bathroom or kitchen is bright. Too much can seem harsh and irritating—think sonic glare. (Chapter 14)

Burls Growth on a tree disrupting natural organization of internal structures producing veneer that has a random grain pattern of small curved lines. (Chapter 5)

C

Calcite-based stones Stones that contain calcite such as marble, limestone, travertine, and some onyx. Calcite can be etched by even mild acids like vinegar, citric acid in grooming products, and fruit juice, which can remove the polish from the stone if left to sit for an extended length of time. (Chapter 11)

Calendering Flattening fabric between rollers, similar to ironing, to produce smooth or visual texture like moiré. (Chapter 3)

Carcinogens Substances known to have links to causes of cancer. (Chapter 1)

Carded Fibers aligned in the same direction. (Chapter 4)

Carved nap A process of carving around a design or motif to enhance the look of the rug. (Chapter 4)

Case goods Furniture and cabinets made of hard materials (like wood, engineered wood products, etc.) as opposed to upholstered furniture. (Chapter 5)

Cellulosic Material that comes from plants and is deconstructed into its chemical parts and recombined to make fabric with properties unlike those of the original plant material. (Chapter 3)

Cement grout A mixture of portland cement, sand or other ingredients and water, which produces a water-resistant, uniformly colored material used to fill joints between tile units. (Chapter 10)

Cementitious Containing finely powdered mixtures of inorganic compounds that, when combined with water, harden by curing. (Chapter 12)

Chalking When paint deteriorates it will sometimes release a white, powdery substance onto its surface. This action is called chalking and is sometimes desired on white exterior paint as the chalking will rinse away in the rain taking dirt with it. (Chapter 2)

Checking
(1) Small cracks in the paint film usually caused when the paint dries out over time and loses its elasticity. (Chapter 2)
(2) A split in solid wood along the direction of the grain, caused by the drying of the wood. (Chapter 2)

Chemical bond Adhering two surfaces of identical material together by applying a glue that interacts with the chemistry of the two halves and, in a sense, chemically welding them together. (Chapter 7)

Chemically strengthened glass Glass that has been heat treated from ion exchange instead of heating and cooling alone. (Chapter 8)

Chintz Cotton, plain weave cloth often printed with large floral designs, calendered, sometimes with wax, to produce a smooth shiny surface. If wax is used during calendering, it is called glazed chintz. (Chapter 3)

Coefficient of friction The ratio of the tangential force that is needed to start or maintain uniform relative motion between two contacting surfaces to the perpendicular force holding them in contact. Essentially, slip resistance. (Chapter 1)

Cold rolled Bringing metal to final thickness and simultaneously finishing it by passing it between heavy rollers without heat. (Chapter 9)

Commercial/contract wallcovering Wallcovering suitable for high-traffic areas, normally available in 48- or 54-inch widths. (Chapter 2)

Commissioning agents Persons responsible for coordinating and carrying out the commissioning process by implementing the commissioning plan and ensuring prior to occupancy that all building systems are operational. (Chapter 1)

Companion/correlated wallcovering A set of wallcoverings designed and colored to be used together in the same or adjoining areas. (Chapter 2)

Courses Continuous horizontal layers of bricks, bonded with mortar in masonry. (Chapter 10)

Crimped Having a waviness of a fiber or yarn. Can be found naturally, as with wool, or can be mechanically produced and heat set in synthetic fiber. (Chapter 3)

Critical radiant flux (CRF) A gas-fueled heater applies heat to a sample to determine the minimum amount of heat required to sustain flame. (Chapter 1)

Crocking Coloring that rubs off and smears. (Chapter 2)

D

Dead The condition of sound in a room when there is a lack of reflection and a lack of reverberation. A space with too much sound absorption will be dead and users will sometimes talk louder in an unconscious effort to normalize the sonic environment. (Chapter 14)

Denier The diameter or thickness of yarn; the lower the number, the finer the yarn. (Chapters 3, 4)

Distressed Texture that gives a timeworn look; might include hand scraping, wire brushing, beating with chains, etc. (Chapter 5)

E

Economies of scale Increased efficiency in production attributable to making a large quantity of the same thing. (Chapter 3)

Ecosystems Inter-related habitats and organisms; healthy ecosystems remain in balance without depletion of resources. (Chapter 1)

Electrochromic (glass) Glass that darkens in color or turns into a mirror when electric current is applied. (Chapter 8)

Embossed A raised effect created by impressing a design into wallcovering using either pressure or heat. (Chapter 2)

Engineered wood Composite product that is made of wood particles or wood flour/sawdust, combined with resins or glues and shaped into new forms. The reason for this production is that these woodlike elements have many of the positive characteristics of wood but are dimensionally stable. (Chapter 5)

Epoxy coatings Highly durable two-part coating system where the two parts are mixed together just before applying. They will cure only after they have been mixed, but then must be applied before they harden. Epoxy coatings for floors are often mixed with colored epoxy chips, but these chips are decorative and contribute little to the performance of the floor coating except perhaps for some slip resistance. (Chapter 2)

F

Faux finish *Faux* is a French word that means fake. These finishes are created by special painters who use translucent glazes to visually imitate other materials, creating surfaces that are faux bois (fake wood), faux marble (fake marble), faux tortoise (fake tortoiseshell), and other imitations along with trompe l'oeil ("fool the eye") murals that look like landscapes or other compositions that may also include faux materials in the rendering. (Chapter 2)

Feathered An area blended into its surroundings. (Chapter 2)

Feathered (edge) Chipping away the body from beneath a facial edge of a tile to miter the back for forming an out-corner. (Chapter 10)

Felted A nonwoven fabric with fibers matted together to form a compact material. It does not fray. (Chapter 3)

Figuring Inherent markings, patterning in the wood caused by growth patterns and conditions. (Chapter 5)

Filaments Single-fiber strands. (Chapter 3)

Flammability A material's tendency to support flame. (Chapter 1)

Flash Uneven gloss, visual texture, or color resulting from an unsealed substrate or failure to maintain recommended temperature during dry time. (Chapter 2)

Flat weaves Weaving in which no knots are used and no pile is created. The weft strands are simply passed through the warp strands; for example, a kilim, cicim, or soumac. (Chapter 4)

Float glass High-optical-quality glass with parallel surfaces having fire-finished brilliance attained without polishing and grinding. Float is fast replacing plate glass. (Chapter 8)

Floats Yarn strands that travel over the surface of the weave, skipping some interlacing to create a smooth, lustrous face. (Chapter 3)

Flocking Finely chopped fibers are sprinkled over, and adhere to, a pattern printed in varnish or other sticky material creating a plush surface pattern. (Chapter 2)

Foil Category of wallcovering that has a thin layer of metal foil adhered to a paper backing. Foil is less common since the development of Mylar wallcovering. It requires a substrate that is in good condition because the reflectivity of foil will highlight every imperfection in the wall surface. (Chapter 2)

Frit Glass particulates that are fused to the face of a sheet of glass altering color and/or transparency. (Chapter 8)

Full-spread adhesive Adhesive is spread across the entire underside of a material, not just the perimeter. (Chapter 6)

G

Galvanized Metal coated with zinc, either by dipping in a bath of molten zinc, pounding zinc onto the surface, or electrolytic action. (Chapter 9)

Gauged Stone ground to produce a uniform thickness of all pieces for material that is to be used together. (Chapter 11)

Glaze A special paint that has lower pigment solids per binder volume so it produces a translucent coating. Glazes are typically built up in layers so their translucency can be exploited to imitate other materials, such as stone, tortoiseshell, or other faux finish surfaces. (Chapter 2)

Glueless tile system Vinyl tiles that are sold as a system including the tile, a rollout underlayment that has a premarked grid pattern that assists with the installation, and the adhesive tabs or spray adhesive. It is easy to place down and easy to pick up again. (Chapter 6)

Gneiss Common kind of granite whose formation generally leaves it with a "granular" distribution of minerals and colors. (Chapter 11)

Grade level The position of the floor structure relative to the ground around it. *Below grade* is below ground level, *on grade* is at ground level, and *above grade* is above ground level. If the floor and the ground are in contact or separated by less than 18 inches of well-ventilated space it is on grade. More than 18 inches of separation constitutes above grade. (Chapter 6)

Grain The composition and texture of particles, crystals, and/or veins in stone, wood, etc. (Chapter 5)

Grain raising The uneven swelling of summer and winter growth of wood caused by absorption of a liquid that makes the wood grain more prominent. Water is very good at causing this. (Chapter 2)

Granite Hard, crystalline rock composed of feldspar, quartz, and other minerals. (Chapter 11)

Green Sustainable materials or practices. (Chapter 1)

Greige goods Undyed and unfinished fabric or carpet. (Chapter 3)

Ground Raw stock onto which a coat of pigment has been applied before the top colors are put on in wallcovering manufacturing. (Chapter 2)

H

Hand

(1) The tactile aesthetic qualities of carpets and textiles. Factors determining how carpets feel to the hand include weight, stiffness, fiber type and denier, density, backing, and latex. Terms like *softness, smoothness, coarseness, crispness, dryness, silkiness, springiness, tightness,* and *looseness* all describe the hand of a fabric/fiber. (Chapter 3)

(2) Description of the location of the hinge side and latch side of the door as judged from the more public side. Left-hand door: has hinges on the left. Right-hand door: has hinges on the right. (Chapter 5)

Heartwood The wood extending from the center core of the trunk (pith) to the sapwood; heartwood is usually darker than sapwood. (Chapter 5)

Heat set Permanent twist or crimp by heat or steam; for twist retention and stabilization of yarn configuration. (Chapter 4)

Heat-strengthened glass Glass that has been formed, cooled, and reheated to just below melting point, and then cooled again increasing its strength. Heat-strengthened glass does not qualify as safety glass. (Chapter 8)

Heat welding The way seams between sheets of linoleum floors or vinyl sheet floors are sealed. Heat welding requires skilled professionals who use specialized tools. (See "Welding rods.") (Chapter 6)

High-density foam Attached carpet cushion made from latex foam having a minimum density of 17 pounds per cubic foot and a minimum weight of 38 ounces per square yard. (Chapter 4)

Hollow core Doors that have an air space, foam insulation, or fibrous honeycomb filler between the door skins. These doors are lighter in weight and lower quality than solid-core doors. (Chapter 5)

Honed Smooth, matte finish. (Chapter 11)

Hot melt Adhesive of thermoplastic polymers and plastics that can be melted and solidified repeatedly, used with carpet tape to seam goods together. (Chapter 4)

I

Inside mount Attach the window covering to the inside/jamb. (Chapter 3)

L

Laminated Thin layers of materials bonded together with adhesive, heat, and pressure. These layers may be the same material, as is the case of plywood, where layers of softwood are glued together. Different materials can also be laminated together, as in the case of veneered surfaces where thin layers of wood are glued to others like particleboard. (Chapters 2, 5)

Laminated glass Two or more sheets with an inner layer of transparent plastic to which the glass adheres if broken. (Chapter 8)

Lap Area where one stroke of the brush or roller overlaps other fresh paint just applied. The painter's objective is to make this juncture without visible lap marks by always working against a wet edge. When wet paint meets dry paint the overlapping areas will be visible. (Chapter 2)

Leadership in Energy and Environmental Design (LEED) Leadership in Energy and Environmental Design Green Building Rating System promotes a whole-building approach to sustainability by recognizing performance in five key areas of human and environmental health: sustainable site development, water savings, energy efficiency, materials selection, and indoor environmental quality. (Chapter 1)

Limestone Calcite-based stone, generally softer than marble. (Chapter 11)

Lippage

(1) A condition where one edge of a tile is higher than an adjacent tile giving the finished surface an uneven appearance. (Chapter 10)

(2) When one edge of a stone is higher than the adjacent edge in an installation. Some lippage is to be expected but typically, in commercial installations, if it is greater than $^{3}/_{32}$ inch it is specified to be ground down to flat. (Chapter 11)

Live (liveliness) Reverberation at middle and high frequencies (above about 350 hertz). A "live" space may still be deficient in bass. If a room is sufficiently reverberant at low frequencies, it is said to sound *warm.* (Chapter 14)

Loose-laid (and modified loose lay) An installation method used for installing the floor where no adhesive is used, or adhesive is used just in strategic spots such as under appliances (modified loose lay). (Chapter 6)

Low-E glass Low-emission glass (Low-E) is a clear glass that allows the sun's light to pass through the glass into the building while blocking heat from leaving. (Chapter 1)

Luster Brightness or reflectivity of fibers or carpets. Luster classifications include bright, semi-bright, semi-dull, and dull. (Chapter 4)

M

Malleable Metal that can be bent cold to a degree. It is easily welded. (Chapter 9)

Marble A crystalline, metamorphic stone typically presenting a veined appearance structure. (Chapter 11)

Mechanically bonded Adhered by roughening two surfaces to be bonded so that the adhesive "grabs" onto each surface because the glue does not interact chemically with the surfaces the way a chemical bond does. (Chapter 7)

Memo sample A piece of fabric representing the fabric pattern, construction, and general colors but is not to be taken as an exact representation of fabric stock on hand. For that kind of exactness in representation you will request a "cutting" from the current lot. (Chapter 3)

Mercerizing Fabric is singed, then passed through a solution of caustic soda and rinsed, making the fibers swell, giving them increased strength and an increased ability to hold dye. (Chapter 3)

Metallic fiber Synthetic fiber made of metal-coated plastic, or plastic-coated metal, as used in small amounts in carpet to dissipate static electricity. (Chapter 4)

Metamorphic stones Any stone that started life as one thing but "morphed" due to heat, pressure, or both to become something else. (Chapter 11)

Mineral streak Wood containing a pocket of mineral matter introduced by sap flow, causing an unnatural color ranging from greenish brown to black. (Chapter 5)

Mock-up A section of an assembly, built full size or to scale, to test its performance, judge its appearance, etc. (Chapter 9)

Monocottura Method of producing tile by a single firing in which body and glazes are fired simultaneously in kilns at temperatures over 2,000°F. (Chapter 10)

Monoculture Single crop grown over a large expanse that disrupts biodiversity, affecting the entire local ecosystem. (Chapter 3)

Mud veins A streak or vein in a stone slab that is composed of minerals that are softer than the surrounding area. Sometimes these areas are unstable and the stone will fracture along the length of the mud vein. These soft veins can be seen when you let the light glance obliquely off of the stone's face because they are not as reflective as surrounding material. (Chapter 11)

Mylar A highly reflective plastic that imitates metallic wallcovering but is more stable than metals that could oxidize. (Chapter 2)

N

Nap Pile face of short fibers that tends to feel smooth when brushed in one direction only. (Chapter 3)

O

Off-grain Fabric having warp and weft yarns oriented other than perpendicular to each other. Off-grain fabric will not drape as expected and will pucker and sag when used for upholstery. (Chapter 3)

Onyx Translucent variety of quartz-based stone. (Chapter 11)

Outgas Volatile compounds that change from a solid or liquid to a gas and float out of the material. (Chapter 1)

Overtufting Tufting process done by hand or machine in which an already tufted and dyed carpet has another yarn system tufted through the back of the fabric to develop a pattern on the surface. (Chapter 4)

Oxidize Develop a coating as the metal combines with oxygen, usually darkening the color. Oxidation can be burnished off (so it can rub off accidentally onto clothing). (Chapter 9)

P

Particulates Suspended solids (dust, grit, etc.) that reduce visibility and can cause lung and eye damage, and respiratory problems. (Chapter 1)

Passive solar System that relies on the natural radiation, convection, and conduction for the transfer of heat or coolness. Dense materials are effective storage for heat and coolness, absorbing heat from the sun, radiating it back out at night to even out indoor temperatures, causing air movement for ventilation or cooling, or storing heat for future use, without the assistance of other energy sources. (Chapter 1)

Patching compounds Compound used to fill or smooth subfloor irregularities in preparation for installing a new vinyl floor. (Chapter 6)

Pecky Small pockets of decay (which has been arrested so will not spread) that create little voids in the wood. (Chapter 5)

Penetrating sealant A protective formula applied to the stone that soaks into the material, coating the capillaries and microfissures. Porous stones will "drink up" more sealer than dense stones and may need more than one application of penetrating sealer to protect them. (Chapter 11)

Pervious Has empty space in it that allows water to percolate down through it rather than causing it to run off into sewer systems. (Chapter 12)

Phenolic Heat-set resin that is hard and abrasion resistant. Historically it was mixed with wood flour to make Bakelite and is used today, fused with paper, to make plastic laminate. (Chapter 7)

Pile The extra yarn that protrudes from the surface of a fabric like velvet or corduroy. (Chapter 3)

Plain-sliced Also called flat-sawn, the log is cut in the direction of its length with all cuts parallel to one another, allowing for a cathedral grain appearance. (Chapter 5)

Plastic Polymers and resins with bio-based or petroleum-based ingredients, softened by heat and fashioned into films, sheets, and forms. (Chapter 7)

Plies Layers of wood, typically used to describe engineered hardwood construction layers. (Chapter 13)

Polished Smoothest, shiniest finish possible for a stone characterized by a gloss or reflective property; high gloss is only possible on hard, dense materials. (Chapter 11)

Polymers Combination of molecules linked and cross-linked to create material with characteristics unlike those of the constituents. (Chapter 7)

Poms Small bundles of yarns measuring less than 2 inches across, having lengths of 2 or 3 inches, dyed to a specified color and used to gain approval of the color before the skeins are dyed for a custom rug or a sample is produced. (Chapter 4)

Portland cement A cement consisting predominantly of calcium silicates that reacts with water to form a hard mass. (Chapter 12)

Prepasted Wallcovering with adhesive applied to the back of it by the manufacturer. Dipping a strip in water before hanging activates the adhesive. (Chapter 2)

Pretrimmed Rolls of wallcovering trimmed at the factory to remove the selvage. (Chapter 2)

Protein Fiber with origins in animal life either as animal hair or the cocoons of silkworms. Leather is not referred to as protein as the term is applied most commonly to fiber products. (Chapter 3)

Q

Quarter-sliced The log is cut in the direction of its length into quarters and the quarters are sliced parallel to one another creating a straight grain with flake. (Chapter 5)

Quartz One of the most common natural substances, found in many forms, such as sand, and in many kinds of stone. (Chapter 7)

Quartzite Hard, dense, metamorphic rock composed of quartz crystals packed very densely, lending both compression and tensile strength to the material. (Chapter 11)

R

Random sheared A carpet texture created by shearing carpet lightly so that only the higher loops are sheared. The sheared yarns appear darker and more matte in their reflectivity than the yarns remaining as loops. (Chapter 4)

Reducer strip Molding that finishes the space between wood or laminate flooring and other thinner flooring surfaces, like vinyl or carpet. (Chapter 6)

Reflective glass Glass with a metallic coating to reduce solar heat gain. (Chapter 8)

Register The alignment of successive screens required to complete a multicolored pattern. If the colors in the pattern are not perfectly aligned, the pattern is described as out of register. (Chapter 2)

Repeat The distance from the center of one motif or pattern to the center of the next. (Chapter 2)

Reverberation Accumulation of many reflections, interacting with one another, so that the sound no longer seems composed of echoes but rather just noise having no identifiable location. (Chapter 14)

Running match When stone slabs are cut from the block, they are polished as they are cut without flipping over every other one. (Chapter 11)

S

Sags Wide drips or runs when the paint flows down, collecting in a raised ridge before drying. If the paint is put on too thickly it will sag before it dries. (Chapter 2)

Seam slippage Tendency of fabric that is not tightly woven to pull apart along stitched seams. Commercial fabrics are typically tested and document the number of pounds of pulling force the fabric can endure before yarns start to slide apart. (Chapter 3)

Sedimentary stone Stone that is built up over time by disintegration of animal, vegetable, and mineral sources. Limestone is an example of a sedimentary stone that you will likely specify. (Chapter 11)

Selvage Also spelled *selvedge*; side edges of a roll of wallcovering carrying no design, intended to protect the design. The thin compressed edge of a woven fabric that runs parallel to the warp yarns and prevents raveling at the sides. It is usually woven, with a tighter construction than the rest of the fabric. (Chapter 2)

Serpentine Metamorphic rock composed of mineral containing serpentinite. (Chapter 11)

Shellac A sealer for sealing knots in woodwork so the resins don't migrate into the paint. (Chapter 2)

Sick building syndrome Health or comfort complaints that appear to be linked to building systems but where no specific illness or cause can be identified. (Chapter 1)

Site-finishing Material stained and sealed at the installation site by the installer, the opposite of prefinishing. (Chapter 13)

Sizing A liquid compound that prevents the surface of the wall from soaking up too much glue or paint. (Chapter 2)

Slabs Stone pieces usually 2 centimeters or 3 centimeters thick and approximately 5' × 8' in length. (Chapter 11)

Slate Fine-grained rock derived from clay and shale, often having a natural cleft; material will often spall off the face, even after installed. (Chapter 11)

Soapstone Variety of talc stones, known for their stain- and heatproof qualities. (Chapter 11)

Spall A chip or splinter in stone. (Chapter 11)

Spalted Figuring caused by initial rot that resembles thin ink lines traced along the natural wood grain. Spalted veneer is cultivated intentionally by burying logs for a number of months, after which the logs are exhumed and the rot arrested by drying the wood. (Chapter 5)

Specification A detailed description of requirements, or characteristics of a product or of labor, to be performed by others. (Chapter 1)

Specify To write a description of characteristics, function, and performance of a material or object that may also include installation instructions. (Chapter 1)

Stackback The amount of space occupied by the open drapery. The general rule is that the stackback will be equal to one-third the width of the window. For a split-draw (half of stackback on each side of the window) just divide the stackback in two and put half on each side. (Chapter 3)

Stock A pattern that is part of a manufactured line. Or *in-stock*, which means it is the inventory on hand. (Chapter 2)

Stretched Carpet installation term for the amount of elongation of carpet when it is stretched over cushion onto tackless strip, generally 1 to 2 percent. (Chapter 4)

Striaé Paint technique in which a base color is painted over with a glaze and before the glaze can set up, it is dragged off the surface with a dry brush, creating fine, parallel lines. (Chapter 2)

Structure-borne sound Sound travels from the source to the receiving space through vibration of the solid materials along the way. This includes sounds generated by impacts to a structure (hammering, drilling, etc.) and sounds from moving parts inside mechanical equipment touching the structure (pumps, motors, fans, etc.). (Chapter 14)

Subfloor Structural layer that flooring is installed on. (Chapter 13)

Substrate The surface underneath a material that holds and supports it. (Chapter 2)

Suspended particle Glass that changes from frosted to clear when an electric current is passed through it. (Chapter 8)

Sustainable Meeting present needs without compromising the ability of future generations to meet their own needs; material sources that can be replenished. (Chapter 1)

Synthesis Combining elements to create a unified product which has different characteristics than the two original components. (Chapter 1)

Synthetic Man-made of petroleum instead of natural material (like the cellulosic fibers). (Chapter 3)

T

Tempered glass Safety glass subjected to heat treatment, followed by rapid cooling, which, if broken, will form cubic beads instead of shards. It is approximately four times stronger than standard annealed glass. (Chapter 8)

Tensile strength The maximum load in pounds per square inch that can be sustained by metal in tension (pulling or bending). (Chapter 9)

Thermal mass Dense material that can absorb radiant heat from the sun during the day and release it at night, to even out heating and cooling loads, saving energy. (Chapter 12)

Thermoplastic Plastic that is softened by heat and can be reheated and bent. (Chapter 7)

Thermoset Plastic that cures with heat and cannot be heated and bent after formation. (Chapter 7)

Third-party An entity or organization that is not associated with parties having interest but is instead only incidentally associated. A second party, on the other hand, is an organization or entity that is once-removed from a monetary interest. For instance, a trade association whose members are manufacturers or installers of a product would be considered a second-party entity to those businesses. (Chapter 1)

Tip sheared Light, shallow shearing to add surface interest to carpet texture. (Chapter 4)

Tolerance An allowable deviation from specs. (Chapter 11)

Tongue and groove The edge profile on flooring planks to allow fastening together. (Chapter 13)

Topdressing A protective coating that sits on top of the stone rather than soaking in (as would a penetrating sealer). These protective coats are applied in addition to penetrating sealers and are often intended to be periodically removed and reapplied. The intention is that if a slight scratch or stain occurs, it is scratching or staining the topdressing and not the stone. Topdressings are softer, so more easily damaged than stone faces, but they are also easier to restore than the stone face. (Chapter 11)

Topping Cement material that is placed on top of a supporting underbed and serves as a surfacing material but is not structural or even self-supporting. (Chapter 12)

Travertine A dense limestone formed by materials deposited as hot springs bubbled up. This explains the holes through cross-cut travertine. Vein-cut travertine does not exhibit the holes of cross-cut material. It has properties in common with marble. Those travertines dense enough to take a polish are sometimes referred to as travertine marbles. (Chapter 11)

Trombe wall High-mass wall that stores heat from solar gain during the day and slowly radiates the heat back into the living space at night. (Chapter 1)

Twill Woven construction that produces the appearance of a diagonal, even though warp and weft are still perpendicular to each other. (Chapter 3)

U

Underlayments Layers of material, usually installed on or over a subfloor, that provide a surface suitable to receive a new floor covering. (Chapter 13)

V

Veneer Slices of wood, thinner than lumber's minimum of ¾-inch finished thickness. Very few trees have a quality that warrants veneer and most are sliced into lumber. A thin layer of material applied to the structure of a supporting surface that it covers. (Chapter 5)

Volatile organic compounds (VOCs) Substances whose state can be changed and that interact with organic systems like ecosystems or individual plants and animals. (Chapter 1)

W

Water-modified alkyd Sustainable alkyd paint that uses plant-based oils instead of petroleum. (Chapter 2)

Wear layer

(1) A layer of material applied to the top surface of vinyl flooring. The thickness of the wear layer varies with each vinyl product collection, or series, and is generally measured in mils. The thickness of a mil is about the same as a page in a phone book. Premium wear layers offer superior resistance to stains, scuffs, and scratches. How long a vinyl floor will look new and fresh is based on the wear layer's performance. (Chapter 6)

(2) The top surface of the laminated product that withstands abrasion. (Chapter 13)

Welding rods Thin rods that are melted with a specialized tool to seal seams on sheet floors. Vinyl floors use vinyl rods, and linoleum floors use linoleum rods, in color-coordinated shades that blend with or accent seams. (See "Heat welding.") (Chapter 6)

Worsted Wool fabric woven from firmly twisted yarns, which are spun from combed long-staple wool, creating a solid, smooth surface with no nap. (Chapter 3)

BASIC METRIC CONVERSION TABLE

Length	
English	**Metric**
1 inch	2.54 centimeters
1 foot	0.3048 meter/30.48 centimeters
1 yard	0.9144 meter
Metric	**English**
1 centimeter	0.3937 inch
1 meter	3.280 feet
Weights	
English	**Metric**
1 ounce	28.35 grams
1 pound	0.45 kilogram
Metric	**English**
1 gram	0.035 ounce
1 kilogram	2.2 pounds

General formula for converting:
Number of Units × Conversion Number = New Number of Units

To convert inches to centimeters:
[number of inches] × 2.54 = [number of centimeters]

To convert centimeters to inches:
[number of centimeters] × 0.3937 = [number of inches]

To convert feet to meters:
[number of feet] × 0.3048 = [number of meters]

To convert meters to feet:
[number of meters] × 3.280 = [number of feet]

To convert yards to meters:
[number of yards] × 0.9144 = [number of meters]

To convert ounces to grams:
[number of ounces] × 28.35 = [number of grams]

To convert grams to ounces:
[number of grams] × 0.035 = [number of ounces]

To convert pounds to kilograms:
[number of pounds] × 0.45 = [number of kilograms]

To convert kilograms to pounds:
[number of kilograms] × 2.2 = [number of pounds]

INDEX